Welfare
Volume 2: Measuring
Social Welfare

Welfare
Volume 2: Measuring
Social Welfare

Dale W. Jorgenson

The MIT Press
Cambridge, Massachusetts
London, England

This book was printed and bound in the United States of America.

Library of Congress Cataloging-in-Publication Data

Jorgenson, Dale Weldeau, 1933–
  Welfare / Dale W. Jorgenson.
   p.   cm.
  Includes bibliographical references and index.
  Contents: v. 1. Aggregate consumer behavior. — v. 2. Measuring social welfare.
  ISBN 0–262–10062–2 (v. 1: alk. paper). — ISBN 0–262–10063–0 (v. 2: alk. paper)
  1. Income distribution. 2. Consumer behavior. 3. Economic policy.
  4. Public welfare. I. Title.
  HB523.J673   1997   96–44875
  361.6′1—dc20   CIP

Contents

List of Tables   ix
Preface   xi
List of Sources   xxix

1   **Aggregate Consumer Behavior and the Measurement
    of Social Welfare**   1
    D.W. Jorgenson
    1.1   Introduction   1
    1.2   Preliminaries   7
    1.3   Modeling Consumer Behavior   13
    1.4   Individual and Social Welfare   20
    1.5   The Standard of Living and its Cost   25
    1.6   Summary and Conclusion   32
    Appendix Table   35

2   **Individual and Social Cost-of-Living Indexes**   39
    D.W. Jorgenson and D.T. Slesnick
    2.1   Introduction   39
    2.2   Aggregate Consumer Behavior   42
    2.3   Econometric Model   51
    2.4   Individual Cost-of-Living Indexes   56
    2.5   Social Welfare Functions   63
    2.6   Social Cost-of-Living Index   75
    2.7   Group Cost-of-Living Indexes   78
    2.8   Summary and Conclusion   85
    Appendix Tables   91

3   **Inequality in the Distribution of Individual Welfare**   99
    D.W. Jorgenson and D.T. Slesnick
    3.1   Introduction   99

3.2 Aggregate Consumer Behavior   102
3.3 Econometric Model   112
3.4 Social Welfare Functions   117
3.5 Indexes of Inequality   127
3.6 Inequality within Groups   133
3.7 Inequality between Groups   137
3.8 Money Metric Inequality   142
3.9 Applications of Money Metric Inequality   149
3.10 Summary and Conclusion   156
Appendix Tables   159

4 General Equilibrium Analysis of Economic Policy   165
D.W. Jorgenson and D.T. Slesnick
4.1 Introduction   165
4.2 Aggregate Consumer Behavior   169
4.3 Econometric Model   180
4.4 Money Metric Individual Welfare   185
4.5 Social Welfare Functions   195
4.6 Money Metric Social Welfare   205
4.7 Efficiency versus Equity   212
4.8 Summary and Conclusion   216

**5 Aggregate Consumer Behavior and Household
    Equivalence Scales   219**
D.W. Jorgenson and D.T. Slesnick
5.1 Introduction   219
5.2 Aggregate Consumer Behavior   222
5.3 Identification and Estimation   228
5.4 Econometric Model   236
5.5 Household Equivalence Scales   238
Appendix A Notation for Instrumental Variables, 1947–1982 244
Appendix B Notation for Cross-Section Results   245
Appendix C Notation for Pooled Estimation Results   249

**6 General Equilibrium Analysis of Natural Gas
    Price Regulation   253**
D.W. Jorgenson and D.T. Slesnick
6.1 Introduction   253
6.2 Aggregate Consumer Behavior   254
6.3 Money Metric Individual Welfare   263
6.4 Social Welfare Functions   271
6.5 Money Metric Social Welfare   279

7   **Redistributional Policy and the Measurement**
    of Poverty   **291**
    D.W. Jorgenson and D.T. Slesnick
    7.1   Introduction   291
    7.2   Poverty and Social Welfare   295
    7.3   Measures of Poverty   301
    7.4   Individual and Social Welfare   305
    7.5   Money Metric Poverty   309
    7.6   Poverty within Groups   314
    7.7   Poverty between Groups   322
    7.8   Alternative Poverty Measures   328
    7.9   Summary and Conclusion   335
    Appendix Tables   337

8   **Inequality and the Standard of Living**   **343**
    D.W. Jorgenson and D.T. Slesnick
    8.1   Introduction   343
    8.2   Individual Welfare   345
    8.3   Social Welfare   347
    8.4   Standard of Living Index   351
    8.5   Real Expenditure per Person   353

9   **Carbon Taxes and Economic Welfare**   **361**
    D.W. Jorgenson, D.T. Slesnick and P.J. Wilcoxen
    9.1   Introduction   361
    9.2   An Overview of the Model   363
    9.3   Welfare Economics   372
    9.4   The Impact of a Carbon Tax   379
    9.5   The Effect of Welfare   388

References   401
Index   415

List of Tables

1.1	The U.S. standard of living and its cost	30
1.A.1	The transcendental logarithmic model of aggregate consumer behavior	35
2.1	Pooled estimation results	53
2.2	Changes in individual cost-of-living indexes (annual percentage rates)	60
2.3	Social cost-of-living index	78
2.4	Change in group cost-of-living indexes	82
2.5	Exact translog cost-of-living index	90
2.A.1	Individual cost-of-living indexes (1972 = 1.000)	91
2.A.2	Group cost-of-living indexes (1972 = 1.0000)	94
3.1	Pooled estimation results	114
3.2	Levels of social welfare	131
3.3	Indexes of inequality	132
3.4	Indexes of group inequality	136
3.5	Indexes of group relative inequality	137
3.6	Decomposition of indexes of inequality	141
3.7	Decomposition of indexes of relative inequality	142
3.8	Money metric social welfare	152
3.9	Money metric inequality	153
3.10	Money metric group inequality	154
3.11	Money metric group relative inequality	155
3.12	Decomposition of money metric inequality	156
3.13	Decomposition of money metric relative inequality	157
3.A.1	Levels of group welfare	159
3.A.2	Indexes of group efficiency	160
3.A.3	Money metric group welfare	161
3.A.4	Money metric group efficiency	162
4.1	Pooled estimation results	182
4.2	Projections of prices and total expenditures	190

4.3	Money metric individual welfare (current prices; Northeast region)	192
4.4	Money metric social welfare (millions of current dollars)	213
4.5	Money metric efficiency (millions of current dollars)	214
4.6	Money metric equity (millions of current dollars)	216
5.1	Age 35–44, Northeast	239
5.2	Size 4, Northeast	241
5.3	Age 35–44, Size 4	243
5.B.1	Cross-section results for energy and food	245
5.B.2	Cross-section results for consumer goods and capital services	246
5.B.3	Cross-section results for consumer services	247
5.C.1	Pooled estimation results—Energy	249
5.C.2	Pooled estimation results—Food	249
5.C.3	Pooled estimation results—Consumer goods	249
5.C.4	Pooled estimation results—Capital services	250
5.C.5	Pooled estimation results—Consumer services	250
6.1	Projections of prices and total expenditure	268
6.2	Money metric individual welfare (constant prices; Northeast region)	270
6.3	Money metric social welfare (millions of constant dollars)	284
6.4	Money metric efficiency (millions of constant dollars)	285
6.5	Money metric equity (millions of constant dollars)	286
7.1	Money measures of social welfare (billions of 1972 dollars)	310
7.2	Money metric poverty (billions of 1972 dollars)	311
7.3	Money metric relative poverty (billions of 1972 dollars)	313
7.4	Money metric group relative poverty (billions of 1972 dollars)	319
7.5	Money metric between-group relative poverty	327
7.6	Head-count ratios of the poor	331
7.7	Utilitarian money metric poverty (billions of 1972 dollars)	332
7.8	Transfers (billions of 1972 dollars)	334
7.A.1	Money metric group poverty (billions of 1972 dollars)	337
7.A.2	Money metric between-group poverty (billions of 1972 dollars)	340
8.1	Standard of living indexes	354
8.2	Biases in real aggregate expenditure per person	357
9.1	Industries used in the model	364
9.2	Carbon emissions data, 1987	370
9.3	Consumer goods used in model	388
9.4	Equivalent variations in wealth upon imposition of a carbon tax (1990 dollars)	394
9.5	Equivalent variations as a percentage of wealth	395
9.6	Change in social welfare	396

Preface

Dale W. Jorgenson

This volume is the second of two volumes containing my empirical studies of consumer behavior and presents a new conceptual framework for normative economics. The first of the two volumes, *Modeling Consumer Behavior*, focuses on econometric modeling at the aggregate level. My initial goal was to incorporate the implications of utility maximization into a model for aggregate time series data, employing the concept of a representative consumer. Subsequently, my objective expanded to include the implications of aggregation over utility-maximizing consumers. This required pooling aggregate time series with cross-section data for individual households.

The new approach to normative economics presented in this volume exploits the econometric model of aggregate consumer behavior that resulted from my earlier investigations. The model takes the form of a system of aggregate demand functions obtained by aggregating over individual demand functions. Measures of welfare are then recovered from the individual demand functions and combined into a single indicator of social welfare, reflecting concepts of horizontal and vertical equity. This approach was summarized in my presidential address to the Econometric Society, published in 1990 and reprinted as chapter 1 below.

Problems of normative economics have a number of common features. The initial step in the solution of each problem is to establish and implement the relevant measure of individual welfare. This is a natural consequence of formulating a model of individual consumer behavior on the basis of utility maximization. However, the theory of consumer behavior that has been the standard since the seminal work of John Hicks and Roy Allen (1934) is based on an ordinal concept of individual welfare that is not comparable among individuals.

Economic policies are commonly compared by means of index numbers representing consumer's surplus. Given the limitations of the traditional index number approach discussed below, attention has shifted toward lineal descendents of Jules Dupuit's (1844) concept of consumer's surplus—the compensating and equivalent variations introduced almost a century later by Hicks (1942). The issue that remains is to relate these changes in individual welfare to changes in social welfare. This is essential if the changes are to be decomposed into changes in economic efficiency and distributional equity.

Since the pioneering work of Anthony Atkinson (1970) and Serge Kolm (1969), the measurement of social welfare has been based on explicit social welfare functions. However, the social welfare functions introduced by Atkinson and Kolm are defined on the distribution of income rather than the distribution of individual welfare. John Muellbauer (1974b) and Kevin Roberts (1980c) have shown that measures of social welfare based on income coincide with measures based on individual welfare if and only if preferences are identical and homothetic for all consumers.

To overcome objections to social welfare functions defined on income, Muellbauer (1974b) has defined social welfare functions on the distribution of Hicks's equivalent variation. Roberts (1980c) has characterized the conditions under which these measures of social welfare coincide with measures based on the distribution of individual welfare. In the absence of restrictions on social welfare functions, individuals must have identical and homothetic preferences. With no restrictions on preferences, the social welfare function must be dictatorial in the sense of Kenneth Arrow (1963).

Dictatorial social welfare functions are obviously unsatisfactory as a conceptual basis for normative economics. The objection to the assumption of identical and homothetic preferences is empirical rather than conceptual. Econometric models of consumer behavior, like the one presented in chapter 1, exhibit income elasticities of demand that are different from unity, implying that preferences are not homothetic. These models also reveal differences in preferences among households with different characteristics, so that the assumption of identical preferences is also empirically untenable.

At this point the literature on normative economics bifurcates. The first branch, at one time denominated the New Welfare Economics, follows Hicks (1940) in applying the "compensation principle." Under this principle any change in policy in which the winners can compensate the losers improves social welfare. Paul Samuelson (1950) demonstrated that this principle gives rise to inconsistent orderings.

John Chipman and James Moore (1973, 1980a) showed that the compensation principle provides a valid indicator of social welfare only if measures of individual welfare are identical and homothetic.

The second branch of normative economics reverts to a much earlier tradition, invoking the Pareto principle. Under this principle a change in policy improves social welfare only if it makes at least one individual better off while leaving other individuals at least as well off. The concept of Pareto optimality plays a central role in the theory of general competitive equilibrium of Arrow and Gerard Debreu (1954) through the two Fundamental Theorems of Welfare Economics, relating Pareto optimality to competitive equilibrium.

By itself the useful idea of Pareto optimality is much too weak to provide a satisfactory foundation for normative economics. On the other hand, the compensation principle depends for its validity on empirically untenable assumptions about individual preferences. Fortunately, the concept of a social welfare function, originated by Abram Bergson (1937) and discussed by Samuelson (1947), provides a means of overcoming these difficulties. As Amartya Sen (1977) has argued persuasively, this requires dispensing with ordinal measures of individual welfare that are not comparable among individuals.

The model of a representative consumer illustrates the essential ideas. The most transparent version of this model is based on identical and homothetic preferences for all individuals. Aggregate demand functions then assume the same form as individual demand functions. Welfare for each individual is proportional to total expenditure and inversely proportional to an index of the cost of living. These measures can be combined into an indicator of social welfare based on Bergson's concept of a social welfare function.

Construction of a model of consumer behavior by aggregation over utility-maximizing consumers is possible without requiring the untenable restrictions of identical and homothetic preferences. However, such a model retains the most important feature of the model of a representative consumer—measures of individual welfare that are cardinal and interpersonally comparable. Obviously, this formulation of the theory of consumer behavior is far more restrictive than that of Hicks and Allen (1934).

While a cardinal measure of individual welfare that is fully comparable among individuals is implicit in the index number approach to welfare economics, differences among individuals are ignored and preferences are assumed to be homothetic. By overcoming these restrictions the econometric approach to normative economics presented in chapter 1 opens up a richer and more satisfactory methodology for comparison of alternative economic policies. This methodology exploits the measurability and comparability of welfare measures for different individuals to construct an indicator of social welfare.

Replacing the ordinal concept of individual welfare that is not comparable among individuals will require a great deal of relearning for generations of economists schooled on Hicks and Allen (1934) and Arrow and Debreu (1954). However, this concept has effectively neutered many of these same economists in debates about economic policy. Only modest consolation is available from the influential teaching of Lionel Robbins (1938) that an economist *qua* economist has little to contribute to these debates—beyond announcing those rare instances when the principle of Pareto optimality can be invoked.

For practitioners of normative economics the application of an econometric model to the measurement of social welfare is a highly innovative but also unfamiliar and even disturbing idea. Multi-million dollar budgets are involved in statistical reporting of price index numbers. This well-established practice does not require explicit modeling of consumer behavior. The index number approach to the cost of living is evaluated in chapter 2 below and, perhaps surprisingly, found to be conceptually sound and empirically robust.

However, the successful implementation of a cost-of-living index is far from trivial. The U.S. Bureau of Labor Statistics compiles a Consumer Price Index (CPI) based on the index number approach. During the period 1964–1989 the CPI incorporated an upward bias of more than ten percent, due to an inconsistent treatment of the cost of owner-occupied housing before and after 1983. More recently, the CPI has been subject to a persistent upward bias of 1.5 percent per year. This experience shows that implementation of price index numbers is highly problematical.

Similarly, the standard of living appears at first glance to be one of the most straightforward ideas in the conceptual toolkit of the normative economist. The value of transactions is divided by a cost-of-living index to obtain an index of the standard of living. The first issue is the scope of the transactions to be included; this issue is implicit in the definition of the cost of living. The second issue is how to allow for changes in distributional equity. A satisfactory resolution of this issue requires combining measures of individual welfare into an overall indicator of social welfare.

The U.S. Bureau of the Census constructs a measure of the standard of living based on median real family income. According to this measure, the U.S. standard of living has been stagnant for the past two decades. The fundamental difficulty with the Census approach is that the standard of living is defined in terms of consumption rather than income. However, the standard of living measure presented in chapter 1 grows more than forty percent faster than a conventional measure based on real consumption per capita. Important biases in this conventional measure can be traced to biases in the CPI, the definition of the population, and the omission of equity considerations.

Given empirically satisfactory measures of individual and social welfare, it is very straightforward to formulate a concept of the standard of living that reflects distributional equity as well as economic efficiency. The measure of equity implied by this formulation is a natural starting point for a measure of inequality that reflects society's willingness to pay for the redistribution of individual welfare. A similar measure of poverty reflects society's willingness to pay for redistributions that bring all individuals to the minimum level of well-being represented by a poverty line.

Inequality is usually measured by considering dispersion in the distribution of "income" for cross sections of individual households, but inequality, like the standard of living, is defined in terms of consumption rather than income. Once again, a critical issue is the scope of transactions pertinent to individual welfare. More sophisticated approaches to inequality take into account differences in the cost of living, especially in comparisons at different points of time. Only rarely do differences in the composition of individual households come into play, but these differences are obviously germane to distributional equity, the central issue in measuring inequality.

The Bureau of the Census publishes a measure of inequality based on a Gini coefficient for family income. This measure shows a widely reported U-turn with decreases in inequality until 1973, followed by a rise in inequality. By contrast the measure of equity presented in chapter 1 shows a steady rise throughout the period 1947–1985. This is due to differences between the distributions of income and consumption and incorporation of an appropriate adjustment for changes in the composition of families.

Poverty measurement traditionally focuses on the head-count ratio of individuals and families below a stipulated poverty line. This initially appears as a problem in the enumeration of the relevant populations. However, comparison of head-count ratios for different points of time or different sub-groups of the population inevitably requires more careful scrutiny of the poverty line itself. Differences in the cost of living and demographic characteristics of the relevant populations immediately come to the fore, just as in the measurement of inequality.

Head-count measures of poverty published by the Bureau of the Census show the same U-turn for poverty as for inequality. These measures are based on real income per household equivalent member. By contrast consumption-based measures of inequality and poverty presented in chapter 7 show that inequality has declined over the period 1947–1985 and poverty has been a declining proportion of inequality. Important biases in the Census measure can be attributed to the use of income rather than consumption, equivalence scales for different family members based on food consumption rather than household budgets for all items, and biases in the CPI.

In short, the econometric approach to normative economics unifies the treatment of inequality, poverty, and the cost and standard of living. However, this approach brings to light some very significant flaws in statistical programs that cover these important areas. The stagnation of the U.S. standard of living and the U-turns in inequality and poverty are revealed as statistical artifacts. The most important deficiency in the Census programs that generate these statistics is the use of income rather than consumption. Serious deficiencies also arise from biases in the CPI and the use of household equivalence scales.

In the studies presented in this volume my objective is to provide a detailed alternative to the empirically untenable index number approach. Dispensing with index numbers will undoubtedly remain an unsettling prospect for many practitioners. However, the reader steeped in traditional methods will find much that is familiar, despite the radical restructuring implied by the econometric approach. For example, I have preserved the logical structure of the index number approach by employing cardinal and interpersonally comparable measures of individual welfare.

The basic concepts of normative economics are introduced in section 1.2 of chapter 1. The concept of individual welfare is derived from the theory of the utility-maximizing household. Individual welfare is transformed into a money metric by defining an individual expenditure function as the minimum expenditure required to attain a given level of individual welfare. All of this is standard apparatus in the theory of consumer behavior, but it is important to note that the individual units are households, which are social entities, rather than biological individuals.

Only ordinal measures of welfare that are not comparable among households are required for applications of the Pareto principle. However, individual welfare depends on the characteristics of households as well as prices and total expenditure. The conditions required for aggregation imply the existence of measures of individual welfare that are cardinal and fully comparable among individuals. In section 1.4 of chapter 1 I present these measures and a class of social welfare functions defined on them.

The first step in determining social welfare is to evaluate individual welfare functions for all households. The second step is to evaluate the social welfare function. Social welfare is transformed into a money metric by defining a social expenditure function in terms of the minimum aggregate expenditure required to attain a given level of welfare, as in section 1.4 of chapter 1. While the social expenditure function is a much less familiar concept than the individual expenditure function, the application of these concepts is precisely analogous.

I decompose social welfare into equity and efficiency components in section 1.2 of chapter 1. Efficiency is the maximum level of social welfare attainable by redistributing aggregate expenditure among individual households. Welfare losses from an inequitable distribution are eliminated by this maximization. The resulting level of welfare can be expressed as a function of prices and aggregate expenditure. Equity reflects the gain in welfare from moving toward a more egalitarian distribution.

To illustrate the basic concepts of the econometric approach to normative economics, I present a model of aggregate consumer behavior in section 1.3. I then recover measures of individual welfare from demand functions and incorporate this information into a social welfare function. The class of social welfare functions I consider combines the average level of welfare with a measure of dispersion. Utilitarian social welfare functions are a limiting case where the dispersion drops out.

I define measures of the standard of living and its cost in chapter 1 and implement these measures for the United States for the period, 1947–1985. My 1983 paper with Daniel Slesnick, reprinted in chapter 2, discusses individual and social cost of living indexes in much greater detail. Slesnick and I present a third concept of the cost of living, defined for sub-groups of the population. For this purpose we introduce group welfare and expenditure functions analogous to the social welfare and expenditure functions of chapter 1. Finally, we present a nonparametric approach to the cost of living based on the price index formula introduced by Leo Tornqvist (1936).

The most striking empirical finding in chapter 2 in that cost-of-living indexes for typical households, indexes for sub-groups of the population, and the social cost-of-living index give nearly identical results for the twenty year period 1958–1978. In short, the cost-of-living index is unaffected by substantial differences in the definition of the group under consideration. In addition, the nonparametric cost-of-living index is very similar, so that the index number approach produces the same results.

Slesnick (1991a) has compared alternative social cost-of-living indexes for the U.S. for the substantially longer period 1947–1988. He shows that those presented in chapters 1 and 2 and others discussed in the literature give similar results. He also presents two different nonparametric indexes—the Laspeyres index used by the U.S. Bureau of Labor Statistics in constructing the Consumer Price Index (CPI) and the Tornqvist index of chapter 2. Again, the index number and econometric approaches produce essentially the same measures of the cost of living.

Erwin Diewert's (1981) theory of exact index numbers suggests a rationale for the empirical results of chapter 2 and Slesnick (1991a). Diewert shows that the Tornqvist index formula is exact for preferences that take the translog parametric form employed in the econometric models of chapters 1 and 2. If the preferences of an individual consumer take this form, the corresponding cost-of-living index can be obtained by applying the Tornqvist formula; econometric modeling is not required.

The social cost-of-living index number of chapter 1 is based on a model of a representative consumer. This model corresponds to the concept of a maximizing society introduced by Samuelson (1956) and discussed by Robert Pollak (1981). The model also underlies the group cost-of-living index in chapter 2. I conclude that the cost-of-living index for an individual consumer provides the conceptual basis for cost-of-living measurement at all levels. The index number approach is conceptually sound as well as empirically robust.

However, empirical implementation of the index number approach to the cost of living has proven to be highly problematical. Slesnick

(1991b) has estimated that the CPI incorporated an upward bias of about ten percent during the period 1964–1989, due to differences in the treatment of the cost of owner-occupied residential housing before and after 1983. More recently, the Advisory Commission to Study the Consumer Price Index (1995) has carefully evaluated the biases in the CPI, revealing a persistent bias of 1.5 percent per year.

The standard of living index presented in chapter 1 is a money measure of actual social welfare. This index can be represented as a product of measures of economic efficiency and distributional equity. Economic efficiency is an indicator of potential social welfare, the maximum that can be attained through redistributions. This can be represented as the ratio of aggregate expenditure to the cost of living and is independent of society's aversion to inequality. Finally, equity is defined as the ratio of money measures of actual and potential social welfare.

Chapter 8, reprinted from my 1989 paper with Slesnick, discusses the social standard of living in more detail. The standard of living measure grows more than forty percent faster than real expenditure per capita. This conventional measure of the standard of living is defined as the ratio of aggregate expenditure per capita to the CPI. Important biases can be traced to the CPI and the head-count definition of the population. In addition, per capita real expenditure omits equity considerations altogether, giving rise to a significant bias.

Slesnick (1991a) has compared alternative social standard of living indexes for the U.S. for the period 1947–1988. By contrast with the cost of living, indexes of the standard of living differ substantially, reflecting different measures of equity. Slesnick (1991b) has compared indexes based on income, like that of the Census, with the consumption-based measures presented in chapters 1 and 8. Consumption-based measures do not exhibit the stagnation of the past two decades reported by the Census.

Chapter 3, reprinted from my 1984 paper with Slesnick, discusses measures of equity and efficiency in detail. In section 3.8 we define a measure of relative inequality as one minus the measure of equity presented in chapter 1. Relative inequality, defined in this way, lies between zero and one and is equal to zero for perfect equality. The money measures of inequality and efficiency that underly this definition are expressed in terms of the social expenditure function introduced in chapter 1. The money measure of inequality expresses society's willingness to pay for perfect equality.

Table 3.9 of chapter 3 contains the important empirical finding that inequality decreases throughout the period 1958–1978. Table 1.1 of chapter 1 gives a parallel result, showing that equity has risen for the longer period 1947–1985. However, growth in equity occurred only during 1958–1978 and 1983–1985. Slesnick (1994) has extended these results to the period 1947–1991, showing little change in inequality since the early 1970s. The widely reported U-turn in inequality, reported by the Census, is not reflected in any of these measures of inequality.

Slesnick (1994) has compared consumption-based measures of inequality with measures based on income, like that of the Census. Important differences between the distributions of income and consumption account for most of the discrepancies. However, changes in the composition of families play a significant role in the measures of inequality presented in chapters 1 and 3. The Census adjusts family income for these changes in measuring poverty, but not in measuring inequality. Biases in the CPI, which contribute to biases in the Census measure of the standard of living, are unimportant for inequality.

The decomposition of a social welfare function presented in chapter 3 is a very significant innovation. The initial step is to define group welfare functions, like those presented in chapter 2, for a set of mutually exclusive and exhaustive groups, for example, age groups. A between group welfare function is then defined on the group welfare functions in the same way a social welfare function is defined on individual welfare functions in chapter 1. Using these concepts and the corresponding expenditure functions we show that relative inequality can be decomposed into the sum of between and within group components.

Focusing on groups defined in terms of age of the head of household, we first consider relative inequality for each group. These measures of inequality have declined over the period 1958–1978, but much of the decline is concentrated in the early part of the period. Overall, inequality within groups falls steadily from 1958 to 1970 and then remains almost unchanged through the remainder of the period. Inequality between groups falls after 1958 and then rises to a peak in 1969, falling gradually through 1978. The great predominance of inequality for U.S. is within rather than between age groups.

Slesnick (1994) has considerably extended the decomposition of inequality between and within groups. Inequality between age groups is a relatively small proportion of overall inequality and changes relatively little over the period 1947–1991. The decline in overall inequality through the 1970s is largely within age groups. Inequality between groups classified by size of household is about half of total inequality, but there is little change during the period. A fall in inequality within size groups accounts for the decline in overall inequality.

Inequality between regions falls sharply over the period 1947–1980, reflecting the rise in the standard of living of the South. However, most of the fall in overall inequality can be attributed to a reduction in inequality within regions. Inequality between farm and nonfarm groups of the population is a very small part of overall inequality and nearly vanishes over the period 1947–1991. Inequality between racial groups is a very modest proportion of total inequality and has not changed over this period. Inequality by gender of the household head is also a very small part of total inequality and has not changed substantially.

The concept of equity presented in chapter 1 rests on society's willingness to pay to eliminate inequality. Chapter 7, reprinted from my 1989 paper with Slesnick, introduces a poverty threshold specified in terms of individual welfare. Holding aggregate expenditure constant, the optimal policy for alleviation of poverty is to transfer expenditure from the most affluent households to households below the poverty threshold. The gain in social welfare from this redistributional policy is a measure of poverty analogous to the measure of inequality presented in chapter 3.

Inequality is measured by the gain in social welfare that results from redistributions of aggregate expenditure to eliminate inequality. This measure of inequality can be represented as the sum of two components. The first is associated with the elimination of poverty, while the second corresponds to the inequality that remains after poverty has been eliminated. Similarly, we decompose relative inequality between relative measures of poverty and the remaining inequality. Finally, we consider the transfers required to eliminate poverty and the remaining inequality.

The most important empirical result of chapter 7 is that poverty has decreased steadily over the period 1947–1985. By the end of the period a transfer of $4.742 billions in constant dollars of 1972, had it been feasible, would have brought about the elimination of poverty. Inequality has declined over the period and poverty has been a declining proportion of inequality. While almost three-quarters of inequality can be attributed to individuals below the poverty line in 1947, less than six percent can be so attributed in 1985.

The advantage of approaching the elimination of poverty in terms of redistributional policy is that poverty and inequality can be viewed from the same perspective. However, measures of poverty are more commonly based on head-count ratios, like those regularly compiled by the Census. Chapter 6 shows that thirty-four percent of households and forty-one percent of individuals fell below the poverty line in 1947, but only slightly more than three percent of households and five percent of individuals fell below the line in 1985.

Slesnick (1993) has compared head-count ratios like those presented in chapter 7 with ratios compiled by the Census for the period 1947–1989. The Census measures fall to a minimum in 1973 and rise afterward, paralleling the U-turn in inequality already discussed. Slesnick traces this to the use of income rather than consumption in measuring poverty, the construction of equivalence scales from food budgets rather than household budgets for all items, and the use of the CPI, which is subject to very substantial biases during the 1970s and 1980s.

In chapter 7 Slesnick and I exploit the decomposition of social welfare into within and between group components. Poverty within groups can be defined in terms of group welfare gains due to redistribution within the group so as to eliminate poverty. Poverty between groups can then be defined in terms of additional gains in social welfare that result from redistribution between groups. Poverty differs substantially among age groups. Gains from allowing redistribution between groups to eliminate inequality are modest, while these gains are negligible for poverty elimination.

One of the common features of the problems of normative economics presented in this volume is adjusting for changes in the composition of families. Chapter 5, reprinted from my 1987 paper with Slesnick, discusses the household equivalence scales used for this purpose in chapters 1, 7, and 8. As a starting point, we take the econometric model of aggregate consumer behavior presented in chapter 1. The individual demand functions that underlly this model incorporate the demographic characteristics of individual households.

To define commodity-specific household equivalence scales we take utility to be a function of effective quantities consumed for all commodities. These quantities are defined as ratios of the actual quantities to commodity-specific equivalence scales. We can define general household equivalence scales by comparing budgets for different households. The key to estimating household equivalence scales is to view households as social entities, rather than collections of biological individuals. Households distribute total expenditure among family members in accordance with socially determined welfare objectives.

General equivalence scales are defined in terms of household expenditure functions by analogy with cost-of-living indexes. The individual cost of living index is the ratio of expenditures required to make a given household equally well off at two different sets of prices. The general equivalence scale defined in chapter 5 is the ratio of expenditures required to make two different households equally well off at a given set of prices. This scale can be interpreted as the number of equivalent members for each household.

Chapter 5 gives general and commodity-specific equivalence scales for households classified by size, age of head, and region of residence. The conditions required for aggregation over individual demand functions imply that equivalence scales are independent of utility levels. This has the important advantage that comparisons between two households require only their characteristics, not their levels of utility. A cost of living index independent of utility levels requires the empirically untenable assumption of homothetic preferences.

The Census employs household equivalence scales in constructing a poverty line for different types of households. Inexplicably, the Census employs household equivalence scales in measuring poverty, but not in measuring inequality or the standard of living. In addition, these scales are based on food consumption, rather than household expenditure on all commodities. Slesnick (1993) shows that this produces a substantial bias in the Census poverty measures and contributes to the statistical artifact that measured poverty rises during the 1970s and 1980s.

The evaluation of alternative economic policies uses the same framework for normative economics as the measurement of inequality, poverty, and the cost and standard of living. Policies can be compared in terms of levels of individual welfare by appealing to the Pareto principle. The econometric model generates measures of individual welfare that can be combined into an indicator of social welfare. Policies can be compared in terms of levels of social welfare and these comparisons can be further decomposed between levels of economic efficiency and distributional equity.

My 1985 paper with Slesnick, reprinted in chapter 4, compares alternative policies for petroleum price regulation and taxation of petroleum production in the United States. We take the prevailing policy as a reference case. Under this policy petroleum price controls were eliminated in 1981; a windfall profits tax was levied on petroleum production at the same time. The alternative policies include continued controls with no taxation of petroleum production and elimination of controls with a reformed windfall profits tax, beginning in 1983. Finally, we consider a third alternative policy of eliminating controls with no tax.

We compare social welfare under under the policy prevailing in 1985 with welfare under each of the three alternative policies and translate these comparisons into money measures. Although the measures depend on American society's degree of aversion to inequality, we find that the comparisons are almost identical in qualitative terms. Under continued controls money metric social welfare is positive for three years and then becomes negative. Eliminating the windfall profits tax reduces welfare for one year, but increases it for all remaining years. Reforming the windfall profits tax is an improvement over the prevailing policy, but produces lower welfare levels than simply eliminating the tax.

Social welfare can be decomposed between efficiency and equity, where efficiency corresponds to the potential gain in welfare. The prevailing policy results in lower efficiency than eliminating the windfall profits tax, except for the initial year of the policy change. While eliminating the tax has a negative impact on equity, this is outweighed by the gains in efficiency. Eliminating the tax produces greater gains in efficiency than either of the alternative policies, but this is partially offset by losses in equity. We conclude that both efficiency and equity comparisons are essential for the evaluation of alternative policies.

My 1987 paper with Slesnick, reprinted as chapter 6, compares alternative policies for natural gas price regulation. The reference case for policy analysis is gradual decontrol of natural gas prices under the National Gas Policy Act of 1978. We also consider continued controls and immediate decontrol, both presented as legislative proposals to the Congress in 1983. Under continued controls the impact on social welfare is positive for the years 1983 to 1989, but then becomes negative. Welfare increases under immediate decontrol throughout the period 1983 to 2000, so that this policy is superior to the prevailing policy and continued controls.

The impact of continued controls on efficiency is positive for the period 1983 to 1989 and negative for the rest of the period, while efficiency gains under immediate decontrol are positive throughout the period. Continued controls also reduce equity for the period 1983 to 1989, while immediate decontrol reduces equity throughout the period. Efficiency and equity move in opposite directions and both are essential for the evaluation of alternative policies.

The comparisons of alternative policies for petroleum taxation and petroleum and natural gas price regulation presented in chapters 4 and 6 are based on simulations of U.S. economic growth under alternative policies. These simulations employ a dynamic general equilibrium model of the U.S. economy that I constructed with Edward Hudson (1974). In my 1992 paper with Slesnick and Peter Wilcoxen, reprinted in chapter 9, we consider simulations of the impact of a carbon tax to reduce emissions of carbon dioxide. For this purpose we use a far more detailed model of the growth of the U.S. economy that I have constructed with Wilcoxen (1990a, 1990b).

To estimate the impact of a carbon tax on the distribution of individual welfare we consider a population of infinitely-lived households or "dynasties." Households are classified by demographic characteristics, as in the earlier chapters, but each household type is linked to similar types in the future through intergenerational altruism. Measures of individual welfare are based on time paths of consumption for the corresponding dynasty. As before, we define social welfare on the distribution of individual welfare over households or dynasties.

We consider a sequence of carbon taxes that holds emissions of carbon dioxide in the U.S. constant at the 1990 level. The direct effect of the tax is to increase purchasers' prices of fossil fuels, which contain carbon, especially coal and crude oil. This results in substitution away from fossil fuels by both producers and consumers, reducing emissions of carbon dioxide fourteen percent by the year 2020. Higher energy prices reduce capital formation and produce a decline in output; about half of this decline is due to lower capital formation and the rest to lower productivity growth.

The welfare cost of a carbon tax is dominated by a loss in efficiency amounting to $234 billion in 1990 dollars. The equity impact of the tax can be positive or negative, depending on the degree of aversion to inequality. The welfare cost must be compared with the benefits of internalizing the externality associated with carbon dioxide emissions.

Of course, this externality affects the whole planet, while a carbon tax is the responsibility of an individual government like the U.S.

The econometric approach to welfare economics summarized in this volume is based on a straightforward extension of the conventional index number approach. The essential idea is that preferences of individual households are revealed by their market behavior. An econometric model of household behavior makes it possible to dispense with the limitation to identical and homothetic preferences that characterizes the index number approach. Using much weaker restrictions required for aggregation over utility-maximizing households, we obtain measures of individual welfare that are cardinal and interpersonally comparable.

Measures of individual welfare can be combined into an indicator of social welfare by means of Bergson's concept of a social welfare function. Changes in social welfare can be decomposed between changes in economic efficiency and distributional equity. This approach has been applied to the measurement of inequality, poverty, and the cost and standard of living. It has also been applied to the evaluation of alternative tax and regulatory policies, separating the impacts of policy changes into impacts on efficiency and equity.

Practitioners of normative economics may be relieved to find that the construction of a consumer price index, perhaps the most important application of the index number approach, is conceptually sound and empirically robust. However, the implementation of this approach in the official statistics leaves a great deal to be desired. The official statistical programs that generate measures of poverty, inequality, and the standard of living are deeply flawed and give highly misleading results. These programs will require a total overhaul.

A great deal remains to be done to exploit the new conceptual framework for normative economics. The new methodology presented in chapter 9 provides comparisons among different growth paths resulting from alternative policies. Economic impacts are summarized in terms of wealth rather than consumption. An important objective that remains is to incorporate labor-leisure choice into a model of aggregate consumer behavior, so that measures of individual welfare depend on leisure as well as goods and services.

Each extension of the econometric approach to normative economics generates new information about individual welfare. This information can be incorporated into an indicator of social welfare by bringing to bear ethical judgements about horizontal and vertical equity. We have found it useful to translate changes in social welfare into monetary terms for the applications presented in this volume. The scope of normative economics will be extended by this research program to encompass a broader and broader range of issues in the evaluation of economic performance.

I would like to thank June Wynn of the Department of Economics at Harvard University for her excellent work in assembling the manuscripts for this volume in machine-readable form. Renate d'Arcangelo of the Editorial Office of the Division of Engineering and Applied Sciences at Harvard edited the manuscripts, proofread the machine-readable versions and prepared them for typesetting. Warren Hrung, then a senior at Harvard College, checked the references and proofread successive versions of the typescript. William Richardson and his associates provided the index. Gary Bisbee of Chiron Incorporated typeset the manuscript and provided camera-ready copy for publication. The staff of The MIT Press, especially Terry Vaughn, Victoria Richardson, and Michael Sims, has been very helpful at every stage of the project. Financial support was provided by the Program on Technology and Economic Policy of the Kennedy School of Government at Harvard. As always, the author retains sole responsibility for any remaining deficiencies in the volume.

List of Sources

1. Dale W. Jorgenson 1990. Aggregate Consumer Behavior and the Measurement of Social Welfare. *Econometrica* 58, No. 5 (September): 1007–1040. Reprinted by permission.

2. Dale W. Jorgenson and Daniel T. Slesnick 1983. Individual and Social Cost-of-Living Indexes. In *Price Level Measurement*, ed. W. E. Diewert and C. Montmarquette. Ottawa, Statistics Canada, Catalogue No. 62–602: 241–323. Reproduced by authority of the Minister responsible for Statistics Canada 1993. Readers wishing further information on data provided through cooperation of Statistics Canada may obtain copies of the related publications by mail from: Publications Sales, Statistics Canada, Ottawa, Ontario, Canada, K1A OT6, by calling 1–613–951–7277 or toll-free 1–800–267–6677. Readers may also facsimile their order by dialing 1–613–951–1584.

3. Dale W. Jorgenson and Daniel T. Slesnick 1984. Inequality and the Distribution of Individual Welfare. In *Advances in Econometrics*, ed. R. L. Basmann and G. Rhodes, vol. 3. Greenwich, CT: JAI Press. Reprinted by permission.

4. Dale W. Jorgenson and Daniel T. Slesnick 1985. General Equilibrium Analysis of Economic Policy. In *New Developments in Applied General Equilibrium Analysis*, ed. J. Piggott and J. Whalley. Cambridge: Cambridge University Press. Reprinted by permission of the Cambridge University Press.

5. Dale W. Jorgenson and Daniel T. Slesnick 1987. Aggregate Consumer Behavior and Household Equivalence Scales. *Journal of Business and Economic Statistics* 5, No. 2 (April): 219–232. Reprinted by permission.

6. Dale W. Jorgenson and Daniel T. Slesnick 1987. General Equilibrium Analysis of Natural Gas Price Regulation. In *Public Regulation*, ed. E. E. Bailey. Cambridge: MIT Press. Reprinted by permission.

7. Dale W. Jorgenson and Daniel T. Slesnick 1989. Redistributional Policy and the Measurement of Poverty. In *Research on Economic Inequality*, ed. D. Slottje, vol. 1. Greenwich, CT: JAI Press. Reprinted by permission.

8. Dale W. Jorgenson and Daniel T. Slesnick 1990. Inequality and the Standard of Living. *Journal of Econometrics* 43, Nos. 1/2 (January/February): 103–120. Reprinted by permission of Elsevier Science Publishers B.V.

9. Dale W. Jorgenson, Daniel T. Slesnick, and Peter J. Wilcoxen 1992. Carbon Taxes and Economic Welfare. *Brookings Papers on Economic Activity: Microeconomics 1992:* 393–431. Reprinted by permission.

Welfare
Volume 2: Measuring
Social Welfare

1

Aggregate Consumer Behavior and the Measurement of Social Welfare

Dale W. Jorgenson

This chapter describes a new approach to normative economics, combining the theory of social choice with econometric modeling of aggregate consumer behavior. We first derive a system of aggregate demand functions by exact aggregation over individual demand functions. Finally, we incorporate these measures into a social welfare function, introducing ethical assumptions based on horizontal and vertical equity. To illustrate the application of this approach, we consider the U.S. standard of living and its cost over the period 1947–1985.

1.1 Introduction

The purpose of this chapter is to describe a remarkable convergence that has occurred between economic theory and econometrics over the past decade. This conjunction has taken place between the theory of social choice and econometric modeling of aggregate consumer behavior. The confluence of these two streams of research has produced a new approach to normative economics. This approach has been successfully applied to the evaluation of economic policy, the measurement of poverty and inequality, and the assessment of the standard of living and its cost.

A common problem in the modeling of consumer behavior and social choice is the representation of individual preferences. In the econometric modeling of aggregate consumer behavior, the primary emphasis has been on simplifying aggregate demand functions. The most familiar approach to this problem is the model of a representative consumer. This model is required to justify applications of the theory of individual consumer behavior to aggregate data on prices and quantities consumed. The simplest version of the model is based on identical homothetic preferences for all individuals.

Under identical homothetic preferences aggregate quantities consumed are functions of aggregate expenditure and prices. These functions have precisely the same properties as demand functions in the theory of individual consumer behavior. The condition of identical homothetic preferences was weakened by Gorman (1953) to permit displacements from the origin for individual demand functions. Gorman showed that a necessary and sufficient condition for aggregate demand functions to depend on aggregate expenditure is that all individuals must have parallel linear Engel curves. This condition has been used repeatedly in modeling aggregate consumer behavior.[1]

Gorman's definition of the concept of a representative consumer was significantly broadened by Muellbauer (1975). In Muellbauer's model of a representative consumer individual preferences are identical, but not necessarily homothetic. Aggregate expenditure shares depend on prices and a function of the distribution of individual expenditure that is not restricted to aggregate expenditure. Engel curves are permitted to be nonlinear, so that aggregate quantities consumed depend on the distribution of total expenditure among individuals.[2]

Lau (1977b) has developed a model of aggregate consumer behavior that does not require the notion of a representative consumer. Aggregate demand functions are obtained by exact aggregation over individual demand functions. Differences in individual preferences are incorporated into individual demand functions through attributes of individuals such as demographic characteristics. Aggregate demand functions depend on the joint distribution of attributes and total expenditure over all consuming units through summary statistics of the distribution.

Within the framework provided by Lau (1977b) and Muellbauer (1975), the assumption of identical homothetic preferences for all individuals appears as a highly oversimplified approach to modeling aggregate consumer behavior. This assumption implies excessively stringent restrictions on individual preferences. The implications of these restrictions for consumer behavior at both individual and aggregate levels have been contradicted by the results of empirical research dating back to Engel (1895). The linearity of Engel curves required by Gorman's concept of a representative consumer is also inconsistent with a substantial body of empirical evidence.[3]

In representing individual preferences for the theory of social choice the primary focus is on the precision of the information available. Measures of individual welfare can be distinguished according to measurability. For example, these measures can be classified between those that are cardinal and those that are ordinal. In addition, measures can be distinguished by interpersonal comparability and classified between those that are comparable among individuals and those that are noncomparable. Interpersonal comparisons require information beyond that available from studies of individual preferences.

The classic result of social choice theory is Arrow's (1963) impossibility theorem, which states that ordinal noncomparability of individual welfare orderings implies that a consistent social ordering must be dictatorial, corresponding to the preferences of a single individual. Ordinal noncomparability requires that a social welfare function must be invariant with respect to monotone increasing transformations of individual welfare functions that may differ among individuals. Sen (1970) has shown that the conclusions of Arrow's impossibility theorem are preserved by replacing ordinal noncompatibility by cardinal noncomparability. This requires that a social welfare ordering is unchanged when individual welfare functions are subjected to positive affine transformations that may differ among individuals.

The introduction of interpersonal comparability of individual welfare orderings greatly broadens the class of possible social orderings. For example, d'Aspremont and Gevers (1977), and Maskin (1978) have shown that cardinal unit comparability implies the existence of a class of social orderings that can be represented by utilitarian social welfare functions. A utilitarian social welfare function is an average of individual welfare functions. Cardinal unit comparability requires that a social welfare function is invariant with respect to positive affine transformations with units that are the same for all individuals.

Roberts (1980a) has shown that the class of possible social orderings can be further extended by cardinal full comparability of individual welfare functions. Cardinal full comparability requires that a social welfare function is invariant with respect to positive affine transformations that are the same for all individuals. The corresponding social orderings can be represented by a class of social welfare functions that are sums of two components. The first is an average of individual welfare functions, as in a utilitarian social welfare function. The second represents a measure of dispersion in individual welfare levels. This is a linear homogeneous function of deviations of individual welfare functions from the average.

Within the framework provided by Roberts (1980a) and Sen (1977, 1979b) the assumption of ordinal noncomparability of individual welfare functions results in an extremely specialized approach to the theory of social choice. This assumption embodies the least precise information about individual orderings; accordingly, the selection of an appropriate social ordering is the most severely limited. By providing additional information about individual welfare orderings, the range of possibilities for a social ordering can be considerably broadened. This provides expended scope for the introduction of ethical judgements about horizontal and vertical equity among individuals.

During the past decade considerable progress has been made in filling the gap between the extreme specialization of the theory of social choice that results from ordinal noncomparability of individual welfare functions and the oversimplification of econometric modeling of aggregate consumer behavior implied by the assumption of identical homothetic preferences for all individuals. As a consequence, both econometric modeling and social choice have been greatly enriched. Perhaps more important, the potential links between the two approaches to representing individual preferences have become more apparent.[4]

The conjunction of econometric modeling of aggregate consumer behavior and the theory of social choice has produced a new approach to applications of normative economics. In this chapter the new approach is presented in summary form, incorporating the results of an extensive and growing body of literature. One strand of this literature is devoted to modeling individual and aggregate consumer behavior. A second strand applies the results to the evaluation of economic policies. In this chapter we illustrate the characteristic features of both econometric modeling and its application to the measurement of social welfare.

In section 1.2 we outline the standard methodology for applications of normative economics. This includes measures of individual and social welfare and methods for translating these measures into monetary terms. At the individual level the primary requisites are the individual welfare function and the individual expenditure function. The individual expenditure function, introduced by McKenzie (1957), is defined by the minimum level of total expenditure required to attain a stipulated level of individual welfare for a given price system. This function can be used to generate a money measure of individual welfare.

The social expenditure function originated by Pollak (1981) is defined by the minimum level of aggregate expenditure required to attain a stipulated level of social welfare for a given price system.

Although the social expenditure function is a less familiar concept than the individual expenditure function, the application of the two concepts is precisely analogous. Just as the individual expenditure function can be employed in translating individual welfare into monetary terms, the social expenditure function can be utilized in generating a money measure of social welfare.

To implement the money measures of individual and social welfare presented in section 1.2 we first develop a measure of individual welfare that reflects observed patterns of consumer behavior. For this purpose we outline a method for constructing indirect utility functions for all consuming units in section 1.3. We derive these measures of individual welfare from systems of individual demand functions. The existence of an indirect utility function for each consuming unit is assured by the requirement that individual demand functions are integrable.

To simplify the econometric modeling of consumer behavior we derive a system of aggregate demand functions from systems of individual demand functions by exact aggregation, following Jorgenson, Lau, and Stoker (1980, 1981, 1982). The aggregate demand system depends on summary statistics of the joint distribution of attributes and total expenditure among individuals. We implement this econometric model by statistical methods for combining aggregate time-series and individual cross-section data developed by Jorgenson and Stoker (1986).

The money measure of individual welfare presented in section 1.2 requires only an ordinal and noncomparable representation of individual preferences. Similarly, the derivation of a system of individual demand functions from the indirect utility function for each consuming unit utilizes only ordinal and noncomparable preferences. However, the construction of an aggregate demand system by exact aggregation over individual demand systems implies restrictions on individual consumer behavior that add precision to the information available for measuring individual welfare.

In section 1.3 we define a cardinal measure of individual welfare that is fully comparable among consuming units. This measure utilizes the information made available by restrictions on indirect utility functions implied by exact aggregation. The incorporation of this information into a social welfare function requires the first ethical assumption of our approach to normative economics. This assumption embodies a notion of horizontal equity among individuals, namely, that every individual must be treated symmetrically with any other individual having the same individual welfare function.

In section 1.4 we present a class of social welfare functions introduced by Jorgenson and Slesnick (1983). These social welfare functions are defined on the distribution of cardinal and interpersonally comparable measures of individual welfare. Every member of this class is the sum of an average of levels of individual welfare and a measure of the dispersion of these welfare levels. The selection of an appropriate measure of dispersion incorporates the second ethical assumption of our approach to normative economics. This assumption embodies a notion of vertical equity among individuals.

To illustrate the application of the new approach to normative economics we consider the problem of measuring the performance of an economic system in section 1.5. The objective of an economic system is to generate the highest possible level of social welfare. We present a quantity index of social welfare that can be interpreted as a measure of the standard of living for a society. By comparing changes in aggregate expenditure with changes in the standard of living, we obtain a measure of the cost of living. The standard of living and its cost can be defined for individuals, groups within society, and society as a whole.

We implement our measures of the standard of living and its cost for the United States over the postwar period, 1947–1985. We present a quantity index of social welfare that provides a measure of the standard of living for the U.S. economy as a whole. This index is defined in terms of the money measure of social welfare given in section 1.2. To implement this measure we first convert two different distributions of total expenditure and two price systems into the corresponding distributions of individual welfare. We then express the resulting measures of social welfare in terms of a common price system.

We find that the standard of living in the United States has grown at 2.92 percent per year during the postwar period. This growth rate is more than forty percent higher than the rate of growth of real personal consumption expenditure per capita, a conventional measure of the standard of living. Important biases in this conventional measure can be traced to biases in the cost-of-living index and the population measure. In addition, a significant bias results from the total omission of equity considerations. Section 1.6 provides a summary and conclusion of the chapter and suggests possible directions for further research.

1.2   Preliminaries

In this section we present money measures of individual and social welfare. Our measures of individual welfare are based on the preference orderings of individual consumers. We represent these orderings by means of real-valued individual welfare functions. Our measure of social welfare is based on preferences over social tastes by all individuals. We represent a social ordering by means of a real-valued social welfare function, defined on the distribution of individual welfare over the whole population.

To represent preferences in a form suitable for measuring individual welfare, we take households as consuming units. We assume that expenditures on individual commodities are allocated so as to maximize a household welfare function. As a consequence, the household behaves in the same way as an individual maximizing a utility function, as demonstrated by Samuelson (1956) and Pollak (1981). This model of household behavior is also employed by Becker (1981). We treat households as individuals in measuring social welfare. All subsequent references to individuals are to households, considered as consuming units.

To provide a money measure of individual welfare we represent preferences by means of an individual expenditure function, using the following notation:

p_n — price of the nth commodity, assumed to be the same for all consuming units.

$p = (p_1, p_2, \ldots, p_N)$ — vector of prices of all commodities.

x_{nk} — quantity of the nth commodity consumed by the kth consuming unit ($n = 1, 2, \ldots, N$; $k = 1, 2, \ldots, K$).

$x_k = (x_{1k}, x_{2k}, \ldots, x_{Nk})$ — vector of quantities of all commodities consumed by the kth consuming unit ($k = 1, 2, \ldots, K$).

$M_k = \sum_{n=1}^{N} p_n x_{nk}$ — total expenditure of the kth consuming unit ($k = 1, 2, \ldots, K$).

A_k — vector of attributes of the kth consuming unit ($k = 1, 2, \ldots, K$).

The *individual expenditure function* gives the minimum total expenditure M_k required for the kth consuming unit to achieve the welfare level W_k, given the prices p ($k = 1, 2, \ldots, K$). More formally, the individual expenditure function $M_k(p, W_k, A_k)$ is defined by

$$M_k(p, W_k, A_k) = \min \left\{ M_k = \sum_{n=1}^{N} p_n x_{nk} : W_k(x_k, A_k) \geq W_k \right\}. \qquad (1.2.1)$$

For a given price system we can translate individual welfare into monetary terms by evaluating the individual expenditure function at that level of welfare.[5] If the level of individual welfare W_k is the maximum attainable at total expenditure M_k, this level of expenditure is a money measure of individual welfare at the current price system p.

The individual welfare function and the individual expenditure function can be used to construct measures of the household standard of living and its cost. We illustrate these concepts geometrically in figure 1.1. This figure represents the indifference map for a consuming unit with expenditure function $M_k(p, W_k, A_k)$. For simplicity we consider the case of two commodities ($N = 2$). Consumer equilibrium in the base period is represented by the point A. The corresponding level of individual expenditure $M_k(p^0, W_k^0, A_k)$, divided by the price of

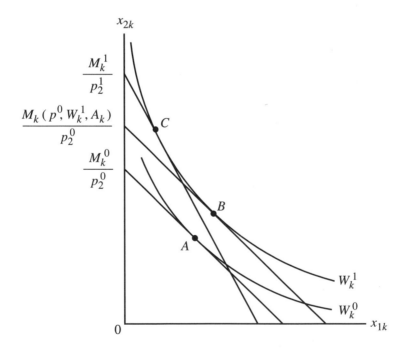

Figure 1.1
Household standard of living and its cost.

the second commodity p_2^0, is given on the vertical axis. This level provides a representation of individual expenditure in terms of units of the second commodity.

Consumer equilibrium in the current period is represented by the point C. To translate the corresponding level of welfare W_k^1 into total expenditure at the prices of the base period, we evaluate the individual expenditure function (1.2.1) at this level of welfare and the base period price system p^0. The resulting level of total expenditure $M_k(p^0, W_k^1, A_k)$ corresponds to consumer equilibrium at the point B. The quantity index given by the ratio between levels of total expenditure $M_k(p^0, W_k^1, A_k)$ and M_k^0 is a measure of the household standard of living. The price index given by the ratio between levels of total expenditure M_k^1 and $M_k(p^0, W_k^1, A_k)$ is a measure of the household cost of living.

Under the Pareto principle a social state represents an improvement over an alternative state if all consuming units are as well off as under the alternative and at least one unit is better off. The Pareto principle provides a partial ordering of social states. This ordering is invariant with respect to monotone increasing transformations of individual welfare that differ among consuming units. Only welfare comparisons that are ordinal and noncomparable among consuming units are required for application of the Pareto principle. The measures of household standard and cost of living we have described are based on comparisons of this type.

The money measure of individual welfare provided by the expenditure function (1.2.1) is a monotone increasing transformation of individual welfare. This transformation depends on the prices faced by the individual consuming unit and on the attributes of the individual. Considered as a measure of individual welfare in its own right, this measure provides all the information about preferences required for applications of the Pareto principle. To obtain a complete ordering of social states we next introduce a social welfare function.

We consider orderings over the set of social states and the set of real-valued individual welfare functions. To describe these social orderings in greater detail we find it useful to introduce the following notation:

x — matrix with N by K elements $\{x_{nk}\}$ describing the social state.

$u = (W_1, W_2, \ldots, W_k)$ — vector of individual welfare functions of all K consuming units.

To represent social orderings in a form suitable for measuring social welfare we consider a class of social welfare functions $W(u, x)$ incorporating a notion of horizontal equity. In particular, we require that if two individuals have identical individual welfare functions, then these functions enter the social welfare functions in the same way. We also incorporate a notion of vertical equity by requiring that the social welfare functions are equity-regarding in the sense of Hammond (1977). This amounts to imposing a version of Dalton's (1920) principle of transfers. This principle requires that a transfer from a household with a high welfare level to a household with a low welfare level that does not reverse their relative positions must increase the level of social welfare.

To provide a money measure of individual welfare, we have found it useful to express individual welfare in terms of total expenditure. Similarly, we find it useful to express social welfare in terms of aggregate expenditure. For this purpose we introduce the *social expenditure function*, defined as the minimum level of total expenditure, $M = \sum_{k=1}^{K} M_k$, required to attain a given level of social welfare, say W, at a specified price system p.[6] More formally, the social expenditure function $M(p, W)$ is defined by

$$M(p, W) = \min \left\{ M = \sum_{k=1}^{K} M_k : W(u, x) \geq W \right\}. \tag{1.2.2}$$

For a given price system we can translate social welfare into monetary terms by evaluating the social expenditure function at that level of welfare. To determine the level of social welfare we first evaluate the individual welfare functions $\{W_k\}$ for all consuming units at the price system p and the distribution of total expenditure $\{M_k\}$. We then evaluate the social welfare function $W(u, x)$. Finally, we express the resulting level of social welfare in terms of a stipulated price system by means of the social expenditure function $M(p, W)$.

Second, we can decompose our money measure of social welfare into money measures of equity and efficiency. Equity reflects the gain in welfare from a more egalitarian distribution of total expenditure. A distribution is more equitable if it is closer to a perfectly egalitarian distribution. Efficiency is the maximum level of social welfare that can be attained by redistributions of aggregate expenditure among individuals. Welfare losses associated with an inequitable distribution of total expenditure are eliminated by this maximization.

To define money measures of equity and efficiency we evaluate the social welfare function at the maximum that can be attained through lump-sum redistributions of aggregate expenditure, $M = \sum_{k=1}^{K} M_k$. This is the maximum level of social welfare that is potentially available and can be taken as a measure of efficiency. Evaluating the social expenditure function at the potential level of welfare, we obtain aggregate expenditure M, so that this level of expenditure is a money measure of efficiency at the current price system p.

Given a money measure of efficiency, we can define a corresponding money measure of equity as the ratio between the money measure of actual social welfare $M(p, W)$ and the money measure of efficiency M. This measure of equity increases as the distribution of total expenditure approaches perfect equality. Using the social expenditure functions, we can express our money measure of social welfare as the product of measures of efficiency and equity

$$M(p, W) = M \cdot \left(\frac{M(p, W)}{M} \right). \tag{1.2.3}$$

The critical feature of this decomposition is that all three measures are expressed in terms of the same price system p.[7]

The social welfare function and the social expenditure function can be employed in defining measures of the social standard of living and its cost. We illustrate these concepts geometrically in figure 1.2. The figure represents the indifference map of a representative consumer with preferences corresponding to the social expenditure function $M(p, W)$. This concept of a representative consumer corresponds to the one proposed by Samuelson (1956) and Pollak (1981). The same concept underlies our model of the household as a consuming unit.

For simplicity we consider the case of two commodities ($N = 2$), as before. Consumer equilibrium at the actual level of social welfare in the base period W^0 is represented by the point A. The corresponding level of aggregate expenditure $M(p^0, W^0)$, divided by the price of the second commodity p_2^0, is given on the vertical axis. This level provides a representation of aggregate expenditure in terms of units of the second commodity. Consumer equilibrium at the level of social welfare in the current period W^1 is represented by the point C. To translate the level of social welfare W^1 into aggregate expenditure at the prices of the base period, we evaluate the social expenditure function (1.2.2) at this level of welfare and the base period price system p^0.

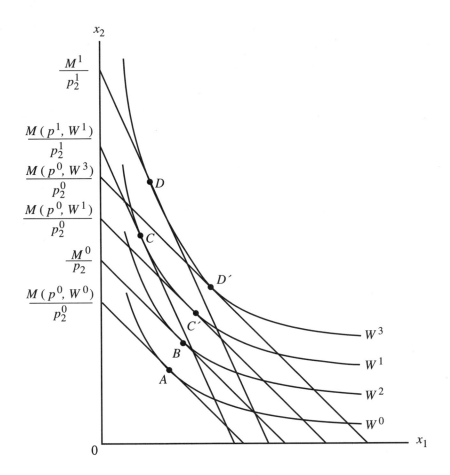

Figure 1.2
Social standard of living and its cost.

The resulting level of aggregate expenditure $M(p^0, W^1)$ corresponds to consumer equilibrium at the point C'.

Aggregate expenditure M^0 is the value of the social expenditure function at the potential level of welfare in the base period, say W^2, expressed in terms of the base period price system p^0. This is the maximum level of welfare that can be attained by lump-sum redistributions of aggregate expenditure. The corresponding consumer equilibrium is represented by the point B. Similarly, consumer equilibrium at the potential level of social welfare in the current period, say W^3, is presented by the point D. This is the maximum level of social welfare that can be attained through lump-sum redistributions of aggregate expenditure M^1 at current prices p^1. We can translate this level of social welfare into aggregate expenditure at the base period price system p^0 by evaluating the expenditure function $M(p^0, W^3)$ at the consumer equilibrium represented by the pint D'.

The quantity index given by the ratio between levels of aggregate expenditure $M(p^0, W^1)$ and $M(p^0, W^0)$ is a measure of the actual standard of living. Similarly, the quantity index represented by the ratio of the levels of aggregate expenditure $M(p^0, W^3)$ and M^0 is the measure of the potential standard of living. The ratio of the actual standard of living to its potential is an index of equity. Finally, the price index given by the ratio between levels of expenditure M^1 and $M(p^0, W^3)$ is the measure of the social cost of living proposed by Pollak (1981).

1.3   Modeling Consumer Behavior

In order to implement the money measures of individual and social welfare presented in section 1.2, we first require individual welfare functions that reflect the preference orderings of individual consuming units. In this section we outline an econometric model of consumer behavior in the United States originated by Jorgenson, Lau, and Stoker (1980, 1981, 1982). A distinctive feature of this model is that it incorporates integrability restrictions for individual demand functions that assure the existence of an indirect utility function for each consuming unit. In section 1.5 below we construct indirect utility functions for all consuming units and utilize the results in developing numerical counterparts for the money measures of individual and social welfare given in figures 1.1 and 1.2.

Our econometric model is based on the theory of exact aggregation. Under exact aggregation the system of aggregate demand functions is obtained by explicit aggregation over individual demand systems. In addition, the aggregate demand system must depend on the attributes and total expenditure of individual consuming units through summary statistics of their joint distribution. Our model incorporates cross-section data on individual quantities consumed, individual total expenditure, and attributes of individual households such as demographic characteristics. We also include time-series data on prices, aggregate quantities consumed, and summary statistics of the joint distribution of total expenditure and attributes of individual households.

Exact aggregation is useful in simplifying the econometric modeling of aggregate consumer behavior. In fact, the special formulations of exact aggregation developed by Gorman (1953) and Muellbauer (1975) were designed precisely for this purpose. Our objective, in addition to modeling aggregate consumer behavior, is to utilize restrictions on individual preferences implied by exact aggregation in generating more precise information for measuring social welfare. For example, we can exploit the exact aggregation restrictions in defining cardinal measures of individual welfare for all consuming units. In addition, we can define interpersonal comparability in terms of these measures of individual welfare. Of course, these properties of individual welfare measures can be utilized for social welfare measurement only in combination with ethical assumptions such as horizontal and vertical equity that we discuss in more detail in section 1.4 below.

To construct an econometric model based on exact aggregation we first represent individual preferences by means of an indirect utility function for each consuming unit, using the following notation:

$w_{nk} = p_n x_{nk}/M_k$ — expenditure share of the nth commodity in the budget of the kth consuming unit $(n = 1, 2, \ldots, N; k = 1, 2, \ldots, K)$.

$w_k = (w_{1k}, w_{2k}, \ldots, w_{Nk})$ — vector of expenditure shares for the kth consuming unit $(k = 1, 2, \ldots, K)$.

$\ln p/M_k = (\ln p_1/M_k, \ln p_2/M_k, \ldots, \ln p_N/M_k)$ — vector of logarithms of ratios of prices to expenditure by the kth consuming unit $(k = 1, 2, \ldots, K)$.

$\ln p = (\ln p_1, \ln p_2, \ldots, \ln p_N)$ — vector of logarithms of prices.

We assume that the kth consuming unit allocates expenditures in accord with the transcendental logarithmic or translog indirect utility function,[8] say V_k, where

$$\ln v_k = G\left(\ln \frac{p'}{M_k} \alpha_p + \frac{1}{2} \ln \frac{p'}{M_k} B_{pp} \ln \frac{p}{M_k} + \ln \frac{p'}{M_k} B_{pA} A_k, A_k\right),$$

$$(k = 1, 2, \ldots, K). \qquad (1.3.1)$$

In this representation the function G is a monotone increasing function of its first argument. The vector α_p and the matrices B_{pp} and B_{pA} are constant parameters that are the same for all consuming units. In addition, the function G depends directly on the attribute vector A_k.[9] This form of the indirect utility function is ordinal and noncomparable among consuming units. Measurability and interpersonal comparability of individual preferences are not required in modeling consumer behavior.

The expenditure shares of the kth consuming unit can be derived by the logarithmic form of Roy's (1943) Identity[10]

$$w_{nk} = \frac{\partial \ln V_k}{\partial \ln(p_n / M_k)} \Big/ \sum_{n=1}^{N} \frac{\partial \ln V_k}{\partial \ln(p_n / M_k)} ,$$

$$(n = 1, 2, \ldots, N; \ k = 1, 2, \ldots, K) . \qquad (1.3.2)$$

Applying this Identity to the translog indirect utility function (1.3.1), we obtain the system of individual expenditure shares

$$w_k = \frac{1}{D_k(p)} \left(\alpha_p + B_{pp} \ln \frac{p}{M_k} + B_{pA} A_k \right), \qquad (k = 1, 2, \ldots, K) , \qquad (1.3.3)$$

where the denominators $\{D_k(p)\}$ take the form

$$D_k(p) = i'\alpha_p + i'B_{pp} \ln \frac{p}{M_k} + i'B_{pA} A_k , \qquad (k = 1, 2, \ldots, K) , \qquad (1.3.4)$$

and i is a vector of ones.

The individual expenditure shares are homogeneous of degree zero in the unknown parameters—α_p, B_{pp}, B_{pA}. By multiplying a given set of these parameters by a constant we obtain another set of parameters that generates the same system of individual budget shares. Accordingly, we can choose a normalization for the parameters without affecting observed patterns of individual expenditure allocation. We find it convenient to employ the normalization

$$i'\alpha_p = -1 .$$

Under this restriction any change in the set of unknown parameters will be reflected in changes in individual expenditure patterns.

The conditions for exact aggregation are that the individual expenditure shares are linear in functions of the attributes $\{A_k\}$ and total expenditures $\{M_k\}$ for all consuming units.[11] These conditions will be satisfied if and only if the terms involving the attributes and expenditures do not appear in the denominators of the expressions for the individual expenditure shares, so that

$i'B_{pp}i = 0$,

$i'B_{pA} = 0$.

The exact aggregation restrictions imply that the denominators $\{D_k(p)\}$ reduce to

$$D(p) = -1 + i'B_{pp} \ln p ,$$

where the subscript k is no longer required, since the denominator is the same for all consuming units. Under these restrictions the individual expenditure shares can be written

$$w_k = \frac{1}{D(p)} (\alpha_p + B_{pp} \ln p - B_{pp}i \cdot \ln M_k + B_{pA}A_k) ,$$

$$(k = 1, 2, \ldots, K) . \qquad (1.3.5)$$

The individual expenditure shares are linear in the logarithms of expenditures $\{\ln M_k\}$ and the attributes $\{A_k\}$, as required by exact aggregation.

To construct an econometric model of aggregate consumer behavior based on exact aggregation we obtain aggregate expenditure shares, say w, by multiplying individual expenditure shares (1.3.5) by expenditure for each consuming unit, adding over all consuming units, and dividing by aggregate expenditure, $M = \sum_{k=1}^{K} M_k$

$$w = \frac{\sum M_k w_k}{M} . \qquad (1.3.6)$$

The aggregate expenditure shares can be written

$$w = \frac{1}{D(p)} \left(\alpha_p + B_{pp} \ln p - B_{pp}i \frac{\sum M_k \ln M_k}{M} + B_{pA} \frac{\sum M_k A_k}{M} \right). \qquad (1.3.7)$$

Aggregate expenditure patterns depend on the distribution of expenditure over all consuming units through summary statistics of the joint distribution of expenditures and attributes—$\sum M_k \ln M_k/M$ and $\{\sum M_k A_k/M\}$. Under exact aggregation systems of individual expenditure shares (1.3.5) for consuming units with identical demographic characteristics can be recovered in one and only one way from the system of aggregate expenditure shares (1.3.7).

The system of individual expenditure shares (1.3.3) can be fitted without requiring that it is generated from an indirect utility function of the form (1.3.1). We say that the system is *integrable* if it can be generated from such an indirect utility function. Since we utilize the indirect utility functions for all consuming units in measuring social welfare, we must impose conditions for integrability on the individual demand functions. A complete set of conditions for integrability[12] is the following:

1. *Homogeneity.* The individual expenditure shares are homogeneous of degree zero in prices and total expenditure.

We can write the individual expenditure shares in the form

$$w_k = \frac{1}{D(p)} \left(\alpha_p + B_{pp} \ln p - B_{pM} \ln M_k + B_{pA} A_k \right), \qquad (k = 1, 2, \ldots, K),$$

where the vector of parameters β_{pM} is constant and the same for all consumer units. Homogeneity implies that this vector must satisfy the restrictions

$$\beta_{pM} = B_{pp} i . \tag{1.3.8}$$

Given the exact aggregation restrictions, there are $N - 1$ restrictions implied by homogeneity.

2. *Summability.* The sum of the individual expenditure shares over all commodity groups is equal to unity

$$i' w_k = 1, \qquad (k = 1, 2, \ldots, K) .$$

We can write the denominator $D(p)$ in (1.3.5) in the form

$$D = -1 + \beta_{Mp} \ln p ,$$

where the vector of parameters β_{Mp} is constant and the same for all commodity groups and all consuming units. Summability implies that this vector must satisfy the restrictions

$$\beta_{Mp} = i' B_{pp} . \tag{1.3.9}$$

Given the exact aggregation restrictions, there are $N - 1$ restrictions implied by summability.

3. *Symmetry.* The matrix of compensated own- and cross-price substitution effects must be symmetric.

If the system of individual expenditure shares can be generated from an indirect utility function of the form (1.3.1), a necessary and sufficient condition for symmetry is that the matrix B_{pp} must be symmetric. Without imposing this condition, we can write the individual expenditure shares in the form

$$w_k = \frac{1}{D(p)} \left(\alpha_p + B_{pp} \ln \frac{p}{M_k} + B_{pA} A_k \right), \qquad (k = 1, 2, \ldots, K) .$$

Symmetry implies that the matrix of parameters B_{pp} must satisfy the restrictions

$$B_{pp} = B'_{pp} . \qquad (1.3.10)$$

The total number of symmetry restrictions is $1/2\, N(N-1)$.

4. *Nonnegativity*. The individual expenditure shares must be non-negative.

By summability the individual expenditure shares sum to unity, so that we can write

$$w_k \geq 0 , \qquad (k = 1, 2, \ldots, K) ,$$

where $w_k \geq 0$ implies $w_{nk} \geq 0$ $(n = 1, 2, \ldots, N)$, and $w_k \neq 0$.

Since the translog indirect utility function is quadratic in the logarithms of prices, we can always choose the prices so that the individual expenditure shares violate the nonnegativity conditions. Accordingly, we cannot impose restrictions on the parameters of the translog indirect utility functions that would imply nonnegativity of the individual expenditure shares for all prices and total expenditure. Instead we consider restrictions on the parameters that imply monotonicity of the system of individual demand functions for all nonnegative expenditure shares.

5. *Monotonicity*. The matrix of compensated own- and cross-price substitution effects must be nonpositive definite.

We introduce the definition due to Martos (1969) of a *strictly merely positive subdefinite matrix*, namely, a real symmetric matrix S such that

$$x'Sx < 0$$

implies $Sx > 0$ or $Sx < 0$. A necessary and sufficient condition for monotonicity is either that the translog indirect utility function is homothetic or that B_{pp}^{-1} exists and is strictly merely positive subdefinite.[13]

In implementing the econometric model of consumer behavior we divide consumer expenditures among five commodity groups. These groups are aggregates defined on a much more detailed classification of commodities, as described by Jorgenson, Slesnick, and Stoker (1987,

1988). We assume that the indirect utility functions ar homothetically separable in prices of the commodities within each group:

1. *Energy*: Expenditures on electricity, natural gas, heating oil, and gasoline.

2. *Food*: Expenditures on all food products, including tobacco and alcohol.

3. *Consumer goods*: Expenditures on all other nondurable goods.

4. *Capital services*: The service flow from consumer durables and housing.

5. *Consumer services*: Expenditures on consumer services, such as car repairs, medical services, entertainment, and so on.

We employ the following demographic characteristics as attributes of individual households:

1. *Family size*: 1, 2, 3, 4, 5, 6, and 7 or more persons.

2. *Age of head*: 16–24, 25–34, 35–44, 45–54, 55–64, 65 and over.

3. *Region of residence*: Northeast, North Central, South, and West.

4. *Race*: White, nonwhite.

5. *Type of residence*: Urban, rural.

Our cross-section observations on individual expenditures for each commodity group and demographic characteristics of individual households are for the year 1973 from the 1972–1973 Survey of Consumer Expenditures (CES).[14] Our time-series observations are based on data on personal consumption expenditures from the U.S. National Income and Product Accounts (NIPA) for the years 1947 to 1985.[15] Price for each commodity group are defined in terms of translog price indexes computed from detailed prices included in NIPA for each year. We employ time-series data on the distribution of expenditures over all households and among demographic groups based on *Current Population Reports*.[16]

In our application we treat the expenditure shares for five commodity groups as endogenous variables, so that we estimate four equations. As unknown parameters we have four elements of the vector α_p, four expenditure coefficients of the vector $B_{pp}i$, sixteen attribute coefficients for each of the four equations in the matrix B_{pA}, and ten price coefficients in the matrix B_{pp}, which is constrained to be symmetric. The expenditure coefficients are sums of price coefficients in the corresponding equation, so that we have a total of 82 unknown parameters. Jorgenson and Slesnick (1990) have estimated the complete model, subject to inequality restrictions implied by monotonicity of the individual expenditure shares, by pooling time-series and cross-section data.[17] The results are given in the appendix to this chapter.

Provided that the parameters of the model of aggregate expenditures are identified, the nonlinear three-stage least squares estimator introduced by Jorgenson and Laffont (1974) could be employed to estimate the unknown parameters from aggregate time-series data alone. A necessary condition for identification is that the number of free parameters in the aggregate model must be less than the total number of instruments, assuming that no multicollinearity exists among the instruments. This condition would require a very large number of instruments to identify all the unknown parameters from our model for aggregate expenditures. Accordingly, we consider methods of estimation that combine individual cross-section data with aggregate time-series data to achieve identification.[18]

To estimate the complete model of individual and aggregate expenditures we employ the method of nonlinear three-stage least squares for pooling time-series and cross-section data introduced by Jorgenson and Stoker (1986). Our objective is to estimate the unknown parameters—α_p, B_{pp}, and B_{pA}—subject to the restrictions implied by integrability. To solve this nonlinear programming problem we utilize the SOL-NPSOL algorithm of Gill, Murray, Saunders, and Wright (1983). This algorithm is based on the solution of a nonlinear programming problem by means of a sequence of quadratic programming problems.

1.4   Individual and Social Welfare

A distinctive feature of the econometric model presented in section 1.3 is that systems of individual demand functions can be recovered uniquely from the aggregate demand system. By requiring that the individual demand functions be integrable, we can recover indirect utility functions for all consuming units. In this section we define cardinal measures of individual welfare that are fully comparable among individuals in terms of these indirect utility functions.

Under exact aggregation the translog indirect utility function for the kth consuming unit V_k can be written

$$\ln V_k = \ln p'\alpha_p + \frac{1}{2} \ln p'B_{pp} \ln p - D(p) \ln[M_k / m_0(p, A_k)] ,$$

$$(k = 1, 2, \ldots, K) . \qquad (1.4.1)$$

In this representation the function $m_0(p, A_k)$ is the *general translog household equivalence scale* and can be interpreted as the number of household equivalent members. This equivalence scale takes the form

$$\ln m_0 = \frac{1}{D(p)}\left[\ln m(A_k)'\alpha_p + \frac{1}{2}\ln m(A_k)'B_{pp}\ln m(A_k) + \ln m(A_k)'B_{pp}\ln p\right],$$

$$(k = 1, 2, \ldots, K), \qquad\qquad (1.4.2)$$

where

$$\ln m(A_k) = B_{pp}^{-1}B_{pA}A_k, \qquad (k = 1, 2, \ldots, K). \qquad\qquad (1.4.3)$$

We refer to the scales $\{m(A_k)\}$ as the *commodity specific translog household equivalence scales.*[19]

Given the indirect utility function (1.4.1) for each consuming unit, we can express total expenditure as a function of prices, the general household equivalence scale, and the level of utility

$$\ln M_k = \frac{1}{D(p)}\left[\ln p'\left(\alpha_p + \frac{1}{2}B_{pp}\ln p\right) - \ln V_k\right] + \ln m_0(p, A_k),$$

$$(k = 1, 2, \ldots, K). \qquad\qquad (1.4.4)$$

We refer to this function as the *translog expenditure function.* The translog expenditure function gives the minimum level of expenditure required for the k*th* consuming unit to achieve the utility level V_k, given the prices p $(k = 1, 2, \ldots, K)$.

The first step in measuring social welfare is to select representations of the individual welfare functions. We define individual welfare for the k*th* consuming unit, say W_k $(k = 1, 2, \ldots, K)$, as the logarithm of the translog indirect utility function (1.4.1)

$$W_k = \ln V_k$$

$$= \ln p'\alpha_p + \frac{1}{2}\ln p'B_{pp}\ln p - D(p)\ln[M_k / m_0(p, A_k)],$$

$$(k = 1, 2, \ldots, K). \qquad\qquad (1.4.5)$$

It is important to emphasize that we have utilized the exact aggregation restrictions given in section 1.3 in this representation of the individual welfare function. These restrictions add precision to the information about individual preferences available from the representation of the indirect utility function (1.3.1).

The appeal of the measures of individual welfare (1.4.5) at an intuitive level is based on the fact that they incorporate three types of information that are obviously relevant to welfare measurement. Total expenditure M_k corresponds to size of the household budget, while the number of household equivalent member $m_0(p, A_k)$ is an indicator of the size of consuming unit. The budget and the size of the household are combined into a "per capita" measure of total expenditure. Transforming expenditure per capita logarithmically implies that increments in individual welfare correspond to proportional changes in the resources of the household. Finally, prices faced by the household enter through a linear transformation that is the same for all consuming units. Household size also depends on prices since the preferences of household members are not necessarily identical.

More formally, individual welfare is a linear function (1.4.5) of the logarithm of total expenditure per household equivalent member $\ln[M_k/m_0(p, A_k)]$ with an intercept and slope coefficient that depend only on prices $p(k = 1, 2, \ldots, K)$. This property is invariant with respect to positive affine transformations that are the same for all consuming units, so that the individual welfare function (1.4.5) provides a cardinal measure of individual welfare that is fully comparable among units.[20] The incorporation of measures of individual welfare based on the individual welfare function (1.4.5) into a social welfare function requires an ethical judgement about horizontal equity among individuals. We assume that every individual should be treated symmetrically with any other individual having the same welfare function.

To represent social orderings in a form suitable for measuring social welfare we consider the class of social welfare functions introduced by Jorgenson and Slesnick (1983)

$$W(u, x) = \ln \bar{V} - \gamma(x) \left[\frac{\sum_{k=1}^{K} m_0(p, A_k) \ln V_k - \ln \bar{V}^{-\rho}}{\sum_{k=1}^{K} m_0(p, A_k)} \right]^{-1/\rho} . \qquad (1.4.6)$$

The first term in the social welfare functions (1.4.6) corresponds to an average of individual welfare levels over all consuming units

$$\ln \bar{V} = \frac{\sum_{k=1}^{K} m_0(p, A_k) \ln V_k}{M_k}$$

$$= \ln p' \left(\alpha_p + \frac{1}{2} B_{pp} \ln p \right) - D(p) \frac{\sum_{k=1}^{K} m_0(p, A_k) \ln[M_k / m_0(p, A_k)]}{\sum_{k=1}^{K} m_0(p, A_k)} .$$

The second term in (1.4.6) is a linear homogeneous function of deviations of levels of individual welfare from the average. This is a measure of dispersion in individual welfare levels. The social welfare functions (1.4.6) are represented in a form that is invariant with respect to positive affine transformations and provide cardinal measures of social welfare.[21]

The parameter ρ in the representation (1.4.6) determines the curvature of the social welfare function in the individual welfare functions $\{W_k(x)\}$. We refer to this parameter as the *degree of aversion to inequality*. By selecting an appropriate value of this parameter, we can incorporate ethical judgements about vertical equity among individuals into the social welfare function. The range of admissible values of ρ is from negative unity to negative infinity. In the limiting case of negative infinity the second term in (1.4.6) vanishes, so that the social welfare functions (1.4.6) reduce to the utilitarian case, corresponding to averages of welfare levels over all consuming units. This limiting case gives the least possible weight to equity considerations. In the applications presented in the following section we take ρ to be negative unity in order to give the greatest possible weight to these consideration.

At this point we have generated a class of social welfare functions capable of expressing the implications of a variety of ethical judgements. The Pareto principle requires that an increase in individual welfare must increase social welfare. This condition implies that the increase in the first term in (1.4.6), representing the average level of individual welfare, must exceed the increase in the second term, representing the dispersion in individual welfare. We assume that the function $\gamma(x)$ in (1.4.6) must take the maximum value consistent with the Pareto principle, so that

$$\gamma(x) = \left\{ \frac{\sum_{k=!\,j}^{K} m_0(p, A_k)}{\sum_{k=1}^{K} m_0(p, A_k)} \left[1 + \left[\frac{\sum_{k=!\,j}^{K} m_0(p, A_k)}{m_0(p, A_j)} \right]^{-(\rho+1)} \right] \right\}^{1/\rho} \qquad (1.4.7)$$

where

$$m_0(p, A_j) = \min_k m_0(p, A_k), \qquad (k = 1, 2, \ldots, K).$$

This assumption gives maximum weight to the second term on (1.4.6), representing equity considerations.

In order to determine the form of the social expenditure function $M(p, W)$ in (1.2.2), we can maximize the social welfare function (1.4.6) for a fixed level of aggregate expenditure by equalizing total expenditure per household equivalent member $[M_k/m_0(p, A_k)\}$ for all consuming units. For the translog indirect utility function the maximum value of social welfare for a given level of aggregate expenditure takes the form

$$\ln \bar{V} = \ln p' \left(\alpha_p + \frac{1}{2} B_{pp} \ln p \right) - D(p) \ln \left[M \Big/ \sum_{k=1}^{K} m^0(p, A_k) \right]. \qquad (1.4.8)$$

As before, this is the maximum level of welfare that is potentially available and can be taken as a measure of efficiency. This measure of efficiency does not depend on the value of the degree of aversion to inequality ρ.

If aggregate expenditure is distributed so as to equalize total expenditure per household equivalent member, the level of individual welfare is the same for all consuming units. For this distribution of total expenditure the social welfare function reduces to the average level of individual welfare $\ln \bar{V}$. The value of social welfare is obtained by evaluating the translog indirect utility function (1.4.1) at total expenditure per household equivalent member $M/\sum_{k=1}^{K} m_0(p, A_k)$ for the economy as a whole. This is an algebraic representation of the preferences of the representative consumer depicted in figure 1.2.

We can express aggregate expenditure as a function of the level of social welfare and prices

$$\ln M(p, W) = \frac{1}{D(p)} \left[\ln p' \left(\alpha_p + \frac{1}{2} B_{pp} \ln p \right) - \right] + \ln \left[\sum_{k=1}^{K} m_0(p, A_k) \right].$$

$$(1.4.9)$$

The value of aggregate expenditure is obtained by evaluating the translog individual expenditure function (1.4.4) at the level of social welfare W and the number of household equivalent members $\sum_{k=1}^{K} m_0(p, A_k)$ for the economy as a whole. This is the form of the social expenditure function (1.2.2) used in constructing numerical counterparts of measures of the social standard of living and its cost represented in figure 1.2.[22]

1.5   The Standard of Living and Its Cost

The measurement of the standard of living and its cost are classic problems in the application of normative economics. Measurement of the standard of living is the objective of the approach to evaluating national income introduced by Hicks (1940) and discussed by Samuelson (1950). Chipman and Moore (1973, 1980b) have demonstrated that the compensation principle proposed by Hicks provides a valid indicator of social welfare only if preferences are identical and homothetic for all consuming units. Sen (1976a, 1979a) has revived interest in this problem, applying rank-order weights to elements of the matrix x that describes the social state. Hammond (1978) has shown that Sen's approach requires preferences of the type considered by Gorman (1953) for its validity.

In this section we illustrate the implementation of the approach to normative economics outlined in section 1.2. For this purpose we consider the problem of measuring the performance of the U.S. economy over the postwar period, 1947–1985. We introduce a quantity index of social welfare that can be interpreted as a measure of the standard of living of a society. We define the quantity index of social welfare, say Q_A, as the ratio of two levels of aggregate expenditure per capita

$$Q_A(p^0, W^0, W^1) = \frac{M(p^0, W^1) \big/ \sum_{k=1}^{K^1} m_0(p^0, A_k)}{M(p^0, W^0) \big/ \sum_{k=1}^{K^0} m_0(p^0, A_k)}. \tag{1.5.1}$$

The numerator of our quantity index of social welfare (1.5.1) is the aggregate expenditure per capita required to attain the current level of social welfare W^1 at the base period price system p^0. The denominator of the index (1.5.1) is the expenditure per capita required to attain the base period level of welfare W^0 at this price system. Our measure of the size of the population in each period is the number of household equivalent members for society as a whole. The current number of households is K^1, while the base period number of households is K^0. The number of households varies over our sample period, 1947–1985, approaching one hundred million by the end of the period.

The social welfare function (1.4.6) and the translog social expenditure function (1.4.9) can be employed in implementing the index of social welfare (1.5.1). To obtain the base level of social welfare W^0, we evaluate the social welfare function at the base period price system p^0 and the base period distribution of total expenditure $\{M_k^0\}$. We can express the current level of social welfare W^1 in terms of the social welfare function by replacing the base period price system and distribution of total expenditure with the current price system p^1 and the current distribution of total expenditure $\{M_k^1\}$. It is important to emphasize that we have the degree of aversion to inequality ρ in (1.4.6) equal to negative unity, which gives maximum weight to equity considerations.

Using the social expenditure function, we can express the quantity index of social welfare (1.5.1) in the form

$$\ln Q_A(p^0, W^{0,}W^1) = \frac{1}{D(p^0)}\,(W^0 - W^1)\,.\qquad (1.5.2)$$

We refer to the index Q_A as the *translog social standard of living index*. If this index is greater than unity, actual social welfare has increased; otherwise, social welfare has remained the same or decreased.

Next, we decompose our quantity index of social welfare (1.5.2) into the product of an index of efficiency and an index of equity. For this purpose we first determine the maximum level of welfare, say W^3, that can be attained through lump-sum redistributions of aggregate total expenditure $M^1 = \sum M_k^1$. Aggregate expenditure must be distributed so as to equalize individual expenditure per capita, so that the social welfare function reduces to average individual welfare (1.4.8)

$$W^3 = \ln \bar{V}^1$$

$$= \ln p^{1'}\!\left(\alpha_p + \frac{1}{2}\,B_{pp}\ln p^1\right) - D(p^1)\ln\!\left[M^1 \Big/ \sum_{k=1}^{K^1} m_0(p_1, A_k)\right].\quad (1.5.3)$$

This is the maximum level of social welfare that is potentially available in the current period and can be taken as a measure of efficiency. This measure does not depend on the degree of aversion to inequality ρ, since the second term in the social welfare function (1.4.6) is identically equal to zero.

We can define the quantity index of efficiency, say Q_p, as the ratio of two levels of aggregate expenditure per capita

$$Q_p(p^0, W^2, W^3) = \frac{M(p^0, W^3) / \sum_{k=1}^{K^1} m_0(p^0, A_k)}{M(p^0, W^2) / \sum_{k=1}^{K^0} m_0(p^0, A_k)}$$

$$= \frac{M(p^0, W^3) / \sum_{k=1}^{K^1} m_0(p, A_k)}{M^0 / \sum_{k=1}^{K^0} m_0(p, A_k)}, \tag{1.5.4}$$

where M^0 is base period expenditure.

The numerator of our quantity index of efficiency (1.5.4) is the aggregate expenditure per capita required to attain the potential level of social welfare in the current period W^3 at the base period price system p^0. The denominator of our index is the expenditure per capita required to attain the potential level of welfare in the base period W^2 at this price system. The quantity index of efficiency (1.5.4) is the ratio of money measures of efficiency in the current period and the base period, both evaluated at the base period price system p^0. This index is independent of the degree of aversion to inequality ρ.

We can express potential levels of social welfare in the base period W^2 and the current period W^3 in terms of average individual welfare (1.4.8). Using the social expenditure function, we can express the quantity index of efficiency (1.5.4) in the form

$$\ln Q_p(p^0, W^2, W^3) = \frac{1}{D(p^0)} (W^2 - W^3). \tag{1.5.5}$$

We refer to the index Q_p as the *translog efficiency index*. If this index is greater than unity, potential social welfare has increased; otherwise, potential welfare has remained the same or decreased.

Finally, we can define a quantity index of equity, say Q_E, as the ratio of the index of social welfare to the index of efficiency

$$Q_E = \frac{Q_A}{Q_P} = \frac{M(p^0, W^1)/M(p^0, W^3)}{M(p^0, W^0)/M^0}. \tag{1.5.6}$$

The numerator of our quantity index of equity (1.5.6) is a money measure of equity in the current period, evaluated at the base period price system p^0. Similarly, the denominator is the money measure of equity in the base period, evaluated at this same price system. These measures depend on the degree of aversion to inequality ρ.

Using the social expenditure function, we express the quantity index of equity (1.5.6) in the form

$$\ln Q_E(p^0, W^0, W^1, W^2, W^3) = \frac{1}{D(p^0)} \, [(W^0 - W^1) - (W^2 - W^3)] \, . \qquad (1.5.7)$$

We refer to the index Q_E as the *translog equity index*. If this index is greater than unity, equity has increased; otherwise, equity has remained the same or decreased.

In section 1.4 we have observed that the social welfare function (1.4.6) provides a cardinal measure of social welfare. Since the logarithms of translog indexes of the standard of living, efficiency, and equity are proportional to differences between values of the social welfare function, they also provide cardinal measures of social welfare. Similarly, growth rates of these indexes, defined in terms of differences between successive logarithms, are cardinal measures of changes in social welfare.

To define a social cost-of-living index we first consider the ratio of nominal expenditure per capita, as follows

$$\ln \frac{M^1 \Big/ \sum_{k=1}^{K^1} m_0(p^1, A_k)}{M^0 \Big/ \sum_{k=1}^{K^0} m_0(p^0, A_k)} = \ln \frac{M(p^1, W^3) \Big/ \sum_{k=1}^{K^1} m_0(p^1, A_k)}{M(p^0, W^2) \Big/ \sum_{k=1}^{0} m_0(p^0, A_k)} \, . \qquad (1.5.8)$$

The base period level of aggregate expenditure M^0 is a money measure of potential social welfare, evaluated at base period prices p^0. Similarly, the current level of aggregate expenditure M^1 is a measure of potential welfare at current prices p^1.

Next, we decompose our index of nominal aggregate expenditure (1.5.8) into the product of an index of efficiency and a social cost-of-living index. We can rewrite the nominal expenditure index (1.5.8) as follows;

$$\ln \frac{M^1 \Big/ \sum_{k=1}^{K^1} m_0(p^1, A_k)}{M^0 \Big/ \sum_{k=1}^{0} m_0(p^0, A_k)} = \ln Q_p + \ln P \, ,$$

where Q_p is the translog index of efficiency (1.5.5) and the index P is the *translog social cost-of-living index* introduced by Jorgenson and Slesnick (1983)

$$\ln P(p^1, p^0, W^3) = \ln M^1 - \frac{1}{D(p^0)} \, [\ln p^0(\alpha_p + B_{pp} \ln p^0) - W^3]$$

$$+ \ln \sum_{k=1}^{K^1} m_0(p^0, A_k) \, . \qquad (1.5.9)$$

To construct the translog social cost-of-living index we first determine the potential level of welfare W^3 from average individual welfare (1.4.8). The social cost-of-living index is the ratio of the aggregate expenditure required to attain the potential level of welfare in the current period W^3 at current prices p^1 to the expenditure required to attain this level of welfare at base period prices p^0. Since this index depends only on the potential level of social welfare W^3, it is independent of the degree of aversion to inequality ρ. If the translog social cost-of-living index is greater than unity and aggregate expenditure is constant, then social welfare is decreased by the change in prices.

As an illustration of the standard of living index Q_A in (1.5.1) and the cost-of-living index P in (1.5.9), we can assess the impact of changes in the price system p and the distribution of total expenditure $\{M_k\}$ on the standard of living and its cost for the U.S. economy. The first column of table 1.1 gives personal consumption expenditures for the U.S. in nominal terms, annually, for the postwar period 1947–1985. This is aggregate expenditure M, the sum of total expenditure over all U.S. households $\sum_{k=1}^{K} M_k$.

To transform aggregate expenditure into a measure of the standard of living the first step is to express total expenditure per capita in real terms. The second column of table 1.1 gives the number of household equivalent members $\sum_{k=1}^{K} m_0(p, A_k)$ of the U.S. population; the third column gives the social cost-of-living index P in (1.5.9). The fourth column of this table presents real expenditure per capita in constant prices of 1982. This is a measure of potential social welfare and is proportional to the translog efficiency index Q_p in (1.5.4).

The final step in constructing a measure of the U.S. standard of living is to transform real expenditure per capita by a measure of equity. The fifth column of table 1.1 gives an index of equity that is proportional to the translog equity index Q_E in (1.5.6). The product of the equity index and real expenditure per capita is the standard of living index presented in the sixth column of the table. This is a measure of actual social welfare and is proportional to the translog social welfare index Q_A in (1.5.2). For the period 1947–1985 the average annual rate of growth of the standard of living is 2.92 percent. The average growth rate of the standard of living during the first half of the period, 1947–1966, is 3.05 percent, while the growth rate during the second half of the period, 1966–1985, is 2.78 percent.

For the postwar period as a whole the average annual growth rate of real expenditure per capita in the U.S. is 2.51 percent, while the

Table 1.1
The U.S. standard of living and its cost

Year	Personal consumption expenditure (billions)	Household equivalent members (millions)	Cost-of-living index (1982 = 1.000)	Real personal consumption expenditures per capita (1982 dollars)	Equity index	Standard of living (1982 dollars)
1947	156.330	161.242	0.2585	3750.81	0.5800	2175.62
1948	171.119	163.591	0.2756	3795.93	0.5755	2184.49
1949	174.723	162.680	0.2750	3905.82	0.5701	2226.54
1950	186.915	164.601	0.2797	4038.26	0.5802	2343.18
1951	206.998	166.169	0.2953	4217.79	0.5769	2433.09
1952	221.747	168.225	0.3029	4351.11	0.5769	2510.22
1953	234.881	170.427	0.3110	4432.16	0.5727	2538.21
1954	241.761	175.073	0.3135	4404.49	0.5725	2521.43
1955	255.346	180.029	0.3160	4488.57	0.5696	2556.90
1956	269.831	180.898	0.3199	4663.36	0.5740	2676.59
1957	286.401	184.160	0.3299	4714.00	0.5678	2676.63
1958	300.039	187.189	0.3370	4756.31	0.5753	2736.25
1959	319.827	186.742	0.3434	4987.02	0.5974	2929.38
1960	334.775	186.471	0.3491	5143.30	0.6036	3104.35
1961	347.838	189.014	0.3524	5221.56	0.6072	3170.45
1962	366.530	193.632	0.3574	5296.98	0.6074	3217.42
1963	384.651	195.504	0.3631	5418.27	0.6147	3330.70
1964	411.260	197.879	0.3683	5643.63	0.6134	3462.04
1965	440.877	198.495	0.3758	5910.95	0.6193	3660.68
1966	475.770	200.017	0.3850	6178.34	0.6289	3885.39
1967	506.624	203.406	0.3944	6315.29	0.6330	3997.63
1968	549.902	203.812	0.4087	6601.39	0.6370	4204.80
1969	596.498	205.916	0.4256	6805.70	0.6400	4355.54
1970	646.614	207.661	0.4453	6993.22	0.6439	4503.04
1971	692.730	210.087	0.4640	7107.06	0.6456	4588.21
1972	755.144	211.358	0.4820	7412.87	0.6490	4810.91
1973	829.853	212.996	0.5091	7653.49	0.6509	4981.76
1974	920.073	214.221	0.5555	7731.73	0.6552	5065.95
1975	1020.559	215.620	0.5993	7898.35	0.6587	5202.82
1976	1126.930	217.266	0.6352	8165.80	0.6631	5414.71
1977	1251.219	218.557	0.6770	8456.41	0.6680	5648.79
1978	1398.152	219.934	0.7232	8790.02	0.6737	5921.93
1979	1569.639	221.262	0.7848	9039.71	0.6699	6055.94
1980	1758.997	227.600	0.8631	8954.41	0.6686	5986.71
1981	1950.728	230.454	0.9424	8982.47	0.6698	6016.18
1982	2100.303	232.600	1.0000	9029.68	0.6735	6081.91
1983	2266.985	235.150	1.0430	9243.11	0.6734	6224.20
1984	2451.936	238.049	1.0863	9481.82	0.6764	6413.26
1985	2626.406	241.594	1.1180	9724.02	0.6782	6594.94

average growth rate of equity is 0.41 percent. Growth in equity is 14 percent of the growth in the U.S. standard of living, while growth in efficiency is 86 percent of welfare growth. It is important to emphasize that we have selected a social welfare function from the class (1.4.6), introduced by Jorgenson and Slesnick (1983), that gives the greatest weight to equity considerations. In particular, we have selected values of $\gamma(x)$ and ρ that give maximum weight to the dispersion in individual welfare levels.

Inspection of the index of equity given in the fifth column of table 1.1 reveals that all of the growth in equity occurred during the periods 1958–1978 and 1983–1985. During the twenty-year period 1958–1978, the average growth rate of the U.S. standard of living is 3.86 percent. The growth rate of real expenditure per capita is 3.07 percent, while the growth rate of equity is 0.79 percent. Growth in equity is 20.5 percent of the growth in the standard of living, while growth in efficiency is 79.5 percent. By contrast the contributions of equity to growth in the U.S. standard of living during the periods 1947–1958 and 1978–1983 are slightly negative.

The problem that remains is to compare the measure of growth in the U.S. standard of living presented in table 1.1 with a more conventional alternative. One alternative measure of the standard of living is real expenditure per capita, where a head-count of the population is used in place of the number of household equivalent members and the consumer price index (CPI) is used in place of the social cost-of-living index. Real expenditure per capita, measured in this way, grows at 2.07 percent per year or only 70.9 percent of the growth in our welfare-based measure of the U.S. standard of living. The bias in the alternative measure grows at 0.85 percent per year or 29.1 percent of standard of living growth. We conclude that the growth of the bias is the same order of magnitude as the growth of the conventional measure of the standard of living.

The first difficulty with the conventional measure of the U.S. standard of living arises from the use of the consumer price index in place of the social cost-of-living index. The consumer price index is based on a model of a representative consumer and is independent of the level of social welfare. This price index measures the social cost of living only under the assumption of identical homothetic preferences for all consuming units. The cost-of-living index presented in the third column of the table grows at 3.85 percent per year for the postwar period 1947–1985. By contrast the consumer price index, compiled by the Bureau of Labor Statistics, grows at 4.14 percent per year. The bias in the consumer price index grows at 0.29 percent per year and accounts for 34.1 percent of the overall bias in the growth of our welfare-based measure of the U.S. standard of living.

The second difficulty with the conventional measure of the U.S. standard of living can be traced to the use of a population head-count in place of the welfare-based number of household equivalent members of the population. The number of household equivalent members presented in the second column of the table grows at 1.06 percent per year for the postwar period 1947–1985. By contrast the U.S. population grows at 1.21 percent per year. This bias in the population head-count, relative to our welfare-based measure grows at 0.15 percent per year and accounts for 17.6 percent of the overall bias in measuring standard of living growth.

Finally, the conventional measure of the U.S. standard of living omits equity considerations altogether. The equity index presented in the fifth column of the table grows at 0.41 percent per year and accounts for 48.2 percent of the overall bias in standard of living growth of 0.85 percent per year. We conclude that the consumer price index, the head-count measure of the population, and the omission of equity considerations are all important sources of bias in the conventional measure of the growth of the U.S. standard of living.

1.6   Summary and Conclusion

In this chapter we have summarized a new approach to applications of normative economics. This approach has resulted from the convergence of the econometric modeling of consumer behavior and the theory of social choice. The key to this conjunction is the development of measures of individual welfare that are cardinal and fully comparable among individuals. These measures incorporate restrictions on preferences implied by exact aggregation. The added precision in representing individual preferences provides the information needed to implement the concept of a social welfare function, originated by Bergson (1938) and discussed by Samuelson (1947).[23]

Since the path-breaking work of Atkinson (1970) and Kolm (1969), the measurement of social welfare has been based on explicit social welfare functions. However, the social welfare functions introduced by Atkinson and Kolm are defined on the distribution of "income" or total expenditure rather than the distribution of individual welfare.[24]

Muellbauer (1974b,c) has defined social welfare functions on the distribution of money measures of individual welfare. This approach has also been employed by Deaton and Muellbauer (1980b), King (1983a,b), and McKenzie (1982).

Roberts (1980c) has derived restrictions on preferences under which measures of social welfare based on the distribution of money measures of individual welfare coincide with measures based on the distribution of individual welfare itself. In the absence of restrictions on the class of social welfare functions, individuals must have identical homothetic preferences. With no restrictions on individual preferences, the social welfare functions must be dictatorial in the sense of Arrow (1963).

It is obvious that the assumption of identical homothetic preferences greatly oversimplifies the modeling of aggregate consumer behavior. The restrictions on preferences implied by exact aggregation are much weaker and permit a more flexible approach to the modeling of consumer behavior. Similarly, the class of dictatorial social welfare functions is too narrow to provide an adequate basis for expressing alternative ethical judgements about horizontal and vertical equity among individuals. We generate a much broader class of social welfare functions by utilizing cardinal full comparability of individual welfare functions.

The approach to normative economics we have presented in this chapter can be applied to the evaluation of alternative economic policies. Jorgenson, Lau, and Stoker (1980, 1981, 1982) have implemented the concept of money metric individual welfare, defined as the difference between money measures of individual welfare corresponding to each policy, expressed in terms of a common price system. This concept of money metric individual welfare includes the compensating and equivalent variations in total expenditure introduced by Hicks (1942).

Money metric individual welfare provides the information required for ranking alternative economic policies on the basis of the Pareto principle. For this purpose only ordinal and noncomparable measures of individual welfare are needed. However, the resulting ordering of policies is incomplete and the possibility of establishing a basis for choice among alternative policies is remote. To provide a complete ordering of economic policies, Jorgenson and Slesnick (1985a) have introduced the concept of money metric social welfare.

Money metric social welfare is defined as the difference between money measures of social welfare corresponding to each policy, expressed in terms of a common price system. By introducing money measures of equity and efficiency, as defined in section 1.2, it is possible to decompose the impact of alternative policies into effects on equity and efficiency. Jorgenson and Slesnick (1985a,c) have employed this approach in evaluating alternative policies for price regulation and taxation of petroleum production in the United States. Jorgenson and Slesnick (1985b, 1987b) have analyzed alternative policies for regulation of natural gas prices in the United States.

The decomposition of money measures of social welfare into components that can be identified with equity and efficiency makes it possible to analyze the impact of redistributional policy on social welfare. Jorgenson and Slesnick (1984a,b) have introduced a money measure of inequality, defined as the difference between the money measures of actual and potential welfare presented in section 1.2. This measure of inequality can be interpreted as the maximum gain to society from lump-sum redistributions of aggregate expenditure among consuming units.

Jorgenson and Slesnick (1989) have considered the elimination of poverty as an objective of redistributional policy. For this purpose a poverty line for individual consuming units can be defined in terms of levels of individual welfare. The optimal policy for the elimination of poverty requires lump-sum transfers of expenditure to consuming units below the poverty line. Measures of inequality can be decomposed into the gains to society from the elimination of poverty and the additional gains from reduction of the remaining inequality.

Our overall conclusion is that the convergence of econometric modeling of aggregate consumer behavior and the theory of social choice has proved to be very fruitful. However, a great deal remains to be done to exploit the remaining possibilities for further research. An immediate objective is to incorporate labor-leisure choice into the modeling of aggregate consumer behavior. A second objective is to embed labor-leisure choice and the allocation of total expenditure among commodity groups into an intertemporal framework. This would facilitate the analysis of fertility choice, as suggested by Pollak and Wales (1979), or other forms of investment in human capital.

Each extension of the econometric framework for modeling aggregate consumer behavior generates new information about individual welfare functions. This information can be incorporated into a social welfare function by bringing to bear ethical judgements about horizontal and vertical equity among individuals. For practical applications—like those we have discussed in section 1.5—the resulting measures of social welfare can be translated into monetary terms. The scope of applied normative economics can be gradually extended by this research program to encompass a broader and broader range of problems in the evaluation of the performance of an economic system.

Appendix Table

Table 1.A.1
The transcendental logarithmic model of aggregate consumer behavior

Notation:		
CONST	=	constant term
ln *PEN*	=	coefficient of log of price of energy
ln *PF*	=	coefficient of log of price of food
ln *PCG*	=	coefficient of log of price of consumer goods
ln *PK*	=	coefficient of log of price of capital services
ln *PCS*	=	coefficient of log of price of consumer services
ln *M*	=	coefficient of log of total expenditure
S2	=	coefficient of dummy for family of size 2
S3	=	coefficient of dummy for family of size 3
S4	=	coefficient of dummy for family of size 4
S5	=	coefficient of dummy for family of size 5
S6	=	coefficient of dummy for family of size 6
S7+	=	coefficient of dummy for family of size 7 or more
A25–34	=	coefficient of dummy for age between 25 and 34
A35–44	=	coefficient of dummy for age between 35 and 44
A45–54	=	coefficient of dummy for age between 45 and 54
A55–64	=	coefficient of dummy for age between 55 and 64
A65+	=	coefficient of dummy for age 65 and older
RNC	=	coefficient of dummy for family living in North Central
RS	=	coefficient of dummy for family living in South
RW	=	coefficient of dummy for family living in West
NW	=	coefficient of dummy for nonwhite family
RUR	=	coefficient of dummy for family living in rural area

$D(p) = -1 - .01355$ ln *PEN* $.05950$ ln *PF* $+ .01999$ ln *PCG* $.01495$ ln *PK* $+ .06801$ ln *PCS*

Table 1.A.1 (continued)

	Energy Estimate	SE	Food Estimate	SE	Consumer goods Estimate	SE	Capital services Estimate	SE	Consumer services Estimate	SE
CONST	-.19542	.00897	-.67894	.02043	.02946	.01000	-.53472	.02420	.37962	.02000
ln PEN	.04057	.00313	-.07313	.00797	.02280	.00592	.03690	.00627	.04069	.00738
ln PF	-.07313	.00797	.17257	.04120	-.08994	.02825	-.07381	.01942	.00481	.02364
ln PCG	.02280	.00592	-.08994	.02825	.14575	.02080	-.06765	.01516	.00903	.01713
ln PK	.03690	.00627	-.07381	.01942	-.06765	.01516	.18465	.01882	-.09504	.01625
ln PCS	-.04069	.00138	.00481	.02364	.00903	.01713	-.09504	.01625	.18990	.02618
ln M	.01355	.00098	.05950	.00224	-.01999	.00108	.01495	.00267	-.06801	.00219
S2	-.01200	.00128	-.02611	.00294	.00072	.00142	.02198	.00350	.01541	.00286
S3	-.01517	.00151	-.03792	.00347	-.00304	.00167	.03465	.00413	.02148	.00337
S4	-.01549	.00161	-.05963	.00369	-.00425	.00178	.04791	.00439	.03146	.00359
S5	-.01454	.00188	-.06411	.00432	-.00491	.00208	.04080	.00514	.04276	.00420
S6	-.01196	.00233	-.09218	.00535	-.00827	.00258	.05493	.00636	.05749	.00520
S7+	-.01309	.00242	-.11214	.00555	-.00900	.00268	.06293	.00660	.07219	.00540
A25–34	-.00029	.00177	-.03498	.00406	.00562	.00195	.04042	.00483	-.01077	.00394
A35–44	-.00153	.00192	-.06812	.00440	.00594	.00212	.06883	.00523	-.00512	.00427
A45–54	-.00166	.00182	-.07214	.00418	.01367	.00202	.07281	.00498	-.01268	.00407
A55–64	-.00326	.00182	-.07030	.00418	.01895	.00201	.07742	.00497	-.02281	.00406
A65+	.00084	.00179	-.06410	.00411	.02204	.00198	.06160	.00489	-.02038	.00399
RNC	-.00838	.00119	.01356	.00274	-.00036	.00132	.00886	.00326	-.01368	.00266
RS	-.00962	.00119	.00326	.00273	-.00312	.00131	.03138	.00324	-.02190	.00265
RW	.00252	.00128	.01097	.00294	-.00190	.00142	-.00514	.00350	-.00645	.00286
NW	.00052	.00149	-.01633	.00341	-.01551	.00164	.04814	.00406	-.01682	.00332
RUR	-.02955	.00119	.00068	.00272	-.00571	.00131	.02707	.00324	.00750	.00264

Cross section SSR = 37263.79; aggregate SSR = 2442.58.

Notes

1. Gorman's condition is satisfied by aggregate demand functions generated from the linear expenditure system implemented by Stone (1954). The condition is also satisfied by such generalizations of the linear expenditure system as the Gorman polar form employed by Blackorby, Boyce, and Russell (1978).
2. Econometric models of aggregate consumer behavior based on Muellbauer's model of a representative consumer have been constructed by Berndt, Darrough, and Diewert (1977) and Deaton and Muellbauer (1980a). Muellbauer (1976b) extends the representative consumer model to individual preferences that are not identical.
3. See, for example, Houthakker (1957), Leser (1963), and Prais and Houthakker (1971).
4. See, for example, Blackorby and Donaldson (1985), Jorgenson and Slesnick (1983), and Roberts (1980c).
5. The individual expenditure function was introduced by McKenzie (1957). Hicks (1942) and Samuelson (1974) have discussed the translation of individual welfare into monetary terms. A detailed characterization of the expenditure function and references to the literature are provided by Diewert (1980).
6. The social expenditure function was introduced by Pollak (1981), Russell (1983) emphasizes that applications of this concept depend on the form of the social welfare function. Surveys of the literature on money measures of social welfare are provided by Diewert (1984) and Sen (1979a).
7. The measure of equity in (1.2.3) lies between zero and unity. By subtracting this measure from unity we obtain the money measure of relative inequality introduced by Jorgenson and Slesnick (1984a,b). Alternative money measures of efficiency and equity are discussed by Arrow and Kalt (1979), Bergson (19980), and Sen (1976a). A survey of the literature is provided by Sen (1979a).
8. The translog indirect utility function was introduced by Christensen, Jorgenson, and Lau (1975) and extended to encompass determinants of expenditure allocation other than prices and total expenditure by Jorgenson and Lau (1975). Alternative approaches to the representation of the effects of prices and total expenditure on expenditure allocation are summarized by Barten (1977), Deaton (1986), and Lau (1986).
9. Alternative approaches to the representation of household characteristics on expenditure allocation are presented by Barten (1964), Gorman (1976), and Prais and Houthakker (1971). A survey of the literature is provided by Deaton (1986).
10. The specifications of a system of individual demand functions by means of Roy's Identity was first employed in econometric modeling of consumer behavior by Houthakker (1960). A detailed review of econometric models based on Roy's Identity is given by Lau (1977a).
11. For further discussion, see Jorgenson, Lau, and Stoker (1982, pp. 113–165), and Lau (1977b, 1982).
12. Conditions for integrability are discussed by Jorgenson and Lau (1979, 1986) and Jorgenson, Lau, and Stoker (1982, pp. 172–187).
13. For further discussion, see Jorgenson, Lau, and Stoker (1982, pp. 175–186).
14. The 1972–1973 Survey of Consumer Expenditures is discussed by Carlson (1974). Detailed imputations on the flow of services from durable goods for individual consuming units are based on an inventory of durable goods for each unit.
15. The U.S. National Income and Product Accounts are constructed by the Bureau of Economic Analysis (1986). We employ aggregate time-series data on the flow of services from durable goods rather than purchases of durable goods.
16. This series is published annually by the U.S. Bureau of the Census.

17. The stochastic specification of the econometric model is discussed in detail by Jorgenson, Lau, and Stoker (1982, pp. 188–192). Econometric methods for pooling time-series and cross-section data are presented by Jorgenson and Stoker (1986).

18. Identification of the econometric model is discussed in detail by Jorgenson, Lau, and Stoker (1982, pp. 192–204). Overidentifying restrictions, such as those generated by integrability and exact aggregation, can be tested empirically. Tests of restrictions based on monotonicity require methods for inequality constraints like those proposed by Wolak (1989).

19. The household equivalence scales used in our measures of individual welfare are discussed by Jorgenson and Slesnick (1987a). Household equivalence scales have been presented by Barten (1964), Muellbauer (1974a, 1977), Deaton and Muellbauer (1986), and many others. Alternative approaches are summarized by Deaton and Muellbauer (1980b).

20. The use of household equivalence scales in evaluating transfers among individuals has been advocated by Deaton and Muellbauer (1980b, esp. pp. 205–212), and Muellbauer (1974a). Pollak and Wales (1979) have presented arguments against the use of household equivalence scales for this purpose.

21. The class of social welfare functions (1.4.6) is distributionally homothetic in the sense of Blackorby and Donaldson (1982).

22. In section 1.3 we have assumed that each household has an indirect utility function (1.3.1). This representation of household preferences can be derived by first assuming that each individual has an indirect utility function of this form. We then assume, in addition, that the household maximizes a household welfare function analogous to (1.4.6). Under these assumptions the distribution of individual welfare with the household is perfectly egalitarian, so that each member of the household has the same level of welfare. The form of the household indirect utility function (1.3.1) is identical to the individual indirect utility function with total expenditure and number of household equivalent members equal to the sum over all individuals. The household welfare function that enters the social welfare function (1.4.6) can be obtained by weighting the welfare function for any member of the household by the number of household equivalent members.

23. The class of social welfare functions introduced by Jorgenson and Slesnick (1983) is defined on a specific vector of individual welfare function u and exemplifies the single profile approach to social choice of Bergson (1938) and Samuelson (1947). The literature on single profile social welfare functions and its relationship to the multiple profile social welfare functions of Arrow (1963) is summarized by Roberts (1980d), Samuelson (1982), and Sen (1977, 1979b).

24. Muellbauer (1974b, p. 498) has shown that measures of social welfare based on "income" coincide with measures based on individual welfare is and only if preferences are identical and homothetic for all consuming units. See also Roberts (1980c).

2   Individual and Social Cost-of-Living Indexes

*Dale W. Jorgenson and
Daniel T. Slesnick*

2.1   Introduction

The purpose of this chapter is to present an econometric approach to cost-of-living measurement. This approach implements the economic theory of individual cost-of-living measurement pioneered by Konüs (1939) almost six decades ago.[1] In this chapter we develop and implement a completely parallel theory of social cost-of-living measurement.

Our approach to cost-of-living measurement is based on an econometric model of aggregate consumer behavior. The novel feature of this model is that systems of individual demand functions can be recovered uniquely from the system of aggregate demand functions. We derive cost-of-living indexes for individual households from systems of individual demand functions.

Our key innovation in the economic theory of cost-of-living measurement is the introduction of an explicit social welfare function. Our social welfare function incorporates measures of individual welfare from our econometric model. In addition, this social welfare function employs normative criteria for evaluating transfers among individuals.

In section 2.2 we outline econometric methodology for developing a model of aggregate consumer behavior. In this model the system of aggregate demand functions depends on summary statistics of the joint distribution of attributes and total expenditures of individual households. Attributes of households such as demographic characteristics enable us to account for differences in preferences.

In section 2.3 we implement our econometric model of aggregate consumer behavior for the United States. For this purpose we employ cross-section data on individual expenditure patterns. We combine these data with time series information on aggregate expenditure patterns. We also employ time series data on the distribution of total expenditures among consuming units.

In section 2.4 we present methods for translating changes in prices into measures of change in the individual cost of living. For this purpose we employ the individual expenditure function. The expenditure function gives the minimum total expenditure required to attain a base level of individual welfare. This minimum expenditure depends on prices and on the attributes of the consuming unit.

Following Konüs (1939), we define the individual cost-of-living index as the ratio between the total expenditure required to attain a base level of individual welfare at current prices and the corresponding base level of expenditure. If the individual cost-of-living index exceeds unity and total expenditure is constant, then the welfare of the consuming unit has decreased relative to the base level.

To implement the individual cost-of-living index the remaining problem is to determine the base level of individual welfare. For this purpose we define individual welfare in terms of the indirect utility function. This function gives utility as a function of prices and of the total expenditure and attributes of the consuming unit.

We calculate individual cost-of-living indexes and rates of inflation for households with different levels of total expenditure and different demographic characteristics for the period 1958–1978. For this purpose we derive indirect utility functions and expenditure functions for all consuming units from our econometric model of aggregate consumer behavior.

In section 2.5 we present methods for evaluating the level of social welfare. For this purpose we construct an explicit social welfare function. Our social welfare function incorporates measures of individual welfare based on indirect utility functions for all consuming units. In addition, this social welfare function employs normative criteria based on horizontal and vertical equity for evaluating transfers among units.

Given indirect utility functions from our econometric model, we can express the level of social welfare as a function of prices and of total expenditures and attributes for all consuming units. We define the social expenditure function as the minimum aggregate expenditure required to attain a base level of social welfare. This minimum level of expenditure depends on prices and on the attributes of all consuming units.

In section 2.6 we present methods for translating changes in prices into measures of change in the social cost of living. Following Pollak

(1981), we define the social cost-of-living index as the ratio between the aggregate expenditure required to attain a base level of social welfare at current prices and the corresponding base level of expenditure. If the social cost-of-living index exceeds unity and aggregate expenditure is constant, then social welfare has decreased relative to the base level.

Our definitions of social and individual cost-of-living indexes are perfectly analogous. In these definitions the roles of the social and individual expenditure functions and the roles of the social and individual welfare functions are completely parallel. We calculate the social cost-of-living index and rates of inflation for the period 1958–1978.

In section 2.7 we extend the concept of a social cost-of-living index to groups of consuming units with common demographic characteristics. Our definition of the group cost-of-living index is analogous to the definition of a social cost-of-living index. To implement a group cost-of-living index we require a group welfare function that is analogous to a social welfare function. We also require a group expenditure function.

Given group welfare and expenditure functions, we calculate cost-of-living indexes and rates of inflation for groups of households with common demographic characteristics for the period 1958–1978. If a group cost-of-living index exceeds unity and group expenditure is constant, then the welfare of the group has decreased relative to the base level.

In section 2.8 we compare the econometric and index number approaches to cost-of-living measurement. The econometric approach incorporates all the information employed in cost-of-living index numbers. An important advantage of the econometric approach is that it summarizes the available information in a concise and readily intelligible way.

In concluding we emphasize that the econometric and index number approaches share a number of significant limitations. These limitations arise from the practical problems of obtaining appropriate data on prices and expenditures. However, the econometric approach has greater flexibility and is easier to apply. These advantages are illustrated by our implementation of individual, social, and group cost-of-living indexes for the United States for the period 1958–1978.

2.2 Aggregate Consumer Behavior

In this section we develop an econometric model of aggregate consumer behavior based on the theory of exact aggregation, following Jorgenson, Lau, and Stoker (1980, 1981, 1982). Our model incorporates time series data on prices and aggregate quantities consumed. We also include cross-section data on individual quantities consumed, individual total expenditure, and attributes of individual households such as demographic characteristics.

To construct an econometric model based on exact aggregation we first represent individual preferences by means of an indirect utility function for each consuming unit, using the following notation:

p_n — price of the nth commodity, assumed to be the same for all consuming units.

$p = (p_1, p_2, \ldots, p_N)$ — the vector of prices of all commodities.

x_{nk} — the quantity of the nth commodity group consumed by the kth consuming unit ($n = 1, 2, \ldots, N$; $k = 1, 2, \ldots, K$).

$M_k = \sum_{n=1}^{N} p_n x_{nk}$ — total expenditure of the kth consuming unit ($k = 1, 2, \ldots, K$).

$w_{nk} = p_n x_{nk} / M_k$ — expenditure share of the nth commodity group in the budget of the kth consuming unit ($n = 1, 2, \ldots, N$; $k = 1, 2, \ldots, K$).

$w_k = (w_{1k}, w_{2k}, \ldots, w_{Nk})$ — vector of expenditure shares for the kth consuming unit ($k = 1, 2, \ldots, K$).

$\ln \dfrac{p}{M_k} = \left(\ln \dfrac{p_1}{M_k}, \ln \dfrac{p_2}{M_k}, \ldots, \ln \dfrac{p_N}{M_k} \right)$ — vector of logarithms of ratios of prices to expenditure by the kth consuming unit ($k = 1, 2, \ldots, K$).

$\ln p = (\ln p_1, \ln p_2, \ldots, \ln p_N)$ — vector of logarithms of prices.

A_k — vector of attributes of the kth consuming unit ($k = 1, 2, \ldots, K$).

We assume that the kth consuming unit allocates expenditures in accord with the transcendental logarithmic or translog indirect utility function,[2] say V_k, where

$$\ln V_k = G\left(\ln \frac{p'}{M_k}\,\alpha_p + \frac{1}{2}\ln \frac{p'}{M_k}\,B_{pp}\,\ln \frac{p}{M_k} + \ln \frac{p'}{M_k}\,B_{pA}A_k,\, A_k\right),$$

$$(k = 1, 2, \ldots, K)\,. \qquad (2.2.1)$$

In this representation the function G is a monotone increasing function of the variable

$$\ln \frac{p'}{M_k}\,\alpha_p + \frac{1}{2}\ln \frac{p'}{M_k}\,B_{pp}\,\ln \frac{p}{M_k} + \ln \frac{p'}{M_k}\,B_{pA}A_k\,.$$

In addition, the function G depends directly on the attribute vector A_k.[3] The vector α_p and the matrices B_{pp} and B_{pA} are constant parameters that are the same for all consuming units.

The expenditure shares of the kth consuming unit can be derived by the logarithmic form of Roy's (1943) Identity[4]

$$w_{nk} = \frac{\partial \ln V_k}{\partial \ln (p_n/M_k)} \Big/ \sum_{n=1}^{N} \frac{\partial \ln V_k}{\partial \ln (p_n/M_k)}\,,$$

$$(n = 1, 2, \ldots, N;\ k = 1, 2, \ldots, K)\,. \qquad (2.2.2)$$

Applying this Identity to the translog indirect utility function (2.2.1), we obtain the system of individual expenditure shares

$$w_k = \frac{1}{D_k(p)}\left(\alpha_p + B_{pp}\,\ln \frac{p}{M_k} + B_{pA}A_k\right), \qquad (k = 1, 2, \ldots, K)\,, \qquad (2.2.3)$$

where the denominators $\{D_k\}$ take the form

$$D_k = i'\alpha_p + i'B_{pp}\,\ln \frac{p}{M_k} + i'B_{pA}A_k\,, \qquad (k = 1, 2, \ldots, K)\,. \qquad (2.2.4)$$

The individual expenditure shares are homogeneous of degree zero in the unknown parameters—α_p, B_{pp}, B_{pA}. By multiplying a given set of these parameters by a constant we obtain another set of parameters that generates the same system of individual budget shares. Accordingly, we can choose a normalization for the parameters without affecting observed patterns of individual expenditure allocation. We find it convenient to employ the normalization

$$i'\alpha_p = -1\,.$$

Under this restriction any change in the set of unknown parameters will be reflected in changes in individual expenditure patterns.

The conditions for exact aggregation are that the individual expenditure shares are linear in functions of the attributes $\{A_k\}$ and total expenditures $\{M_k\}$ for all consuming units.[5] These conditions will be satisfied if and only if the terms involving the attributes and expenditures do not appear in the denominators of the expressions given above for the individual expenditure shares, so that

$$i' B_{pp} i = 0 ,$$
$$i' B_{pA} = 0 .$$

The exact aggregation restrictions imply that the denominators $\{D_k\}$ reduce to

$$D = -1 + i' B_{pp} \ln p ,$$

where the subscript k is no longer required, since the denominator is the same for all consuming units. Under these restrictions the individual expenditure shares can be written

$$w_k = \frac{1}{D(p)} (\alpha_p + B_{pp} \ln p - B_{pp} i \cdot \ln M_k + B_{pA} A_k) ,$$

$$(k = 1, 2, \ldots, K) . \qquad (2.2.5)$$

The individual expenditure shares are linear in the logarithms of expenditures $\{\ln M_k\}$ and in the attributes $\{A_k\}$, as required by exact aggregation.

Under exact aggregation the indirect utility function for each consuming unit can be represented in the form

$$\ln V_k = F(A_k) + \ln p' \left(\alpha_p + \frac{1}{2} B_{pp} \ln p + B_{pA} A_k \right) - D(p) \ln M_k ,$$

$$(k = 1, 2, \ldots, K) . \quad (2.2.6)$$

In this representation the indirect utility function is linear in the logarithm of total expenditure $\ln M_k$ with a coefficient that depends on the prices p ($k = 1, 2, \ldots, K$). This property is invariant with respect to positive affine transformations, but is not preserved by arbitrary monotone increasing transformations. We conclude that the indirect utility function (2.2.6) provides a cardinal measure of individual welfare for each consuming unit.

If a system of individual expenditure shares (2.2.3) can be generated from an indirect utility function of the form (2.2.1) we say that the system is *integrable*. A complete set of conditions for integrability[6] is the following:

1. *Homogeneity*. The individual expenditure shares are homogeneous of degree zero in prices and total expenditure.

We can write the individual expenditure shares in the form

$$\beta_{pM} = B_{pp} i .\tag{2.2.7}$$

Given the exact aggregation restrictions, there are $N - 1$ restrictions implied by homogeneity.

2. *Summability*. The sum of the individual expenditure shares over all commodity groups is equal to unity

$$i' w_k = 1 , \quad (k = 1, 2, \ldots, K) .$$

We can write the denominator $D(p)$ in (2.2.4) in the form

$$D = -1 + \beta_{Mp} \ln p ,$$

where the vector of parameters β_{Mp} is constant and the same for all commodity groups and all consuming units. Summability implies that this vector must satisfy the restrictions

$$\beta_{Mp} = i' B_{pp} .\tag{2.2.8}$$

Given the exact aggregation restrictions, there are $N - 1$ restrictions implied by summability.

3. *Symmetry*. The matrix of compensated own- and cross-price substitution effects must be symmetric.

If the system of individual expenditure shares can be generated from an indirect utility function of the form (2.2.1), a necessary and sufficient condition for symmetry is that the matrix B_{pp} must be symmetric. Without imposing this condition, we can write the individual expenditure shares in the form

$$w_k = \frac{1}{D(p)} \left(\alpha_p + B_{pp} \ln \frac{p}{M_k} + B_{pA} A_k \right), \quad (k = 1, 2, \ldots, K) .$$

Symmetry implies that the matrix of parameters B_{pp} must satisfy the restrictions

$$B_{pp} = B'_{pp} \, . \tag{2.2.9}$$

The total number of symmetry restrictions is $1/2N(N-1)$.

4. *Nonnegativity*. The individual expenditure shares must be non-negative.

By summability the individual expenditure shares sum to unity, so that we can write

$$w_k \geqq 0 \, , \quad (k = 1, 2, \ldots, K) \, ,$$

where $w_k \geqq 0$ implies $w_{nk} \geq 0$, $(n = 1, 2, \ldots, N)$, and $w_k \neq 0$.

Since the translog indirect utility function is quadratic in the logarithms of prices, we can always choose the prices so that the individual expenditure shares violate the nonnegativity conditions. Accordingly, we cannot impose restrictions on the parameters of the translog indirect utility functions that would imply nonnegativity of the individual expenditure shares. Instead we consider restrictions on the parameters that imply monotonicity of the system of individual demand functions for all nonnegative expenditure shares.

5. *Monotonicity*. The matrix of compensated own- and cross-price substitution effects must be nonpositive definite.

We introduce the definition due to Martos (1969) of a *strictly merely positive subdefinite matrix*, namely, a real symmetric matrix S such that

$$xSx < 0$$

implies $Sx > 0$ or $Sx < 0$. A necessary and sufficient condition for monotonicity is either that the translog indirect utility function is homothetic or that B_{pp}^{-1} exists and is strictly merely positive subdefinite.[7]

To provide a basis for evaluating the impact of transfers among households on social welfare, we find it useful to represent household preferences by means of a utility function that is the same for all consuming units. For this purpose, we assume that the kth consuming unit maximizes its utility, say U_k, where

$$U_k = U\left[\frac{x_{1k}}{m_1(A_k)}, \frac{x_{2k}}{m_2(A_k)}, \ldots, \frac{x_{Nk}}{m_N(A_k)} \right], \quad (k = 1, 2, \ldots, K) \, , \tag{2.2.10}$$

subject to the budget constraint

$$M_k = \sum_{n=1}^{N} p_n\, x_{nk}\,, \qquad (k = 1, 2, \ldots, K)\,.$$

In this representation of consumer preferences the quantities $\{x_{nk}/m_n(A_k)\}$ can be regarded as *effective quantities consumed*, as proposed by Barten (1964). The crucial assumption embodied in this representation is that differences in preferences among consumers enter the utility function U only through differences in the commodity specific household equivalence scales $\{m_n(A_k)\}$.[8]

Consumer equilibrium implies the existence of an indirect utility function, say V, that is the same for all consuming units. The level of utility for the kth consuming unit, say V_k, depends on the prices of individual commodities, the household equivalence scales, and the level of total expenditure

$$V_k = V\left[\frac{p_1\, m_1(A_k)}{M_k},\, \frac{p_2\, m_2(A_k)}{M_k},\, \ldots,\, \frac{p_N\, m_N(A_k)}{M_k} \right],$$

$$(k = 1, 2, \ldots, K)\,. \qquad (2.2.11)$$

In this representation the prices $\{p_n\, m_n(A_k)\}$ can be regarded as *effective prices*. Differences in preferences among consuming units enter this indirect utility function only through the household equivalence scales $\{m_n(A_k)\}$ $(k = 1, 2, \ldots, K)$.

To represent the translog indirect utility function (2.2.1) in terms of household equivalence scales, we require some additional notation:

$\ln \dfrac{pm(A_k)}{M_k}$ — vector of logarithms of ratios of effective prices $\{p_n\, m_n(A_k)\}$ to total expenditure M_k of the kth consuming unit $(k = 1, 2, \ldots, K)$.

$\ln m(A_k) = (\ln m_1(A_k), \ln m_2(A_k), \ldots, \ln m_N(A_k))$ — vector of logarithms of the household equivalence scales of the kth consuming unit $(k = 1, 2, \ldots, K)$.

We assume, as before, that the kth consuming unit allocates its expenditures in accord with the translog indirect utility function (2.2.1). However, we also assume that this function, expressed in terms of the effective prices $\{p_n\, m_n(A_k)\}$ and total expenditure M_k, is the *same for all* consuming units. The indirect utility function takes the form

$$\ln V_k = \ln \frac{pm(A_k)'}{M_k} \alpha_p + \frac{1}{2} \ln \frac{pm(A_k)'}{M_k} B_{pp} \ln \frac{pm(A_k)}{M_k} ,$$

$$(k = 1, 2, \ldots, K) . \qquad (2.2.12)$$

Taking logarithms of the effective prices $\{p_n\, m_n(A_k)\}$, we can rewrite the indirect utility function (2.2.12) in the form

$$\ln V_k = \ln m(A_k)'\alpha_p + \frac{1}{2} \ln m(A_k)' B_{pp} \ln m(A_k) + \ln \frac{p'}{M_k} \alpha_p + \frac{1}{2} \ln \frac{p'}{M_k} B_{pp}$$

$$\times \ln \frac{p}{M_k} + \ln \frac{p'}{M_k} B_{pp} \ln m(A_k) , \quad (k = 1, 2, \ldots, K) . \qquad (2.2.13)$$

Comparing the representation (2.2.13) with the representation (2.2.6), we see that the term involving only the household equivalent scales must take the form

$$F(A_k) = \ln m(A_k)' \, \alpha_p + \frac{1}{2} \ln m(A_k)' \, B_{pp} \ln m(A_k) , \quad (k = 1, 2, \ldots, K) (2.2.14)$$

Second, the term involving ratios of prices to total expenditure and the household equivalence scales must satisfy

$$\ln \frac{p'}{M_k} B_{pA} A_k = \ln \frac{p'}{M_k} B_{pp} \ln m(A_k) , \quad (k = 1, 2, \ldots, K) , \qquad (2.2.15)$$

for all prices and total expenditure.

The household equivalence scales $\{m_n(A_k)\}$ defined by (2.2.15) must satisfy the equation

$$B_{pA} A_k = B_{pp} \ln m(A_k) , \quad (k = 1, 2, \ldots, K) . \qquad (2.2.16)$$

Under monotonicity of the individual expenditure shares the matrix B_{pp} has an inverse, so that we can express the household equivalence scales in terms of the parameters of the translog indirect utility function—B_{pp}, B_{pA}—and the attributes $\{A_k\}$

$$\ln m(A_k) = B_{pp}^{-1} B_{pA} A_k , \quad (k = 1, 2, \ldots, K) . \qquad (2.2.17)$$

We can refer to these scales as the *commodity specific translog household equivalence scales.*

Substituting the commodity specific equivalence scales (2.2.16) into the indirect utility function (2.2.13) we obtain a representation of the indirect utility function in terms of the attributes $\{A_k\}$

$$\ln V_k = A'_k\, B'_{pA}\, B^{-1}_{pp}\, \alpha_p + \frac{1}{2}\, A'_k\, B'_{pA}\, B^{-1}_{pp}\, B_{pA}\, A_k$$

$$+ \ln p' \left(\alpha_p + \frac{1}{2}\, B_{pp}\, \ln p + B_{pA}\, A_k \right) - D(p) \ln M_k \,,$$

$$(k = 1, 2, \ldots, K) \,. \qquad (2.2.18)$$

This form of the translog indirect utility function is equivalent to the form (2.2.1) in that both generate the same system of individual demand functions. By requiring that the attributes A_k enter only through the commodity specific household equivalence scales, we have provided a specific form for the function $F(A_k)$ in (2.2.6).

Given the indirect utility function (2.2.18) for each consuming unit, we can express total expenditure as a function of prices, consumer attributes, and the level of utility

$$\ln M_k = \frac{1}{D(p)} \left[A'_k\, B'_{pA}\, B^{-1}_{pp}\, \alpha_p + \frac{1}{2}\, A'_k\, B'_{pA}\, B^{-1}_{pp}\, B_{pA}\, A_k \right.$$

$$\left. + \ln p' \left(\alpha_p + \frac{1}{2}\, B_{pp}\, \ln p + B_{pA}\, A_k \right) - \ln V_k \right], \quad (k = 1, 2, \ldots, K) \,. \quad (2.2.19)$$

We can refer to this function as the *translog expenditure function*. The translog expenditure function gives the minimum expenditure required for the kth consuming unit to achieve the utility level V_k, given prices p ($k = 1, 2, \ldots, K$).

We find it useful to introduce household equivalence scales that are not specific to a given commodity.[9] Following Deaton and Muellbauer (1980b), we define a general household equivalence scale, say m_0, as follows

$$m_0 = \frac{M_k[pm(A_k), V^0_k]}{M_0(p, V^0_k)} \,, \qquad (k = 1, 2, \ldots, K) \,, \qquad (2.2.20)$$

where M_k is the expenditure function for the kth household, M_0 is the expenditure function for a reference household with commodity specific equivalence scales equal to unity for all commodities, and $pm(A_k)$ is a vector of effective prices $\{p_n\, m_n(A_k)\}$.

The general household equivalence scale m_0 is the ratio between total expenditures required by the kth household and by the reference household required for the same level of utility V^0_k ($k = 1, 2, \ldots, K$). This scale can be interpreted as the number of household equivalent members. The number of members depends on the attributes A_k of the consuming unit and on the prices p.

If each household has a translog indirect utility function, then the general household equivalence scale for the kth household takes the form

$$\ln m_0 = \ln M_k - \ln M_0$$

$$= \frac{1}{D(p)}\left[\ln m(A_k)'\alpha_p + \frac{1}{2}\ln m(A_k)'B_{pp}\ln m(A_k) + \ln m(A_k)'B_{pp}\ln p\right],$$

$$(k = 1, 2, \ldots, K). \qquad (2.2.21)$$

We can refer to this scale as the *general translog household equivalence scale*. The translog equivalence scale depends on the attributes A_k of the kth household and the prices p of all commodities, but is independent of the level of utility V_k^0.

Given the general translog equivalence scale, we can rewrite the indirect utility function (2.2.18) in the form

$$\ln V_k = \ln p'\alpha_p + \frac{1}{2}\ln p'B_{pp}\ln p - D(p)\ln[M_k/m_0(p, A_k)],$$

$$(k = 1, 2, \ldots, K). \qquad (2.2.22)$$

The level of utility for the kth consuming unit depends on prices p and total expenditure per household equivalent member $M_k/m_0(p, A_k)$ $(k = 1, 2, \ldots, K)$. Similarly, we can rewrite the expenditure function (2.2.19) in the form

$$\ln M_k = \frac{1}{D(p)}\left[\ln p'\left(\alpha_p + \frac{1}{2}B_{pp}\ln p\right) - \ln V_k\right] + \ln m_0(p, A_k),$$

$$(k = 1, 2, \ldots, K). \qquad (2.2.23)$$

Total expenditure required by the kth consuming unit to attain the level of utility V_k depends on prices p and the number of household equivalent members $m_0(p, A_k)$, $(k = 1, 2, \ldots, K)$.

To construct an econometric model of aggregate consumer behavior based on exact aggregation we obtain aggregate expenditure shares, say w, by multiplying individual expenditure shares (2.2.5) by expenditure for each consuming unit, adding over all consuming units, and dividing by aggregate expenditure, $M = \sum_{k=1}^{K} M_k$

$$w = \frac{\sum M_k \, w_k}{M} \, . \tag{2.2.24}$$

The aggregate expenditure shares can be written

$$w = \frac{1}{D(p)} \left(\alpha_p + B_{pp} \ln p - B_{pp} i \, \frac{\sum M_k \ln M_k}{M} + B_{pA} \, \frac{\sum M_k \, A_k}{M} \right). \tag{2.2.25}$$

The aggregate expenditure patterns depend on the distribution of expenditure over all consuming units through summary statistics of the joint distribution of expenditures and attributes—$\sum M_k \ln M_k / M$ and $\{\sum M_k \, A_k / M\}$. Systems of individual expenditure shares (2.2.5) for consuming units with identical demographic characteristics can be recovered in one and only one way from the system of aggregate expenditure shares (2.2.25).

To summarize: Systems of individual expenditure shares (2.2.5) can be recovered in one and only one way from the system of aggregate expenditure shares (2.2.25). Given a system of individual expenditure shares (2.2.5) that is integrable, we can recover the indirect utility function (2.2.22). This indirect utility function provides a cardinal measure of utility. We obtain measures of utility for all consuming units by deriving indirect utility functions from the fitted systems of individual expenditure shares.

2.3   Econometric Model

In this section we present the empirical results of implementing the econometric model of consumer behavior described in section 2.2. We divide consumer expenditures among five commodity groups:

1. *Energy*: Expenditures on electricity, natural gas, heating oil, and gasoline.

2. *Food*: Expenditures on all food products, including tobacco and alcohol.

3. *Consumer goods*: Expenditures on all other nondurable goods included in consumer expenditures.

4. *Capital services*: The service flow from consumer durables and the service flow from housing.

5. *Consumer services*: Expenditures on consumer services, such as car repairs, medical services, entertainment, and so on.

We employ the following demographic characteristics as attributes of individual households:

1. *Family size*: 1, 2, 3, 4, 5, 6, and 7 or more persons.
2. *Age of head*: 16–24, 25–34, 35–44, 45–54, 55–64, 65 and over.
3. *Region of residence*: Northeast, North Central, South, and West.
4. *Race*: White, nonwhite.
5. *Type of residence*: Urban, rural.

Our cross-section observations on individual expenditures for each commodity group and on demographic characteristics of individual households are for the year 1972 from the 1972–1973 Survey of Consumer Expenditures (CES).[10] Our time series observations are based on data on personal consumption expenditures from the United States National Income and Product Accounts (NIPA) for the years 1958 to 1974.[11] Prices for each commodity group are defined in terms of translog price indexes computed from detailed prices included in NIPA for each year. We employ time series data on the distribution of expenditures over all households and among demographic groups based on *Current Population Reports.*[12]

In our application we treat the expenditure shares for five commodity groups as endogenous variables, so that we estimate four equations. As unknown parameters we have four elements of the vector α_p, four expenditure coefficients of the vector $B_{pp}i$, sixteen attribute coefficients for each of the four equations in the matrix B_{pA}, and ten price coefficients in the matrix B_{pp}, which is constrained to be symmetric. The expenditure coefficients are sums of price coefficients in the corresponding equation, so that we have a total of eighty-two unknown parameters. We estimate the complete model, subject to inequality restrictions implied by monotonicity of the individual expenditure shares, by pooling time series and cross-section data.[13] The results are given in table 2.1.

The impacts of changes in total expenditures and in demographic characteristics of the individual household are estimated very precisely. This reflects the fact that estimates of the expenditure and demographic effects incorporate a relatively large number of cross-section observations. The impacts of prices enter through the denominator of the equations for expenditure shares; these price coefficients are estimated very precisely since they also incorporate cross-section data. Finally, the price impacts also enter through the numerators of equations for the expenditure shares. These parameters are estimated somewhat less precisely, since they are based on a much smaller number of time series observations on prices.

Table 2.1
Pooled estimation results

Notation:		
CONST	=	constant term
ln PEN	=	coefficient of log of price of energy
ln PF	=	coefficient of log of price of food
ln PCG	=	coefficient of log of price of consumer goods
ln PK	=	coefficient of log of price of capital services
ln PCS	=	coefficient of log of price of consumer services
ln M	=	coefficient of log of total expenditure
S2	=	coefficient of dummy for family of size 2
S3	=	coefficient of dummy for family of size 3
S4	=	coefficient of dummy for family of size 4
S5	=	coefficient of dummy for family of size 5
S6	=	coefficient of dummy for family of size 6
S7 +	=	coefficient of dummy for family of size 7 or more
A25–34	=	coefficient of dummy for age between 25 and 34
A35–44	=	coefficient of dummy for age between 35 and 44
A45–54	=	coefficient of dummy for age between 45 and 54
A55–64	=	coefficient of dummy for age between 55 and 64
A65 +	=	coefficient of dummy for age 65 and older
RNC	=	coefficient of dummy for family living in North Central
RS	=	coefficient of dummy for family living in South
RW	=	coefficient of dummy for family living in West
BLK	=	coefficient of dummy for nonwhite family
RUR	=	coefficient of dummy for family living in rural area

$D(p) = -1$ $-0.03491 \ln PEN$ $-0.08171 \ln PF$ $+0.06189 \ln PCG$
  (0.000997) (0.00238) (0.00214)
  $-0.02060 \ln PK$ $+0.05679 \ln PCS$
  (0.00300) (0.00233)

Table 2.1 (continued)

	Energy		Food			Consumer Goods		
Parameter	Estimate	Standard Error	Parameter	Estimate	Standard Error	Parameter	Estimate	Standard Error
CONST	-.3754	.00923	CONST	-.8917	.0215	CONST	.4053	.0194
ln PEN	.09151	.0134	ln PEN	-.1441	.0214	ln PEN	-.06455	.0127
ln PF	-.1441	.0214	ln PF	.3118	.0428	ln PF	.3118	.0428
ln PCG	-.06455	.0127	ln PCG	.05547	.0215	ln PCG	.05547	.0215
ln PK	.07922	.0171	ln PK	-.1982	.0334	ln PK	-.1056	.0195
ln PCS	.003061	.0138	ln PCS	-.1066	.0259	ln PCS	-.05354	.0271
ln M	.03491	.000997	ln M	.08171	.00238	ln M	-.06189	.00214
S2	-.02402	.00139	S2	-.04859	.00333	S2	-.005594	.00300
S3	-.02971	.00163	S3	-.06730	.00390	S3	-.006290	.00351
S4	-.03144	.00178	S4	-.08881	.00428	S4	-.001941	.00385
S5	-.03255	.00206	S5	-.1108	.00496	S5	.004522	.00446
S6	-.03606	.00249	S6	-.1185	.00598	S6	.01059	.00539
S7+	-.02977	.00266	S7+	-.1471	.00639	S7+	.01495	.00575
A25-34	.0002010	.00197	A25-34	-.04393	.00474	A25-34	-.02311	.00426
A35-44	-.006703	.00210	A35-44	-.08221	.00504	A35-44	-.01916	.00454
A45-54	-.01155	.00199	A45-54	-.09604	.00478	A45-54	-.005279	.00431
A55-64	-.01372	.00199	A55-64	-.1034	.00477	A55-64	-.009068	.00429
A65+	-.005487	.00196	A65+	-.08833	.00470	A65+	-.01722	.00423
RNC	-.003277	.00131	RNC	.08173	.00315	RNC	-.02098	.00283
RS	.0001280	.00131	RS	.01213	.00314	RS	-.03553	.00283
RW	.01281	.00140	RW	.01856	.00337	RW	-.009928	.00304
BLK	.01300	.00170	BLK	.006274	.00409	BLK	-.02648	.00368
RUR	-.03057	.00134	RUR	-.001793	.00323	RUR	-.01122	.00290

Table 2.1 (continued)

	Capital Services			Consumer Services	
Parameter	Estimate	Standard Error	Parameter	Estimate	Standard Error
CONST	-.4658	.0270	CONST	.3277	.0211
ln PEN	.07922	.0171	ln PEN	.003061	.0138
ln PF	-.1982	.0334	ln PF	-.1066	.0259
ln PCG	-.1056	.0195	ln PCG	-.05354	.0271
ln PK	.2038	.0368	ln PK	.01869	.0165
ln PCS	.01869	.0165	ln PCS	.1952	.0375
ln M	.002060	.00300	ln M	-.05679	.00233
S2	.07355	.00421	S2	.004666	.00327
S3	.09982	.00493	S3	.003483	.00383
S4	.1148	.00541	S4	.007338	.00420
S5	.1253	.00626	S5	.01357	.00486
S6	.1284	.00756	S6	.01561	.00587
S7+	.1369	.00807	S7+	.02508	.00627
A25–34	.04362	.00599	A25–34	.02321	.00465
A35–44	.08503	.00637	A35–44	.02304	.00495
A45–54	.1166	.00605	A45–54	-.003805	.00470
A55–64	.1395	.00603	A55–64	-.01332	.00468
A65+	.1296	.00595	A65+	-.01863	.00462
RNC	.02767	.00398	RNC	-.02214	.00309
RS	.05528	.00397	RS	-.03200	.00308
RW	-.004132	.00427	RW	-.01731	.00331
BLK	-.003539	.00517	BLK	.01074	.00401
RUR	.05588	.00408	RUR	-.01229	.00317

Convergence after 3 iterations.
SSR = 37387. 12.
Convergence criterion = .00001.

To summarize: We have implemented an econometric model of aggregate consumer behavior by combining time series and cross-section data for the United States. This model allocates personal consumption expenditures among five commodity groups—energy, food, other consumer goods, capital services, and other consumer services. Households are classified by five sets of demographic characteristics—family size, age of head, region of residence, race, and urban versus rural residence.

2.4   Individual Cost-of-Living Indexes

In this section we outline a methodology for translating changes in prices into measures of change in the individual cost of living. The first step in measuring the cost of living for an individual consuming unit is to select a representation for the individual welfare function. We assume that individual welfare for the kth consuming unit, say W_k ($k = 1, 2, \ldots, K$), is equal to the logarithm of the translog indirect utility function (2.2.22)

$$W_k = \ln V_k$$
$$= \ln p'\alpha_p + \frac{1}{2} \ln p' B_{pp} \ln p - D(p) \ln [M_k/m_0(p, A_k)] \,,$$
$$(k = 1, 2, \ldots, K) \,. \qquad (2.4.1)$$

Following Konüs (1939), we define the cost-of-living index for the kth consuming unit, say P_k ($k = 1, 2, \ldots, K$), as the ratio of two levels of total expenditure

$$P_k(p^1, p^0, W_k^0, A_k) = \frac{M_k(p^1, W_k^0, A_k)}{M_k(p^0, W_k^0, A_k)} \,, \qquad (k = 1, 2, \ldots, K) \,. \qquad (2.4.2)$$

In this ratio the numerator is the expenditure required to attain the base level of individual welfare W_k^0 at the current price system p^1; the denominator is the base level of expenditure M_k^0.

The translog indirect utility function (2.2.22) and the translog expenditure function (2.2.23) can be employed in implementing the individual cost-of-living index (2.4.2).[14] First, we can express the base level of individual welfare W_k^0 in terms of the translog indirect utility function

$$W_k^0 = \ln p^{0'} \alpha_p + \frac{1}{2} \ln p^{0'} B_{pp} p^0 - D(p^0) \ln [M_k^0 / m_0(p^0, A_k)] ,$$

$$(k = 1, 2, \ldots, K) . \qquad (2.4.3)$$

In this expression $m_0(p^0, A_k)$ is the base level of the general translog household equivalence scale (2.2.21) and M_k^0 is the base level of total expenditure.

Using the translog expenditure function, we can express the individual cost-of-living index (2.4.2) in the form

$$\ln P_k(p^1, p^0, W_k^0, A_k) = \frac{1}{D(p^1)} \left[\ln p^{1'} \left(\alpha_p + \frac{1}{2} B_{pp} \ln p^1 \right) - W_k^0 \right]$$
$$+ \ln m_0(p^1, A_k) - \ln M_k^0 , \qquad (k = 1, 2, \ldots, K) \ (2.4.4)$$

We can refer to the index P_k as the *translog individual cost-of-living index*. If the translog index is greater than unity and total expenditure is constant, then the welfare of the consuming unit is decreased by the change in prices.

We can illustrate the measurement of the individual cost-of-living index by representing the impact of a change in prices in diagrammatic form. For simplicity we consider the case of two commodities ($N = 2$). In figure 2.1 we have depicted the indifference map of the kth household. Consumer equilibrium at the base price system p^0 is represented by the point A with base level of individual welfare W_k^0. The corresponding level of total expenditure M_k^0, divided by the base price of the second commodity p_2^0, is given on the vertical axis. This axis provides a representation of total expenditure in terms of units of the second commodity.

Consumer equilibrium after the change in prices is represented by the point B with associated level of individual welfare W_k^1. The level of total expenditure associated with the change in prices M_k^1, divided by the current price of the second commodity p_2^1, is given, as before, on the vertical axis. Finally, the level of total expenditure required to attain the base level of individual welfare W_k^0 at current prices $M(p^1, W_k^0, A_k)$ corresponds to consumer equilibrium at the point C. The individual cost-of-living index is given by ratio of the distances on the vertical axis corresponding to the consumer equilibrium at points C and A, multiplied by the ratio of prices of the second commodity at the two points p_2^1 / p_2^0.

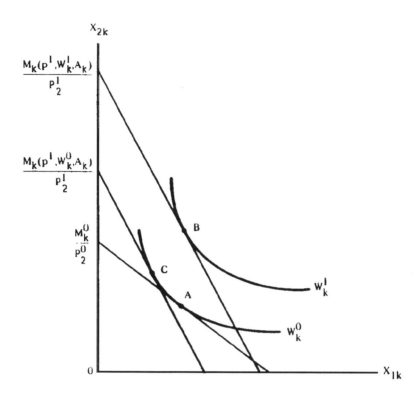

Figure 2.1
Individual Cost-of-Living Index.

As a further illustration of the individual cost-of-living index, we analyze the changes in prices over the period 1958–1978, using prices for 1972 as the base price system. For this purpose we employ the econometric model of aggregate consumer behavior presented in section 2.3. This model is based on time series and cross-section data on personal consumption expenditures for the United States, broken down by five commodity groups. The five commodity groups are energy, food, other consumer goods, capital services, and other consumer services.

Using the translog individual cost-of-living index (2.4.4), we can assess the impact of price changes on households with different base levels of individual welfare and different demographic characteristics. For this purpose we set the base level of individual welfare at the levels attained in 1972 with half mean expenditure in that year or $4,467, mean expenditure or $8,934, and twice mean expenditure or $17,868. We present translog individual cost-of-living indexes for the period 1958–1978 for white and nonwhite households with urban and rural residences in appendix table 2.A.1. Within each of these groups we consider families of size five with a head of household aged 35–44, living in the Northeast region of the United States.

We present rates of inflation calculated from the translog individual cost-of-living indexes in table 2.2. For example, the change in the logarithm of the translog index between 1958 and 1959 for a white, urban family with total expenditure equal to $4,467 in 1972 is −0.02 percent. The corresponding change for a white, rural family is 0.24 percent. For nonwhite households the change in cost of living for urban households is −0.05 percent, while the change for rural households is 0.21 percent. If we compare translog individual cost-of-living indexes for households with different base levels of total expenditure, we find that rates of inflation are greater for higher levels of expenditure for the periods 1958–1963, 1966–1971, and 1974–1977. For the remainder of the period—1963–1966, 1971–1974, and 1977–1978—rates of inflation are greater for lower levels of expenditure.

We can compare rates of inflation for households with different demographic characteristics. For example, a nonwhite, urban family with mean base level of expenditure experienced a change of 8.15 percent in the cost of living between 1973 and 1974. By comparison a white, rural household at the same level of expenditure had a change of 9.61 percent over the same period. On the basis of the results presented in table 2.2 we conclude that there are substantial differences in rates of inflation for households with different base levels of individual welfare and with different demographic characteristics.

To summarize: We have defined the individual cost-of-living index as the ratio of the total expenditure required to attain a base level of individual welfare at current prices to the base level of expenditure. Using the translog indirect utility function (2.2.22) and the translog expenditure function (2.2.23), we implement this definition by means of the translog individual cost-of-living index (2.4.4). We find that changes in the individual cost of living vary substantially for households with different base levels of welfare and different demographic characteristics over the period 1958–1978.

Table 2.2
Changes in individual cost-of-living indexes (annual
percentage rates)

Year	Urban		Rural	
	White	Nonwhite	White	Nonwhite
1959	−0.02	−0.05	0.24	0.21
1960	2.94	2.95	2.67	2.68
1961	0.84	0.83	0.86	0.85
1962	1.03	1.02	1.01	1.00
1963	0.46	0.46	0.62	0.62
1964	2.19	2.23	1.91	1.95
1965	3.26	3.26	2.94	2.93
1966	2.97	2.95	3.01	2.99
1967	0.73	0.74	1.09	1.10
1968	3.16	3.21	3.24	3.29
1969	6.18	6.23	5.76	5.80
1970	1.48	1.43	2.15	2.10
1971	3.78	3.76	3.77	3.75
1972	7.05	7.07	6.29	6.31
1973	8.21	8.14	8.00	7.93
1974	8.87	8.56	10.33	10.03
1975	4.65	4.60	5.40	5.34
1976	6.39	6.43	6.10	6.14
1977	8.36	8.31	7.91	7.86
1978	7.04	7.02	6.90	6.88

Region = Northeast
Size = 5
Age = 35–44
Expenditure = $4,467 in 1972

Table 2.2 (continued)

Year	Urban White	Urban Nonwhite	Rural White	Rural Nonwhite
1959	0.08	0.06	0.35	0.33
1960	2.97	2.97	2.69	2.70
1961	0.84	0.83	0.86	0.86
1962	1.06	1.05	1.04	1.03
1963	0.49	0.49	0.65	0.65
1964	2.21	2.24	1.93	1.96
1965	3.18	3.17	2.85	2.84
1966	2.86	2.84	2.90	2.88
1967	0.86	0.87	1.23	1.24
1968	3.26	3.31	3.35	3.39
1969	6.21	6.25	5.79	5.83
1970	1.49	1.44	2.16	2.10
1971	3.91	3.89	3.90	3.88
1972	6.96	6.97	6.20	6.22
1973	7.71	7.63	7.50	7.43
1974	8.15	7.84	9.61	9.31
1975	4.68	4.63	5.43	5.37
1976	6.79	6.82	6.50	6.53
1977	8.48	8.43	8.03	7.98
1978	6.70	6.68	6.55	6.53

Region = Northeast
Size = 5
Age = 35–44
Expenditure = $8,934 in 1972

Table 2.2 (continued)

Year	Urban White	Urban Nonwhite	Rural White	Rural Nonwhite
1959	0.20	0.17	0.47	0.44
1960	2.99	2.99	2.72	2.72
1961	0.84	0.84	0.87	0.86
1962	1.08	1.07	1.07	1.06
1963	0.52	0.52	0.68	0.68
1964	2.23	2.26	1.95	1.98
1965	3.09	3.08	2.76	2.75
1966	2.75	2.73	2.79	2.78
1967	1.00	1.01	1.37	1.38
1968	3.37	3.42	3.45	3.50
1969	6.24	6.28	5.81	5.85
1970	1.50	1.44	2.16	2.11
1971	4.04	4.02	4.03	4.01
1972	6.86	6.88	6.11	6.12
1973	7.21	7.13	7.00	6.92
1974	7.43	7.12	8.90	8.59
1975	4.71	4.66	5.45	5.40
1976	7.18	7.21	6.89	6.92
1977	8.59	8.55	8.15	8.10
1978	6.35	6.33	6.21	6.19

Region = Northeast
Size = 5
Age = 35–44
Expenditure = $17,868 in 1972

2.5 Social Welfare Functions

Our next objective is to generate a class of possible social welfare functions that can provide the basis for social cost-of-living measurement. For this purpose we must choose social welfare functions capable of expressing the implications of a variety of different ethical judgements. To facilitate comparisons with alternative approaches, we employ the axiomatic framework for social choice used by Arrow (1963), Sen (1970), and Roberts (1980a) in proving the impossibility of a nondictatorial social ordering.

We consider the set of all possible social orderings over the set of social states, say X, and the set of all possible real-valued individual welfare functions, say W_k, $(k = 1, 2, \ldots, K)$. A social ordering, say R, is a complete, reflexive, and transitive ordering of social states. A social state is described by the quantities consumed of N commodity groups by K individuals. The individual welfare function for the kth individual W_k, $(k = 1, 2, \ldots, K)$ is defined on the set of social states X and gives the level of individual welfare for that individual in each state.

To describe social orderings in greater detail we find it useful to introduce the following notation:

x_{nk} — the quantity of the nth commodity group consumed by the kth consuming unit $(n = 1, 2, \ldots, N; \ k = 1, 2, \ldots, K)$.

x — a matrix with elements $\{x_{nk}\}$ describing the social state.

$u = (W_1, W_2, \ldots, W_K)$ — a vector of individual welfare functions of all K individuals.

Following Sen (1970, 1977) and Hammond (1976) we define a *social welfare functional*, say f, as a mapping from the set of individual welfare functions to the set of social orderings, such that $f(u') = f(u)$ implies $R' = R$, where

$$u = [W_1(x), W_2(x), \ldots, W_K(x)] ,$$
$$u' = [W_1'(x), W_2'(x), \ldots, W_K'(x)] ,$$

for all $x \in X$. Similarly, we define L_k, $(k = 1, 2, \ldots, K)$ as the *set of admissible individual welfare functions* for the kth individual and L as the Cartesian product $\prod_{k=1}^{K} L_k$. Finally, let $\mathbf{L}$ be the partition of L such that all elements of $\mathbf{L}$ yield the same social ordering.

We can describe a social ordering in terms of the following properties of a social welfare functional:

1. *Unrestricted domain.* The social welfare functional f is defined for all possible vectors of individual welfare functions u.

2. *Independence of irrelevant alternatives.* For any subset A contained in X, if $u(x) = u'(x)$ for all $x \in A$, then $R: A = R': A$, where $R = f(u)$ and $R' = f(u')$ and $R: A$ is the social ordering over the subset A.

3. *Positive association.* For any vectors of individual welfare functions u and u', if for all y in $X - x$, such that

$$W_k'(y) = W_k(y) \,,$$

$$W_k'(x) > W_k(x) \,, \quad (k = 1, 2, \ldots, K) \,,$$

then xPy implies $xP'y$ and $yP'x$ implies yPx, where P is a strict ordering of social states.

4. *Nonimposition.* For all x, y in X there exist u, u' such that xPy and $yP'x$.

5. *Cardinal full comparability.* The set of admissible individual welfare functions that yield the same social ordering $\mathbf{L}$ is defined by

$$\mathbf{L} = \{u': \ W_k'(x) = \alpha + \beta W_k(x) \,, \ \beta > 0 \,, \ k = 1, 2, \ldots, K\} \,,$$

and $f(u') = f(u)$ for all $u' \in \mathbf{L}$.

Cardinal full comparability implies that social orderings are invariant with respect to any positive affine transformation of the individual welfare functions $\{W_k\}$ that is the same for all individuals. By contrast Arrow requires ordinal noncomparability,[15] which implies that social orderings are invariant with respect to monotone increasing transformations of the individual welfare functions that may differ among individuals:

5'. *Ordinal noncomparability.* The set of individual welfare functions that yield the same social ordering $\mathbf{L}$ is defined by

$$\mathbf{L} = \{u': \ W_k'(x) = \phi_k[W_k(x)] \,, \ \phi_k \ \text{increasing} \,, \ k = 1, 2, \ldots, K\} \,,$$

and $f(u') = f(u)$ for all u' in $\mathbf{L}$.

The properties of a social welfare functional corresponding to unrestricted domain and independence of irrelevant alternatives are used by Arrow in proving the impossibility of a nondictatorial social ordering:

4'. *Nondictatorship.* There is no individual k such that for all x, $y \in X$, $W_k(x) > W_k(y)$ implies xPy.

Under ordinal noncomparability the assumptions of positive association and nonimposition employed by Arrow imply the weak Pareto principle:

3'. *Pareto principle.* For any x, $y \in X$, if $W_k(x) > W_k(y)$ for all individuals $(k = 1, 2, \ldots, K)$, then xPy.

If a social welfare functional f has the properties of unrestricted domain, independence of irrelevant alternatives, the weak Pareto principle, and ordinal noncomparability, then no nondictatorial social ordering is possible. This result is Arrow's impossibility theorem. Since it is obvious that the class of dictatorial social orderings is too narrow to provide an adequate basis for expressing the implications of alternative ethical judgements, we propose to generate a class of social welfare functions suitable for the evaluation of alternative economic policies by weakening Arrow's assumptions.

We first consider weakening the assumption of ordinal noncomparability of individual welfare functions. Sen (1970) has shown that Arrow's conclusion that no nondictatorial social ordering is possible is preserved by replacing ordinal noncomparability by cardinal noncomparability. This implies that social orderings are invariant with respect to positive affine transformations of the individual welfare functions that may differ among individuals:

5''. *Cardinal noncomparability.* The set of individual welfare functions that yield the same social ordering $\mathbf{L}$ is defined by

$$\mathbf{L} = \{ u' : \ W_k'(x) = \alpha_k + \beta_k W_k(x) \, , \ \ \beta_k > 0 \, , \ \ k = 1, 2, \ldots, K \} \, ,$$

and $f(u') = f(u)$ for all u' in $\mathbf{L}$.

However, d'Aspremont and Gevers (1977), Deschamps and Gevers (1978), Maskin (1978), and Roberts (1980b) have shown that we obtain an interesting class of nondictatorial social orderings by requiring cardinal unit comparability of individual welfare functions, which implies that social orderings are invariant with respect to positive affine transformations with units that are the same for all individuals:

5'''. *Cardinal unit comparability.* The set of individual welfare functions that yield the same social ordering $\mathbf{L}$ is defined by

$$\mathbf{L} = \{ u' : \ W_k'(x) = \alpha_k + \beta W_k(x) \, , \ \ \beta > 0 \, , \ \ k = 1, 2, \ldots, K \} \, ,$$

and $f(u') = f(u)$ for all u' in $\mathbf{L}$.

If a social welfare functional f has the properties of unrestricted domain, independence of irrelevant alternatives, the weak Pareto

principle, and cardinal unit comparability, there exist social orderings
and a continuous real-valued social welfare function, say W, such that
if $W[u(x)] > W[u(y)]$, then xPy. Furthermore, the social welfare function can be represented in the form

$$W[u(x)] = \sum_{k=1}^{K} a_k \, W_k(x) . \tag{2.5.1}$$

If we add the assumption that the social welfare function has the
property of anonymity, that is, no individual is given greater weight
than any other individual in determining the level of social welfare,
then the social welfare function W in (2.5.1) must be symmetric in the
individual welfare functions $\{W_k\}$. The property of anonymity incorporates a notion of horizontal equity into the representation of social
orderings.

Under anonymity the function W in (2.5.1) reduces to the sum of
individual welfare functions and takes the form of a utilitarian social
welfare function. Utilitarian social welfare functions have been
employed extensively in applications of welfare economics, especially
in the measurement of inequality by methods originated by Atkinson
(1970) and Kolm (1969, 1976a, b), in the design of optimal income tax
schedules along the lines pioneered by Mirrlees (1971), and in the
evaluation of alternative economic policies by Arrow and Kalt (1979).

The approach to the measurement of social welfare based on a utilitarian social welfare function provides a worthwhile starting point for
applications. Harsanyi (1976) and Ng (1975) have pointed out that
distributional considerations can be incorporated into a utilitarian
social welfare function through the representation of individual welfare functions. However, Sen (1973, p. 18) has argued that a utilitarian
social welfare function does not take appropriate account of the distribution of welfare among individuals:

The distribution of welfare between persons is a relevant aspect of any problem of income distribution, and our evaluation of inequality will obviously
depend on whether we are concerned only with the loss of the sum of individual utilities through a bad distribution of income, or also with the inequality
of welfare levels of different individuals.

To broaden the range of possible social orderings we can require
cardinal full comparability of individual welfare functions, as defined
above. Roberts (1980b) has shown that a social welfare functional f
with the properties of unrestricted domain, independence of irrele-

vant alternatives, the weak Pareto principle, and cardinal full comparability implies the existence of a social welfare function that takes the form

$$W[u(x)] = \bar{W}(x) + g[u(x) - \bar{W}(x) \, i] \,, \tag{2.5.2}$$

where i is a vector of ones, the function $\bar{W}(x)$ corresponds to average individual welfare

$$\bar{W}(x) = \sum_{k=1}^{K} a_k \, W_k(x) \,,$$

and $g(x)$ is a linear homogeneous function of deviations of levels of individual welfare from the average.[16]

If the function $g(x)$ in the representation (2.5.2) of the social welfare function is identically equal to zero, then the social welfare function reduces to the form (2.5.1). If the function $g(x)$ is not identically zero, then the social welfare function incorporates both a measure of average individual welfare and a measure of inequality in the distribution of individual welfare. We conclude that the class of possible social welfare functions (2.5.2) includes utilitarian welfare functions, but also includes functions that are not subject to the objections that can be made to utilitarianism.

Although Roberts (1980b) has succeeded in broadening the class of possible social welfare functions beyond those consistent with utilitarianism, the social welfare functions (2.5.2) are subject to an objection raised by Sen (1973).[17] Information about alternative social states enters only through the individual welfare functions $\{W_k\}$. Sen refers to this property of a social welfare functional f as *welfarism*. Welfarism rules out characteristics of a social state that are conceivably relevant for social orderings, but that cannot be incorporated into the social welfare function through the individual welfare functions.

Roberts (1980b) has suggested the possibility of further weakening of Arrow's assumptions in order to incorporate nonwelfare characteristics of social states.[18] For this purpose we can replace the weak Pareto principle by positive association and nonimposition, as defined above. We retain the assumptions of unrestricted domain, independence of irrelevant alternatives, and cardinal full comparability of measures of individual welfare. We can partition the set of social states X into subsets, such that all states within each subset have the same nonwelfare characteristics. For each subset there exists a social ordering that can be represented by a social welfare function of the form (2.5.2).

Under the assumptions we have outlined there exists a social ordering for the set of all social states that can be represented by a social welfare function of the form

$$W(u, x) = F\{\bar{W}(x) + g[x, u(x) - \bar{W}(x) i] , x\} ,\qquad(2.5.3)$$

where the function $\bar{W}(x)$ corresponds to average individual welfare

$$\bar{W}(x) = \sum_{k=1}^{K} a_k(x) W_k(x) .$$

As before, the function g is a linear homogeneous function of deviations of levels of individual welfare from average welfare.

The class of social welfare functions (2.5.3) incorporates nonwelfare characteristics of social states through the weights $\{a_k(x)\}$ in average individual welfare $\bar{W}(x)$, through the function $g(x)$, which depends directly on the social state x as well as on deviations of levels of individual welfare from the average welfare, and through the function F, which depends directly on the social state x and on the sum of the functions $\bar{W}(x)$ and $g(x)$. This class includes social welfare functions that are not subject to the objections that can be made to welfarism.

At this point we have generated a class of possible social welfare functions capable of expressing the implications of a variety of different ethical judgements. In order to choose a specific social welfare function, we must narrow the range of possible ethical judgements by imposing further requirements on the class of possible social welfare functions. First, we must limit the dependence of the function $F(x)$ in (2.5.3) on the characteristics of alternative social states. Second, we must select a form for the function $g(x)$ in (2.5.3), which depends on deviations of levels of individual welfare from average welfare $\bar{W}(x)$. Finally, we must choose representations of the individual welfare functions $\{W_k(x)\}$ that provide cardinal full comparability.

We first rule out the dependence of the function $F(x)$ in (2.5.3) on characteristics of social states that do not enter through the functions $\bar{W}(x)$ and $g(x)$. This restriction reduces F to a function of a single variable $\bar{W} + g$. We obtain an ordinal measure of social welfare by permitting the function F to be any monotone increasing transformation. To obtain a cardinal measure of social welfare we observe that the function $\bar{W}(x) + g$ is homogeneous of degree one in the individual welfare functions $\{W_k(x)\}$. All representations of the social welfare function that preserve this property can be written in the form

$$W(u, x) = \beta[\bar{W}(x) + g(x)], \quad \beta > 0. \tag{2.5.4}$$

We conclude that only positive, homogeneous, affine transformations are permitted.

The restrictions embodied in the class of social welfare functions (2.5.4) do not reduce social welfare to a function of the individual welfare functions $\{W_k(x)\}$ alone, since the weights $\{a_k(x)\}$ in average individual welfare $\bar{W}(x)$ and the function g(x) depend on nonwelfare characteristics of the social state x. However, these social welfare functions are homogeneous of degree one in levels of individual welfare. This implies that doubling the welfare of each individual will double social welfare, holding nonwelfare characteristics of the social state constant. Blackorby and Donaldson (1982) refer to this class of social welfare functions as *distributionally homothetic*.[19]

We impose a second set of requirements on the class of social welfare functions (2.5.3) by selecting an appropriate form for the function $g(x)$. In particular, we require that this function is additive in deviations of individual welfare functions $\{W_k(x)\}$ from average welfare $\bar{W}(x)$. Since the function $g(x)$ is homogeneous of degree one, it must be a mean value function of order $\rho(x)$:[20]

$$g[x, u(x) - \bar{W}(x) i] = -\gamma(x)\left[\sum_{k=1}^{K} b_k(x) |W_k - \bar{W}|^{-\rho(x)}\right]^{-1/\rho(x)}, \tag{2.5.5}$$

where

$$\gamma(x) > 0, \quad \rho(x) \leq -1, \quad \sum_{k=1}^{K} b_k(x) = 1, \quad 0 < b_k(x) < 1, \quad (k = 1, 2, \ldots, K).$$

Under these restrictions the function $g(x)$ is negative, except at the point of perfect equality $W_k = \bar{W}, (k = 1, 2, \ldots, K)$, where it is zero.

The function (x) in the representation (2.5.5) determines the curvature of the social welfare function in the individual welfare functions $\{W_k(x)\}$. We can refer to this function as the *degree of aversion to inequality*. We assume that this function is constant, so that the corresponding social welfare function $W(u, x)$ is characterized by a constant degree of aversion to inequality. To complete the selection of an appropriate form for the social welfare function we must choose appropriate weights $\{a_k(x)\}$ for average individual welfare $\bar{W}(x)$ and $\{b_k(x)\}$ for the measure of equality $g(x)$. We find it natural to require that the two sets of weights are the same.

To incorporate a notion of horizontal equity into the social welfare functions (2.5.5) we can impose a weak form of the property of anonymity. In particular, we require that no individual is given greater weight in the social welfare function than any other individual with an identical individual welfare function. This implies that the social welfare function is symmetric in the levels of individual welfare for identical individuals. The weights $\{a_k(x)\}$ in average welfare $\bar{W}(x)$ and the measure of equality $g(x)$ must be the same for identical individuals.

Under the restrictions presented up to this point the social welfare function W takes the form

$$W(u, x) = \bar{W} - \gamma(x) \left[\sum_{k=1}^{K} a_k(x) \, |W_k - \bar{W}|^{-\rho} \right]^{-1/\rho} \tag{2.5.6}$$

where

$$\bar{W}(x) = \sum_{k=1}^{K} a_k(x) \, W_k(x) \, .$$

The condition of positive association requires that an increase in all levels of individual welfare must increase social welfare. This condition implies that the average level of individual welfare $\bar{W}$ must increase by more than the function $g(x)$, whatever the initial distribution of individual welfare. We assume that the function $\gamma(x)$ in (2.5.6) must take the maximum value consistent with positive association, so that

$$\gamma(x) = \left\{ 1 + \left[\frac{\sum_{k=1}^{K} a_k(x)}{a_j(x)} \right]^{-(\rho+1)} \right\}^{1/\rho} , \tag{2.5.7}$$

where

$$a_j(x) = \min_k a_k(x) \, , \quad (k = 1, 2, \ldots, K) \, .$$

for the social state x.

To complete the selection of a social welfare function $W(u, x)$ we require that the individual welfare functions $\{W_k\}$ in (2.5.3) must be invariant with respect to any positive affine transformation that is the same for all households.[21] Under this assumption the logarithm of the translog indirect utility function is a cardinal measure of individual welfare with full comparability among households. The social welfare function takes the form

$$W(u, x) = \ln \bar{V} - \gamma(x) \left[\sum_{k=1}^{K} a_k(x) \mid \ln V_k - \ln \bar{V} \mid^{-\rho} \right]^{-1/\rho} , \qquad (2.5.8)$$

where

$$\ln \bar{V} = \sum_{k=1}^{K} a_k(x) \ln V_k \left[\frac{pm(A_k)}{M_k} \right] .$$

We can complete the specification of a social welfare function $W(u, x)$ by choosing a set of weights $\{a_k(x)\}$ for the levels of individual welfare $\{\ln V_k[pm(A_k)/M_k]\}$ in (2.5.8). For this purpose we must appeal to a notion of vertical equity. Following Hammond (1977), we define a distribution of total expenditure $\{M_k\}$ as more *equitable* than another distribution $\{M'_k\}$ if

(i) $M_i + M_j = M'_i + M'_j$,

(ii) $M_k = M'_k$ for $k \neq i, j$,

(iii) $\ln V_i \left[\frac{pm(A_i)}{M'_i} \right] > \ln V_i \left[\frac{pm(A_i)}{M_i} \right] > \ln V_j \left[\frac{pm(A_j)}{M_j} \right]$

$$> \ln V_j \left[\frac{pm(A_j)}{M'_j} \right] .$$

We say that a social welfare function $W(u, x)$ is *equity-regarding* if it is larger for a more equitable distribution of total expenditure.

We require that the social welfare functions (2.5.8) must be equity-regarding. This amounts to imposing a version of Dalton's (1920) principle of transfers. This principle requires that a transfer of total expenditures from a rich household to a poor household that does not reverse their relative positions in the distribution of total expenditure must increase the level of social welfare.

If the social welfare functions (2.5.8) are required to be equity-regarding, then the weights $\{a_k(x)\}$ associated with the individual welfare functions $\{\ln V_k[pm(A_k)/M_k]\}$ must take the form

$$a_k(x) = \frac{m_0(p, A_k)}{\sum_{k=1}^{K} m_0(p, A_k)}, \qquad (k = 1, 2, \ldots, K). \tag{2.5.9}$$

We conclude that an equity-regarding social welfare function of the class (2.5.8) must take the form

$$W(u, x) = \ln \bar{V} - \gamma(x) \left[\frac{\sum_{k=1}^{K} m_0(p, A_k) \, | \ln V_k - \ln \bar{V} |^{-\rho}}{\sum_{k=1}^{K} m_0(p, A_k)} \right]^{-1/\rho}, \tag{2.5.10}$$

where

$$\ln \bar{V} = \frac{\sum_{k=1}^{K} m_0(p, A_k) \ln V_k \left[\dfrac{pm(A_k)}{M_k} \right]}{\sum_{k=1}^{K} m_0(p, A_k)}$$

$$= \ln p' \left(\alpha_p + \frac{1}{2} B_{pp} \ln p \right) - D(p) \frac{\sum_{k=1}^{K} m_0(p, A_k) \ln [M_k/m_0(p, A_k)]}{\sum_{k=1}^{K} m_0(p, A_k)}.$$

Furthermore, the condition of positive association implies that the function $\gamma(x)$ in (2.5.10) must take the form

$$\gamma(x) = \left\{ 1 + \left[\frac{\sum_{k=1}^{K} m_0(p, A_k)}{m_0(p, A_j)} \right]^{-(\rho+1)} \right\}^{1/\rho}, \tag{2.5.11}$$

where

$$m_0(p, A_j) = \min_{k} m_0(p, A_k), \qquad (k = 1, 2, \ldots, K).$$

In order to formulate a social cost-of-living index, we can introduce the social expenditure function, defined as the minimum level of aggregate expenditure $M = \sum_{k=1}^{K} M_k$ required to attain a given level of social welfare, say W, at a specified price system p.[22] More formally, the social expenditure function $M(p, W)$ is defined by

$$M(p, W) = \min \left\{ M : W(u, x) \geq W; \ M = \sum_{k=1}^{K} M_k \right\}. \tag{2.5.12}$$

The social expenditure function (2.5.12) is precisely analogous to the individual expenditure function (2.2.19). The individual expenditure function gives the minimum level of individual expenditure required to attain a stipulated level of individual welfare; the social expenditure function gives the minimum level of aggregate expenditure required to attain a stipulated level of social welfare. Just as the individual expenditure function and the indirect utility function can be employed in measuring the individual cost of living, the social expenditure function and the social welfare function can be employed in measuring the social cost of living.

To construct a social expenditure function we first maximize social welfare for a fixed level of aggregate expenditure. We can maximize the average level of individual welfare for a given level of aggregate expenditure by means of the Lagrangian

$$
\begin{aligned}
Z &= \ln \bar{V} + \lambda \left[\sum_{k=1}^{K} M_k - M \right], \\
&= \ln p' \left(\alpha_p + \frac{1}{2} B_{pp} \ln p \right) - D(p) \, \frac{\sum_{k=1}^{K} m_0(p, A_k) \ln [M_k/m_0(p, A_k)]}{\sum_{k=1}^{K} m_0(p, A_k)} \\
&\quad + \lambda \left[\sum_{k=1}^{K} M_k - M \right].
\end{aligned} \tag{2.5.13}
$$

The first-order conditions for a constrained maximum of average individual welfare are

$$
\frac{D(p)}{\sum_{k=1}^{K} m_0(p, A_k)} \cdot \frac{m_0(p, A_k)}{M_k} = \lambda \,,
$$

$$
\sum_{k=1}^{K} M_k = M \,, \quad (k = 1, 2, \ldots, K) \,,
$$

so that total expenditure per household equivalent member $\{M_k/m_0(p, A_k)\}$ is the same for all consuming units.

Next we consider the class of social welfare functions (2.5.8). Since the function $g(x, u - \bar{W}i)$ is nonpositive, we obtain a maximum of the social welfare function (2.5.8) if the function $g(x, u - \bar{W}i)$ can be made equal to zero while the average level of individual welfare $\bar{W}$ is a maximum. If total expenditure per household equivalent member $\{M_k/m_0(p, A_k)\}$ is the same for all consuming units, the function $g(x, u - \bar{W}i)$ is equal to zero, so that the social welfare function $W(u, x)$ in (2.5.8) is a maximum.

If aggregate expenditure is distributed so as to equalize total expenditure per household equivalent member, the level of individual welfare is the same for all consuming units. For this distribution of total expenditure the social welfare functions (2.5.8) reduce to the average level of individual welfare $\ln \bar{V}$. For the translog indirect utility function the maximum value of social welfare for a given level of aggregate expenditure takes the form

$$W(x, u) = \ln \bar{V} . \tag{2.5.14}$$

$$= \ln p' \left(\alpha_p + \frac{1}{2} B_{pp} \ln p \right) - D(p) \ln \left[M \Big/ \sum_{k=1}^{K} m_0(p, A_k) \right].$$

This value of social welfare is obtained by evaluating the translog indirect utility function (2.2.22) at total expenditure per household equivalent member $M / \sum_{k=1}^{K} m_0(p, A_k)$ for the economy as a whole. We can solve for aggregate expenditure as a function of the level of social welfare and prices

$$\ln M(p, W) = \frac{1}{D(p)} \left[\ln p' \left(\alpha_p + \frac{1}{2} B_{pp} \ln p \right) - W \right]$$

$$+ \ln \left[\sum_{k=1}^{K} m_0(p, A_k) \right]. \tag{2.5.15}$$

We can refer to this function as the *translog social expenditure function*. The value of aggregate expenditure is obtained by evaluating the translog individual expenditure function (2.2.23) at the level of social welfare W and the number of household equivalent members $\sum_{k=1}^{K} m_0(p, A_k)$ for the economy as a whole.

To summarize: We have generated a class of social welfare functions (2.5.3) that has the properties of unrestricted domain, independence of irrelevant alternatives, positive association, nonimposition, and cardinal full comparability. By imposing the additional assumption that the degree of aversion to inequality is constant and requiring the social welfare function to satisfy requirements of horizontal and vertical equity, we obtain the social welfare functions (2.5.10). Finally, we have derived a social expenditure function (2.5.15) giving the minimum aggregate expenditure required to attain a base level of social welfare.

2.6 Social Cost-of-Living Index

In this section we present methods for translating changes in prices into measures of change in the social cost of living. Following Pollak (1981), we define the social cost-of-living index, say P, as the ratio of two levels of aggregate expenditure

$$P(p^1, p^0, W^0) = \frac{M(p^1, W^0)}{M(p^0, W^0)} .$$ (2.6.1)

In this ratio the numerator is the aggregate expenditure required to attain the base level of social welfare W^0 at the current price system p^1; the denominator is the expenditure required to attain this level of social welfare at the base price system p^0 .

The social welfare functions (2.5.10) and the translog social expenditure function (2.5.15) can be employed in implementing the social cost-of-living index (2.6.1). First, we can express the base level of social welfare W^0 in terms of the social welfare functions

$$W^0 = \ln \bar{V}^0 - \left\{ 1 + \left[\frac{\sum_{k=1}^{K} m_0(p^0, A_k)}{m_0(p^0, A_j)} \right]^{-1(\rho-1)} \right\}^{1/\rho}$$

$$\times \left[\frac{\sum_{k=1}^{K} m_0(p^0, A_k) \,|\ln V_k^0 - \ln \bar{V}^0|^{-\rho}}{\sum_{k=1}^{K} m_0(p^0, A_k)} \right]^{-1/\rho} ,$$ (2.6.2)

where

$$\ln \bar{V}^0 = \frac{\sum_{k=1}^{K} m_0(p^0, A_k) \ln V_k \left[p^0 m(A_k)/M_k^0 \right]}{\sum_{k=1}^{K} m_0(p^0, A_k)} ,$$

and

$$\ln V_k^0 = \ln p^{0\prime} \left(\alpha_p + \frac{1}{2} B_{pp} \ln p^0 \right) - D(p^0) \ln [M_k^0/m_0(p^0, A_k)], \, (k = 1, 2, \ldots, K) .$$

Using the translog social expenditure function (2.5.15), we can express the social cost-of-living index (2.6.1) in the form

$$\ln P(p^1, p^0, W^0) = \frac{1}{D(p^1)} \left[\ln p^{1\prime} \left(\alpha_p + \frac{1}{2} B_{pp} \ln p^1 \right) - W^0 \right]$$

$$+ \ln \left[\sum_{k=1}^{K} m_0(p^1, A_k) \right] - \ln M^0 . \tag{2.6.3}$$

We can refer to the index P as the *translog social cost-of-living index*. If the translog index is greater than unity and aggregate expenditure is constant, then social welfare is decreased by the change in prices.

The translog social expenditure function (2.5.15) has the same form as the translog individual expenditure function (2.2.23). We can express the level of social welfare as a function of the price system p and aggregate expenditure M. We can take this level of social welfare to be the average level of individual welfare $\bar{W}$, obtained by redistributing aggregate expenditure among households so as to equalize total expenditure per household equivalent member. Under this assumption society behaves in the same way as an individual maximizing a utility function, as demonstrated by Samuelson (1956) and Pollak (1981). We can represent social welfare in terms of the indifference map for a single representative consumer, as in figure 2.1 above.

In figure 2.2 we have depicted the indifference map of the representative consumer with indirect utility function given by the average level of utility $\ln \bar{V}$ in (2.5.14). As before, we consider the case of two commodities ($N = 2$) for simplicity. Equilibrium of the representative consumer at the base price system p^0 is represented by the point A with base level of average welfare $\bar{W}^0$. The corresponding level of aggregate expenditure M^0, divided by the base price of the second commodity p_2^0, is given on the vertical axis. This axis provides a representation of aggregate expenditure in terms of units of the second commodity.

Equilibrium of the representative consumer after the change in prices is represented by the point B with associated level of average welfare $\bar{W}^{-1}$. The level of aggregate expenditure associated with the change in prices M^1, divided by the current price of the second commodity p_2^1, is given, as before, on the vertical axis. Finally, the level of aggregate expenditure required to attain the base level of average welfare $\bar{W}^0$ at current prices $M(p^1, \bar{W}^0)$, corresponds to equilibrium of the representative consumer at the point C. The social cost-of-living index is given by the ratio of the distances on the vertical axis corresponding

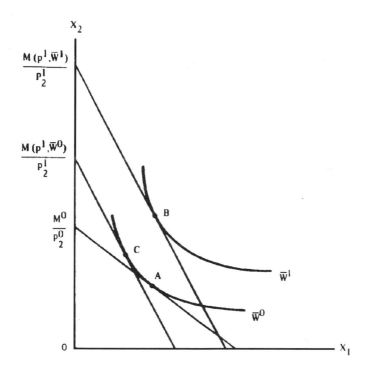

Figure 2.2
Social Cost-of-Living Index.

to consumer equilibrium at points C and A, multiplied by the ratio of prices of the second commodity at the two points p_2^1 / p_2^0.

As a further illustration of the social cost-of-living index, we analyze the changes in prices over the period 1958–1978, using prices for 1972 as the base price system. As before, we employ the econometric model of aggregate consumer behavior presented in section 2.3 for this purpose. Using the translog social cost-of-living index (2.6.3), we can assess the impact of price changes on the U.S. economy as a whole. We present the social cost-of-living index and rates of inflation corresponding to this index in table 2.3. Over the twenty-year period 1958–1978 this index has risen from .6928 to 1.5214 with 1972 equal to 1.0000.

To summarize: We have defined the social cost-of-living index as the ratio of the aggregate expenditure required to attain a base level of social welfare at current prices to the base level of expenditure. Using the average level of social welfare (2.5.14) and the translog social

Table 2.3
Social cost-of-living index

Year	Social Cost-of-Living Index (1972 = 1.0000)	Inflation Rate (annual percentage rates)
1958	0.6928	0.00
1959	0.6946	0.25
1960	0.7156	2.96
1961	0.7217	0.85
1962	0.7296	1.09
1963	0.7335	0.53
1964	0.7497	2.17
1965	0.7731	3.07
1966	0.7947	2.75
1967	0.8030	1.03
1968	0.8303	3.34
1969	0.8831	6.16
1970	0.8972	1.58
1971	0.9344	4.06
1972	1.0000	6.77
1973	1.0748	7.21
1974	1.1619	7.79
1975	1.2194	4.83
1976	1.3101	7.17
1977	1.4281	8.61
1978	1.5214	6.33

expenditure function (2.5.15), we implement this definition by means of the translog social cost-of-living index (2.6.3). We illustrate the translog index by analyzing changes in prices over the period 1958–1978 for the U.S. economy as a whole.

2.7   Group Cost-of-Living Indexes

In sections 2.4 and 2.6 we have presented cost-of-living indexes for individual households and for the U.S. economy as a whole. In this section our objective is to provide measures of the cost of living for groups of households. For this purpose we introduce group welfare and expenditure functions that are precisely analogous to the social welfare and expenditure functions of section 2.5. We consider a group of G individuals, where $1 \leq G \leq K$; without loss of generality we can take the group to be comprised of the first G individuals in society.

To describe group orderings we find it useful to introduce the following notation:

x_{ng} — the quantity of the nth commodity group consumed by the gth consuming unit $(n = 1, 2, \ldots, N; \; g = 1, 2, \ldots, G)$.

x_G — a matrix with elements $\{x_{ng}\}$ describing the group state.

$u_G = (W_1, W_2, \ldots, W_G)$ — a vector of individual welfare functions for all G individuals.

We can define a group welfare functional as a mapping from the set of individual welfare functions to the set of group orderings. We can describe a group ordering in terms of properties of a group welfare functional that are precisely analogous to the properties of a social welfare functional considered in section 2.5: unrestricted domain, independence of irrelevant alternatives, positive association, nonimposition, and cardinal full comparability. Under these assumptions there exists a group ordering for the set of all group states that can be represented by a group welfare function analogous to the social welfare function (2.5.3)

$$W_G(u_G, x_G) = F\{\bar{W}_G(x_G) + g[x_G, u_G(x_G) - \bar{W}_G(x_G) \, i], x_G\} , \qquad (2.7.1)$$

where the function $\bar{W}_G(x_G)$ corresponds to average individual welfare

$$\bar{W}_G(x_G) = \sum_{g=1}^{G} a_g(x_G) \, W_g(x_G) .$$

As before, the function g is a linear homogeneous function of deviations of levels of individual welfare from average welfare for the group.

We can rule out the direct dependence of the function $F(x_G)$ in (2.7.1) on characteristics of group states x_G. As in section 2.5, this results in a cardinal representation of group welfare. To complete the selection of a group welfare function $W_G(u_G, x_G)$ we require, as before, that the individual welfare functions $\{W_g(x_G)\}$ must be invariant with respect to any positive affine transformation that is the same for all households. Second, we require that the group welfare function is equity-regarding. Under these assumptions the group welfare function must take forms analogous to (2.5.10).

In order to formulate a group cost-of-living index, we can introduce a group expenditure function, defined as the minimum level of group expenditure $M_G = \sum_{g=1}^{G} M_g$ required to attain a given level of group welfare, say W_G, at a specified price system p. We can maximize group welfare for a fixed level of group expenditure by equalizing total expenditure per household equivalent member. For the translog indirect utility function the group welfare function takes the form

$$W_G(u_G, x_G) = \ln \bar{V}_G \, ,$$

$$= \ln p' \left(\alpha_p + \frac{1}{2} B_{pp} \ln p \right) - D(p) \ln \left[M_G \Big/ \sum_{g=1}^{G} m_0(p, A_g) \right], \quad (2.7.2)$$

where $\ln \bar{V}_G$ is the average level of individual welfare.

We can solve for group expenditure as a function of the level of group welfare and prices

$$\ln M_G(p, W_G) = \frac{1}{D(p)} \left[\ln p' \left(\alpha_p + \frac{1}{2} B_{pp} \ln p \right) - W_G \right]$$

$$+ \ln \left[\sum_{g=1}^{G} m_0(p, A_g) \right]. \quad (2.7.3)$$

We can refer to this function as the *translog group expenditure function.* The value of group expenditure is obtained by evaluating the translog individual expenditure function (2.2.23) at the level of group welfare W_G and the number of household equivalent members $\sum_{g=1}^{G} m_0(p, A_g)$ for the group as a whole.

We can define the group cost-of-living index, say P_G, as the ratio of two levels of group expenditure

$$P_G(p^1, p^0, W_G^0) = \frac{M_G(p^1, W_G^0)}{M_G(p^0, W_G^0)} \, . \quad (2.7.4)$$

In this ratio the numerator is the group expenditure required to attain the base level of group welfare W_G^0 at the current price system p^1; the denominator is the expenditure required for this level of welfare at the base price system p^0. Using the translog group expenditure function (2.7.3), we can express the group cost-of-living index (2.7.4) in the form

$$\ln P_G(p^1, p^0, W_G^0) = \frac{1}{D(p^1)} \left[\ln p^1 \left(\alpha_p + \frac{1}{2} B_{pp} \ln p^1 \right) - W_G^0 \right]$$

$$+ \ln \left[\sum_{g=1}^{G} m_0(p^1, A_g) \right] - \ln M_G^0 \, . \quad (2.7.5)$$

We can refer to the index P_G as the *translog group cost-of-living index*. If the translog index is greater than unity and group expenditure is constant, then group welfare is decreased by the change in prices.

The translog group expenditure function (2.7.3) has the same form as the translog social expenditure function (2.5.15). To obtain the group expenditure function from the social expenditure function, we replace social welfare W and the number of household equivalent members for society as a whole $\sum_{k=1}^{K} m_0(p, A_k)$ by group welfare W_G and the number of household equivalent members for the group $\sum_{g=1}^{G} m_0(p, A_g)$.

We can express the level of group welfare as a function of the price system p and group expenditure M_G. We can take this level of welfare to be the average level of individual welfare $\bar{W}_G$, obtained by equalizing total expenditure per household equivalent member among all households in the group. Under this assumption the group behaves like an individual maximizing a utility function. We can represent group welfare in terms of the indifference map for a single representative consumer, just as we represented social welfare function in terms of such an indifference map in figure 2.2.

We can illustrate the group cost-of-living index by analyzing the changes in prices over the period 1958–1978, using prices for 1972 as a base price system. We have calculated cost-of-living indexes for twenty-one different groups of households, classified by demographic characteristics. These demographic characteristics include size of household, age of head of household, region of residence, race, and urban versus rural residence. For this purpose we set the base level of group welfare at the level the group attained in 1972. We present translog group cost-of-living indexes for the period 1958–1978 in appendix table 2.A.2.

We present rates of inflation calculated from the translog group cost-of-living indexes for seven family size groups in table 2.4. In virtually every year the rates of inflation increase or decrease monotonically with family size. The most dramatic changes occur between unattached individuals, families of size one, and families of size two or more. For example, in 1975 unattached individuals had an inflation rate of only 3.65 percent, while households of size two experienced an inflation rate of 4.78 percent and households with seven or more members had an inflation rate of 5.31 percent. At the opposite extreme, individuals experienced an increase in cost of living of 7.98

Table 2.4
Change in group cost-of-living indexes

Year	Family Size						
	1	2	3	4	5	6	7+
1959	−0.16	0.26	0.31	0.32	0.34	0.33	0.34
1960	3.43	3.00	2.94	2.90	2.82	2.82	2.73
1961	0.79	0.85	0.85	0.85	0.87	0.87	0.88
1962	1.09	1.09	1.09	1.09	1.08	1.08	1.08
1963	0.21	0.51	0.55	0.57	0.62	0.62	0.67
1964	2.54	2.18	2.14	2.12	2.08	2.07	2.03
1965	3.63	3.09	3.02	2.98	2.92	2.93	2.87
1966	2.63	2.72	2.73	2.76	2.82	2.84	2.93
1967	0.40	1.02	1.10	1.13	1.18	1.17	1.22
1968	3.06	3.32	3.36	3.39	3.42	3.40	3.45
1969	6.76	6.19	6.12	6.08	6.00	6.00	5.92
1970	0.38	1.50	1.64	1.73	1.93	1.93	2.17
1971	4.07	4.09	4.09	4.07	4.03	4.01	3.96
1972	7.98	6.82	6.67	6.60	6.46	6.47	6.33
1973	7.68	7.15	7.08	7.10	7.18	7.25	7.36
1974	6.23	7.68	7.84	7.95	8.28	8.38	8.69
1975	3.65	4.78	4.91	4.99	5.14	5.14	5.31
1976	7.71	7.30	7.24	7.13	6.92	6.86	6.57
1977	9.50	8.72	8.60	8.49	8.31	8.29	8.05
1978	6.58	6.27	6.24	6.26	6.34	6.38	6.50

Table 2.4 (continued)

	Age of Head					
Year	16–24	25–34	35–44	45–54	55–64	65+
1959	−0.27	0.02	0.30	0.37	0.39	0.21
1960	3.62	3.20	2.92	2.83	2.83	3.00
1961	0.76	0.81	0.85	0.87	0.87	0.85
1962	1.07	1.06	1.08	1.10	1.10	1.09
1963	0.07	0.36	0.57	0.62	0.63	0.50
1964	2.63	2.36	2.16	2.07	2.05	2.19
1965	3.82	3.34	2.99	2.92	2.91	3.13
1966	2.50	2.66	2.74	2.82	2.81	2.77
1967	0.21	0.73	1.13	1.19	1.21	0.96
1968	2.93	3.21	3.42	3.40	3.40	3.28
1969	6.94	6.46	6.13	6.00	5.97	6.20
1970	−0.12	0.91	1.68	1.95	1.97	1.51
1971	4.10	4.03	4.06	4.06	4.07	4.06
1972	8.35	7.36	6.64	6.45	6.42	6.89
1973	7.71	7.41	7.05	7.15	7.12	7.36
1974	5.81	7.00	7.66	8.30	8.40	7.86
1975	3.25	4.21	4.92	5.16	5.20	4.74
1976	8.08	7.47	7.18	6.97	6.98	7.14
1977	9.90	9.01	8.49	8.37	8.38	8.69
1978	6.55	6.44	6.25	6.30	6.27	6.41

Table 2.4 (continued)

Year	| Region |||				| Race ||		| Residence ||	
	NE	NC	S	W	White	Non- White	Urban	Rural
1959	0.13	0.29	0.40	0.12	0.26	0.19	0.23	0.62
1960	3.06	2.95	2.81	3.14	2.97	2.92	2.99	2.63
1961	0.84	0.85	0.87	0.83	0.85	0.84	0.85	0.88
1962	1.08	1.09	1.08	1.10	1.09	1.06	1.09	1.08
1963	0.46	0.54	0.63	0.43	0.53	0.54	0.51	0.75
1964	2.26	2.14	2.04	2.32	2.17	2.17	2.19	1.85
1965	3.21	3.03	2.88	3.25	3.07	3.07	3.09	2.63
1966	2.76	2.74	2.79	2.70	2.75	2.81	2.75	2.78
1967	0.87	1.08	1.24	0.83	1.04	1.01	1.00	1.53
1968	3.27	3.35	3.42	3.28	3.34	3.35	3.33	3.50
1969	6.30	6.12	5.95	6.40	6.17	6.14	6.19	5.67
1970	1.32	1.62	1.98	1.17	1.57	1.62	1.52	2.42
1971	4.03	4.08	4.05	4.10	4.07	3.96	4.06	4.09
1972	7.06	6.69	6.36	7.20	6.77	6.75	6.83	5.82
1973	7.42	7.14	7.07	7.26	7.19	7.41	7.24	6.78
1974	7.53	7.90	8.40	6.93	7.77	8.05	7.70	9.23
1975	4.56	4.90	5.23	4.40	4.82	4.85	4.77	5.74
1976	7.19	7.21	6.98	7.44	7.20	6.92	7.19	6.93
1977	8.76	8.60	8.32	8.94	8.63	8.42	8.65	8.08
1978	6.46	6.27	6.25	6.35	6.31	6.50	6.35	6.04

percent in 1972, while households of size two had a rate of 6.82 percent and households of size seven or more had only 6.33 percent.

We present the impact of changes in prices on measures of the group cost of living for age groups in table 2.4. We observe that rates of inflation increase or decrease monotonically with age up to the age group 55–64. In fact, the pattern of inflation rates for different age groups is similar to that for different family sizes. The reason for this is that there is a sizable correlation between family size and age of the head of household. Younger and older age groups are associated with smaller family sizes, while families in the middle of the age range are associated with larger sizes. Finally, we present rates of inflation for groups living in different regions, the two racial groups, and urban versus rural residents in table 2.4. Regional differences and differences between urban and rural residents are substantial, while racial differences are not.

To summarize: We have generated group welfare functions that are analogous to the social welfare functions (2.5.10). Second, we have derived a group expenditure function (2.7.3), giving the minimum group expenditure required to attain a base level of group welfare. Finally, we have defined a group cost-of-living indexes in terms of the ratio of the group expenditure required to attain a base level of group welfare at current prices to the base level of expenditure. We illustrate group cost-of-living indexes by comparing rates of inflation among twenty-one demographic groups for the period 1958–1978.

2.8 Summary and Conclusion

In this chapter we have presented an econometric approach to individual, group, and social cost-of-living measurement. The key to our approach is provided by the translog indirect utility function (2.2.22) and the translog individual expenditure function (2.2.23). In section 2.2 we show how the translog indirect utility and expenditure functions can be determined from a system of individual expenditure shares (2.2.5) that is integrable. We also demonstrate how the individual expenditure shares (2.2.5) can be recovered uniquely from the system of aggregate expenditure shares (2.2.25).

In section 2.3 we fit an econometric model of aggregate consumer behavior that incorporates the restrictions implied by integrability of the individual expenditure shares. In section 2.4 we define a cost-of-living index for the individual consuming unit. We implement this index for the period 1958–1978, using translog indirect utility and expenditure functions for all consuming units.

We define and implement a cost-of-living index for the U.S. economy as a whole for the period 1958–1978 in section 2.6. This definition is precisely analogous to the definition of an individual cost-of-living index. The role of the indirect utility function is played by an explicit social welfare function introduced in section 2.5. The role of the individual expenditure function is played by the translog social expenditure function (2.5.15). This expenditure function is simply the translog individual expenditure function, evaluated at aggregate expenditure per household equivalent member.

In section 2.7 we extend the concept of a social cost-of-living index to groups of individuals. We obtain a translog group cost-of-living index that can be expressed in terms of group welfare and expenditure functions. The group expenditure function is the translog individual expenditure function, evaluated at group expenditure per household equivalent member. We present cost-of-living indexes for twenty-one demographic groups for the period 1958–1978.

Next, we find it useful to compare the information required for implementation of the econometric approach to cost-of-living measurement with that required for conventional cost-of-living index numbers.[23] Our cross-section data set, the Survey of Consumer Expenditures for 1972, was assembled for the purpose of providing weights for the Consumer Price Index in the United States. We have employed this data set in estimating the impact of total expenditures and demographic characteristics of households on individual expenditure patterns.

Conventional cost-of-living index numbers are based on weighted averages of price relatives for individual commodity groups. The weights are based on averages of expenditure shares for groups of consumers. Measures of the cost of living for different groups can be constructed by compiling weights for each group. These weights require cross-section data like those collected in the Survey of Consumer Expenditures.

By contrast, the econometric approach is based on sample moments of cross-section data on individual expenditures on specific commodities, total expenditures, and the demographic characteristics of individual households. These sample moments are combined with time series data on prices and aggregate expenditure patterns to estimate the parameters of our econometric model. Estimates like those presented in section 2.3 summarize the cross-section and time series data in a concise and readily intelligible way.

We have found it convenient to employ price data for commodity groups from the U.S. national accounts. These data are based largely on price information compiled for the Consumer Price Index published by the Bureau of Labor Statistics. Our approach could be implemented for price data taken directly from the Consumer Price Index. This would have the advantage of providing greater comparability between the results of the econometric approach and the index number approach employed currently.

Our econometric model employs time series data on the level of aggregate expenditure, its distribution over commodity groups, and its distribution over the population and among demographic groups. We have constructed these data from the *Current Population Survey*, which is conducted monthly in the United States. The necessary information is contained in the summary statistics of the joint distribution of expenditures and attributes—$\sum M_k \ln M_k/M$ and $\{\sum M_k\ A_k/M\}$ — presented in section 2.2.

Although the econometric approach to cost-of-living measurement requires more data than the conventional index number approach, the econometric approach has overwhelming practical advantages. First and foremost, it allows for substitution among commodities in response to price changes. To achieve similar results by means of conventional index numbers, it would be necessary to have surveys of consumer expenditures at the same frequency as the intervals used for reporting the cost-of-living index, which would be far too burdensome.

A second advantage of the econometric approach to cost-of-living measurement is in flexibility and ease of application. We have implemented a social cost-of-living index for the United States in section 2.6. In addition, we have compared cost-of-living increases for typical consuming units in section 2.4. Finally, we have made comparisons among cost-of-living increases for groups of consuming units in section 2.7. Our approach could also be used to construct special cost-of-living indexes for groups such as low income households receiving government transfer payments or aged households living on pensions.

While the econometric approach has important advantages over the conventional index number approach, it is important to emphasize that the two approaches share a number of limitations. In principle prices for commodity groups must be compiled for goods and services of constant quality. In actuality statisticians are faced with rapidly changing commodity specifications and with the introduction of new commodities. As an illustration, the addition of pollution control equipment to automobiles poses exactly the same problems for the two approaches.

A second set of problems common to the econometric and the index number approaches is posed by consumption not associated with direct purchases of goods and services. As an illustration, the imputed value of home produced goods such as food produced on farms must be included in total expenditure. Similarly, an imputation is required for flows of services from owner-occupied housing and owner-utilized transportation equipment and other consumer durables. A more complex range of problems is posed by goods and services consumed collectively, such as police protection and environmental quality.

Finally, the implementation of the econometric approach described in this chapter has important limitations of its own. We have employed prices for all commodity groups compiled at the national level. A more detailed implementation incorporating regional and other differences in prices actually paid would be useful in many applications. In addition, it would be very desirable to provide a more detailed commodity breakdown. These limitations can be overcome by expenditure of greater resources of human effort and computer time. Fortunately, existing data bases will be adequate for the construction of far more detailed econometric models than the model we have presented.

Up to this point we have compared the econometric approach with the conventional index number approach, such as that employed by the Bureau of Labor Statistics in the United States or by Statistics Canada. It is also interesting to compare the econometric approach with a more sophisticated index number approach proposed by Diewert (1976, 1981). Diewert's approach is based on exact index numbers.[24] Exact index numbers do not require an econometric model, but reproduce exactly the individual cost-of-living index derived from an individual expenditure function.

An important example of the sophisticated index number approach is the exact translog cost-of-living index considered by Törnqvist (1936)

$$\ln P_k(p^1, p^0, V_k^*) = \overline{w_k'} \, \Delta \ln p \,, \qquad (k = 1, 2, \ldots, K) \,, \qquad (2.8.1)$$

where V_k^* is the base level of individual welfare

$$V_k^* = (V_k^1 V_k^0)^{1/2} \,, \qquad (k = 1, 2, \ldots, K) \,,$$

and

$$\bar{w}_k = \frac{1}{2} \, (w_k^1 + w_k^0) \,, \qquad (k = 1, 2, \ldots, K) \,,$$
$$\Delta \ln p = \ln p^1 - \ln p^0 \,.$$

Diewert (1976, 1981) has shown that this cost-of-living index is exact for a translog individual expenditure function similar but not identical to our expenditure function (2.2.23).

The data required for implementation of the exact index number approach are far more extensive than those required for the econometric approach. For example, the exact translog cost-of-living index (2.8.1) would require data on individual expenditure shares for each period in which a cost-of-living comparison is needed. An annual time series of comparisons would require that a panel of consumers would have to be surveyed annually.

It is important to note that the exact index number approach is not limited to individual cost-of-living measurement. For social or group cost-of-living measurement a translog cost-of-living index could be defined on the basis of the corresponding translog social or group expenditure functions. The individual budget shares in the index (2.8.1) could be replaced by aggregate or group expenditure shares.

In order to apply the exact translog cost-of-living index (2.8.1) to society as a whole, it would be necessary to obtain aggregate expenditure shares from an econometric model. These shares would correspond to those of a representative consumer, constructed by equalizing aggregate expenditure per household equivalent member over all consuming units. Data on aggregate expenditure shares employed in fitting an econometric model would not be appropriate for this purpose. These expenditure shares correspond to the actual distribution of total expenditure over the population.

Similarly, the exact translog cost-of-living index (2.8.1) could be applied to groups, but only by calculating expenditure shares for the group for an econometric model. As before, these shares would correspond to those of a representative consumer. The demand system for the representative consumer would be obtained by equalizing group expenditure per household equivalent member over the households included in the group.

Despite the limitations of the exact index number approach, we find it useful to present an exact translog social cost-of-living index calculated from the Törnqvist formula (2.8.1) in table 2.5. This index can be compared with the translog social cost-of-living index presented in table 2.3. The two indexes are similar, but not identical. An important difference between the two is that the exact translog index is a chain index with base welfare levels changing from period to period, while the translog index presented in table 2.3 employs the level of welfare in 1972 as a base.

Table 2.5
Exact translog cost-of-living index

Year	Exact Cost-of-living index (1972 = 1.0000)	Inflation rate (annual percentage rates)
1958	0.6934	—
1959	0.6952	0.26
1960	0.7156	2.89
1961	0.7216	0.83
1962	0.7293	1.06
1963	0.7334	0.56
1964	0.7490	2.10
1965	0.7730	3.15
1966	0.7939	2.67
1967	0.8018	0.99
1968	0.8295	3.40
1969	0.8823	6.17
1970	0.8981	1.77
1971	0.9353	4.06
1972	1.0000	6.69
1973	1.0755	7.28
1974	1.1632	7.84
1975	1.2310	5.66
1976	1.3142	6.54
1977	1.4330	8.65
1978	1.5254	6.25

Our final conclusion is that the econometric approach has very substantial advantages over both conventional and sophisticated index number approaches. However, the econometric approach is not a panacea for the solution of all the practical problems of cost-of-living measurement. As better solutions to these problems become available, the results can be incorporated into an econometric model like that we have presented.

Appendix Tables

Table 2.A.1
Individual cost-of-living indexes (1972 = 1.0000)

Year	Urban		Rural	
	White	Nonwhite	White	Nonwhite
1958	0.6969	0.6968	0.7002	0.7001
1959	0.6967	0.6964	0.7019	0.7016
1960	0.7176	0.7173	0.7209	0.7207
1961	0.7236	0.7233	0.7272	0.7269
1962	0.7311	0.7308	0.7346	0.7342
1963	0.7345	0.7341	0.7392	0.7389
1964	0.7508	0.7507	0.7535	0.7534
1965	0.7758	0.7756	0.7760	0.7758
1966	0.7992	0.7989	0.7998	0.7994
1967	0.8051	0.8048	0.8086	0.8084
1968	0.8310	0.8311	0.8353	0.8354
1969	0.8840	0.8845	0.8849	0.8854
1970	0.8973	0.8973	0.9042	0.9042
1971	0.9319	0.9317	0.9390	0.9388
1972	1.0000	1.0000	1.0000	1.0000
1973	1.0856	1.0848	1.0834	1.0826
1974	1.1864	1.1818	1.2014	1.1968
1975	1.2430	1.2375	1.2681	1.2625
1976	1.3251	1.3197	1.3479	1.3425
1977	1.4407	1.4341	1.4590	1.4524
1978	1.5459	1.5385	1.5633	1.5558

Region = Northeast
Size = 5
Age = 35–44
Expenditure = $4,467

Appendix Table 2.A.1 (continued)

Year	Urban		Rural	
	White	Nonwhite	White	Nonwhite
1958	0.6946	0.6945	0.6978	0.6978
1959	0.6952	0.6949	0.7004	0.7001
1960	0.7162	0.7159	0.7195	0.7193
1961	0.7222	0.7219	0.7258	0.7255
1962	0.7299	0.7296	0.7334	0.7330
1963	0.7335	0.7332	0.7382	0.7379
1964	0.7500	0.7498	0.7527	0.7525
1965	0.7742	0.7740	0.7745	0.7743
1966	0.7967	0.7964	0.7973	0.7970
1967	0.8037	0.8034	0.8072	0.8069
1968	0.8304	0.8305	0.8348	0.8349
1969	0.8836	0.8841	0.8845	0.8850
1970	0.8969	0.8970	0.9039	0.9039
1971	0.9328	0.9326	0.9398	0.9397
1972	1.0000	1.0000	1.0000	1.0000
1973	1.0802	1.0794	1.0780	1.0771
1974	1.1720	1.1675	1.1868	1.1823
1975	1.2282	1.2228	1.2530	1.2475
1976	1.3145	1.3092	1.3372	1.3318
1977	1.4309	1.4244	1.4491	1.4425
1978	1.5301	1.5228	1.5473	1.5399

Region = Northeast
Size = 5
Age = 35–44
Expenditure = $8,934

Appendix Table 2.A.1 (continued)

Year	Urban		Rural	
	White	Nonwhite	White	Nonwhite
1958	0.6923	0.6922	0.6955	0.6954
1959	0.6937	0.6934	0.6988	0.6986
1960	0.7148	0.7145	0.7181	0.7179
1961	0.7209	0.7206	0.7244	0.7241
1962	0.7287	0.7284	0.7322	0.7318
1963	0.7326	0.7322	0.7373	0.7369
1964	0.7491	0.7490	0.7518	0.7517
1965	0.7727	0.7724	0.7729	0.7727
1966	0.7943	0.7939	0.7948	0.7945
1967	0.8023	0.8020	0.8058	0.8055
1968	0.8298	0.8299	0.8342	0.8343
1969	0.8833	0.8837	0.8842	0.8846
1970	0.8966	0.8966	0.9035	0.9035
1971	0.9336	0.9335	0.9407	0.9405
1972	1.0000	1.0000	1.0000	1.0000
1973	1.0748	1.0740	1.0725	1.0717
1974	1.1577	1.1533	1.1724	1.1679
1975	1.2137	1.2083	1.2382	1.2327
1976	1.3041	1.2988	1.3266	1.3212
1977	1.4212	1.4147	1.4392	1.4327
1978	1.5145	1.5073	1.5315	1.5242

Region = Northeast
Size = 5
Age = 35–44
Expenditure = $17,864

Table 2.A.2
Group cost-of-living indexes (1972 = 1.0000)

	Family Size						
Year	1	2	3	4	5	6	7+
1958	0.6917	0.6927	0.6930	0.6930	0.6932	0.6935	0.6932
1959	0.6906	0.6946	0.6952	0.6953	0.6956	0.6958	0.6956
1960	0.7147	0.7157	0.7160	0.7158	0.7156	0.7157	0.7148
1961	0.7204	0.7219	0.7221	0.7219	0.7218	0.7220	0.7212
1962	0.7283	0.7298	0.7301	0.7299	0.7297	0.7299	0.7291
1963	0.7299	0.7336	0.7341	0.7341	0.7343	0.7344	0.7340
1964	0.7487	0.7498	0.7500	0.7499	0.7497	0.7498	0.7492
1965	0.7764	0.7733	0.7730	0.7726	0.7720	0.7722	0.7710
1966	0.7971	0.7947	0.7944	0.7942	0.7941	0.7945	0.7940
1967	0.8004	0.8029	0.8033	0.8033	0.8036	0.8038	0.8037
1968	0.8252	0.8300	0.8308	0.8311	0.8316	0.8317	0.8320
1969	0.8830	0.8831	0.8832	0.8832	0.8831	0.8831	0.8828
1970	0.8864	0.8965	0.8979	0.8987	0.9003	0.9004	0.9021
1971	0.9232	0.9340	0.9354	0.9361	0.9374	0.9373	0.9386
1972	1.0000	1.0000	1.0000	1.0000	1.0000	1.0000	1.0000
1973	1.0798	1.0741	1.0734	1.0736	1.0744	1.0752	1.0764
1974	1.1493	1.1600	1.1610	1.1624	1.1672	1.1692	1.1742
1975	1.1921	1.2168	1.2195	1.2219	1.2288	1.2309	1.2382
1976	1.2877	1.3090	1.3111	1.3123	1.3169	1.3184	1.3224
1977	1.4161	1.4283	1.4290	1.4287	1.4310	1.4325	1.4333
1978	1.5125	1.5208	1.5210	1.5211	1.5247	1.5270	1.5295

Appendix Table 2.A.2 (continued)

	Age of Head					
Year	16–24	25–34	35–44	45–54	55–64	65+
1958	0.6930	0.6938	0.6926	0.6926	0.6928	0.6927
1959	0.6911	0.6940	0.6947	0.6952	0.6956	0.6943
1960	0.7166	0.7165	0.7153	0.7152	0.7156	0.7154
1961	0.7221	0.7224	0.7214	0.7215	0.7219	0.7216
1962	0.7299	0.7301	0.7293	0.7295	0.7299	0.7295
1963	0.7305	0.7328	0.7335	0.7341	0.7345	0.7332
1964	0.7500	0.7503	0.7495	0.7494	0.7497	0.7495
1965	0.7792	0.7758	0.7723	0.7717	0.7719	0.7734
1966	0.7990	0.7967	0.7938	0.7938	0.7939	0.7952
1967	0.8008	0.8026	0.8029	0.8034	0.8036	0.8028
1968	0.8246	0.8288	0.8308	0.8312	0.8314	0.8297
1969	0.8839	0.8842	0.8834	0.8826	0.8826	0.8828
1970	0.8828	0.8923	0.8984	0.9000	0.9003	0.8962
1971	0.9198	0.9290	0.9357	0.9374	0.9377	0.9333
1972	1.0000	1.0000	1.0000	1.0000	1.0000	1.0000
1973	1.0802	1.0769	1.0730	1.0741	1.0738	1.0763
1974	1.1448	1.1550	1.1585	1.1671	1.1680	1.1644
1975	1.1827	1.2048	1.2170	1.2290	1.2304	1.2210
1976	1.2823	1.2982	1.3076	1.3177	1.3194	1.3114
1977	1.4159	1.4207	1.4236	1.4328	1.4349	1.4306
1978	1.5119	1.5154	1.5154	1.5261	1.5278	1.5254

Dale W. Jorgenson and Daniel T. Slesnick

Appendix Table 2.A.2 (continued)

Year	NE	NC	S	W	White	Non-white	Urban	Rural
1958	0.6927	0.6932	0.6936	0.6910	0.6927	0.6942	0.6927	0.6953
1959	0.6937	0.6953	0.6964	0.6919	0.6945	0.6956	0.6943	0.6997
1960	0.7152	0.7161	0.7162	0.7140	0.7155	0.7162	0.7154	0.7184
1961	0.7213	0.7222	0.7225	0.7200	0.7216	0.7223	0.7215	0.7248
1962	0.7292	0.7302	0.7304	0.7280	0.7296	0.7300	0.7294	0.7327
1963	0.7325	0.7342	0.7351	0.7312	0.7335	0.7340	0.7332	0.7383
1964	0.7493	0.7501	0.7503	0.7484	0.7496	0.7501	0.7495	0.7521
1965	0.7738	0.7732	0.7722	0.7732	0.7730	0.7735	0.7731	0.7722
1966	0.7954	0.7947	0.7942	0.7944	0.7946	0.7956	0.7947	0.7940
1967	0.8024	0.8034	0.8041	0.8011	0.8029	0.8037	0.8028	0.8063
1968	0.8291	0.8308	0.8322	0.8278	0.8302	0.8311	0.8300	0.8351
1969	0.8831	0.8833	0.8833	0.8826	0.8830	0.8838	0.8831	0.8838
1970	0.8949	0.8978	0.9010	0.8930	0.8971	0.8983	0.8967	0.9055
1971	0.9317	0.9352	0.9383	0.9304	0.9344	0.9346	0.9339	0.9434
1972	1.0000	1.0000	1.0000	1.0000	1.0000	1.0000	1.0000	1.0000
1973	1.0770	1.0740	1.0733	1.0753	1.0745	1.0769	1.0750	1.0701
1974	1.1612	1.1623	1.1674	1.1525	1.1614	1.1672	1.1612	1.1737
1975	1.2154	1.2207	1.2302	1.2044	1.2188	1.2252	1.2179	1.2432
1976	1.3060	1.3119	1.3192	1.2974	1.3099	1.3130	1.3087	1.3324
1977	1.4256	1.4299	1.4336	1.4189	1.4281	1.4284	1.4270	1.4446
1978	1.5209	1.5225	1.5262	1.5119	1.5211	1.5244	1.5206	1.5346

Notes

1. The literature on the individual cost-of-living index is summarized by Deaton and Muellbauer (1980b), pp. 170–178, and by Diewert (1981).

2. The translog indirect utility function was introduced by Christensen, Jorgenson, and Lau (1975) and extended to encompass determinants of expenditure allocation other than prices and total expenditure by Jorgenson and Lau (1975). Alternative approaches to the representation of the effects of prices and total expenditure on expenditure allocation are summarized by Barten (1977), Deaton and Muellbauer (1980b), pp. 60–85, and Lau (1977a).

3. Alternative approaches to the representation of household characteristics on expenditure allocation are presented by Barten (1964), Gorman (1976), and Prais and Houthakker (1971). Empirical evidence on the impact of demographic characteristics on expenditure allocation is given by Lau, Lin, and Yotopoulos (1978), Muellbauer (1977), Parks and Barten (1973), Pollak and Wales (1980, 1981), and Ray (1982).

4. The specification of a system of individual demand functions by means of Roy's Identity was first employed in econometric modeling of consumer behavior by Houthakker (1960). A detailed review of econometric models based on Roy's Identity is given by Lau (1977a).

5. For further discussion, see Lau (1977b, 1982) and Jorgenson, Lau, and Stoker (1980, 1981, 1982).

6. Conditions for integrability are discussed by Jorgenson and Lau (1979) and by Jorgenson, Lau, and Stoker (1982).

7. For further discussion see Jorgenson, Lau, and Stoker (1982), esp. pp. 175–186.

8. Household equivalence scales are discussed by Barten (1964), Lazear and Michael (1980), Muellbauer (1974a, 1977, 1980), and Prais and Houthakker (1971), among others. Alternative approaches are summarized by Deaton and Muellbauer (1980b).

9. The use of household equivalence scales in evaluating transfers among individuals has been advocated by Deaton and Muellbauer (1980b), esp. pp. 205–212, and by Muellbauer (1974a). Pollak and Wales (1979) have presented arguments against the use of household equivalence scales for this purpose.

10. The 1972–3 Survey of Consumer Expenditures is discussed by Carlson (1974).

11. We employ data on the flow of services from durable goods rather than purchases of durable goods. Personal consumption expenditures in the U.S. National Income and Product Accounts are based on purchases of durable goods.

12. This series is published annually by the U.S. Bureau of the Census.

13. A detailed discussion of the stochastic specification of our model and of econometric methods for pooling time series and cross-section data is presented by Jorgenson, Lau and Stoker (1982), section 2.6. This stochastic specification implies that time series data must be adjusted for heteroscedasticity by multiplying each observation by the statistic

$$\rho = \frac{(\sum M_k)^2}{\sum M_k^2} \, .$$

14. An alternative approach to implementation of the individual cost-of-living index (2.4.2) is to bound this index on the basis of observable data. Bounds have been developed by Allen (1949), Frisch (1936), and Konüs (1939) and, more recently, by Afriat (1977), Pollak (1971, 1981), and Samuelson and Swamy (1974), among many others. This approach is reviewed by Deaton and Muellbauer (1980b), pp. 170–178, and by Diewert (1981).

15. Arrow (1977, p. 225) has defended noncomparability in the following terms: "...the autonomy of individuals, an element of mutual incommensurability among people seems denied by the possibility of interpersonal comparisons".

16. It is important to note that the social welfare function in (2.5.2) represents a social ordering over all possible individual orderings and exemplifies the multiple profile approach to social choice of Arrow (1963) rather than the single profile approach employed by Bergson (1938) and Samuelson (1947). The literature on the existence of single profile social welfare functions is discussed by Roberts (1980d), Samuelson (1982), and Sen (1979b).

17. See Sen (1977, 1979b) for further discussion.

18. See Roberts (1980b), esp. pp. 434–436.

19. The implications of distributional homotheticity are discussed by Kolm (1976b) and Blackorby and Donaldson (1978).

20. Mean value functions were introduced into economics by Bergson (1936) and have been employed, for example, by Arrow, Chenery, Minhas, and Solow (1961) and Atkinson (1970). Properties of mean value functions are discussed by Hardy, Littlewood, and Polya (1959).

21. This assumption implies that individual welfare increases with total expenditure at a rate that is inversely proportional to total expenditure. This is also implied by the utilitarian social welfare function employed by Arrow and Kalt (1979).

22. The social expenditure function was introduced by Pollak (1981). Alternative money measures of social welfare are discussed by Arrow and Kalt (1979), Bergson (1980), Deaton and Muellbauer (1980b), pp. 214–239, Roberts (1980c), and Sen (1976). A survey of the literature is presented by Sen (1979a).

23. The conventional index number approach is summarized in Statistics Canada (1982).

24. Exact index numbers are discussed by Lau (1979), Pollak (1971), and Samuelson and Swamy (1974).

3

Inequality in the Distribution of Individual Welfare

Dale W. Jorgenson and
Daniel T. Slesnick

3.1 Introduction

The purpose of this chapter is to present an econometric approach to the measurement of inequality in the distribution of individual welfare. This approach meets the objectives of inequality measurement identified by Dalton (1920) more than sixty years ago: "For the economist is primarily interested, not in the distribution of income as such, but in the effects of the distribution of income upon the distribution and total amount of economic welfare, which may be derived from income."[1]

Since the pioneering work of Atkinson (1970) and Kolm (1969, 1976a, b), inequality measurement has been based on explicit social welfare functions. However, the resulting measures of inequality have been defined on the distribution of individual income rather than the distribution of individual welfare, "... which may be derived from income." Muellbauer (1974b, c) and Roberts (1980c) have shown that measures of inequality based on income rather than welfare are subject to very stringent limitations.

Measures of social welfare defined on the distribution of individual income coincide with measures defined on the distribution of individual welfare if and only if preferences are identical and homothetic for all consumers.[2] However, homothetic preferences are inconsistent with well established empirical regularities in the behavior of individual consumers.[3] Further, identical preferences are inconsistent with empirical findings that expenditure patterns depend on the demographic characteristics of consumers.[4]

Our approach to inequality measurement is based on an econometric model of aggregate consumer behavior. The novel feature of this model is that systems of individual demand functions can be recovered uniquely from the system of aggregate demand functions. By requiring that the individual demand functions are integrable, we can also recover indirect utility functions for all consumers. Finally, we can define measures of individual welfare in terms of these indirect utility functions.

In section 3.2 we outline an econometric methodology for developing a model of aggregate consumer behavior. In this model, systems of individual demand functions depend on the prices faced by all households. These systems also depend on total expenditures and attributes such as demographic characteristics that vary among households. We obtain aggregate demand functions by summing over individual demand functions. The resulting system of aggregate demand functions depends on summary statistics of the joint distribution of total expenditures and attributes among all households.

In section 3.3 we implement our econometric model of aggregate consumer behavior for the United States. For this purpose we employ cross-section data on individual expenditure patterns. We combine these data with time-series data on aggregate expenditure patterns and prices for all commodities. We also employ time-series data on the distribution of total expenditures among households.

In section 3.4 we present methods for evaluating the level of social welfare. For this purpose we construct an explicit social welfare function. This social welfare function incorporates measures of individual welfare based on indirect utility functions for all consumer units. In addition, this social welfare function employs normative criteria based on horizontal and vertical equity for evaluating transfers among units.

In section 3.5 we develop indexes of inequality in the distribution of individual welfare. For this purpose we express the measures of social welfare presented in section 3.4 as the sum of measures of efficiency and equity. Efficiency is the maximum level of social welfare that is potentially available through redistributions of aggregate expenditure. Equity is the difference between the actual level of social welfare and the measure of efficiency.

We can define an absolute index of inequality as the negative of the measure of equity. This index reflects the differences between a perfectly egalitarian distribution of individual welfare and the actual welfare distribution. Similarly, we can define a relative measure of inequality as the ratio between the absolute index of inequality and the measure of efficiency. We implement these measures of inequality for the United States for the years 1958–1978.

In section 3.6 we develop indexes of inequality within subgroups of the population. For this purpose we introduce group welfare functions that are precisely analogous to the social welfare functions of section 3.4. We decompose these measures of group welfare into measures of group efficiency and equity. Finally, we implement the resulting absolute and relative measures of group inequality for subgroups of the U.S. population, classified by age of head of household, for the years 1958–1978.

In section 3.7 we decompose indexes of inequality in the distribution of individual welfare into the sum of indexes of inequality between and within subgroups of the population. The index of inequality between groups represents the loss in social welfare owing to an inequitable distribution of welfare between groups. The index of inequality within groups represents the loss in social welfare owing to an inequitable distribution within each group. We implement these indexes for age groups of the U.S. population for the years 1958–1978.

In order to quantify the gains to society that can accrue from redistributional policies, we find it useful to express social welfare in terms of aggregate expenditure. For this purpose we introduce the social expenditure function, defined as the minimum level of aggregate expenditure required to attain a given level of social welfare. The social expenditure function is analogous to the individual expenditure function, which gives the minimum level of individual expenditure required to attain a stipulated level of utility.

In section 3.8 we define money metric inequality as the difference between money measures of potential and actual social welfare. This measure is the amount that society as a whole would gain from a perfectly egalitarian distribution of aggregate expenditure. We also consider money measures of group inequality, corresponding to the amounts that each group would gain from an egalitarian distribution within the group. Finally, we decompose money metric inequality into the sum of money measures of between- and within-group inequality. These measures provide the amounts society would gain from redistribution between and within groups.

In section 3.9 we implement the money measures of inequality presented in section 3.8. We first present money metric inequality for the U.S. population as a whole for the years 1958–1978. We find that society as a whole can gain the equivalent of 30–40% of aggregate expenditure by redistributional policies. Second, we decompose money measures of inequality between- and within-age groups. We find that redistribution between age groups could produce gains of 6–8% of aggregate expenditure, whereas redistribution within age groups could produce gains of 23–26%.

3.2   Aggregate Consumer Behavior

In this section we develop an econometric model of aggregate consumer behavior based on the theory of exact aggregation, following Jorgenson, Lau, and Stoker (1980, 1981, 1982). Our model incorporates time-series data on prices and aggregate quantities consumed. We also include cross-section data on individual quantities consumed, individual total expenditure, and attributes of individual households such as demographic characteristics.

To represent preferences for all individuals in a form suitable for measuring individual welfare, we take households as consuming units. We assume that expenditures on individual commodities are allocated so as to maximize a household welfare function. As a consequence, the household behaves in the same way as an individual maximizing a utility function, as demonstrated by Samuelson (1956) and Pollak (1981). By assuming that each household maximizes a household welfare function, we can focus on the distribution of welfare among households rather than the distribution among individuals within households.

To construct an econometric model based on exact aggregation we first represent individual preferences by means of an indirect utility function for each consuming unit, using the following notation:

p_n — price of the nth commodity, assumed to be the same for all consuming units.

$p = (p_1, p_2, \ldots, p_N)$ — the vector of prices of all commodities.

x_{nk} — the quantity of the nth commodity group consumed by the kth consuming unit ($n = 1, 2, \ldots, N$; $k = 1, 2, \ldots, K$).

$M_k = \sum_{n=1}^{N} p_n x_{nk}$ — total expenditure of the kth consuming unit ($k = 1, 2, \ldots, K$).

$w_{nk} = p_n x_{nk}/M_k$ — expenditure share of the nth commodity group in the budget of the kth consuming unit ($n = 1, 2, \ldots, N$; $k = 1, 2, \ldots, K$).

$w_k = (w_{1k}, w_{2k}, \ldots, w_{Nk})$ — vector of expenditure shares for the kth consuming unit ($k = 1, 2, \ldots, K$).

$\ln (p/M_k) = [\ln (p_1/M_k), \ln (p_2/M_k), \ldots, \ln (p_N/M_k)]$ — vector of logarithms of ratios of prices to expenditure by the kth consuming unit ($k = 1, 2, \ldots, K$).

$\ln p = (\ln p_1, \ln p_2, \ldots, \ln p_N)$ — vector of logarithms of prices.

A_k — vector of attributes of the kth consuming unit ($k = 1, 2, \ldots, K$).

We assume that the kth consuming unit allocates expenditures in accord with the transcendental logarithmic or translog indirect utility function,[5] say V_k, where

$$\ln V_k = G\left(\ln \frac{p'}{M_k} \alpha_p + \frac{1}{2} \ln \frac{p'}{M_k} B_{pp} \ln \frac{p}{M_k} + \ln \frac{p'}{M_k} B_{pA} A_k, A_k\right),$$
$$(k = 1, 2, \ldots, K) . \qquad (3.2.1)$$

In this representation the function G is a monotone increasing function of the variable

$$\ln \frac{p'}{M_k} \alpha_p + \frac{1}{2} \ln \frac{p'}{M_k} B_{pp} \ln \frac{p}{M_k} + \ln \frac{p'}{M_k} B_{pA} A_k .$$

In addition, the function G depends directly on the attribute vector A_k.[6] The vector α_p and the matrices B_{pp} and B_{pA} are constant parameters that are the same for all consuming units.

The expenditure shares of the kth consuming unit can be derived by the logarithmic form of Roy's (1943) Identity[7]

$$w_{nk} = \frac{\partial \ln V_k}{\partial \ln (p_n/M_k)} \Big/ \sum_{n=1}^{N} \frac{\partial \ln V_k}{\partial \ln (p_n/M_k)} ,$$
$$(n = 1, 2 \ldots N; \; k = 1, 2, \ldots, K) . \qquad (3.2.2)$$

Applying this Identity to the translog indirect utility function (3.2.1), we obtain the system of individual expenditure shares

$$w_k = \frac{1}{D_k(p)} \left(\alpha_p + B_{pp} \ln \frac{p}{M_k} + B_{pA} A_k\right), \quad (k = 1, 2, \ldots, K), \qquad (3.2.3)$$

where the denominators $\{D_k\}$ take the form

$$D_k = i'\alpha_p + i'B_{pp} \ln \frac{p}{M_k} + i'B_{pA} A_k , \quad (k = 1, 2, \ldots, K) . \qquad (3.2.4)$$

The individual expenditure shares are homogeneous of degree zero in the unknown parameters—α_p, B_{pp}, B_{pA}. By multiplying a given set of these parameters by a constant we obtain another set of parameters that generates the same system of individual budget shares. Accordingly, we can choose a normalization for the parameters without affecting observed patterns of individual expenditure allocation. We find it convenient to employ the normalization

$$i'\alpha_p = -1 .$$

Under this restriction any change in the set of unknown parameters will be reflected in changes in individual expenditure patterns.

The conditions for exact aggregation are that the individual expenditure shares are linear in functions of the attributes $\{A_k\}$ and total expenditures $\{M_k\}$ for all consuming units.[8] These conditions will be satisfied if and only if the terms involving the attributes and expenditures do not appear in the denominators of the expressions given above for the individual expenditure shares, so that

$$i'B_{pp}i = 0 ,$$

and

$$i'B_{pA} = 0 .$$

The exact aggregation restrictions imply that the denominators $\{D_k\}$ reduce to

$$D = -1 + i'B_{pp} \ln p ,$$

where the subscript k is no longer required, since the denominator is the same for all consuming units. Under these restrictions the individual expenditure shares can be written

$$w_k = \frac{1}{D(p)} (\alpha_p + B_{pp} \ln p - B_{pp} i \ln M_k + B_{pA} A_k) ,$$

$$(k = 1, 2, \ldots, K) . \qquad (3.2.5)$$

The individual expenditure shares are linear in the logarithms of expenditures $\{\ln M_k\}$ and in the attributes $\{A_k\}$, as required by exact aggregation.

Under exact aggregation the indirect utility function for each consuming unit can be represented in the form

$$\ln V_k = F(A_k) + \ln p' \left(\alpha_p + \frac{1}{2} B_{pp} \ln p + B_{pA} A_k \right) - D(p) \ln M_k ,$$

$$(k = 1, 2, \ldots, K) . \qquad (3.2.6)$$

In this representation the indirect utility function is linear in the logarithm of total expenditure $\ln M_k$ with a coefficient that depends on the prices p $(k = 1, 2, \ldots, K)$. This property is invariant with respect to positive affine transformations, but is not preserved by arbitrary monotone increasing transformations. We conclude that the indirect utility function (3.2.6) provides a cardinal measure of utility for each consuming unit.

If a system of individual expenditure shares (3.2.3) can be generated from an indirect utility function of the form (3.2.1) we say that the system is *integrable*. A complete set of conditions for integrability[9] is the following:

1. *Homogeneity.* The individual expenditure shares are homogeneous of degree zero in prices and total expenditure.

We can write the individual expenditure shares in the form

$$\beta_{pM} = B_{pp} i . \tag{3.2.7}$$

Given the exact aggregation restrictions, there are $N - 1$ restrictions implied by homogeneity.

2. *Summability.* The sum of the individual expenditure shares over all commodity groups is equal to unity

$$i' w_k = 1 , \quad (k = 1, 2, \ldots, K) .$$

We can write the denominator $D(p)$ in (3.2.4) in the form

$$D = -1 + \beta_{Mp} \ln p ,$$

where the vector of parameters β_{Mp} is constant and the same for all commodity groups and all consuming units. Summability implies that this vector must satisfy the restrictions

$$\beta_{Mp} = i' B_{pp} . \tag{3.2.8}$$

Given the exact aggregation restrictions, there are $N - 1$ restrictions implied by summability.

3. *Symmetry.* The matrix of compensated own- and cross-price substitution effects must be symmetric.

If the system of individual expenditure shares can be generated from an indirect utility function of the form (3.2.1), a necessary and sufficient condition for symmetry is that the matrix B_{pp} must be symmetric. Without imposing this condition, we can write the individual expenditure shares in the form

$$w_k = \frac{1}{D(p)} \left(\alpha_p + B_{pp} \ln \frac{p}{M_k} + B_{pA} A_k \right), \quad (k = 1, 2, \dots, K).$$

Symmetry implies that the matrix of parameters B_{pp} must satisfy the restrictions

$$B_{pp} = B'_{pp} .$$ (3.2.9)

The total number of symmetry restrictions is $1/2\, N(N - 1)$.

4. *Nonnegativity.* The individual expenditure shares must be non-negative.

By summability the individual expenditure shares sum to unity, so that we can write

$$w_k \geq 0, \quad (k = 1, 2, \dots, K) ,$$

where $w_k \geq 0$ implies $w_{nk} \geq 0$, $(n = 1, 2, \dots, N)$, and $w_k \neq 0$.

Since the translog indirect utility function is quadratic in the logarithms of prices, we can always choose the prices so that the individual expenditure shares violate the nonnegativity conditions. Accordingly, we cannot impose restrictions on the parameters of the translog indirect utility functions that would imply nonnegativity of the individual expenditure shares. Instead we consider restrictions on the parameters that imply monotonicity of the system of individual demand functions for all nonnegative expenditure shares.

5. *Monotonicity.* The matrix of compensated own- and cross-price substitution effects must be nonpositive definite.

We introduce the definition owing to Martos (1969) of a *strictly merely positive subdefinite matrix*, namely, a real symmetric matrix S such that

$$xSx < 0$$

implies $Sx > 0$ or $Sx < 0$. A necessary and sufficient condition for monotonicity is either that the translog indirect utility function is homothetic or that B_{pp}^{-1} exists and is strictly merely positive subdefinite.[10]

To provide a basis for evaluating the impact of transfers among households on social welfare, we find it useful to represent household preferences by means of a utility function that is the same for all consuming units. For this purpose, we assume that the kth consuming unit maximizes its utility, say U_k, where

$$U_k = U \left[\frac{x_{1k}}{m_1(A_k)}, \frac{x_{2k}}{m_2(A_k)}, \ldots, \frac{x_{Nk}}{m_N(A_k)} \right], \quad (k = 1, 2, \ldots, K), \quad (3.2.10)$$

subject to the budget constraint

$$M_k = \sum_{n=1}^{N} p_n x_{nk}, \quad (k = 1, 2, \ldots, K).$$

In this representation of consumer preferences the quantities $\{x_{nk}/m_n(A_k)\}$ can be regarded as *effective quantities consumed,* as proposed by Barten (1964). The crucial assumption embodied in this representation is that differences in preferences among consumers enter the utility function U only through differences in the commodity specific household equivalence scales $\{m_n(A_k)\}$.[11]

Consumer equilibrium implies the existence of an indirect utility function, say V, that is the same for all consuming units. The level of utility for the kth consuming unit, say V_k, depends on the prices of individual commodities, the household equivalence scales, and the level of total expenditure

$$V_k = V \left[\frac{p_1 \, m_1(A_k)}{M_k}, \frac{p_2 \, m_2(A_k)}{M_k}, \ldots, \frac{p_N \, m_N(A_k)}{M_k} \right],$$

$$(k = 1, 2, \ldots, K). \quad (3.2.11)$$

In this representation the prices $\{p_n \, m_n(A_k)\}$ can be regarded as *effective prices.* Differences in preferences among consuming units enter this indirect utility function only through the household equivalence scales $\{m_n(A_k)\}$ $(k = 1, 2, \ldots, K)$.

To represent the translog indirect utility function (3.2.1) in terms of household equivalence scales, we require some additional notation:

$\ln [p\dot{m}(A_k)/M_k]$ — vector of logarithms of ratios of effective prices

$\{p_n m_n(A_k)\}$ to total expenditure M_k of the kth consuming unit $(k = 1, 2, \ldots, K)$.

$\ln m(A_k) = (\ln m_1(A_k), \ln m_2(A_k), \ldots, \ln m_N(A_k))$ — vector of logarithms of the household equivalence scales of the kth consuming unit $(k = 1, 2, \ldots, K)$.

We assume, as before, that the kth consuming unit allocates its expenditures in accord with the translog indirect utility function (3.2.1). However, we also assume that this function, expressed in terms of the effective prices $\{p_n\, m_n(A_k)\}$ and total expenditure M_k, is the same for all consuming units. The indirect utility function takes the form

$$\ln V_k = \ln \frac{pm(A_k)'}{M_k}\, \alpha_p + \frac{1}{2}\ln \frac{pm(A_k)'}{M_k}\, B_{pp}\, \ln \frac{pm(A_k)}{M_k}\,,$$

$$(k = 1, 2, \ldots, K)\,. \qquad (3.2.12)$$

Taking logarithms of the effective prices $\{p_n\, m_n(A_k)\}$, we can rewrite the indirect utility function (3.2.12) in the form

$$\ln V_k = \ln m(A_k)'\alpha_p + \frac{1}{2}\ln m(A_k)' B_{pp}\, \ln m(A_k) + \ln \frac{p'}{M_k}\, \alpha_p$$

$$+\frac{1}{2}\ln \frac{p'}{M_k}\, B_{pp}\, \ln \frac{p}{M_k} + \ln \frac{p'}{M_k}\, B_{pp}\, \ln m(A_k)\,,$$

$$(k = 1, 2, \ldots, K)\,. \qquad (3.2.13)$$

Comparing the representation (3.2.13) with the representation (3.2.6), we see that the term involving only the household equivalent scales must take the form

$$F(A_k) = \ln m(A_k)'\, \alpha_p + \frac{1}{2}\ln m(A_k)'\, B_{pp}\, \ln m(A_k)\,,$$

$$(k = 1, 2, \ldots, K)\,. \qquad (3.2.14)$$

Second, the term involving ratios of prices to total expenditure and the household equivalence scales must satisfy

$$\ln \frac{p'}{M_k}\, B_{pA}\, A_k = \ln \frac{p'}{M_k}\, B_{pp}\, \ln m(A_k)\,, \quad (k = 1, 2, \ldots, K), \qquad (3.2.15)$$

for all prices and total expenditure.

The household equivalence scales $\{m_n(A_k)\}$ defined by (3.2.15) must satisfy the equation

$$B_{pA}\, A_k = B_{pp}\, \ln m(A_k)\,, \quad (k = 1, 2, \ldots, K). \qquad (3.2.16)$$

Under monotonicity of the individual expenditure shares the matrix B_{pp} has an inverse, so that we can express the household equivalence scales in terms of the parameters of the translog indirect utility function, namely B_{pp} and B_{pA}, and the attributes $\{A_k\}$

$$\ln m(A_k) = B_{pp}^{-1} B_{pA} A_k, \quad (k = 1, 2, \ldots, K). \tag{3.2.17}$$

We can refer to these scales as the *commodity specific translog household equivalence scales*.

Substituting the commodity specific equivalence scales (3.2.16) into the indirect utility function (3.2.13) we obtain a representation of the indirect utility function in terms of the attributes $\{A_k\}$

$$\ln V_k = A_k' B_{pA}' B_{pp}^{-1} \alpha_p + \frac{1}{2} A_k' B_{pA}' B_{pp}^{-1} B_{pA} A_k$$

$$+ \ln p' \left(\alpha_p + \frac{1}{2} B_{pp} \ln p + B_{pA} A_k \right) - D(p) \ln M_k,$$

$$(k = 1, 2, \ldots, K). \tag{3.2.18}$$

This form of the translog indirect utility function is equivalent to the form (3.2.1) in that both generate the same system of individual demand functions. By requiring that the attributes A_k enter only through the commodity specific household equivalence scales, we have provided a specific form for the function $F(A_k)$ in (3.2.6).

Given the indirect utility function (3.2.18) for each consuming unit, we can express total expenditure as a function of prices, consumer attributes, and the level of utility

$$\ln M_k = \frac{1}{D(p)} \left[A_k' B_{pA}' B_{pp}^{-1} \alpha_p + \frac{1}{2} A_k' B_{pA}' B_{pp}^{-1} B_{pA} A_k \right.$$

$$\left. + \ln p' \left(\alpha_p + \frac{1}{2} B_{pp} \ln p + B_{pA} A_k \right) - \ln V_k \right],$$

$$(k = 1, 2, \ldots, K). \tag{3.2.19}$$

We can refer to this function as the *translog expenditure function*. The translog expenditure function gives the minimum expenditure required for the kth consuming unit to achieve the utility level V_k, given prices p $(k = 1, 2, \ldots, K)$.

We find it useful to introduce household equivalence scales that are not specific to a given commodity.[12] Following Muellbauer (1974a), we define a general household equivalence scale, say m_0, as follows

$$m_0 = \frac{M_k[pm(A_k), V_k^0]}{M_0(p, V_k^0)}, \quad (k = 1, 2, \ldots, K), \quad (3.2.20)$$

where M_k is the expenditure function for the kth household, M_0 is the expenditure function for a reference household with commodity specific equivalence scales equal to unity for all commodities, and $pm(A_k)$ is a vector of effective prices $\{p_n \, m_n(A_k)\}$.

The general household equivalence scale m_0 is the ratio between total expenditures required by the kth household and by the reference household required for the same level of utility V_k^0 $(k = 1, 2, \ldots, K)$. This scale can be interpreted as the number of household equivalent members. The number of members depends on the attributes A_k of the consuming unit and on the prices p.

If each household has a translog indirect utility function, then the general household equivalence scale for the kth household takes the form

$$\ln m_0 = \ln M_k - \ln M_0$$

$$= \frac{1}{D(p)} \left[\ln m(A_k)' \alpha_p + 1/2 \ln m(A_k)' B_{pp} \ln m(A_k) \right.$$

$$\left. + \ln m(A_k)' B_{pp} \ln p \right], \quad (k = 1, 2, \ldots, K) . \quad (3.2.21)$$

We can refer to this scale as the *general translog household equivalence scale*. The translog equivalence scale depends on the attributes A_k of the kth household and the prices p of all commodities, but is independent of the level of utility V_k^0.

Given the general translog equivalence scale, we can rewrite the indirect utility function (3.2.18) in the form

$$\ln V_k = \ln p' \alpha_p + \frac{1}{2} \ln p' B_{pp} \ln p - D(p) \ln \left[\frac{M_k}{m_0} (p, A_k) \right],$$

$$(k = 1, 2, \ldots, K) . \quad (3.2.22)$$

The level of utility for the kth consuming unit depends on prices p and total expenditure per household equivalent member $M_k/m_0(p, A_k)$ $(k = 1, 2, \ldots, K)$. Similarly, we can rewrite the expenditure function (3.2.19) in the form

$$\ln M_k = \frac{1}{D(p)}\left[\ln p'\left(\alpha_p + \frac{1}{2}B_{pp}\ln p\right) - \ln V_k\right] + \ln m_0(p, A_k),$$

$$(k = 1, 2, \ldots, K). \qquad (3.2.23)$$

Total expenditure required by the kth consuming unit to attain the level of utility V_k depends on prices p and the number of household equivalent members $m_0(p, A_k)$ $(k = 1, 2, \ldots, K)$.

To construct an econometric model of aggregate consumer behavior based on exact aggregation we obtain aggregate expenditure shares, say w, by multiplying individual expenditure shares (3.2.5) by expenditure for each consuming unit, adding over all consuming units, and dividing by aggregate expenditure, $M = \sum_{k=1}^{K} M_k$

$$w = \frac{\sum M_k \, w_k}{M}. \qquad (3.2.24)$$

The aggregate expenditure shares can be written

$$w = \frac{1}{D(p)}\left(\alpha_p + B_{pp}\ln p - B_{pp}i\frac{\sum M_k \ln M_k}{M} + B_{pA}\frac{\sum M_k A_k}{M}\right). \qquad (3.2.25)$$

The aggregate expenditure patterns depend on the distribution of expenditure over all consuming units through summary statistics of the joint distribution of expenditures and attributes—$\sum M_k \ln M_k/M$ and $\{\sum M_k A_k/M\}$. Systems of individual expenditure shares (3.2.5) for consuming units with identical demographic characteristics can be recovered in one and only one way from the system of aggregate expenditure shares (3.2.25).

The first step in analyzing inequality in the distribution of individual welfare is to select a representation of the individual welfare function. We assume that individual welfare for the kth consuming unit, say W_k $(k = 1, 2, \ldots, K)$, is equal to the logarithm of the translog indirect utility function (3.2.22)[13]

$$W_k = \ln V_k$$

$$= \ln p'\alpha_p + \frac{1}{2}\ln p'B_{pp}\ln p - D(p)\ln\left[\frac{M_k}{m_0}(p, A_k)\right],$$

$$(k = 1, 2, \ldots, K). \qquad (3.2.26)$$

To summarize: For our econometric model a system of individual expenditure shares (3.2.5) can be recovered in one and only one way from the system of aggregate expenditure shares (3.2.25). Given a system of individual expenditure shares (3.2.5) that is integrable, we can recover the translog indirect utility function (3.2.22). This indirect utility function provides a cardinal measure of utility. We obtain a cardinal measure of individual welfare for each consuming unit (3.2.26) by setting this measure equal to the logarithm of the indirect utility function.

3.3   Econometric Model

In this section we present the empirical results of implementing the econometric model of consumer behavior described in section 3.2. We divide consumer expenditures among five commodity groups:

1. *Energy:* Expenditures on electricity, natural gas, heating oil, and gasoline.

2. *Food:* Expenditures on all food products, including tobacco and alcohol.

3. *Consumer goods:* Expenditures on all other nondurable goods included in consumer expenditures.

4. *Capital services:* The service flow from consumer durables and the service flow from housing.

5. *Consumer services:* Expenditures on consumer services, such as car repairs, medical services, entertainment, and so on.

We employ the following demographic characteristics as attributes of individual households:

1. *Family size:* 1, 2, 3, 4, 5, 6, and 7 or more persons.

2. *Age of head:* 16–24, 25–34, 35–44, 45–54, 55–64, 65 and over.

3. *Region of residence:* Northeast, North Central, South, and West.

4. *Race:* White, nonwhite.

5. *Type of residence:* Urban, rural.

Our cross-section observations on individual expenditures for each commodity group and on demographic characteristics of individual households are for the year 1972 from the 1972–193 Survey of Consumer Expenditures (CES).[14] Our time-series observations are based on data on personal consumption expenditures from the United States National Income and Product Accounts (NIPA) for the years 1958 to 1974.[15] Prices for each commodity group are defined in terms of translog price indexes computed from detailed prices included in

NIPA for each year. We employ time-series data on the distribution of expenditures over all households and among demographic groups based on *Current Population Reports*.[16]

In our application we treat the expenditure shares for five commodity groups as endogenous variables, so that we estimate four equations. As unknown parameters we have four elements of the vector α_p, four expenditure coefficients of the vector $B_{pp}i$, sixteen attribute coefficients for each of the four equations in the matrix B_{pA}, and ten price coefficients in the matrix B_{pp}, which is constrained to be symmetric. The expenditure coefficients are sums of price coefficients in the corresponding equation, so that we have a total of 82 unknown parameters. We estimate the complete model, subject to inequality restrictions implied by monotonicity of the individual expenditure shares, by pooling time-series and cross-section data.[17] The results are given in table 3.1.

The impacts of changes in total expenditures and in demographic characteristics of the individual household are estimated very precisely. This reflects the fact that estimates of the expenditure and demographic effects incorporate a relatively large number of cross-section observations. The impacts of prices enter through the denominator of the equations for expenditure shares; these price coefficients are estimated very precisely since they also incorporate cross-section data. Finally, the price impacts also enter through the numerators of equations for the expenditure shares. These parameters are estimated somewhat less precisely, since they are based on a much smaller number of time-series observations on prices.

To summarize: We have implemented an econometric model of aggregate consumer behavior by combining time-series and cross-section data for the United States. This model allocates personal consumption expenditures among five commodity groups—energy, food, other consumer goods, capital services, and other consumer services. Households are classified by five sets of demographic characteristics—family size, age of head, region of residence, race, and urban versus rural residence.

Table 3.1
Pooled estimation results

Notation:		
CONST	=	constant term
ln *PEN*	=	coefficient of log of price of energy
ln *PF*	=	coefficient of log of price of food
ln *PCG*	=	coefficient of log of price of consumer goods
ln *PK*	=	coefficient of log of price of capital services
ln *PCS*	=	coefficient of log of price of consumer services
ln *M*	=	coefficient of log of total expenditure
S2	=	coefficient of dummy for family of size 2
S3	=	coefficient of dummy for family of size 3
S4	=	coefficient of dummy for family of size 4
S5	=	coefficient of dummy for family of size 5
S6	=	coefficient of dummy for family of size 6
S7 +	=	coefficient of dummy for family of size 7 or more
A25–34	=	coefficient of dummy for age between 25 and 34
A35–44	=	coefficient of dummy for age between 35 and 44
A45–54	=	coefficient of dummy for age between 45 and 54
A55–64	=	coefficient of dummy for age between 55 and 64
A65 +	=	coefficient of dummy for age 65 and older
RNC	=	coefficient of dummy for family living in North Central
RS	=	coefficient of dummy for family living in South
RW	=	coefficient of dummy for family living in West
BLK	=	coefficient of dummy for nonwhite family
RUR	=	coefficient of dummy for family living in rural area

$$D(p) = -1 \quad \begin{array}{lll} -0.03491 \ln PEN & -0.08171 \ln PF & +0.06189 \ln PCG \\ (0.000997) & (0.00238) & (0.00214) \\ -0.02060 \ln PK & +0.05679 \ln PCS & \\ (0.00300) & (0.00233) & \end{array}$$

Table 3.1 (continued)

	Energy		Food			Consumer Goods		
Parameter	Estimate	Standard Error	Parameter	Estimate	Standard Error	Parameter	Estimate	Standard Error
CONST	-.3754	.00923	CONST	-.8917	.0215	CONST	.4053	.0194
ln PEN	.09151	.0134	ln PEN	-.1441	.0214	ln PEN	-.06455	.0127
ln PF	-.1441	.0214	ln PF	.3118	.0428	ln PF	.05547	.0215
ln PCG	-.06455	.0127	ln PCG	.05547	.0215	ln PCG	.2301	.0269
ln PK	.07922	.0171	ln PK	-.1982	.0334	ln PK	-.1056	.0195
ln PCS	.003061	.0138	ln PCS	-.1066	.0259	ln PCS	-.05354	.0271
ln M	.03491	.000997	ln M	.08171	.00238	ln M	-.06189	.00214
S2	-.02402	.00139	S2	-.04859	.00333	S2	-.005594	.00300
S3	-.02971	.00163	S3	-.06730	.00390	S3	-.006290	.00351
S4	-.03144	.00178	S4	-.08881	.00428	S4	-.001941	.00385
S5	-.03255	.00206	S5	-.1108	.00496	S5	.004522	.00446
S6	-.03606	.00249	S6	-.1185	.00598	S6	.01059	.00539
S7+	-.02977	.00266	S7+	-.1471	.00639	S7+	.01495	.00575
A25–34	.0002010	.00197	A25–34	-.04393	.00474	A25–34	-.02311	.00426
A35–44	-.006703	.00210	A35–44	-.08221	.00504	A35–44	-.01916	.00454
A45–54	-.01155	.00199	A45–54	-.09604	.00478	A45–54	-.005279	.00431
A55–64	-.01372	.00199	A55–64	-.1034	.00477	A55–64	-.009068	.00429
A65+	-.005487	.00196	A65+	-.08833	.00470	A65+	-.01722	.00423
RNC	-.003277	.00131	RNC	.08173	.00315	RNC	-.02098	.00283
RS	.0001280	.00131	RS	.01213	.00314	RS	-.03553	.00283
RW	.01281	.00140	RW	.01856	.00337	RW	-.009928	.00304
BLK	.01300	.00170	BLK	.006274	.00409	BLK	-.02648	.00368
RUR	-.03057	.00134	RUR	-.001793	.00323	RUR	-.01122	.00290

Table 3.1 (continued)

	Capital Services			Consumer Services		
	Parameter	Estimate	Standard Error	Parameter	Estimate	Standard Error
	CONST	-.4658	.0270	CONST	.3277	.0211
	ln PEN	.07922	.0171	ln PEN	.003061	.0138
	ln PF	-.1982	.0334	ln PF	-.1066	.0259
	ln PCG	-.1056	.0195	ln PCG	-.05354	.0271
	ln PK	.2038	.0368	ln PK	.01869	.0165
	ln PCS	.01869	.0165	ln PCS	.1952	.0375
	ln M	.002060	.00300	ln M	-.05679	.00233
	S2	.07355	.00421	S2	.004666	.00327
	S3	.09982	.00493	S3	.003483	.00383
	S4	.1148	.00541	S4	.007338	.00420
	S5	.1253	.00626	S5	.01357	.00486
	S6	.1284	.00756	S6	.01561	.00587
	S7+	.1369	.00807	S7+	.02508	.00627
	A25–34	.04362	.00599	A25–34	.02321	.00465
	A35–44	.08503	.00637	A35–44	.02304	.00495
	A45–54	.1166	.00605	A45–54	-.003805	.00470
	A55–64	.1395	.00603	A55–64	-.01332	.00468
	A65+	.1296	.00595	A65+	-.01863	.00462
	RNC	.02767	.00398	RNC	-.02214	.00309
	RS	.05528	.00397	RS	-.03200	.00308
	RW	-.004132	.00427	RW	-.01731	.00331
	BLK	-.003539	.00517	BLK	.01074	.00401
	RUR	.05588	.00408	RUR	-.01229	.00317

Convergence after 3 iterations.
SSR = 37387. 12.
Convergence criterion = .00001.

3.4   Social Welfare Functions

Our next objective is to generate a class of possible social welfare functions that can provide the basis for analyzing inequality in the distribution of individual welfare. For this purpose we must choose social welfare functions capable of expressing the implications of a variety of different ethical judgments. To facilitate comparisons with alternative approaches, we employ the axiomatic framework for social choice used by Arrow (1963), Sen (1970), and Roberts (1980a) in proving the impossibility of a nondictatorial social ordering.

We consider the set of all possible social orderings over the set of social states, say X, and the set of all possible real-valued individual welfare functions, say W_k ($k = 1, 2, \ldots, K$). A social ordering, say R, is a complete, reflexive, and transitive ordering of social states. A social state is described by the quantities consumed of N commodity groups by K individuals. The individual welfare function for the kth individual W_k ($k = 1, 2, \ldots, K$) is defined on the set of social states X and gives the level of individual welfare for that individual in each state.

To describe social orderings in greater detail we find it useful to introduce the following notation:

x — a matrix with elements $\{x_{nk}\}$ describing the social state.

$u = (W_1, W_2, \ldots, W_K)$ — a vector of individual welfare functions of all K individuals.

Following Sen (1970, 1977) and Hammond (1976) we define a *social welfare functional*, say f, as a mapping from the set of individual welfare functions to the set of social orderings, such that $f(u') = f(u)$ implies $R' = R$, where

$$u = [W_1(x), W_2(x), \ldots, W_K(x)] ,$$

and

$$u' = [W_1'(x), W_2'(x), \ldots, W_K'(x)] ,$$

for all $x \in X$. Similarly, we define L_k ($k = 1, 2, \ldots, K$) as the *set of admissible individual welfare functions* for the kth individual and L as the Cartesian product $\prod_K^{k=1} L_k$. Finally, let **L** be the partition of L such that all elements of **L** yield the same social ordering.

We can describe a social ordering in terms of the following properties of a social welfare functional:

1. *Unrestricted domain.* The social welfare functional f is defined for all possible vectors of individual welfare functions u.

2. *Independence of irrelevant alternatives.* For any subset A contained in X, if $u(x) = u'(x)$ for all $x \in A$, then $R: A = R': A$, where $R = f(u)$ and $R' = f(u')$ and $R: A$ is the social ordering over the subset A.

3. *Positive association.* For any vectors of individual welfare functions u and u', if for all y in $X - x$, such that

$$W'_k(y) = W_k(y) ,$$

$$W'_k(x) > W_k(x) , \quad (k = 1, 2, \ldots, K),$$

then xPy implies $xP'y$ and $yP'x$ implies yPx, where P is a strict ordering of social states.

4. *Nonimposition.* For all x, y in X there exist u, u' such that xPy and $yP'x$.

5. *Cardinal full comparability.* The set of admissible individual welfare functions that yield the same social ordering $\mathbf{L}$ is defined by

$$\mathbf{L} = \{u': \ W'_k(x) = \alpha + \beta W_k(x) , \ \beta > 0 , \ k = 1, 2, \ldots, K\} ,$$

and $f(u') = f(u)$ for all $u' \in \mathbf{L}$.

Cardinal full comparability implies that social orderings are invariant with respect to any positive affine transformation of the individual welfare functions $\{W_k\}$ that is the same for all individuals. By contrast Arrow requires ordinal noncomparability,[18] which implies that social orderings are invariant with respect to monotone increasing transformations of the individual welfare functions that may differ among individuals:

5'. *Ordinal noncomparability.* The set of individual welfare functions that yield the same social ordering $\mathbf{L}$ is defined by

$$\mathbf{L} = \{u': \ W'_k(x) = \phi_k[W_k(x)] , \ \phi_k \text{ increasing} , \ k = 1, 2, \ldots, K\},$$

and $f(u') = f(u)$ for all u' in $\mathbf{L}$.

The properties of a social welfare functional corresponding to unrestricted domain and independence of irrelevant alternatives are used by Arrow in proving the impossibility of a nondictatorial social ordering:

4'. *Nondictatorship.* There is no individual k such that for all x, $y \in X$, $W_k(x) > W_k(y)$ implies xPy.

Under ordinal noncomparability the assumptions of positive association and nonimposition employed by Arrow imply the weak Pareto principle:

3'. *Pareto principle.* For any x, $y \in X$, if $W_k(x) > W_k(y)$ for all individuals $(k = 1, 2, \ldots, K)$, then xPy.

If a social welfare functional f has the properties of unrestricted domain, independence of irrelevant alternatives, the weak Pareto principle, and ordinal noncomparability, then no nondictatorial social ordering is possible. This result is Arrow's impossibility theorem. Since it is obvious that the class of dictatorial social orderings is too narrow to provide an adequate basis for expressing the implications of alternative ethical judgments, we propose to generate a class of social welfare functions suitable for the evaluation of alternative economic policies by weakening Arrow's assumptions.

We first consider weakening the assumption of ordinal noncomparability of individual welfare functions. Sen (1970) has shown that Arrow's conclusion that no nondictatorial social ordering is possible is preserved by replacing ordinal noncomparability by cardinal noncomparability. This implies that social orderings are invariant with respect to positive affine transformations of the individual welfare functions that may differ among individuals:

5''. *Cardinal noncomparability.* The set of individual welfare functions that yield the same social ordering $\mathbf{L}$ is defined by

$$\mathbf{L} = \{u': \ W'_k(x) = \alpha_k + \beta_k W_k(x) , \quad \beta_k > 0 , \quad k = 1, 2, \ldots, K\} ,$$

and $f(u') = f(u)$ for all u' in $\mathbf{L}$.

However, d'Aspremont and Gevers (1977), Deschamps and Gevers (1978), Maskin (1978), and Roberts (1980b) have shown that we obtain an interesting class of nondictatorial social orderings by requiring cardinal unit comparability of individual welfare functions, which implies that social orderings are invariant with respect to positive affine transformations with units that are the same for all individuals:

5'''. *Cardinal unit comparability.* The set of individual welfare functions that yield the same social ordering $\mathbf{L}$ is defined by

$$\mathbf{L} = \{u': \ W'_k(x) = \alpha_k + \beta W_k(x) ; \quad \beta > 0 ; \quad k = 1, 2, \ldots, K\} ,$$

and $f(u') = f(u)$ for all u' in $\mathbf{L}$.

If a social welfare functional f has the properties of unrestricted domain, independence of irrelevant alternatives, the weak Pareto principle, and cardinal unit comparability, there exist social orderings and a continuous real-valued social welfare function, say W, such that if $W[u(x)] > W[u(y)]$, then xPy. Furthermore, the social welfare function can be represented in the form

$$W[u(x)] = \sum_{k=1}^{K} a_k W_k(x) . \qquad (3.4.1)$$

If we add the assumption that the social welfare function has the property of anonymity, that is, no individual is given greater weight than any other individual in determining the level of social welfare, then the social welfare function W in (3.4.1) must be symmetric in the individual welfare functions $\{W_k\}$. The property of anonymity incorporates a notion of horizontal equity into the representation of social orderings.

Under anonymity the function W in (3.4.1) reduces to the sum of individual welfare functions and takes the form of a utilitarian social welfare function. Utilitarian social welfare functions have been employed extensively in applications of welfare economics, especially in the measurement of inequality by methods originated by Atkinson (1970) and Kolm (1969, 1976a, b), in the design of optimal income tax schedules along the lines pioneered by Mirrlees (1971), and in the evaluation of alternative economic policies by Arrow and Kalt (1979).

The approach to the measurement of social welfare based on a utilitarian social welfare function provides a worthwhile starting point for applications. Harsanyi (1976) and Ng (1975) have pointed out that distributional considerations can be incorporated into a utilitarian social welfare function through the representation of individual welfare functions. However, Sen (1973, p. 18) has argued that a utilitarian social welfare function does not take appropriate account of the distribution of welfare among individuals:

The distribution of welfare between persons is a relevant aspect of any problem of income distribution, and our evaluation of inequality will obviously depend on whether we are concerned only with the loss of the sum of individual utilities through a bad distribution of income, or also with the inequality of welfare levels of different individuals.

To broaden the range of possible social orderings we can require cardinal full comparability of individual welfare functions, as defined above. Roberts (1980b) has shown that a social welfare functional f with the properties of unrestricted domain, independence of irrelevant alternatives, the weak Pareto principle, and cardinal full comparability implies the existence of a social welfare function that takes the form

$$W[u(x)] = \bar{W}(x) + g[u(x) - \bar{W}(x) \, i] \,, \qquad (3.4.2)$$

where i is a vector of ones, the function $\bar{W}(x)$ corresponds to average individual welfare

$$\bar{W}(x) = \sum_{k=1}^{K} a_k W_k(x) \,;$$

and $g(x)$ is a linear homogeneous function of deviations of levels of individual welfare from the average.[19]

If the function $g(x)$ in the representation (3.4.2) of the social welfare function is identically equal to zero, then the social welfare function reduces to the form (3.4.1). If the function $g(x)$ is not identically zero, then the social welfare function incorporates both a measure of average individual welfare and a measure of inequality in the distribution of individual welfare. We conclude that the class of possible social welfare functions (3.4.2) includes utilitarian welfare functions, but also includes functions that are not subject to the objections that can be made to utilitarianism.

Although Roberts (1980b) has succeeded in broadening the class of possible social welfare functions beyond those consistent with utilitarianism, the social welfare functions (3.4.2) are subject to an objection raised by Sen (1973).[20] Information about alternative social states enters only through the individual welfare functions $\{W_k\}$. Sen refers to this property of a social welfare functional f as *welfarism*. Welfarism rules out characteristics of a social state that are conceivably relevant for social orderings, but that cannot be incorporated into the social welfare function through the individual welfare functions.

Roberts (1980b) has suggested the possibility of further weakening Arrow's assumptions in order to incorporate nonwelfare characteristics of social states.[21] For this purpose we can replace the weak Pareto principle by positive association and nonimposition, as defined above. We retain the assumptions of unrestricted domain, independence of irrelevant alternatives, and cardinal full comparability of measures of individual welfare. We can partition the set of social states X into subsets, such that all states within each subset have the same nonwelfare characteristics. For each subset there exists a social ordering that can be represented by a social welfare function of the form (3.4.2).

Under the assumptions we have outlined there exists a social ordering for the set of all social states that can be represented by a social welfare function of the form

$$W(u, x) = F\{\bar{W}(x) + g[x, u(x) - \bar{W}(x) i], x\},\tag{3.4.3}$$

where the function $\bar{W}(x)$ corresponds to average individual welfare

$$\bar{W}(x) = \sum_{k=1}^{K} a_k(x)\, W_k(x).$$

As before, the function g is a linear homogeneous function of deviations of levels of individual welfare from average welfare.

The class of social welfare functions (3.4.3) incorporates nonwelfare characteristics of social states through the weights $\{a_k(x)\}$ in average individual welfare $\bar{W}(x)$, through the function $g(x)$, which depends directly on the social state x as well as on deviations of levels of individual welfare from the average welfare, and through the function F, which depends directly on the social state x and on the sum of the functions $\bar{W}(x)$ and $g(x)$. This class includes social welfare functions that are not subject to the objections that can be made to welfarism.

At this point we have generated a class of possible social welfare functions capable of expressing the implications of a variety of different ethical judgments. In order to choose a specific social welfare function, we must narrow the range of possible ethical judgments by imposing further requirements on the class of possible social welfare functions. First, we must limit the dependence of the function $F(x)$ in (3.4.3) on the characteristics of alternative social states. Second, we must select a form for the function $g(x)$ in (3.4.3), which depends on deviations of levels of individual welfare from average welfare $\bar{W}(x)$. Finally, we must choose representations of the individual welfare functions $\{W_k(x)\}$ that provide cardinal full comparability.

We first rule out the dependence of the function $F(x)$ in (3.4.3) on characteristics of social states that do not enter through the functions $\bar{W}(x)$ and $g(x)$. This restriction reduces F to a function of a single variable $\bar{W} + g$. We obtain an ordinal measure of social welfare by permitting the function F to be any monotone increasing transformation. To obtain a cardinal measure of social welfare we observe that the function $\bar{W}(x) + g$ is homogeneous of degree one in the individual welfare functions $\{W_k(x)\}$. All representations of the social welfare function that preserve this property can be written in the form

$$W(u, x) = \beta[\bar{W}(x) + g(x)] , \quad (\beta > 0) . \qquad (3.4.4)$$

We conclude that only positive, homogeneous, affine transformations are permitted.

The restrictions embodied in the class of social welfare functions (3.4.4) do not reduce social welfare to a function of the individual welfare functions $\{W_k(x)\}$ alone, since the weights $\{a_k(x)\}$ in average individual welfare $\bar{W}(x)$ and the function $g(x)$ depend on nonwelfare characteristics of the social state x. However, these social welfare functions are homogeneous of degree one in levels of individual welfare. This implies that doubling the welfare of each individual will double social welfare, holding nonwelfare characteristics of the social state constant. Blackorby and Donaldson (1982) refer to this class of social welfare functions as *distributionally homothetic*.[22]

We impose a second set of requirements on the class of social welfare functions (3.4.3) by selecting an appropriate form for the function $g(x)$. In particular, we require that this function is additive in deviations of individual welfare functions $\{W_k(x)\}$ from average welfare $\bar{W}(x)$. Since the function $g(x)$ is homogeneous of degree one, it must be a mean value function of order $\rho(x)$:[23]

$$g[x, u(x) - \bar{W}(x) i] = -\gamma(x)\left[\sum_{k=1}^{K} b_k(x) |W_k - \bar{W}|^{-\rho(x)}\right]^{-1/\rho(x)} , \qquad (3.4.5)$$

where

$$\gamma(x) > 0 ; \quad \rho(x) \leqq -1 ; \quad \sum_{k=1}^{K} b_k(x) = 1 ; \quad 0 < b_k(x) < 1, \quad (k = 1, 2, \ldots, K).$$

Under these restrictions the function $g(x)$ is negative, except at the point of perfect equality $W_k = \bar{W}(x)$ $(k = 1, 2, \ldots, K)$, where it is zero. The function $\rho(x)$ in the representation (3.4.5) determines the curvature of the social welfare function in the individual welfare functions $\{W_k(x)\}$. We can refer to this function as the *degree of aversion to inequality*. We assume that the degree of inversion to inequality is constant. To complete the selection of an appropriate form for the social welfare function we must choose appropriate weights $\{a_k(x)\}$ for average individual welfare $\bar{W}(x)$ and $\{b_k(x)\}$ for the measure of equality $g(x)$. We find it natural to require that the two sets of weights are the same.

To incorporate a notion of horizontal equity into the social welfare functions (3.4.5) we can impose a weak form of the property of anonymity. In particular, we require that no individual is given greater weight in the social welfare function than any other individual with an identical individual welfare function. This implies that the social welfare function is symmetric in the levels of individual welfare for identical individuals. The weights $\{a_k(x)\}$ in average welfare $\bar{W}(x)$ and the measure of $g(x)$ must be the same for identical individuals.

Under the restrictions presented up to this point the social welfare function W takes the form

$$W(u, x) = \bar{W} - \gamma(x) \left[\sum_{k=1}^{K} a_k(x) \, |W_k - \bar{W}|^{-\rho} \right]^{-1/\rho} \qquad (3.4.6)$$

where

$$\bar{W}(x) = \sum_{k=1}^{K} a_k(x) \, W_k(x) \,.$$

The condition of positive association requires that an increase in all levels of individual welfare must increase social welfare. This condition implies that the average level of individual welfare $\bar{W}$ must increase by more than the function $g(x)$, whatever the initial distribution of individual welfare. We assume that the function $\gamma(x)$ in (3.4.6) must take the maximum value consistent with positive association, so that:

$$\gamma(x) = \left\{ 1 + \left[\frac{\sum_{k=1}^{K} a_k(x)}{a_j(x)} \right]^{-(\rho+1)} \right\}^{1/\rho}, \qquad (3.4.7)$$

where

$$a_j(x) = \min_k a_k(x) \,, \qquad (k = 1, 2, \ldots, K) \,,$$

for the social state x.

To complete the selection of a social welfare function $W(u, x)$ we require that the individual welfare functions $\{W_k\}$ in (3.4.3) must be invariant with respect to any positive affine transformation that is the same for all households.[24] Under this assumption the logarithm of the translog indirect utility function is a cardinal measure of individual welfare with full comparability among households. The social welfare function takes the form

$$W(u, x) = \ln \bar{V} - \gamma(x) \left[\sum_{k=1}^{K} a_k(x) \, |\ln V_k - \ln \bar{V}|^{-\rho} \right]^{-1/\rho}. \tag{3.4.8}$$

where

$$\ln \bar{V} = \sum_{k=1}^{K} a_k(x) \ln V_k \left[\frac{pm(A_k)}{M_k} \right].$$

We can complete the specification of a social welfare function $W(u, x)$ by choosing a set of weights $\{a_k(x)\}$ for the levels of individual welfare $\{\ln V_k[pm(A_k) / M_k]\}$ in (3.4.8). For this purpose we must appeal to a notion of vertical equity. Following Hammond (1977), we define a distribution of total expenditure $\{M_k\}$ as more *equitable* than another distribution $\{M'_k\}$ if:

(i) $M_i + M_j = M'_i + M'_j$;

(ii) $M_k = M'_k$ (for $k \neq i, j$) ;

(iii) $\ln V_i \left[\dfrac{pm(A_i)}{M'_i} \right] > \ln V_i \left[\dfrac{pm(A_i)}{M_i} \right] > \ln V_j \left[\dfrac{pm(A_j)}{M_j} \right]$

$$> \ln V_j \left[\frac{pm(A_j)}{M'_j} \right].$$

We say that a social welfare function $W(u, x)$ is an *equity-regarding* function if it is larger for a more equitable distribution of total expenditure.

We require that the social welfare functions (3.4.8) must be equity-regarding functions. This amounts to imposing a version of Dalton's (1920) principle of transfers. This principle requires that a transfer of total expenditures from a rich household to a poor household that does not reverse their relative positions in the distribution of total expenditure must increase the level of social welfare.

If the social welfare functions (3.4.8) are required to be equity-regarding functions, then the weights $\{a_k(x)\}$ associated with the individual welfare functions $\{\ln V_k[pm(A_k) / M_k]\}$ must take the form

$$a_k(x) = \frac{m_0(p, A_k)}{\sum_{k=1}^{K} m_0(p, A_k)}, \qquad (k = 1, 2, \ldots, K). \qquad (3.4.9)$$

We conclude that an equity-regarding social welfare function of the class (3.4.8) must take the form

$$W(u, x) = \ln \bar{V} - \gamma(x) \left[\frac{\sum_{k=1}^{K} m_0(p, A_k) \, |\ln V_k - \ln \bar{V}|^{-\rho}}{\sum_{k=1}^{K} m_0(p, A_k)} \right]^{-1/\rho}, \qquad (3.4.10)$$

where

$$\ln \bar{V} = \frac{\sum_{k=1}^{K} m_0(p, A_k) \ln V_k \left[pm(A_k)/M_k \right]}{\sum_{k=1}^{K} m_0(p, A_k)},$$

$$= \ln p' \left(\alpha_p + \frac{1}{2} B_{pp} \ln p \right) - D(p) \frac{\sum_{k=1}^{K} m_0(p, A_k) \ln \left[M_k/m_0(p, A_k) \right]}{\sum_{k=1}^{K} m_0(p, A_k)}.$$

Furthermore, the condition of positive association implies that the function $\gamma(x)$ in (3.4.8) must take the form

$$\gamma(x) = \left\{ 1 + \left[\frac{\sum_{k=1}^{K} m_0(p, A_k)}{m_0(p, A_j)} \right]^{-(\rho+1)} \right\}^{-1/\rho}, \qquad (3.4.11)$$

where

$$m_0(p, A_j) = \min_k m_0(p, A_k), \qquad (k = 1, 2, \ldots, K).$$

To summarize: We have generated a class of social welfare functions (3.4.3) that has the properties of unrestricted domain, independence of irrelevant alternatives, positive association, nonimposition, and cardinal full comparability. By imposing the additional assumption that the degree of aversion to inequality is constant and requiring the social welfare function to satisfy requirements of horizontal and vertical equity, we obtain the social welfare functions (3.4.10).

3.5   Indexes of Inequality

In this section we develop indexes of inequality in the distribution of individual welfare. For this purpose we decompose the measures of social welfare presented in section 3.4 into measures of efficiency and measures of equity. Efficiency can be defined as the maximum level of welfare that is potentially available through redistributions of aggregate expenditure. We define an absolute index of inequality as the difference between the measure of efficiency and the actual level of social welfare.[25] Finally, we define a relative measure of inequality as the ratio between the absolute index of inequality and the measure of efficiency.[26]

In order to decompose social welfare into measures of efficiency and equity, we first maximize social welfare for a fixed level of aggregate expenditure. We can maximize the average level of individual welfare for a given level of aggregate expenditure by means of the Lagrangian

$$
Z = \ln \bar{V} + \lambda \left[\sum_{k=1}^{K} M_k - M \right]
$$

$$
= \ln p' \left(\alpha_p + \frac{1}{2} B_{pp} \ln p \right) - D(p) \frac{\sum_{k=1}^{K} m_0(p, A_k) \ln \left[M_k / m_0(p, A_k) \right]}{\sum_{k=1}^{K} m_0(p, A_k)}
$$

$$
+ \lambda \left[\sum_{k=1}^{K} M_k - M \right]. \tag{3.5.1}
$$

The first-order conditions for a constrained maximum of average individual welfare are

$$
\left. \begin{array}{c} \dfrac{D(p)}{\displaystyle\sum_{k=1}^{K} m_0(p, A_k)} \cdot \dfrac{m_0(p, A_k)}{M_k} = \lambda \\[2em] \displaystyle\sum_{k=1}^{K} M_k = M \end{array} \right\}, \quad (k = 1, 2, \ldots, K),
$$

so that total expenditure per household equivalent member $\{M_k / m_0(p, A_k)\}$ is the same for all consuming units.

Next we consider the class of social welfare functions (3.4.6). Since the function $g(x, u - \bar{W}i)$ is nonpositive, we obtain a maximum of the social welfare function if the function $g(x, u - \bar{W}i)$ can be made equal to zero while the average level of individual welfare $\bar{W}$ is a maximum. If total expenditure per household equivalent member $\{M_k/m_0(p, A_k)\}$ is the same for all consuming units, the function $g(x, u - \bar{W}i)$ is equal to zero, so that the social welfare function $W(u, x)$ in (3.4.6) is a maximum.

If aggregate expenditure is distributed so as to equalize total expenditure per household equivalent member, the level of individual welfare is the same for all consuming units. For this distribution of total expenditure the social welfare functions (3.4.6) reduce to the average level of individual welfare $\ln \bar{V}$. For the translog indirect utility function the social welfare function takes the form

$$E(x, u) = \ln \bar{V} ,$$

$$= \ln p' \left(\alpha_p + \frac{1}{2} B_{pp} \ln p \right) - D(p) \ln \left[\frac{M}{\sum_{k=1}^{K} m_0(p, A_k)} \right]. \qquad (3.5.2)$$

This is the maximum level of welfare that is potentially available and can be taken as a measure of efficiency. We can refer to this measure as the *translog index of efficiency*. The translog index is equal to the translog indirect utility function (3.2.22), evaluated at aggregate expenditure per household equivalent member for society as a whole.

Given the translog index of efficiency (3.5.2), defined in terms of the social welfare function, we can define a measure of inequality as the difference between the translog index of efficiency and the actual value of the social welfare function

$$I(x, u) = E(x, u) - W(x, u) . \qquad (3.5.3)$$

We can refer to this measure as the *translog index of inequality*. Since the index of efficiency is always greater than or equal to the social welfare function $W(u, x)$, the index of inequality $I(x, u)$ is nonnegative. This index is equal to zero only at the point of perfect equality, where total expenditure per household equivalent member is the same for all consuming units. Finally, the social welfare function can be decomposed into the sum of measures of efficiency and equity

$$W(u, x) = E(u, x) - I(u, x) . \qquad (3.5.4)$$

Similarly, we can define a relative measure of inequality, say $J(x)$, as

$$J(x) = 1 - \frac{W(u, x)}{E(u, x)} = \frac{I(u, x)}{E(u, x)} \ .$$

We can refer to this measure as the *translog index of relative inequality*. The index of relative inequality lies between zero and one and is zero only at the point of perfect equality. It is important to note that measures of inequality are usually defined in terms of the distribution of income or total expenditure, rather than the distribution of individual welfare.[27] The indexes of inequality I and J are defined in terms of the distribution of individual welfare.[28]

To illustrate the measurement of inequality in the distribution of individual welfare we can represent the indexes of inequality I and J in diagrammatic form. For simplicity we consider the case of a society consisting of two identical individuals ($K = 2$). In figure 3.1 we have depicted the contours of a concave social welfare function. The 45° line through the origin represents distributions of individual welfare characterized by perfect equality ($W_1 = W_2$). Under anonymity the contours of the social welfare function are symmetric around the line of perfect equality. Under distributional homotheticity distances between contours are in the same proportion along any ray from the origin.

We can represent the actual distribution of individual welfare by the point A with level of social welfare W^0. To measure the potential level of social welfare we consider levels of individual welfare corresponding to all possible lump sum redistributions of aggregate expenditure $M = M_1 + M_2$. The maximum level of social welfare is attained at the point B corresponding to perfect equality in the distribution of individual welfare. The potential level of social welfare is W^1.

In figure 3.1 the point A' represents perfect equality in the distribution of individual welfare at the same level of social welfare W^0 as at point A. The actual level of social welfare W^0 can be represented by the distance OA'. The level of efficiency W^1 can be represented by the distance OB. The absolute index of inequality I is represented by the distance $OB - OA' = A'B$. The relative index of inequality J is represented by the ratio $A'B/OB$. Under distributional homotheticity, this ratio is the same for distances between the contours corresponding to social welfare levels W^0 and W^1 along any ray from the origin.

We can also illustrate the measurement of inequality in the distribution of individual welfare by considering actual and potential levels of social welfare over the period 1958–1978. The first step in measuring

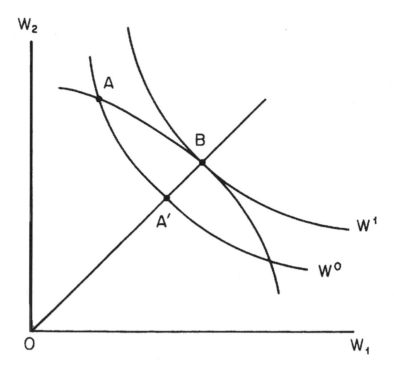

Figure 3.1
Indexes of inequality.

inequality is to evaluate the actual level of social welfare. Levels of
social welfare for alternative values of the degree of aversion to
inequality ρ are presented in table 3.2. The first term in the social welfare functions (3.4.10) represents an average of individual welfare levels over all consuming units, while the second term in these functions
is a measure of dispersion in individual welfare levels. The unit for
measurement of individual welfare is the level of welfare of a white
household with one family member, aged 16–24, living in the Northeast region of the United States in an urban residence, facing prices
equal to unity, and having the log of total expenditure equal to unity.
Social welfare is measured in the same units as individual welfare.

To decompose each measure of social welfare into measures of efficiency and equity we maximize social welfare for a fixed level of
aggregate expenditure to obtain a measure of efficiency or potential
social welfare. The maximum value results from equalizing total

Table 3.2
Levels of social welfare

Year	Actual levels of social welfare		Translog index of efficiency
	$\rho = -1$	$\rho = -2$	
1958	7.08032	7.32138	7.49464
1959	7.12603	7.35945	7.52364
1960	7.15476	7.38594	7.54755
1961	7.16900	7.39788	7.55669
1962	7.18551	7.41395	7.57203
1963	7.21120	7.43712	7.59225
1964	7.24447	7.47186	7.62946
1965	7.29288	7.51858	7.67355
1966	7.33922	7.56292	7.71515
1967	7.35314	7.57707	7.73013
1968	7.39051	7.61350	7.76569
1969	7.41633	7.63909	7.79087
1970	7.44096	7.66264	7.81313
1971	7.45043	7.67184	7.82248
1972	7.49446	7.71466	7.86315
1973	7.53176	7.75304	7.90208
1974	7.52867	7.75005	7.89760
1975	7.53466	7.75673	7.90548
1976	7.56748	7.78750	7.93436
1977	7.60081	7.81870	7.96333
1978	7.63985	7.85778	8.00183

expenditure per household equivalent member over all households. This provides a translog index of efficiency that is independent of the value of the degree of aversion to inequality ρ. An index of efficiency for the years 1958–1978 is presented in table 3.2.

We can define the translog index of inequality as the difference between the translog index of efficiency and the actual value of the social welfare function. This index of inequality is nonnegative and equal to zero under perfect equality with total expenditure per household equivalent member the same for all households. Since the value of the social welfare function depends on the degree of aversion to inequality ρ, we have presented measures of inequality for alternative values of this parameter for the years 1958–1978 in table 3.3.

We find it useful to present our measures of inequality in relative form by means of the translog index of relative inequality. We have defined this index as the ratio of the translog index of inequality to the translog index of efficiency. This ratio varies between zero and one and is equal to zero under perfect equality. Translog indexes of rela-

Table 3.3
Indexes of inequality

Year	Translog index of inequality		Translog index of relative inequality	
	$\rho = -1$	$\rho = -2$	$\rho = -1$	$\rho = -2$
1958	.41432	.17326	.05528	.02312
1959	.39761	.16419	.05285	.02182
1960	.39280	.16161	.05204	.02141
1961	.38769	.15881	.05130	.02102
1962	.38652	.15808	.05105	.02088
1963	.38105	.15513	.05019	.02043
1964	.38499	.15760	.05046	.02066
1965	.38067	.15496	.04961	.02019
1966	.37593	.15224	.04873	.01973
1967	.37699	.15306	.04877	.01980
1968	.37518	.15219	.04831	.01960
1969	.37454	.15178	.04807	.01948
1970	.37216	.15049	.04763	.01926
1971	.37205	.15064	.04756	.01926
1972	.36869	.14849	.04689	.01888
1973	.37032	.14904	.04686	.01868
1974	.36893	.14755	.04671	.01868
1975	.37082	.14875	.04691	.01882
1976	.36688	.14686	.04624	.01851
1977	.36253	.14463	.04552	.01816
1978	.36198	.14405	.04524	.01800

tive inequality are presented for alternative values of the degree of aversion to inequality ρ for the years 1958–1978 in table 3.3.

To summarize: In order to analyze inequality in the distribution of individual welfare we can decompose the measures of social welfare (3.4.10) into measures of efficiency and equity. Our measure of efficiency is the translog indirect utility function (3.5.2), evaluated at aggregate expenditure per household equivalent member for society as a whole. The translog index of inequality is the difference between the translog index of efficiency and the actual value of the social welfare function. The translog index of relative inequality is the ratio between the translog index of inequality and the translog index of efficiency.

3.6 Inequality within Groups

In section 3.5 we have presented indexes of inequality in the distribution of individual welfare for the U.S. economy as a whole. In this section our objective is to develop indexes of inequality in the distribution of individual welfare within subgroups of the U.S. population. For this purpose we introduce group welfare functions that are precisely analogous to the social welfare functions of section 3.4. We consider a group of G individuals, where $1 \leq G \leq K$; without loss of generality we can take the group to be comprised of the first G individuals in the society.

To describe group orderings we find it useful to introduce the following notation:

x_{ng} — the quantity of the nth commodity group consumed by the gth consuming unit ($n = 1, 2, \ldots, N$; $g = 1, 2, \ldots, G$).

x_G — a matrix with elements $\{x_{ng}\}$ describing the group state.

$u_G = (W_1, W_2, \ldots, W_G)$ — a vector of individual welfare functions for all G individuals.

We can define a group welfare functional as a mapping from the set of individual welfare functions to the set of group orderings. We can describe a group ordering in terms of properties of a group welfare functional that are precisely analogous to the properties of a social welfare functional considered in section 3.4: unrestricted domain, independence of irrelevant alternatives, positive association, nonimposition, and cardinal full comparability. Under these assumptions there exists a group ordering for the set of all group states that can be represented by a group welfare function analogous to the social welfare function (3.4.3)

$$W_G(u_G, x_G) = F\{\bar{W}_G(x_G) + g[x_G, u_G(x_G) - \bar{W}_G(x_G)\ i], x_G\} , \qquad (3.6.1)$$

where the function $\bar{W}_G(x_G)$ corresponds to average individual welfare

$$\bar{W}_G(x_G) = \sum_{g=1}^{G} a_g(x_G)\ W_g(x_G) .$$

As before, the function g is a linear homogeneous function of deviations of levels of individual welfare from average welfare for the group.

We can rule out the direct dependence of the function $F(x_G)$ in (3.6.1) on characteristics of group states x_G. As in section 3.4, this results in a cardinal representation of group welfare. To complete the selection of a group welfare function $W_G(u_G, x_G)$ we require, as before, that the individual welfare functions $\{W_g(x_G)\}$ must be invariant with respect to any positive affine transformation that is the same for all households. Second, we require that the group welfare function be an equity-regarding function. Under these assumptions the group welfare function must take forms analogous to (3.4.10).

Our next objective is to decompose group welfare into measures of efficiency and equity. For this purpose we can maximize group welfare for a fixed level of group expenditure $M_G = \sum_{g=1}^{G} M_g$ by equalizing total expenditure per household equivalent member for all households in the group. The maximum value of the group welfare function, say E_G, takes the form

$$E_G(u_G, x_G) = \ln \bar{V}_G$$

$$= \ln p' \left(\alpha_p + \frac{1}{2} B_{pp} \ln p \right) - D(p) \left[\frac{\ln M_G}{\sum_{g=1}^{G} m_0(p, A_g)} \right], \qquad (3.6.2)$$

where $\ln \bar{V}_G$ is the average level of individual welfare for the group. We can refer to the maximum value of group welfare that is potentially available E_G as the *translog index of group efficiency*. The translog index is equal to the translog indirect utility function (3.2.22), evaluated at group expenditure per household equivalent member.

Given the translog index of group efficiency (3.6.2), defined in terms of the group welfare function (3.6.1), we can define a measure of group inequality as the difference between the index of efficiency and the actual level of social welfare

$$I_G(u_G, x_G) = E_G(u_G, x_G) - W_G(u_G, x_G) . \qquad (3.6.3)$$

The translog index of group inequality I_G is nonnegative and equal to zero only at the point of perfect equality, where total expenditure per household equivalent member is the same for all households in the group. The group welfare function can be decomposed into the sum of measures of group efficiency and group equity

$$W_G(u_G, x_G) = E_G(u_G, x_G) - I_G(u_G, x_G) . \qquad (3.6.4)$$

We can define a translog index of group relative inequality, say $J_G(u_G, x_G)$, as

$$J_G(u_G, x_G) = 1 - \frac{W_G(u_G, x_G)}{E_G(u_G, x_G)} = \frac{I_G(u_G, x_G)}{E_G(u_G, x_G)}. \qquad (3.6.5)$$

The group index of relative inequality lies between zero and one and is zero only at the point of perfect equality within the group. We can represent the indexes of group inequality I_G and J_G in the same way as in figure 3.1. If we consider contours of the group welfare function, say W_G^0 and W_G^1, rather than contours of the social welfare function, W^0 and W^1, we obtain diagrammatic interpretation of the indexes I_G and J_G that is precisely analogous to the interpretation of the indexes I and J given in section 3.5.

We can also illustrate the measurement of group inequality by considering actual and potential levels of group welfare for subgroups of the U.S. population classified by age of head of the household. The first step in measuring group inequality is to evaluate the actual level of group welfare. Levels of group welfare for six age groups are presented for the years 1958–1978 in the appendix (table 3.A.1). We take the degree of aversion to inequality ρ to be minus unity in order to simplify the presentation. It would be possible to evaluate the level of group welfare for alternative values of this parameter.

To decompose each measure of group welfare into sums of measures of group efficiency and equity we maximize group welfare for a fixed level of group expenditure. The maximum value results from equalizing total expenditure per household equivalent member over all households in the group. This provides a translog index of group efficiency that is independent of the degree of aversion to inequality ρ. Indexes of group efficiency for six age groups of the U.S. population are presented in the appendix (table 3.A.2) for the years 1958–1978.

We can define the translog index of group inequality as the difference between the translog index of group efficiency and the actual value of the group welfare function. This index of group inequality is equal to zero under perfect equality. Indexes of group inequality for six age groups of the U.S. population are presented in table 3.4 for the years 1958–1978. As before, we take the degree of aversion to inequality ρ equal to minus unity.

We have defined the translog index of group relative inequality as the ratio of the translog index of group inequality to the translog index of group efficiency. This ratio varies between zero and one and

Table 3.4
Indexes of group inequality

	Age groups					
Year	16–24	25–34	35–44	45–54	55–64	65+
1958	.32704	.39062	.38851	.41726	.39114	.39456
1959	.32212	.37565	.36677	.40085	.38088	.38831
1960	.31762	.36945	.36389	.39578	.37478	.38181
1961	.31584	.36889	.36084	.39368	.37202	.37807
1962	.31769	.37194	.35975	.39129	.37147	.37510
1963	.31319	.36615	.35213	.38694	.36633	.37152
1964	.31347	.37040	.35762	.39017	.36462	.36858
1965	.31009	.36402	.35127	.38439	.36200	.36701
1966	.30624	.35897	.34543	.37989	.35618	.36232
1967	.30606	.35916	.34372	.37810	.35350	.35930
1968	.30847	.36035	.34245	.37653	.35130	.35639
1969	.30855	.35728	.33800	.37295	.34990	.35607
1970	.30832	.35709	.33745	.37053	.34604	.35264
1971	.30868	.35670	.33874	.37107	.34570	.35196
1972	.30306	.35147	.33627	.36666	.34301	.35075
1973	.30649	.35353	.33720	.36759	.34458	.35270
1974	.31004	.35267	.33694	.36598	.34580	.35486
1975	.31299	.35414	.34175	.36789	.34555	.35497
1976	.31094	.35045	.33620	.36364	.34326	.35336
1977	.30782	.34617	.33244	.35975	.34006	.35083
1978	.31048	.34570	.33167	.35857	.34118	.35307

is equal to zero under perfect equality. Translog indexes of group relative inequality for six age groups of the U.S. population are presented in table 3.5 for the years 1958–1978. Again, we take the degree of aversion to inequality ρ equal to minus unity.

To summarize: In this section we have developed measures of inequality within subgroups of the U.S. population. For this purpose we have introduced translog indexes of group inequality and relative inequality that are analogous to the indexes for the U.S. population as a whole presented in section 3.5. To illustrate the application of measures of inequality within subgroups we have presented translog indexes for six age groups for the years 1958–1978. Our methodology could also be used to provide measures of inequality within subgroups classified by the other demographic characteristics employed in the econometric model of section 3.3. These characteristics include family size, region of residence, race, and urban versus rural residence.

Table 3.5
Indexes of group relative inequality

| Year | Age groups | | | | | |
	16–24	25–34	35–44	45–54	55–64	65+
1958	.04198	.05113	.05095	.05666	.05302	.05381
1959	.04160	.04907	.04788	.05433	.05128	.05250
1960	.04088	.04816	.04731	.05339	.05048	.05138
1961	.04071	.04804	.04693	.05295	.04995	.05073
1962	.04086	.04844	.04665	.05246	.04970	.05039
1963	.04011	.04744	.04561	.05175	.04884	.04980
1964	.03986	.04775	.04602	.05198	.04852	.04905
1965	.03929	.04665	.04492	.05083	.04790	.04874
1966	.03860	.04572	.04394	.04990	.04691	.04792
1967	.03856	.04563	.04353	.04960	.04649	.04758
1968	.03867	.04571	.04313	.04921	.04590	.04698
1969	.03872	.04521	.04233	.04856	.04561	.04689
1970	.03849	.04506	.04216	.04812	.04495	.04629
1971	.03876	.04506	.04218	.04812	.04488	.04607
1972	.03799	.04429	.04161	.04726	.04433	.04566
1973	.03832	.04436	.04148	.04717	.04431	.04567
1974	.03877	.04437	.04148	.04701	.04442	.04587
1975	.03911	.04449	.04202	.04720	.04448	.04573
1976	.03879	.04395	.04118	.04645	.04401	.04534
1977	.03838	.04339	.04056	.04570	.04340	.04488
1978	.03848	.04323	.04028	.04529	.04330	.04492

3.7 Inequality between Groups

We have presented indexes of inequality in the distribution of individual welfare within subgroups of the U.S. population in section 3.6. In this section our objective is to develop indexes of inequality between subgroups. For this purpose we introduce between-group welfare functions that are precisely analogous to the social welfare functions of section 3.4. We first partition the population into B mutually exclusive and exhaustive groups. We suppose that the bth group has G_b individuals ($b = 1, 2, \ldots, B$). The sum of the number of individuals over all groups, say $\sum G_b$, is equal to the total population K.

We can express the potential level of welfare for each group as a function of the price system p and the level of group expenditure, say M_{G_b} ($b = 1, 2, \ldots, B$). This level of welfare can be attained by equalizing total expenditure per household equivalent member within the group. The potential level of group welfare corresponds to the value of the translog indirect utility function (3.6.2) at group expenditure per household equivalent member for the group as a whole. When actual group welfare is equal to potential group welfare, the group behaves like an individual household with a number of household equivalent members equal to the total for all households in the group.

To describe between-group orderings we find it useful to introduce the following notation:

x_{nb} — the quantity of the nth commodity group consumed by the bth group with actual group welfare equal to potential group welfare $(n = 1, 2, \ldots, N; \ b = 1, 2, \ldots, B)$.

x_B — a matrix with elements $\{x_{nb}\}$ describing the between group state.

$u_B = (E_{G_1}, E_{G_2} \cdots E_{G_B})$ — a vector of potential group welfare functions for all B groups.

We can define a between-group welfare functional as a mapping from the set of group welfare functions to the set of between-group orderings. We can describe a between-group ordering in terms of properties of a between-group welfare functional that are precisely analogous to the properties of a social welfare functional considered in section 3.4. There exists a between-group ordering for the set of all between-group states that can be represented by a between-group welfare function analogous to the social welfare function (3.4.3)

$$W_B(u_B, x_B) = F\{\bar{W}_B(x_b) + g[x_B, u_B(x_B) - \bar{W}_B(x_B) \, i], x_B\} , \qquad (3.7.1)$$

where the function $\bar{W}_B (x_B)$ corresponds to the average level of potential group welfare,

$$\bar{W}_B(x_B) = \sum_{b=1}^{B} a_b(x_B) \, E_{G_b} ,$$

and the function g is a linear homogeneous function of deviations of levels of potential group welfare from average potential group welfare.

Ruling out direct dependence of the function $F(x_B)$ in (3.7.1) on characteristics of between-group states x_B results in a cardinal representation of between-group welfare. We can require that potential group welfare functions $\{E_{G_b}\}$ must be invariant with respect to any positive affine transformation that is the same for all households and that the between-group welfare function is an equity-regarding function. Under these assumptions the between-group welfare function must take forms analogous to (3.4.10).

The translog index of efficiency (3.5.2) is expressed in terms of the social state x and the vector u of individual welfare functions for all K individuals. We can also define such an index, say E_B, in terms of the between-group state x_B and the vector u_B of potential group welfare functions for all B groups. Both indexes correspond to the potential level of social welfare and both are equal to the translog indirect utility function (3.3.13), evaluated at aggregate expenditure per household equivalent member for society as a whole.

Given the translog index of efficiency E_B, we can define a measure of between-group inequality as the difference between the translog index of efficiency and the value of the between-group welfare function

$$I_B(u_B, x_B) = E_B(u_B, x_{B)} - W_B(u_B, x_B) . \tag{3.7.2}$$

The *translog index of between-group inequality* I_B is nonnegative and equal to zero only where group expenditure per household equivalent member is the same for all groups. The between-group social welfare function can be decomposed into the sum of measures of efficiency and between-group equity

$$W_B(u_B, x_B) = E_B(u_B, x_{B)} - I_B(u_B, x_B) . \tag{3.7.3}$$

Given the between-group welfare function (3.7.1), we can define a measure of within-group inequality, say I_W, as the difference between the actual values of the between-group welfare function and the social welfare function

$$I_W(u, x; u_B, x_B) = W_B(u_B, x_B) - W(u, x) . \tag{3.7.4}$$

The *translog index of within-group inequality* I_W is nonnegative and equal to zero only where group expenditure per household equivalent member is the same for all households within each group. The translog index of inequality I can be decomposed into the sum of measures of inequality between and within groups

$$\begin{aligned} I(u, x) &= I_B(u_B, x_B) + I_W(u, x; u_B, x_B) \\ &= [E_B(u_B, x_B) - W_B(u_B, x_B)] + [W_B(u_B, x_B) - W(u, x)] . \end{aligned} \tag{3.7.5}$$

Similarly, we can define a *translog index of between-group relative inequality*, say J_B, as

$$J_B(u_B, x_B) = 1 - \frac{W_B(u_B, x_B)}{E_B(u_B, x_B)} = \frac{I_B(u_B, x_B)}{E_B(u_B, x_B)} . \qquad (3.7.6)$$

The between-group index of relative inequality lies between zero and one and is zero only at the point of perfect equality among groups. We can also define a *translog index of within-group relative inequality*, say J_W, as

$$J_W(u, x; u_B, x_B) = \frac{W_B(u_B, x_B) - W(u, x)}{E(u, x)} = \frac{I_W(u, x; u_B, x_B)}{E(u, x)} . \qquad (3.7.7)$$

The within-group index lies between zero and one and is zero only at the point of perfect equality within each group. The translog index of relative inequality J can be decomposed into the sum of measures of relative inequality between and within groups

$$
\begin{aligned}
J(u, x) &= J_B(u_B, x_B) + J_W(u, x; u_B, x_B) \\
&= \frac{I_B(u_B, x_B)}{E_B(u_B, x_B)} + \frac{I_W(u, x; u_B, x_B)}{E(u, x)} .
\end{aligned} \qquad (3.7.8)
$$

The translog indexes of inequality presented in table 3.3 can be decomposed into the sum of translog indexes of inequality between and within groups.[29] The index of between-group inequality is equal to zero where group expenditure per household equivalent member is the same for all groups. The index of within-group inequality is equal to zero only where group expenditure per household equivalent member is the same for all households within each group. Indexes of between- and within-group inequality for the U.S. population divided among six subgroups classified by age of head of household are presented in table 3.6 for the years 1958–1978. To simplify the presentation we take the degree of aversion to inequality ρ equal to minus unity.

Similarly, the translog indexes of relative inequality presented in table 3.3 can be decomposed into the sum of translog indexes of relative inequality between and within groups. Both indexes lie between zero and one. The translog index of relative between-group inequality is equal to zero only at the point of perfect equality among groups. The translog index of relative within-group inequality is equal to zero only at the point of perfect equality within each group. Relative

Table 3.6
Decomposition of indexes of inequality

	Translog indexes of inequality		
Year	Total	Between groups	Within groups
1958	.41432	.07881	.33551
1959	.39761	.07474	.32287
1960	.39280	.07523	.31757
1961	.38769	.06806	.31962
1962	.38652	.06743	.31909
1963	.38105	.06738	.31366
1964	.38499	.07261	.31239
1965	.38067	.07360	.30707
1966	.37593	.07482	.30111
1967	.37699	.08152	.29546
1968	.37518	.08038	.29479
1969	.37454	.08437	.29018
1970	.37216	.08371	.28846
1971	.37205	.08246	.28959
1972	.36869	.08113	.28756
1973	.37032	.08161	.28871
1974	.36893	.07683	.29210
1975	.37082	.07791	.29291
1976	.36688	.07536	.29151
1977	.36253	.07118	.29134
1978	.36198	.06768	.29430

indexes of between- and within-group inequality for the U.S. population are presented in table 3.7 for the years 1958–1978. As before, we take the degree of aversion to inequality ρ equal to minus unity.

To summarize: In this section we have developed measures of inequality between and within subgroups of the U.S. population. For this purpose we have introduced a between-group welfare function that is analogous to the social welfare function presented in section 3.4 above. The translog index of between-group inequality is the difference between the translog index of efficiency for the society as a whole and the actual value of the between-group welfare function. The translog index of within-group inequality is the difference between the actual values of the between-group welfare function and the social welfare function.

To illustrate the decomposition of the translog indexes of inequality and relative inequality for society as a whole we have presented

Table 3.7
Decomposition of indexes of relative inequality

	Translog indexes of relative inequality		
Year	Total	Between groups	Within groups
1958	.05528	.01052	.04477
1959	.05285	.00993	.04291
1960	.05204	.00997	.04208
1961	.05130	.00901	.04230
1962	.05105	.00891	.04214
1963	.05019	.00888	.04131
1964	.05046	.00952	.04094
1965	.04961	.00959	.04002
1966	.04873	.00970	.03903
1967	.04877	.01055	.03822
1968	.04831	.01035	.03796
1969	.04807	.01083	.03725
1970	.04763	.01071	.03692
1971	.04756	.01054	.03702
1972	.04689	.01032	.03657
1973	.04686	.01033	.03654
1974	.04671	.00973	.03699
1975	.04691	.00985	.03705
1976	.04624	.00950	.03674
1977	.04552	.00894	.03659
1978	.04524	.00846	.03678

indexes of between-group and within-group inequality for the U.S. population classified by age of head of household for the years 1958–1978. Our methodology could also be used to decompose the measures of inequality by the other demographic characteristics employed in the econometric model of section 3.3.

3.8 Money Metric Inequality

In order to quantify gains to society from redistributional policies we find it useful to express measures of inequality in terms of equivalent levels of aggregate expenditure. For this purpose we introduce the social expenditure function, defined as the minimum level of aggregate expenditure $M = \sum_{k=1}^{K} M_k$ required to attain a given level of social welfare, say W, at a specified price system p.[30] More formally, the social expenditure function $M(p, W)$ is defined by

$$M(p, W) = \min\left\{M: \ W(u, x) \geq W \ ; \ \ M = \sum_{k=1}^{K} M_k\right\}.$$ (3.8.1)

The social expenditure function (3.8.1) is precisely analogous to the individual expenditure function (3.2.23). The individual expenditure function gives the minimum level of individual expenditure required to attain a level of individual welfare; the social expenditure function gives the minimum level of aggregate expenditure required to attain a level of social welfare.

To construct a social expenditure function we maximize social welfare for a fixed level of aggregate expenditure by equalizing total expenditure per household equivalent member for all consuming units. The maximum level of welfare (3.5.2) is equal to the translog indirect utility function (3.2.22), evaluated at total expenditure per household equivalent member $M/\sum_{k=1}^{K} m_0(p, A_k)$ for the economy as a whole. We can solve for aggregate expenditure as a function of the level of social welfare and prices

$$\ln M(p, W) = \frac{1}{D(p)}\left[\ln p'\left(\alpha_p + \frac{1}{2} B_{pp} \ln p\right) - W\right]$$
$$+ \ln\left[\sum_{k=1}^{K} m_0(p, A_k)\right].$$ (3.8.2)

We can refer to this function as the *translog social expenditure function*. The value of aggregate expenditure is obtained by evaluating the translog individual expenditure function (3.2.23) at the level of social welfare W and the number of household equivalent members $\sum_{k=1}^{K} m_0(p, A_k)$ for the economy as a whole.

To obtain a money measure of the actual level of social welfare, say W^0, we first evaluate the social welfare function at prices actually prevailing, say p^0, and at the actual distribution of total expenditure $\{M_k^0\}$

$$W^0 = \ln \bar{V}^0 - \left\{1 + \left[\frac{\sum_{k=1}^{K} m_0(p^0, A_k)}{m_0(p^0, A_j)}\right]^{-(\rho+1)}\right\}^{-1/\rho}$$
$$\times \left[\frac{\sum_{k=1}^{K} m_0(p^0, A_k) \, |\ln V_k^0 - \ln \bar{V}^0|^{-\rho}}{\sum_{k=1}^{K} m_0(p^0, A_k)}\right]^{-1/\rho},$$ (3.8.3)

where

$$\ln \bar{V}^0 = \frac{\sum_{k=1}^{K} m_0(p^0, A_k) \ln V_k \left[\dfrac{p^0 m(A_k)}{M_k^0} \right]}{\sum_{k=1}^{K} m_0(p^0, A_k)},$$

and

$$\ln V_k^0 = \ln p^{0'} \left(\alpha_p + \frac{1}{2} B_{pp} \ln p^0 \right) D(p^0) \ln \left[\frac{M_k^0}{m_0(p^0, A_k)} \right], \quad (k = 1, 2, \ldots, K).$$

We can express the actual level of social welfare W^0 in terms of aggregate expenditure by means of the social expenditure function

$$\ln M(p^0, W^0) = \frac{1}{D(p^0)} \left[\ln p^{0'} \left(\alpha_p + \frac{1}{2} B_{pp} \ln p^0 \right) - W^0 \right]$$
$$+ \ln \left[\sum_{k=1}^{K} m_0(p^0, A_k) \right]. \tag{3.8.4}$$

Second, we can decompose our measure of social welfare into measures of efficiency and equity. For this purpose we evaluate the social welfare function at the maximum level, say W^2, that can be attained through lump sum redistributions of aggregate expenditure $M^0 = \sum_{k=1}^{K} M_k^0$. Total expenditure per household equivalent member must be equalized for all consuming units, so that the social welfare function reduces to average individual welfare

$$W^2 = \ln \bar{V}^2$$
$$= \ln p^{0'} \left(\alpha_p + \frac{1}{2} B_{pp} \ln p^0 \right) - D(p^0) \ln \left[\frac{M^0}{\sum_{k=1}^{K} m_0(p^0, A_k)} \right]. \tag{3.8.5}$$

This is the maximum level of social welfare that is potentially available and can be taken as a measure of efficiency. Evaluating the social expenditure function at the potential level of welfare, W^2 we obtain

$$M(p^0, W^2) = M^0, \tag{3.8.6}$$

so that aggregate total expenditure M^0 is the resulting money measure of efficiency.

Given a money measure of efficiency (3.8.6), defined in terms of the social expenditure function, we can define a money measure of inequality, say $M^I(p^0, W^0)$, as the difference between the money measure of potential social welfare M^0 and the money measure of actual social welfare $M(p^0, W^0)$

$$M^I(p^0, W^0) = M^0 - M(p^0, W^0) . \qquad (3.8.7)$$

This measure of inequality is nonnegative and equal to zero only for perfect equality in the distribution of individual welfare. The money measure of inequality M^I is the amount that society as a whole would gain from a perfectly egalitarian distribution of aggregate expenditure M^0.

Using the social expenditure function, our money measure of social welfare $M(p^0, W^0)$ can be decomposed into money measures of efficiency M^0 and equity $-M^I$

$$M(p^0, W^0) = M^0 - M^I(p^0, W^0) . \qquad (3.8.8)$$

The level of aggregate expenditure M^0 is the amount society would be willing to pay for the level of social welfare that is potentially available. The money measure of equity $-M^I$ is the loss to society that results from an inequitable distribution of aggregate expenditure among individual households. The critical feature of this decomposition is that all three money measures are expressed in terms of the same set of prices p^0.

Similarly, we can define a money measure of relative inequality, say $M^J(p^0, W^0)$, as

$$M^J(p^0, W^0) = 1 - \frac{M(p^0, W^0)}{M^0} = \frac{M^I(p^0, W^0)}{M^0} . \qquad (3.8.9)$$

This money measure of relative inequality lies between zero and one and is zero only at the point of perfect equality. The money measure of relative inequality M^I is the proportion of aggregate expenditure M^0 lost owing to an inequitable distribution of aggregate expenditure.

In order to quantify gains to subgroups of the U.S. population from redistributional policies we find it useful to express measures of group inequality in terms of equivalent levels of group expenditure. For this purpose we introduce group expenditure functions that are precisely analogous to the social expenditure function (3.8.1). The group expenditure function is defined as the minimum level of group expenditure $M_G = \sum_{g=1}^{G} M_g$ required to attain a given level of group welfare W_G at a specified price system p. The group expenditure function gives the minimum level of group expenditure required to attain a stipulated level of group welfare.

To construct a group expenditure function we can maximize group welfare for a fixed level of group expenditure by equalizing total expenditure per household equivalent member for all households in the group. The maximum level of group welfare (3.6.2) is equal to the translog indirect utility function (3.2.22) evaluated at group expenditure per household equivalent member $M_G/\sum_{g=1}^{G} m_0(p, A_g)$ for the group as a whole. We can solve for group expenditure as a function of the level of social welfare and prices

$$\ln M_G(p, W_G) = \frac{1}{D(p)}\left[\ln p'\left(\alpha_p + \frac{1}{2} B_{pp} \ln p\right) - W_G\right]$$

$$+ \ln\left[\sum_{g=1}^{G} m_0(p, A_g)\right]. \tag{3.8.10}$$

The *translog group expenditure function* is obtained by evaluating the translog individual expenditure function (3.2.23) at the level of group welfare W_G and the number of household equivalent members $\sum_{g=1}^{G} m_0(p, A_g)$ for the group as a whole.

To obtain a money measure of the actual level of group welfare, say W_G^0, we first evaluate the group welfare function at prices p^0 and the actual distribution of total expenditure within the group. We then express this level of welfare in terms of group expenditure by means of the group expenditure function (3.8.10). We can decompose this money measure of group welfare, say $M_G(p^0, W_G^0)$ into money measures of group efficiency and equity. The level of group expenditure, say M_G^0 is a money measure of efficiency, so that we can define a money measure of group inequality, say $M_G^I(p^0, W_G^0)$, as follows

$$M_G^I(p^0, W_G^0) = M_G^0 - M_G(p^0, W_G^0). \tag{3.8.11}$$

This measure is nonnegative and equal to zero only for perfect equality in the distribution of individual welfare within the group. The money measure of group inequality M_G^I is the amount that the group would gain from a perfectly egalitarian distribution of group expenditure.

Using the group expenditure function, our money measure of group welfare $M_G(p^0, W_G^0)$ can be decomposed into money measures of group efficiency M_G^0 and equity $-M_G^0$

$$M_G(p^0, W_G^0) = M_G^0 - M_G^I(p^0, W^0) .$$ (3.8.12)

The level of group expenditure M_G^0 is the amount the group would be willing to pay for the level of group welfare that is potentially available. The money measure of group equity $-M_G^I$ is the loss to the group that results from an inequitable distribution of expenditure among households within the group. We can define a money measure of relative group inequality, say $M_G^J(p^0, W_G^0)$, as follows

$$M_G^J(p^0, W_G^0) = \frac{M_G^I(p^0, W^0)}{M_G^0} ,$$ (3.8.13)

This measure represents the proportion of aggregate expenditure M_G^0 lost owing to an inequitable distribution within the group.

Finally, we can decompose money measures of inequality into the sum of money measures of inequality between and within groups. For this purpose we first express differences in between-group welfare in terms of differences in aggregate expenditure. The between-group expenditure function gives the minimum level of aggregate expenditure required to attain a stipulated level of between-group welfare. We can construct this function by equalizing group expenditure per household equivalent member among all groups or total expenditure per household equivalent member among all households. We obtain the translog index of efficiency (3.5.2), which is equal to the translog utility function (3.2.13), evaluated at aggregate expenditure per household equivalent member for society as a whole. We can solve for aggregate expenditure as a function of the level of social welfare and prices, obtaining the translog social expenditure function (3.8.2).

To obtain a money measure of the actual level of between-group welfare, say W_B^0, we first evaluate the between-group welfare function at prices p^0 and the actual distribution of aggregate expenditure among groups. We then express this level of welfare in terms of aggregate expenditure by means of the social expenditure function (3.8.2). We can decompose this money measure of between-group welfare, say $M(p^0, W_B^0)$ into money measures of efficiency and between-group equity. The level of aggregate expenditure M^0 is a money measure of efficiency, so that we can define a money measure of between-group inequality, say $M_B^I(p^0, W_B^0)$, as follows

$$M_B^I(p^0, W_B^0) = M^0 - M(p^0, W_B^0) \,. \tag{3.8.14}$$

This measure of between-group inequality is nonnegative and equal to zero only for perfect equality in the distribution of aggregate expenditure among groups.

Given the money measure of between-group welfare $M(p^0, W_B^0)$, we can define a money measure of within-group inequality, say M_W^I (p^0, W_B^0, W^0), as the difference between money measures of between-group welfare and the actual level of social welfare

$$M_W^I\ (p^0, W_B^0, W^0) = M(p^0, W_B^0) - M(p^0, W^0) \,. \tag{3.8.15}$$

This measure of within-group inequality is nonnegative and equal to zero only for perfect equality in the distribution of group expenditure within each group. The money measure of inequality $M^I(p^0, W^0)$ can be decomposed into the sum of money measures of inequality between and within groups

$$M^I(p^0, W^0) = M_B^I\ (p^0, W_B^0) + M_W^I\ (p^0, W_B^0, W^0) \,,$$

$$= [M^0 - M(p^0, W_B^0)] + [M(p^0, W_B^0) - M(p^0, W^0)] \,. \tag{3.8.16}$$

The money measure of between-group inequality M_B^I is the amount that society as a whole would gain from a perfectly egalitarian distribution of aggregate expenditure among groups. The money measure of within-group inequality M_W^I is the amount society would gain from a perfectly egalitarian distribution of group expenditure within each group.

We can define a money measure of relative between-group inequality, say $M_B^J(p^0, W_B^0)$, as follows

$$M_B^J\ (p^0, W_B^0) = \frac{M_B^I(p^0, W_B^0)}{M^0} \,. \tag{3.8.17}$$

This measure represents the proportion of aggregate expenditure M^0 lost owing to an inequitable distribution of aggregate expenditure among groups. We can also define a money measure of relative within-group inequality, say $M_W^J(p^0, W_B^0, W^0)$, as follows

$$M_W^J(p^0, W_B^0, W^0) = \frac{M_W^I(p^0, W_B^0, W^0)}{M^0} . \tag{3.8.18}$$

This measure represents the proportion of aggregate expenditure lost owing to an inequitable distribution of group expenditure among households within each group. The money measure of relative inequality $M^J(p^0, W^0)$ can be decomposed as the sum of money measures of relative inequality between and within groups

$$M^J(p^0, W^0) = M_B^J(p^0, W_B^0) + M_W^J(p^0, W_B^0, W^0) . \tag{3.8.19}$$

To summarize: In this section we have developed methods for expressing differences in levels of social welfare in terms of differences in aggregate expenditure. These methods are useful in quantifying gains to society from redistributional policies. Money metric inequality can be defined as the difference between money measures of potential and actual social welfare. This measure of inequality is the amount that society as a whole would gain from a perfectly egalitarian distribution of aggregate expenditure. We also consider money measures of group inequality, corresponding to the amounts groups would gain from an egalitarian distribution. Finally, we decompose money metric inequality into the sum of money measures of between- and within-group inequality. These measures correspond to gains to society from redistribution between and within groups.

3.9 Applications of Money Metric Inequality

To illustrate the application of the money measures of inequality presented in section 3.8 we observe that the translog social expenditure function (3.8.2) has the same form as the translog individual expenditure function (3.2.23). We can express the level of social welfare as a function of the price system and aggregate expenditure M. We take this level of social welfare to be the level obtained by equalizing total expenditure per household equivalent member among all households. Under this assumption society behaves in the same way as an individual maximizing a utility function, so that we can represent social welfare in terms of the indifference map for a single representative consumer.[31]

In figure 3.2 we have depicted the indifference map of the representative consumer with indirect utility function given by the average level of utility $\ln \bar{V}$ in (3.5.2). For simplicity we consider the case of

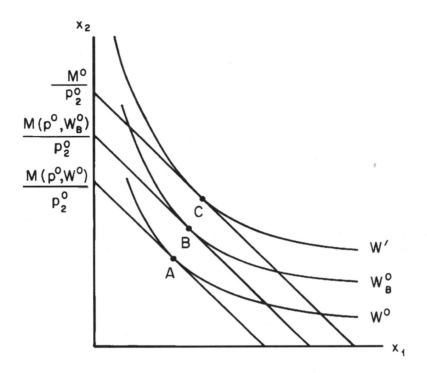

Figure 3.2
Indexes of group inequality.

two commodities ($N = 2$). Consumer equilibrium at the actual level of social welfare W^0 is represented by the point A. The corresponding level of aggregate expenditure $M(p^0, W^0)$, divided by the price of the second commodity p_2^0, is given the vertical axis. This axis provides a representation of aggregate expenditure in terms of units of the second commodity.

Aggregate expenditure M^0 is the value of the social expenditure function at the potential level of welfare W^1. This is the maximum level of welfare that can be obtained by lump sum redistributions of aggregate expenditure. The corresponding consumer equilibrium is represented by the point C. A money measure of the loss in social welfare owing to inequality, expressed in terms of units of the second commodity, is provided by the distance along the x_2 axis between aggregate expenditure M^0/p_2^0 and the value of the social expenditure function $M(p^0, W^0)/p_2^0$. This distance represents the money measure of inequality $M^I(p^0, W^0)$, divided by the price of the second commodity.

The ratio between this distance and the distance corresponding to aggregate expenditure M^0/p_2^0 is the money measure of relative inequality $M^J(p^0, W^0)$.

Since the translog group expenditure function (3.8.11) is precisely analogous to the translog social and individual expenditure functions, we can also express group welfare in terms of the indifference map for a representative consumer. By interpreting the consumer equilibria A and C in figure 3.2 as those corresponding to actual and potential group welfare, we obtain a representation of money measures of group inequality and relative inequality. These measures are analogous to the money measures of inequality for society as a whole that we have already described.

Finally, we can decompose money measures of inequality into the sum of measures of inequality between and within groups. The level of between-group welfare W_B^0 can be attained by equalizing group expenditure per household equivalent member within each group. The corresponding consumer equilibrium is represented by the point B. A money measure of the loss in social welfare owing to inequality in the distribution of aggregate expenditure among groups is provided by the distance along the x_2 axis between the level of aggregate expenditure and the value of the social expenditure function $M(p^0, W_B^0)/p_2^0$. This distance represents the money measure of between-group inequality $M_B^I(p^0, W_B^0)$, divided by the price of the second commodity. Similarly, the loss in social welfare owing to inequality within groups $M_W^I(p^0, W_B^0, W^0)$, divided by the price of the second commodity, is the distance between the value of the social expenditure function $M(p^0, W_B^0)/p_2^0$ and the value at the actual level of social welfare $M(p^0, W^0)/p_2^0$. Ratios between these distances and the distance corresponding to aggregate expenditure M^0/p_2^0 represent money measures of relative between-group and within-group inequality, $M_B^J(p^0, W_B^0)$ and $M_W^J(p^0, W_B^0, W^0)$, respectively.

We can also illustrate money measures of inequality in the distribution of individual welfare by considering money measures of actual and potential levels of social welfare over the period 1958–1978. We first present money measures of social welfare for alternative values of the degree of aversion to inequality ρ in table 3.8. The money measure of potential social welfare is independent of the degree of aversion to inequality ρ. Money metric efficiency for the years 1958–1978 is presented in table 3.8. Money metric social welfare and efficiency are measured in prices of 1972.

Table 3.8
Money metric social welfare

	Money metric social welfare		Money metric efficiency
Year	$\rho = -1$	$\rho = -2$	
1958	247351.78	314780.43	374327.96
1959	261652.47	330441.39	389406.41
1960	269947.79	340158.88	399823.92
1961	278505.80	350136.05	410397.88
1962	288739.03	362839.33	424980.25
1963	299392.61	375280.84	438255.18
1964	313877.64	394017.70	461276.74
1965	331406.26	415320.71	484934.29
1966	350819.84	438765.73	510915.29
1967	362386.95	453337.89	528319.68
1968	378768.96	473387.80	551204.43
1969	393892.71	492177.76	572848.77
1970	408149.04	509437.21	592170.79
1971	417450.60	520910.67	605599.08
1972	439859.27	548209.69	635967.11
1973	461234.37	575467.36	667958.55
1974	463423.37	578257.88	670199.13
1975	470846.24	587924.63	682218.56
1976	491298.65	612206.60	709051.25
1977	513076.66	637987.81	737266.40
1978	538670.09	669837.30	773622.09

Money metric inequality is defined as the difference between money metric efficiency and money metric social welfare. This measure of inequality is the amount that society as a whole would gain from a perfectly egalitarian distribution of aggregate expenditure. Since money metric social welfare depends on the degree of aversion to inequality ρ, we have presented money metric inequality for different values of this parameter for the years 1958–1978 in table 3.9. We also present the corresponding values of money metric relative inequality in table 2.9. This measure is the proportion of aggregate expenditure lost owing to an inequitable distribution among households.

Similarly, we can illustrate money measures of group inequality in the distribution of individual welfare. For this purpose we consider money measures of actual and potential group welfare for subgroups of the U.S. population classified by age of head of household. The first step in constructing money measures of group inequality is to present

Table 3.9
Money metric inequality

Year	Money metric inequality		Money metric relative inequality	
	$\rho = -1$	$\rho = -2$	$\rho = -1$	$\rho = -2$
1958	126976.18	59547.53	.33921	.15908
1959	127753.94	58965.02	.32807	.15142
1960	129876.13	59665.04	.32483	.14923
1961	131892.08	60261.83	.32138	.14684
1962	136241.21	62140.92	.32058	.14622
1963	138862.56	62974.34	.31685	.14369
1964	147398.10	67258.04	.31954	.14581
1965	153528.02	69613.58	.31660	.14355
1966	160095.44	72149.56	.31335	.14122
1967	165932.73	74981.79	.31408	.14193
1968	172435.46	77816.63	.31283	.14118
1969	178956.06	80671.01	.31240	.14082
1970	184021.75	82733.58	.31076	.13971
1971	188148.48	84688.42	.31068	.13984
1972	196107.84	87757.42	.30836	.13799
1973	206724.18	92491.19	.30949	.13847
1974	206775.76	91941.25	.30853	.13718
1975	211372.32	94293.93	.30983	.13822
1976	217752.60	96844.65	.30710	.13658
1977	224190.74	99278.59	.30408	.13466
1978	234952.00	103784.79	.30370	.13415

money measures of group welfare for six age groups for the years 1958–1978 in appendix table 3.A.3. We take the degree of aversion to inequality ρ equal to minus unity in order to simplify the presentation. The money measure of potential group welfare is independent of the degree of aversion to inequality. Money metric group efficiency for the six age groups for the years 1958–1978 is presented in appendix table 3.A.4. Money metric group welfare and efficiency are given in prices of 1972.

Money metric group inequality is defined as the difference between money metric group efficiency and money metric group welfare. These money measures of inequality are the amounts that each group would gain from a perfectly egalitarian distribution of group expenditure. Money metric inequality for six age groups of the U.S. population is presented in table 3.10 for the years 1958–1978. We present the corresponding values of money metric group relative inequality in table 3.11. These measures are the proportions of group expenditure

Table 3.10
Money metric group inequality

Year	Age groups					
	16–24	25–34	35–44	45–54	55–64	65+
1958	3447.98	20882.64	37115.51	28561.99	18468.05	13463.39
1959	3450.47	20096.69	37058.78	28308.07	19304.58	14597.27
1960	3618.72	20228.31	37473.17	29546.45	19381.75	14520.44
1961	3510.88	19797.20	37499.23	29736.95	20649.46	16245.49
1962	3619.39	19589.07	39636.20	30584.01	21632.02	16658.31
1963	3905.83	20166.12	39518.31	31338.80	22221.36	16981.93
1964	4404.91	21401.11	41552.57	33702.20	22913.60	17950.81
1965	4592.21	22587.32	42612.89	35324.76	23919.78	18520.36
1966	4880.51	23642.38	43825.51	37145.06	24759.44	19381.34
1967	4945.80	24806.21	45198.83	37891.49	25858.45	19554.78
1968	5849.16	26551.55	45830.74	38786.11	27249.57	20327.16
1969	6093.08	27708.48	47038.63	39930.96	28207.82	20909.23
1970	6915.97	28721.44	47790.69	41001.96	28905.09	21552.45
1971	7206.44	30283.43	47933.48	41622.81	29193.02	22759.84
1972	7532.08	31963.75	50143.83	42634.63	30045.18	24063.55
1973	8314.51	34780.78	52362.30	44160.97	31100.97	25692.54
1974	8265.53	35286.63	52007.73	43177.97	31754.93	26697.57
1975	8539.16	36755.43	53651.22	43093.50	31709.12	28003.10
1976	8842.40	38198.84	55219.22	43788.36	32818.55	28894.73
1977	8978.27	39241.68	57744.27	43869.41	34408.20	29820.61
1978	9923.73	40399.85	60924.00	45116.37	36005.96	32220.40

lost owing to an inequitable distribution among households within the group.

Finally, we can illustrate the decomposition of the money measures of inequality presented in table 3.9 into money measures of inequality between and within subgroups of the U.S. population. Money metric between-group inequality is defined as the differences between money metric efficiency and money metric between-group welfare. This measure is the amount that society as a whole would gain from a perfectly egalitarian distribution of aggregate expenditure among groups. Money metric within-group inequality is defined as the difference between money metric between-group welfare and money metric social welfare. This measure is the amount that society as a whole would gain from a perfectly egalitarian distribution of group expenditure within each group.

Money measures of between- and within-group inequality for the U.S. population divided among six groups classified by age of head of

Table 3.11
Money metric group relative inequality

	Age groups					
Year	16–24	25–34	35–44	45–54	55–64	65+
1958	.27894	.32336	.32193	.34115	.32372	.32603
1959	.27539	.31316	.30703	.33025	.31674	.32180
1960	.27212	.30889	.30503	.32684	.31256	.31737
1961	.27082	.30850	.30291	.32543	.31066	.31482
1962	.27217	.31061	.30215	.32382	.31028	.31278
1963	.26889	.30660	.29681	.32087	.30673	.31031
1964	.26909	.30954	.30066	.32306	.30554	.30828
1965	.26662	.30512	.29621	.31913	.30372	.30720
1966	.26379	.30160	.29209	.31606	.29966	.30394
1967	.26366	.30174	.29087	.31484	.29777	.30184
1968	.26543	.30257	.28997	.31376	.29623	.29980
1969	.26549	.30042	.28681	.31130	.29524	.29957
1970	.26532	.30029	.28642	.30963	.29252	.29717
1971	.26558	.30002	.28734	.31000	.29228	.29669
1972	.26145	.29634	.28557	.30696	.29037	.29584
1973	.26397	.29780	.28624	.30760	.29148	.29721
1974	.26658	.29719	.28605	.30648	.29235	.29873
1975	.26874	.29822	.28947	.30781	.29217	.29880
1976	.26724	.29563	.28552	.30486	.29055	.29767
1977	.26495	.29261	.28283	.30215	.28827	.29590
1978	.26690	.29228	.28228	.30133	.28907	.29747

household are presented in table 3.12 for the years 1958–1978. To simplify the presentation we take the degree of aversion to inequality ρ equal to minus unity. Money metric between- and within-group inequality are measured in prices of 1972. We present the corresponding money measures of between- and within-group relative inequality in table 3.13. These measures are the proportions of aggregate expenditure lost owing to inequitable distributions between and within groups.

To summarize: In this section we have illustrated the application of the money measures of inequality presented in section 3.8. We have first presented money metric inequality for the U.S. population as a whole for the years 1958–1978. This money measure of inequality is the difference between money metric efficiency and money metric social welfare. Second, to illustrate the application of money measures of inequality within subgroups we have presented money metric group inequality for six groups, classified by age of head of house-

Table 3.12
Decomposition of money metric inequality

	Money metric inequality		
Year	Total	Between groups	Within groups
1958	126976.18	28369.72	98606.47
1959	127753.94	28043.54	99710.40
1960	129876.13	28973.54	100902.60
1961	131892.08	27004.28	104887.80
1962	136241.21	27711.82	108529.39
1963	138862.56	28558.46	110304.11
1964	147398.10	32305.03	115093.07
1965	153528.02	34409.54	119118.49
1966	160095.44	36832.11	123263.33
1967	165932.73	41362.07	124570.67
1968	172435.46	42574.35	129861.11
1969	178956.06	46346.13	132609.92
1970	184021.75	47550.88	136470.87
1971	188148.48	47934.36	140214.12
1972	196107.84	49559.65	146548.18
1973	206776.76	52347.22	154376.95
1974	206775.76	49565.48	157210.29
1975	211372.32	51131.44	160240.88
1976	217752.60	51472.64	166279.96
1977	224190.74	50656.93	173533.81
1978	234952.00	50628.34	184323.66

hold. Finally, we have decomposed money measures of inequality for the U.S. population as a whole into money measures of inequality between and within age groups. Our methodology could also be used to decompose money measures of inequality by the other demographic characteristics employed in the econometric model of section 3.3.

3.10   Summary and Conclusion

In this chapter we have presented an econometric approach to the measurement of inequality in the distribution of individual welfare. The first step in analyzing inequality is to select a representation for individual welfare. We assume that individual welfare is equal to the logarithm of the translog indirect utility function (3.2.22). The indirect utility function enables us to express individual welfare in terms of the price system and the level of total expenditure.

Table 3.13
Decomposition of money metric relative inequality

Year	Total	Between groups	Within groups
		Money metric relative inequality	
1958	.33921	.07579	.26342
1959	.32807	.07202	.25606
1960	.32483	.07247	.25237
1961	.32138	.06580	.25558
1962	.32058	.06521	.25538
1963	.31685	.06516	.25169
1964	.31954	.07003	.24951
1965	.31660	.07096	.24564
1966	.31335	.07209	.24126
1967	.31408	.07829	.23579
1968	.31283	.07724	.23560
1969	.31240	.08090	.23149
1970	.31076	.08030	.23046
1971	.31068	.07915	.23153
1972	.30836	.07793	.23043
1973	.30949	.07837	.23112
1974	.30853	.07396	.23457
1975	.30983	.07495	.23488
1976	.30710	.07259	.23451
1977	.30408	.06871	.23537
1978	.30370	.06544	.23826

In section 3.2 we show how the translog indirect utility function can be determined from a system of individual expenditure shares (3.2.5) that is integrable. We also demonstrate how the individual expenditure shares (3.2.5) can be recovered uniquely from the system of aggregate expenditure shares (3.2.25). In section 3.3 we fit an econometric model of aggregate consumer behavior that incorporates the restrictions implied by integrability of the individual expenditure shares.

In section 3.4 we generate a class of possible social welfare functions that provides the basis for analyzing inequality in the distribution of individual welfare. Each of these social welfare functions can be represented as the sum of two terms. The first term represents an average of individual welfare levels over all consuming units. The second term is a measure of dispersion in individual welfare levels. Using indirect utility functions for all households we can express social welfare in terms of the price system and the distribution of aggregate expenditure among individuals.[32]

In section 3.5 we develop indexes of inequality in the distribution of individual welfare. For this purpose we decompose the measures of social welfare presented in section 3.4 into measures of efficiency and equity. Our measure of efficiency is the translog indirect utility function (3.5.2), evaluated at aggregate expenditure per household equivalent member for society as a whole. Our measure of equity is the difference between the actual level of social welfare and the measure of efficiency.

In section 3.5 we define the translog index of inequality as the difference between the measure of efficiency given by the translog indirect utility function (3.5.2) and the actual level of social welfare. Similarly, we define the translog index of relative inequality as the ratio between the translog index of inequality and the measure of efficiency. We implement our measures of inequality for the U.S. population as a whole for the years 1958–1978.

In section 3.6 we extend our measures of inequality to the distribution of individual welfare within subgroups of the U.S. population. We first introduce group welfare functions that are precisely analogous to the social welfare functions of section 3.4. We define measures of group inequality and group relative inequality that are analogous to those for the U.S. population as a whole. We implement these measures of inequality for six groups, classified by age of head of household, for the years 1958–1978.

In section 3.7 we develop measures of inequality between subgroups of the U.S. population. We introduce between-group welfare functions that are analogous to the social welfare functions of section 3.4. We define the translog index of inequality between groups as the difference between our measure of efficiency for the population as a whole and the value of the between-group welfare function. Similarly, we define the translog index of equality within groups as the difference between the values of the between-group welfare function and the social welfare functions. We implement these measures of between-group and within-group inequality for six age groups for the years 1958–1978.

For applications to the evaluation of redistributional policies we find it useful to express our measures of inequality in terms of aggregate expenditure. For this purpose we introduce the social expenditure function in section 3.8, giving the minimum level of aggregate expenditure required to attain a stipulated level of social welfare. This value of aggregate expenditure is obtained by evaluating the translog individual expenditure function (3.2.23) at the actual level of social welfare per household equivalent member for the U.S. population as a whole.

We define money metric inequality as the difference between money measures of potential and actual social welfare. This measure is the amount that society as a whole would gain from a perfectly egalitarian distribution of income. We also consider money measures of group inequality and we decompose money metric inequality into the sum of money measures of between- and within-group inequality. In section 3.9 we implement these money measures of inequality for the U.S. population as a whole and for six age groups for the years 1958–1978.

Appendix

Table 3.A.1
Levels of group welfare

| | Age Groups | | | | | |
Year	16–24	25–34	35–44	45–54	55–64	65+
1958	7.46383	7.24867	7.23708	6.94668	6.98630	6.93805
1959	7.42142	7.27994	7.29390	6.97660	7.04650	7.00746
1960	7.45163	7.30163	7.32777	7.01759	7.04965	7.04909
1961	7.44188	7.31046	7.32835	7.04101	7.07588	7.07469
1962	7.45703	7.30572	7.35136	7.06735	7.10265	7.06861
1963	7.49431	7.35187	7.36828	7.09042	7.13424	7.08863
1964	7.55130	7.38741	7.41328	7.11530	7.15032	7.14529
1965	7.58140	7.43842	7.46820	7.17822	7.19604	7.16284
1966	7.62703	7.49181	7.51662	7.23272	7.23630	7.19830
1967	7.63029	7.51182	7.55249	7.24482	7.24975	7.19195
1968	7.66930	7.52383	7.59684	7.27459	7.30294	7.23013
1969	7.65965	7.54540	7.64671	7.30685	7.32121	7.23765
1970	7.70156	7.56736	7.66603	7.32931	7.35256	7.26543
1971	7.65429	7.55899	7.69283	7.34005	7.35739	7.28777
1972	7.67454	7.58487	7.74624	7.39180	7.39525	7.33059
1973	7.69195	7.61637	7.79261	7.42522	7.43223	7.36972
1974	7.68761	7.59547	7.78677	7.41857	7.43980	7.38154
1975	7.68898	7.60510	7.79119	7.42690	7.42387	7.40681
1976	7.70511	7.62282	7.82817	7.46432	7.45696	7.44067
1977	7.71316	7.63288	7.86335	7.51239	7.49471	7.46625
1978	7.75827	7.65057	7.90188	7.55815	7.53805	7.50680

Table 3.A.2
Indexes of group efficiency

Year	Age groups					
	16–24	25–34	35–44	45–54	55–64	65+
1958	7.79087	7.63928	7.62559	7.36394	7.37744	7.33262
1959	7.74355	7.65559	7.66067	7.37745	7.42739	7.39577
1960	7.76925	7.67108	7.69166	7.41337	7.42443	7.43090
1961	7.75772	7.67935	7.68919	7.43469	7.44790	7.45276
1962	7.77472	7.67767	7.71111	7.45865	7.47412	7.44371
1963	7.80750	7.71802	7.72040	7.47736	7.50057	7.46015
1964	7.85476	7.75781	7.77090	7.50548	7.51494	7.51387
1965	7.89149	7.80244	7.81947	7.56261	7.55804	7.52985
1966	7.93327	7.85078	7.86205	7.61261	7.59249	7.56062
1967	7.93636	7.87098	7.89621	7.62292	7.60325	7.55125
1968	7.97777	7.88418	7.93929	7.65112	7.65423	7.58652
1969	7.96821	7.90267	7.98472	7.67980	7.67111	7.59371
1970	8.00988	7.92445	7.00349	7.69984	7.69860	7.61807
1971	7.96297	7.91569	8.03157	7.71112	7.70310	7.63973
1972	7.97761	7.93633	8.08251	7.75846	7.73827	7.68134
1973	7.99844	7.96990	8.12982	7.79281	7.77680	7.72243
1974	7.99765	7.94814	8.12371	7.78455	7.78560	7.73640
1975	8.00197	7.95924	8.13294	7.79479	7.76941	7.76178
1976	8.01605	7.97326	8.16437	7.82797	7.80022	7.79403
1977	8.02099	7.97906	8.19579	7.87214	7.83477	7.81708
1978	8.06875	7.99627	8.23355	7.91673	7.87923	7.85986

Table 3.A.3
Money metric group welfare

Year						

	Age groups					
Year	16–24	25–34	35–44	45–54	55–64	65+
1958	8912.91	43697.32	78173.49	55160.54	38581.93	27832.00
1959	9078.85	44078.05	83640.86	57409.79	41642.57	30763.98
1960	9679.34	45259.73	85376.60	60852.64	42628.57	31231.56
1961	9452.87	44375.69	86296.51	61640.31	45820.08	35357.00
1962	9678.72	43478.15	91545.49	63864.28	48084.99	36600.34
1963	10620.00	45607.15	93625.97	66329.05	50224.78	37742.90
1964	11964.68	47737.11	96652.48	70619.79	52081.00	40277.61
1965	12631.71	51439.72	101249.40	75364.58	54836.40	41767.87
1966	13620.83	54746.84	106217.51	80378.70	57866.63	44385.93
1967	13812.41	57404.54	110192.36	82460.31	60981.14	45231.33
1968	16187.51	61202.96	112220.80	84830.94	64739.29	47474.80
1969	16857.30	64523.80	116968.74	88341.78	67333.43	48887.09
1970	19150.49	66923.74	119067.10	91419.11	69909.84	50973.22
1971	19928.00	70654.50	118887.06	92642.51	70688.50	53951.55
1972	21277.23	75896.27	125446.69	96260.59	73426.66	57276.64
1973	23183.24	82012.37	130571.12	99405.94	75599.71	60751.80
1974	22740.29	83446.93	129805.90	97703.93	76865.29	62672.90
1975	23235.10	86492.54	131689.92	96908.15	76821.80	65714.11
1976	24244.86	91014.62	138177.96	99845.53	80135.68	68174.14
1977	24907.82	94867.34	146423.37	101320.31	84951.80	70960.20
1978	27257.49	97825.11	154904.95	104608.89	88552.72	76094.14

Table 3.A.4
Money metric group efficiency

	Age groups					
Year	16–24	25–34	35–44	45–54	55–64	65+
1958	12360.89	64579.96	115289.00	83722.53	57049.98	41295.38
1959	12592.32	64175.73	120699.64	85717.86	60947.15	45361.25
1960	13298.06	65488.04	122849.77	90399.09	62010.32	45752.00
1961	12963.75	64172.88	123795.74	91377.26	66469.54	51602.49
1962	13298.11	63067.22	131181.69	94448.29	69717.01	53258.65
1963	14525.83	65773.27	133144.28	97667.85	72446.14	54724.82
1964	16369.60	69138.22	138205.05	104321.99	74994.60	58228.42
1965	17223.92	74027.04	143862.29	110689.34	78756.18	60288.23
1966	18501.33	78389.22	150043.02	117523.76	82626.08	63767.27
1967	18758.21	82210.75	155391.19	120351.80	86839.60	64786.11
1968	22036.66	87754.51	158051.53	123617.05	91988.86	67801.96
1969	22950.38	92232.28	164007.37	128272.75	95541.25	69796.32
1970	26066.45	95645.18	166857.79	132421.07	98814.93	72525.67
1971	27134.44	100937.92	166820.54	134265.32	99881.52	76711.39
1972	28809.31	107860.02	175590.52	138895.22	103471.85	81340.19
1973	31497.75	116793.15	182933.42	143566.90	106700.68	86444.34
1974	31005.82	118733.56	181813.64	140881.90	108620.22	89370.47
1975	31774.26	123247.97	185341.13	140001.65	108530.92	93717.21
1976	33087.26	129213.46	193397.17	143633.89	112954.22	97068.87
1977	33886.09	134109.02	204167.64	145189.72	119360.00	100780.81
1978	37181.22	138224.97	215828.95	149725.26	124558.68	108314.54

Notes

1. Dalton (1920), p. 348, as quoted by Atkinson (1983b), p. 3. These objectives have also been emphasized by Bentzel (1970) and Tinbergen (1970).

2. See, for example, Muellbauer (1974b), p. 498.

3. Evidence on the nonhomotheticity of preferences is presented by Houthakker (1957), Leser (1963), Muellbauer (1976a), Pollak and Wales (1978), and Prais and Houthakker (1971).

4. Evidence on the impact of demographic characteristics on expenditure allocation is given by Lau, Lin, and Yotopoulos (1978), Muellbauer (1977), Parks and Barten (1973), Pollak and Wales (1980, 1981), and Ray (1982).

5. The translog indirect utility function was introduced by Christensen, Jorgenson, and Lau (1975) and extended to encompass determinants of expenditure allocation other than prices and total expenditure by Jorgenson and Lau (1975). Alternative approaches to the representation of the effects of prices and total expenditure on expenditure allocation are summarized by Barten (1977), Deaton and Muellbauer (1980), pp. 60–85, and Lau (1977a).

6. Alternative approaches to the representation of household characteristics in expenditure allocation are presented by Barten (1964), Gorman (1976), and Prais and Houthakker (1971). A review of the literature is presented by Deaton and Muellbauer (1980), pp. 191–213.

7. The specification of a system of individual demand functions by means of Roy's Identity was first employed in econometric modeling of consumer behavior by Houthakker (1960). A detailed review of econometric models based on Roy's Identity is given by Lau (1977a).

8. For further discussion, see Lau (1977b, 1982) and Jorgenson, Lau, and Stoker (1980, 1981, 1982).

9. Conditions for integrability are discussed by Jorgenson and Lau (1979) and Jorgenson, Lau, and Stoker (1982).

10. For further discussion see Jorgenson, Lau, and Stoker (1982), esp. pp. 175–186.

11. Household equivalence scales are discussed by Barten (1964), Lazear and Michael (1980), Muellbauer (1974a, 1977, 1980), and Prais and Houthakker (1971), among others. Alternative approaches are summarized by Deaton and Muellbauer (1980).

12. The use of household equivalence scales in evaluating transfers among individuals has been advocated by Deaton and Muellbauer (1980), esp. pp. 205–212, and by Muellbauer (1974a). Pollak and Wales (1979) have presented arguments against the use of household equivalence scales for this purpose.

13. Deaton and Muellbauer (1980), pp. 227–239, King (1983a, b), McKenzie (1982), and Muellbauer (1974b, c) present approaches to inequality measurement based on the distribution of "real expenditure." Measures of "real expenditure" could be derived from the individual expenditure function (3.2.23) by varying the level of utility V_k for a fixed set of prices p $(k = 1, 2, \ldots, K)$. Restrictions on preferences under which measures of inequality defined on the distribution of real expenditure coincide with measures defined on the distribution of individual welfare are given by Roberts (1980c).

14. The 1972–1973 Survey of Consumer Expenditures (CES) is discussed by Carlson (1974).

15. We employ data on the flow of services from durable goods rather than purchases of durable goods. Personal consumption expenditures in the U.S. National Income and Product Accounts (NIPA) are based on purchases of durable goods.

16. This series is published annually by the U.S. Bureau of the Census.

17. A detailed discussion of the stochastic specification of our model and of econometric methods for pooling time-series and cross-section data is presented by Jorgenson, Lau and Stoker (1982), section 3.6. This stochastic specification implies that time-series data must be adjusted for heteroscedasticity by multiplying each observation by the statistic

$$\rho = \frac{\left(\sum M_k \right)^2}{\sum M_k^2} \,.$$

18. Arrow (1977, p. 225) has defended noncomparability in the following terms: "...the autonomy of individuals, an element of mutual incommensurability among people[,] seems denied by the possibility of interpersonal comparisons."

19. It is important to note that the social welfare function in (3.5.2) represents a social ordering over all possible individual orderings and exemplifies the multiple profile approach to social choice of Arrow (1963) rather than the single profile approach employed by Bergson (1938) and Samuelson (1947). The literature on the existence of single profile social welfare functions is discussed by Roberts (1980d), Samuelson (1982), and Sen (1979b).

20. See Sen (1977, 1979b) for further discussion.

21. See Roberts (1980b), esp. pp. 434–36.

22. The implications of distributional homotheticity are discussed by Kolm (1976b) and Blackorby and Donaldson (1978).

23. Mean value functions were introduced into economics by Bergson (1936) and have been employed, for example, by Arrow, Chenery, Minhas, and Solow (1961) and Atkinson (1970). Properties of mean value functions are discussed by Hardy, Littlewood, and Polya (1959).

24. This assumption implies that individual welfare increases with total expenditure at a rate that is inversely proportional to total expenditure. This is also implied by the utilitarian social welfare function employed by Arrow and Kalt (1979).

25. An absolute index of inequality is invariant with respect to equal additions to the levels of individual welfare. See Blackorby and Donaldson (1980) and Kolm (1976a, b) for further discussion.

26. A relative index of inequality is homogeneous of degree zero in the levels of individual welfare. See Blackorby and Donaldson (1978) and Kolm (1976a, b) for further discussion.

27. A bibliography of applications of the approach to inequality measurement originated by Atkinson (1970) and Kolm (1969, 1976a, b) is given by Atkinson (1983a), pp. 32–36.

28. The relationship between measures of inequality and social welfare functions is discussed by Atkinson (1970), Blackorby and Donaldson (1978, 1980), Dasgupta, Sen and Starrett (1973), Kolm (1969, 1976a, b), Roberts (1980b, d), and Sen (1973). Alternative approaches to measuring efficiency and equity are discussed by Arrow and Kalt (1979) and Sen (1979a).

29. References on the decomposition of inequality measures by subgroups of the population are listed by Atkinson (1983a), pp. 34–35.

30. The social expenditure function was introduced by Pollak (1981). Alternative money measures of social welfare are discussed by Arrow and Kalt (1979), Bergson (1980), Deaton and Muellbauer (1980, pp. 214–239), Roberts (1980c), and Sen (1976a). A survey of the literature is presented by Sen (1979a).

31. The indifference map for society as a whole corresponds to that for a consumer with an indirect utility function given by the translog index of efficiency (3.5.2). In section 3.3 above we have assumed that each household has a translog indirect utility function (3.2.22). We can derive this representation of household preferences by first assuming that each individual has a translog indirect utility function of this form. We then assume, in addition, that the household maximizes a household welfare function of the form (3.4.10). Under these assumptions the distribution of individual welfare within each household is perfectly egalitarian. The household indirect utility function has the same form as the individual indirect utility functions (3.2.22) with the number of household equivalent members equal to the sum over all individuals. The translog indexes of inequality I and J in section 3.5 can be interpreted as measures of inequality in the distribution of individual welfare between households by analogy with the translog indexes of between-group inequality I_B and J_B in section 3.7. For further discussion, see Pollak (1981) and Samuelson (1956).

32. Atkinson and Bourguignon (1982), p. 184, have pointed out that this approach has the effect of reducing multidimensional inequality measures, defined on the multivariate distribution of all commodities among individual households, to a single dimensional inequality measure, defined on the univariate distribution of individual welfare. References on multidimensional inequality measures are listed by Atkinson (1983a), p. 36.

4

General Equilibrium Analysis of Economic Policy

Dale W. Jorgenson and
Daniel T. Slesnick

4.1   Introduction

The purpose of this chapter is to present a new approach to the general equilibrium analysis of economic policy. Our objective is to provide an ordering of alternative economic policies. The most desirable economic policy is the policy yielding the highest level of social welfare. This principle can be used to evaluate a specific policy change or to select the optimal policy from a set of alternatives.

Dupuit (1969) originated the appraisal of alternative economic policies on the basis of their impact on consumer welfare. He proposed to measure individual welfare on the basis of preferences revealed by consumer behavior. The prices faced by the consumer and the corresponding quantities demanded were used to obtain estimates of consumer's surplus. (Dupuit's approach to welfare economics has generated a voluminous literature. Key references include Harberger (1971), Hicks (1942), Hotelling (1938), and Marshall (1920).)

Hicks (1942) introduced measures of consumer's surplus based on compensating and equivalent variations in income or total expenditure. The intuition underlying Hicks's approach to welfare economics is straightforward. Levels of welfare before and after a change in economic policy can be ordered by comparing the required levels of total expenditure. For Hicks's compensating variation the difference in total expenditure is evaluated at prices prevailing after the change in policy. For the equivalent variation the difference is evaluated at prices before the policy change.

Chipman and Moore (1980a) have shown that a necessary and sufficient condition for Hicks's compensating variation to provide an appropriate ordering of economic policies is that individual preferences are homothetic. Chipman and Moore recommend Hicks's equivalent variation, since homothetic preferences are inconsistent with well established regularities in the behavior of individual consumers, such as those reviewed by Houthakker (1957). (Evidence on the nonhomotheticity of preferences is presented by Houthakker (1957), Leser (1963), Muellbauer (1976a), Pollak and Wales (1978), and Prais and Houthakker (1971).)

The individual expenditure function introduced by McKenzie (1957) provides the simplest approach for implementing Hicks's measures of welfare. The expenditure function gives the minimum level of total expenditure required to attain a stipulated level of utility as a function of the prices faced by the consumer. This level of expenditure can be derived from the indirect utility function, which gives the maximum attainable utility level as a function of prices and total expenditure.

The approach to welfare measurement originated by Dupuit is limited to individual welfare. Under the Pareto principle a change in economic policy can be recommended if all consuming units are at least as well off under the policy change and at least one consuming unit is better off. This principle provides a partial ordering of economic policies. To obtain a complete ordering we require the concept of a social welfare function originated by Bergson (1938) and discussed by Samuelson (1947, 1982).

A social welfare function gives the level of social welfare as a function of the distribution of individual welfare over the population of consumers. The social welfare function incorporates the effects of changes in economic policy on the welfare of individual consumers. A requirement often imposed on social welfare functions is that they must obey the Pareto principle. A social welfare function also includes the impacts of policy changes on horizontal and vertical equity among consumers.

Since the pioneering work of Atkinson (1970) and Kolm (1969), the measurement of social welfare has been based on explicit social welfare functions. However, the social welfare functions introduced by Atkinson and Kolm are defined on the distribution of income rather than the distribution of individual welfare. Muellbauer (1974b) and Roberts (1980c) have shown that measures of social welfare based on income coincide with measures based on individual welfare if and only if preferences are identical and homothetic for all consumers. (See, for example, Muellbauer (1974b), p. 498.)

Identical preferences are inconsistent with empirical findings on consumer behavior, such as those of Prais and Houthakker (1971), showing that expenditure patterns depend on the demographic characteristics on individual consuming units. (Evidence on the impact of demographic characteristics on expenditure allocation is given by Lau *et al.* (1978), Muellbauer (1977), Parks and Barten (1973), Pollak and Wales (1980, 1981), and Ray (1982).) Muellbauer (1974) has defined social welfare functions on the distribution of Hicks's equivalent variation or money metric individual welfare. This approach has also been employed by Deaton and Muellbauer (1980b), King (1983a, b), and McKenzie (1982).

Roberts (1980c) has derived restrictions on preferences under which measures of social welfare based on the distribution of money metric individual welfare coincide with measures based on the distribution of individual welfare. In the absence of restrictions on social welfare functions, individuals must have identical homothetic preferences. Roberts (1980c) also considers possible restrictions on the class of social welfare functions. With no restrictions on individual preferences, the social welfare functions must be dictatorial in the sense of Arrow (1963) and Roberts (1980a).

Our approach to policy evaluation is based on an econometric model of aggregate consumer behavior. The novel feature of this model is that systems of individual demand functions can be recovered uniquely from the system of aggregate demand functions. By requiring that the individual demand functions are integrable, we can also recover indirect utility functions and individual expenditure functions for all consumers. Finally, we can define measures of individual welfare in terms of these indirect utility and individual expenditure functions.

In section 4.2 we outline an econometric methodology for developing a model of aggregate consumer behavior. In this model systems of individual demand functions depend on the prices faced by all households. These systems also depend on total expenditures and attributes such as demographic characteristics that vary among households. We obtain aggregate demand functions by summing over individual demand functions. The resulting system of aggregate demand functions depends on summary statistics of the joint distribution of total expenditures and attributes among all households.

In section 4.3 we implement our econometric model of aggregate consumer behavior for the United States. For this purpose we employ cross-section data on individual expenditure patterns. We combine these data with time-series data on aggregate expenditure patterns and prices for all commodities. We also employ time-series data on the distribution of total expenditures among households.

In section 4.4 we present methods for evaluating the impact of alternative economic policies on the distribution of individual welfare. We illustrate these methods by comparing alternative regulatory and tax policies for petroleum production in the United States. For this purpose we require projections of prices and total expenditure under each policy. We obtain these projections from the Dynamic General Equilibrium Model (DGEM) of the U.S. economy, constructed by Hudson and Jorgenson (1974, 1976, 1978a, b). This model is based on a breakdown of the U.S. economy into nine industrial sectors, including five energy sectors and four aggregates of the nonenergy sectors.

Our approach to the measurement of individual welfare is based on the indirect utility function and the individual expenditure function for each consuming unit. The indirect utility function can be used to generate measures of individual welfare. The individual expenditure function can then be employed to translate these measures of individual welfare into money metric individual welfare. Money metric individual welfare provides a monotone increasing transformation of individual welfare that is not full comparable among consuming units. This measure can be used in evaluating economic policies by constructing partial orderings of these policies on the basis of the Pareto principle.

In section 4.5 we introduce a class of social welfare functions capable of expressing a variety of ethical judgements. This class is based on the distribution of individual welfare over the population of consuming units. In measuring social welfare we employ cardinal measures of individual welfare that are fully comparable among units. To translate comparisons among economic policies into money measures of social welfare, we introduce the social expenditure function in section 4.6. This function gives the minimum level of aggregate expenditure required to attain a stipulated level of social welfare as a function of the prices faced by all consumers.

The social expenditure function can be used to translate changes in social welfare based on a social welfare function into money metric social welfare. The concept of money metric social welfare can be used in comparing alternative economic policies on the basis of the aggregate expenditure required for each policy. As a measure of efficiency we introduce the maximum level of social welfare that can be attained by lump sum redistributions of aggregate expenditure among consuming units. Using this measure, we can decompose money metric social welfare into the sum of money metric equity and money metric efficiency.

In section 4.7 we present an evaluation of alternative regulatory and fiscal policies for petroleum production in the United States, based on projections of prices and the distribution of total expenditure from the DGEM model of the U.S. economy. On the basis of these projections we first construct the distribution of measures of individual welfare for each policy. We then evaluate the corresponding level of social welfare and translate the differences in levels of social welfare among policies into money measures of changes in efficiency and changes in equity. Section 4.8 of the paper provides a summary and conclusion.

4.2 Aggregate Consumer Behavior

In this section we develop an econometric model of aggregate consumer behavior based on the theory of exact aggregation, following Jorgenson, Lau, and Stoker (1980, 1981, 1982). Our model incorporates time-series data on prices and aggregate quantities consumed. We also include cross-section data on individual quantities consumed, individual total expenditure, and attributes of individual households such as demographic characteristics.

To represent preferences for all individuals in a form suitable for measuring individual welfare, we take households as consuming units. We assume that expenditures on individual commodities are allocated so as to maximize a household welfare function. As a consequence, the household behaves in the same way as an individual maximizing a utility function, as demonstrated by Samuelson (1956) and Pollak (1981). By assuming that each household maximizes a household welfare function, we can focus on the distribution of welfare among households rather than the distribution among individuals within households.

To construct an econometric model based on exact aggregation we first represent individual preferences by means of an indirect utility function for each consuming unit, using the following notation:

p_n — price of the nth commodity, assumed to be the same for all consuming units.

$p = (p_1, p_2, \ldots, p_N)$ — the vector of prices of all commodities.

x_{nk} — the quantity of the nth commodity group consumed by the kth consuming unit ($n = 1, 2, \ldots, N; k = 1, 2, \ldots, K$).

$M_k = \sum_{n=1}^{N} p_n x_{nk}$ — total expenditure of the kth consuming unit ($k = 1, 2, \ldots, K$).

$w_{nk} = p_n x_{nk} / M_k$ — expenditure share of the nth commodity group in the budget of the kth consuming unit ($n = 1, 2, \ldots, N; k = 1, 2, \ldots, K$).

$w_k = (w_{1k}, w_{2k}, \ldots, w_{Nk})$ — vector of expenditure shares for the kth consuming unit ($k = 1, 2, \ldots, K$).

$\ln \dfrac{p}{M_k} = \left(\ln \dfrac{p_1}{M_k}, \ln \dfrac{p_2}{M_k}, \ldots, \ln \dfrac{p_N}{M_k} \right)$ — vector of logarithms of ratios of prices to expenditure by the kth consuming unit ($k = 1, 2, \ldots, K$).

$\ln p = (\ln p_1, \ln p_2, \ldots, \ln p_N)$ — vector of logarithms of prices.

A_k — vector of attributes of the kth consuming unit ($k = 1, 2, \ldots, K$).

We assume that the kth consuming unit allocates expenditures in accord with the transcendental logarithmic or translog indirect utility function, say V_k, where

$$\ln V_k = G\left(\ln \frac{p'}{M_k} \alpha_p + \frac{1}{2} \ln \frac{p'}{M_k} B_{pp} \ln \frac{p}{M_k} + \ln \frac{p'}{M_k} B_{pA} A_k, A_k \right),$$
$$(k = 1, 2, \ldots, K) . \tag{4.2.1}$$

In this representation the function G is a monotone increasing function of the variable $(\ln p'/M_k)\alpha_p + \frac{1}{2} (\ln p'/M_k) B_{pp} (\ln p/M_k) + (\ln p'/M_k) B_{pA} A_k$. In addition, the function G depends directly on the attribute vector A_k. The vector α_p and the matrices B_{pp} and B_{pA} are constant parameters that are the same for all consuming units.

(The translog indirect utility function was introduced by Christensen, Jorgenson, and Lau (1975) and extended to encompass determinants of expenditure allocation other than prices and total expenditure by Jorgenson and Lau (1975). Alternative approaches to the representation of the effects of prices and total expenditure on expenditure allocation are summarized by Barten (1977), Deaton and Muellbauer (1980b, pp. 60–85), and Lau (1977a). Alternative approaches to the representation of household characteristics in expenditure allocation are presented by Barten (1964), Gorman (1976), and Prais and

Houthakker (1971). A review of the literature is presented by Deaton and Muellbauer (1980b, pp. 191–213.)

The expenditure shares of the kth consuming unit can be derived by the logarithmic form of Roy's Identity (1943). (The specification of a system of individual demand functions by means of Roy's Identity was first employed in econometric modeling of consumer behavior by Houthakker (1960). A detailed review of econometric models based on Roy's Identity is given by Lau (1977a).)

$$w_{nk} = \frac{\partial \ln V_k}{\partial \ln (p_n/M_k)} \Big/ \sum_{n=1}^{N} \frac{\partial \ln V_k}{\partial \ln (p_n/M_k)} ,$$
$$(n = 1, 2 \ldots, N; \; k = 1, 2, \ldots, K) . \qquad (4.2.2)$$

Applying this Identity to the translog indirect utility function (4.2.1), we obtain the system of individual expenditure shares

$$w_k = \frac{1}{D_k(p)} \left(\alpha_p + B_{pp} \ln \frac{p}{M_k} + B_{pA} A_k \right), \qquad (k = 1, 2, \ldots, K) , \qquad (4.2.3)$$

where the denominators $\{D_k\}$ take the form

$$D_k = i'\alpha_p + i'B_{pp} \ln \frac{p}{M_k} + i'B_{pA} A_k , \qquad (k = 1, 2, \ldots, K) . \qquad (4.2.4)$$

The individual expenditure shares are homogeneous of degree zero in the unknown parameters—α_p, B_{pp}, B_{pA}. By multiplying a given set of these parameters by a constant we obtain another set of parameters that generates the same system of individual budget shares. Accordingly, we can choose a normalization for the parameters without affecting observed patterns of individual expenditure allocation. We find it convenient to employ the normalization

$$i'\alpha_p = -1 .$$

Under this restriction any change in the set of unknown parameters will be reflected in changes in individual expenditure patterns.

The conditions for exact aggregation are that the individual expenditure shares are linear in functions of the attributes $\{A_k\}$ and total expenditures $\{M_k\}$ for all consuming units. (For further discussion, see Lau (1977b, 1982) and Jorgenson, Lau, and Stoker (1980, 1981, 1982).) These conditions will be satisfied if and only if the terms involving the attributes and expenditures do not appear in the denominators of the expressions given above for the individual expenditure shares, so that

$$i'B_{pp}i = 0 \; ,$$

and

$$i'B_{pA} = 0 \; .$$

The exact aggregation restrictions imply that the denominators $\{D_k\}$ reduce to

$$D = -1 + i'B_{pp} \ln p \; ,$$

where the subscript k is no longer required, since the denominator is the same for all consuming units. Under these restrictions the individual expenditure shares can be written

$$w_k = \frac{1}{D(p)} (\alpha_p + B_{pp} \ln p - B_{pp} \, i \cdot \ln M_k + B_{pA}A_k),$$

$$(k = 1, 2, \ldots, K) \; . \tag{4.2.5}$$

The individual expenditure shares are linear in the logarithms of expenditures $\{\ln M_k\}$ and in the attributes $\{A_k\}$, as required by exact aggregation.

Under exact aggregation the indirect utility function for each consuming unit can be represented in the form

$$\ln V_k = F(A_k) + \ln p'\left(\alpha_p + \frac{1}{2} B_{pp} \ln p + B_{pA}A_k\right) - D(p) \ln M_k \; ,$$

$$(k = 1, 2, \ldots, K). \tag{4.2.6}$$

In this representation the indirect utility function is linear in the logarithm of total expenditure $\ln M_k$ with a coefficient that depends on the prices p $(k = 1, 2, \ldots, K)$. This property is invariant with respect to positive affine transformations, but is not preserved by arbitrary monotone increasing transformations. We conclude that the indirect utility function (4.2.6) provides a cardinal measure of utility for each consuming unit.

If a system of individual expenditure shares (4.2.3) can be generated from an indirect utility function of the form (4.2.1) we say that the system is *integrable*. A complete set of conditions for integrability (discussed by Jorgenson and Lau (1979) and Jorgenson, Lau, and Stoker (1982)) is the following:

1. *Homogeneity*. The individual expenditure shares are homogeneous of degree zero in prices and total expenditure.

We can write the individual expenditure shares in the form

$$\beta_{pM} = B_{pp}i . \qquad (4.2.7)$$

Given the exact aggregation restrictions, there are $N - 1$ restrictions implied by homogeneity.

2. *Summability*. The sum of the individual expenditure shares over all commodity groups is equal to unity

$$i'w_k = 1 , \qquad (k = 1, 2, \ldots, K) .$$

We can write the denominator $D(p)$ in (4.2.4) in the form

$$D = -1 + \beta_{Mp} \ln p ,$$

where the vector of parameters β_{Mp} is constant and the same for all commodity groups and all consuming units. Summability implies that this vector must satisfy the restrictions

$$\beta_{Mp} = i'B_{pp} . \qquad (4.2.8)$$

Given the exact aggregation restrictions, there are $N - 1$ restrictions implied by summability.

3. *Symmetry*. The matrix of compensated own- and cross-price substitution effects must be symmetric.

If the system of individual expenditure shares can be generated from an indirect utility function of the form (4.2.1), a necessary and sufficient condition for symmetry is that the matrix B_{pp} must be symmetric. Without imposing this condition, we can write the individual expenditure shares in the form

$$w_k = \frac{1}{D(p)} \left(\alpha_p + B_{pp} \ln \frac{p}{M_k} + B_{pA}A_k \right), \qquad (k = 1, 2, \ldots, K) .$$

Symmetry implies that the matrix of parameters B_{pp} must satisfy the restrictions

$$B_{pp} = B'_{pp} . \qquad (4.2.9)$$

The total number of symmetry restrictions is $1/2 \, N(N - 1)$.

4. *Nonnegativity.* The individual expenditure shares must be nonnegative.

By summability the individual expenditure shares sum to unity, so that we can write

$$w_k \geq 0, \qquad (k = 1, 2, \ldots, K),$$

where $w_k \geq 0$ implies $w_{nk} \geq 0$, $(n = 1, 2, \ldots, N)$, and $w_k \neq 0$.

Since the translog indirect utility function is quadratic in the logarithms of prices, we can always choose the prices so that the individual expenditure shares violate the nonnegativity conditions. Accordingly, we cannot impose restrictions on the parameters of the translog indirect utility functions that would imply nonnegativity of the individual expenditure shares. Instead we consider restrictions on the parameters that imply monotonicity of the system of individual demand functions for all nonnegative expenditure shares.

5. *Monotonicity.* The matrix of compensated own- and cross-price substitution effects must be nonpositive definite.

We introduce the definition due to Martos (1969) of a *strictly merely positive subdefinite matrix,* namely, a real symmetric matrix S such that

$$xSx < 0$$

implies $Sx > 0$ or $Sx < 0$. A necessary and sufficient condition for monotonicity is either that the translog indirect utility function is homothetic or that B_{pp}^{-1} exists and is strictly merely positive subdefinite. (For further discussion see Jorgenson, Lau, and Stoker (1982, esp. pp. 175–186).)

To provide a basis for evaluating the impact of transfers among households on social welfare, we find it useful to represent household preferences by means of a utility function that is the same for all consuming units. For this purpose, we assume that the kth consuming unit maximizes its utility, say U_k, where

$$U_k = U \left[\frac{x_{1k}}{m_1(A_k)}, \frac{x_{2k}}{m_2(A_k)}, \ldots, \frac{x_{Nk}}{m_N(A_k)} \right], \qquad (k = 1, 2, \ldots, K), \quad (4.2.10)$$

subject to the budget constraint

$$M_k = \sum_{n=1}^{N} p_n \, x_{nk} \,, \qquad (k = 1, 2, \ldots, K) \,.$$

In this representation of consumer preferences the quantities $\{x_{nk}/m_n(A_k)\}$ can be regarded as *effective quantities consumed*, as proposed by Barten (1964). The crucial assumption embodied in this representation is that differences in preferences among consumers enter the utility function U only through differences in the commodity specific household equivalence scales $\{m_n(A_k)\}$. (Household equivalence scales are discussed by Barten (1964), Van der Gaag and Smolensky (1982), Kakwani (1977), Lazear and Michael (1980), Muellbauer (1974a, 1977, 1980), and Prais and Houthakker (1971), among others. Alternative approaches are summarized by Deaton and Muellbauer (1980b).)

Consumer equilibrium implies the existence of an indirect utility function, say V, that is the same for all consuming units. The level of utility for the kth consuming unit, say V_k, depends on the prices of individual commodities, the household equivalence scales, and the level of total expenditure

$$V_k = V \left[\frac{p_1 m_1(A_k)}{M_k}, \frac{p_2 m_2(A_k)}{M_k}, \ldots, \frac{p_N m_N(A_k)}{M_k} \right], \qquad (k = 1, 2, \ldots, K) \,.$$

(4.2.11)

In this representation the prices $\{p_n m_n(A_k)\}$ can be regarded as *effective prices*. Differences in preferences among consuming units enter this indirect utility function only through the household equivalence scales $\{m_n(A_k)\}$ $(k = 1, 2, \ldots, K)$.

To represent the translog indirect utility function (4.2.1) in terms of household equivalence scales, we require some additional notation:

$\ln pm(A_k)/M_k$ — vector of logarithms of ratios of effective prices.

$\{p_n m_n(A_k)\}$ to total expenditure M_k of the kth consuming unit $(k = 1, 2, \ldots, K)$.

$\ln m(A_k) = (\ln m_1(A_k), \ln m_2(A_k), \ldots, \ln m_N(A_k))$ — vector of logarithms of the household equivalence scales of the kth consuming unit $(k = 1, 2, \ldots, K)$.

We assume, as before, that the kth consuming unit allocates its expenditures in accord with the translog indirect utility function (4.2.1). However, we also assume that this function, expressed in terms of the effective prices $\{p_n m_n(A_k)\}$ and total expenditure M_k, is

the same for all consuming units. The indirect utility function takes
the form

$$\ln V_k = \ln \frac{pm(A_k)'}{M_k} \, \alpha_p + \frac{1}{2} \ln \frac{pm(A_k)'}{M_k} \, B_{pp} \ln \frac{pm(A_k)}{M_k} \, ,$$

$$(k = 1, 2, \ldots, K) \, . \tag{4.2.12}$$

Taking logarithms of the effective prices $\{p_n m_n(A_k)\}$, we can rewrite
the indirect utility function (4.2.12) in the form

$$\ln V_k = \ln m(A_k)' \alpha_p + \frac{1}{2} \ln m(A_k)' B_{pp} \ln m(A_k) + \ln \frac{p'}{M_k} \alpha_p$$

$$+ \frac{1}{2} \ln \frac{p'}{M_k} B_{pp} \ln \frac{p}{M_k} + \ln \frac{p'}{M_k} B_{pp} \ln m(A_k) \, ,$$

$$(k = 1, 2, \ldots, K) \, . \tag{4.2.13}$$

Comparing the representation (4.2.13) with the representation
(4.2.6), we see that the term involving only the household equivalent
scales must take the form

$$F(A_k) = \ln m(A_k)' \, \alpha_p + \frac{1}{2} \ln m(A_k)' \, B_{pp} \ln m(A_k) \, , \tag{4.2.14}$$

$$(k = 1, 2, \ldots, K) \, .$$

Second, the term involving ratios of prices to total expenditure and
the household equivalence scales must satisfy

$$\ln \frac{p'}{M_k} B_{pA} A_k = \ln \frac{p'}{M_k} B_{pp} \ln m(A_k) \, , \qquad (k = 1, 2, \ldots, K) \, , \tag{4.2.15}$$

for all prices and total expenditure.

The household equivalence scales $\{m_n(A_k)\}$ defined by (4.2.15) must
satisfy the equation

$$B_{pA} A_k = B_{pp} \ln m(A_k) \, , \qquad (k = 1, 2, \ldots, K) \, . \tag{4.2.16}$$

Under monotonicity of the individual expenditure shares the matrix
B_{pp} has an inverse, so that we can express the household equivalence
scales in terms of the parameters of the translog indirect utility
function—B_{pp}, B_{pA}— and the attributes $\{A_k\}$

$$\ln m(A_k) = B_{pp}^{-1} B_{pA} A_k \, , \qquad (k = 1, 2, \ldots, K) \, . \tag{4.2.17}$$

We can refer to these scales as the *commodity specific translog household
equivalence scales*.

Substituting the commodity specific equivalence scales (4.2.16) into the indirect utility function (4.2.13) we obtain a representation of the indirect utility function in terms of the attributes $\{A_k\}$

$$\ln V_k = A_k' \, B_{pA}' \, B_{pp}^{-1} \, \alpha_p + \frac{1}{2} \, A_k' \, B_{pA}' \, B_{pp}^{-1} \, B_{pA} \, A_k$$

$$+ \ln p' \left(\alpha_p + \frac{1}{2} \, B_{pp} \ln p + B_{pA} \, A_k \right) - D(p) \ln M_k \,,$$

$$(k = 1, 2, \ldots, K) \,. \tag{4.2.18}$$

This form of the translog indirect utility function is equivalent to the form (4.2.1) in that both generate the same system of individual demand functions. By requiring that the attributes A_k enter only through the commodity specific household equivalence scales, we have provided a specific form for the function $F(A_k)$ in (4.2.6).

Given the indirect utility function (4.2.18) for each consuming unit, we can express total expenditure as a function of prices, consumer attributes, and the level of utility

$$\ln M_k = \frac{1}{D(p)} \left[A_k' \, B_{pA}' \, B_{pp}^{-1} \, \alpha_p + \frac{1}{2} \, A_k' \, B_{pA}' \, B_{pp}^{-1} \, B_{pA} \, A_k \right.$$

$$\left. + \ln p' \left(\alpha_p + \frac{1}{2} \, B_{pp} \ln p + B_{pA} \, A_k \right) - \ln V_k \right],$$

$$(k = 1, 2, \ldots, K) \,. \tag{4.2.19}$$

We can refer to this function as the *translog expenditure function*. The translog expenditure function gives the minimum expenditure required for the kth consuming unit to achieve the utility level V_k, given prices p $(k = 1, 2, \ldots, K)$.

We find it useful to introduce household equivalence scales that are not specific to a given commodity. (The use of household equivalence scales in evaluating transfers among individuals has been advocated by Deaton and Muellbauer (1980b, esp. pp. 205–212), and by Muellbauer (1974a). Pollak and Wales (1979) have presented arguments against the use of household equivalence scales for this purpose.) Following Muellbauer (1974a), we define a general household equivalence scale, say m_0, as follows

$$m_0 = \frac{M_k[pm(A_k), V_k^0]}{M_0(p, V_k^0)}, \qquad (k = 1, 2, \ldots, K) , \qquad\qquad (4.2.20)$$

where M_k is the expenditure function for the kth household, M_0 is the expenditure function for a reference household with commodity specific equivalence scales equal to unity for all commodities, and $pm(A_k)$ is a vector of effective prices $\{p_n m_n(A_k)\}$.

The general household equivalence scale m_0 is the ratio between total expenditures required by the kth household and by the reference household required for the same level of utility V_k^0 $(k = 1, 2, \ldots, K)$. This scale can be interpreted as the number of household equivalent members. The number of members depends on the attributes A_k of the consuming unit and on the prices p.

If each household has a translog indirect utility function, then the general household equivalence scale for the kth household takes the form

$$\ln m_0 = \ln M_k - \ln M_0 ,$$

$$= \frac{1}{D(p)} \left[\ln m(A_k)' \alpha_p + \frac{1}{2} \ln m(A_k)' B_{pp} \ln m(A_k) + \ln m(A_k)' B_{pp} \ln p \right],$$

$$(k = 1, 2, \ldots, K) . \qquad\qquad (4.2.21)$$

We can refer to this scale as the *general translog household equivalence scale*. The translog equivalence scale depends on the attributes A_k of the kth household and the prices p of all commodities, but is independent of the level of utility V_k^0.

Given the general translog equivalence scale, we can rewrite the indirect utility function (4.2.18) in the form

$$\ln V_k = \ln p' \alpha_p + \frac{1}{2} \ln p' B_{pp} \ln p - D(p) \ln [M_k/m_0(p, A_k)] ,$$

$$(k = 1, 2, \ldots, K) . \qquad\qquad (4.2.22)$$

The level of utility for the kth consuming unit depends on prices p and total expenditure per household equivalent member $M_k/m_0(p, A_k)$ $(k = 1, 2, \ldots, K)$. Similarly, we can rewrite the expenditure function (4.2.19) in the form

$$\ln M_k = \frac{1}{D(p)} \left[\ln p' \left(\alpha_p + \frac{1}{2} B_{pp} \ln p \right) - \ln V_k \right] + \ln m_0(p, A_k) ,$$

$$(k = 1, 2, \ldots, K) . \tag{4.2.23}$$

Total expenditure required by the kth consuming unit to attain the level of utility V_k depends on prices p and the number of household equivalent members $m_0(p, A_k)$ ($k = 1, 2, \ldots, K$).

To construct an econometric model of aggregate consumer behavior based on exact aggregation we obtain aggregate expenditure shares, say w, by multiplying individual expenditure shares (4.2.5) by expenditure for each consuming unit, adding over all consuming units, and dividing by aggregate expenditure, $M = \sum_{k=1}^{K} M_k$

$$w = \frac{\sum M_k w_k}{M} . \tag{4.2.24}$$

The aggregate expenditure shares can be written

$$w = \frac{1}{D(p)} \left(\alpha_p + B_{pp} \ln p - B_{pp} i \frac{\sum M_k \ln M_k}{M} + B_{pA} \frac{\sum M_k A_k}{M} \right). \tag{4.2.25}$$

The aggregate expenditure patterns depend on the distribution of expenditure over all consuming units through summary statistics of the joint distribution of expenditures and attributes—$\sum M_k \ln M_k / M$ and $\{\sum M_k A_k / M\}$. Systems of individual expenditure shares (4.2.5) for consuming units with identical demographic characteristics can be recovered in one and only one way from the system of aggregate expenditure shares (4.2.25).

The first step in analyzing inequality in the distribution of individual welfare is to select a representation of the individual welfare function. We assume that individual welfare for the kth consuming unit, say W_k ($k = 1, 2, \ldots, K$), is equal to the logarithm of the translog indirect utility function (4.2.22)

$$W_k = \ln V_k$$

$$= \ln p' \alpha_p + \frac{1}{2} \ln p' B_{pp} \ln p - D(p) \ln [M_k / m_0(p, A_k)] ,$$

$$(k = 1, 2, \ldots, K) . \tag{4.2.26}$$

(Deaton and Muellbauer (1980b, pp. 227–239), King (1983a, b), McKenzie (1982), and Muellbauer (1974b) present approaches to welfare measurement based on the distribution of "real expenditure."

Measures of "real expenditure" could be derived from the individual expenditure function (4.2.23) by varying the level of utility V_k for a fixed set of prices p $(k = 1, 2, \ldots, K)$. Restrictions on preferences under which measures of social welfare defined on the distribution of real expenditure coincide with measures defined on the distribution of individual welfare are given by Roberts (1980c).)

To summarize: For our econometric model a system of individual expenditure shares (4.2.5) can be recovered in one and only one way from the system of aggregate expenditure shares (4.2.25). Given a system of individual expenditure shares (4.2.5) that is integrable, we can recover the translog indirect utility function (4.2.22). This indirect utility function provides a cardinal measure of utility. We obtain a cardinal measure of individual welfare for each consuming unit (4.2.26) by setting this measure equal to the logarithm of the indirect utility function.

4.3   Econometric Model

In this section we present the empirical results of implementing the econometric model of consumer behavior described in section 4.2. We divide consumer expenditures among five commodity groups:

1. *Energy*: Expenditures on electricity, natural gas, heating oil, and gasoline.

2. *Food*: Expenditures on all food products, including tobacco and alcohol.

3. *Consumer goods*: Expenditures on all other nondurable goods included in consumer expenditures.

4. *Capital services*: The service flow from consumer durables and the service flow from housing.

5. *Consumer services*: Expenditures on consumer services, such as car repairs, medical services, entertainment, and so on.

We employ the following demographic characteristics as attributes of individual households:

1. *Family size*: 1, 2, 3, 4, 5, 6, and 7 or more persons.

2. *Age of head*: 16–24, 25–34, 35–44, 45–54, 55–64, 65 and over.

3. *Region of residence*: Northeast, North Central, South, and West.

4. *Race*: White, nonwhite.

5. *Type of residence*: Urban, rural.

Our cross-section observations on individual expenditures for each commodity group and on demographic characteristics of individual households are for the year 1972 from the 1972–1973 Survey of Consumer Expenditures (CES). (The 1972–1973 Survey of Consumer Expenditures is discussed by Carlson (1974).) Our time-series observations are based on data on personal consumption expenditures from the United States National Income and Product Accounts (NIPA) for the years 1958 to 1974. (We employ data on the flow of services from durable goods rather than purchases of durable goods. Personal consumption expenditures in the U.S. National Income and Product Accounts are based on purchases of durable goods.) Prices for each commodity group are defined in terms of translog price indexes computed from detailed prices included in NIPA for each year. We employ time series data on the distribution of expenditures over all households and among demographic groups based on *Current Population Reports*. (This series is published annually by the U.S. Bureau of the Census.)

In our application we treat the expenditure shares for five commodity groups as endogenous variables, so that we estimate four equations. As unknown parameters we have four elements of the vector α_p, four expenditure coefficients of the vector $B_{pp}i$, sixteen attribute coefficients for each of the four equations in the matrix B_{pA}, and ten price coefficients in the matrix B_{pp}, which is constrained to be symmetric. The expenditure coefficients are sums of price coefficients in the corresponding equation, so that we have a total of eighty-two unknown parameters. We estimate the complete model, subject to inequality restrictions implied by monotonicity of the individual expenditure shares, by pooling time-series and cross-section data. (A detailed discussion of the stochastic specification of our model and of econometric methods for pooling time series and cross-section data is presented by Jorgenson, Lau and Stoker (1982), section 4.6. This stochastic specification implies that time series data must be adjusted for heteroscedasticity by multiplying each observation by the statistic

$$\rho = \frac{(\sum M_k)^2}{\sum M_k^2} \cdot)$$

The results are given in table 4.1.

The impacts of changes in total expenditures and in demographic characteristics of the individual household are estimated very precisely. This reflects the fact that estimates of the expenditure and demographic effects incorporate a relatively large number of cross-section observations. The impacts of prices enter through the

Table 4.1
Pooled estimation results

Notation:	
CONST	= constant term
ln *PEN*	= coefficient of log of price of energy
ln *PF*	= coefficient of log of price of food
ln *PCG*	= coefficient of log of price of consumer goods
ln *PK*	= coefficient of log of price of capital services
ln *PCS*	= coefficient of log of price of consumer services
ln *M*	= coefficient of log of total expenditure
S2	= coefficient of dummy for family of size 2
S3	= coefficient of dummy for family of size 3
S4	= coefficient of dummy for family of size 4
S5	= coefficient of dummy for family of size 5
S6	= coefficient of dummy for family of size 6
S7 +	= coefficient of dummy for family of size 7 or more
A25–34	= coefficient of dummy for age between 25 and 34
A35–44	= coefficient of dummy for age between 35 and 44
A45–54	= coefficient of dummy for age between 45 and 54
A55–64	= coefficient of dummy for age between 55 and 64
A65 +	= coefficient of dummy for age of 65 and over
RNC	= coefficient of dummy for family living in the Northcentral
RS	= coefficient of dummy for family living in the South
RW	= coefficient of dummy for family living in the West
NW	= coefficient of dummy for nonwhite family
RUR	= coefficient of dummy for family living in rural area

$$D(p) = -1 \quad \begin{array}{lll} -.007900 \ln PEN & -.06479 \ln PF & +.02752 \ln PC \\ -.005559 \ln PK & +.05023 \ln PCS & \end{array}$$

Table 4.1 (continued)

	Energy			Food			Consumer goods	
Parameter	Estimate	Standard error	Parameter	Estimate	Standard error	Parameter	Estimate	Standard error
CONST	-.1418	.0106	CONST	-.7138	.0235	CONST	.1015	.0137
ln PEN	.04021	.00374	ln PEN	-.06449	.0106	ln PEN	.03769	.0112
ln PF	-.06449	.0105	ln PF	.1354	.0418	ln PF	-.1229	.0434
ln PCG	.03769	.0112	ln PCG	-.1229	.0434	ln PCG	.2761	.0512
ln PK	.03041	.00817	ln PK	-.02709	.0296	ln PK	-.1909	.0336
ln PCS	-.05172	.00651	ln PCS	.01479	.0198	ln PCS	.02753	.0191
ln M	.007900	.00116	ln M	.06429	.0258	ln M	-.02752	.00149
S2	-.01448	.00147	S2	-.03419	.00324	S2	.002259	.00186
S3	-.01686	.00174	S3	-.04442	.00383	S3	-.005487	.00220
S4	-.01669	.00185	S4	-.06991	.00408	S4	-.007615	.00234
S5	-.01519	.00217	S5	-.07268	.00480	S5	-.007393	.00275
S6	-.01265	.00270	S6	-.1040	.00596	S6	-.008864	.00342
S7+	-.01080	.00283	S7+	-.1194	.00623	S7+	-.006818	.00358
A25-34	-.002054	.00203	A25-34	-.04683	.00447	A25-34	-.003208	.00257
A35-44	-.005095	.00220	A35-44	-.09233	.00484	A35-44	-.00008580	.00278
A45-54	-.008143	.00208	A45-54	-.09846	.00459	A45-54	.006572	.00263
A55-64	-.01364	.00208	A55-64	-.1011	.00458	A55-64	.007436	.00263
A65+	-.009532	.00207	A65+	-.09010	.00455	A65+	.002513	.00261
RNC	-.008130	.00137	RNC	.01461	.00303	RNC	.001349	.00174
RS	-.008457	.00137	RS	.004641	.00301	RS	-.001261	.00173
RW	.007488	.00148	RW	.01406	.00325	RW	.003393	.00186
NW	.002603	.00171	NW	-.006326	.00377	NW	-.01331	.00216
RUR	-.03145	.00138	RUR	.09619	.00304	RUR	.006909	.00174

Table 4.1 (continued)

	Capital services			Consumer services		
Parameter	Estimate	Standard error	Parameter	Estimate	Standard error
CONST	−.5354	.0264	CONST	.2895	.0197
ln PEN	.03041	.00817	ln PEN	−.05172	.00651
ln PF	−.02709	.0296	ln PF	.01479	.0198
ln PCG	−.1909	.0336	ln PCG	.02753	.0191
ln PK	.3618	.0271	ln PK	−.1798	.0184
ln PCS	−.1798	.0184	ln PCS	.2394	.0260
ln M	.005559	.00293	ln M	−.05023	.00216
S2	.03686	.00368	S2	.009544	.00269
S3	.04804	.00436	S3	.01873	.00319
S4	.06821	.00464	S4	.02600	.00339
S5	.06445	.00546	S5	.03081	.00399
S6	.08742	.00678	S6	.03810	.00496
S7+	.09841	.00709	S7+	.03859	.00518
A25–34	.04087	.00509	A25–34	.01122	.00372
A35–44	.08380	.00551	A35–44	.01371	.00402
A45–54	.1074	.00523	A45–54	−.007396	.00382
A55–64	.1286	.00521	A55–64	−.02128	.00381
A65+	.1433	.00518	A65+	−.04615	.00378
RNC	.0009652	.00345	RNC	−.008790	.00252
RS	.02319	.00342	RS	−.01811	.00250
RW	−.009788	.00370	RW	−.01515	.00270
NW	.02840	.00429	NW	−.01137	.00314
RUR	.02125	.00346	RUR	−.006330	.00253

Cross section SSR = 38059.56;
convergence after 149 iterations;
aggregate SSR = 2165.14.

denominator of the equations for expenditure shares; these price coefficients are estimated very precisely since they also incorporate cross-
section data. Finally, the price impacts also enter through the numerators of equations for the expenditure shares. These parameters are
estimated somewhat less precisely, since they are based on a much
smaller number of time-series observations on prices.

To summarize: We have implemented an econometric model of
aggregate consumer behavior by combining time-series and cross-
section data for the United States. This model allocates personal consumption expenditures among five commodity groups—energy, food,
other consumer goods, capital services, and other consumer services.
Households are classified by five sets of demographic characteristics—family size, age of head, region of residence, race, and urban versus rural residence.

4.4   Money Metric Individual Welfare

The translog indirect utility function (4.2.22) and the translog individual expenditure function (4.2.23) can be employed in assessing the
impacts of alternative economic policies on individual welfare. To
analyze the impact of economic policy on the welfare of the kth household, we first evaluate the indirect utility function after the change in
policy has taken place. Suppose that prices are p^1 and expenditure for
the kth household is M_k^1 ($k = 1, 2, \ldots, K$). The level of individual welfare for the kth consuming unit after the policy change W_k^1 is given by

$$W_k^1 = \ln V_k^1 ,$$

$$= \ln p^{1'} \left(\alpha_p + \frac{1}{2} B_{pp} \ln p^1 \right) - D(p^1) \ln [M_k^1/m_0(p^1, A_k)] ,$$

$$(k = 1, 2, \ldots, K) . \qquad (4.4.1)$$

To evaluate the impact of alternative economic policies we must
compare the total expenditure required to attain the individual welfare resulting from each policy at prices prevailing before any change,
say p^0. For this purpose we can define *money metric individual welfare*
for the kth household, say N_k, as the difference between the total
expenditure required to attain W_k^1 and the expenditure required to
attain W_k^0, the level before the policy change. Both are evaluated at
prices p^0

$$N_k = M_k(p^0, W_k^1, A_k) - M_k(p^0, W_k^0, A_k)$$
$$= M_k(p^0, W_k^1, A_k) - M_k^0, \qquad (k = 1, 2, \ldots, K), \qquad (4.4.2)$$

where M_k^0 is total expenditure before the policy change. If money metric individual welfare is positive, the welfare of the consuming unit is increased; otherwise, the welfare of the consuming unit is decreased or left unaffected.

(This concept of money metric individual welfare coincides with the concept of net equivalent variation employed by Jorgenson, Lau, and Stoker (1982). Measures of equivalent variations based on the translog indirect utility function were introduced by Jorgenson, Lau, and Stoker (1981). The corresponding measures of compensating variations were introduced by Jorgenson, Lau, and Stoker (1980). The concepts of equivalent and compensating variations are due to Hicks (1942) and have been discussed by Chipman and Moore (1980a), Deaton and Muellbauer (1980b, pp. 184–190), Diamond and McFadden (1974), Hausman (1981), and Hurwicz and Uzawa (1971), among others. An individual ordering based on money metric individual welfare is identical to that based on Samuelson's (1974) concept of money metric utility.)

We illustrate the concept of money metric individual welfare geometrically in figure 4.1. This diagram represents the indifference map for a consuming unit with indirect utility function (4.2.22). For simplicity we consider the case of two commodities ($N = 2$). Consumer equilibrium before the policy change is represented by the point A. The corresponding level of total expenditure $M_k^0(p^0, W_k^0)$, divided by the price of the second commodity p_2^0, is given on the vertical axis. This axis gives total expenditure in units of the second commodity.

Similarly, consumer equilibrium after the policy change is represented by the point C. To translate the corresponding level of welfare into total expenditure at the prices before the change, we evaluate the expenditure function (4.2.23) at this level of welfare and at the prices p^0. The resulting level of total expenditure $M_k(p^0, W_k^1, A_k)$ corresponds to consumer equilibrium at the point B. Money metric individual welfare is the difference between the levels of total expenditure $M_k(p^0, W_k^1, A_k)$ and M_k^0.

To illustrate the measurement of individual welfare we undertake a comparison of alternative policies for regulation of petroleum prices and taxation of petroleum production in the United States. These policies have been analyzed by the Office of Policy, Planning, and

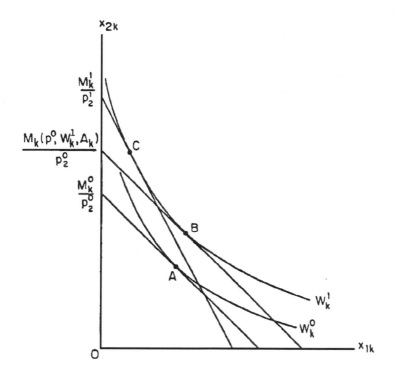

Figure 4.1
Money metric individual welfare.

Analysis of the U.S. Department of Energy (DOE). Our reference case for policy analysis is the policy of petroleum price decontrol instituted in January 1981. Under this policy price controls were eliminated on all petroleum products, but petroleum production is taxed under the provisions of the windfall profits tax. Our base case for policy analysis is the behavior of the U.S. economy under these policies with the regime of low world petroleum prices.

Alternatives to current regulatory and fiscal policies for petroleum considered by DOE are the following:

Continued petroleum price controls. Under this policy petroleum price controls would be continued, essentially in the form that prevailed prior to the beginning of petroleum price decontrol in May 1980.

Elimination of the windfall profits tax. Under this policy the windfall profits tax would be eliminated on domestic petroleum production after 1980.

Reform of the windfall profits tax. Under this policy the windfall profits tax would be reduced on certain categories of petroleum production, beginning in 1983.

We have analyzed the three alternatives to current regulatory and fiscal policy for petroleum production in the United States listed above. We analyze modifications of the windfall profits tax under the assumption that the shortfall in government revenue is added to the government deficit. To evaluate alternatives to current regulatory and fiscal policy for petroleum considered by DOE, we require projections of prices and total expenditure under each policy. We obtain these projections from the Dynamic General Equilibrium Model (DGEM) of the U.S. economy, constructed by Hudson and Jorgenson (1974, 1976, 1978a, b). This model is based on a nine sector breakdown of the U.S. economy:

1. Agriculture, nonfuel mining, construction
2. Manufacturing, except for petroleum
3. Transportation
4. Communications, trade, and services
5. Coal mining
6. Crude petroleum and gas extraction
7. Refined petroleum products
8. Electric utilities
9. Gas utilities.

The first step in analyzing alternative policies for petroleum price regulation and taxation is to establish projections of prices and total expenditure for all consuming units under current policy. To simulate the impact of alternatives to current regulatory and fiscal policy, projections of the resulting changes in prices of petroleum to the individual industrial sectors and to final demand are incorporated into DGEM. Financial flows resulting from the alternatives to current policy are also projected and incorporated into the model.

Changes in demand for petroleum by manufacturing industries and by electric utilities are projected and incorporated into DGEM, while changes in demand by the other sectors of the economy are determined endogenously within the model. The response of domestic petroleum supply to changes in regulatory and fiscal policy are specified exogenously. Total domestic supply is required to be equal to total domestic demand plus losses in transportation, plus the petroleum demands of petroleum producers, and less imports.

Projections of prices for each of the five commodities included in our model of aggregate consumer behavior—energy, food, consumer goods, capital services, and consumer services—are presented in table 4.2 for the reference case corresponding to current regulatory and fiscal policy and for alternative policies. (These price projections are based on the projections of the U.S. economy under alternative regulatory and fiscal policies for petroleum production by Goettle and Hudson (1983).) Table 4.2 presents projections of total expenditure per household for the U.S. economy for each of the alternative regulatory and fiscal policies that we consider. The projections of prices and total expenditure cover the period 1980–1995. It is important to note that the prices given in table 4.2 are purchasers' prices for the five commodity groups. Price projections from DGEM are given in terms of producers' prices and must be transformed by incorporating trade and transportation margins to obtain purchasers' prices.

Under continued petroleum price controls we find that the price of energy is lower than under the current policy of petroleum price decontrol. However, the prices of all nonenergy commodities are higher under continued controls than under current policy. We also find that total expenditure per household is higher under a policy of continued controls than under current policy. It is not obvious whether individual welfare is higher or lower under continued controls than under the reference case.

To evaluate the change in individual welfare for typical households, we employ prices in the reference case as a basis for calculating money metric individual welfare (4.4.2). We make the simplifying assumption that total expenditure changes in the same proportion for all consuming units. Changes in relative levels of individual welfare are the result of differential impacts of price changes associated with changes in regulatory and fiscal policy.

The dollar value of changes in individual welfare under a policy of continued controls is given for typical households in table 4.3. We present results for families of size five, with age of head 35–44, living in the Northeast region of the United States, and with average total expenditure in each year. Under continued controls all types of households gain during the period 1980 and 1981 and rural households continue to gain in 1982. However, all types of families lose under continued controls beginning 1983. For example, a white urban family living in the Northeast loses $236.03 in 1983. This loss rises to

Table 4.2
Projections of prices and total expenditures

	Prices (equal to 1.000 in 1972)				
Year	Energy	Food	Consumer goods	Capital services	Consumer services
			Current policy		
1980	2.0019	1.6798	1.6646	1.8775	1.6356
1981	2.2669	1.8198	1.8022	2.0811	1.7721
1982	2.4852	1.9376	1.9182	2.2236	1.8924
1983	2.6410	2.0497	2.0269	2.4174	1.9901
1984	2.8150	2.1510	2.1252	2.6214	2.0816
1985	3.0286	2.2851	2.2549	2.8160	2.1995
1986	3.2194	2.4129	2.3788	2.9718	2.3169
1987	3.4299	2.5222	2.4830	3.1971	2.4051
1988	3.6352	2.6279	2.5842	3.4167	2.4951
1989	3.8746	2.7779	2.7279	3.6420	2.6212
1990	4.0730	2.9013	2.8456	3.7904	2.7270
1991	4.2992	3.0299	2.9665	4.0128	2.8273
1992	4.5396	3.1525	3.0830	4.2405	2.9354
1993	4.7774	3.2901	3.2123	4.4543	3.0468
1994	5.0559	3.4799	3.3897	4.5830	3.1929
1995	5.2784	3.6089	3.5086	4.7954	3.2895
			Continued controls		
1980	1.9387	1.7183	1.7025	1.9322	1.6686
1981	2.1202	1.8872	1.8689	2.1934	1.8304
1982	2.3417	2.0183	1.9981	2.3731	1.9641
1983	2.5448	2.1408	2.1170	2.6035	2.0728
1984	2.7290	2.2492	2.2222	2.8407	2.1714
1985	2.9448	2.3913	2.3598	3.0680	2.2965
1986	3.1356	2.5259	2.4903	3.2521	2.4205
1987	3.3428	2.6414	2.6004	3.5116	2.5135
1988	3.5379	2.7509	2.7053	3.7589	2.6063
1989	3.7709	2.9073	2.8551	4.0159	2.7375
1990	3.9585	3.0357	2.9775	4.1878	2.8472
1991	4.1747	3.1681	3.1020	4.4377	2.9500
1992	4.3967	3.2912	3.2189	4.6785	3.0578
1993	4.6247	3.4329	3.3519	4.9127	3.1719
1994	4.8879	3.6321	3.5381	5.0613	3.3249
1995	5.1040	3.7651	3.6608	5.2964	3.4241

Table 4.2 (continued)

		Prices (equal to 1.000 in 1972)		
Year	Energy	Food	Consumer goods	Capital services	Consumer services
		No windfall profits tax		
1980	1.9865	1.6744	1.6593	1.8753	1.6304
1981	2.2499	1.8114	1.7939	2.0802	2.7641
1982	2.4670	1.9274	1.9080	2.2239	1.8825
1983	2.6152	2.0401	2.0173	2.4226	1.9806
1984	2.7934	2.1429	2.1171	2.6335	2.0736
1985	3.0100	2.2785	2.2484	2.8347	2.1931
1986	3.2098	2.4088	2.3746	2.9983	3.3130
1987	3.4271	2.5208	2.4815	2.2330	2.4039
1988	3.6371	2.6290	2.5852	3.4626	2.4963
1989	3.8823	2.7816	2.7314	3.6975	2.6248
1990	4.0824	2.8070	2.8510	3.8528	2.7324
1991	4.3183	3.0387	2.9749	4.0842	2.8359
1992	4.5605	3.1636	3.0937	4.3192	2.9461
1993	4.8045	3.3034	3.2251	4.5388	3.0595
1994	5.0851	3.4948	3.4040	4.6702	3.2070
1995	5.3105	3.6248	3.5240	4.8855	3.3046
		Reformed windfall profits tax		
1980	2.0019	1.6798	1.6646	1.8775	1.6356
1981	2.2669	1.8198	1.8022	2.0811	1.7721
1982	2.4852	1.9376	1.9182	2.2236	1.8924
1983	2.6392	2.0492	2.0264	2.4170	1.9896
1984	2.8123	2.1499	2.1241	2.6207	2.0805
1985	3.0209	2.2830	2.2529	2.8141	2.1974
1986	3.2148	2.4109	2.3768	2.9701	2.3149
1987	3.4253	2.5201	2.4809	3.1954	2.4030
1988	3.6273	2.6252	2.5816	3.4144	2.4924
1989	3.8665	2.7749	2.7251	3.6396	2.6183
1990	4.0645	2.8984	2.8428	3.7881	2.7240
1991	4.2939	3.0275	2.9642	4.0114	2.8250
1992	4.5332	3.1505	3.0810	4.2396	2.9333
1993	4.7744	3.2887	3.2109	4.4544	3.0454
1994	5.0521	3.4786	3.3884	4.5834	3.1915
1995	5.2782	3.6080	3.5078	4.7966	3.2887

Table 4.2 (continued)

Total expenditure per household (current prices)

Year	Current policy	Continued controls	No tax	Reformed tax
1980	20895.20	21656.03	20820.57	20895.20
1981	22913.16	23945.35	22948.26	22913.16
1982	24554.57	25509.16	24638.97	24554.57
1983	26096.65	26989.83	26246.48	26094.74
1984	28004.82	28805.27	28219.38	27996.21
1985	29672.51	30410.93	29925.72	29649.17
1986	31123.50	31811.41	31422.85	31113.34
1987	32759.69	33459.28	33106.60	32752.48
1988	34776.13	35453.27	35160.68	34760.77
1989	36835.98	37526.38	37245.01	36823.05
1990	38341.84	39040.83	38740.92	38332.59
1991	40331.78	41031.39	40730.46	40336.98
1992	43361.01	43983.71	43725.01	43363.93
1993	45861.79	46513.24	46207.58	45875.05
1994	48075.13	48839.90	48400.22	48080.81
1995	50414.99	51237.25	50734.36	50430.82

Table 4.3
Money metric individual welfare (current prices; Northeast region)

	Urban		Rural	
Year	White	Nonwhite	White	Nonwhite
	Continued controls			
1980	338.99	340.32	378.54	379.86
1981	248.39	253.60	324.65	329.93
1982	−22.86	−13.06	54.51	64.30
1983	−236.03	−222.10	−169.49	−155.41
1984	−406.19	−389.74	−340.17	−323.49
1985	−518.20	−499.65	−452.06	−433.26
1986	−599.82	−579.39	−533.27	−512.58
1987	−629.25	−607.57	−561.47	−539.45
1988	−665.92	−643.48	−595.77	−572.92
1989	−684.77	−661.19	−613.58	−589.56
1990	−696.44	−671.71	−623.54	−598.36
1991	−705.12	−679.41	−630.94	−605.03
1992	−745.09	−719.94	−668.28	−642.59
1993	−743.30	−717.77	−665.33	−639.23
1994	−723.81	−697.18	−643.95	−616.80
1995	−712.22	−685.06	−631.65	−603.93

Table 4.3 (continued)

Year	Urban		Rural	
	White	Nonwhite	White	Nonwhite
No windfall profits tax				
1980	−12.33	−11.36	−8.47	−7.50
1981	109.06	111.47	112.77	115.18
1982	156.27	159.56	159.78	163.06
1983	190.85	195.06	197.06	201.29
1984	206.99	212.47	213.20	218.70
1985	199.28	205.53	205.53	211.80
1986	187.54	194.87	192.87	199.83
1987	179.79	187.63	184.96	192.82
1988	168.05	176.82	173.62	182.41
1989	146.18	155.45	151.80	161.10
1990	115.76	125.18	121.85	131.29
1991	83.20	92.81	88.72	98.34
1992	41.69	51.39	47.79	57.52
1993	12.38	21.96	18.17	27.78
1994	−11.87	−2.60	−6.04	3.24
1995	−21.79	−12.72	−16.17	−7.09
Reformed windfall profits tax				
1980	0.00	0.00	0.00	0.00
1981	0.00	0.00	0.00	0.00
1982	0.00	0.00	0.00	0.00
1983	3.89	3.93	4.22	4.26
1984	4.19	4.32	4.57	4.70
1985	4.31	4.39	5.50	5.59
1986	10.40	10.58	10.92	11.10
1987	12.64	12.87	13.10	13.33
1988	12.85	13.09	13.77	14.02
1989	15.00	15.27	15.85	16.13
1990	16.54	16.83	17.42	17.72
1991	18.44	18.80	18.92	19.27
1992	15.32	15.68	16.04	16.40
1993	14.73	15.13	15.06	15.46
1994	10.03	10.38	10.47	10.83
1995	10.30	10.69	10.35	10.74

$745.09 by 1992. The time pattern of losses for a nonwhite ur.
household living in the Northeast is similar to that for a white family.

With elimination of the windfall profits tax we find that the price of
energy is lower through 1987 and higher for the remaining period
1988–1995. Elimination of the tax reduces prices of nonenergy commodities at the beginning of the period of our study. However, prices
of these commodities rise more rapidly with elimination of the tax.
We also find that total expenditure per household is lower in 1980 and
higher for all subsequent years. Again, it is not obvious whether individual welfare is higher or lower with elimination of the tax than
under the reference case. As before, we employ prices of the reference
case as a basis for calculating money metric individual welfare (4.4.2).

The dollar value of changes in welfare under a policy of eliminating
the windfall profits tax is given for various types of households in
table 4.3. Under elimination of the tax all households experience a
slight decline in welfare in 1980 and substantial gains in welfare for
the period 1981–1993; urban households in 1994 and 1995 undergo a
slight decline in welfare for those years. As before, the time pattern of
gains and losses in welfare is similar for urban and rural households
and for white and nonwhite households living in the Northeast.

The final alternative to current regulatory and fiscal policy that we
consider is reform of the windfall profits tax beginning in 1983. This
policy results in slightly lower energy prices for the period 1983–1995.
The changes in prices of nonenergy commodities are relatively small
under reform of the windfall profits tax. Total expenditure per household is lower under this policy than under current policy through
1990. For the remainder of the period 1991–1995 total expenditure per
household is higher. The dollar value of the change in welfare for various types of households is nonnegative for the entire period of our
study. However, the gains in welfare are small by comparison with
those for eliminating the windfall profits tax after 1983.

To summarize: Most of the households we have considered would
be better off with elimination of the windfall profits tax than under
current policy. Continued controls would result in welfare losses for
most households, while reform of the windfall profits tax would produce welfare gains that are positive but smaller in magnitude than
elimination of the tax. However, these comparisons do not hold uniformly for all households and all years.

4.5   Social Welfare Functions

Under the Pareto principle an economic policy can be recommended if all consuming units are as well off as under any alternative policy and at least one unit is better off. The Pareto principle provides a partial ordering of economic policies. This ordering is invariant with respect to monotone increasing transformations of individual welfare that differ among consuming units. Only welfare comparisons that are ordinal and not comparable among consuming units are required.

Money metric individual welfare (4.5.2) is a monotone increasing transformation of the measure of individual welfare (4.2.26). This transformation depends on the prices faced by all consuming units and on the attributes of the individual consuming unit. Considered as a measure of individual welfare in its own right, money metric individual welfare provides all the information about consumer preferences required for application of the Pareto principle. To obtain a complete ordering of economic policies we next introduce a social welfare function.

We consider the set of all possible social orderings over the set of social states, say X, and the set of all possible real-valued individual welfare functions, say W_k ($k = 1, 2, \ldots, K$). A social ordering, say R, is a complete, reflexive, and transitive ordering of social states. A social state is described by the quantities consumed of N commodity groups by K individuals. The individual welfare function for the kth individual W_k ($k = 1, 2, \ldots, K$) is defined on the set of social states X and gives the level of individual welfare for that individual in each state.

To describe social orderings in greater detail we find it useful to introduce the following notation:

x — a matrix with elements $\{x_{nk}\}$ describing the social state.

$u = (W_1, W_2, \ldots, W_K)$ — a vector of individual welfare functions of all K individuals.

Following Sen (1970, 1977) and Hammond (1976) we define a *social welfare functional*, say f, as a mapping from the set of individual welfare functions to the set of social orderings, such that $f(u') = f(u)$ implies $R' = R$, where

$$u = [W_1(x), W_2(x), \ldots, W_K(x)] \,,$$
$$u' = [W_1'(x), W_2'(x), \ldots, W_K'(x)] \,,$$

for all $x \in X$. Similarly, we define L_k ($k = 1, 2, \ldots, K$) as the *set of admissible individual welfare functions* for the kth individual and L as the Cartesian product $\prod_{k=1}^{K} L_k$. Finally, let **L** be the partition of L such that all elements of **L** yield the same social ordering.

We can describe a social ordering in terms of the following properties of a social welfare functional:

1. *Unrestricted domain.* The social welfare functional f is defined for all possible vectors of individual welfare functions u.

2. *Independence of irrelevant alternatives.* For any subset A contained in X, if $u(x) = u'(x)$ for all $x \in A$, then $R : A = R' : A$, where $R = f(u)$ and $R' = f(u')$ and $R : A$ is the social ordering over the subset A.

3. *Positive association.* For any vectors of individual welfare functions u and u', if for all y in $X - x$, such that

$$W_k'(y) = W_k(y) \, ,$$

$$W_k'(x) > W_k(x) \, , \qquad (k = 1, 2, \ldots, K) \, ,$$

then xPy implies $xP'y$ and $yP'x$ implies yPx, where P is a strict ordering of social states.

4. *Nonimposition.* For all $x, y \in X$ there exist u, u' such that xPy and $yP'x$.

5. *Cardinal full comparability.* The set of admissible individual welfare functions that yield the same social ordering **L** is defined by

$$\mathbf{L} = \{u' : W_k'(x) = \alpha + \beta W_k(x) \, , \ \beta > 0 \, , \ k = 1, 2, \ldots, K\} \, ,$$

and $f(u') = f(u)$ for all $u' \in \mathbf{L}$.

Cardinal full comparability implies that social orderings are invariant with respect to any positive affine transformation of the individual welfare functions $\{W_k\}$ that is the same for all individuals. Arrow (1967, p. 225) has defended noncomparability in the following terms:

... the autonomy of individuals, an element of mutual incommensurability among people seems denied by the possibility of interpersonal comparisons.

He requires ordinal noncomparability, which implies that social orderings are invariant with respect to monotone increasing transformations of the individual welfare functions that may differ among individuals:

5′. *Ordinal noncomparability.* The set of individual welfare functions that yield the same social ordering **L** is defined by

$\mathbf{L} = \{u': W_k'(x) = \phi_k[W_k(x)], \ \phi_k \text{ increasing, } k = 1, 2, \ldots, K\}$,

and $f(u') = f(u)$ for all $u' \in \mathbf{L}$.

The properties of a social welfare functional corresponding to unrestricted domain and independence of irrelevant alternatives are used by Arrow in proving the impossibility of a nondictatorial social ordering:

4′. *Nondictatorship.* There is no individual k such that for all x, $y \in X$, $W_k(x) > W_k(y)$ implies xPy.

Under ordinal noncomparability the assumptions of positive association and nonimposition employed by Arrow imply the weak Pareto principle:

3′. *Pareto principle.* For any x, $y \in X$, if $W_k(x) > W_k(y)$ for all individuals ($k = 1, 2, \ldots, K$), then xPy.

If a social welfare functional f has the properties of unrestricted domain, independence of irrelevant alternatives, the weak Pareto principle, and ordinal noncomparability, then no nondictatorial social ordering is possible. This result is Arrow's impossibility theorem. Since it is obvious that the class of dictatorial social orderings is too narrow to provide an adequate basis for expressing the implications of alternative ethical judgements, we propose to generate a class of social welfare functions suitable for the evaluation of alternative economic policies by weakening Arrow's assumptions.

We first consider weakening the assumption of ordinal noncomparability of individual welfare functions. Sen (1970) has shown that Arrow's conclusion that no nondictatorial social ordering is possible is preserved by replacing ordinal noncomparability by cardinal noncomparability. This implies that social orderings are invariant with respect to positive affine transformations of the individual welfare functions that may differ among individuals:

5″. *Cardinal noncomparability.* The set of individual welfare functions that yield the same social ordering $\mathbf{L}$ is defined by

$\mathbf{L} = \{u': W_k'(x) = \alpha_k + \beta_k W_k(x), \ \beta_k > 0, \ k = 1, 2, \ldots, K\}$,

and $f(u') = f(u)$ for all u' in $\mathbf{L}$.

However, d'Aspremont and Gevers (1977), Deschamps and Gevers (1978), Maskin (1978), and Roberts (1980b) have shown that we obtain an interesting class of nondictatorial social orderings by requiring cardinal unit comparability of individual welfare functions, which implies that social orderings are invariant with respect to positive affine transformations with units that are the same for all individuals:

5'''. *Cardinal unit comparability.* The set of individual welfare functions that yield the same social ordering **L** is defined by

$$\mathbf{L} = \{u': W_k'(x) = \alpha_k + \beta W_k(x), \beta > 0, k = 1, 2, \ldots, K\} \,,$$

and $f(u') = f(u)$ for all u' in **L**.

If a social welfare functional f has the properties of unrestricted domain, independence of irrelevant alternatives, the weak Pareto principle, and cardinal unit comparability, there exist social orderings and a continuous real-valued social welfare function, say W, such that if $W[u(x)] > W[u(y)]$, then xPy. Furthermore, the social welfare function can be represented in the form

$$W[u(x)] = \sum_{k=1}^{K} a_k W_k(x) \,. \tag{4.5.1}$$

If we add the assumption that the social welfare function has the property of anonymity, that is, no individual is given greater weight than any other individual in determining the level of social welfare, then the social welfare function W in (4.5.1) must be symmetric in the individual welfare functions $\{W_k\}$. The property of anonymity incorporates a notion of horizontal equity into the representation of social orderings.

Under anonymity the function W in (4.5.1) reduces to the sum of individual welfare functions and takes the form of a utilitarian social welfare function. Utilitarian social welfare functions have been employed extensively in applications of welfare economics, especially in the measurement of inequality by methods originated by Atkinson (1970) and Kolm (1969, 1976a, b), in the design of optimal income tax schedules along the lines pioneered by Mirrlees (1971), and in the evaluation of alternative economic policies by Arrow and Kalt (1979).

The approach to the measurement of social welfare based on a utilitarian social welfare function provides a worthwhile starting point for applications. Harsanyi (1976) and Ng (1975) have pointed out that distributional considerations can be incorporated into a utilitarian social welfare function through the representation of individual welfare functions. However, Sen (1973, p. 18) has argued that a utilitarian social welfare function does not take appropriate account of the distribution of welfare among individuals:

The distribution of welfare between persons is a relevant aspect of any problem of income distribution, and our evaluation of inequality will obviously depend on whether we are concerned only with the loss of the sum of individual utilities through a bad distribution of income, or also with the inequality of welfare levels of different individuals.

To broaden the range of possible social orderings we can require cardinal full comparability of individual welfare functions, as defined above. Roberts (1980b) has shown that a social welfare functional f with the properties of unrestricted domain, independence of irrelevant alternatives, the weak Pareto principle, and cardinal full comparability implies the existence of a social welfare function that takes the form

$$W[u(x)] = \bar{W}(x) + g[u(x) - \bar{W}(x)i] , \qquad (4.5.2)$$

where i is a vector of ones, the function $\bar{W}(x)$ corresponds to average individual welfare:

$$\bar{W}(x) = \sum_{k=1}^{K} a_k W_k(x) ,$$

and $g(x)$ is a linear homogeneous function of deviations of levels of individual welfare from the average. (It is important to note that the social welfare function in (4.5.2) represents a social ordering over all possible individual orderings and exemplifies the multiple profile approach to social choice of Arrow (1963) rather than the single profile approach employed by Bergson (1938) and Samuelson (1947). The literature on the existence of single profile social welfare functions is discussed by Roberts (1980d), Samuelson (1982), and Sen (1979b).)

If the function $g(x)$ in the representation (4.5.2) of the social welfare function is identically equal to zero, then the social welfare function reduces to the form (4.5.1). If the function $g(x)$ is not identically zero, then the social welfare function incorporates both a measure of average individual welfare and a measure of inequality in the distribution of individual welfare. We conclude that the class of possible social welfare functions (4.5.2) includes utilitarian welfare functions, but also includes functions that are not subject to the objections that can be made to utilitarianism.

Although Roberts (1980b) has succeeded in broadening the class of possible social welfare functions beyond those consistent with utilitarianism, the social welfare functions (4.5.2) are subject to an objection raised by Sen (1973). (See Sen (1977, 1979b) for further discussion.) Information about alternative social states enters only through the individual welfare functions $\{W_k\}$. Sen refers to this property of a social welfare functional f as *welfarism*. Welfarism rules out characteristics of a social state that are conceivably relevant for social orderings, but that cannot be incorporated into the social welfare function through the individual welfare functions.

Roberts (1980b) has suggested the possibility of further weakening Arrow's assumptions in order to incorporate nonwelfare characteristics of social states. (See Roberts (1980b, esp. pp. 434–436).) For this purpose we can replace the weak Pareto principle by positive association and nonimposition, as defined above. We retain the assumptions of unrestricted domain, independence of irrelevant alternatives, and cardinal full comparability of measures of individual welfare. We can partition the set of social states X into subsets, such that all states within each subset have the same nonwelfare characteristics. For each subset there exists a social ordering that can be represented by a social welfare function of the form (4.5.2).

Under the assumptions we have outlined there exists a social ordering for the set of all social states that can be represented by a social welfare function of the form

$$W(u, x) = F\{\bar{W}(x) + g[x, u(x) - \bar{W}(x)i], x\} , \qquad (4.5.3)$$

where the function $\bar{W}(x)$ corresponds to average individual welfare

$$\bar{W}(x) = \sum_{k=1}^{K} a_k(x) \, W_k(x) .$$

As before, the function g is a linear homogeneous function of deviations of levels of individual welfare from average welfare.

The class of social welfare functions (4.5.3) incorporates nonwelfare characteristics of social states through the weights $\{a_k(x)\}$ in average individual welfare $\bar{W}(x)$, through the function $g(x)$, which depends directly on the social state x as well as on deviations of levels of individual welfare from the average welfare, and through the function F, which depends directly on the social state x and on the sum of the functions $\bar{W}(x)$ and $g(x)$. This class includes social welfare functions that are not subject to the objections that can be made to welfarism.

At this point we have generated a class of possible social welfare functions capable of expressing the implications of a variety of different ethical judgements. In order to choose a specific social welfare function, we must narrow the range of possible ethical judgements by imposing further requirements on the class of possible social welfare functions. First, we must limit the dependence of the function $F(x)$ in (4.5.3) on the characteristics of alternative social states. Second, we must select a form for the function $g(x)$ in (4.5.3), which depends on deviations of levels of individual welfare from average welfare $\bar{W}(x)$. Finally, we must choose representations of the individual welfare functions $\{W_k(x)\}$ that provide cardinal full comparability.

We first rule out the dependence of the function $F(x)$ in (4.5.3) on characteristics of social states that do not enter through the functions $\bar{W}(x)$ and g(x). This restriction reduces F to a function of a single variable $\bar{W} + g$. We obtain an ordinal measure of social welfare by permitting the function F to be any monotone increasing transformation. To obtain a cardinal measure of social welfare we observe that the function $\bar{W}(x) + g$ is homogeneous of degree one in the individual welfare functions $\{W_k(x)\}$. All representations of the social welfare function that preserve this property can be written in the form

$$W(u, x) = \beta[\bar{W}(x) + g(x)] , \quad \beta > 0 . \tag{4.5.4}$$

We conclude that only positive, homogeneous, affine transformations are permitted.

The restrictions embodied in the class of social welfare functions (4.5.4) do not reduce social welfare to a function of the individual welfare functions $\{W_k(x)\}$ alone, since the weights $\{a_k(x)\}$ in average individual welfare $\bar{W}(x)$ and the function $g(x)$ depend on nonwelfare characteristics of the social state x. However, these social welfare functions are homogeneous of degree one in levels of individual welfare. This implies that doubling the welfare of each individual will double social welfare, holding nonwelfare characteristics of the social state constant. Blackorby and Donaldson (1982) refer to this class of social welfare functions as *distributionally homothetic*. (The implications of distributional homotheticity are discussed by Kolm (1976b) and Blackorby and Donaldson (1978).)

We impose a second set of requirements on the class of social welfare functions (4.5.3) by selecting an appropriate form for the function $g(x)$. In particular, we require that this function is additive in deviations of individual welfare functions $\{W_k(x)\}$ from average welfare $\bar{W}(x)$. Since the function $g(x)$ is homogeneous of degree one, it must be a mean value function of order $\rho(x)$

$$g[x, u(x) - \bar{W}(x) \, i] = -\gamma(x) \left[\sum_{k=1}^{K} b_k(x) \, |W_k - \bar{W}|^{-\rho(x)} \right]^{-\frac{1}{\rho(x)}}, \tag{4.5.5}$$

where

$$\gamma(x) > 0, \, \rho(x) \lessgtr -1, \, \sum_{k=1}^{K} b_k(x) = 1, \, 0 < b_k(x) < 1, \qquad (k = 1, 2, \dots, K).$$

Under these restrictions the function $g(x)$ is negative, except at the point of perfect equality $W_k = \bar{W}$ $(k = 1, 2, \dots, K)$, where it is zero. (Mean value functions were introduced into economics by Bergson (1936) and have been employed, for example, by Arrow, Chenery, Minhas, and Solow (1961) and Atkinson (1970). Properties of mean value functions are discussed by Hardy, Littlewood, and Polya (1959).)

The function $\rho(x)$ in the representation (4.5.5) determines the curvature of the social welfare function in the individual welfare functions $\{W_k(x)\}$. We can refer to this function as the *degree of aversion to inequality*. We assume that this function is constant, so that the corresponding social welfare function $W(u, x)$ is characterized by a constant degree of aversion to inequality. To complete the selection of an appropriate form for the social welfare function we must choose appropriate weights $\{a_k(x)\}$ for average individual welfare $\bar{W}(x)$ and $\{b_k(x)\}$ for the measure of equality $g(x)$. We find it natural to require that the two sets of weights are the same.

To incorporate a notion of horizontal equity into the social welfare functions (4.5.5) we can impose a weak form of the property of anonymity. In particular, we require that no individual is given greater weight in the social welfare function than any other individual with an identical individual welfare function. This implies that the social welfare function is symmetric in the levels of individual welfare for identical individuals. The weights $\{a_k(x)\}$ in average welfare $\bar{W}(x)$ and the measure of equality $g(x)$ must be the same for identical individuals.

Under the restrictions presented up to this point the social welfare function W takes the form

$$W(u, x) = \bar{W} - \gamma(x) \left[\sum_{k=1}^{K} a_k(x) |W_k - \bar{W}|^{-\rho} \right]^{-1/\rho} \tag{4.5.6}$$

where

$$\bar{W}(x) = \sum_{k=1}^{K} a_k(x) \, W_k(x).$$

The condition of positive association requires that an increase in all levels of individual welfare must increase social welfare. This condition implies that the average level of individual welfare $\bar{W}$ must increase by more than the function $g(x)$, whatever the initial distribution of individual welfare. We assume that the function $\gamma(x)$ in (4.5.6) must take the maximum value consistent with positive association, so that

$$\gamma(x) = \left\{ 1 + \left[\frac{\sum_{k=1}^{K} a_k(x)}{a_j(x)} \right]^{-(\rho+1)} \right\}^{1/\rho}, \tag{4.5.7}$$

where

$$a_j(x) = \min_k a_k(x), \qquad (k = 1, 2, \ldots, K),$$

for the social state x.

To complete the selection of a social welfare function $W(u, x)$ we require that the individual welfare functions $\{W_k\}$ in (4.5.3) must be invariant with respect to any positive affine transformation that is the same for all households. (This assumption implies that individual welfare increases with total expenditure at a rate that is inversely proportional to total expenditure. This is also implied by the utilitarian social welfare function employed by Arrow and Kalt (1979).) Under this assumption the logarithm of the translog indirect utility function is a cardinal measure of individual welfare with full comparability among households. The social welfare function takes the form

$$W(u, x) = \ln \bar{V} - \gamma(x) \left[\sum_{k=1}^{K} a_k(x) | \ln V_k - \ln \bar{V} |^{-\rho} \right]^{-1/\rho}. \tag{4.5.8}$$

where

$$\ln \bar{V} = \sum_{k=1}^{K} a_k(x) \ln V_k \left[\frac{pm(A_k)}{M_k} \right].$$

We can complete the specification of a social welfare function $W(u, x)$ by choosing a set of weights $\{a_k(x)\}$ for the levels of individual welfare $\{\ln V_k[pm(A_k)/M_k]\}$ in (4.5.8). For this purpose we must appeal to a notion of vertical equity. Following Hammond (1977), we define a distribution of total expenditure $\{M_k\}$ as more *equitable* than another distribution $\{M_k'\}$ if

(i) $M_i + M_j = M_i' + M_j'$,

(ii) $M_k = M_k'$ for $k \neq i, j$,

(iii) $\ln V_i[pm(A_i)/M_i'] > \ln V_i[pm(A_i)/M_i] > \ln V_j[pm(A_j)/M_j] > \ln V_j[pm(A_j)/M_j']$,

We say that a social welfare function $W(u, x)$ is *equity-regarding* if it is larger for a more equitable distribution of total expenditure.

We require that the social welfare functions (4.5.8) must be equity-regarding. This amounts to imposing a version of Dalton's (1920) principle of transfers. This principle requires that a transfer of total expenditures from a rich household to a poor household that does not reverse their relative positions in the distribution of total expenditure must increase the level of social welfare.

If the social welfare functions (4.5.8) are required to be equity-regarding, then the weights $\{a_k(x)\}$ associated with the individual welfare functions $\{\ln V_k[pm(A_k)/M_k]\}$ must take the form

$$a_k(x) = \frac{m_0(p, A_k)}{\sum_{k=1}^{K} m_0(p, A_k)}, \qquad (k = 1, 2, \ldots, K). \qquad (4.5.9)$$

We conclude that an equity-regarding social welfare function of the class (4.5.8) must take the form

$$W(u, x) = \ln \bar{V} - \gamma(x) \left[\frac{\sum_{k=1}^{K} m_0(p, A_k) |\ln V_k - \ln \bar{V}|^{-\rho}}{\sum_{k=1}^{K} m_0(p, A_k)} \right]^{-1/\rho}, \qquad (4.5.10)$$

where

$$\ln \bar{V} = \frac{\sum_{k=1}^{K} m_0(p, A_k) \ln V_k [pm(A_k)/M_k]}{\sum_{k=1}^{K} m_0(p, A_k)},$$

$$= \ln p' \left(\alpha_p + \frac{1}{2} B_{pp} \ln p \right) - D(p) \frac{\sum_{k=1}^{K} m_0(p, A_k) \ln [M_k/m_0(p, A_k)]}{\sum_{k=1}^{K} m_0(p, A_k)}.$$

Furthermore, the condition of positive association implies that the function $\gamma(x)$ in (4.5.8) must take the form

$$\gamma(x) = \left\{ 1 + \left[\frac{\sum_{k=1}^{K} m_0(p, A_k)}{m_0(p, A_j)} \right]^{-(\rho+1)} \right\}^{-1/\rho},$$

(4.5.11)

where

$$m_0(p, A_j) = \min_k m_0(p, A_{k)}, \qquad (k = 1, 2, \ldots, K).$$

To summarize: We have generated a class of social welfare functions (4.5.3) that has the properties of unrestricted domain, independence of irrelevant alternatives, positive association, nonimposition, and cardinal full comparability. By imposing the additional assumption that the degree of aversion to inequality is constant and requiring the social welfare function to satisfy requirements of horizontal and vertical equity, we obtain the social welfare functions (4.5.10).

4.6 Money Metric Social Welfare

In assessing the impact of changes in economic policy on levels of individual welfare for each consuming unit, we have found it useful to express the change in welfare in terms of the change in total expenditure. Similarly, to provide a basis for comparisons among social states $\{x_{nk}\}$ we propose to formulate a money measure of social welfare. (Alternative money measures of social welfare are discussed by Arrow and Kalt (1979), Bergson (1980), Deaton and Muellbauer (1980b, pp. 214–239), Roberts (1980c), and Sen (1976). A survey of the literature is presented by Sen (1979a).) Following Pollak (1981), we can define the *social expenditure function* as the minimum level of total expenditure $M = \sum_{k=1}^{K} M_k$ required to attain a given level of social welfare, say W, at a specified price system p. More formally, the social expenditure function $M(p, W)$ is defined by

$$M(p, W) = \min \left\{ M: W(u, x) \geqq W; M = \sum_{k=1}^{K} M_k \right\}.$$

(4.6.1)

The social expenditure function (4.6.1) is precisely analogous to the individual expenditure function (4.2.23). The individual expenditure function gives the minimum level of expenditure required to attain a stipulated level of individual welfare; the social expenditure function gives the minimum level of aggregate expenditure required to attain a stipulated level of social welfare. The individual expenditure function and the indirect utility function can be employed in assessing the impact of alternative economic policies on individual welfare. Similarly, the social expenditure function and the social welfare function can be employed in assessing the impacts of alternative policies on social welfare.

We can translate any level of social welfare into monetary terms by evaluating the social expenditure function at that level of welfare for a given price system p. Two different levels of social welfare can be compared with reference to a single price system by determining the minimum level of aggregate expenditure required to attain each level of social welfare for the reference prices. In addition, changes in social welfare can be decomposed into changes in efficiency and changes in equity. Money measures of both components of the change in social welfare can be defined in terms of the social expenditure function and the social welfare function.

In order to determine the form of the social expenditure function $M(p, W)$ in (4.6.1), we can maximize the social welfare function (4.5.10) for a fixed level of aggregate total expenditure by equalizing total expenditure per household equivalent member $\{M_k/m_0(p, A_k)\}$ for all consuming units. If aggregate total expenditure is distributed so as to equalize total expenditure per household equivalent member, the level of individual welfare is the same for all consuming units. For this distribution of total expenditure the social welfare function reduces to the average level of individual welfare $\ln \bar{V}$.

For the translog indirect utility function the maximum value of social welfare for a given level of aggregate expenditure takes the form

$$W(x, u) = \ln \bar{V} \ .$$

$$= \ln p' \left(\alpha_p + \frac{1}{2} B_{pp} \ln p \right) - D(p) \ln \left[M / \sum_{k=1}^{K} m_0(p, A_k) \right]. \qquad (4.6.2)$$

This maximum value of social welfare reduces to average individual welfare. The average is obtained by evaluating the translog indirect utility function (4.2.22) at total expenditure per household equivalent member $M / \sum_{k=1}^{K} m_0(p, A_k)$ for the economy as a whole.

We can solve for aggregate expenditure as a function of the level of social welfare and prices

$$\ln M(p, W) = \frac{1}{D(p)} \left[\ln p' \left(\alpha_p + \frac{1}{2} B_{pp} \ln p \right) - W \right]$$

$$+ \ln \left[\sum_{k=1}^{K} m_0(p, A_k) \right]. \tag{4.6.3}$$

We can refer to this function as the *translog social expenditure function*. The value of aggregate expenditure is obtained by evaluating the translog individual expenditure function (4.2.23) at the level of social welfare W and the number of household equivalent members $\sum_{k=1}^{K} m_0(p, A_k)$ for the economy as a whole.

To obtain a money measure of social welfare we first evaluate the social welfare function (4.5.10) at prices p^0 and distribution of total expenditure $\{M_k^0\}$ prevailing before any change in policy. We can express the level of social welfare before any change in policy, say W^0, in terms of the social expenditure function

$$\ln M(p^0, W^0) = \frac{1}{D(p^0)} \left[\ln p^{0\prime} (\alpha_p + \frac{1}{2} B_{pp} \ln p^0) - W^0 \right]$$

$$+ \ln \left[\sum_{k=1}^{K} m_0(p^0, A_k) \right]. \tag{4.6.4}$$

Second, we can decompose our money measure of social welfare into money measures of efficiency and equity. (Alternative money measures of efficiency and equity are discussed by Arrow and Kalt (1979), Bergson (1980), and Sen (1976a, 1979a).) For this purpose we evaluate the social welfare function at the maximum level, say W^2, that can be attained through lump sum redistributions of aggregate expenditure $M^0 = \sum_{k=1}^{K} M_k^0$. Total expenditure per household equivalent member must be equalized for all consuming units, so that the social welfare function (4.5.10) reduces to average individual welfare (4.6.2). This is the maximum level of social welfare that is potentially available and can be taken as a measure of efficiency. Evaluating the social expenditure function at the potential level of welfare, say W^2, we obtain

$$M(p^0, W^2) = M^0, \tag{4.6.5}$$

so that aggregate total expenditure M^0 is the resulting money measure of efficiency.

Given a money measure of efficiency, we can define the corresponding money measure of equity as the difference between the money measure of actual social welfare $M(p^0, W^0)$ and the money measure of potential social welfare M^0. This measure of equity is nonpositive and equal to zero only for perfect equality in the distribution of individual welfare. Under perfect equality total expenditure per household equivalent member is equalized among all consuming units. Using the social expenditure function, we can express our money measure of social welfare $M(p^0, W^0)$ as the sum of a money measure of efficiency M^0 and a money measure of equity $M(p^0, W^0) - M^0$

$$M(p^0, W^0) = M^0 + [M(p^0, W^0) - M^0] . \tag{4.6.6}$$

The critical feature of this decomposition is that all three money measures are expressed in terms of the same set of prices p^0.

Finally, to analyze the impact of a change in economic policy on social welfare, we can evaluate the social welfare function (4.5.10) at prices p^1 and distribution of total expenditure $\{M_k^1\}$ after the change in policy has taken place. In order to evaluate the impact of a change in economic policy on social welfare, we must compare the levels of aggregate total expenditure required to attain the actual levels of social welfare before and after the policy change at prices prevailing before the change. For this purpose we define *money metric social welfare*, say M_A, as the difference between the total expenditure required to attain the actual level of welfare after the policy change, say W^1, and the expenditure required to attain the actual level of welfare before the policy change W^0 at prices prevailing before the policy change p^0

$$M_A(p^0, W^0, W^1) = M(p^0, W^1) - M(p^0, W^0). \tag{4.6.7}$$

If money metric social welfare is positive, the level of social welfare is increased by the policy change; otherwise, social welfare is decreased or left unaffected.

We can decompose our money measure of social welfare after the change in economic policy into money measures of efficiency and equity. For this purpose we first determine the maximum level of welfare, say W^3, that can be attained through lump sum redistributions of aggregate total expenditure $M^1 = \sum_{k=1}^{K} M_k^1$. As before, aggregate expenditure must be distributed so as to equalize individual expenditure per household equivalent member, so that the social welfare function (4.5.10) reduces to average individual welfare (4.6.2). This is the maximum level of social welfare that is potentially available after the change in economic policy and can be taken as a measure of efficiency.

To preserve comparability between money measures of actual social welfare W^1 and potential welfare W^3 after the change in economic policy, we can evaluate the measure of potential welfare at prices prevailing before the change in policy p^0, using the social expenditure function

$$\ln M(p^0, W^3) = \frac{1}{D(p^0)} \left[\ln p^{0\prime} \left(\alpha_p + \frac{1}{2} B_{pp} \ln p^0 \right) - W^3 \right]$$

$$+ \ln \left[\sum_{k=1}^{K} m_0(p^0, A_k) \right]. \tag{4.6.8}$$

The corresponding money measure of equity in terms of prices prevailing before the change in policy is given by the difference between the money measure of actual social welfare after the policy change $M(p^0, W^1)$ and the money measure of potential social welfare after the policy change $M(p^0, W^3)$. Our money measure of actual social welfare $M(p^0, W^1)$ is the sum of money measures of efficiency and equity. All three measures are evaluated at prices prevailing before the change in policy p^0

$$M(p^0, W^1) = M(p^0, W^3) + [M(p^0, W^1) - M(p^0, W^3)]. \tag{4.6.9}$$

Finally, we can decompose money metric social welfare (4.6.8) into the sum of money metric efficiency and money metric equity. *Money metric efficiency*, say M_P, can be defined as the difference between the total expenditure required to attain the potential level of welfare after the policy change W^3 and the expenditure required to attain the potential level of welfare before the policy change W^2. Both are evaluated at prices prevailing before the policy change p^0

$$M_P(p^0, W^2, W^3) = M(p^0, W^3) - M^0. \tag{4.6.10}$$

Similarly, *money metric equity*, say M_E, can be defined as the difference between money measures of equity before and after the policy change, evaluated at prices before the change p^0

$$M_E(p^0, W^0, W^1, W^2, W^3) = [M(p^0, W^1) - M(p^0, W^3)]$$
$$- [M(p^0, W^0) - M^0] . \qquad (4.6.11)$$

Money metric social welfare is the sum of money metric efficiency and money metric equity

$$M_A(p^0, W^0, W^1) = M_P(p^0, W^2, W^3) + M_E(p^0, W^0, W^1, W^2, W^3) . \qquad (4.6.12)$$

All three money measures of social welfare in this decomposition are expressed in terms of the same set of prices p^0.

To illustrate the measurement of social welfare we can represent the concept of money metric social welfare geometrically, as in figure 4.2. In this diagram we have depicted a representative consumer with indirect utility function given by the average level of utility $\ln \bar{V}$ in (4.6.2). As before, we consider the case of two commodities ($N = 2$) for simplicity. Consumer equilibrium at the actual level of social welfare W^0 before the policy change is represented by the point A. The corresponding level of aggregate expenditure $M(p^0, W^0)$, divided by the price of the second commodity p_2^0, is given on the vertical axis. This axis provides a representation of aggregate expenditure in terms of units of the second commodity.

Aggregate expenditure M^0 is the value of the social expenditure function at the potential level of welfare W^1. This is the maximum level of welfare that can be obtained by lump sum redistributions of aggregate expenditure. The corresponding consumer equilibrium is represented by the point B. A money measure of efficiency, expressed in terms of units of the second commodity, is given by the level of aggregate expenditure M^0/p_2^0. The corresponding money measure of equity is provided by the distance along the x_2 axis between aggregate expenditure M^0/p_2^0 and the value of the social expenditure function $M(p^0, W^{0)}/p_2^0$; each is divided by the price of the second commodity. The money measure of social welfare at A is the sum of money measures of efficiency and equity.

As before, consumer equilibrium at the level of social welfare W^1 after the policy change is represented by the point C. In (4.6.7) we have determined this level of welfare by evaluating the social welfare

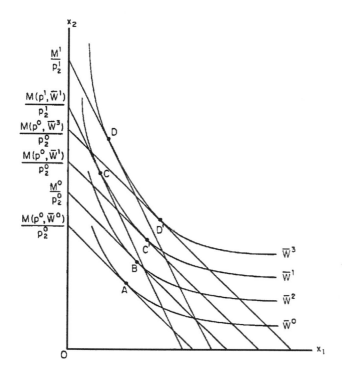

Figure 4.2
Money metric social welfare.

function (4.5.10) at the prices p^1 and the distribution of total expenditure $\{M_k^1\}$ after the change in policy has taken place. To translate the level of social welfare W^1 into aggregate expenditure at the prices prevailing before the policy change, we evaluate the social expenditure function (4.6.3) at this level of social welfare and the prices before the changes p^0. The resulting level of aggregate expenditure $M(p^0, W^1)$ corresponds to consumer equilibrium at the point C'.

The money measure of social welfare at C' is the sum of money measures of efficiency and equity that are precisely analogous to those we have defined for the measure of welfare at A. We can decompose our money measure of social welfare by first determining the maximum level of social welfare, say W^3, that can be obtained through lump sum distributions to aggregate expenditure M^1 at prices p^1. The corresponding consumer equilibrium is represented by the point D. We can translate this level of social welfare into aggregate expenditure at prices prevailing before the change p^0 by evaluating the social welfare function $M(p^0, W^3)$ at the point D'.

Money metric social welfare, expressed in units of the second commodity, is represented by the distance along the x_2 axis between aggregate expenditure $M(p^0, W^1)/p_2$ and expenditure $M(p^0, W^0)/p_2$, each divided by the price of the second commodity. Similarly, money metric efficiency is represented by the distance between aggregate expenditure $M(p^0, W^3)/p_2$ and expenditure M^0/p_2. Finally, money metric equity is represented by the difference between the distances $[M(p^0, W^1) - M(p^0, W_3)]/p_2$ and $[M(p^0, W^0) - M^0]/p_2$. The distance corresponding to money metric social welfare is the sum of the distances corresponding to money metric efficiency and money metric equity.

To summarize: In this section we have developed methods for expressing changes in economic policy. We can decompose our money measure of changes in social welfare into money measures of efficiency and equity. Money metric efficiency is defined in terms of changes in the potential level of social welfare. Money metric equity is defined in terms of changes in the difference between potential and actual levels of social welfare.

4.7   Efficiency versus Equity

Given methods for measuring social welfare, we are in a position to evaluate alternative policies for petroleum price regulation and taxation of petroleum production in the United States. As a basis for comparison of levels of social welfare associated with alternative policies, we take current policy as a reference case. Under this policy petroleum price controls were eliminated in January 1981; a windfall profits tax is levied on petroleum production. We employ the behavior of the U.S. economy under these policies with a regime of low oil prices as a base case for policy analysis.

The value of social welfare depends on prices for each of the five commodities included in our model of aggregate consumer behavior—energy, food, consumer goods, capital services, and consumer services. In addition, it depends on total expenditure for the U.S. economy as a whole. As before, we make the simplifying assumption that total expenditure changes in the same proportion for all consuming units. We employ the projections of prices and total expenditure based on the Dynamic General Equilibrium Model (DGEM) of the U.S. economy given in table 4.2.

We can translate our evaluation of alternative policies for petroleum price regulation into money measures of social welfare by employing the social expenditure function introduced in section 4.6. In table 4.4 we present money metric social welfare for the three alternatives to current policy described in section 4.4 above. Although the magnitude of money metric social welfare depends on the degree of aversion to inequality, we find that the qualitative features of comparisons among alternative policies for different values of this parameter are almost identical. We present money metric social welfare for all three alternatives to the base case for the degree of aversion to inequality ρ equal to one.

Under continued controls money metric social welfare is positive for the years 1980, 1981, and 1982, and becomes negative for the rest of the period. Money metric social welfare under elimination of the windfall profits tax is slightly negative for the year 1980. For all subsequent years included in our study money metric social welfare is positive, reaching a maximum of $10.524 billion dollars in 1984. Reforming the windfall profits tax has no impact on social welfare

Table 4.4
Money metric social welfare (millions of current dollars)

Year	Continued controls	No tax	Reformed tax
1980	17359.914	−412.867	0.000
1981	14289.919	5509.200	0.000
1982	1732.022	7836.263	0.000
1983	−8386.252	9642.212	198.001
1984	−16326.843	10524.042	221.431
1985	−21510.685	10224.960	244.202
1986	−25253.311	9699.709	526.232
1987	−26531.095	9404.192	636.930
1988	−28165.957	8933.008	660.231
1989	−28953.384	7932.562	764.214
1990	−29377.805	6501.736	840.548
1991	−29711.136	4943.447	926.703
1992	−31584.172	2977.254	783.785
1993	−31444.095	1554.040	748.735
1994	−30377.851	367.070	522.893
1995	−29766.946	−131.788	528.650

during 1980, 1981, and 1982, since the reform does not take effect until 1983.

Beginning in 1983 a reformed windfall profits tax produces a gain in social welfare, relative to the base case, but produces lower social welfare levels than elimination of the windfall profits tax for this entire period. Our analysis of current regulatory and fiscal policy for petroleum and the three alternative policies appears to justify change in policy to eliminate the windfall profits tax. This policy is superior to current policy and to a policy of continued price controls. It is also superior to a reformed windfall profits tax.

Money metric social welfare is the sum of money metric efficiency and money metric equity. Money metric efficiency corresponds to the gain in potential social welfare associated with a change in regulatory and fiscal policy and is independent of the degree of aversion to inequality ρ. We present money metric efficiency for all three alternatives to the base case in table 4.5.

Under continued controls money metric efficiency is positive for 1980–1982 and negative for the rest of the period 1983–1995. Money metric efficiency under elimination of the windfall profits tax is slightly negative for the year 1980. For the period 1981–1993 money

Table 4.5
Money metric efficiency (millions of current dollars)

Year	Continued controls	No tax	Reformed tax
1980	30705.080	−951.504	0.000
1981	23801.790	9734.482	0.000
1982	311.309	13904.026	0.000
1983	−18387.854	17047.828	350.182
1984	−33176.097	18529.671	381.874
1985	−42890.709	17903.877	409.799
1986	−49954.218	16892.739	932.365
1987	−52461.101	16263.804	1130.191
1988	−55596.050	15296.033	1161.109
1989	−57190.454	13411.956	1349.977
1990	−58134.560	10767.518	1487.271
1991	−58857.002	7910.025	1648.278
1992	−62325.187	4284.953	1380.887
1993	−62143.559	1698.934	1321.890
1994	−60361.396	−442.609	909.944
1995	−59323.376	−1330.389	926.484

metric social welfare is positive, reaching a maximum of $18.530 billion dollars in 1987. Reforming the windfall profits tax produces no gains in efficiency for the years 1980, 1981, and 1982, but produces relative modest efficiency gains for the period 1983–1995. Money metric efficiency is higher for elimination of the windfall profits tax than for reform of this tax for the period 1981–1993.

Gains in potential welfare under a policy of eliminating the windfall profits tax are greater than under continued controls or under reform of the windfall profits tax for the period 1982–1994. Current policy results in lower efficiency than a policy of elimination of the windfall profits tax, except for 1980. A common practice in welfare economics is to recommend the policy with the greatest efficiency. On these grounds the policy of elimination of the windfall profits tax would be judged superior to current policy and to continued controls and reform of the windfall profits tax.

We next consider money measures of equity for all three alternatives to current regulatory policy. Money metric equity is defined as the difference between actual and potential gains in social welfare resulting from a change in regulatory and fiscal policy. Money metric equity, unlike money metric efficiency, depends on the degree of aversion to inequality ρ. We have found, as before, that the qualitative features of comparisons among alternative policies are almost identical for different values of this parameter, so that we present money metric equity for the three alternatives to current regulatory policy in table 4.6 for degree of aversion to inequality ρ equal to one.

Money metric equity for a policy of continued petroleum price controls is negative for 1980 and 1981 and positive for the remainder of the period 1982–1995, reaching a level of $30.741 billion dollars in 1995. By contrast a policy of eliminating the windfall profits tax improves equity in 1980 and after 1992, but worsens equity for the period 1981–1993. A policy of reforming the windfall profits taxes worsens equity through the period covered by our study.

Finally, by comparing the results presented in tables 4.4 and 5.5 we can see that money metric efficiency and equity can move in the same direction or in opposite directions. For example, a policy of eliminating the windfall profits tax is preferred to all other policies for the period 1982–1993. During the period 1982–1993 money metric efficiency under elimination of the windfall profits tax dominates that for the alternative policies. However, money metric equity under elimi-

Table 4.6
Money metric equity (millions of current dollars)

Year	Continued controls	No tax	Reformed tax
1980	−13345.166	538.637	0.000
1981	−9511.871	−4225.283	0.000
1982	1420.713	−6067.762	0.000
1983	10001.602	−7405.616	−152.181
1984	16849.254	−8005.630	−160.443
1985	21380.025	−7678.917	−165.597
1986	24700.906	−7193.029	−406.133
1987	25930.005	−6859.612	−493.261
1988	27430.094	−6363.025	−500.878
1989	28237.070	−5479.394	−585.763
1990	28756.755	−4265.782	−646.723
1991	29145.867	−2966.579	−721.575
1992	30741.014	−1307.699	−597.101
1993	30699.465	−144.894	−573.155
1994	29983.545	809.679	−387.051
1995	29556.429	1198.601	−397.834

nation of the tax is lower than that for current policy, for continued controls and for reform of the tax for the period 1982–1992.

To summarize: We have translated comparisons among alternative policies for petroleum price regulation and taxation into money measures of social welfare. Money metric social welfare for a policy of eliminating the windfall profits tax is higher than for any of the alternative policies we have considered. Finally, we have decomposed money metric social welfare into money metric equity and money metric efficiency. We have found that money metric equity and money metric efficiency are both essential to the determination of money metric social welfare.

4.8   Summary and Conclusion

We can summarize our approach to the general equilibrium analysis of economic policy as follows: First we introduce a measure of individual welfare based on the indirect utility function for each consuming unit. We assume that individual welfare is equal to the logarithm of the translog indirect utility function (4.2.22). The indirect utility function enables us to express individual welfare in terms of the price system and the level of total expenditure.

In section 4.2 we show how the translog indirect utility function can be determined from a system of individual expenditure shares (4.2.5) that is integrable. We also demonstrate how the individual expenditure shares (4.2.5) can be recovered uniquely from the system of aggregate expenditure shares (4.2.25). In section 4.3 we fit an econometric model of aggregate consumer behavior that incorporates the restrictions implied by integrability of the individual expenditure shares.

In section 4.4 we employ the translog individual expenditure function (4.2.23) to translate changes in individual welfare into money metric individual welfare. Money metric individual welfare provides a monotone increasing transformation of individual welfare that is not fully comparable among consuming units. This measure can be used in evaluating economic policies by constructing partial orderings of these policies based on the Pareto principle. We illustrate the application of money metric individual welfare by analyzing the impact of alternative policies for regulation and taxation of domestic petroleum production in the United States.

A complete ordering of economic policies requires a social welfare function. In section 4.5 we have introduced a class of social welfare functions capable of expressing a variety of ethical judgements. This class is based on the distribution of individual welfare over the population of consuming units. In measuring social welfare we require cardinal measures of individual welfare that are fully comparable among units. For this purpose we employ translog indirect utility functions for all units.

In section 4.6 we introduce a social expenditure function. This function can be used to translate changes in social welfare into money metric social welfare. The concept of money metric social welfare can be used in comparing alternative economic policies on the basis of the aggregate expenditure required for each policy. In addition, we introduce the maximum level of social welfare that can be attained by lump sum redistributions of aggregate expenditure among consuming units as a measure of efficiency. Using this measure, we can decompose money metric social welfare into the sum of money metric equity and money metric efficiency.

In section 4.7 we compare the impact of alternative policies for regulation and taxation of domestic petroleum production in the United States on social welfare. We find that continued controls would produce gains in equity, but that these would be offset by losses in efficiency, resulting in a loss in social welfare. By contrast dropping the windfall profits tax would produce gains in efficiency that outweigh losses in equity, resulting in a gain in social welfare.

The approach to general equilibrium analysis of economic policy we have presented has been fruitful in generating interesting and useful applications. However, a great deal of important and worthwhile research remains to be done. Completion of this line of research promises to restore normative economics to its rightful place—as an equal partner of positive economics in the general equilibrium analysis of economic policies.

5

Aggregate Consumer Behavior and Household Equivalence Scales

Dale W. Jorgenson and
Daniel T. Slesnick

This chapter presents estimates of household equivalence scales broken down by demographic characteristics of U.S. households. Separate estimates are given by family size, age of head, region, race, and urban versus rural residence. Commodity-specific scales are presented for five separate commodity groups—energy, food, consumer goods, capital services, and other services. The estimates are obtained from an econometric model of aggregate consumer behavior. The parameters of this model are estimated by combining aggregate time-series and individual cross-section data.

5.1 Introduction

Household equivalence scales provide an economical way of incorporating the impact of demographic change into models for the allocation of aggregate consumer expenditure. Equivalence scales are also useful in welfare economics for comparing levels of welfare among households with different demographic characteristics. In this chapter we provide a novel methodology for estimating household equivalence scales by combining time-series and cross-section observations.

Our first objective is to represent preferences for consuming units in a form suitable for estimating equivalence scales. For this purpose we take households rather than individuals as consuming units. We assume that household expenditures on individual commodities are allocated so as to maximize a household social welfare function. As a consequence, the household behaves in the same way as an individual maximizing a utility function, as demonstrated by Samuelson (1956) and Pollak (1981).

Differences in preferences among consuming units can be incorporated into the representation of preferences by means of commodity-specific household equivalence scales. Following Barten (1964), we take utility to be a function of effective quantities consumed for all commodities. Effective quantities are defined as ratios of actual quantities to the corresponding equivalence scales. The same utility function is used to characterize the preferences of all consuming units. This results in a parsimonious description of demographic effects on expenditure allocation.

Consumer equilibrium implies the existence of an indirect utility function for each consuming unit. The indirect utility function gives the level of utility as a function of actual prices of individual commodities, household equivalence scales, and total expenditure. Under the assumption that the utility function is the same for all consuming units, the indirect utility function can be taken to be the same function of effective prices and total expenditure for all units, where effective prices are defined as products of actual prices and the corresponding household equivalence scales.

To compare levels of individual welfare among consuming units, we find it useful to combine commodity-specific household equivalence scales into a general household equivalence scale. Following Deaton and Muellbauer (1980b, 1986), we define a general scale in terms of the expenditure required for each consuming unit to attain a stipulated level of individual welfare. The problem that remains is to derive an empirical representation of commodity-specific and general household equivalence scales for all consuming units.

The analysis of the impact of demographic characteristics of households on expenditure patterns was initiated by Engel (1895). He specified that expenditure on each commodity per household equivalent member is a function of total expenditure per household equivalent member. This approach, while suggestive, is excessively restrictive, because it does not permit commodity-specific demographic effects.

Prais and Houthakker (1971) have generalized Engel's approach by introducing both commodity-specific household equivalence scales and a general scale for deflating total expenditure. Muellbauer (1980) showed that the Prais-Houthakker specification does not permit substitution among commodities, since it requires fixed proportions among commodity groups. More fundamentally, the Prais-Houthakker specification is characterized by an identification problem. The general household equivalence scale is not defined in terms of commodity-specific scales, as in Barten's specification.

Muellbauer (1974a) has shown that commodity-specific household equivalence scales introduced by Barten cannot be identified from cross-section data alone. Identification is achieved by introducing price variation among observations. This approach was implemented by Muellbauer (1977) using PIGL and PIGLOG demand systems and by Muellbauer and Pashardes (1982) and Ray (1982) using the AIDS specification of Deaton and Muellbauer (1980b). These estimates are based on a time series of cross-section observations on individual expenditure patterns for the United Kingdom.

Household equivalence scales were discussed by Gorman (1976), Lazear and Michael (1980), and Muellbauer (1974a), among many others. Empirical evidence on the impact of demographic characteristics on expenditure allocation was given by Lau, Lin, and Yotopoulos (1978), Muellbauer (1977), Parks and Barten (1973), and Pollak and Wales (1980, 1981). Comparisons of welfare levels among households by means of equivalence scales was discussed by Deaton and Muellbauer (1980b, esp. pp. 205–212). Pollak and Wales (1979) have pointed out important limitations of these comparisons.

The first step in estimating household equivalence scales is to derive a system of individual demand functions from the indirect utility function for each consuming unit. For this purpose, we represent the level of utility as a function of the actual prices of all commodities, total expenditure, and attributes of the consuming unit such as demographic characteristics that are associated with differences in preferences among units. Given the indirect utility function for each consuming unit, we can construct the corresponding system of individual demand functions by means of Roy's (1943) Identity.

Following Jorgenson, Lau and Stoker (1980, 1981, 1982), section 5.2 we develop an econometric model of aggregate consumer behavior based on the theory of exact aggregation. Our approach combines time-series data on prices and aggregate quantities consumed and cross-section data on individual quantities consumed, individual total expenditures, and attributes of individual households, such as demographic characteristics. We define commodity-specific and general household equivalence scales in terms of this econometric model.

In section 5.3 we outline the estimation and identification of our econometric model of aggregate consumer behavior. We first specify the stochastic structure of models for individual cross-section data and aggregate time-series data. We show that identification of household equivalence scales requires price variation among observations. We estimate unknown parameters of our model by the nonlinear three stage least squares (NL3SLS) method for pooling cross-section and time-series data proposed by Jorgenson and Stoker (1986).

In section 5.4 we implement our econometric model of aggregate consumer behavior. We employ cross-section data on individual expenditures for the year 1973 from the 1972–1973 Survey of Consumer Expenditures. We combine these data with time-series data on aggregate expenditures from the U.S. National Income and Product Accounts for the years 1947 to 1982. We also employ time-series data on the distribution of total expenditures over all households and among demographic groups based on the Current Population Survey.

In section 5.5 we present household equivalence scales for individual households, classified by demographic characteristics such as family size, age of head, region, race, and urban versus rural residence. We present commodity-specific equivalence scales for energy, food, other consumer goods, capital services, and other consumer services. We also present general household equivalence scales for demographic groups.

5.2   Aggregate Consumer Behavior

To construct an econometric model based on exact aggregation, we first represent individual preferences by means of an indirect utility function for each consuming unit, using the following notation:

p_n — price of the nth commodity, assumed to be the same for all consuming units.

$p = (p_1, p_2, \ldots, p_N)$ — the vector of prices of all commodities.

x_{nk} — the quantity of the nth commodity group consumed by the kth consuming unit ($n = 1, 2, \ldots, N$; $k = 1, 2, \ldots, K$).

$M_k = \sum_{n=1}^{N} p_n x_{nk}$ — total expenditure of the kth consuming unit ($k = 1, 2, \ldots, K$).

$w_{nk} = p_n x_{nk} / M_k$ — expenditure share of the nth commodity group in the budget of the kth consuming unit ($n = 1, 2, \ldots, N$; $k = 1, 2, \ldots, K$).

$w_k = (w_{1k}, w_{2k}, \ldots, w_{Nk})$ — vector of expenditure shares for the kth consuming unit ($k = 1, 2, \ldots, K$).

$\ln(p/M_k) = (\ln(p_1/M_k), \ln(p_2/M_k), \ldots, \ln(p_N/M_k))$ — vector of logarithms of ratios of prices to expenditure by the kth consuming unit ($k = 1, 2, \ldots, K$).

$\ln p = (\ln p_1, \ln p_2, \ldots, \ln p_N)$ — vector of logarithms of prices.

A_k — vector of attributes of the kth consuming unit ($k = 1, 2, \ldots, K$).

We assume that the kth consuming unit allocates expenditures in accord with the transcendental logarithmic or translog indirect utility function, introduced by Christensen, Jorgenson and Lau (1975) and discussed by Jorgenson and Lau (1975). The indirect utility function, say V_k, takes the form

$$\ln V_k = \ln\left(\frac{p}{M_k}\right)' \alpha_p + \frac{1}{2} \ln\left(\frac{p}{M_k}\right)' B_{pp} \ln\left(\frac{p}{M_k}\right) + \ln\left(\frac{p}{M_k}\right)' B_{pA} A_k ,$$

$$(k = 1, 2, \ldots, K) . \qquad (5.2.1)$$

In this representation differences among consumers are introduced through the attribute vector A_k. The vector α_p and the matrices B_{pp} and B_{pA} are constant parameters that are the same for all consuming units. Alternative representations of the effects of prices and total expenditure on expenditure allocation were summarized by Barten (1977), Deaton and Muellbauer (1980b, pp. 60–85), and Lau (1977a).

The expenditure shares of the kth consuming unit can be derived by the logarithmic form of Roy's (1943) Identity

$$w_{nk} = \frac{\partial \ln V_k}{\partial \ln (p_n/M_k)} \Big/ \sum_{n=1}^{N} \frac{\partial \ln V_k}{\partial \ln (p_n/M_k)} , \quad (n = 1, 2, \ldots, N;$$

$$k = 1, 2, \ldots, K) . \qquad (5.2.2)$$

Applying this Identity to the translog indirect utility function (5.2.1), we obtain the system of individual expenditure shares

$$w_k = \frac{1}{D_k(p)}\left(\alpha_p + B_{pp} \ln\left(\frac{p}{M_k}\right) + B_{pA} A_k\right), \quad (k = 1, 2, \ldots, K) , \qquad (5.2.3)$$

where the denominators $\{D_k\}$ take the form

$$D_k = i'\alpha_p + i' B_{pp} \ln\left(\frac{p}{M_k}\right) + i' B_{pA} A_k , \quad (k = 1, 2, \ldots, K) . \qquad (5.2.4)$$

The individual expenditure shares are homogeneous of degree zero in the unknown parameters—α_p, B_{pp}, B_{pA}. By multiplying a given set of these parameters by a constant we obtain another set of parameters that generates the same system of individual budget shares. Accordingly, we can choose a normalization for the parameters without affecting observed patterns of individual expenditure allocation. We find it convenient to employ the normalization $i'\alpha_p = -1$. Under this restriction any change in the set of unknown parameters will be reflected in changes in individual expenditure patterns.

The conditions for exact aggregation obtained by Lau (1977b, 1982) are that the individual expenditure shares are linear in functions of the attributes $\{A_k\}$ and total expenditures $\{M_k\}$ for all consuming units. These conditions will be satisfied if and only if the terms involving the attributes and expenditures do not appear in the denominators of the expressions given previously for the individual expenditure shares, so $i'B_{pp}i = 0$, and $i'B_{pA} = 0$. The exact aggregation restrictions imply that the denominators $\{D_k\}$ reduce to $D = -1 + i'B_{pp} \ln p$, where the subscript k is no longer required, since the denominator is the same for all consuming units. Under these restrictions the individual expenditure shares can be written as

$$w_k = \frac{1}{D(p)} \, (\alpha_p + B_{pp} \ln p - B_{pp}i \cdot \ln M_k + B_{pA}A_k),$$

$$(k = 1, 2, \ldots, K) . \tag{5.2.5}$$

The individual expenditure shares are linear in the logarithms of expenditures $\{\ln M_k\}$ and in the attributes $\{A_k\}$, as required by exact aggregation.

To construct an econometric model of aggregate consumer behavior based on exact aggregation we obtain aggregate expenditure shares, say w, by multiplying individual expenditure shares (5.2.5) by expenditure for each consuming unit, adding overall consuming units, and dividing by aggregate expenditure, $M = \sum_{k=1}^{K} M_k$:

$$w = \sum M_k w_k / M . \tag{5.2.6}$$

The aggregate expenditure shares can be written

$$w = \frac{1}{D(p)} \left(\alpha_p + B_{pp} \ln p - B_{pp}i \, \frac{\sum M_k \ln M_k}{M} + B_{pA} \, \frac{\sum M_k A_k}{M} \right). \tag{5.2.7}$$

The aggregate expenditure patterns depend on the distribution of expenditure over all consuming units through statistics of the joint distribution of expenditures and attributes—$\sum M_k \ln M_k / M$ and $\{\sum M_k A_k / M\}$.

To provide a basis for determining household equivalence scales, we find it useful to represent household preferences by means of a utility function that is the same for all consuming units. We assume that the kth consuming unit maximizes its utility, say U_k, where

$$U_k = U\left[\frac{x_{1k}}{m_1(A_k)}, \frac{x_{2k}}{m_2(A_k)}, \ldots, \frac{x_{Nk}}{m_N(A_k)}\right], \qquad (k = 1, 2, \ldots, K), \qquad (5.2.8)$$

subject to the budget constraint

$$M_k = \sum_{n=1}^{N} p_n x_{nk}, \qquad (k = 1, 2, \ldots, K).$$

In this representation of consumer preferences the quantities $\{x_{nk}/m_n(A_k)\}$ can be regarded as *effective quantities consumed*, as proposed by Barten (1964). The crucial assumption embodied in this representation is that differences in preferences among consumers enter the utility function U only through differences in the commodity-specific household equivalence scales $\{m_n(A_k)\}$.

Consumer equilibrium implies the existence of an indirect utility function, say V, that is the same for all consuming units. The level of utility for the kth consuming unit, say V_k, depends on the prices of individual commodities, the household equivalence scales, and the level of total expenditure:

$$V_k = V\left[\frac{p_1\, m_1(A_k)}{M_k}, \frac{p_2 m_2(A_k)}{M_k}, \ldots, \frac{p_N m_N(A_k)}{M_k}\right],$$

$$(k = 1, 2, \ldots, K). \qquad (5.2.9)$$

In this representation the prices $\{p_n m_n(A_k)\}$ can be regarded as *effective prices*. Differences in preferences among consuming units enter this indirect utility function only through the household equivalence scales $\{m_n(A_k)\}$ $(k = 1, 2, \ldots, K)$.

To represent the translog indirect utility function (5.2.1) in terms of household equivalence scales, we require some additional notation:

$\ln[pm(A_k)/M_k]$ — vector of logarithms of ratios of effective prices $\{p_n m_n(A_k)\}$ to total expenditure M_k of the kth consuming unit $(k = 1, 2, \ldots, K)$.

$\ln m(A_k) = (\ln m_1(A_k), \ln m_2(A_k), \ldots, \ln m_N(A_k))$ — vector of logarithms of the household equivalence scales of the kth consuming unit $(k = 1, 2, \ldots, K)$.

We assume, as before, that the kth consuming unit allocates its expenditures in accord with the translog indirect utility function (5.2.1). We also assume, however, that this function, expressed in terms of the effective prices $\{p_n m_n(A_k)\}$ and total expenditure M_k, is the same for all consuming units. The indirect utility function takes the form

$$\ln V_k = \ln \frac{pm(A_k)'}{M_k} \alpha_p + \frac{1}{2} \ln \frac{pm(A_k)'}{M_k} B_{pp} \ln \frac{pm(A_k)}{M_k} ,$$

$$(k = 1, 2, \ldots, K). \qquad (5.2.10)$$

Taking logarithms of the effective prices $\{p_n m_n(A_k)\}$, we can rewrite the indirect utility function (5.2.10) in the form

$$\ln V_k = \ln m(A_k)' \alpha_p + \frac{1}{2} \ln m(A_k)' B_{pp} \ln m(A_k) + \ln\left(\frac{p}{M_k}\right)' \alpha_p$$

$$+ \frac{1}{2} \ln\left(\frac{p}{M_k}\right)' B_{pp} \ln\left(\frac{p}{M_k}\right) + \ln\left(\frac{p}{M_k}\right)' B_{pp} \ln m(A_k) ,$$

$$(k = 1, 2, \ldots, K) . \qquad (5.2.11)$$

Comparing the indirect utility function (5.2.11) with the function (5.2.1), we see that the term involving ratios of prices to total expenditure and the household equivalence scales must satisfy

$$\ln\left(\frac{p}{M_k}\right)' B_{pA} A_k = \ln\left(\frac{p}{M_k}\right)' B_{pp} \ln m(A_k) , \qquad (k = 1, 2, \ldots, K) , \qquad (5.2.12)$$

for all prices and total expenditure.

The household equivalence scales $\{m_n(A_k)\}$ defined by (5.2.12) must satisfy the equation

$$B_{pA} A_k = B_{pp} \ln m(A_k), \qquad (k = 1, 2, \ldots, K) . \qquad (5.2.13)$$

Under monotonicity of the individual expenditure shares the matrix B_{pp} has an inverse, so that we can express the household equivalence scales in terms of the parameters of the translog indirect utility function—B_{pp}, B_{pA}—and the attributes $\{A_k\}$

$$\ln m(A_k) = B_{pp}^{-1} B_{pA} A_k , \qquad (k = 1, 2, \ldots, K) . \qquad (5.2.14)$$

We can refer to these scales as the *commodity-specific translog household equivalence scales*.

Given the indirect utility function (5.2.11) for each consuming unit, we can express total expenditure as a function of prices, the household equivalence scales, and the level of utility

$$\ln M_k = \frac{1}{D(p)} \left[\ln m(A_k)' \alpha_p + \frac{1}{2} \ln m(A_k)' B_{pp} \ln m(A_k) + \ln p' B_{pp} \ln m(A_k) \right.$$

$$\left. + \ln p' \alpha_p + \frac{1}{2} \ln p' B_{pp} \ln p - \ln V_k \right], \quad (k = 1, 2, \dots, K) . \text{ (5.2.15)}$$

We can refer to this function as the *translog expenditure function*. The translog expenditure function gives the minimum expenditure required for the kth consuming unit to achieve the individual welfare level V_k, given prices p $(k = 1, 2, \dots, K)$.

We find it useful to introduce household equivalence scales that are not specific to a given commodity. Following Deaton and Muellbauer (1980b, 1986), we define a general household equivalence scale, say m_0, as follows

$$m_0 = M_k[pm(A_k), V_k^0]/M_0(p, V_k^0), \quad (k = 1, 2, \dots, K), \quad (5.2.16)$$

where M_k is the expenditure function for the kth household, M_0 is the expenditure function for a reference household with commodity-specific equivalence scales equal to unity for all commodities, and $p[m(A_k)]$ is a vector of effective prices $\{p_n m_n(A_k)\}$.

The general household equivalence scale m_0 is the ratio between total expenditures required by the kth household and by the reference household required for the same level of utility V_k^0 $(k = 1, 2, \dots, K)$. This scale can be interpreted as the number of household equivalent members. The number of members depends on the attributes A_k of the consuming unit and on the prices p.

If each household has a translog indirect utility function, then the general household equivalence scale for the kth household takes the form

$$\ln m_0 = \ln M_k - \ln M_0$$

$$= \frac{1}{D(p)} \left[\ln m(A_k)' \alpha_p + \frac{1}{2} \ln m(A_k)' B_{pp} \ln m(A_k) + \ln m(A_k)' B_{pp} \ln p \right],$$

$$(k = 1, 2, \dots K) . \quad (5.2.17)$$

We can refer to this scale as the *general translog household equivalence scale*. The translog equivalence scale depends on the attributes A_k of the kth household and the prices p of all commodities, but is independent of the level of utility V_k^0.

Given the general translog equivalence scale, we can rewrite the indirect utility function (5.2.11) in the form

$$\ln V_k = \ln p'\alpha_p + \frac{1}{2} \ln p' B_{pp} \ln p - D(p) \ln [M_k/m_0(p, A_k)],$$

$$(k = 1, 2, \ldots, K). \tag{5.2.18}$$

The level of utility for the kth consuming unit depends on prices p and total expenditure per household equivalent member $M_k/m_0(p, A_k)$ $(k = 1, 2, \ldots, K)$. Similarly, we can rewrite the expenditure function (5.2.15) in the form

$$\ln M_k = \frac{1}{D(p)} \left[\ln p' \left(\alpha_p + \frac{1}{2} B_{pp} \ln p \right) - \ln V_k \right] + \ln m_0(p, A_k). \tag{5.2.19}$$

Total expenditure required by the kth consuming unit to attain the level of utility V_k depends on prices p and the number of household equivalent members $m_0(p, A_k)$ $(k = 1, 2, \ldots, K)$.

5.3   Identification and Estimation

In this section we outline the implementation of the econometric model of aggregate consumer behavior presented in section 5.2. This model is generated from a translog indirect utility function for each consuming unit. We formulate an econometric model of consumer behavior by adding a stochastic component to the equations for the individual expenditure shares. We associate this component with unobservable random disturbances at the level of the individual consuming unit.

To represent our econometric model we first introduce some additional notation. We consider observations on expenditure patterns by K consuming units, indexed by $k = 1, 2, \ldots, K$, for T time periods, indexed by $t = 1, 2, \ldots, T$:

p_{nt} — price of the nth commodity in the tth time period, assumed to be the same for all consuming units $(n = 1, 2, \ldots, N; t = 1, 2, \ldots, T)$.

$p_t = (p_{1t}, p_{2t}, \ldots, p_{Nt})$ — the vector of prices of all commodities in the tth time period $(t = 1, 2, \ldots, T)$.

M_{kt} — total expenditure for the kth consuming unit in the tth time period $(k = 1, 2, \ldots, K; t = 1, 2, \ldots, T)$.

w_{nkt} — expenditure share of the nth commodity group in the budget of the kth consuming unit in the tth time period ($n = 1, 2, \ldots, N$; $k = 1, 2, \ldots, K$; $t = 1, 2, \ldots, T$).

w_{kt} — vector of expenditure shares for the kth consuming unit in the tth time period ($k = 1, 2, \ldots, K$; $t = 1, 2, \ldots, T$).

$\ln p_t / M_{kt}$ — vector of logarithms of ratios of prices to expenditure by the kth consuming unit in the tth time period ($k = 1, 2, \ldots, K$; $t = 1, 2, \ldots, T$).

$\ln p_t$ — vector of logarithms of prices in the tth time period ($t = 1, 2, \ldots, T$).

Using our new notation the individual expenditure shares for all commodities can be written as

$$w_{kt} = \frac{1}{D_t} [\alpha_p + B_{pp} \ln p_t - B_{pp} i \ln M_{kt} + B_{pn} A_k] + \mu_{kt} ,$$

$$(k = 1, 2, \ldots, K; \ t = 1, 2, \ldots, T), \qquad (5.3.1)$$

where

$$D_t = -1 + B_{pp} i \ln p_t, \qquad (t = 1, 2, \ldots, T),$$

and μ_{kt} ($k = 1, 2, \ldots, K$; $t = 1, 2, \ldots, T$) is the vector of unobservable random disturbances for the kth consuming unit and the tth time period. Since the individual expenditure shares sum to unity for each consuming unit in each time period

$$i' \mu_{kt} = 0, \quad (k = 1, 2, \ldots, K; t = 1, 2, \ldots, T), \qquad (5.3.2)$$

the disturbances are not distributed independently.

We assume that the unobservable random disturbances for all commodities have expected value equal to zero for all observations

$$E(\mu_{kt}) = 0, \quad (k = 1, 2, \ldots, K; t = 1, 2, \ldots, T) . \qquad (5.3.3)$$

We also assume that these disturbances have the same covariance matrix for all observations

$$V(\mu_{kt}) = \Omega_\mu, \quad (k = 1, 2, \ldots, K; t = 1, 2, \ldots, T).$$

Since the disturbances sum to zero for each observation, this matrix is nonnegative definite with rank at most equal to $N - 1$. We assume that the covariance matrix has rank equal to $N - 1$. Finally, we assume that disturbances corresponding to distinct observations are uncorrelated. Under this assumption the covariance matrix of the disturbances for all commodities at a given point of time has a Kronecker product form for all consuming units. The covariance matrix of the disturbances for all time periods has a similar form for a given consuming unit.

The data for individual consuming units and for the aggregate of all consuming units are based on the same definitions, but the aggregate data are not obtained by summing over the data for individuals. Individual observations are based on a random sample from the population of all consuming units, while aggregate observations are constructed from data on production of all commodities and on consumption by households and other consuming units such as businesses, governments, and the rest of the world. Accordingly, we introduce an additional source of random error in the equations for the aggregate expenditure shares, corresponding to errors of measurement.

Denoting the vector of aggregate expenditure shares at time t by w_t $(t = 1, 2, \ldots, T)$, we can express these shares in the form

$$
w_t = \frac{1}{D_t} \left[\alpha_p + B_{pp} \ln p_t + B_{pp} i \, \frac{\sum M_{kt} \ln M_{kt}}{\sum M_{kt}} + B_{pA} \, \frac{\sum M_{kt} A_k}{\sum M_{kt}} \right] + \mu_t \,,
$$

$$
(t = 1, 2, \ldots, T) \,, \tag{5.3.4}
$$

where μ_t $(t = 1, 2, \ldots, T)$ is the vector of unobservable random disturbances for the tth time period. The aggregate disturbances can be expressed in the form

$$
\mu_t = \frac{\sum_{k=1}^{K} M_{kt} \, \mu_{kt}}{\sum_{k=1}^{K} M_{kt}} + \frac{\sum_{k=1}^{K} M_{kt} \, \eta_{kt}}{\sum_{k=1}^{K} M_{kt}} \,, \qquad (t = 1, 2, \ldots, T), \tag{5.3.5}
$$

where η_{kt} $(k = 1, 2, \ldots, K; t = 1, 2, \ldots, T)$ is the vector of errors of measurement for all commodities. Since the random disturbances sum to zero for each individual in each time period

$$
i' \eta_{kt} = 0, \qquad (k = 1, 2, \ldots, K; t = 1, 2, \ldots, T), \tag{5.3.6}
$$

these disturbances are not distributed independently.

We assume that the errors of measurement that underlie the data on the aggregate expenditure shares for all commodities have expected value equal to zero for all observations

$E(\eta_{kt}) = 0, \quad (k = 1, 2, \ldots, K; t = 1, 2, \ldots, T).$

We also assume that these errors have the same covariance matrix for all observations

$V(\eta_{kt}) = \Omega_\eta, \quad (k = 1, 2, \ldots, K; t = 1, 2, \ldots, T).$

and that the rank of this matrix is equal to $N - 1$.

If the errors of measurement are distributed independently of total expenditure and of the disturbances in the equations for the individual expenditure shares of all commodities, the aggregate disturbances have expected value equal to zero for all time periods

$$E(\mu_t) = 0, \qquad (t = 1, 2, \ldots, T), \tag{5.3.7}$$

and have a covariance matrix given by

$$V(\mu_t) = \frac{\sum_{k=1}^{K} M_{kt}^2}{\left(\sum_{k=1}^{K} M_{kt}\right)^2} \Omega_\mu + \frac{\sum_{k=1}^{K} M_{kt}^2}{\left(\sum_{k=1}^{K} M_{kt}\right)^2} \Omega_\eta, \qquad (t = 1, 2, \ldots, T),$$

so that the aggregate disturbances for different time periods are heteroscedastic.

We can correct the aggregate disturbances for heteroscedasticity by transforming the observations on the aggregate expenditure shares as follows

$$\rho_t \, w_t = \frac{\rho_t}{D_t}\left[\alpha_p + B_{pp} \ln p_t - B_{pp}i \frac{\sum M_{kt} \ln M_{kt}}{\sum M_{kt}} + B_{pA} \frac{\sum M_{kt} A_k}{\sum M_{kt}}\right] + \rho_t \mu_t \,,$$

$$(t = 1, 2, \ldots, T), \tag{5.3.8}$$

where

$$\rho_t^2 = \left(\sum_{k=1}^{K} M_{kt}\right)^2 \Big/ \sum_{k=1}^{K} M_{kt}^2, \qquad (t = 1, 2, \ldots, T).$$

The covariance matrix of the transformed disturbances, say Ω, becomes $V(\rho_t \mu_t) = \Omega_\mu + \Omega_\eta = \Omega$. This matrix is nonnegative definite with rank equal to $N - 1$; we assume that errors of measurement corresponding to distinct observations are uncorrelated. Under this assumption the covariance matrix of the transformed disturbances at all points of time has a Kronecker product form.

We can now discuss the identification and estimation of the model of aggregate consumer behavior, combining cross-section observations on individual expenditure patterns with time-series observations on aggregate expenditure patterns. We first consider a random sample of observations on individual expenditures on all commodities at a given point of time. The model for individual expenditures (5.3.1) takes the form

$$-w_k = \delta_p - B_{pp}i \ln M_k + B_{pA}A_k + \mu_k , \qquad (k = 1, 2, \dots, K) , \qquad (5.3.9)$$

where we drop the time subscript. The prices for all commodities are the same for all consumers. We assume that the data matrix with $(1, \ln M_k, A_k)$ as its kth row is of full rank.

The parameters δ_p, $B_{pp}i$, and B_{pA} are identified in the cross section. Moreover, the model (5.3.9) is a multivariate regression model, except that the vector μ_k has a singular distribution. If this vector is normally distributed, the maximum likelihood estimator (MLE) is obtained by dropping one equation and estimating the remaining $N - 1$ equations by maximum likelihood. Estimates of the parameters of the omitted equation are derived from estimates of the parameters for the $N - 1$ equations not omitted. This results in a linear, multivariate regression model, so the unique, minimum variance, unbiased estimator of the unknown parameters is obtained by applying ordinary least squares (OLS) to each equation separately.

We can write the cross-section model (5.3.9) in the form

$$y_1 = X \beta_1 + \varepsilon_1 , \qquad y_2 = X \beta_2 + \varepsilon_2 ,$$

$$y_{N-1} = X\beta_{N-1} + \varepsilon_{N-1} , \qquad (5.3.10)$$

where y_i $(i = 1, 2, \dots, N - 1)$ is the vector of observations on the individual expenditure shares of the ith commodity for all individuals, X is a matrix of observations on the independent variables, and ε_i $(i = 1, 2, \dots, N - 1)$ is a vector of unobservable random disturbances.

We can stack the equations in (5.3.10) in the usual way, obtaining

$$y = [I \otimes X] \beta + \varepsilon , \qquad (5.3.11)$$

where $\otimes$ is the Kronecker product and

$$
y = \begin{bmatrix} y_1 \\ y_2 \\ \vdots \\ y_{N-1} \end{bmatrix}, \qquad \beta = \begin{bmatrix} \beta_1 \\ \beta_2 \\ \vdots \\ \beta_{N-1} \end{bmatrix}, \qquad \varepsilon = \begin{bmatrix} \varepsilon_1 \\ \varepsilon_2 \\ \vdots \\ \varepsilon_{N-1} \end{bmatrix}. \tag{5.3.12}
$$

The matrix X is of full rank and the random vector ε is distributed normally with mean zero and covariance matrix $\Sigma_\varepsilon \otimes I$, where Σ_ε is obtained from the covariance matrix Ω_ε by striking the row and column corresponding to the omitted equation.

The MLE of the vector of parameters β from the cross-section model is

$$
\hat{\beta} = [I \otimes (X'X)^{-1} X'] \, y, \tag{5.3.13}
$$

which is equivalent to the least squares estimator applied to each equation individually. This estimator has covariance matrix

$$
V(\hat{\beta}) = \Sigma_\varepsilon \otimes (X'X)^{-1}. \tag{5.3.14}
$$

The LS estimator is a consistent estimator of the vector of unknown parameters β; the probability limit of this estimator as the number of cross-section observations K tends to infinity is equal to β.

Our model of aggregate consumer behavior is given by the vector equation (5.3.4). To estimate the parameters of this model we can employ time-series observations on the prices of all commodities p_t, statistics of the joint distribution of total expenditures and attributes $\sum M_{kt} \ln M_{kt} / \sum M_{kt}$ and $\sum M_{kt} A_k / \sum M_{kt}$, and the heteroscedasticity adjustment ρ_t $(t = 1, 2, \dots, T)$. This model might appear to be a nonlinear regression model with additive errors. Prices of all commodities may be treated as endogenous, however, so we can consider limited information techniques using instrumental variables. We introduce a sufficient number of instrumental variables to identify all parameters. As before, we drop one equation to deal with the singularity of the distribution of the disturbance vector.

We can write the model for aggregate expenditure shares of all commodities (5.3.4) in the form

$$
v_1 = f_1(\beta, \gamma) + v_1, \qquad v_2 = f_2(\beta, \gamma) + v_2, \tag{5.3.15}
$$
$$
v_{N-1} = f_{N-1}(\beta, \gamma) + v_{N-1},
$$

where v_i $(i = 1, 2, \ldots, N - 1)$ is the vector of observations on the aggregate expenditure shares of the ith commodity for all time periods, transformed to eliminate heteroscedasticity, f_i $(i = 1, 2, \ldots, N - 1)$ is a vector of nonlinear functions of the parameters β that enter the cross-section model and the vector of parameters γ that enter the time-series model and v_i $(i = 1, 2, \ldots, N - 1)$ is a vector of unobservable random disturbances, transformed to eliminate heteroscedasticity.

As before, we can stack the equations in (5.3.15), obtaining

$$
\begin{aligned}
v &= f(\beta, \gamma) + v , \\
&= f(\delta) + v ,
\end{aligned}
\tag{5.3.16}
$$

where

$$
v = \begin{bmatrix} v_1 \\ v_2 \\ \vdots \\ v_{N-1} \end{bmatrix}, \quad
f = \begin{bmatrix} f_1 \\ f_2 \\ \vdots \\ f_{N-1} \end{bmatrix}, \quad
\delta = \begin{bmatrix} \beta \\ \gamma \end{bmatrix}, \quad
v = \begin{bmatrix} v_1 \\ v_2 \\ \vdots \\ v_{N-1} \end{bmatrix}.
\tag{5.3.17}
$$

By the assumptions listed previously, the random vector v is distributed normally with mean zero and covariance matrix $\Sigma_v \otimes I$, where Σ_v is obtained from the covariance matrix Ω by striking the row and column corresponding to the omitted equation.

NL3SLS introduced by Jorgenson and Laffont (1974) can be employed to estimate all parameters of the model of aggregate expenditures, provided that the parameters are identified. A necessary condition for identification is that

$$
(N - 1)(1 + P)[(N + 1)N/2] - 1 < (N - 1) \min(V, T)
\tag{5.3.18}
$$

where N is the number of commodities, P is the number of components of the attribute vector A_k, and V is the number of instrumental variables for the aggregate model. The instruments for the cross section are the microdata themselves; for the aggregate model we employ the list of instrumental variables given in appendix A. The left side of (5.3.18) is the number of free parameters in the aggregate model and the right side is the total number of instruments, assuming that no multicollinearity exists among the instruments. This condition fails to hold in our application, so that not all parameters are identified in the model for aggregate expenditures.

We next consider methods of estimation using individual cross-section data together with aggregate time-series data to obtain identification. Cross-section data can be used to identify the constants δ_p, the coefficients of total expenditure $B_{pp}i$, and the demographic coefficients B_{pA}. The price coefficients B_{pp} must be identified from aggregate time-series data. A necessary condition for identification of these parameters is

$$\frac{1}{2}(N-1)(N+1) < (N-1)\min(V,T). \tag{5.3.19}$$

This condition is met in our application. Sufficient conditions for identification are given hereafter.

Estimation of the complete model requires the method of NL3SLS for pooling time-series and cross-section data introduced by Jorgenson and Stoker (1986). Our objective is* to estimate the unknown parameters—α_p, B_{pp}, and B_{pA}—subject to the restrictions implied by integrability. The pooled NL3SLS estimator is found by minimizing the following with respect to the vector unknown parameters δ

$$SSR\ (\delta) = [y - Y\delta]'[\hat{\Sigma}_\varepsilon^{-1} \otimes I][y - Y\delta]$$

$$+ [v - f(\delta)]'[\hat{\Sigma}^{-1} \otimes Z(Z'Z)^{-1}Z'][v - f(\delta)] \tag{5.3.20}$$

where

$$Y = \begin{bmatrix} I \otimes X & 0 \\ 0 & 0 \end{bmatrix}.$$

is a matrix of observations on the independent variables in (5.3.11) and Z is a matrix of instrumental variables for the aggregate model (5.3.16).

We choose estimates that minimize the objective function (5.3.20), subject to constraints implied by integrability. These constraints were described in detail by Jorgenson and Lau (1979, 1986) and by Jorgenson, Lau, and Stoker (1982). To solve this nonlinear programming problem we employ the SOL/NPSOL algorithm of Gill, Murray, Saunders, and Wright (1983). This algorithm is based on the solution of a nonlinear programming problem by a sequence of quadratic programming problems.

The NL3SLS estimator obtained by minimizing the function (5.3.20), subject to the integrability constraints, is a consistent estimator of the vector of unknown parameters δ. This requires taking the probability limit of the estimator as the number of cross-section observations K and the number of time-series observations T tend to infinity. This estimator has the symptotic covariance matrix

$$V(\hat{\delta}) = \left\{ Y'[\Sigma_\varepsilon^{-1} \otimes I]Y + \frac{\partial f}{\partial \delta}(\delta)'[\Sigma^{-1} \otimes Z[Z'Z]^{-1}Z'] \frac{\partial f}{\partial \delta}(\delta) \right\}^{-1}. \qquad (5.3.21)$$

We obtain a consistent estimator of this matrix by inserting the estimators $\hat{\delta}$, $\hat{\Sigma}_\varepsilon$ and $\hat{\Sigma}$ in place of the parameters δ, Σ_ε and Σ. A necessary and sufficient condition for identifiability of the vector of unknown parameters δ in the model for pooling time-series and cross-section data is the nonsingularity of the following matrix in a neighborhood of the true parameter value

$$Y'[\Sigma_\varepsilon^{-1} \otimes I]Y + \frac{\partial f}{\partial \delta}(\delta)'[\Sigma^{-1} \otimes Z(Z'Z)^{-1}Z'] \frac{\partial f}{\partial \delta}(\delta). \qquad (5.3.22)$$

5.4 Econometric Model

In this section we present the empirical results of implementing the econometric model of consumer behavior described in section 5.2. We divide consumer expenditures among five commodity groups:

1. *Energy*: Expenditures on electricity, natural gas, heating oil, and gasoline.

2. *Food*: Expenditures on all food products, including tobacco and alcohol.

3. *Consumer goods*: Expenditures on all other nondurable goods included in consumer expenditures.

4. *Capital services*: The service flow from consumer durables and the service flow from housing.

5. *Consumer services*: Expenditures on consumer services, such as car repairs, medical services, entertainment, and so on.

We employ the following demographic characteristics as attributes of individual households:

1. *Family size*: 1, 2, 3, 4, 5, 6, and 7 or more persons.

2. *Age of head*: 16–24, 25–34, 35–44, 45–54, 55–64, 65 and over.

3. *Region of residence*: Northeast, North Central, South, and West.

4. *Race*: White, nonwhite.

5. *Type of residence*: Urban, rural.

Our cross-section observations on individual expenditures for each commodity group and on demographic characteristics of individual households are for the year 1973 from the 1972–1973 Survey of Consumer Expenditures (CES) described by Carlson (1974). Our time-series observations are based on data on personal consumption expenditures from the U.S. National Income and Product Accounts (NIPA) for the years 1947 to 1982. We employ data on the flow of services from durable goods rather than purchases of durable goods. Prices for each commodity group are defined in terms of translog price indexes computed from detailed prices included in NIPA for each year. We employ time-series data on the distribution of expenditures over all households and among demographic groups based on *Current Population Reports*, published annually by the Bureau of the Census.

In our application we treat the expenditure shares for five commodity groups as endogenous variables, so we estimate four equations. As unknown parameters we have four elements of the vector α_p, four expenditure coefficients of the vector B_{pA}, and ten price coefficients in the matrix B_{pp}, which is constrained to be symmetric. The expenditure coefficients are sums of price coefficients in the corresponding equation, so we have a total of 82 unknown parameters. We obtain initial estimates of the expenditure and attribute coefficients from the cross-section data alone. The results are given in appendix B. We estimate the complete model, subject to inequality restrictions implied by monotonicity of the individual expenditure shares, by pooling time-series and cross-section data in the same way as Jorgenson, Lau, and Stoker (1982, pp. 175–186). The results are given in appendix A.

The impacts of changes in total expenditures and in demographic characteristics of the individual household are estimated very precisely. This reflects the fact that estimates of the expenditure and demographic effects incorporate a relatively large number of cross-section observations. The impacts of prices enter through the denominator of the equations for expenditure shares; these price coefficients are estimated very precisely since they also incorporate cross-section data. Finally, the price impacts also enter through the numerators of equations for the expenditure shares. These parameters are estimated somewhat less precisely, since they are based on a much smaller number of time-series observations on prices.

5.5   Household Equivalence Scales

We are now in a position to calculate household equivalence scales for any of the 672 household types included in our model. The commodity-specific translog household equivalence scales are calculated using equation (5.2.14). This formula indicates the importance of pooling individual cross-section data and aggregate time-series data to the identification of the commodity-specific equivalence scales. Unless there is price variation in the data, we cannot identify the parameters of the matrix of price coefficients B_{pp}. Without this matrix, estimation of by the formula (5.2.14) of the equivalence scales is impossible.

We begin by considering a consuming unit with head of household aged between 35 and 44 and living in the Northeast. The reference household is one of size four, the head of which is white and living in an urban area. Commodity-specific equivalence scales for each of the five commodities included in our model and the general household equivalence scales are given in table 5.1. The household equivalence scales for the reference household are set equal to unity for all commodities.

The commodity-specific household equivalence scales can be interpreted as the number of members of the household in terms of the consumption of each good. Consequently, one would expect the scales to be monotonically increasing with family size. This is the case for all goods. The commodity-specific translog household equivalence scales for energy, food, consumer goods, capital services, and consumer services increase with each additional member of the family. The increase of family sizes from one to two is less than proportional for energy, food, and consumer services, indicating economies of scale in consumption. Two individuals forming a family of size two do not need twice as much of each of these commodities in order to be as well off as a single person.

The household equivalence scales for consumer goods and capital services indicate diseconomies of scale. An urban, white household of size 2, with the head aged 35–44 years, would have to have 2.32 times as much housing and consumers' durables to produce the same level of effective capital services as a similar household of size 1. The household equivalence scale for consumer goods increases by 2.19 times between family sizes 1 and 2. A household of size 2 requires 2.19 times as many consumer goods to produce the same effective level of consumption.

Table 5.1
Age 35–44, Northeast

	White		Nonwhite	
	Urban	Rural	Urban	Rural
Size 1				
EN	0.75	0.37	0.70	0.35
F	0.33	0.65	0.37	0.74
CG	0.26	0.71	0.32	0.85
K	0.22	0.61	0.31	0.84
CS	0.37	0.57	0.42	0.65
M_{ok}	0.30	0.60	0.37	0.72
Size 2				
EN	0.75	0.38	0.71	0.35
F	0.60	1.19	0.69	1.36
CG	0.57	1.53	0.69	1.85
K	0.51	1.38	0.70	1.90
CS	0.61	0.96	0.69	1.08
M_{ok}	0.58	1.13	0.69	1.35
Size 3				
EN	0.79	0.40	0.75	0.37
F	0.76	1.51	0.88	1.74
CG	0.75	2.02	0.91	2.45
K	0.71	1.92	0.98	2.65
CS	0.76	1.19	0.86	1.35
M_{ok}	0.75	1.45	0.90	1.73
Size 4				
EN	1.00	0.50	0.94	0.47
F	1.00	1.98	1.15	2.28
CG	1.00	2.69	1.21	3.26
K	1.00	2.70	1.38	3.72
CS	1.00	1.56	1.13	1.77
M_{ok}	1.00	1.94	1.20	2.30
Size 5				
EN	1.14	0.57	1.08	0.54
F	1.08	2.14	1.24	2.45
CG	1.04	2.79	1.26	3.38
K	1.06	2.86	1.46	3.94
CS	1.10	1.71	1.24	1.94
M_{ok}	1.07	2.09	1.29	2.47

Table 5.1 (continued)

	White		Nonwhite	
	Urban	Rural	Urban	Rural
Size 6				
EN	1.70	0.85	1.60	0.80
F	1.45	2.88	1.67	3.31
CG	1.36	3.66	1.65	4.43
K	1.51	4.09	2.08	5.63
CS	1.52	2.38	1.73	2.70
M_{ok}	1.48	2.88	1.77	3.41
Size 7				
EN	2.19	1.10	2.06	1.03
F	1.93	3.82	2.21	4.39
CG	1.80	4.84	2.18	5.87
K	2.11	5.71	2.91	7.86
CS	2.03	3.18	2.30	3.60
M_{ok}	1.99	3.86	2.38	4.56

The general translog household equivalence scales are the measures of household size which are critical to welfare comparisons across households with different demographic characteristics. From equation (5.2.18), it is observed that the general equivalence scales indicate the amount that expenditure of the given household must change relative to the reference household in order to attain the same level of utility. The general household equivalence scale increases sharply in moving from one to two individuals and there are relatively smaller increases thereafter. This is a reflection of the fact that, although the second household member is often an adult, additional members are frequently children. Further, the increase in the scale occurs at a slower rate than the increase in the number of family members so there are economies of scale. In other words, less than five times the total expenditure of an unattached individual is needed for a family of five to attain the same level of well-being.

Household equivalence scales by age of head are reported in table 5.2. The impact of age on equivalence scales is through the ages of members of the family such as children. The equivalence scale for food increases monotonically with the age of the head of the household as the children grow up and require more food. When the head of the household is 65 or older, the scale falls, perhaps as a result of both the lower needs of an elderly couple and the children's nominal

Table 5.2
Size 4, Northeast

	White		Nonwhite	
	Urban	Rural	Urban	Rural
Age 16–24				
EN	0.71	0.35	0.67	0.33
F	0.48	0.95	0.55	1.09
CG	0.37	0.99	0.44	1.20
K	0.34	0.91	0.46	1.26
CS	0.51	0.80	0.58	0.91
M_{ok}	0.43	0.84	0.52	1.01
Age 25–34				
EN	0.77	0.39	0.73	0.36
F	0.67	1.34	0.77	1.53
CG	0.62	1.67	0.75	2.02
K	0.58	1.58	0.80	2.17
CS	0.69	1.07	0.78	1.21
M_{ok}	0.64	1.26	0.78	1.50
Age 35–44				
EN	1.00	0.50	0.94	0.47
F	1.00	1.98	1.15	2.28
CG	1.00	2.69	1.21	3.26
K	1.00	2.70	1.38	3.72
CS	1.00	1.56	1.13	1.77
M_{ok}	1.00	1.94	1.20	2.30
Age 45–54				
EN	0.78	0.39	0.74	0.37
F	1.06	2.10	1.21	2.41
CG	1.23	3.31	1.49	4.01
K	1.17	3.16	1.61	4.35
CS	0.99	1.55	1.12	1.75
M_{ok}	1.08	2.07	1.29	2.45
Age 55–64				
EN	0.61	0.31	0.57	0.29
F	1.05	2.09	1.21	2.39
CG	1.37	3.69	1.66	4.47
K	1.24	3.35	1.71	4.62
CS	0.93	1.45	1.05	1.65
M_{ok}	1.08	2.06	1.29	2.43

Table 5.2 (continued)

	White		Nonwhite	
	Urban	Rural	Urban	Rural
Age 65+				
EN	0.67	0.34	0.63	0.32
F	0.88	1.75	1.01	2.01
CG	1.07	2.88	1.30	3.49
K	0.93	2.52	1.28	3.46
CS	0.81	1.27	0.92	1.44
M_{ok}	0.89	1.72	1.07	2.04

attachment to the family. Both consumer goods and capital services follow the same pattern—equivalence scales increase as the age of the head of the household increases. At age 65, there is a drop in the equivalence scales that can be accounted for in the same way as for food.

For the first three age groups, the equivalence scales for energy and consumer services increase slightly. As children get older, they add to the consumption of commodities such as medical and dental services as well as the consumption of fuel for transportation. The estimated household size begins to decline, however, when the head of household reaches the age of 45. This can be explained by the fact that transportation and services play a smaller role as the children grow up and become more independent. Finally, the overall measure of family size given by the general household equivalence scales increases for all age groups until the family head is 65 or over.

Household equivalence scales by region, race, and urban versus rural residence are given in table 5.3. The scales for energy are lower for rural areas as opposed to urban areas for all family sizes. Thus rural families obtain more effective energy than urban families from the same actual quantity of energy. This is undoubtedly the result of rural household's greater needs for transportation. All other commodity-specific household equivalence scales are larger for rural families than for urban families.

For all commodities except energy, families in the South are the "largest" in household equivalent size. Southern families have the largest household equivalence scales for food, consumer goods, capital services, and consumer services and the smallest levels for energy. The families in the West have the smallest equivalence scales for food, consumer goods, capital services, and consumer services. Families in the Northeast have the largest equivalence scales for energy.

Table 5.3
Age 35–44, Size 4

	White		Nonwhite	
	Urban	Rural	Urban	Rural
Northeast				
EN	1.0	0.50	0.94	0.47
F	1.0	1.98	1.15	2.28
CG	1.0	2.69	1.21	3.26
K	1.0	2.70	1.38	3.72
CS	1.0	1.56	1.13	1.77
M_{ok}	1.0	1.94	1.20	2.30
North Central				
EN	0.61	0.31	0.58	0.29
F	1.01	2.00	1.16	2.30
CG	1.16	3.13	1.41	3.79
K	1.12	3.03	1.54	4.17
CS	0.92	1.44	1.04	1.63
M_{ok}	1.01	1.92	1.20	2.28
South				
EN	0.58	0.29	0.55	0.27
F	1.12	2.23	1.29	2.56
CG	1.38	3.72	1.68	4.51
K	1.38	3.72	1.90	5.13
CS	1.00	1.56	1.13	1.77
M_{ok}	1.15	2.17	1.36	2.56
West				
EN	0.99	0.50	0.93	0.47
F	0.80	1.59	0.92	1.82
CG	0.75	2.01	0.90	2.43
K	0.74	2.00	1.02	2.76
CS	0.83	1.30	0.94	1.47
M_{ok}	0.79	1.55	0.95	1.84

Appendix A   Notation for Instrumental Variables, 1947–1982

$I1$ =   constant

$I2$ =   effective tax rate, labor services

$I3$ =   effective tax rate, noncompetitive imports

$I4$ =   time available for labor services

$I5$ =   U.S. population, millions of individuals

$I6$ =   implicit deflator, supply of labor services

$I7$ =   implicit deflator, government purchases of labor services

$I8$ =   exogeneous income, which equals government transfers to persons (excepting social insurance) less personal transfers to foreigners and personal nontax payments to government

$I9$ =   private national wealth, lagged one period

$I10$ =   potential time for labor services; rate of Harrod neutral change

$I11$ =   total imports

$I12$ =   implicit deflator, noncompetitive imports

$I13$ =   corrected deflator for labor services

$I14$ =   time, set to 0 in 1972

Appendix B   Notation for Cross-Section Results

Table 5.B.1
Cross-section results for energy and food

	Energy		Food	
Parameter	Estimate	Standard error	Estimate	Standard error
CONST	−0.2026	0.00853	−0.7087	0.0196
ln M	0.01562	0.000983	0.06360	0.00225
S2	−0.01581	0.00128	−0.02877	0.00294
S3	−0.02150	0.00152	−0.04209	0.00348
S4	−0.02289	0.00161	−0.06460	0.00370
S5	−0.02548	0.00189	−0.07043	0.00433
S6	−0.02524	0.00234	−0.09970	0.00536
S7+	−0.02829	0.00243	−0.1205	0.00556
A25–34	0.002500	0.00177	−0.03491	0.00406
A35–44	0.002091	0.00192	−0.06894	0.00440
A45–54	−0.001935	0.00183	−0.07381	0.00419
A55–64	−0.003437	0.00182	−0.07176	0.00418
A65+	0.002470	0.00179	−0.06420	0.00411
RNC	−0.007384	0.00119	0.01431	0.00274
RS	−0.005951	0.00119	0.004910	0.00273
RW	0.005457	0.00128	0.01192	0.00294
NW	0.004700	0.00149	−0.01343	0.00342
RUR	−0.02980	0.00119	0.001392	0.00273

NOTE: For energy, the standard error is 0.04024 and $R^2 = 0.1407$; for food, the standard error is 0.09225 and $R^2 = 0.1623$.

Table 5.B.2
Cross-section results for consumer goods and capital services

Parameter	Consumer goods		Capital services	
	Estimate	Standard error	Estimate	Standard error
CONST	0.08297	0.00942	−0.5624	0.0233
ln M	−0.01881	0.00109	0.01243	0.00268
S2	0.0004038	0.00142	0.02945	0.00350
S3	−0.003124	0.00167	0.04719	0.00414
S4	−0.004619	0.00178	0.06292	0.00440
S5	−0.005278	0.00208	0.06365	0.00515
S6	−0.008552	0.00258	0.08296	0.00638
S7+	−0.009932	0.00268	0.09511	0.00662
A25–34	0.005329	0.00196	0.03344	0.00483
A35–44	0.005605	0.00212	0.06082	0.00524
A45–54	0.01324	0.00202	0.07282	0.00499
A55–64	0.01864	0.00201	0.07740	0.00497
A65+	0.02199	0.00198	0.05842	0.00489
RNC	−0.0004717	0.00132	0.006494	0.00366
RS	−0.003629	0.00131	0.02360	0.00325
RW	−0.002315	0.00142	−0.01136	0.00350
NW	−0.01545	0.00165	0.03956	0.00407
RUR	−0.005047	0.00131	0.02733	0.03324

NOTE: For consumer goods, the standard error is 0.4445 and R^2 = 0.1077; for capital services, the standard error is 0.1098 and R^2 = 0.1535.

Table 5.B.3
Cross-section results for consumer services

Parameter	Estimate	Standard error
CONST	0.3907	0.0190
ln M	−0.07284	0.00219
S2	0.01473	0.00286
S3	0.01953	0.00338
S4	0.02918	0.00359
S5	0.03754	0.00420
S6	0.05054	0.00521
S7+	0.06362	0.00540
A25–34	−0.006657	0.00395
A35–44	0.004254	0.00428
A45–54	−0.01031	0.00407
A55–64	−0.02083	0.00406
A65+	−0.01869	0.00399
RNC	−0.01295	0.00266
RS	−0.01893	0.00265
RW	−0.003705	0.00286
NW	−0.01537	0.00332
RUR	0.006130	0.00265

NOTE: The standard error is 0.08961 and $R^2 = 0.1359$,

$$\hat{\Sigma}_\varepsilon = \begin{bmatrix} 0.001616 & & & \\ -0.0004492 & 0.008494 & & \\ -0.0001572 & -0.0002804 & 0.001970 & \\ -0.0005068 & -0.005316 & -0.001338 & 0.01203 \end{bmatrix},$$

and the cross-section SSR = 37,108.07.

Table Notation

CONST	=	constant term
ln *M*	=	coefficient of log to total expenditure
S2	=	coefficient of dummy for family of size 2
S3	=	coefficient of dummy for family of size 3
S4	=	coefficient of dummy for family of size 4
S5	=	coefficient of dummy for family of size 5
S6	=	coefficient of dummy for family of size 6
S7+	=	coefficient of dummy for family of size 7 or more
A25–34	=	coefficient of dummy for age between 25 and 34
A35–44	=	coefficient of dummy for age between 35 and 44
A45–54	=	coefficient of dummy for age between 45 and 54
A55–64	=	coefficient of dummy for age between 55 and 64
A65+	=	coefficient of dummy for age 65 and over
RNC	=	coefficient of dummy for family residing in North Central
RS	=	coefficient of dummy for family residing in South
RW	=	coefficient of dummy for family residing in West
NW	=	coefficient of dummy for nonwhite family
RUR	=	coefficient of dummy for family residing in rural area

See Tables 5.B.1–5.B.3 for cross-section results.

Appendix C   Notation for Pooled Estimation Results

Table 5.C.1			Table 5.C.2			Table 5.C.3		
Pooled estimation results—Energy			Pooled estimation results—Food			Pooled estimation results—Consumer goods		
Parameter	Estimate	Standard error	Parameter	Estimate	Standard error	Parameter	Estimate	Standard error
CONST	-0.1786	0.00878	CONST	-0.7334	0.0202	CONST	0.003297	0.0101
ln PEN	0.03893	0.00393	ln PEN	-0.07029	0.0107	ln PEN	0.01500	0.0111
ln PF	-0.07029	0.0107	ln PF	0.1637	0.0422	ln PF	-0.08137	0.0430
ln PCG	0.01500	0.0111	ln PCG	-0.08137	0.0430	ln PCG	0.1664	0.0501
ln PK	0.05099	0.00830	ln PK	-0.08271	0.0297	ln PK	-0.1216	0.0333
ln PCS	-0.04566	0.00691	ln PCS	0.006689	0.0202	ln PCS	0.03870	0.0188
ln M	0.01103	0.000974	ln M	0.06401	0.00224	ln M	-0.01711	0.00108
S2	-0.01258	0.00128	S2	-0.02784	0.00294	S2	-0.0008115	0.00142
S3	-0.01635	0.00151	S3	-0.04078	0.00347	S3	-0.005105	0.00167
S4	-0.01707	0.00161	S4	-0.06251	0.00369	S4	-0.006910	0.00178
S5	-0.01788	0.00188	S5	-0.06664	0.00432	S5	-0.008385	0.00208
S6	-0.01629	0.00233	S6	-0.09490	0.00535	S6	-0.01227	0.00258
S7+	-0.01823	0.00242	S7+	-0.1149	0.00555	S7+	-0.01416	0.00268
A25-34	0.002064	0.00177	A25-34	-0.03663	0.00406	A25-34	0.005777	0.00195
A35-44	0.001753	0.00192	A35-44	-0.07106	0.00440	A35-44	0.006068	0.00212
A45-54	-0.0002350	0.00182	A45-54	0.07433	0.00418	A45-54	0.01271	0.00202
A55-64	-0.002076	0.00182	A55-64	-0.07201	0.00418	A55-64	0.01822	0.00201
A65+	0.001808	0.00179	A65+	-0.06451	0.00411	A65+	0.02233	0.00198
RNC	-0.007964	0.00119	RNC	0.01407	0.00274	RNC	-0.0002035	0.00132
RS	-0.008123	0.00119	RS	0.004529	0.00273	RS	-0.002689	0.00131
RW	0.003936	0.00128	RW	0.01182	0.00294	RW	-0.001727	0.00131
NW	0.001469	0.00149	NW	-0.01446	0.00341	NW	-0.01424	0.00164
RUR	-0.02987	0.00119	RUR	0.008474	0.00272	RUR	-0.005057	0.00131

Table 5.C.4

Table 5.C.5

	Pooled estimation results—Capital services		Pooled estimation results—Consumer services	
Parameter	Estimate	Standard error	Estimate	Standard error
CONST	-0.5663	0.0239	0.4750	0.0197
ln PEN	0.05099	0.00830	-0.04566	0.00691
ln PF	-0.08271	0.0297	0.006689	0.0202
ln PCG	-0.1216	0.0333	0.03870	0.0188
ln PK	0.3208	0.0272	-0.1795	0.0183
ln PCS	-0.1795	0.0183	0.2497	0.0241
ln M	0.01208	0.00267	-0.07000	0.00219
S2	0.02727	0.00350	0.01397	0.00286
S3	0.04310	0.00413	0.01914	0.00337
S4	0.05821	0.00440	0.02829	0.00359
S5	0.05620	0.00514	0.03670	0.00420
S6	0.07393	0.00637	0.04953	0.00520
S7+	0.08459	0.00661	0.06272	0.00540
A25–34	0.03604	0.00483	-0.007251	0.00394
A35–44	0.06341	0.00523	-0.0001688	0.00427
A45–54	0.07308	0.00498	-0.01122	0.00407
A55–64	0.07739	0.00497	-0.02152	0.00406
A65+	0.05915	0.00489	-0.01877	0.00399
RNC	0.007170	0.00326	-0.01307	0.00266
RS	0.02610	0.00324	-0.01981	0.00265
RW	-0.009427	0.00350	-0.004598	0.00286
NW	0.04240	0.00406	-0.01517	0.00332
RUR	0.02660	0.00324	0.007475	0.00264

NOTE: Cross-section SSR = 37,165.98;
aggregate SSR = 1,781.84.
SSR failed to improve after 95 iterations.

Table Notation		
CONST	=	constant term
ln PEN	=	coefficient of log of price of energy
ln PF	=	coefficient of log of price of food
ln PCG	=	coefficient of log of price of consumer goods
ln PK	=	coefficient of log of price of capital services
ln PCS	=	coefficient of log of price of consumer services
ln M	=	coefficient of log to total expenditure
S2	=	coefficient of dummy for family of size 2
S3	=	coefficient of dummy for family of size 3
S4	=	coefficient of dummy for family of size 4
S5	=	coefficient of dummy for family of size 5
S6	=	coefficient of dummy for family of size 6
S7+	=	coefficient of dummy for family of size 7 or more
A25–34	=	coefficient of dummy for age between 25 and 34
A35–44	=	coefficient of dummy for age between 35 and 44
A45–54	=	coefficient of dummy for age between 45 and 54
A55–64	=	coefficient of dummy for age between 55 and 64
A65+	=	coefficient of dummy for age 65 and over
RNC	=	coefficient of dummy for family residing in North Central
RS	=	coefficient of dummy for family residing in South
RW	=	coefficient of dummy for family residing in West
NW	=	coefficient of dummy for nonwhite family
RUR	=	coefficient of dummy for family residing in rural area

See Tables 5.C.1–5.C.5 for the pooled estimation results.

6   General Equilibrium
Analysis of Natural
Gas Price Regulation

Dale W. Jorgenson and
Daniel T. Slesnick

6.1   Introduction

In this chapter we present a new approach to the general equilibrium
analysis of economic policy. Our objective is to provide a complete
ordering of alternative economic policies. The most desirable economic policy is the policy yielding the highest level of social welfare.
This principle can be used to evaluate a specific policy change or to
select the optimal policy from a set of alternatives.

We begin with a much less informative approach to the general
equilibrium analysis of economic policy based on the Pareto principle.
Under this principle a change in economic policy can be recommended if all consuming units are at least as well off under the policy
change and at least one consuming unit is better off. The Pareto
principle does not employ the concept of social welfare and provides
only a partial ordering of economic policies rather than a complete
ordering.

We extend the partial ordering of alternative economic policies
implied by the Pareto principle to a complete ordering. For this purpose we employ the concept of a social welfare function originated by
Bergson (1938) and discussed by Samuelson (1947, 1982). A social
welfare function gives the level of social welfare as a function of the
distribution of individual welfare over the population of consuming
units. Our approach to economic policy evaluation requires measures
of individual welfare that are cardinal and fully comparable among
consuming units.

By contrast, the comparison of alternative economic policies by
means of the Pareto principle requires only ordinal information about
individual preferences. Also, this principle does not require interpersonal comparability of preferences. To extend the partial ordering
of economic policies based on the Pareto principle to the complete

ordering represented by a social welfare function, we introduce additional information about individual preferences. This information provides measures of individual welfare that are cardinal and interpersonally comparable.

Our measures of individual welfare are derived from a model of aggregate consumer behavior. In this model systems of individual demand functions depend on the prices faced by all households. These systems also depend on levels of total expenditure and on attributes of households such as demographic characteristics. We obtain aggregate demand functions by exact aggregation over individual demand functions. The resulting system of aggregate demand functions depends on summary statistics of the joint distribution of total expenditures and attributes among consuming units.

The restrictions on individual preferences required for exact aggregation imply cardinal measures of utility that are fully comparable among individuals. The level of utility for each consuming unit can be expressed as a linear function of a single variable that incorporates the total expenditures and the attributes of the consuming unit. We define cardinal and interpersonally comparable measures of individual welfare in terms of this level of utility.

Our approach to the measurement of individual welfare is based on the indirect utility function and the individual expenditure function for each consuming unit. The indirect utility function gives the maximum attainable utility level as a function of the prices faced by the consuming unit and the level of total expenditure. The expenditure function gives the minimum level of total expenditure required to attain a stipulated level of utility as a function of the prices.

6.2   Aggregate Consumer Behavior

In this section we develop an econometric model of aggregate consumer behavior based on the theory of exact aggregation, following Jorgenson, Lau, and Stoker (1980, 1981, 1982). Our model incorporates time-series data on prices and aggregate quantities consumed. We also include cross-section data on individual quantities consumed, individual total expenditure, and attributes of individual households such as demographic characteristics.

To represent preferences for all individuals in a form suitable for measuring individual welfare, we take households as consuming units. We assume that expenditures on individual commodities are allocated so as to maximize a household welfare function. As a consequence, the household behaves in the same way as an individual maximizing a utility function, as demonstrated by Samuelson (1956) and Pollak (1981). By assuming that each household maximizes a household welfare function, we can focus on the distribution of welfare among households rather than the distribution among individuals within households.

To construct an econometric model based on exact aggregation we first represent individual preferences by means of an indirect utility function for each consuming unit, using the following notation:

p_n — price of the nth commodity, assumed to be the same for all consuming units.

$\mathbf{p} = (p_1, p_2, \ldots, p_N)$ — the vector of prices of all commodities.

x_{nk} — quantity of the nth commodity group consumed by the kth consuming unit ($n = 1, 2, \ldots, N; k = 1, 2, \ldots, K$).

$M_k = \sum_{n=1}^{N} p_n x_{nk}$ — total expenditure of the kth consuming unit ($k = 1, 2, \ldots, K$).

$w_{nk} = p_n x_{nk} / M_k$ — expenditure share of the nth commodity group in the budget of the kth consuming unit ($n = 1, 2, \ldots, N; k = 1, 2, \ldots, K$).

$\mathbf{w}_k = (w_{1k}, w_{2k}, \ldots, w_{Nk})$ — vector of expenditure shares for the kth consuming unit ($k = 1, 2, \ldots, K$).

$\ln(\mathbf{p}/M_k) = [\ln(p_1/M_k), \ln(p_2/M_k), \ldots, \ln(p_N/M_k)]$ — vector of logarithms of ratios of prices to expenditure by the kth consuming unit ($k = 1, 2, \ldots, K$).

$\ln p = (\ln p_1, \ln p_2, \ldots, \ln p_N)$ — vector of logarithms of prices.

$\mathbf{A}_k$ — vector of attributes of the kth consuming unit ($k = 1, 2, \ldots, K$).

We assume that the kth consuming unit allocates expenditures in accord with the transcendental logarithmic or translog indirect utility function,[1] say V_k, where

$$\ln V_k = G\left(\ln \frac{\mathbf{p}'}{M_k} \alpha_p + \frac{1}{2} \ln \frac{\mathbf{p}'}{M_k} B_{pp} \ln \frac{\mathbf{p}}{M_k} + \ln \frac{\mathbf{p}'}{M_k} B_{pA} \mathbf{A}_k, \mathbf{A}_k\right),$$

$$(k = 1, 2, \ldots, K). \qquad (6.1)$$

In this representation the function G is a monotone increasing function of the variable

$$\ln \frac{\mathbf{p}'}{M_k} \alpha_p + \frac{1}{2} \ln \frac{\mathbf{p}'}{M_k} B_{pp} \ln \frac{\mathbf{p}}{M_k} + \ln \frac{\mathbf{p}'}{M_k} B_{pA} A_k \; .$$

In addition, the function G depends directly on the attribute vector A_k.[2] The vector α_p and the matrices B_{pp} and B_{pA} are constant parameters that are the same for all consuming units.

The expenditure shares of the kth consuming unit can be derived by the logarithmic form of Roy's (1943) Identity[3]

$$w_{nk} = \frac{\partial \ln V_k / [\partial \ln (p_n/M_k)]}{\sum_{n=1}^{N} \partial \ln V_k / [\partial \ln (p_n/M_k)]}, \quad (n = 1, 2, \ldots, N; \; k = 1, 2, \ldots, K). \quad (6.2)$$

Applying this Identity to the translog indirect utility function (6.1), we obtain the system of individual expenditure shares

$$\mathbf{w}_k = \frac{1}{D_k(p)} \left(\alpha_p + B_{pp} \ln \frac{\mathbf{p}}{M_k} + B_{pA} \mathbf{A}_k \right), \quad (k = 1, 2, \ldots, K), \quad (6.3)$$

where the denominators $\{D_k\}$ take the form

$$D_k = i' \alpha_p + i' B_{pp} \ln \frac{\mathbf{p}}{M_k} + i' B_{pA} \mathbf{A}_k, \quad (k = 1, 2, \ldots, K). \quad (6.4)$$

The individual expenditure shares are homogeneous of degree zero in the unknown parameters—α_p, B_{pp}, B_{pA}. By multiplying a given set of these parameters by a constant we obtain another set of parameters that generates the same system of individual budget shares. Accordingly, we can choose a normalization for the parameters without affecting observed patterns of individual expenditure allocation. We find it convenient to employ the normalization

$$i' \alpha_p = -1 \; .$$

Under this restriction any change in the set of unknown parameters will be reflected in changes in individual expenditure patterns.

The conditions for exact aggregation are that the individual expenditure shares are linear in functions of the attributes $\{A_k\}$ and total expenditures $\{M_k\}$ for all consuming units.[4] These conditions will be satisfied if and only if the terms involving the attributes and expenditures do not appear in the denominators of the expressions given above for the individual expenditure shares, so that

$$\mathbf{i}'B_{pp}\mathbf{i} = 0 \,,$$

$$\mathbf{i}'B_{pA} = 0 \,.$$

The exact aggregation restrictions imply that the denominators $\{D_k\}$ reduce to

$$D = -1 + \mathbf{i}'B_{pp} \ln \mathbf{p} \,,$$

where the subscript k is no longer required, since the denominator is the same for all consuming units. Under these restrictions the individual expenditure shares can be written

$$\mathbf{w}_k = \frac{1}{D(\mathbf{p})} \left(\alpha_p + B_{pp} \ln \mathbf{p} - B_{pp}\mathbf{i} \cdot \ln M_k + B_{pA}\mathbf{A}_k\right) \,,$$

$$(k = 1, 2, \ldots, K) \,. \qquad (6.5)$$

The individual expenditure shares are linear in the logarithms of expenditures $\{\ln M_k\}$ and in the attributes $\{\mathbf{A}_k\}$, as required by exact aggregation.

To construct an econometric model of aggregate consumer behavior based on exact aggregation we obtain aggregate expenditure shares, say $\mathbf{w}$, by multiplying individual expenditure shares (6.5) by expenditure for each consuming unit, adding over all consuming units, and dividing by aggregate expenditure, $M = \sum_{k=1}^{K} M_k$

$$\mathbf{w} = \frac{\sum M_k \mathbf{w}_k}{M} \,. \qquad (6.6)$$

The aggregate expenditure shares can be written

$$\mathbf{w} = \frac{1}{D(\mathbf{p})} \left(\alpha_p + B_{pp} \ln \mathbf{p} - B_{pp}\mathbf{i} \frac{\sum M_k \ln M_k}{M} + B_{pA} \frac{\sum M_k \mathbf{A}_k}{M}\right). \qquad (6.7)$$

The aggregate expenditure patterns depend on the distribution of expenditure over all consuming units through summary statistics of the joint distribution of expenditures and attributes—$\sum M_k \ln M_k / M$ and $\{\sum M_k \mathbf{A}_k / M\}$. Systems of individual expenditure shares (6.5) for consuming units with identical demographic characteristics can be recovered in one and only one way from the system of aggregate expenditure shares (6.7).

Under exact aggregation the indirect utility function for each consuming unit can be represented in the form

$$\ln V_k = F(\mathbf{A}_k) + \ln \mathbf{p}' \left(\alpha_p + \frac{1}{2} B_{pp} \ln \mathbf{p} + B_{pA} \mathbf{A}_k \right) - D(\mathbf{p}) \ln M_k \,,$$

$$(k = 1, 2, \dots, K) \,. \qquad (6.8)$$

In this representation the indirect utility function is linear in the logarithm of total expenditure $\ln M_k$ with a coefficient that depends on the prices $\mathbf{p}$ $(k = 1, 2, \dots, K)$. This property is invariant with respect to positive affine transformations, but is not preserved by arbitrary monotone increasing transformations. We conclude that the indirect utility function (6.8) provides a cardinal measure of utility for each consuming unit.

To provide a basis for evaluating the impact of transfers among households on social welfare, we find it useful to represent household preferences by means of a utility function that is the same for all consuming units. For this purpose, we assume that the kth consuming unit maximizes its utility, say U_k, where

$$U_k = U \left[\frac{x_{1k}}{m_1(\mathbf{A}_k)} , \frac{x_{2k}}{m_2(\mathbf{A}_k)} , \dots , \frac{x_{Nk}}{m_N(\mathbf{A}_k)} \right] , \qquad (k = 1, 2, \dots, K) , \qquad (6.9)$$

subject to the budget constraint

$$M_k = \sum_{n=1}^{N} p_n x_{nk} \,, \qquad (k = 1, 2, \dots, K).$$

In this representation of consumer preferences the quantities $\{x_{nk}/m_n(\mathbf{A}_k)\}$ can be regarded as *effective quantities consumed*, as proposed by Barten (1964). The crucial assumption embodied in this representation is that differences in preferences among consumers enter the utility function U only through differences in the commodity specific household equivalence scales $\{m_n(\mathbf{A}_k)\}$.[5]

Consumer equilibrium implies the existence of an indirect utility function, say V, that is the same for all consuming units. The level of utility for the kth consuming unit, say V_k, depends on the prices of individual commodities, the household equivalence scales, and the level of total expenditure

$$V_k = V \left[\frac{p_1 m_1(\mathbf{A}_k)}{M_k} , \frac{p_2 m_2(\mathbf{A}_k)}{M_k} , \dots , \frac{p_N m_N(\mathbf{A}_k)}{M_k} \right] ,$$

$$(k = 1, 2, \dots, K) \,. \qquad (6.10)$$

In this representation the prices $\{p_n m_n(\mathbf{A}_k)\}$ can be regarded as *effective prices*. Differences in preferences among consuming units enter this indirect utility function only through the household equivalence scales

$$\{m_n(\mathbf{A}_k)\}, \quad (k = 1, 2, \ldots, K).$$

To represent the translog indirect utility function (6.1) in terms of household equivalence scales, we require some additional notation

$\ln \dfrac{\mathbf{pm}(\mathbf{A}_k)}{M_k}$ — vector of logarithms of ratios of effective prices. $\{p_n m_n(\mathbf{A}_k)\}$ to total expenditure M_k of the kth consuming unit $(k = 1, 2, \ldots, K)$.

$\ln \mathbf{m}(\mathbf{A}_k) = (\ln m_1(\mathbf{A}_k), \ln m_2(\mathbf{A}_k), \ldots, \ln m_N(\mathbf{A}_k))$ — vector of logarithms of the household equivalence scales of the kth consuming unit $(k = 1, 2, \ldots, K)$.

We assume, as before, that the kth consuming unit allocates its expenditures in accord with the translog indirect utility function (6.1). However, we also assume that this function, expressed in terms of the effective prices $\{p_n m_n(\mathbf{A}_k)\}$ and total expenditure M_k, is the same for all consuming units. The indirect utility function takes the form

$$\ln V_k = \ln \frac{\mathbf{pm}(\mathbf{A}_k)'}{M_k} \alpha_p + \frac{1}{2} \ln \frac{\mathbf{pm}(\mathbf{A}_k)'}{M_k} B_{pp} \ln \frac{\mathbf{pm}(\mathbf{A}_k)}{M_k},$$

$$(k = 1, 2, \ldots, K). \qquad (6.11)$$

Taking logarithms of the effective prices $\{p_n m_n(\mathbf{A}_k)\}$, we can rewrite the indirect utility function (6.11) in the form

$$\ln V_k = \ln \mathbf{m}(\mathbf{A}_k)' \alpha_p + \frac{1}{2} \ln \mathbf{m}(\mathbf{A}_k)' B_{pp} \ln \mathbf{m}(\mathbf{A}_k) + \ln \frac{\mathbf{p}'}{M_k} \alpha_p$$

$$+ \frac{1}{2} \ln \frac{\mathbf{p}'}{M_k} B_{pp} \ln \frac{\mathbf{p}}{M_k} + \ln \frac{\mathbf{p}'}{M_k} B_{pp} \ln \mathbf{m}(\mathbf{A}_k),$$

$$(k = 1, 2, \ldots, K). \qquad (6.12)$$

Comparing the representation (6.12) with the representation (6.8), we see that the term involving only the household equivalence scales must take the form

$$F(\mathbf{A}_k) = \ln \mathbf{m}(\mathbf{A}_k)'\alpha_p + \frac{1}{2} \ln \mathbf{m}(\mathbf{A}_k)'B_{pp} \ln \mathbf{m}(\mathbf{A}_k) ,$$
$$(k = 1, 2, \ldots, K) . \tag{6.13}$$

Second, the term involving ratios of prices to total expenditure and the household equivalence scales must satisfy

$$\ln \frac{\mathbf{p}'}{M_k} B_{pA}\mathbf{A}_k = \ln \frac{\mathbf{p}'}{M_k} B_{pp} \ln \mathbf{m}(\mathbf{A}_k) . \tag{6.14}$$

for all prices and total expenditure.

The household equivalence scales $\{m_n(\mathbf{A}_k)\}$ defined by (6.14) must satisfy the equations

$$B_{pA}\mathbf{A}_K = B_{pp} \ln \mathbf{m}(\mathbf{A}_k) , \quad (k = 1, 2, \ldots, K) . \tag{6.15}$$

Under monotonicity of the individual expenditure shares the matrix B_{pp} has an inverse, so we can express the household equivalence scales in terms of the parameters of the translog indirect utility function (B_{pp}, B_{pA}) and the attributes $\{\mathbf{A}_k\}$

$$\ln \mathbf{m}(\mathbf{A}_k) = B_{pp}^{-1} B_{pA}\mathbf{A}_k , \quad (k = 1, 2, \ldots, K) . \tag{6.16}$$

We can refer to these scales as the *commodity-specific translog household equivalence scales*.

Given the indirect utility function (6.12) for each consuming unit, we can express total expenditure as a function of prices, the commodity-specific household equivalence scales, and the level of utility

$$\ln M_k = \frac{1}{D(\mathbf{p})} \left\{ \ln \mathbf{m}(\mathbf{A}_k)'\alpha_p + \frac{1}{2} \ln \mathbf{m}(\mathbf{A}_k)'B_{pp} \ln \mathbf{m}(\mathbf{A}_k) \right.$$
$$\left. + \ln \mathbf{p}' \left[\alpha_p + \frac{1}{2} B_{pp} \ln \mathbf{p} + B_{pp} \ln \mathbf{m}(\mathbf{A}_k) \right] - \ln V_k \right\} ,$$
$$(k = 1, 2, \ldots, K) . \tag{6.17}$$

We can refer to this function as the *translog expenditure functon*. The translog expenditure function gives the minimum required for the kth consuming unit to achieve the utility level V_k, given the prices $\mathbf{p}$ $(k = 1, 2, \ldots, K)$.

We find it useful to introduce household equivalence scales that are not specific to a given commodity.[6] Following Muellbauer (1974a), we define a general household equivalence scale, say m_0, as follows

$$m_0 = \frac{M_k[\mathbf{pm}(\mathbf{A}_k), V_k^0]}{M_0(\mathbf{p}, V_k^0)}, \qquad (k = 1, 2, \ldots, K),$$ (6.18)

where M_k is the expenditure function for the kth household, M_0 is the expenditure function for a reference household with commodity-specific equivalence scales equal to unity for all commodities, and $\mathbf{pm}(\mathbf{A}_k)$ is a vector of effective prices $\{p_n m_n(\mathbf{A}_k)\}$.

The general household equivalence scale m_0 is the ratio between total expenditures required by the kth household and by the reference household required for the same level of utility V_k^0 $(k = 1, 2, \ldots, K)$. This scale can be interpreted as the number of household equivalent members. The number of members depends on the attributes $\mathbf{A}_k$ of the consuming unit and on the prices p.

If each household has a translog indirect utility function, then the general household equivalence scale for the kth household takes the form

$$\ln m_0 = \ln M_k - \ln M_0$$

$$= \frac{1}{D(\mathbf{p})} \left[\ln \mathbf{m}(\mathbf{A}_k)' \alpha_p + \frac{1}{2} \ln \mathbf{m}(\mathbf{A}_k)' B_{pp} \ln \mathbf{m}(\mathbf{A}_k) \right.$$

$$\left. + \ln \mathbf{m}(\mathbf{A}_k)' B_{pp} \ln \mathbf{p} \right], \qquad (k = 1, 2, \ldots, K).$$ (6.19)

We can refer to this scale as the *general translog household equivalence scale*. The translog equivalence scale depends on the attributes $\mathbf{A}_k$ of the kth household and the prices $\mathbf{p}$ of all commodities, but is independent of the level of utility V_k^0.

Given the general translog equivalence scale, we can rewrite the indirect utility function (6.8) in the form

$$\ln V_k = \ln \mathbf{p}' \alpha_p + \frac{1}{2} \ln \mathbf{p}' B_{pp} \ln \mathbf{p} - D(\mathbf{p}) \ln \left[\frac{M_k}{m_0(\mathbf{p}, \mathbf{A}_k)} \right],$$

$$(k = 1, 2, \ldots, K).$$ (6.20)

The level of utility for the kth consuming unit depends on prices p and total expenditure per household equivalent member $M_k/m_0(\mathbf{p}, \mathbf{A}_k)$ $(k = 1, 2, \ldots, K)$. Similarly, we can rewrite the expenditure function (6.17) in the form

$$\ln M_k = \frac{1}{D(\mathbf{p})} \left[\ln \mathbf{p}' \left(\alpha_p + \frac{1}{2} B_{pp} \ln \mathbf{p} \right) - \ln V_k \right] + \ln m_0(\mathbf{p}, \mathbf{A}_k) ,$$

$$(k = 1, 2, \ldots, K) . \qquad (6.21)$$

Total expenditure required by the kth consuming unit to attain the level of utility V_k depends on prices p and the number of household equivalent members $m_0(\mathbf{p}, \mathbf{A}_k)$ $(k = 1, 2, \ldots, K)$.

The first step in analyzing the impact of alternative economic policies on the distribution of individual welfare is to select a representation of the individual welfare function. We assume that individual welfare for the kth consuming unit, say W_k $(k = 1, 2, \ldots, K)$, is equal to the logarithm of the translog indirect utility function (6.20)[7]

$$W_k = \ln V_k$$

$$= \ln \mathbf{p}' \alpha_p + \frac{1}{2} \ln \mathbf{p}' B_{pp} \ln \mathbf{p} - D(\mathbf{p}) \ln \left[\frac{M_k}{m_0(\mathbf{p}, \mathbf{A}_k)} \right] ,$$

$$(k = 1, 2, \ldots, K) . \qquad (6.22)$$

In implementing the econometric model of consumer behavior we divide consumer expenditures among five commodity groups:

1. *Energy*: Expenditures on electricity, natural gas, heating oil, and gasoline.

2. *Food*: Expenditures on all food products, including tobacco and alcohol.

3. *Consumer goods*: Expenditures on all other nondurable goods included in consumer expenditures.

4. *Capital services*: The service flow from consumer durables and the service flow from housing.

5. *Consumer services*: Expenditures on consumer services, such as car repairs, medical services, and entertainment.

We employ the following demographic characteristics as attributes of individual households

1. *Family size*: 1, 2, 3, 4, 5, 6, and 7 or more persons.

2. *Age of head*: 16–24, 25–34, 35–44, 45–54, 55–64, 65 and over.

3. *Region of residence*: Northeast, North Central, South, and West.

4. *Race*: White, nonwhite.

5. *Type of residence*: Urban, rural.

Our cross-sectional observations on individual expenditures for each commodity group and on demographic characteristics of individual households are for the year 1973 from the 1972–1973 Survey of Consumer Expenditures (CES).[8] Our time series observations are based on data on personal consumption expenditures from the U.S. National Income and Product Accounts (NIPA) for the years 1947 to 1982.[9] Prices for each commodity group are defined in terms of translog price indexes computed from detailed prices included in NIPA for each year. We employ time series data on the distribution of expenditures over all households and among demographic groups based on *Current Population Reports.*[10]

In our application we treat the expenditure shares for five commodity groups as endogenous variables, so that we estimate four equations. As unknown parameters we have four elements of the vector α_p, four expenditure coefficients of the vector $B_{pp}\mathbf{i}$, sixteen attribute coefficients for each of the four equations in the matrix B_{pA}, and ten price coefficients in the matrix B_{pp}, which is constrained to be symmetric. The expenditure coefficients are sums of price coefficients in the corresponding equation, so we have a total of eighty-two unknown parameters. We estimate the complete model, subject to inequality restrictions implied by monotonicity of the individual expenditure shares, by pooling time-series and cross-section data.[11]

In summary, for our econometric model a system of individual expenditure shares (6.5) can be recovered in only one way from the system of aggregate expenditure shares (6.7). Given a system of individual expenditure shares (6.5) that is integrable, we can recover the translog indirect utility function (6.20). This indirect utility function provides a cardinal measure of utility. We obtain a cardinal measure of individual welfare for each consuming unit (6.22) by setting this measure equal to the logarithm of the indirect utility function.

6.3   Money Metric Individual Welfare

The translog indirect utility function (6.20) and the translog individual expenditure function (6.21) can be employed in assessing the impacts of alternative economic policies on individual welfare. To analyze the impact of economic policy on the welfare of the kth household, we first evaluate the indirect utility function after the change in policy has taken place. Suppose that prices are $\mathbf{p}^1$ and expenditure for the kth household is M_k^1 $(k = 1, 2, \ldots, K)$. The level of individual welfare for the kth consuming unit after the policy change W_k^1 is given by

$$W_k^1 = \ln V_k^1$$

$$= \ln \mathbf{p}^{1\prime} \left(\alpha_p + \frac{1}{2} B_{pp} \ln \mathbf{p}^1 \right) - D(\mathbf{p}^1) \ln \left[\frac{M_k^1}{m_0(\mathbf{p}^1, \mathbf{A}_k)} \right],$$

$$(k = 1, 2, \ldots, K) . \qquad (6.23)$$

To evaluate the impact of alternative economic policies we must compare the total expenditure required to attain the individual welfare resulting from each policy at prices prevailing before any change, say $\mathbf{p}^0$. For this purpose we can define *money metric individual welfare* for the kth household, say N_k, as the difference between the total expenditure required to attain W_k^1 and the expenditure required to attain W_k^0, the level before the policy change. Both are evaluated at prices $\mathbf{p}^{0}$:[12]

$$N_k = M_k(\mathbf{p}^0, W_k^1, \mathbf{A}_k) - M_k(\mathbf{p}^0, W_k^0, \mathbf{A}_k)$$

$$= M_k(\mathbf{p}^0, W_k^1, \mathbf{A}_k) - M_k^0 , \quad (k = 1, 2, \ldots, K) , \qquad (6.24)$$

where M_k^0 is total expenditure before the policy change. If money metric individual welfare is positive, the welfare of the consuming unit is increased; otherwise, the welfare of the consuming unit is decreased or left unaffected.

We illustrate the concept of money metric individual welfare geometrically in figure 6.1. This diagram represents the indifference map for a consuming unit with indirect utility function (6.20). For simplicity we consider the case of two commodities ($N = 2$). Consumer equilibrium before the policy change is represented by the point A. The corresponding level of total expenditure $M_k^0(\mathbf{p}^0, W_k^0)$, divided by the price of the second commodity p_2^0, is given on the vertical axis. This axis gives total expenditure in units of the second commodity.

Similarly, consumer equilibrium after the policy change is represented by the point C. To translate the corresponding level of welfare into total expenditure at the prices before the change, we evaluate the expenditure function (6.21) at this level of welfare and at the prices $\mathbf{p}^0$. The resulting level of total expenditure $M_k(\mathbf{p}^0, W_k^1, \mathbf{A}_k)$ corresponds to consumer equilibrium at the point B. Money metric individual welfare is the difference between the levels of total expenditure $M_k(\mathbf{p}^0, W_k^1, \mathbf{A}_k)$ and M_k^0.

To illustrate the measurement of individual welfare we undertake a comparison of alternative policies for regulation of natural gas prices

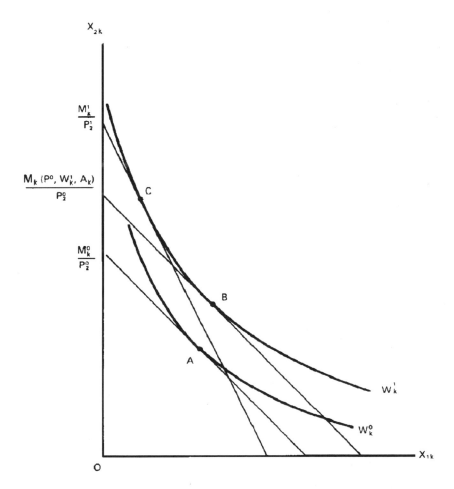

Figure 6.1
Money metric individual welfare.

in the United States. These policies have been analyzed by the Office of Policy, Planning, and Analysis of the U.S. Department of Energy (DOE). Our reference case for policy analysis is the policy of natural gas price decontrol called for in the Natural Gas Policy Act (NGPA) of 1978. Under this policy price controls on natural gas remained until 1985, when prices on some types of natural gas were decontrolled. Our base case for policy analysis is the behavior of the U.S. economy under this policy.

Alternatives to current regulatory policy for natural gas prices considered by DOE are the following:

1. *Continued controls.* Under this policy price controls on natural gas would have continued beyond 1985 and an effort would have been made to shift consumption from domestic to imported natural gas. This policy was embodied in the Gephardt bill presented to Congress in 1983.

2. *Immediate decontrol.* Under this policy, price controls would have been maintained on some types of natural gas until 1985; at this time decontrol would occur for prices on most types of natural gas. This policy was embodied in a Senate-Administration bill presented to Congress in 1983.

We have analyzed the two alternatives to current regulatory policy for natural gas prices in the United States. To evaluate these alternatives, we require projections of prices and total expenditure under each policy. We obtain these projections from the Dynamic General Equilibrium Model (DGEM) of the U.S. economy, constructed by Hudson and Jorgenson (1974, 1976, 1978a, b). This model is based on a nine-sector breakdown of the U.S. economy

1. Agriculture, nonfuel mining, construction
2. Manufacturing, except for petroleum
3. Transportation
4. Communications, trade, and services
5. Coal mining
6. Crude petroleum and gas extraction
7. Refined petroleum products
8. Electric utilities
9. Gas utilities.

The first step in analyzing alternative policies for regulation of natural gas prices is to establish projections of prices and total expenditure for all consuming units under current policy. To simulate the impact of alternatives to current regulatory policy, projections of the resulting changes in prices of natural gas to the individual industrial sectors and to final demand are incorporated into DGEM. Financial flows resulting from the alternatives to current policy are also projected and incorporated into the model.

Changes in demand for natural gas by manufacturing industries and by electric utilities are projected and incorporated into DGEM, whereas changes in demand by the other sectors of the economy are determined endogenously within the model. The response of domestic natural gas supply to changes in regulatory policy are specified exogenously. Total domestic supply is required to be equal to total domestic demand plus losses in transportation, plus the natural gas demands of natural gas producers, and less imports.

Projections of prices for each of the five commodities included in our model of aggregate consumer behavior—energy, food, consumer goods, capital services, and consumer services—are presented in table 6.1 for the reference case corresponding to current regulatory policy and for alternative policies.[13] Table 6.1 presents projections of total expenditure per household for the U.S. economy for each of the alternative regulatory policies that we consider. The projections of prices and total expenditure cover the period 1983 to 2000. It is important to note that the prices given in table 6.1 are purchasers' prices for the five commodity groups. Price projections from DGEM are given in terms of producers' prices and must be transformed by incorporating trade and transportation margins to obtain purchasers' prices.

Under continued natural gas price controls we find that the price of energy is lower than under the current policy for only two years. In addition, the prices of all nonenergy commodities are higher under continued controls than under current policy after 1986. We also find that total expenditure per household is higher under a policy of continued controls than under current policy. It is not obvious whether individual welfare is higher or lower under continued controls than under the reference case.

To evaluate the change in individual welfare for typical households, we employ prices in the reference case as a basis for calculating money metric individual welfare (6.24). We make the simplifying assumption that total expenditure changes in the same proportion for all consuming units. Changes in relative levels of individual welfare are the result of differential impacts of price changes associated with changes in regulatory policy.

The dollar value of changes in individual welfare under a policy of continued controls is given for typical households in table 6.2. We present results for families of size five, with age of head 35–44, living in the Northeast region of the United States, and with average total expenditure in each year. Under continued controls all types of households gain during the period 1983 to 1989 and nonwhite households continue to gain in 1990. However, all types of families lose under continued controls beginning 1991. For example, a white urban family living in the Northeast gains $23.43 in 1983. This gain falls to $6.90 by 1989 and then becomes negative for the rest of the period.

Table 6.1
Projections of prices and total expenditure

a. Prices (equal to 1.000 in 1972)

Year	Energy	Food	Consumer goods	Capital services	Consumer services
Current policy					
1983	2.8452	1.8190	1.8039	2.5335	1.8067
1984	3.0394	1.8756	1.8591	2.7261	1.8620
1985	3.2794	1.9599	1.9406	2.9447	1.9394
1986	3.5175	2.0843	2.0610	3.1321	2.0553
1987	3.7893	2.1797	2.1521	3.3958	2.1332
1988	4.0712	2.2594	2.2289	3.6776	2.2051
1989	4.4023	2.3550	2.3206	3.9783	2.2877
1990	4.6296	2.5114	2.4699	4.1261	2.4232
1991	4.9263	2.6357	2.5874	4.3868	2.5240
1992	5.3241	2.7454	2.6933	4.7239	2.6297
1993	5.7350	2.8835	2.8248	5.0564	2.7503
1994	6.1258	3.1212	3.0476	5.1710	2.9395
1995	6.5515	3.3017	3.2157	5.4501	3.0855
1996	6.9604	3.3937	3.3025	5.8803	3.1774
1997	7.5162	3.5340	3.4335	6.3149	3.2962
1998	7.9925	3.7491	3.6339	6.6225	3.4783
1999	8.5172	3.9303	3.8004	7.0004	3.6230
2000	9.0189	4.1287	3.9858	7.3203	3.8061
Continued controls					
1983	2.8096	1.8182	1.8032	2.5334	1.8049
1984	3.0311	1.8753	1.8588	2.7265	1.8614
1985	3.2242	1.9575	1.9381	2.9437	1.9355
1986	3.4993	2.0826	2.0593	3.1328	2.0533
1987	3.7926	2.1794	2.1519	3.3998	2.1331
1988	4.0783	2.2598	2.2293	3.6837	2.2058
1989	4.4098	2.3556	2.3212	3.9857	2.2886
1990	4.6363	2.5122	2.4708	4.1346	2.4244
1991	4.9396	2.6371	2.5888	4.3967	2.5258
1992	5.3243	2.7463	2.6942	4.7342	2.6307
1993	5.7463	2.8851	2.8264	5.0683	2.7522
1994	6.1355	3.1229	3.0493	5.1831	2.9415
1995	6.5579	3.3034	3.2174	5.4626	3.0874
1996	6.9674	3.3955	3.3042	5.8934	3.1793
1997	7.5220	3.5358	3.4353	6.3287	3.2982
1998	7.9988	3.7510	3.6358	6.6366	3.4803
1999	8.5219	3.9322	3.8023	7.0149	3.6250
2000	9.0241	4.1308	3.9877	7.3351	3.8082

Table 6.1 (continued)

a. Prices (equal to 1.000 in 1972)

Year	Energy	Food	Consumer goods	Capital services	Consumer services
Immediate decontrol					
1983	2.8063	1.8181	1.8031	2.5335	1.8047
1984	3.0214	1.8752	1.8587	2.7264	1.8611
1985	3.2564	1.9595	1.9401	2.9451	1.9383
1986	3.4979	2.0840	2.0607	3.1328	2.0544
1987	3.7713	2.1795	2.1520	3.3968	2.1325
1988	4.0573	2.2596	2.2291	3.6792	2.2048
1989	4.3918	2.3552	2.3208	3.9802	2.2876
1990	4.6217	2.5118	2.4703	4.1284	2.4233
1991	4.9195	2.6360	2.5877	4.3896	2.5240
1992	5.3231	2.7462	2.6941	4.7278	2.6304
1993	5.7462	2.8850	2.8263	5.0614	2.7521
1994	6.1084	3.1215	3.0480	5.1747	2.9394
1995	6.5313	3.3021	3.2162	5.4542	3.0853
1996	6.9399	3.3940	3.3027	5.8847	3.1770
1997	7.4963	3.5344	3.4339	6.3199	3.2960
1998	7.9738	3.7496	3.6344	6.6278	3.4783
1999	8.4976	3.9308	3.8009	7.0062	3.6229
2000	8.9984	4.1293	3.9864	7.3265	3.8061

b. Total expenditure per household (current prices)

Year	Current policy	Continued controls	Immediate decontrol
1983	24,576	24,572	24,573
1984	26,214	26,239	26,224
1985	28,442	28,427	28,456
1986	30,993	31,028	31,012
1987	33,141	33,188	33,165
1988	35,324	35,367	35,357
1989	37,692	37,722	37,723
1990	40,214	40,238	40,246
1991	42,765	42,795	42,786
1992	45,647	45,657	45,677
1993	48,761	48,785	48,808
1994	52,722	52,743	52,731
1995	56,927	56,945	56,933
1996	61,125	61,143	61,149
1997	65,535	65,551	65,556
1998	69,982	69,998	70,002
1999	74,618	74,634	74,636
2000	79,804	79,821	79,821

Table 6.2
Money metric individual welfare (constant prices; Northeast region)

	Urban		Rural	
Year	White	Nonwhite	White	Nonwhite
Continued controls				
1983	23.43	23.61	32.07	32.26
1984	29.96	30.34	31.96	32.33
1985	37.79	38.58	49.83	50.67
1986	51.53	52.75	55.49	56.72
1987	33.30	34.92	33.42	35.04
1988	19.98	21.82	19.80	21.64
1989	6.90	8.81	6.90	8.81
1990	−1.25	0.71	−0.87	1.09
1991	−4.78	−2.77	−5.24	−3.23
1992	−9.16	−7.07	−7.52	−5.43
1993	−9.67	−7.62	−9.48	−7.43
1994	−12.53	−10.45	−11.98	−9.90
1995	−13.64	−11.56	−12.59	−10.51
1996	−13.92	−11.88	−12.91	−10.88
1997	−14.40	−12.39	−13.20	−11.18
1998	−14.87	−12.90	−13.70	−11.72
1999	−14.45	−12.49	−13.09	−11.12
2000	−14.54	−12.62	−13.22	−11.29
Immediate decontrol				
1983	27.05	27.29	36.51	36.76
1984	21.58	21.88	25.84	26.15
1985	26.72	27.09	31.92	32.31
1986	26.46	26.88	30.76	31.20
1987	26.73	27.21	30.53	31.03
1988	26.93	27.49	29.86	30.45
1989	22.09	22.69	24.31	24.93
1990	18.77	19.35	20.54	21.13
1991	11.13	11.84	12.71	13.43
1992	9.34	10.08	10.12	10.86
1993	8.98	9.64	8.13	8.78
1994	3.70	4.41	6.63	7.37
1995	1.65	2.38	4.90	5.66
1996	11.88	12.81	15.09	16.05
1997	8.50	9.46	11.56	12.56
1998	6.22	7.16	9.06	10.03
1999	4.83	5.80	7.70	8.71
2000	3.66	4.64	6.57	7.58

The time pattern of gains and losses for a nonwhite urban household living in the Northeast is similar to that for a white family.

With immediate decontrol of natural gas prices we find that the price of energy is lower throughout the period 1983 to 2000. Elimination of controls has very little impact on the prices of nonenergy commodities during the period of our study. We also find that total expenditure per household is slightly higher under immediate decontrol. As before, we employ prices of the reference case as a basis for calculating money metric individual welfare (6.24).

The dollar value of changes in welfare under a policy of immediate decontrol is given for various types of households in table 6.2. Under decontrol all households experience a gain in welfare throughout the period 1983 to 2000. As before, the time pattern of gains in welfare is similar for urban and rural households and for white and nonwhite households in the Northeast.

In summary, most of the households we have considered would be better off with immediate decontrol of natural gas prices than under current policy. Continued controls would eventually result in welfare losses for most households. However, these comparisons do not hold uniformly for all households and all years.

6.4   Social Welfare Functions

Under the Pareto principle an economic policy can be recommended if all consuming units are as well off as under any alternative policy and at least one unit is better off. The Pareto principle provides a partial ordering of economic policies. This ordering is invariant with respect to monotone increasing transformations of individual welfare that differ among consuming units. Only welfare comparisons that are ordinal and not comparable among consuming units are required.

Money metric individual welfare (6.24) is a monotone increasing transformation of the measure of individual welfare (6.22). This transformation depends on the prices faced by all consuming units and on the attributes of the individual consuming unit. Considered as a measure of individual welfare in its own right, money metric individual welfare provides all the information about consumer preferences required for application of the Pareto principle. To obtain a complete ordering of economic policies we next introduce a social welfare function.

We consider the set of all possible social orderings over the set of social states, say X, and the set of all possible real-valued individual welfare functions, say W_k $(k = 1, 2, \ldots, K)$. A social ordering, say R, is a complete, reflexive, and transitive ordering of social states. A social state is described by the quantities consumed of N commodity groups by K individuals. The individual welfare function for the kth individual W_k $(k = 1, 2, \ldots, K)$ is defined on the set of social states X and gives the level of individual welfare for that individual in each state.

To describe social orderings in greater detail we find it useful to introduce the following notation:

x — a matrix with elements $\{x_{nk}\}$ describing the social state.

$\mathbf{u} = (W_1, W_2, \ldots, W_K)$ — a vector of individual welfare functions of all K individuals.

Following Sen (1970, 1977) and Hammond (1976) we define a *social welfare functional*, say f, as a mapping from the set of individual welfare functions to the set of social orderings, such that $f(\mathbf{u}') = f(\mathbf{u})$ implies $R' = R$, where

$$\mathbf{u} = [W_1(x), W_2(x), \ldots, W_K(x)]$$
$$\mathbf{u}' = [W_1'(x), W_2'(x), \ldots, W_K'(x)] \, ,$$

for all $x \in X$. Similarly, we define L_k $(k = 1, 2, \ldots, K)$ as the *set of admissible individual welfare functions* for the kth individual and L as the Cartesian product $\Pi_{k=1}^{K} L_k$. Finally, let $\mathbf{L}$ be the partition of L such that all elements of $\mathbf{L}$ yield the same social ordering.

We can describe a social ordering in terms of the following properties of a social welfare functional

1. *Unrestricted domain.* The social welfare functional f is defined for all possible vectors of individual welfare functions $\mathbf{u}$.

2. *Independence of irrelevant alternatives.* For any subset A contained in X, if $\mathbf{u}(x) = \mathbf{u}'(x)$ for all $x \in A$, then $R: A = R': A$, where $R = f(\mathbf{u})$ and $R' = f(\mathbf{u}')$ and $R: A$ is the social ordering over the subset A.

3. *Positive association.* For any vectors of individual welfare functions $\mathbf{u}$ and $\mathbf{u}'$, if for all y in $X - x$, such that

$$W_k'(y) = W_k(y) \, ,$$
$$W_k'(x) > W_k(x) \, , \quad (k = 1, 2, \ldots, K) \, ,$$

then xPy implies $xP'y$ and $yP'x$ implies yPx, where P is a strict ordering of social states.

4. *Nonimposition.* For all x, y in X there exist $\mathbf{u}$, $\mathbf{u}'$ such that xPy and $yP'x$.

5. *Cardinal full comparability.* The set of admissible individual welfare functions that yield the same social ordering $\mathbf{L}$ is defined by

$$\mathbf{L} = \{\mathbf{u}': W_k'(x) = \alpha + \beta W_k(x), \quad \beta > 0, \quad k = 1, 2, \ldots, K\},$$

and $f(\mathbf{u}') = f(\mathbf{u})$ for all $\mathbf{u}' \in \mathbf{L}$.

Cardinal full comparability implies that social orderings are invariant with respect to any positive affine transformation of the individual welfare functions $\{W_k\}$ that is the same for all individuals. By contrast Arrow requires ordinal noncomparability,[14] which implies that social orderings are invariant with respect to monotone increasing transformations of the individual welfare functions that may differ among individuals:

5′. *Ordinal noncomparability.* The set of individual welfare functions that yield the same social ordering $\mathbf{L}$ is defined by

$$\mathbf{L} = \{\mathbf{u}': W_k'(x) = \phi_k[W_k(x)], \quad \phi_k \text{ increasing}, \quad k = 1, 2, \ldots, K\},$$

and $f(\mathbf{u}') = f(\mathbf{u})$ for all u' in $\mathbf{L}$.

The properties of a social welfare functional corresponding to unrestricted domain and independence of irrelevant alternatives are used by Arrow in proving the impossibility of a nondictatorial social ordering:

4′. *Nondictatorship.* There is no individual k such that for all x, $y \in X$, $W_k(x) > W_k(y)$ implies xPy.

Under ordinal noncomparability the assumptions of positive association and nonimposition employed by Arrow imply the weak Pareto principle:

3′. *Pareto principle.* For any x, $y \in X$, if $W_k(x) > W_k(y)$ for all individuals $(k = 1, 2, \ldots, K)$, then xPy.

If a social welfare functional f has the properties of unrestricted domain, independence of irrelevant alternatives, the weak Pareto principle, and ordinal noncomparability, then no nondictatorial social ordering is possible. This result is Arrow's impossibility theorem. Since it is obvious that the class of dictatorial social orderings is too narrow to provide an adequate basis for expressing the implications of alternative ethical judgements, we propose to generate a class of social welfare functions suitable for the evaluation of alternative economic policies by weakening Arrow's assumptions.

If a social welfare functional f has the properties of unrestricted domain, independence of irrelevant alternatives, the weak Pareto principle, and cardinal unit comparability, there exist social orderings and a continuous real-valued social welfare function, say W, such that if $W[\mathbf{u}(x)] > W[\mathbf{u}(y)]$, then xPy. To represent the social orderings appropriate for comparing alternative economic policies, we consider the class of social welfare functions

$$W(\mathbf{u}, x) = \bar{W} - \gamma(x) \left[\sum_{k=1}^{K} a_k(x) |W_k - \bar{W}|^{-\rho} \right]^{-1/\rho} \tag{6.25}$$

where the function $\bar{W}(x)$ corresponds to average individual welfare

$$\bar{W}(x) = \sum_{k=1}^{K} a_k(x) \, W_k(x).$$

The second part of the function $W(\mathbf{u}, x)$ is a linear homogeneous function of deviations of levels of individual welfare from the average.[15]

At this point we have generated a class of possible social welfare functions capable of expressing the implications of a variety of ethical judgements. In order to choose a specific social welfare function, we must narrow the range of possible ethical judgements by imposing further requirements on the class of social welfare functions. The parameter ρ in the representation (6.25) determines the curvature of the social welfare function in the individual welfare functions $\{W_k(x)\}$. We refer to this parameter as the *degree of aversion to inequality*. By selecting an appropriate value for this parameter, we can incorporate ethical judgements about inequality in the distribution of individual welfare.

If we add the assumption that the social welfare function has the property of anonymity—that is, no individual is given greater weight than any other individual in determining the level of social welfare—then the social welfare functions W in (6.25) must be symmetric in the individual welfare functions $\{W_k(x)\}$. To incorporate a notion of horizontal equity into the social welfare functions (6.25) we can impose a weak form of the property of anonymity. In particular, we require that no individual is given greater weight in the social welfare function than any other individual with an identical individual welfare function. This implies that the social welfare function is symmetric in the levels of individual welfare for identical individuals. The weights $\{a_k(x)\}$ in the social welfare functions (6.25) must be the same for identical individuals.

To complete the selection of a social welfare function $W(\mathbf{u}, x)$ we require that the individual welfare functions $\{W_k\}$ in (6.25) must be invariant with respect to any positive affine transformation that is the same for all households.[16] Under this assumption the logarithm of the translog indirect utility function is a cardinal measure of individual welfare with full comparability among households. The social welfare function takes the form

$$W(\mathbf{u}, x) = \ln \bar{V} - \gamma(x) \left[\sum_{k=1}^{K} a_k(x) |\ln V_k - \ln \bar{V}|^{-\rho} \right]^{-1/\rho}. \tag{6.26}$$

where

$$\ln \bar{V} = \sum_{k=1}^{K} a_k(x) \ln V_k \left[\frac{\mathbf{pm}(\mathbf{A}_k)}{M_k} \right].$$

We can complete the specification of a social welfare function $W(u, x)$ by choosing a set of weights $\{a_k(x)\}$ for the levels of individual welfare $\{\ln V_k[\mathbf{pm}(\mathbf{A}_k) / M_k]\}$ in (6.26). For this purpose we must appeal to a notion of vertical equity. Following Hammond (1977), we define a distribution of total expenditure $\{M_k\}$ as more *equitable* than another distribution $\{M'_k\}$ if

(i) $M_i + M_j = M'_i + M'_j$,

(ii) $M_k = M'_k$ for $k \neq i, j$,

(iii) $\ln V_i \left[\dfrac{\mathbf{pm}(\mathbf{A}_i)}{M'_i} \right] > \ln V_i \left[\dfrac{\mathbf{pm}(\mathbf{A}_i)}{M_i} \right] > \ln V_j \left[\dfrac{\mathbf{pm}(\mathbf{A}_j)}{M_j} \right]$

$> \ln V_i \left[\dfrac{\mathbf{pm}(\mathbf{A}_i)}{M'_j} \right].$

We say that a social welfare function $W(\mathbf{u}, x)$ is *equity-regarding* if it is larger for a more equitable distribution of total expenditure.

We require that the social welfare functions (6.26) must be equity-regarding. This amounts to imposing a version of Dalton's (1920) principle of transfers. This principle requires that a transfer of total expenditures from a rich household to a poor household that does not reverse their relative positions in the distribution of total expenditure must increase the level of social welfare.

If the social welfare functions (6.26) are required to be equity-regarding, then the weights $\{a_k(x)\}$ associated with the individual welfare functions $\{\ln V_k[\mathbf{pm}(\mathbf{A}_k) / M_k]\}$ must take the form

$$a_k(x) = \frac{m_0(\mathbf{p}, \mathbf{A}_k)}{\sum_{k=1}^{K} m_0(\mathbf{p}, \mathbf{A}_k)}, \qquad (k = 1, 2, \ldots, K). \qquad (6.27)$$

We conclude that an equity-regarding social welfare function of the class (6.26) must take the form

$$W(\mathbf{u}, x) = \ln \bar{V} - \gamma(x) \left[\frac{\sum_{k=1}^{K} m_0(\mathbf{p}, \mathbf{A}_k) |\ln V_k - \ln \bar{V}|^{-\rho}}{\sum_{k=1}^{K} m_0(\mathbf{p}, \mathbf{A}_k)} \right]^{-1/\rho}, \qquad (6.28)$$

where

$$\ln \bar{V} = \frac{\sum_{k=1}^{K} m_0(\mathbf{p}, \mathbf{A}_k) \ln V_k[\mathbf{pm}(\mathbf{A}_k) / M_k]}{\sum_{k=1}^{K} m_0(\mathbf{p}, \mathbf{A}_k)}$$

$$= \ln \mathbf{p}' \left(\alpha_p + \frac{1}{2} B_{pp} \ln \mathbf{p} \right) - D(\mathbf{p}) \frac{\sum_{k=1}^{K} m_0(\mathbf{p}, \mathbf{A}_k) \ln [M_k / m_0(\mathbf{p}, \mathbf{A}_k)]}{\sum_{k=1}^{K} m_0(\mathbf{p}, \mathbf{A}_k)}.$$

Furthermore, the condition of positive association implies that the function $\gamma(x)$ in (6.28) must take the form

$$\gamma(x) = \left\{ \frac{\sum_{k \neq j}^{K} m_0(\mathbf{p}, \mathbf{A}_k)}{\sum_{k=1}^{K} m_0(\mathbf{p}, \mathbf{A}_k)} \left[1 + \left[\frac{\sum_{k \neq j}^{K} m_0(\mathbf{p}, \mathbf{A}_k)}{m_0(\mathbf{p}, \mathbf{A}_j)} \right]^{-(\rho+1)} \right] \right\}^{1/\rho} \qquad (6.29)$$

where

$$m_0(\mathbf{p}, \mathbf{A}_j) = \min_k m_0(\mathbf{p}, \mathbf{A}_k), \qquad (k = 1, 2, \ldots, K).$$

In assessing the impact of changes in economic policy on levels of individual welfare for each consuming unit, we have found it useful to express the change in welfare in terms of the change in total expenditure. Similarly, to provide a basis for comparisons among social states $\{x_{nk}\}$ we propose to formulate a money measure of social welfare.[17] Following Pollak (1981), we can define the *social expenditure function* as the minimum level of total expenditure $M = \sum_{k=1}^{K} M_k$ required to attain a given level of social welfare, say W, at a specified price system $\mathbf{p}$. More formally, the social expenditure function $M(\mathbf{p}, W)$ is defined by

$$M(\mathbf{p}, W) = \min \left\{ M: W(\mathbf{u}, x) \geqq W; \, M = \sum_{k=1}^{K} M_k \right\}. \tag{6.30}$$

The social expenditure function (6.30) is precisely analogous to the individual expenditure function (6.21). The individual expenditure function gives the minimum level of expenditure required to attain a stipulated level of individual welfare; the social expenditure function gives the minimum level of aggregate expenditure required to attain a stipulated level of social welfare. The individual expenditure function and the indirect utility function can be employed in assessing the impact of alternative economic policies on individual welfare. Similarly, the social expenditure function and the social welfare function can be employed in assessing the impacts of alternative policies on social welfare.

We can translate any level of social welfare into monetary terms by evaluating the social expenditure function at that level of welfare for a given price system p. Two different levels of social welfare can be compared with reference to a single price system by determining the minimum level of aggregate expenditure required to attain each level of social welfare for the reference prices. In addition, changes in social welfare can be decomposed into changes in efficiency and changes in equity. Money measures of both components of the change in social welfare can be defined in terms of the social expenditure function and the social welfare function.

In order to determine the form of the social expenditure function $M(p, W)$ in (6.30), we can maximize the social welfare function (6.28) for a fixed level of aggregate total expenditure by equalizing total expenditure per household equivalent member $\{M_k/m_0(\mathbf{p}, \mathbf{A}_k)\}$ for all consuming units. If aggregate total expenditure is distributed so as to equalize total expenditure per household equivalent member, the level of individual welfare is the same for all consuming units. For this distribution of total expenditure the social welfare function reduces to the average level of individual welfare $\ln \bar{V}$.

For the translog indirect utility function the maximum value of social welfare for a given level of aggregate expenditure takes the form

$W(x, \mathbf{u}) = \ln \bar{V}$.

$$= \ln \mathbf{p}'\left(\alpha_p + \frac{1}{2} B_{pp} \ln \mathbf{p}\right) - D(\mathbf{p}) \ln\left[\frac{M}{\sum_{k=1}^{K} m_0(\mathbf{p}, \mathbf{A}_k)}\right]. \qquad (6.31)$$

This maximum value of social welfare reduces to average individual welfare. The average is obtained by evaluating the translog indirect utility function (6.20) at total expenditure per household equivalent member $M / \sum_{k=1}^{K} m_0(\mathbf{p}, \mathbf{A}_k)$ for the economy as a whole.

We can solve for aggregate expenditure as a function of the level of social welfare and prices

$$\ln M(\mathbf{p}, W) = \frac{1}{D(\mathbf{p})}\left[\ln \mathbf{p}'\left(\alpha_p + \frac{1}{2} B_{pp} \ln \mathbf{p}\right) - W\right] + \ln\left[\sum_{k=1}^{K} m_0(\mathbf{p}, \mathbf{A}_k)\right]. \qquad (6.32)$$

We can refer to this function as the *translog social expenditure function*. The value of aggregate expenditure is obtained by evaluating the translog individual expenditure function (6.21) at the level of social welfare W and the number of household equivalent members $\sum_{k=1}^{K} m_0(\mathbf{p}, \mathbf{A}_k)$ for the economy as a whole.

To obtain a money measure of social welfare we first evaluate the social welfare function (6.28) at prices $\mathbf{p}^0$ and distribution of total expenditure $\{M_k^0\}$ prevailing before any change in policy. We can express the level of social welfare before any change in policy, say W^0, in terms of the social expenditure function

$$\ln M(\mathbf{p}^0, W^0) = \frac{1}{D(\mathbf{p}^0)}\left[\ln \mathbf{p}^{0'}\left(\alpha_p + \frac{1}{2} B_{pp} \ln \mathbf{p}^0\right) - W^0\right]$$
$$+ \ln\left[\sum_{k=1}^{K} m_0(\mathbf{p}^0, \mathbf{A}_k)\right]. \qquad (6.33)$$

Second, we can decompose our money measure of social welfare into money measures of efficiency and equity.[18] For this purpose we evaluate the social welfare function at the maximum level, say W^2, that can be attained through lump sum redistributions of aggregate expenditure $M^0 = \sum_{k=1}^{K} M_k^0$. Total expenditure per household equivalent member must be equalized for all consuming units, so that the social welfare function (6.28) reduces to average individual welfare (6.31). This is the maximum level of social welfare that is potentially available and can be taken as a measure of efficiency. Evaluating the social expenditure function at the potential level of welfare, say W^2, we obtain

$$M(\mathbf{p}^0, W^2) = M^0 , \tag{6.34}$$

so that aggregate total expenditure M^0 is the resulting money measure of efficiency.

Given a money measure of efficiency, we can define the corresponding money measure of equity as the difference between the money measure of actual social welfare $M(\mathbf{p}^0, W^0)$ and the money measure of potential social welfare M^0. This measure of equity is nonpositive and equal to zero only for perfect equality in the distribution of individual welfare. Under perfect equality total expenditure per household equivalent member is equalized among all consuming units. Using the social expenditure function, we can express our money measure of social welfare $M(\mathbf{p}^0, W^0)$ as the sum of a money measure of efficiency M^0 and a money measure of equity $M(\mathbf{p}^0, W^0) - M^0$

$$M(\mathbf{p}^0, W^0) = M^0 + [M(\mathbf{p}^0, W^0) - M^0] . \tag{6.35}$$

The critical feature of this decomposition is that all three money measures are expressed in terms of the same set of prices $\mathbf{p}^0$.

In summary, we have generated a class of social welfare functions (6.25) that has the properties of unrestricted domain, independence of irrelevant alternatives, positive association, nonimposition, and cardinal full comparability. We can translate social welfare into a money metric by evaluating the social expenditure function (6.32) at the level of social welfare for a given price system. We can decompose money metric social welfare into money measures of efficiency and equity.

6.5 Money Metric Social Welfare

To analyze the impact of a change in economic policy on social welfare, we can evaluate the social welfare function (6.28) at prices $\mathbf{p}^1$ and distribution of total expenditure $\{M_k^1\}$ after the change in policy has taken place. In order to evaluate the impact of a change in economic policy on social welfare, we must compare the levels of aggregate total expenditure required to attain the actual levels of social welfare before and after the policy change at prices prevailing before the change. For this purpose we define *money metric social welfare*, say M_A, as the difference between the total expenditure required to attain the actual level of welfare after the policy change, say W^1, and the expenditure required to attain the actual level of welfare before the policy change W^0 at prices prevailing before the policy change $\mathbf{p}^0$

$$M_A(\mathbf{p}^0, W^0, W^1) = M(\mathbf{p}^0, W^1) - M(\mathbf{p}^0, W^0) . \qquad (6.36)$$

If money metric social welfare is positive, the level of social welfare is increased by the policy change; otherwise, social welfare is decreased or left unaffected.

We can decompose our money measure of social welfare after the change in economic policy into money measures of efficiency and equity. For this purpose we first determine the maximum level of welfare, say W^3, that can be attained through lump sum redistributions of aggregate total expenditure $M^1 = \sum_{k=1}^{K} M_k^1$. As before, aggregate expenditure must be distributed so as to equalize individual expenditure per household equivalent member, so that the social welfare function (6.28) reduces to average individual welfare (6.31). This is the maximum level of social welfare that is potentially available after the change in economic policy and can be taken as a measure of efficiency.

To preserve comparability between money measures of actual social welfare W^1 and potential welfare W^3 after the change in economic policy, we can evaluate the measure of potential welfare at prices prevailing before the change in policy $\mathbf{p}^0$, using the social expenditure function

$$\ln M(\mathbf{p}^0, W^3) = \frac{1}{D(\mathbf{p}^0)} \left[\ln \mathbf{p}^{0'} \left(\alpha_p + \frac{1}{2} B_{pp} \ln \mathbf{p}^0 \right) - W^3 \right]$$
$$+ \ln \left[\sum_{k=1}^{K} m_0(\mathbf{p}^0, A_k) \right] . \qquad (6.37)$$

The corresponding money measure of equity in terms of prices prevailing before the change in policy is given by the difference between the money measure of actual social welfare after the policy change $M(\mathbf{p}^0, W^1)$ and the money measure of potential social welfare after the policy change $M(\mathbf{p}^0, W^3)$. Our money measure of actual social welfare $M(\mathbf{p}^0, W^1)$ is the sum of money measures of efficiency and equity. All three measures are evaluated at prices prevailing before the change in policy $\mathbf{p}^0$

$$M(\mathbf{p}^0, W^1) = M(\mathbf{p}^0, W^3) + [M(\mathbf{p}^0, W^1) - M(\mathbf{p}^0, W^3)] \,. \tag{6.38}$$

Finally, we can decompose money metric social welfare (6.36) into the sum of money metric efficiency and money metric equity. *Money metric efficiency*, say M_P, can be defined as the difference between the total expenditure required to attain the potential level of welfare after the policy change W^3 and the expenditure required to attain the potential level of welfare before the policy change W^2. Both are evaluated at prices prevailing before the policy change $\mathbf{p}^0$

$$M_P(\mathbf{p}^0, W^2, W^3) = M(\mathbf{p}^0, W^3) - M^0 \,. \tag{6.39}$$

Similarly, *money metric equity*, say M_E, can be defined as the difference between money measures of equity before and after the policy change, evaluated at prices before the change $\mathbf{p}^0$

$$M_E(\mathbf{p}^0, W^0, W^1, W^2, W^3) = [M(\mathbf{p}^0, W^1) - M(\mathbf{p}^0, W^3)]$$
$$- [M(\mathbf{p}^0, W^0) - M^0] \,. \tag{6.40}$$

Money metric social welfare is the sum of money metric efficiency and money metric equity

$$M_A(\mathbf{p}^0, W^0, W^1) = M_P(\mathbf{p}^0, W^2, W^3) + M_E(\mathbf{p}^0, W^0, W^1, W^2, W^3) \,. \tag{6.41}$$

All three money measures of social welfare in this decomposition are expressed in terms of the same set of prices $\mathbf{p}^0$.

To illustrate the measurement of social welfare we can represent the concept of money metric social welfare geometrically, as in figure 6.2. In this figure we have depicted a representative consumer with indirect utility function given by the average level of utility $\ln \bar{V}$ in (6.31). As before, we consider the case of two commodities ($N = 2$) for simplicity. Consumer equilibrium at the actual level of social welfare W^0 before the policy change is represented by the point A. The corresponding level of aggregate expenditure $M(\mathbf{p}^0, W^0)$, divided by the price of the second commodity $\mathbf{p}^0_2$, is given on the vertical axis. This axis provides a representation of aggregate expenditure in terms of units of the second commodity.

Aggregate expenditure M^0 is the value of the social expenditure function at the potential level of welfare W^2. This is the maximum level of welfare that can be obtained by lump-sum redistributions of

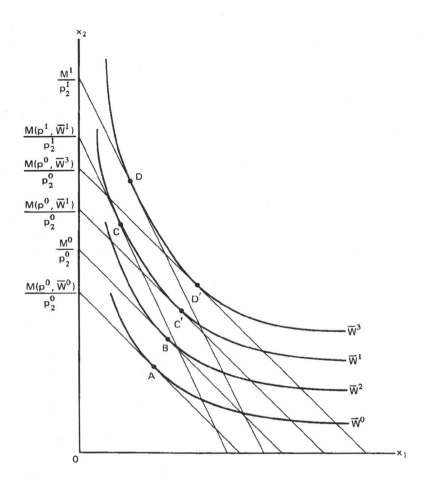

Figure 6.2
Money metric social welfare.

aggregate expenditure. The corresponding consumer equilibrium is represented by the point B. A money measure of efficiency, expressed in terms of units of the second commodity, is given by the level of aggregate expenditure $M^0/\mathbf{p}_2^0$. The corresponding money measure of equity is provided by the distance along the x_2 axis between aggregate expenditure $M^0/\mathbf{p}_2^0$ and the value of the social expenditure function $M(p^0, W^0)/p_2^0$; each is divided by the price of the second commodity. The money measure of social welfare at A is the sum of money measures of efficiency and equity.

As before, consumer equilibrium at the level of social welfare W^1 after the policy change is represented by the point C. In (6.36) we have determined this level of welfare by evaluating the social welfare function (6.28) at the prices $\mathbf{p}^1$ and the distribution of total expenditure $\{M_k^1\}$ after the change in policy has taken place. To translate the level of social welfare W^1 into aggregate expenditure at the prices prevailing before the policy change, we evaluate the social expenditure function (6.32) at this level of social welfare and the prices before the changes $\mathbf{p}^0$. The resulting level of aggregate expenditure $M(\mathbf{p}^0, W^1)$ corresponds to consumer equilibrium at the point C'.

The money measure of social welfare at C' is the sum of money measures of efficiency and equity that are precisely analogous to those we have defined for the measure of welfare at A. We can decompose our money measure of social welfare by first determining the maximum level of social welfare, say W^3, that can be obtained through lump-sum distributions to aggregate expenditure M^1 at prices $\mathbf{p}^1$. The corresponding consumer equilibrium is represented by the point D. We can translate this level of social welfare into aggregate expenditure at prices prevailing before the change $\mathbf{p}^0$ by evaluating the social welfare function $M(\mathbf{p}^0, W^3)$ at the point D.

Money metric social welfare, expressed in units of the second commodity, is represented by the distance along the x_2 axis between aggregate expenditure $M(\mathbf{p}^0, W^1)/p_2^0$ and expenditure $M(\mathbf{p}^0, W^0)/p_2^0$, each divided by the price of the second commodity. Similarly, money metric efficiency is represented by the distance between aggregate expenditure $M(\mathbf{p}^0, W^3)/p_2^0$ and expenditure M^0/p_2^0. Finally, money metric equity is represented by the difference between the distances $[M(\mathbf{p}^0, W^1) - M(\mathbf{p}^0, W_3)]/p_2^0$ and $[M(\mathbf{p}^0, W^0) - M^0]/p_2^0$. The distance corresponding to money metric social welfare is the sum of the distances corresponding to money metric efficiency and money metric equity.

Given methods for measuring social welfare, we are in a position to evaluate alternative policies for natural gas price regulation in the United States. As a basis for comparison of levels of social welfare associated with alternative policies, we take current policy as a reference case. Under this policy price controls are eliminated on some types of natural gas in 1985. We employ the behavior of the U.S. economy under this policy as a base case for policy analysis.

The value of social welfare depends on prices for each of the five commodities included in our model of aggregate consumer behavior—energy, food, consumer goods, capital services, and consumer services. In addition, it depends on total expenditure for the U.S. economy as a whole. As before, we make the simplifying assumption that total expenditure changes in the same proportion for all consuming units. We employ the projections of prices and total expenditure based on the Dynamic General Equilibrium Model (DGEM) of the U.S. economy given in table 6.1.

We can translate our evaluation of alternative policies for natural gas price regulation into money measures of social welfare by employing the social expenditure function introduced in section 6.4. In table 6.3 we present money metric social welfare for the two alternatives to current policy described in section 6.3 above. Although the magnitude of money metric social welfare depends on the degree of aversion to inequality ρ, we find that the qualitative features of comparisons among alternative policies for different values of this parameter are almost identical. We present money metric social welfare for both

Table 6.3
Money metric social welfare (millions of constant dollars)

Year	Continued controls	Immediate decontrol
1983	1,492.520	1,717.652
1984	1,799.619	1,332.337
1985	2,401.407	1,650.275
1986	3,117.486	1,625.640
1987	2,004.577	1,636.300
1988	1,221.106	1,640.076
1989	452.995	1,346.813
1990	−20.729	1,144.807
1991	−239.067	695.305
1992	−467.214	579.660
1993	−519.304	532.518
1994	−681.827	276.191
1995	−740.451	160.032
1996	−759.793	768.837
1997	−786.539	569.036
1998	−816.259	429.719
1999	−789.273	349.180
2000	−796.057	280.520

alternatives to the base case for the degree of aversion to inequality ρ equal to minus one.

Under continued controls money metric social welfare is positive for the years 1983 to 1989, and becomes negative for the rest of the period. Money metric social welfare under immediate decontrol is positive throughout the period 1983 to 2000. Gains in social welfare under immediate decontrol exceed those under continued controls in 1983 and for all years after 1988. Our analysis of current regulatory policy for natural gas prices and the two alternative policies appears to justify immediate decontrol of natural gas prices. This policy is superior to current policy and to a policy of continued price controls.

Money metric social welfare is the sum of money metric efficiency and money metric equity. Money metric efficiency corresponds to the gain in potential social welfare associated with a change in regulatory policy and is independent of the degree of aversion to inequality ρ. We present money metric efficiency for both alternatives to the base case in table 6.4.

Table 6.4
Money metric efficiency (millions of constant dollars)

Year	Continued controls	Immediate decontrol
1983	2,162.315	2,492.543
1984	2,695.706	1,963.536
1985	3,483.171	2,434.154
1986	4,641.808	2,405.515
1987	2,978.186	2,424.443
1988	1,783.287	2,437.363
1989	611.950	1,998.672
1990	−114.416	1,697.490
1991	−438.714	1,012.105
1992	−808.774	843.876
1993	−872.335	790.947
1994	−1,125.599	361.113
1995	−1,219.799	180.499
1996	−1,246.097	1,099.865
1997	−1,287.569	797.594
1998	−1,331.449	587.833
1999	−1,291.577	464.389
2000	−1,300.480	358.882

Under continued controls money metric efficiency is positive for 1983 to 1989 and negative for the rest of the period. Money metric efficiency under immediate decontrol is positive throughout the period. Money metric efficiency is higher for immediate decontrol than for continued controls for 1983 and 1988 to 2000. A common practice in welfare economics is to recommend the policy with the greatest efficiency. On these grounds the policy of immediate decontrol would be judged superior to current policy and to continued controls.

We next consider money measures of equity for both alternatives to current regulatory policy. Money metric equity is defined as the difference between actual and potential gains in social welfare resulting from a change in regulatory policy. Money metric equity, unlike money metric efficiency, depends on the degree of aversion to inequality ρ. We have found, as before, that the qualitative features of comparisons among alternative policies are almost identical for different values of this parameter, so that we present money metric equity for

Table 6.5
Money metric equity (millions of constant dollars)

Year	Continued controls	Immediate decontrol
1983	−669.794	−774.890
1984	−896.087	−631.199
1985	−1,081.765	−783.880
1986	−1,524.322	−779.875
1987	−973.610	−788.143
1988	−562.181	−797.286
1989	−158.954	−651.859
1990	93.687	−552.683
1991	199.647	−316.800
1992	341.560	−264.216
1993	353.031	−258.429
1994	443.771	−84.922
1995	479.348	−20.467
1996	486.304	−331.028
1997	501.030	−228.557
1998	515.190	−158.114
1999	502.305	−115.209
2000	504.423	−78.363

the two alternatives to current regulatory policy in table 6.5 for degree of aversion to inequality ρ equal to minus one.

Money metric equity for a policy of continued natural gas price controls is negative for the period 1983 to 1989 and positive for the remainder of the period 1990 to 2000, reaching a level of $515 millions in 1998. By contrast a policy of immediate decontrol reduces equity throughout the period 1983 to 2000.

Finally, by comparing the results presented in tables 6.4 and 6.5, we can see that money metric efficiency and equity move in opposite directions. For example, a policy of immediate decontrol of natural gas prices is preferred to all other policies for the period 1983 to 2000. Throughout this period money metric efficiency under immediate decontrol is positive; however money metric equity under this policy is lower than that for current policy. Under continued controls money metric efficiency is greater than under current policy through 1989 and less than under current policy for the period 1990 to 2000. By contrast money metric equity is lower than under current policy through 1989 and greater for 1990 to 2000.

In summary, we have translated comparisons among alternative policies for natural gas price regulation into money measures of social welfare. Money metric social welfare for a policy of immediate decontrol of natural gas prices is higher than under current policy or continued controls. Finally, we have decomposed money metric social welfare into money metric equity and money metric efficiency. We have found that money metric equity and money metric efficiency are both essential to the determination of money metric social welfare.

Notes

1. The translog indirect utility function was introduced by Christensen, Jorgenson, and Lau (1975) and extended to encompass determinants of expenditure allocation other than prices and total expenditure by Jorgenson and Lau (1975). Alternative approaches to the representation of the effects of prices and total expenditure on expenditure allocation are summarized by Barten (1977), Deaton and Muellbauer (1980b, pp. 60–85), and Lau (1977a).

2. Alternative approaches to the representation of household characteristics in expenditure allocation are presented by Barten (1964), Gorman (1976), and Prais and Houthakker (1971). A review of the literature is presented by Deaton and Muellbauer (1980b, pp. 191–213).

3. The specification of a system of individual demand functions by means of Roy's Identity was first employed in econometric modeling of consumer behavior by Houthakker (1960). A detailed review of econometric models based on Roy's Identity is given by Lau (1977a).

4. For further discussion, see Lau (1977b, 1982) and Jorgenson, Lau, and Stoker (1980, 1981, 1982).

5. Household equivalence scales are discussed by Barten (1964), van der Gaag and Smolensky (1982), Kakwani (1977), Lazear and Michael (1980), Muellbauer (1974a, 1977, 1980), and Prais and Houthakker (1971), among others. Alternative approaches are summarized by Deaton and Muellbauer (1980b).

6. The use of household equivalence scales in evaluating transfers among individuals has been advocated by Deaton and Muellbauer (1980b, esp. pp. 205–212), and by Muellbauer (1974a). Pollak and Wales (1979) have presented arguments against the use of household equivalence scales for this purpose.

7. Deaton and Muellbauer (1980b, pp. 227–239), King (1983a, b), McKenzie (1982), and Muellbauer (1974a, c) present approaches to welfare measurement based on the distribution of "real expenditure." Measures of "real expenditure" could be derived from the individual expenditure function (6.23) by varying the level of utility V_k for a fixed set of prices $\mathbf{p}$ $(k = 1, 2, \ldots, K)$. Restrictions on preferences under which measures of social welfare defined on the distribution of real expenditure coincide with measures defined on the distribution of individual welfare are given by Roberts (1980c).

8. The 1972–1973 Survey of Consumer Expenditures is discussed by Carlson (1974).

9. We employ data on the flow of services from durable goods rather than purchases of durable goods. Personal consumption expenditures in the U.S. National Income and Product Accounts are based on purchases of durable goods.

10. This series is published annually by the U.S. Bureau of the Census.

11. A detailed discussion of the stochastic specification of our model and of econometric methods for pooling time-series and cross-section data is presented by Jorgenson, Lau and Stoker (1982). This stochastic specification implies that time-series data must be adjusted for heteroscedasticity by multiplying each observation by the statistic

$$\rho = \frac{(\sum M_k)^2}{\sum M_k^2} \, .$$

12. This concept of money metric individual welfare coincides with the concept of net equivalent variation employed by Jorgenson, Lau, and Stoker (1982). Measures of equivalent variations based on the translog indirect utility function were introduced by Jorgenson, Lau, and Stoker (1981). The corresponding measures of compensating variations were introduced by Jorgenson, Lau, and Stoker (1980). The concepts of equivalent and compensating variations are due to Hicks (1942) and have been discussed by Chipman and Moore (1980a), Deaton and Muellbauer (1980b, pp. 184–190), Diamond and McFadden (1974), Hausman (1981), and Hurwicz and Uzawa (1971), among others. An individual ordering based on money metric individual welfare is identical to that based on Samuelson's (1974) concept of money metric utility.

13. These price projections are based on the projections of the U.S. economy under alternative regulatory policies for natural gas production by Goettle, Hudson, Jorgenson, and Slesnick (1983).

14. Arrow (1967, p. 225) has defended noncomparability in the following terms "...the autonomy of individuals, an element of mutual incommensurability among people seems denied by the possibility of interpersonal comparisons."

15. It is important to note that the social welfare function in (6.25) represents a social ordering over all possible individual orderings and exemplifies the multiple profile approach to social choice of Arrow (1963) rather than the single profile approach employed by Bergson (1938) and Samuelson (1947). The literature on the existence of single profile social welfare functions is discussed by Roberts (1980d), Samuelson (1982), and Sen (1979b).

16. This assumption implies that individual welfare increases with total expenditure at a rate that is inversely proportional to total expenditure. This is also implied by the utilitarian social welfare function employed by Arrow and Kalt (1979).

17. Alternative money measures of social welfare are discussed by Arrow and Kalt (1979), Bergson (1980), Deaton and Muellbauer (1980b, pp. 214–239), Roberts (1980c), and Sen (1976a). A survey of the literature is presented by Sen (1979a).

18. Alternative money measures of efficiency and equity are discussed by Arrow and Kalt (1979), Bergson (1980), and Sen (1976a, 1979).

7 Redistributional Policy and the Measurement of Poverty

Dale W. Jorgenson and
Daniel T. Slesnick

7.1 Introduction

The purpose of this chapter is to present an approach to the measurement of poverty based on potential gains to society from redistributional policy. The elimination of poverty requires that all consuming units enjoy a level of welfare that exceeds a stipulated poverty threshold. Our measure of poverty represents the maximum social benefit from a redistribution of aggregate expenditure so as to achieve this objective.

In order to assess the gains to society from redistributional policy we employ the concept of a social welfare function, originated by Bergson (1938) and discussed by Samuelson (1947, 1982). The social welfare function is defined on the distribution of individual welfare over the population of all consuming units. Measures of poverty are frequently defined in terms of the distribution of individual welfare only for those consuming units below the poverty threshold.

Redistributional policy is based on transfers of expenditure from the relatively affluent to the relatively poor. The net benefits to society from redistribution can be measured by comparing the gains of the poor with the losses of the rich. By defining poverty in terms of the distribution of individual welfare over all consuming units, we can integrate the measurement of poverty with the evaluation of redistributional policy.

Although the elimination of poverty can be assigned high priority in the formulation of redistributional policy, reduction of the inequality remaining after poverty has been eliminated is also an important policy objective. By combining the measurement of poverty with the measurement of the remaining inequality, we can treat both objectives of redistributional policy within the framework for inequality measurement introduced by Jorgenson and Slesnick (1984a,b).

Our measures of individual welfare incorporate differences in preferences among consuming units associated with demographic characteristics, such as family size and age of head of household. These measures also depend on the prices faced by each consuming unit. We employ an econometric model of consumer behavior to derive cardinal measures of individual welfare that are fully comparable among consuming units.

Since our measures of individual welfare depend on the demographic characteristics of each consuming unit, we can compare poverty levels for populations that differ in demographic composition. Similarly, our measures of poverty incorporate both changes in the distribution of total expenditure and changes in prices. We can compare poverty levels for populations that differ in the distribution of total expenditure and that confront different price systems.

In section 7.2 we develop a measure of poverty based on the distribution of individual welfare over all consuming units. For this purpose we introduce a poverty threshold, defined in terms of individual welfare. It is important to note that the poverty threshold is usually defined in terms of income or total expenditure rather than individual welfare. Our definition exploits the comparability of welfare measures among consuming units.

The elimination of poverty requires the redistribution of aggregate expenditure from consuming units above the poverty threshold to units below the threshold. Optimal redistributional policy requires that this level of expenditure should be collected from consuming units with the highest levels of individual welfare by means of lump-sum taxes. The expenditure should then be distributed by means of lump-sum transfers to units with the lowest levels of individual welfare.

Our measure of poverty is based on the maximum gain in social welfare that is potentially available from the elimination of poverty. In section 7.3 we provide a measure of society's willingness to pay for the benefits of redistributional policy in monetary terms. We first introduce a money metric measure of poverty, defined as the difference between a money measure of social welfare resulting from the elimination of poverty and a corresponding measure of actual welfare. This difference is the amount that society as a whole would gain from the elimination of poverty.

Similarly, we introduce a money metric measure of the inequality remaining after poverty has been eliminated. This measure is defined as the difference between a money measure of welfare associated with perfect equality and welfare resulting from the elimination of poverty. This difference is the additional amount that society would gain from achieving perfect equality after poverty has been eliminated. The sum of our money metric measures of poverty and the remaining inequality is the money metric measure of inequality introduced by Jorgenson and Slesnick (1984a,b).

In section 7.4 we outline the implementation of our measures of poverty and the remaining inequality. We first present an econometric model of aggregate consumer behavior. The distinctive feature of this model is that systems of individual demand functions can be recovered uniquely from the aggregate demand system. By requiring that the individual demand functions are integrable, we recover indirect utility functions for all consuming units. We define measures of individual welfare in terms of these indirect utility functions.

To represent social orderings in a form suitable for measuring poverty and the remaining inequality, we consider the class of social welfare functions introduced by Jorgenson and Slesnick (1983). These social welfare functions incorporate notions of both horizontal and vertical equity. The social welfare functions can be expressed in terms of the average level of individual welfare for all consuming units and the dispersion of individual welfare levels from the overall average.

We illustrate the application of measures of society's willingness to pay for the benefits of redistributional policy in section 7.5. We consider the gains in social welfare that would have resulted from the elimination of poverty and the remaining inequality in the United States over the postwar period, 1947–1985. We find that poverty, defined in this way, has declined substantially. However, the downward trend in poverty has recently slowed. Sizable potential gains from the elimination of poverty remain at the end of the period.

The gains in social welfare that would have resulted from achieving perfect equality after poverty has been eliminated have risen steadily over the postwar period. Poverty accounts for the predominant share of society's willingness to pay for the benefits of redistributional policy at the beginning the postwar period. By the end of the period the share of inequality remaining after poverty has been eliminated greatly predominates. These developments have taken place against a backdrop of the gradually declining relative importance of inequality.

In section 7.6 we extend our measures of poverty and the remaining inequality to groups within the U.S. population. To assess the gains to each group from reallocation of expenditure within the group, we employ group welfare functions that are perfectly analogous to social welfare functions. We provide measures of each group's willingness to pay for the benefits of redistributional policy in monetary terms. We introduce money metric measures of inequality, poverty, and the inequality remaining within each group.

We illustrate the application of measures of each group's willingness to pay for the benefits of redistributional policy by dividing the U.S. population among groups of consuming units classified by age of head of household. Except for the youngest group, corresponding to age of head 16–24 years, the gains in group welfare that would have resulted from the elimination of poverty and the remaining inequality largely reflect corresponding gains for the population as a whole.

In section 7.7 we develop measures of poverty and the remaining inequality within and between groups for the population as a whole. These measures enable us to compare the impacts of redistributional policies that are limited to reallocations within groups to those that also permit reallocations between groups. Our measure of poverty within groups is the maximum gain in social welfare resulting from the elimination of poverty by reallocations within each group. Our measure of poverty between groups is the additional gain resulting from further redistribution of expenditure so as to eliminate poverty for the population as a whole.

We illustrate the applications of measures of society's willingness to pay for the benefits of redistributional policies within and between groups. For this purpose we divide the U.S. population among groups of consuming units classified by age of head, as before. We find that gains in social welfare from reallocations within groups are very similar to the gains from reallocations among the whole population. The additional gains from the elimination of poverty by redistribution of expenditure among groups are negligible by the end of the postwar period.

In section 7.8 we compare our measure of poverty with alternative approaches considered in the literature. For this purpose we specialize to a utilitarian social welfare function. A utilitarian social welfare function is additively decomposable in measures of individual welfare. For a utilitarian social welfare function we can express our measure of poverty as a function of a head-count ratio, defined as the number of individuals below the poverty threshold, divided by the total population. Our measure also depends on the distribution of the poverty gap, defined as the difference between the level of individual welfare and the poverty threshold.

We consider the sensitivity of our measures of poverty to alternative formulations of the head-count ratio. Our measure of the head count is based on the number of household equivalent members of all consuming units. Alternative formulations have utilized the number of individuals or the number of households in the population. We also compare our money measures of poverty and the remaining inequality with the sum of transfers among consuming units required to eliminate poverty and the remaining inequality. Section 7.9 provides a summary and conclusion of the paper.

7.2   Poverty and Social Welfare

In this section we develop measures of poverty based on optimal redistributional policy. We introduce a poverty threshold defined in terms of individual welfare. The elimination of poverty requires the redistribution of aggregate expenditure from consuming units above the poverty threshold to units below the threshold. Our measure of poverty is the maximum gain in social welfare available from the elimination of poverty. A measure of the remaining inequality can be defined as the maximum gain in welfare that can be attained by redistributional policy after poverty is eliminated.

To represent preferences in a form suitable for measuring individual welfare, we take households as consuming units. We assume that expenditures on individual commodities are allocated so as to maximize a household welfare function. As a consequence, the household behaves in the same way as an individual maximizing a utility function, as demonstrated by Samuelson (1956) and Pollak (1981). We assume further that the household welfare function provides a cardinal measure of individual welfare that is fully comparable among consuming units.

In order to define measures of poverty and the remaining inequality, we first introduce the *poverty threshold*, say W_L. We then consider the group of households with levels of individual welfare W_k ($k = 1, 2, \ldots, K$) below the poverty threshold. Without loss of generality we can take this group to be comprised of the first K_L consuming units, so that

$$W_L - W_k \geq 0 , \qquad (k = 1, 2, \ldots, K_L) , \tag{7.2.1}$$

where $0 \leq K_L \leq K$. We refer to this group collectively as the *poor*. Similarly, we refer to the difference between the poverty threshold and the level of individual welfare for a poor household as the *poverty gap*. It is important to note that the poverty gap is usually defined in terms of income or total expenditure rather than individual welfare.[1]

To provide a money measure of individual welfare we represent preferences by means of an individual expenditure function, using the following notation:

p_n — price of the nth commodity, assumed to be the same for all consuming units.

$p = (p_1, p_2, \ldots, p_N)$ — the vector of prices of all commodities.

x_{nk} — the quantity of the nth commodity group consumed by the kth consuming unit ($n = 1, 2, \ldots, N; \ k = 1, 2, \ldots, K$).

$M_k = \sum_{n=1}^{N} p_n x_{nk}$ — total expenditure of the kth consuming unit ($k = 1, 2, \ldots, K$).

The individual expenditure function gives the minimum level of expenditure M_k required for the kth consuming unit to achieve the welfare level W_k, given the prices p ($k = 1, 2, \ldots, K$). The level of total expenditure required to raise a poor household to the poverty threshold is given by the individual expenditure function for that household

$$M_k(p, W_L) - M_k(p, W_k) \geq 0 , \qquad (k = 1, 2, \ldots, K_L). \tag{7.2.2}$$

The difference between the levels of total expenditure required for the poverty threshold W_L and for the level of individual welfare W_k is a money measure of the individual poverty gap. Both levels of total expenditure depend on the price system p.

The elimination of poverty can be accomplished by a lump-sum transfer of total expenditure to each poor household, equal to the money measure of the poverty gap (7.2.2) for that household. The total expenditure required to eliminate poverty, say M^E, is the sum of these transfers over all poor households

$$M^E(p, W_L) = \sum_{k=1}^{K_L} [M_k(p, W_L) - M_k(p, W_k)] . \tag{7.2.3}$$

This is a money measure of the aggregate poverty gap.

We next consider orderings over the set of social states and the set of real-valued individual welfare functions. To describe these social orderings in greater detail we find it useful to introduce the following notation:

x — a matrix with elements $\{x_{nk}\}$ describing the social state.

$u = (W_1, W_2, \ldots, W_K)$ — a vector of individual welfare functions of all K consuming units.

To represent social orderings in a form suitable for measuring poverty we consider a class of social welfare functions $W(u, x)$ incorporating a notion of horizontal equity. In particular, we require that every individual has the same weight in the social welfare function as any other individual with the same individual welfare function. We also incorporate a notion of vertical equity by requiring that the social welfare functions are equity-regarding in the sense of Hammond (1977). This amounts to imposing a version of Dalton's (1920) principle of transfers. This principle requires that a transfer from a rich household to a poor household that does not reverse their relative position must increase the level of social welfare.

The elimination of poverty requires the redistribution of aggregate expenditure from consuming units above the poverty threshold to poor households. The optimal policy for redistribution corresponds to the maximum level of social welfare that can be attained through lump-sum transfers. For optimal reallocation of aggregate expenditure the total expenditure required to eliminate poverty (7.2.3) must be collected by lump-sum taxes on consuming units with the highest levels of individual welfare.[2]

To represent lump-sum taxes on the households with the highest levels of individual welfare we introduce the *threshold of affluence*, say W_U. We consider the group of households with a level of individual welfare above the threshold of affluence. Without loss of generality we can take this group to be the last $K - K_U$ consuming units, so that

$$W_k - W_U \geq 0, \qquad (k = K_U + 1, \ldots, K), \qquad (7.2.4)$$

where $K_L \leq K_U \leq K$. We refer to this group collectively as the *rich*. Similarly, we refer to the difference between the level of individual welfare for a rich household and the threshold of affluence as the *margin of affluence*.

The difference between the total expenditure required for the level of individual welfare W_k and for the threshold of affluence W_U is given by the individual expenditure function

$$M_k(p, W_k) - M_k(p, W_U) \geq 0 , \qquad (k = K_U + 1, \dots, K) . \qquad (7.2.5)$$

This difference is a money measure of the margin of affluence. As before, both levels of total expenditure depend on the price system p.

Optimal redistributional policy requires that the total of lump-sum transfers required to bring all poor households up to the poverty threshold is equal to the total of lump-sum taxes, say M^A, that will bring all rich households down to the margin of affluence

$$M^A(p, W_U) = \sum_{k=K_U+1}^{K} [M_k(p, W_k) - M_k(p, W_U)] = M^E(p, W_L) . \qquad (7.2.6)$$

This equality makes it possible to express the threshold of affluence as a function of the poverty threshold.

As a limiting case we must consider the possibility that reallocation of the available total expenditure is insufficient to bring all poor households up to the poverty threshold. In this case we define the optimal policy for redistribution in terms of the maximum level of social welfare that can be attained through lump-sum transfers, as before. This policy results in perfect equality in levels of individual welfare for all consuming units. The threshold of affluence is equal to this level of individual welfare and lies below the poverty threshold. We find it convenient to refer to this limiting case as the elimination of poverty, since it corresponds to the maximum level of social welfare available through redistributional policy.

Given the level of social welfare that results from the elimination of poverty, say $W(u, x, W_L)$, we can define a measure of poverty as the difference between this level of social welfare and the actual value of the social welfare function

$$P(u, x, W_L) - W(u, x) . \qquad (7.2.7)$$

The index of poverty is nonnegative, since the social welfare level resulting from the elimination of poverty is greater than or equal to the actual level of social welfare. This index is equal to zero only if the level of individual welfare for all consuming units is above the poverty threshold.

Given the elimination of poverty, aggregate expenditure can be further redistributed to eliminate the remaining inequality in the distribution of individual welfare. This results in the maximum value of welfare that is potentially available and can be taken as a measure of efficiency, say $E(u, x)$. The index of inequality introduced by Jorgenson and Slesnick (1984a,b), say $I(u, x)$, can be defined as the difference between the measure of efficiency and the actual value of social welfare

$$I(u, x) = E(u, x) - W(u, x) .$$

Given the index of inequality, we can define a measure of remaining inequality, say $R(u, x, W_L)$, as the difference between indexes of inequality and poverty

$$
\begin{aligned}
R(u, x, W_L) &= I(u, x) - P(u, x, W_L) \\
&= [E(u, x) - W(u, x)] - [W(u, x, W_L) - W(u, x)] \\
&= E(u, x) - W(u, x, W_L) .
\end{aligned}
\tag{7.2.8}
$$

The index of remaining inequality is the difference between potential social welfare and the level of welfare resulting from the elimination of poverty. This index is nonnegative since the welfare level associated with the elimination of poverty is always less than or equal to potential welfare. The index is equal to zero at the point of perfect equality.

To illustrate the measurement of poverty and the remaining inequality we can represent the index of poverty and the index of remaining inequality in diagrammatic form. For simplicity we consider the case of a society consisting of two identical individuals ($K = 2$), one poor (W_1) and the other rich (W_2). In figure 7.1 we have depicted the contours of a concave social welfare function. The forty-five degree line through the origin represents distributions of individual welfare characterized by perfect equality ($W_1 = W_2$).

We can represent the actual distribution of individual welfare by a point A with welfare level $W(u, x) = W^0$. To measure the level of social welfare that results from the elimination of poverty, we first consider the poverty threshold W_L. Next, we consider the locus of individual welfare levels corresponding to all possible lump-sum redistributions of aggregate expenditure $M = M_1 + M_2$. We refer to this as the *redistribution locus*. The level of social welfare resulting from the elimination of poverty, $W(u, x, W_L) = W^1$, corresponds to the point B. This point is

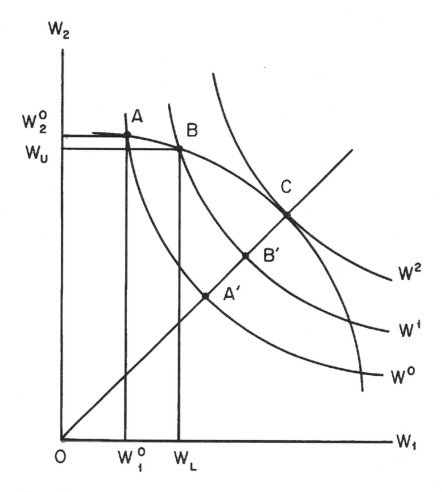

Figure 7.1
Indexes of poverty and the remaining inequality.

the intersection of the redistribution locus and the poverty threshold. The poverty threshold W_L provides one coordinate of the point B, while the threshold of affluence W_U provides the other. The poverty gap corresponds to the distance $W_L - W_1^0$, while the margin of affluence corresponds to $W_2^0 - W_U$.

To measure the level of social welfare that results from the elimination of inequality in the distribution of individual welfare, we continue along the redistribution locus to the point C. This is the maximum level of social welfare, $E(u, x) = W^2$, that can be attained by lump-sum redistributions and corresponds to perfect equality in the distribution of individual welfare. In figure 7.1 the point A' represents perfect equality in the distribution of individual welfare at the same level of social welfare W^0 as at point A. Similarly, the point B' represents perfect equality at the same level of welfare W^1 as at point B.

The actual level of social welfare W^0 can be represented by the distance OA', while the potential level of welfare W^2 can be represented by the distance OC. The level of welfare corresponding to the elimination of poverty can be represented by the distance OB'. The index of poverty P is represented by the distance $OB' - OA' = A'B'$. The index of inequality remaining after the elimination of poverty R is represented by the distance $OC - OB' = B'C$. Finally, the index of inequality I is represented by the distance $OC - OA' = A'C$; this index is the sum of the poverty index and the index of remaining inequality, $A'C = A'B' + B'C$.

7.3 Measures of Poverty

We find it useful to express the gains to society from the elimination of poverty in terms of equivalent levels of aggregate expenditure. For this purpose we introduce the *social expenditure function*, defined as the minimum level of total expenditure, $M = \sum_{k=1}^{K} M_k$, required to attain a given level of social welfare, say W, at a specified price system p.[3] More formally, the social expenditure function $M(p, W)$ is defined by

$$M(p, W) = \min \left\{ M: W(u, x) \geq W; M = \sum_{k=1}^{K} M_k \right\}. \tag{7.3.1}$$

We can translate any level of social welfare into monetary terms by evaluating the social expenditure function at that level of welfare for a given price system p. For example, potential social welfare, W^2 in figure 7.1, is the maximum level of welfare attainable from a given level of aggregate expenditure. The corresponding level of aggregate expenditure M is a money measure of potential social welfare at the current price system P.

Two different levels of social welfare can be compared with reference to a single price system by determining the minimum level of aggregate expenditure required to attain each level of social welfare for the reference prices. For example, we can define a money metric measure of poverty, say $M^P(p, W^0, W^1)$, as the difference between the money measure of welfare resulting from the elimination of poverty, W^1, and a money measure of actual social welfare, W^0, in figure 7.1

$$M^P(p, W^0, W^1) = M(p, W^1) - M(p, W^0) .$$ (7.3.2)

This measure of poverty is nonnegative and equal to zero only when all consuming units are above the poverty threshold. The money metric measure of poverty M^P is the amount that society as a whole would gain from the elimination of poverty.

Similarly, we can define a money metric measure of the inequality remaining after the elimination of poverty, say $M^R(p, W^1, W^2)$, as the difference between the level of aggregate expenditure M, which is a money measure of potential social welfare W^2, and the money measure of welfare resulting from the elimination of poverty W^1

$$M^R(p, W^1, W^2) = M - M(p, W^1) .$$ (7.3.3)

This measure of remaining inequality is nonnegative and equal to zero for perfect equality in the distribution of individual welfare. The money metric measure of remaining inequality M^R is the additional amount the society would gain from a perfectly egalitarian distribution of individual welfare, given the elimination of poverty.

The money metric measure of inequality introduced by Jorgenson and Slesnick (1984a,b), say $M^I(p, W^0, W^2)$, is defined as the difference between money measures of potential and actual social welfare.[4] This measure of inequality can be decomposed into the sum of measures of poverty and the remaining inequality

$$M^I(p, W^0, W^2) = M^P(p, W^0, W^1) + M^R(p, W^1, W^2) .$$ (7.3.4)

We can define a money metric measure of relative poverty, say $M^Q(p, W^0, W^1, W^2)$, as follows

$$\begin{aligned} M^Q(p, W^0, W^1, W^2) &= \frac{M^P(p, W^0, W^1)}{M} \\ &= \frac{M(p, W^1) - M(p, W^0)}{M} . \end{aligned}$$ (7.3.5)

This measure represents the proportion of aggregate expenditure lost due to failure to eliminate poverty.

We can also define a money metric measure of relative remaining inequality, say $M^S(p, W^0, W^1, W^2)$, as follows

$$M^S(p, W^0, W^1, W^2) = \frac{M^R(p, W^1, W^2)}{M}$$

$$= \frac{M - M(p, W^1)}{M} . \qquad (7.3.6)$$

This measure represents the proportion of aggregate expenditure lost due to an inequitable distribution of individual welfare, given the elimination of poverty.

The money metric measure of relative inequality, introduced by Jorgenson and Slesnick (1984a,b), say $M^J(p, W^0, W^2)$, can be defined as the ratio of the money metric measure of inequality $M^I(p, W^0, W^2)$ to the money measure of potential welfare M. This measure of relative inequality can be decomposed into the sum of measures of relative poverty and relative remaining inequality

$$M^J(p, W^0, W^2) = M^Q(p, W^0, W^1, W^2) + M^S(p, W^0, W^1, W^2) . \qquad (7.3.7)$$

To illustrate the application of our money measures of poverty we can express the level of social welfare as a function of the price system p and aggregate expenditure M. We take the level of social welfare to be the potential level obtained by maximizing the social welfare function for a fixed price system and fixed aggregate expenditure. Under this assumption society behaves in the same way as an individual maximizing a utility function, as Samuelson (1956) and Pollak (1981) have pointed out. The individual expenditure function for this representative consumer corresponds to the social expenditure function.

In figure 7.2 we have depicted the indifference map of the representative consumer with individual expenditure function given by the social expenditure function (7.3.1). For simplicity we consider the case of two commodities ($N = 2$). Consumer equilibrium at the actual level of social welfare W^0 is represented by the point A. The corresponding level of aggregate expenditure $M(p, W^0)$, divided by the price of the second commodity p_2, is given the vertical axis. This axis provides a representation of aggregate expenditure in terms of units of the second commodity.

Aggregate expenditure M is the value of the social expenditure function at the potential level of welfare W^2. This is the maximum level of welfare that can be obtained by lump-sum redistributions of aggregate expenditure. The corresponding consumer equilibrium is represented by the point C. A money measure of the loss in social

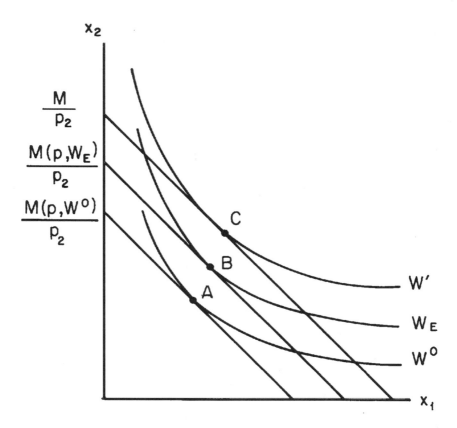

Figure 7.2
Money metric poverty.

welfare due to inequality, expressed in terms of units of the second commodity, is provided by the distance along the x_2 axis between aggregate expenditure M/p_2 and the value of the social expenditure function $M(p, W^0)/p_2$. This distance represents the money measure of inequality $M^I(p, W^0)$, divided by the price of the second commodity. The ratio between this distance and the distance corresponding to aggregate expenditure M/p_2 is the money measure of relative inequality $M^J(p, W^0)$.

We can decompose a money measure of inequality into the sum of measures of poverty and the remaining inequality. The level of social welfare that results from the elimination of poverty W^1 can be attained by raising poor households to the poverty threshold and reducing rich households to the threshold of affluence. The corresponding consumer equilibrium is represented by the point B. A money measure of the loss in social welfare due to failure to eliminate poverty is provided by the distance along the x_2 axis between the value of the social expenditure function $M(p, W^1)/p_2$ and the value at the actual level of social welfare $M(p, W^0)/p_2$. This distance represents the money measure of poverty $M^P(p, W^0, W^1)$, divided by the price of the second commodity. Similarly, the loss in social welfare due to failure to eliminate the inequality remaining $M^R(p, W^1, W^2)$, is the distance between the level of aggregate expenditure and the value of the social expenditure function $M(p, W^1)/p_2$, divided by the price of the second commodity. Ratios between these distances and the distance corresponding to aggregate expenditure M/p_2 represent money measures of relative poverty and relative remaining inequality, $M^Q(p, W^0, W^1, W^2)$ and $M^S(p, W^0, W^1, W^2)$.

7.4   Individual and Social Welfare

In order to implement our measures of poverty we utilize the econometric model constructed by Jorgenson and Slesnick (1987a) to evaluate levels of individual welfare. To measure individual welfare we represent individual preferences by means of an indirect utility function for each consuming unit, using the following notation:

$\ln p = (\ln p_1, \ln p_2, \ldots, \ln p_N)$ — vector of logarithms of prices.

A_k — vector of attributes of the kth consuming unit $(k = 1, 2, \ldots, K)$.

We assume that the kth consuming unit allocates expenditures in accord with the transcendental logarithmic or translog indirect utility function,[5] say V_k, under exact aggregation

$$\ln V_k = \ln p' \alpha_p + \frac{1}{2} \ln p' B_{pp} \ln p - D(p) \ln [M_k/m_0(p, A_k)] ,$$

$$(k = 1, 2, \ldots, K). \qquad (7.4.1)$$

In this representation the function $m_0(p, A_k)$ is the *general translog household equivalence scale* and can be interpreted as the number of household equivalent members.[6] This equivalence scale takes the form

$$\ln m_0 = \frac{1}{D(p)}\left[\ln m(A_k)'\alpha_p + \frac{1}{2}\ln m(A_k)'B_{pp}\ln m(A_k) + \ln m(A_k)'B_{pp}\ln p\right],$$

$$(k = 1, 2, \ldots, K). \qquad (7.4.2)$$

where

$$\ln m(A_k) = B_{pp}^{-1}B_{pA}A_k, \qquad (k = 1, 2, \ldots, K). \qquad (7.4.3)$$

We refer to the scales $\{m(A_k)\}$ as the *commodity specific translog house-hold equivalence scales*.[7] The function $D(p)$ takes the form

$$D(p) = -1 + iB_{pp}\ln p.$$

To construct an econometric model of consumer behavior based on exact aggregation we generate the expenditure shares of the kth consuming unit by Roy's (1943) Identity. The individual expenditure shares are linear in the logarithms of expenditures $\{\ln M_k\}$ and in the attributes $\{A_k\}$, as required by exact aggregation.[8] We obtain aggregate expenditure shares by multiplying the individual expenditure shares by expenditure for each consuming unit, adding over all units, and dividing by aggregate expenditure, $M = \sum_{k=1}^{K} M_k$. Indirect utility functions (7.4.1) for consuming units with identical demographic characteristics can be recovered in one and only one way from the system of aggregate expenditure shares.[9]

Given the indirect utility function (7.4.1) for each consuming unit, we can express total expenditure as a function of prices, the general household equivalence scale, and the level of utility

$$\ln M_k = \frac{1}{D(p)}\left[\ln p'\left(\alpha_p + \frac{1}{2}B_{pp}\ln p\right) - \ln V_k\right] + \ln m_0(p, A_k),$$

$$(k = 1, 2, \ldots, K). \qquad (7.4.4)$$

We refer to this function as the *translog expenditure function*. The translog expenditure function gives the minimum level of expenditure required for the kth consuming unit to achieve the utility level V_k, given the prices p ($k = 1, 2, \ldots, K$).

The first step in measuring social welfare is to select a representation of the individual welfare function. We define individual welfare for the kth consuming unit, say W_k ($k = 1, 2, \ldots, K$), as the logarithm of the translog indirect utility function (7.4.1):[10]

$W_k = \ln V_k$

$$= \ln p'\alpha_p + \frac{1}{2} \ln p'B_{pp} \ln p - D(p) \ln [M_k / m_0(p, A_k)] ,$$

$$(k = 1, 2, \ldots, K) . \qquad (7.4.5)$$

Individual welfare is a linear function (7.4.5) of the logarithm of total expenditure per household equivalent member $\ln[M_k/m_0(p, A_k)]$ with an intercept and slope coefficient that depend only on prices p ($k = 1, 2, \ldots, K$). This property is invariant with respect to positive affine transformations that are the same for all consuming units, so that the individual welfare function (7.4.5) provides a cardinal measure of individual welfare that is fully comparable among units.[11]

To represent social orderings in a form suitable for measuring poverty we consider the class of social welfare functions introduced by Jorgenson and Slesnick (1983)

$$W(u, x) = \ln \bar{V} - \gamma(x) \left[\frac{\sum_{k=1}^{K} m_0(p, A_k) | \ln V_k - \ln \bar{V}|^{-\rho}}{\sum_{k=1}^{K} m_0(p, A_k)} \right]^{-1/\rho} . \qquad (7.4.6)$$

The first term in the social welfare functions (7.4.6) corresponds to an average of individual welfare levels over all consuming units

$$\ln \bar{V} = \frac{\sum_{k=1}^{K} m_0(p, A_k) \ln V_k[pm(A_k) / M_k]}{\sum_{k=1}^{K} m_0(p, A_k)}$$

$$= \ln p' \left(\alpha_p + \frac{1}{2} B_{pp} \ln p \right) - D(p) \frac{\sum_{k=1}^{K} m_0(p, A_k) \ln [M_k / m_0(p, A_k)]}{\sum_{k=1}^{K} m_0(p, A_k)} .$$

The second term in (7.4.6) is a linear homogeneous function of deviations of levels of individual welfare from the average. This is a measure of dispersion in individual welfare levels. The social welfare functions (7.4.6) are represented in a form that is invariant with respect to positive affine transformations and provide cardinal measures of social welfare.[12]

The Pareto principle requires that an increase in individual welfare must increase social welfare. This condition implies that the increase in the first term in (7.4.6), representing the average level of individual welfare, must exceed the increase in the second term, representing the dispersion in individual welfare. We assume that the function $\gamma(x)$ in (7.4.6) must take the maximum value consistent with the Pareto principle, so that

$$\gamma(x) = \left\{ \frac{\sum_{k \neq j}^{K} m_0(p, A_k)}{\sum_{k=1}^{K} m_0(p, A_k)} \left[1 + \left(\frac{\sum_{k \neq j}^{K} m_0(p, A_k)}{m_0(p, A_j)} \right)^{-(\rho+1)} \right] \right\}^{1/\rho} \qquad (7.4.7)$$

where

$$m_0(p, A_j) = \min_{k} m_0(p, A_k), \qquad (k = 1, 2, \ldots, K).$$

At this point we have generated a class of social welfare functions capable of expressing the implications of a variety of ethical judgments. The parameter ρ in the representation (7.4.6) determines the curvature of the social welfare function in the individual welfare functions $\{W_k(x)\}$. We refer to this parameter as the *degree of aversion to inequality*. By selecting an appropriate value of this parameter, we can incorporate ethical judgments about inequality in the distribution of individual welfare into the social welfare function.

In order to determine the form of the social expenditure function $M(p, W)$ in (7.3.1), we can maximize the social welfare function (7.4.6) for a fixed level of aggregate expenditure by equalizing total expenditure per household equivalent member $\{M_k/m_0(p, A_k)\}$ for all consuming units. For the translog indirect utility function the maximum value of social welfare for a given level of aggregate expenditure takes the form

$$\ln \bar{V} = \ln p' \left(\alpha_p + \frac{1}{2} B_{pp} \ln p \right) - D(p) \ln \left[M \bigg/ \sum_{k=1}^{K} m_0(p, A_k) \right]. \qquad (7.4.8)$$

As before, this is the maximum level of welfare that is potentially available and can be taken as a measure of efficiency.

If aggregate expenditure is distributed so as to equalize total expenditure per household equivalent member, the level of individual welfare is the same for all consuming units. For this distribution of total expenditure the social welfare function reduces to the average level of individual welfare $\ln \bar{V}$. The value of social welfare is obtained by evaluating the translog indirect utility function (7.4.1) at total expenditure per household equivalent member $M / \sum_{k=1}^{K} m_0(p, A_k)$ for the economy as a whole.

We can express aggregate expenditure as a function of the level of social welfare and prices

$$\ln M(p, W) = \frac{1}{D(p)} \left[\ln p' \left(\alpha_p + \frac{1}{2} B_{pp} \ln p \right) - W \right] + \ln \left[\sum_{k=1}^{K} m_0(p, A_k) \right].$$

$$(7.4.9)$$

The value of aggregate expenditure is obtained by evaluating the translog individual expenditure function (7.4.4) at the level of social welfare W and the number of household equivalent members $\sum_{k=1}^{K} m_0(p, A_k)$ for the economy as a whole.

7.5 Money Metric Poverty

We can illustrate money measures of poverty and the remaining inequality by considering money measures of actual and potential levels of welfare and the level of welfare that would result from the elimination of poverty over the period 1947–1985. For this purpose we take the poverty threshold to be the level of individual welfare of a household of size four, with the head of household age 25–34 and food consumption corresponding to 75 percent of the Low Cost Food Plan in 1964.[13]

We first present a money measure of social welfare corresponding to degree of aversion to inequality equal to −1 in table 7.1. This form of the social welfare function (7.4.6) gives the greatest possible weight to equity considerations, since the degree of aversion to inequality is assigned its maximum value. Next, we present a money measure of the level of social welfare that results from the elimination of poverty. Finally, we give the level of aggregate expenditure, which is a money measure of potential social welfare and is independent of the degree of aversion to inequality. All three money measures of social welfare are presented for the years 1947–1985 in constant prices of 1972.

Money metric inequality is defined as the difference between money metric efficiency and money metric social welfare. This measure of inequality is the amount that society as a whole would gain from a perfectly egalitarian distribution of aggregate expenditure. Money metric poverty is the difference between the money measure of social welfare that results from the elimination of poverty and money metric social welfare. This measure of poverty is the gain to society from the elimination of poverty. Money metric remaining inequality is the difference between money metric inequality and money metric poverty. This measure is the additional gain to society from achieving perfect equality after poverty is eliminated. All three measures are presented for the years 1947–1985 in table 7.2.

Table 7.1
Money measures of social welfare (billions of 1972 dollars)

Year	Actual social welfare	Elimination of poverty	Potential social welfare
1947	165.499	255.164	286.672
1948	168.519	260.343	294.234
1949	171.110	262.952	301.627
1950	182.310	270.191	315.677
1951	191.038	278.291	332.748
1952	199.607	286.281	347.642
1953	204.757	292.950	359.271
1954	209.078	300.343	366.989
1955	218.275	311.887	385.047
1956	229.986	320.144	402.629
1957	234.159	327.091	414.419
1958	243.405	334.526	425.130
1959	264.583	344.564	444.849
1960	275.568	350.871	458.562
1961	285.430	359.534	472.122
1962	296.849	372.158	490.829
1963	310.448	382.057	507.158
1964	326.796	396.505	534.983
1965	346.863	411.781	562.635
1966	371.199	430.228	592.635
1967	388.858	445.189	616.738
1968	410.327	462.327	646.719
1969	429.712	479.598	674.039
1970	448.365	495.410	698.969
1971	462.683	508.843	719.407
1972	488.254	531.295	755.144
1973	508.370	549.287	783.917
1974	519.041	558.395	795.072
1975	536.749	573.966	817.783
1976	563.806	597.672	853.292
1977	592.301	622.656	889.794
1978	624.784	651.206	930.553
1979	641.820	668.358	961.374
1980	652.226	679.727	978.949
1981	663.525	690.856	994.120
1982	677.665	703.653	1,009.562
1983	702.047	726.921	1,046.134
1984	732.524	754.990	1,086.687
1985	764.715	785.135	1,131.343

Table 7.2
Money metric poverty (billions of 1972 dollars)

Year	Money metric inequality	Money metric poverty	Money metric remaining inequality
1947	121.173	89.664	31.508
1948	125.716	91.825	33.891
1949	130.516	91.841	38.675
1950	133.368	87.881	45.487
1951	141.710	87.253	54.456
1952	148.035	86.674	61.361
1953	154.514	88.193	66.321
1954	157.911	91.266	66.646
1955	166.772	93.612	73.160
1956	172.643	90.157	82.486
1957	180.260	92.932	87.328
1958	181.725	91.121	90.604
1959	180.266	79.981	100.285
1960	182.994	75.303	107.691
1961	186.692	74.104	112.588
1962	193.980	75.309	118.671
1963	196.710	71.608	125.101
1964	208.187	69.709	138.479
1965	215.548	64.919	150.630
1966	221.437	59.029	162.408
1967	227.880	56.331	171.549
1968	236.392	52.001	184.391
1969	244.327	49.887	194.440
1970	250.603	47.045	203.558
1971	256.724	46.160	210.565
1972	266.890	43.041	223.850
1973	275.547	40.917	234.630
1974	276.031	39.355	236.677
1975	281.034	37.217	243.817
1976	289.486	33.866	255.620
1977	297.493	30.355	267.138
1978	305.769	26.422	279.347
1979	319.554	26.538	293.016
1980	326.723	27.501	299.222
1981	330.595	27.331	303.264
1982	331.897	25.988	305.908
1983	344.087	24.874	319.213
1984	354.163	22.466	331.697
1985	366.628	20.420	346.208

We can express money metric measures of inequality, poverty, and the remaining inequality in relative form by dividing each index by aggregate expenditure. Money metric measures of relative inequality, relative poverty, and relative remaining inequality are presented for the years 1947–1985 in table 7.3. These measures lie between zero and one. The measure of relative inequality represents the proportion of aggregate expenditure lost due to inequality in the distribution of individual welfare. The measure of poverty represents the proportion of aggregate expenditure lost due to failure to eliminate poverty. The measure of relative inequality remaining is the proportion of aggregate expenditure lost due to inequality remaining after the elimination of poverty.

Money metric inequality is a measure of the difference between potential and actual levels of social welfare. This measure reflects the maximum gain to society from the elimination of inequality. Money metric inequality rises steadily throughout the period 1947–1985. In relative terms money metric inequality falls from 42.27 percent of aggregate expenditure in 1947 to 32.41 percent in 1985. This fall is concentrated in the period 1958–1978. From 1947 to 1958 and again from 1978 to 1983 the relative importance of inequality rises slightly.

Money metric poverty is a measure of the difference between levels of social welfare with and without the elimination of poverty. This measure reflects the willingness of society to pay for the elimination of poverty, since it gives the maximum gain to society from raising the welfare of all poor households to the poverty threshold. Money metric poverty rises slightly from 1947 to 1958 and then declines precipitously through 1978. After a brief rise to 1980, this measure declines again through 1985. Society's willingness to pay for the elimination of poverty is still substantial at the end of the period in 1985 at a level of 20.420 billions of 1972 dollars.

In relative terms money metric poverty declines from 31.28 percent of aggregate expenditure in 1947 to only 1.80 percent in 1985. At the beginning of the period in 1947 poverty accounts for 74.00 percent of inequality, but by the end of the period in 1985 poverty accounts for only 5.55 percent. Money metric remaining inequality rises sharply over the period; in relative terms most of the increase takes place before 1970 with only modest increases through 1985. The inequality remaining after poverty is eliminated rises from only 26.00 percent of inequality in 1947 to 94.45 percent in 1985.

Table 7.3
Money metric relative poverty (billions of 1972 dollars)

Year	Money metric relative inequality	Money metric relative poverty	Money metric remaining inequality
1947	.4227	.3128	.1099
1948	.4273	.3121	.1152
1949	.4327	.3045	.1282
1950	.4225	.2784	.1441
1951	.4259	.2622	.1637
1952	.4258	.2493	.1765
1953	.4301	.2455	.1846
1954	.4303	.2487	.1816
1955	.4331	.2431	.1900
1956	.4288	.2239	.2049
1957	.4350	.2242	.2107
1958	.4275	.2143	.2131
1959	.4052	.1798	.2254
1960	.3991	.1642	.2348
1961	.3954	.1570	.2385
1962	.3952	.1534	.2418
1963	.3879	.1412	.2467
1964	.3891	.1303	.2588
1965	.3833	.1154	.2678
1966	.3736	.0996	.2740
1967	.3695	.0913	.2782
1968	.3655	.0804	.2851
1969	.3625	.0740	.2885
1970	.3585	.0673	.2912
1971	.3569	.0642	.2927
1972	.3534	.0570	.2964
1973	.3515	.0522	.2993
1974	.3472	.0495	.2977
1975	.3437	.0455	.2981
1976	.3393	.0397	.2996
1977	.3343	.0341	.3002
1978	.3286	.0284	.3002
1979	.3324	.0276	.3048
1980	.3337	.0281	.3057
1981	.3326	.0275	.3051
1982	.3288	.0257	.3030
1983	.3289	.0238	.3051
1984	.3259	.0207	.3052
1985	.3241	.0180	.3060

7.6   Poverty within Groups

In this section we extend our measures of poverty to groups within the U.S. population. For this purpose we employ group welfare functions that are precisely analogous to the social welfare functions introduced in section 7.2. Our measure of poverty within each group is the maximum gain in group welfare available from the elimination of poverty by reallocation of expenditure within the group. Our measure of the inequality remaining within the group is the additional gain in welfare attainable by further redistribution within the group.

We consider a group of G individuals, where $1 \leq G \leq K$. Without loss of generality we can take this group to be composed of the first G consuming units in the society. We then consider the subgroup of households with levels of individual welfare below the poverty threshold. We take this subgroup of the poor to be the first G_L consuming units, where $0 \leq G_L \leq G$.

As before, we describe preferences by means of individual expenditure functions, using the following notation:

x_{ng}—the quantity of the nth commodity group consumed by the gth consuming unit ($n = 1, 2, \ldots, N$; $g = 1, 2, \ldots, G$).

$M_g = \sum_{n=1}^{N} P_n x_{ng}$ — total expenditure of the gth consuming unit ($g = 1, 2, \ldots, G$).

We can express the poverty gap (7.2.1) in monetary terms (7.2.2) by using the individual expenditure function for each household.

The total expenditure required to eliminate poverty within the group, say M_G^E, is the sum of money measures of the poverty gap over all households within the group

$$M_G^E (p, W_L) = \sum_{g=1}^{G_L} [M_g(p, W_L) - M_g(p, W_g)] . \qquad (7.6.1)$$

This is a money measure of the group poverty gap.

To represent group orderings in a form suitable for measuring poverty within each group, we find it useful to introduce the following notation:

x_G — a matrix with elements $\{x_{ng}\}$ describing the group state.

$u_G = (W_1, W_2, \ldots, W_G)$ — a vector of individual welfare functions for all G consuming units.

We consider a class of group welfare functions $W_G(u_G, x_G)$ that is strictly analogous to the class of social welfare functions $W(u, x)$ introduced in section 7.2.

As before, the elimination of poverty within each group can be accomplished by a lump-sum transfer of total expenditure to each poor household, equal to the money measure of the poverty gap (7.2.2) for that household. The optimal reallocation of group expenditure requires that the total expenditure required to eliminate poverty within the group (7.6.1) be collected by lump-sum taxes on consuming units with the highest levels of individual welfare.

The total of lump-sum transfers within each group required to bring all poor households up to the poverty threshold is equal to the total of lump-sum taxes, say M_G^A, that will bring all rich households down to the margin of affluence, say W_U^G, within the group

$$M_G^A (p, W_U^G) = \sum_{g=G_U+1}^{G} [M_g(p, W_g) - M_g(p, W_U^G)] = M_G^E(p, W_L) , \qquad (7.6.2)$$

where the rich are the last $G - G_U$ consuming units in the group, $G_L \leq G_U \leq G$. This equality makes it possible to express the threshold of affluence within each group as a function of the poverty threshold.

As a limiting case, we must consider the possibility that reallocation of expenditure within the group is insufficient to bring all poor households up to the poverty threshold. As before, the maximum level of social welfare that can be attained through lump-sum transfers results in perfect equality in levels of individual welfare for all consuming units within the group. We find it convenient to refer to this limiting case as the elimination of poverty within the group, since it corresponds to the maximum level of group welfare available through redistribution.

The measurement of group poverty and the inequality remaining within the group can be illustrated as in figure 7.1, above, by interpreting welfare contours in terms of a group welfare function $W_G(u_G, x_G)$. In order to express the gains to each group from the elimination of poverty in monetary terms, we can introduce a *group expenditure function*, defined as the minimum level of group expenditure, $M_G = \sum_{g=1}^{G} M_G$, required to attain a given level of group welfare $W_G(u_G, x_G)$ at a specified price system p. Group expenditure M_G is a money measure of potential group welfare at the current price system.

We can define a money metric measure of group poverty, say $M_G^P(p, W_G^0, W_G^1)$, as the difference between the money measure of group welfare resulting from the elimination of poverty W_G^1 and a money measure of actual group welfare W_G^0

$$M_G^P(p, W_G^1, W_G^0) = M_G(p, W_G^1) - M_G(p, W_G^0). \tag{7.6.3}$$

Similarly, we can define a money metric measure of inequality remaining within the group, say $M_G^R(p, W_G^1, W_G^2)$, as the difference between group expenditure M_G, a money measure of potential group welfare W_G^2, and the money measure of welfare resulting from the elimination of poverty

$$M_G^R(p, W_G^1, W_G^2) = M_G - M_G(p, W_G^1). \tag{7.6.4}$$

The money metric measure of group inequality introduced by Jorgenson and Slesnick (1984b), say $M_G^I(p, W_G^0, W_G^2)$, is the sum of money metric measures of group poverty and the remaining inequality

$$\begin{aligned} M_G^I(p, W_G^0, W_G^2) &= M_G^P(p, W_G^0, W_G^1) + M_G^R(p, W_G^1, W_G^2) \\ &= M_G - M_G(p, W_G^0). \end{aligned} \tag{7.6.5}$$

This is the difference between money measures of potential and actual social welfare. All three indexes are nonnegative. The measure of group poverty is equal to zero only when all consuming units are above the poverty threshold. This measure can be interpreted as the amount that the group would gain from the redistribution of group expenditure to eliminate poverty. Similarly, the measure of the remaining inequality is the additional amount the group would gain from a perfectly egalitarian distribution of individual welfare within the group after poverty is eliminated.

As before, we can define a money metric measure of group relative poverty, say $M_G^Q(p, W_G^0, W_G^1, W_G^2)$, as the proportion of group expenditure lost due to failure to eliminate poverty

$$M_G^Q(p, W_G^0, W_G^1, W_G^2) = \frac{M_G^P(p, W_G^0, W_G^1)}{M_G}. \tag{7.6.6}$$

Similarly, the proportion of group expenditure lost due to an inequitable distribution of individual welfare, given the elimination of poverty, say $M_G^S(p, W_G^1, W_G^2)$, is a money metric measure of relative inequality remaining within the group

$$M_G^S(p, W_G^1, W_G^2) = \frac{M_G^R(p, W_G^1, W_G^2)}{M_G} .$$
(7.6.7)

The money metric measure of group relative inequality introduced by Jorgenson and Slesnick (1984b), say $M_G^J(p, W_G^0, W_G^2)$, is the sum of money metric measures of group poverty and inequality remaining within the group

$$M_G^J(p, W_G^0, W_G^2) = M_G^Q(p, W_G^0, W_G^1, W_G^2) + M_G^S(p, W_G^1, W_G^2) .$$
(7.6.8)

These measures can be illustrated as in figure 7.2. Levels of expenditure can be interpreted in terms of a group expenditure function $M_G(p, W_G)$, where W_G is the level of group welfare. We can represent group welfare in terms of the indifference map of a representative consumer.

We can also illustrate money metric measures of group poverty and the inequality remaining within each group by implementing money measures of actual and potential group welfare and the level of group welfare resulting from the elimination of poverty. For this purpose we utilize the econometric model outlined in section 7.4. We define individual welfare for the gth consuming unit, say W_g ($g = 1, 2, \ldots, G$), as the logarithm of the translog indirect utility function (7.4.5).

We consider a class of group welfare functions $W_G(x_G, u_G)$, that is analogous to the social welfare functions (7.4.6). As before, the first term corresponds to an average of individual welfare functions within the group, while the second is a function of deviations of levels of individual welfare from the group average. Choice of the degree of aversion to inequality ρ provides a means of incorporating ethical judgments about inequality in the distribution of individual welfare into the group welfare function.

The group expenditure function $M_G(p, W_G)$ enables us to express group expenditure as a function of the level of group welfare and prices

$$\ln M_G(p, W_G) = \frac{1}{D(p)} \left[\ln p' \left(\alpha_p + \frac{1}{2} B_{pp} \ln p \right) - W_G \right]$$

$$+ \ln \sum_{g=1}^{G} [m_0(p, A_g)] ,$$
(7.6.9)

where A_g is a vector of attributes for the gth consuming unit $(g = 1, 2, \ldots, G)$. The value of group expenditure is obtained by evaluating the translog individual expenditure function (7.4.11) at the level of group welfare W_G and the number of household equivalent members $\sum_{g=1}^{G} m_0(p, A_g)$ for the group as a whole.

To illustrate the application of our money metric measures of group poverty and inequality remaining within each group we consider subgroups of the U.S. population classified by age of head of household. We present money metric measures of relative inequality, poverty, and the remaining inequality corresponding to degree of aversion to inequality minus unity for the period 1947–1985 in table 7.4. Money metric measures of inequality, poverty, and the remaining inequality are given in appendix table 7.A.1.

In relative terms inequality is similar for all age groups, except the youngest, corresponding to age of head of household 16–24 years. For this group relative inequality is the lowest for any group at the beginning of the period in 1947. For all groups relative inequality declines during the period. The largest decline is for the oldest group with age of head 65 years and older. For this group the proportion of group expenditure lost due to an unequal distribution of individual welfare is 42.57 percent at the beginning of the period. This proportion falls to 30.94 percent by the end of the period, the lowest for any group. Relative inequality for the group reaches a maximum of 43.63 percent of group expenditure in 1949 and a minimum of 30.82 percent in 1984. By contrast group relative inequality for the youngest age group is 31.13 percent of group expenditure in 1985 after reaching a minimum of 31.05 percent in 1978.

At the beginning of the period, poverty is a large proportion of relative group inequality for all groups. Poverty accounts for the predominant proportion of relative inequality for all age groups except the youngest in 1947, where it accounts for only 30.02 percent. Poverty declines as a proportion of inequality for all age groups over the postwar period 1947–1985. The most dramatic gains are for the age group 45–54 years, for which relative poverty falls from 38.12 percent of group expenditure in 1947 to only 2.39 percent in 1985, a minimum for the period. At the end of the period in 1985, poverty is a minimum for the oldest age group, at 1.07 percent of group expenditure, and a maximum for the age group 45–54, years at 2.39 percent.

By contrast with poverty the inequality remaining within each group is a relatively small proportion of inequality at the beginning of

Table 7.4
Money metric group relative poverty (billions of 1972 dollars)

	Age 16–24			Age 25–34		
Year	Money metric inequality	Money metric poverty	Money metric remaining inequality	Money metric inequality	Money metric poverty	Money metric remaining inequality
1947	.3464	.1040	.2424	.3966	.2455	.1511
1948	.3470	.0952	.2519	.4003	.2314	.1689
1949	.3578	.1219	.2360	.4100	.2222	.1878
1950	.3479	.0957	.2523	.3995	.2042	.1953
1951	.3486	.0621	.2865	.3998	.1745	.2254
1952	.3481	.0719	.2762	.4034	.1741	.2293
1953	.3532	.0861	.2671	.4091	.1666	.2426
1954	.3490	.0594	.2896	.4059	.1758	.2301
1955	.3543	.0642	.2901	.4105	.1776	.2328
1956	.3525	.0508	.3017	.4049	.1509	.2540
1957	.3521	.0525	.2996	.4140	.1504	.2636
1958	.3439	.0474	.2966	.4034	.1405	.2629
1959	.3407	.0535	.2872	.3847	.1199	.2648
1960	.3322	.0452	.2870	.3780	.1092	.2688
1961	.3328	.0473	.2855	.3766	.1050	.2716
1962	.3388	.0486	.2902	.3798	.1085	.2712
1963	.3313	.0425	.2888	.3723	.0951	.2772
1964	.3271	.0337	.2934	.3749	.0874	.2875
1965	.3266	.0310	.2956	.3697	.0767	.2930
1966	.3199	.0265	.2934	.3609	.0645	.2963
1967	.3156	.0253	.2904	.3580	.0582	.2998
1968	.3157	.0218	.2939	.3561	.0536	.3026
1969	.3192	.0223	.2969	.3533	.0492	.3041
1970	.3146	.0192	.2954	.3505	.0451	.3054
1971	.3142	.0220	.2923	.3485	.0444	.3041
1972	.3133	.0199	.2934	.3560	.0407	.3053
1973	.3161	.0197	.2964	.3466	.0375	.3091
1974	.3150	.0193	.2956	.3421	.0374	.3047
1975	.3113	.0183	.2930	.3385	.0347	.3039
1976	.3123	.0169	.2954	.3364	.0313	.3051
1977	.3117	.0160	.2957	.3335	.0278	.3056
1978	.3105	.0130	.2976	.3288	.0239	.3049
1979	.3139	.0116	.3024	.3315	.0219	.3096
1980	.3149	.0111	.3039	.3337	.0238	.3099
1981	.3158	.0143	.3016	.3346	.0245	.3101
1982	.3164	.0144	.3020	.3312	.0192	.3120
1983	.3165	.0153	.3011	.3320	.0217	.3103
1984	.3121	.0137	.2984	.3283	.0179	.3104
1985	.3113	.0119	.2995	.3274	.0164	.3110

Table 7.4 (continued)

	Age 35–44			Age 45–54		
Year	Money metric inequality	Money metric poverty	Money metric remaining inequality	Money metric inequality	Money metric poverty	Money metric remaining inequality
1947	.4242	.3403	.0838	.4237	.3812	.0425
1948	.4302	.3405	.0897	.4274	.3702	.0572
1949	.4350	.3349	.1001	.4312	.3596	.0715
1950	.4279	.2933	.1346	.4219	.3408	.0811
1951	.4313	.2833	.1480	.4241	.3171	.1070
1952	.4308	.2727	.1582	.4256	.3081	.1175
1953	.4344	.2676	.1668	.4298	.2971	.1327
1954	.4329	.2683	.1646	.4311	.2935	.1377
1955	.4359	.2599	.1759	.4345	.2874	.1471
1956	.4297	.2315	.1982	.4289	.2762	.1527
1957	.4358	.2290	.2068	.4366	.2790	.1577
1958	.4300	.2212	.2087	.4303	.2679	.1624
1959	.4042	.1806	.2236	.4082	.2349	.1734
1960	.4010	.1652	.2359	.4036	.2137	.1899
1961	.3976	.1620	.2356	.4007	.2016	.1992
1962	.3957	.1536	.2422	.4015	.1961	.2054
1963	.3862	.1428	.2435	.3937	.1821	.2115
1964	.3893	.1288	.2605	.3949	.1728	.2221
1965	.3830	.1125	.2705	.3896	.1517	.2380
1966	.3732	.0864	.2769	.3802	.1312	.2490
1967	.3684	.0840	.2844	.3761	.1226	.2534
1968	.3647	.0725	.2922	.3719	.1110	.2609
1969	.3611	.0637	.2974	.3682	.1024	.2658
1970	.3582	.0585	.2997	.3644	.0944	.2701
1971	.3584	.0540	.3044	.3635	.0903	.2733
1972	.3559	.0475	.3084	.3602	.0805	.2797
1973	.3536	.0433	.3103	.3575	.0752	.2823
1974	.3495	.0420	.3075	.3532	.0718	.2814
1975	.3495	.0395	.3100	.3502	.0661	.2841
1976	.3430	.0341	.3090	.3443	.0573	.2870
1977	.3376	.0297	.3079	.3381	.0478	.2903
1978	.3304	.0246	.3057	.3311	.0395	.2916
1979	.3351	.0241	.3110	.3344	.0395	.2949
1980	.3367	.0253	.3113	.3356	.0397	.2958
1981	.3368	.0258	.3110	.3338	.0383	.2955
1982	.3314	.0259	.3055	.3289	.0362	.2927
1983	.3328	.0231	.3097	.3283	.0313	.2970
1984	.3282	.0207	.3075	.3247	.0280	.2967
1985	.3249	.0178	.3071	.3225	.0239	.2986

Table 7.4 (continued)

	Age 55–64			Age 65+		
Year	Money metric inequality	Money metric poverty	Money metric remaining inequality	Money metric inequality	Money metric poverty	Money metric remaining inequality
1947	.4206	.2872	.1334	.4257	.2587	.1669
1948	.4275	.2998	.1276	.4309	.2921	.1389
1949	.4326	.2955	.1371	.4363	.2786	.1577
1950	.4198	.2735	.1463	.4196	.2592	.1604
1951	.4192	.2618	.1574	.4192	.2686	.1506
1952	.4211	.2405	.1807	.4171	.2255	.1916
1953	.4261	.2446	.1816	.4230	.2247	.1983
1954	.4296	.2507	.1789	.4252	.2366	.1886
1955	.4335	.2418	.1916	.4279	.2292	.1987
1956	.4269	.2279	.1990	.4222	.2275	.1947
1957	.4310	.2279	.2031	.4222	.2299	.1922
1958	.4224	.2112	.2111	.4109	.2183	.1926
1959	.4038	.1744	.2294	.3912	.1737	.2175
1960	.3947	.1651	.2296	.3798	.1497	.2301
1961	.3920	.1561	.2358	.3748	.1379	.2369
1962	.3932	.1514	.2418	.3746	.1416	.2330
1963	.3872	.1390	.2482	.3677	.1304	.2372
1964	.3850	.1327	.2523	.3622	.1128	.2495
1965	.3799	.1198	.2600	.3565	.1048	.2517
1966	.3707	.1065	.2641	.3461	.0898	.2563
1967	.3666	.0993	.2673	.3414	.0868	.2547
1968	.3617	.0856	.2760	.3365	.0763	.2602
1969	.3599	.0830	.2778	.3351	.0734	.2617
1970	.3543	.0732	.2811	.3291	.0652	.2639
1971	.3537	.0713	.2823	.3293	.0611	.2682
1972	.3496	.0650	.2846	.3266	.0538	.2728
1973	.3473	.0599	.2874	.3241	.0490	.2751
1974	.3440	.0548	.2891	.3230	.0448	.2781
1975	.3393	.0522	.2870	.3172	.0376	.2796
1976	.3361	.0463	.2898	.3151	.0331	.2820
1977	.3320	.0403	.2917	.3127	.0293	.2833
1978	.3266	.0339	.2927	.3084	.0237	.2847
1979	.3293	.0333	.2959	.3091	.0233	.2857
1980	.3302	.0342	.2960	.3111	.0217	.2894
1981	.3287	.0328	.2959	.3109	.0189	.2920
1982	.3254	.0317	.2938	.3098	.0165	.2934
1983	.3247	.0290	.2957	.3098	.0144	.2955
1984	.3224	.0253	.2971	.3082	.0115	.2968
1985	.3214	.0221	.2993	.3094	.0107	.2986

the period for all age groups except the youngest. For this group relative remaining inequality is 24.24 percent of group expenditure at the
beginning of the period in 1947 or 69.98 percent of inequality. Relative
remaining inequality within the group rises to 29.95 percent of group
expenditure by the end of the period in 1985, or 96.21 percent of
inequality. The group corresponding to age of head 45–54 years provides the most striking illustration of trends that are visible in less
dramatic form in other groups. Inequality remaining within the
group rises from 4.25 percent at the beginning of the period to 29.86
percent of group expenditure or 92.59 percent of inequality at the end
of the period in 1985.

7.7 Poverty between Groups

In section 7.6 we have presented measures of poverty and inequality
remaining within groups of the U.S. population classified by age of
head of household. In this section we develop measures of poverty
and the remaining inequality within and between groups for the population as a whole. These measures enable us to compare the impacts
of redistributional policies that are limited to reallocations of expenditure within groups to those that also permit reallocations between
groups.

Our measure of poverty within groups is the maximum gain in
social welfare available by reallocation of expenditure within groups
so as to eliminate poverty within each group. Our measure of poverty
between groups is the additional gain in social welfare that results
from further redistribution of expenditure between groups so as to
eliminate poverty for the population as a whole. Similarly, we
develop a measure of the inequality remaining within groups. This is
based on the gain in social welfare available from achieving equality
of individual welfare within each group after poverty is eliminated
within the group. Our measure of inequality remaining between
groups is based on the additional gain that results from achieving perfect equality for the population as a whole.

We can partition the population into B mutually exclusive and
exhaustive groups. As an example, we can consider the six age
groups employed in the preceding section. We suppose that the bth
group contains G_b consuming units ($b = 1, 2, \ldots, B$), where the sum of
the numbers of units over all groups is equal to the total population,
$\sum_{b=1}^{B} G_b = K$. We first consider a restricted form of redistributional

policy in which the transfers required to eliminate poverty within each group are collected by lump-sum taxes on consuming units within the group.

The optimal policy for redistribution, subject to the constraint that the reallocation of expenditure must take place within the group, is to collect lump-sum taxes from consuming units having the highest levels of individual welfare. Under this policy the total of lump-sum transfers within each group is equal to the total of lump-sum taxes within the group. The taxes will bring all rich households down to the margin of affluence, say W_U^b ($b = 1, 2, \ldots, B$), within the group. These margins of affluence may differ among groups.

Given the level of social welfare that results from the elimination of poverty by reallocation of expenditure within each group, say $W^3(u, x, W_L)$, we can define a money metric measure of poverty within groups, say $M_W^P(p, W^0, W^3)$, as the difference between the money measure of welfare resulting from the elimination of poverty within groups W^3 and the money measure of actual social welfare W^0

$$M_W^P(p, W^0, W^3) = M(p, W^{3)} - M(p, W^0) . \qquad (7.7.1)$$

This measure of poverty is the amount that society as a whole would gain from the elimination of poverty by redistribution within groups.

Given the elimination of poverty within each group, group expenditure can be further reallocated so as to eliminate the remaining inequality in the distribution of individual welfare within the group. This results in perfect equality within each group; however, the levels of individual welfare at which equality is attained may differ among groups. The index of within group inequality introduced by Jorgenson and Slesnick (1984b) is the difference between the level of social welfare resulting from perfect equality within each group, say $W^4(u, x)$, and the actual level of social welfare W^0.

We can define a money metric measure of the inequality remaining within groups after the elimination of poverty, say $M_W^R(p, W^3, W^4)$, as the difference between the money measure of social welfare resulting from perfect equality within each group W^4 and the money measure of welfare resulting from the elimination of poverty W^3

$$M_W^R(p, W^3, W^4) = M(p, W^{4)} - M(p, W^3). \qquad (7.7.2)$$

This measure of the inequality remaining within each group is the amount that society as a whole would gain from elimination of inequality by redistribution within groups.

The money metric measure of inequality within groups introduced by Jorgenson and Slesnick (1984b), say $M_W^I(p, W^0, W^4)$, is defined as the difference between money measures of the level of social welfare resulting from perfect equality within each group W^4 and actual social welfare W^0 . This money metric measure of inequality within groups can be decomposed into the sum of money metric measures of poverty and the inequality remaining within groups

$$M_W^I(p, W^0, W^4) = M_W^P(p, W^0, W^3) + M_W^R(p, W^3, W^4). \qquad (7.7.3)$$

If we remove the constraint that the elimination of poverty within each group must result from reallocation of expenditure within the group, optimal redistributional policy takes the form we have described in section 7.2. The lump-sum taxes required to eliminate poverty must be collected from consuming units having the highest levels of individual welfare for the population as a whole. These taxes will bring all rich households down to a single margin of affluence W_U for the whole society.

We can define a money metric measure of poverty between groups, say $M_B^P(p, W^1, W^3)$, as the difference between the money measure of the level of social welfare resulting from the elimination of poverty W^1 for the society as a whole and the money measure of the welfare that results from elimination of poverty within each group W^3

$$M_B^P (p, W^1, W^3) = M(p, W^1) - M(p, W^3), \qquad (7.7.4)$$

This measure of poverty is the amount that society would gain from redistribution among groups, given that poverty is eliminated within each group.

The money metric measure of poverty $M^P(p, W^0, W^1)$ introduced in section 7.3, is defined as the difference between the money measure of social welfare resulting from the elimination of poverty W^1 and actual social welfare W^0. This money metric measure of poverty can be decomposed into the sum of money metric measures of poverty within and between groups

$$M^P(p, W^0, W^1) = M_W^P(p, W^3, W^0) + M_B^P(p, W^1, W^3). \qquad (7.7.5)$$

The money metric measure of inequality between groups introduced by Jorgenson and Slesnick (1984b), say $M_B^I(p, W^2, W^4)$, is defined as the difference between money measures of the level of social welfare resulting from perfect equality for the society as a whole, W^2, and the welfare resulting from perfect equality within each group, W^4

$$M_B^I(p, W^2, W^4) = M - M(p, W^4) . \qquad (7.7.6)$$

The money metric measure of inequality (7.3.4) can be decomposed into the sum of money metric measures of inequality within and between groups

$$M^I(p, W^0, W^2) = M_W^I(p, W^0, W^4) + M_B^I(p, W^2, W^4) . \qquad (7.7.7)$$

The money metric measure of inequality between groups $M_B^I(p, W^2, W^4)$ can be decomposed into the sum of money metric measures of poverty and the inequality remaining between groups

$$M_B^I(p, W^2, W^4) = M_B^P(p, W^1, W^3) + M_B^R(p, W^1, W^2, W^3, W^4). \qquad (7.7.8)$$

The money metric measure of remaining inequality $M^R(p, W^1, W^2)$ introduced in section 7.3, is defined as the difference between the money measures of potential social welfare, W^2, and the level of social welfare resulting from the elimination of poverty, W^1. This money metric measure of remaining inequality can be decomposed into the sum of money metric measures of remaining inequality within and between groups

$$M^R(p, W^1, W^2) = M_W^R(p, W^3, W^4) + M_B^R(p, W^1, W^2, W^3, W^4) . \qquad (7.7.9)$$

We can define money metric measures of relative poverty within and between groups, say M_W^Q and M_B^Q, as ratios of the corresponding measures of poverty, M_W^P and M_B^P, to aggregate expenditure. These measures of relative poverty represent the proportion of aggregate expenditure lost due to failure to eliminate poverty within and between groups. Similarly, we can define money metric measures of relative remaining inequality within and between groups, say M_W^S and M_B^S, as ratios of the corresponding measures of remaining inequality, M_W^R and M_B^R, to aggregate expenditure. These measures represent the proportion of aggregate expenditure lost due to an inequitable distribution of individual welfare within and between groups, given the elimination of poverty within and between groups.

We can define money metric measures of relative inequality within and between groups, say M_W^J and M_B^J, as ratios of the corresponding money measures of inequality, M_W^I and M_B^I, to aggregate expenditure.

The money metric measures of relative inequality within and between groups are sums of the corresponding measures of relative poverty and relative remaining inequality, respectively, within and between groups. Similarly, the money metric measures of relative poverty (7.3.5) and remaining inequality (7.3.6) are sums of the corresponding measures of relative poverty and remaining inequality, respectively, within and between groups.

To illustrate the application of our money metric measures of poverty and remaining inequality within and between groups we consider groups of the U.S. population classified by age of head of household, as in section 7.6. We present money metric measures of relative inequality, poverty, and the remaining inequality within and between groups for the period 1947–1985 in table 7.5. These measures correspond to degree of aversion to inequality minus unity and give maximum weight to equity considerations. Money metric measures of poverty and the remaining inequality within and between groups are given in the appendix in table 7.A.2.

In relative terms, inequality and poverty are far more important within groups than between groups. At the beginning of the period in 1947 inequality between groups is 11.52 percent of total inequality, given in table 7.3, above. By the end of the period in 1985 inequality between groups has fallen to 8.42 percent of total inequality. Poverty between groups is only 0.74 percent of total poverty in 1947 and falls to a miniscule proportion of the total by the end of the period in 1985. By contrast remaining inequality between groups is 42.22 percent of remaining inequality in 1947 and falls to only 8.92 percent of the total by the end of the period.

Money metric measures of relative inequality, poverty, and inequality remaining within groups reflect the behavior of the corresponding relative measures given in table 7.3. Money metric relative inequality between groups declines much more rapidly than relative inequality within groups. Money metric relative poverty between groups almost disappears during the postwar period. Finally, money metric relative inequality remaining between groups declines slightly during the period.

Our overall conclusion is that gains in social welfare from redistribution within groups comprise a much greater proportion of aggregate expenditure than the additional gains from redistribution between groups. This conclusion is valid whether the focus of redistributional policy is on poverty or on inequality as a whole. By the

Table 7.5
Money metric between-group relative poverty

	Within			Between		
Year	Money metric inequality	Money metric poverty	Money metric remaining inequality	Money metric inequality	Money metric poverty	Money metric remaining inequality
1947	.3740	.3105	.0635	.0487	.0023	.0464
1948	.3832	.3101	.0731	.0441	.0020	.0421
1949	.3857	.3026	.0831	.0470	.0019	.0451
1950	.3829	.2758	.1061	.0396	.0016	.0380
1951	.3820	.2605	.1215	.0439	.0017	.0421
1952	.3790	.2479	.1311	.0468	.0014	.0454
1953	.3860	.2442	.1418	.0441	.0013	.0428
1954	.3909	.2475	.1434	.0394	.0012	.0382
1955	.3951	.2422	.1529	.0380	.0010	.0371
1956	.3877	.2227	.1649	.0411	.0012	.0399
1957	.3918	.2230	.1688	.0431	.0012	.0419
1958	.3834	.2132	.1702	.0440	.0011	.0429
1959	.3640	.1789	.1850	.0413	.0008	.0404
1960	.3616	.1635	.1980	.0375	.0007	.0368
1961	.3574	.1564	.2010	.0380	.0005	.0374
1962	.3616	.1530	.2087	.0336	.0005	.0331
1963	.3501	.1407	.2094	.0377	.0005	.0373
1964	.3508	.1298	.2210	.0383	.0005	.0379
1965	.3470	.1151	.2319	.0363	.0004	.0359
1966	.3378	.0993	.2385	.0359	.0003	.0356
1967	.3307	.0911	.2397	.0387	.0003	.0385
1968	.3243	.0802	.2441	.0412	.0002	.0410
1969	.3191	.0738	.2453	.0434	.0002	.0432
1970	.3151	.0671	.2480	.0434	.0002	.0432
1971	.3152	.0640	.2512	.0416	.0002	.0415
1972	.3131	.0569	.2562	.0403	.0001	.0402
1973	.3098	.0521	.2577	.0417	.0001	.0416
1974	.3093	.0494	.2599	.0379	.0001	.0378
1975	.3095	.0454	.2641	.0341	.0001	.0340
1976	.3069	.0396	.2673	.0324	.0001	.0323
1977	.3058	.0341	.2717	.0285	.0000	.0285
1978	.3019	.0284	.2735	.0267	.0000	.0267
1979	.3004	.0276	.2728	.0320	.0000	.0320
1980	.3063	.0281	.2782	.0275	.0000	.0274
1981	.3069	.0275	.2794	.0257	.0000	.0256
1982	.3027	.0257	.2770	.0261	.0000	.0260
1983	.3022	.0238	.2784	.0267	.0000	.0267
1984	.2980	.0207	.2773	.0280	.0000	.0279
1985	.2968	.0180	.2787	.0273	.0000	.0273

end of the postwar period the additional gains from reallocation of expenditure between groups contributes very little to the potential social benefits from eliminating poverty. The corresponding gains from eliminating inequality between groups have declined substantially over the postwar period but remain at nonnegligible levels at the end of the period in 1985.

7.8   Alternative Poverty Measures

In section 7.5 we have analyzed the impact of redistributional policy on social welfare. For this purpose we have introduced an index of poverty based on the increase in social welfare that would result from the elimination of poverty. We also introduced an index of the remaining inequality, representing the additional increase in welfare that would result from achieving perfect equality after poverty is eliminated.

The most common alternative approach to the measurement of poverty is based on the head-count ratio, defined as the number of individuals in households below the poverty threshold divided by the total population. Official government statistics on the number of individuals in poverty are published annually by the U.S. Bureau of the Census. The poverty thresholds used in the official statistics depend on family size and composition. These thresholds were originally established for the year 1963 by Orshansky (1965) and have been moved forward by inflating them by the consumer price index compiled by the Bureau of Labor Statistics.

Under additional restrictions to be specified below, we can express our measure of poverty, based on the impact of redistributional policy, as a function of an appropriately defined head-count ratio. We first specialize the class of social welfare functions (7.4.6) by considering the limiting form as the degree of aversion to inequality ρ goes to negative infinity. This limiting form gives the least possible weight to equity considerations

$$W(u, x) = \ln \bar{V} , \tag{7.8.1}$$

where the function $\ln \bar{V}$ corresponds to average individual welfare.

The limiting form of the social welfare function (7.8.1) is a weighted average of individual welfare functions $\{\ln V_k\}$ and is, therefore, a utilitarian social welfare function.[14] We next consider the index of poverty (7.2.7) for a utilitarian social welfare function. Before the elimination of poverty the actual value of the social welfare function is the following

$$W(u, x) =$$

$$\frac{\sum_{k=1}^{K_L} m_0(p, A_k) \ln V_k + \sum_{k=K_L+1}^{K_U} m_0(p, A_k) \ln V_k + \sum_{k=K_U+1}^{K} m_0(p, A_k) \ln V_k}{\sum_{k=1}^{K} m_0(p, A_k)}.$$

The level of social welfare resulting from the elimination of poverty takes the form

$$W(u, x, W_L) =$$

$$\frac{\sum_{k=1}^{K_L} m_0(p, A_k) \ln V_L + \sum_{k=K_L+1}^{K_U} m_0(p, A_k) \ln V_k + \sum_{k=K_U+1}^{K} m_0(p, A_k) \ln V_U}{\sum_{k=1}^{K} m_0(p, A_k)}.$$

Finally, the index of poverty (7.2.7) can be written

$$P(u, x, W_L) = \frac{\sum_{k=1}^{K_L} m_0(p, A_k)}{\sum_{k=1}^{K} m_0(p, A_k)} \frac{\sum_{k=1}^{K_L} m_0(p, A_k)(\ln V_L - \ln V_k)}{\sum_{k=1}^{K_L} m_0(p, A_k)}$$

$$+ \frac{\sum_{k=K_U+1}^{K} m_0(p, A_k)}{\sum_{k=1}^{K} m_0(p, A_k)} \frac{\sum_{k=K_U+1}^{K} m_0(p, A_k)(\ln V_U - \ln V_k)}{\sum_{k=K_U+1}^{K} m_0(p, A_k)}. \qquad (7.8.2)$$

We refer to this index as the *utilitarian index of poverty*.

The utilitarian index of poverty (7.8.2) is the sum of two terms. The first term involves the proportion of the population that falls below the poverty line, say H_L/H

$$H_L / H = \sum_{k=1}^{K_L} m_0(p, A_k) \bigg/ \sum_{k=1}^{K} m_0(p, A_k), \qquad (7.8.3)$$

where H is the number of household equivalent members in the population as a whole and H_L is the number of household equivalent members in consuming units that fall below the poverty line. We refer to this ratio as the *household equivalent head-count ratio of the poor*.

The first term in the utilitarian index of poverty (7.8.2) also involves a weighted average of poverty gaps, defined in terms of individual welfare (7.4.5), say G_L, where

$$G_L = \sum_{k=1}^{K_L} m_0(p, A_k)(\ln V_L - \ln V_k) \bigg/ \sum_{k=1}^{K} m_0(p, A_k). \qquad (7.8.4)$$

The first term is the product of the household equivalent head-count ratio of the poor (7.8.3) and the weighted average of poverty gaps (7.8.4). The second term is the product of a household equivalent head-count ratio of the rich and a weighted average of margins of affluence.

The household equivalent head-count ratio of the poor (7.8.3) is defined in terms of numbers of household equivalent members of the poverty population and the population as a whole. By contrast the official statistics on poverty give the number of households below the poverty threshold and the number of individuals living in those households. To illustrate the differences among alternative head-count ratios of the poor, we present ratios based on the numbers of household equivalent members, individuals, and households in table 7.6.

Head-count ratios of the poor based on household equivalent family members are higher than those based on individuals in all but four years. Ratios based on individuals are, in turn, uniformly higher than those based on households. Substitution of head-count ratios based on the number of individuals in poverty for ratios based on the number of household equivalent family members would bias our utilitarian index of poverty downward. Substitution of head-count ratios based on the number of households would increase this bias. We conclude that the head-count ratios employed in the U.S. official statistics on poverty underestimate the head-count ratios appropriate for evaluating the impact of redistributional policy.

We have defined a money metric measure of poverty (7.3.2) that represents the amount that society as a whole would gain from the elimination of poverty. This measure can be defined in terms of the utilitarian social welfare function (7.8.1). We present money metric inequality, poverty, and remaining inequality indexes in table 7.7. These indexes are defined in precisely the same way as in table 7.2, except that the utilitarian social welfare function (7.8.1) is used in place of a social welfare function with degree of aversion to inequality equal to minus unity.

Utilitarian money metric measures of poverty and the remaining inequality lie below the corresponding money metric measures presented in table 7.2. In table 7.2 the degree of aversion to inequality ρ in the class of social welfare functions (7.4.6) is assigned its maximum value of minus one. The resulting gains in social welfare give the greatest possible weight to equity considerations. The measures of individual welfare (7.4.5) employed in table 7.2 are precisely the same as those used for the utilitarian measures presented in table 7.7.

We conclude that the money metric measures of poverty and the remaining inequality presented in tables 7.2 and 7.7 are sensitive to

Table 7.6
Head-count ratios of the poor

Year	Household equivalent members	Individuals	Households
1947	.4838	.4130	.3409
1948	.4784	.4046	.3429
1949	.4526	.3860	.3213
1950	.4365	.3779	.3099
1951	.4192	.3623	.2934
1952	.4049	.3527	.2771
1953	.3998	.3492	.2704
1954	.3905	.3351	.2657
1955	.3876	.3291	.2639
1956	.3633	.3047	.2435
1957	.3634	.3082	.2396
1958	.3577	.3044	.2361
1959	.3183	.2745	.2137
1960	.3006	.2655	.2003
1961	.2916	.2603	.1905
1962	.2833	.2517	.1874
1963	.2700	.2399	.1759
1964	.2508	.2262	.1549
1965	.2302	.2094	.1414
1966	.2043	.1875	.1251
1967	.1934	.1748	.1194
1968	.1730	.1579	.1039
1969	.1633	.1480	.0983
1970	.1506	.1373	.0873
1971	.1438	.1312	.0829
1972	.1291	.1187	.0750
1973	.1183	.1093	.0672
1974	.1146	.1072	.0667
1975	.1061	.1009	.0605
1976	.0953	.0905	.0541
1977	.0856	.0833	.0491
1978	.0737	.0733	.0491
1979	.0716	.0717	.0412
1980	.0763	.0732	.0442
1981	.0738	.0729	.0430
1982	.0680	.0677	.0391
1983	.0659	.0677	.0386
1984	.0586	.0600	.0340
1985	.0520	.0529	.0301

Table 7.7
Utilitarian money metric poverty (billions of 1972 dollars)

Year	Money metric inequality	Money metric poverty	Money metric remaining inequality
1947	62.963	58.262	4.701
1948	65.526	60.146	5.380
1949	68.354	61.332	7.022
1950	69.203	59.685	9.518
1951	73.891	60.859	13.032
1952	77.229	61.377	15.852
1953	81.011	63.116	17.894
1954	82.703	65.011	17.692
1955	87.724	67.432	20.292
1956	90.557	65.935	24.621
1957	95.466	68.687	26.778
1958	95.368	67.261	28.107
1959	92.254	59.375	32.878
1960	93.046	56.347	36.699
1961	94.487	55.571	38.916
1962	98.164	56.610	41.554
1963	98.569	53.949	44.620
1964	104.599	53.208	51.391
1965	107.491	49.882	57.609
1966	108.900	45.498	63.403
1967	111.605	43.607	47.998
1968	115.284	40.537	74.747
1969	118.723	39.039	79.684
1970	121.072	36.919	84.153
1971	123.794	36.236	87.558
1972	128.002	33.947	94.055
1973	131.768	32.456	99.312
1974	130.901	31.179	99.721
1975	132.538	29.508	103.031
1976	135.759	26.904	108.855
1977	138.596	24.169	114.427
1978	141.110	21.078	120.031
1979	148.064	21.202	126.862
1980	151.851	21.987	129.864
1981	153.357	21.876	131.481
1982	153.270	20.700	132.570
1983	158.962	19.864	139.098
1984	162.828	17.980	144.847
1985	168.322	16.394	151.928

changes in the degree of aversion to inequality ρ. The measure of poverty (7.8.2) and the corresponding measure of the remaining inequality are additively decomposable in measures of individual welfare. This restriction, which is commonly employed in the measurement of poverty, gives the least possible weight to equity considerations. The resulting money metric measures of poverty and the remaining inequality, presented in table 7.7, provide lower bounds for society's willingness to pay for the benefits of redistributional policy. By contrast the measures of poverty and the remaining inequality presented in table 7.2 provide upper bounds for these benefits.

A further alternative to our money measure of poverty is the aggregate expenditure required to eliminate poverty (7.2.3). This is the total of the lump-sum transfers from the rich to the poor required to eliminate poverty and is equal to the total of the lump-sum taxes (7.2.6) that will bring all rich households down to the threshold of affluence. This total provides a money measure of the aggregate poverty gap. Similarly, an alternative to our measure of the remaining inequality is the total of transfers required to achieve perfect equality, given the elimination of poverty.

To illustrate the transfers involved in eliminating poverty and the remaining inequality, we present both levels of aggregate expenditure and the sum of the two in table 7.8. These levels of expenditure can be compared with money metric measures of poverty and the remaining inequality. Measures based on a utilitarian social welfare function are given in table 7.7; similar measures based on a social welfare function with degree of aversion to inequality equal to minus unity are presented in table 7.2.

The transfers required to eliminate poverty move in parallel to the money metric measure of poverty presented in tables 7.2 and 7.7. The aggregate poverty gap rises slightly from 1947 to 1948, reaching a maximum of $48.437 billions and declines to a minimum level in 1985 of $4.742 billions. It is important to emphasize that the aggregate poverty gap represents the total of lump-sum transfers from the rich to the poor, while the money metric measures of poverty correspond to the net benefit to society from these transfers. The aggregate poverty gap is independent of the degree of aversion to inequality; by contrast the gains from redistributional policy depend on the value of this parameter.

Similarly, the transfers required to eliminate the remaining inequality largely parallel the money metric measures of remaining inequal-

Table 7.8
Transfers (billions of 1972 dollars)

Year	Transfers required to eliminate:		
	Inequality	Poverty	Remaining inequality
1947	76.485	47.856	28.630
1948	79.045	48.437	30.608
1949	81.056	46.668	34.388
1950	83.536	43.717	39.819
1951	88.648	41.945	46.703
1952	92.574	40.590	51.984
1953	96.320	40.604	55.716
1954	98.079	42.003	56.076
1955	103.326	42.352	60.974
1956	107.061	39.394	67.667
1957	111.757	40.303	71.454
1958	113.180	39.283	73.897
1959	113.609	33.209	80.400
1960	116.012	30.567	85.445
1961	118.514	29.645	88.869
1962	123.013	29.626	93.387
1963	125.432	27.741	97.691
1964	132.987	26.198	106.789
1965	138.010	23.367	114.643
1966	142.421	20.411	122.011
1967	147.248	19.157	128.090
1968	153.170	16.960	136.210
1969	158.221	15.766	142.456
1970	162.632	14.513	148.210
1971	166.601	13.955	152.646
1972	173.383	12.516	160.867
1973	179.337	11.616	167.720
1974	179.849	11.052	168.797
1975	183.434	10.241	173.193
1976	189.945	9.061	180.884
1977	196.151	7.866	188.285
1978	202.762	6.632	196.129
1979	211.289	6.500	204.788
1980	216.592	6.821	209.772
1981	219.624	6.781	212.843
1982	221.530	6.383	215.147
1983	229.807	5.989	223.818
1984	237.760	5.305	232.455
1985	247.485	4.742	242.742

ity presented in tables 7.2 and 7.5. These transfers rise from $28.630 billions in 1947 to $242.742 billions in 1985. The money metric measures of remaining inequality represent the net benefit to society from transfers to achieve perfect equality after poverty has been eliminated. By contrast the transfers correspond to the money that is redistributed. The gains from redistributional policy depend on the degree of aversion to inequality, while the corresponding transfers do not.

7.9   Summary and Conclusion

In this paper we have presented a new approach to the measurement of poverty, based on the willingness of society to pay for the benefits of redistributional policy. The elimination of poverty involves the redistribution of aggregate expenditure so as to raise the level of individual welfare for all consuming units to a fixed poverty threshold. The gains to the poor households that are the beneficiaries of redistributional policy must be weighed against the losses to affluent households that are required to finance the necessary transfers.

The distinctive feature of our approach to the evaluation of redistributional policy is that net benefits to society are defined in terms of social welfare functions. These welfare functions are defined on the distribution of individual welfare over the population of all consuming units.[15] An alternative approach that also incorporates society's ability to pay for the elimination of poverty is the measure of relative poverty presented by Plotnick and Skidmore (1975). This measure is based on a relative poverty threshold that depends on median individual welfare for the population as a whole.

Our measures of poverty incorporate many of the elements employed in more conventional measures, such as the head-count ratios for individuals reported in official U.S. government statistics on poverty. Our measures also incorporate the distribution of poverty gaps over the population of consuming units below the poverty threshold, as proposed in Sen's (1976b) pioneering approach to poverty measurement. Finally, our measures are based on the monetary value of the aggregate poverty gap—the total of lump-sum transfers to poor households required to eliminate poverty.

By defining poverty in terms of society's willingness to pay for the benefits of redistributional policy, we are able to integrate poverty measurement with the measurement of inequality. The reduction of the inequality remaining after poverty has been eliminated is a significant objective of redistributional policy. Our empirical results show that the relative importance of eliminating poverty and reducing the remaining inequality have been reversed over the postwar period. Poverty predominates at the beginning of the period, while the remaining inequality is more important at the end of the period.

The distinctive feature of our approach to the measurement of individual welfare is that our measures are comparable among consuming units with different demographic characteristics and between situations characterized by different price systems. The implementation of this approach requires an econometric model of individual and aggregate consumer behavior. We define individual welfare in terms of indirect utility functions derived from systems of individual demand functions.

The official U.S. poverty statistics published by the U.S. Bureau of the Census incorporate differences in demographic characteristics of individual households into the underlying poverty thresholds. These thresholds are adjusted by the consumer price index at different times. The general household equivalence scales presented by Jorgenson and Slesnick (1987a) provide an adjustment for demographic characteristics based on the actual expenditure patterns of individual consuming units. The price indexes given by Jorgenson and Slesnick (1983) reflect differences in preferences among consuming units. These differences are not incorporated into the consumer price index used in the official poverty thresholds.

It is important to emphasize that our framework for evaluating the benefits of redistributional policy could be applied to alternative measures of individual welfare, such as those employed in the official poverty statistics. Levels of social welfare could be determined for these alternative measures. A social expenditure function could be used to translate differences in welfare levels into money measures of society's willingness to pay for the benefits of redistributional policy.

Similarly, our measures of individual welfare could be used in compiling alternative measures of poverty, such as that proposed by Sen (1976b), the subsequent proposals reviewed by Foster (1984) and Sen (1981), or the recent proposals by Pyatt (1987). Our measures make it possible to overcome important objections to the measures of individual welfare employed in the official poverty statistics. These objections are that differences in preferences among households or differences in the impact of price changes on households in different circumstances are not taken into account in an appropriate way.

Appendix

Table 7.A.1
Money metric group poverty (billions of 1972 dollars)

	Age 16–24			Age 25–34		
Year	Money metric inequality	Money metric poverty	Money metric remaining inequality	Money metric inequality	Money metric poverty	Money metric remaining inequality
1947	2.940	0.882	2.057	19.148	11.853	7.295
1948	3.470	0.951	2.518	20.735	11.986	8.749
1949	3.545	1.207	2.338	22.149	12.002	10.147
1950	3.435	0.945	2.490	22.134	11.314	10.820
1951	3.678	0.655	3.023	25.151	10.975	14.177
1952	3.700	0.765	2.935	25.408	10.968	14.440
1953	3.472	0.846	2.626	26.733	10.884	15.850
1954	3.897	0.663	3.234	25.169	10.899	14.271
1955	3.955	0.717	3.238	26.433	11.439	14.994
1956	4.659	0.672	3.987	28.635	10.674	17.961
1957	4.697	0.700	3.997	30.438	11.048	19.380
1958	4.721	0.650	4.071	29.478	10.270	19.209
1959	4.752	0.747	4.005	28.025	8.735	19.289
1960	4.955	0.674	4.282	28.284	8.171	20.113
1961	4.867	0.691	4.176	27.687	7.718	19.968
1962	5.117	0.734	4.383	27.537	7.871	19.666
1963	5.433	0.697	4.736	28.154	7.189	20.964
1964	6.112	0.630	5.481	29.926	6.976	22.951
1965	6.477	0.614	5.863	31.695	6.575	25.119
1966	6.777	0.562	6.215	32.793	5.863	26.930
1967	6.776	0.543	6.233	34.229	5.563	28.665
1968	7.995	0.552	7.443	36.515	5.493	31.023
1969	8.549	0.597	7.952	38.336	5.340	32.996
1970	9.444	0.575	8.868	39.323	5.064	34.259
1971	9.884	0.691	9.193	41.529	5.296	36.232
1972	10.678	0.678	10.000	44.322	5.209	39.113
1973	11.737	0.733	11.004	47.689	5.162	42.526
1974	11.451	0.703	10.748	48.049	5.256	42.792
1975	11.528	0.677	10.850	49.599	5.082	44.518
1976	12.208	0.659	11.549	52.007	4.832	47.174
1977	12.672	0.652	12.021	53.851	4.494	49.357
1978	13.864	0.478	13.286	54.675	3.974	50.701
1979	14.352	0.529	13.824	59.753	3.942	55.811
1980	14.828	0.521	14.307	61.814	4.400	57.414
1981	13.337	0.602	12.735	61.974	4.534	57.439
1982	12.437	0.565	11.872	53.206	3.726	60.480
1983	11.916	0.478	11.338	63.105	4.125	58.980
1984	11.965	0.526	11.439	64.529	3.513	61.016
1985	12.269	0.468	11.801	66.894	3.354	63.539

Table 7.A.1 (continued)

	Age 35–44			Age 45–54		
Year	Money metric inequality	Money metric poverty	Money metric remaining inequality	Money metric inequality	Money metric poverty	Money metric remaining inequality
1947	36.723	29.464	7.258	26.769	24.084	2.685
1948	38.730	30.658	8.072	26.959	23.353	3.606
1949	38.561	29.690	8.871	28.631	23.883	4.748
1950	40.639	27.844	12.783	28.878	23.327	5.551
1951	44.409	29.168	14.241	28.746	21.492	7.254
1952	44.796	28.352	16.444	31.258	22.626	8.633
1953	47.986	29.564	18.423	32.822	22.688	10.135
1954	48.929	30.322	18.607	34.061	23.183	10.877
1955	51.439	30.678	20.761	37.143	24.571	12.573
1956	53.783	28.980	24.803	37.430	24.106	13.325
1957	56.044	29.449	26.596	40.154	25.656	14.498
1958	56.493	29.069	27.424	40.970	25.511	15.460
1959	55.945	24.997	30.948	40.081	23.059	17.021
1960	56.667	23.340	33.326	41.924	22.198	19.726
1961	56.758	23.125	33.634	42.247	21.252	20.995
1962	60.191	23.357	36.834	43.846	21.414	22.431
1963	59.734	22.078	37.656	44.615	20.641	23.974
1964	62.685	20.734	41.950	47.886	20.952	26.935
1965	64.162	18.845	45.317	50.073	19.490	30.583
1966	65.051	16.794	48.257	51.863	17.892	33.970
1967	66.963	15.272	51.691	52.933	17.262	35.671
1968	67.766	13.469	54.297	54.063	16.139	37.924
1969	69.770	12.310	57.459	55.577	15.455	40.122
1970	70.663	11.544	59.119	57.161	14.802	42.359
1971	71.137	10.721	60.416	58.195	14.450	43.744
1972	74.212	9.903	64.309	59.408	13.272	46.136
1973	75.776	9.274	66.502	60.140	12.656	47.484
1974	75.129	9.034	66.095	59.181	12.025	47.156
1975	77.481	8.762	68.719	59.132	11.169	47.963
1976	79.673	7.909	71.764	59.776	9.942	49.833
1977	82.932	7.297	75.635	59.382	8.396	50.986
1978	85.431	6.374	79.057	59.707	7.119	52.588
1979	91.234	6.558	84.676	60.072	7.095	52.977
1980	92.824	6.987	85.837	59.290	7.020	52.270
1981	96.850	7.409	89.442	57.894	6.643	51.251
1982	96.740	7.556	89.184	55.862	6.148	49.715
1983	104.511	7.247	97.264	58.381	5.563	52.817
1984	108.465	6.846	101.620	58.708	5.064	53.644
1985	113.483	6.225	107.258	61.688	4.568	57.120

Table 7.A.1 (continued)

	Age 55–64			Age 65+		
Year	Money metric inequality	Money metric poverty	Money metric remaining inequality	Money metric inequality	Money metric poverty	Money metric remaining inequality
1947	19.796	13.518	6.278	14.054	8.542	5.512
1948	20.265	14.214	6.051	13.705	9.289	4.416
1949	21.269	14.528	6.742	14.542	9.286	5.256
1950	22.079	14.385	7.693	14.356	8.868	5.488
1951	21.991	13.732	8.259	15.044	9.640	5.404
1952	23.161	13.224	9.937	17.284	9.345	7.940
1953	23.664	13.582	10.082	17.574	9.335	8.239
1954	24.946	14.556	10.390	18.509	10.298	8.210
1955	26.097	14.561	11.537	19.503	10.447	9.056
1956	25.864	13.805	12.059	19.200	10.347	8.853
1957	26.657	14.095	12.562	18.977	10.336	8.641
1958	27.372	13.690	13.682	19.206	10.205	9.001
1959	28.173	12.165	16.008	20.153	8.946	11.206
1960	28.118	11.759	16.359	19.832	7.817	12.016
1961	29.952	11.929	18.023	22.193	8.164	14.029
1962	31.680	12.197	19.483	22.914	8.661	14.253
1963	32.510	11.668	20.841	23.161	8.216	14.945
1964	33.496	11.548	21.948	24.265	7.554	16.711
1965	34.656	10.931	23.725	24.732	7.270	17.462
1966	35.546	10.215	25.331	25.545	6.628	18.916
1967	37.236	10.087	27.149	25.758	6.545	19.213
1968	39.141	9.268	29.873	26.707	6.054	20.653
1969	40.469	9.226	31.243	27.508	6.028	21.480
1970	41.501	8.576	32.924	28.140	5.574	22.566
1971	42.138	8.498	33.640	29.993	5.566	24.427
1972	42.958	7.988	34.971	31.567	5.201	26.366
1973	43.465	7.496	35.969	32.925	4.978	27.947
1974	44.529	7.101	37.429	34.361	4.770	29.591
1975	44.510	6.852	37.658	35.725	4.238	31.487
1976	45.960	6.328	39.632	36.873	3.872	33.001
1977	47.990	5.829	42.161	38.105	3.575	34.529
1978	49.038	5.090	43.948	40.285	3.092	37.192
1979	49.465	5.009	44.456	41.212	3.112	38.100
1980	50.322	5.209	45.113	44.156	3.076	41.079
1981	50.897	5.084	45.813	46.918	2.945	44.073
1982	50.488	4.911	45.577	49.454	2.632	46.822
1983	51.789	4.624	47.166	51.762	2.402	49.360
1984	52.446	4.120	48.327	54.819	2.041	52.778
1985	52.810	3.630	49.180	56.562	1.964	54.598

340   Dale W. Jorgenson and Daniel T. Slesnick

Table 7.A.2
Money metric between-group poverty (billions of 1972 dollars)

	Within			Between		
Year	Money metric inequality	Money metric poverty	Money metric remaining inequality	Money metric inequality	Money metric poverty	Money metric remaining inequality
1947	107.211	89.014	18.197	13.962	0.651	13.311
1948	112.746	91.240	21.506	12.969	0.584	12.385
1949	116.345	91.278	25.067	14.171	0.563	13.608
1950	120.880	87.390	33.490	12.488	0.491	11.997
1951	127.108	86.674	40.434	14.602	0.580	14.022
1952	131.764	86.176	45.588	16.271	0.498	15.773
1953	138.688	87.744	50.944	15.826	0.449	15.377
1954	143.467	90.841	52.625	14.445	0.424	14.020
1955	152.125	93.244	58.882	14.647	0.368	14.278
1956	156.080	89.669	66.511	16.563	0.489	16.075
1957	162.381	92.417	69.965	17.879	0.515	17.364
1958	163.004	90.645	72.360	17.721	0.476	18.245
1959	161.914	79.605	82.308	18.352	0.376	17.976
1960	165.802	74.997	90.805	17.192	0.306	16.887
1961	168.759	73.845	94.914	17.933	0.259	17.674
1962	177.500	75.083	102.417	16.480	0.226	16.254
1963	177.569	71.370	106.199	19.140	0.238	18.902
1964	187.683	69.455	118.227	20.505	0.253	20.251
1965	195.147	64.711	130.436	20.401	0.208	20.194
1966	200.181	58.848	141.332	21.256	0.181	21.075
1967	203.985	56.156	147.829	23.895	0.175	23.720
1968	209.719	51.846	157.873	26.673	0.155	26.518
1969	215.076	49.736	165.340	29.251	0.151	29.100
1970	220.259	46.911	173.348	30.345	0.134	30.210
1971	226.781	46.041	180.740	29.944	0.119	29.825
1972	236.435	42.902	193.493	30.455	0.099	30.356
1973	242.864	40.822	202.042	32.683	0.095	32.356
1974	245.908	39.278	206.630	30.123	0.077	30.046
1975	253.122	37.149	215.973	27.912	0.068	27.844
1976	261.857	33.811	228.046	27.629	0.055	27.574
1977	272.095	30.320	241.775	25.398	0.035	25.363
1978	280.915	26.398	254.517	24.854	0.024	24.830
1979	288.806	26.508	262.298	30.748	0.030	30.717
1980	299.832	27.473	272.359	26.891	0.028	26.863
1981	305.074	27.307	277.767	25.522	0.024	25.497
1982	305.582	25.957	279.625	26.315	0.031	26.283
1983	316.105	24.856	291.249	27.982	0.018	27.963
1984	323.783	22.446	301.337	30.380	0.020	30.360
1985	335.742	20.405	315.337	30.886	0.015	30.871

Notes

1. Surveys of the literature on poverty measurement are given by Foster (1984) and Sen (1981).
2. The measures of poverty introduced by Sen (1976b) depend only on the economic circumstances of the poor. Sen (1979c, 1981) presents arguments against an approach to poverty measurement based on redistributional policy.
3. The social expenditure function was originated by Pollak (1981). Alternative money measures of social welfare are discussed by Arrow and Kalt (1979), Bergson (1980), Deaton and Muellbauer (1980b, pp. 214–239), Roberts (1980c), and Sen (1976a). A survey of the literature is presented by Sen (1979a).
4. Alternative money measures of efficiency and equity, which is the reverse of inequality, are discussed by Arrow and Kalt (1979), Bergson (1980), and Sen (1976a, 1979a).
5. The translog indirect utility function was introduced by Christensen, Jorgenson, and Lau (1975) and extended to encompass determinants of expenditure allocation other than prices and total expenditure by Jorgenson and Lau (1975). Alternative approaches to the representation of the effects of prices and total expenditure on expenditure allocation are summarized by Barten (1977), Deaton and Muellbauer (1980b, pp. 60–85), and Lau (1977a).
6. The household equivalence scales used in our measures of individual welfare are presented by Jorgenson and Slesnick (1987a). Household equivalence scales are discussed by Barten (1964), Muellbauer (1974a, 1977), and many others. Alternative approaches are summarized by Deaton and Muellbauer (1980b).
7. Alternative approaches to the representation of household characteristics in expenditure allocation are presented by Barten (1964), Gorman (1976), and Prais and Houthakker (1971). A review of the literature is given by Deaton and Muellbauer (1980b, pp. 191–213).
8. For further discussion, see Lau (1977b, 1982) and Jorgenson, Lau, and Stoker (1980, 1981, 1982).
9. The econometric model employed in this study is presented by Jorgenson and Slesnick (1987a).
10. Deaton and Muellbauer (1980, pp. 227–239), King (1983a,b), McKenzie (1982), and Muellbauer (1974b,c) present approaches to welfare measurement based on quantity indexes of individual welfare. These indexes are derived from the individual expenditure function (7.4.4) by varying the level of utility V_k for a fixed set of prices p ($k = 1, 2, \ldots, K$). Restrictions on preferences and social welfare functions under which measures of social welfare defined on the distribution of quantity indexes of individual welfare coincide with measures defined on the distribution of individual welfare itself are given by Roberts (1980c).
11. The use of household equivalence scales in evaluating transfers among individuals has been advocated by Deaton and Muellbauer (1980b, see pp. 205–212), and by Muellbauer (1974a). Pollak and Wales (1979) have presented arguments against the use of household equivalence scales for this purpose.
12. The class of social welfare functions (7.4.6) is *distributionally homothetic* in the sense of Blackorby and Donaldson (1982). The implications of distributional homotheticity are discussed by Kolm (1976b) and Blackorby and Donaldson (1978).
13. The Low Cost Food Plan has been developed by the U.S. Department of Agriculture and is based on the minimal nutritional needs of various types of households. Official estimates of the head-count ratio for individuals in poverty have been compiled by Danziger, Haveman, and Plotnick (1986) for the period 1964–1986. Comparable estimates have been constructed for the period 1939–1979 by Ross, Danziger, and Smolensky (1985).

14. Utilitarian social welfare functions have been employed extensively in applications of welfare economics, especially in the measurement of inequality by methods originated by Atkinson (1970) and Kolm (1969, 1976a,b), in the design of optimal income tax schedules along the lines pioneered by Mirrlees (1971), and in the evaluation of alternative economic policies by Arrow and Kalt (1979). These welfare functions are additively decomposable. Additively decomposable poverty measures are presented by Foster, Greer, and Thorbecke (1984).

15. Social welfare functions defined on the distribution of individual welfare over the population of all consuming units were suggested as a basis for poverty measurement by Watts (1968). Social welfare functions defined on measures of individual welfare truncated at the poverty threshold are employed by Pyatt (1987) and Takayama (1979).

8 Inequality and the Standard of Living

Dale W. Jorgenson and
Daniel T. Slesnick

This chapter presents an econometric approach to the normative analysis of economic growth. The approach has the crucial advantage over national accounting measures that both equity and efficiency considerations are brought to bear. To illustrate our methodology we assess the impact of price changes and changes in the distribution of total expenditure on the U.S. standard of living. Focusing on the period 1947–1985, we find that growth in equity accounts for 14.2 percent of the growth in the standard of living. However, equity growth is concentrated in the period 1958–1978. Equity actually declined from 1947–1958 and from 1978–1983.

8.1   Introduction

The purpose of this chapter is to present an econometric approach to the normative analysis of economic growth. Our approach is based on the concept of a social welfare function, originated by Bergson (1938) and discussed by Samuelson (1947, 1982). This has the crucial advantage over approaches based solely on national accounting information that both equity and efficiency considerations are brought to bear on the measurement of the standard of living.

Since the path-breaking work of Atkinson (1970) and Kolm (1969), the measurement of inequality has been based on explicit social welfare functions. However, the social welfare functions introduced by Atkinson and Kolm are defined on the distribution of "income" or total expenditure rather than the distribution of individual welfare.[1] Muellbauer (1974b) has defined social welfare functions on the distribution of money metric individual welfare. This approach has also been employed by Deaton and Muellbauer (1980b), King (1983a), and McKenzie (1982).

Roberts (1980c) has derived restrictions on preferences under which measures of social welfare based on the distribution of money metric individual welfare coincide with measures based on the distribution of individual welfare itself. In the absence of restrictions on the class of social welfare functions, individuals must have identical homothetic preferences. With no restrictions on individual preferences, the social welfare functions must be dictatorial in the sense of Arrow (1963).

Since it is obvious that the class of dictatorial social welfare functions is too narrow to provide an adequate basis for expressing alternative ethical judgments, we generate a less restrictive class by requiring cardinal full comparability of individual welfare functions. This implies that social orderings are invariant with respect to affine transformations of measures of individual welfare that are the same for all consuming units. Each member of this class of social welfare functions is homogeneous of degree one in levels of individual welfare and provides a cardinal measure of social welfare.

To translate comparisons among social welfare levels into monetary terms, we employ the social expenditure function introduced by Pollak (1981). This function gives the minimum level of aggregate expenditure required to attain a stipulated level of social welfare as a function of the prices faced by all consumers. The social expenditure function can be used to translate changes in social welfare into money measures of social welfare. The concept of money metric social welfare can be used in comparing alternative levels of social welfare on the basis of the aggregate expenditure associated with each level.

We define a social standard of living index as the ratio of two levels of aggregate expenditure.[2] The first is the aggregate expenditure required to attain the current level of social welfare at the base period price system. The second is the level of expenditure required for the base period level of welfare at this same price system. We decompose our standard of living index into the product of an index of efficiency and an index of equity. We define a quantity index of efficiency as the ratio of money metric efficiency in the current period to money metric efficiency in the base period, both evaluated at base period prices. We define a quantity index of equity as the ratio of our standard of living index to the index of efficiency.

To illustrate the application of our social standard of living index we assess the impact of changes in the price system and the distribution of total expenditure on the growth of the U.S. economy over the postwar period, 1947–1985. We find that both efficiency and equity have grown substantially. The growth of equity accounts for 14.2 percent of growth in the standard of living; however, equity growth is concentrated in the twenty-year period 1958–1978. During the periods 1947–1958 and 1978–1983 equity actually declined.

Finally, we show that our quantity index of efficiency can be represented as the ratio of an index of nominal aggregate expenditure per capita and the social cost-of-living index introduced by Jorgenson and Slesnick (1983). We evaluate the biases involved in substituting an index of real aggregate expenditure per person for our index of efficiency. We also evaluate the biases that would result from using real aggregate expenditure per person as a normative measure of economic growth. The biases are almost as important as real expenditure itself in measuring growth in the social standard of living index.

8.2 Individual Welfare

In this section we outline an econometric model of aggregate consumer behavior. The distinctive feature of this model is that systems of individual demand functions can be recovered uniquely from the aggregate demand system. This feature is assured by requiring that the individual demand functions satisfy the restrictions implied by exact aggregation.[3] By requiring, in addition, that the individual demand functions are integrable, we can recover indirect utility functions for all consuming units. Finally, we define cardinal measures of individual welfare that are fully comparable among individuals in terms of these indirect utility functions.

To measure individual welfare we represent individual preferences by means of an indirect utility function for each consuming unit, using the following notation:

p_n — price of the nth commodity, assumed to be the same for all consuming units.

$p = (p_1, p_2, \ldots, p_N)$ — the vector of prices of all commodities.

x_{nk} — the quantity of the nth commodity group consumed by the kth consuming unit ($n = 1,2,\ldots,N$; $k = 1,2,\ldots,K$).

$M_k = \sum_{n=1}^{N} p_n x_{nk}$ — total expenditure of the kth consuming unit ($k = 1, 2, \ldots, K$).

$\ln p = (\ln p_1, \ln p_2, \ldots, \ln p_N)$ — vector of logarithms of prices.

A_k — vector of attributes of the kth consuming unit ($k = 1, 2, \ldots, K$).

The first step in measuring social welfare is to select a representation of the individual welfare function. We define the individual welfare function for the kth consuming unit, say W_k $(k = 1, 2, \ldots, K)$, as the logarithm of the translog[4] indirect utility function

$$W_k = \ln V_k$$

$$= \ln p'\alpha_p + \frac{1}{2} \ln p' B_{pp} \ln p - D(p) \ln [M_k/m_0(p, A_k)] ,$$

$$(k = 1, 2, \ldots, K) . \qquad (8.2.1)$$

The indirect utility function expresses individual welfare in terms of prices p and the level of total expenditure M_k.

In the representation (8.2.1) of the translog indirect utility function the vector α_p and the matrices B_{pp} and B_{pA} are constant parameters that are the same for all consuming units. Differences among consuming units are introduced through the vector of attributes A_k $(k = 1, 2, \ldots, K)$. The exact aggregation conditions require that

$$i' B_{pp} i = 0 , \qquad i' B_{pA} = 0 .$$

The function $D(p)$ takes the form

$$D(p) = -1 + i' B_{pp} \ln p.$$

In this representation the indirect utility function is linear in the logarithm of total expenditure $\ln M_k$ with a coefficient that depends on the prices p $(k = 1, 2, \ldots, K)$, but not on the attributes A_k $(k = 1, 2, \ldots, K)$. This property is invariant with respect to positive affine transformations that are the same for all consuming units, but is not preserved by arbitrary monotone increasing transformations or affine transformations that differ among units. We conclude that the indirect utility function (8.2.1) provides a cardinal measure of individual welfare that is fully comparable among consuming units. Finally, in this representation the function $m_0(p, A_k)$ is the *general translog household equivalence scale* introduced by Jorgenson and Slesnick (1987a) and can be interpreted as the number of household equivalent members.[5]

In implementing the econometric model of consumer behavior we divide consumer expenditures among five commodity groups:

1. *Energy*: Expenditures on electricity, natural gas, heating oil, and gasoline,

2. *Food*: Expenditures on all food products, including tobacco and alcohol,

3. *Consumer goods*: Expenditures on all other nondurable goods included in consumer expenditures,

4. *Capital services*: The service flow from consumer durables and the service flow from housing,

5. *Consumer services*: Expenditures on consumer services, such as car repairs, medical services, entertainment, and so on.

We employ the following demographic characteristics as attributes of individual households:

1. *Family size*: 1,2, 3, 4, 5, 6, and 7 or more persons.

2. *Age of head*: 16–24, 25–34, 35–44, 45–54, 55–64, 65 and over.

3. *Region of residence*: Northeast, North Central, South, and West.

4. *Race*: White, nonwhite.

5. *Type of residence*: Urban, rural.

Our cross-section observations on individual expenditures for each commodity group and on demographic characteristics of individual households are for the year 1973 from the 1972–1973 Survey of Consumer Expenditures (CES).[6] Our time-series observations are based on data on personal consumption expenditures from the United States National Income and Product Accounts (NIPA) for the years 1947 to 1985.[7] Prices for each commodity group are defined in terms of translog price indexes computed from detailed prices included in NIPA for each year. We employ time-series data on the distribution of expenditures over all households and among demographic groups based on *Current Population Reports*.[8]

In our application we treat the expenditure shares for five commodity groups as endogenous variables, so that we estimate four equations. As unknown parameters we have four elements of the vector α_p, four expenditure coefficients of the vector $B_{pp}i$, sixteen attribute coefficients for each of the four equations in the matrix B_{pA}, and ten price coefficients in the matrix B_{pp}, which is constrained to be symmetric. The expenditure coefficients are sums of price coefficients in the corresponding equation, so that we have a total of 82 unknown parameters. We estimate the complete model, subject to inequality restrictions implied by monotonicity of the individual expenditure shares, by pooling time-series and cross-section data.[9]

8.3 Social Welfare

We next consider orderings over the set of social states and the set of real-valued individual welfare functions $\{W_k\}$. A social state is described by the quantities consumed of N commodity groups by K individuals. The individual welfare function for the kth individual W_k

$(k = 1, 2, \ldots, K)$ is defined on the set of social states and gives the level of individual welfare for that individual in each state.

To describe social orderings in greater detail we find it useful to introduce the following notation:

x — a matrix with elements $\{x_{nk}\}$ describing the social state.

$u = (W_1, W_2, \ldots, W_K)$ — a vector of individual welfare functions of all K individuals.

We require that social orderings must be invariant with respect to any positive affine transformation of the individual welfare functions $\{W_k\}$ that is the same for all households.[10] Under this assumption the logarithms of the translog indirect utility functions (8.2.1) are cardinal measures of individual welfare with full comparability among households. To represent social orderings in a form suitable for measuring social welfare we consider the class of social welfare functions introduced by Jorgenson and Slesnick (1983)

$$
W(u, x) = \ln \bar{V} - \gamma(x) \left[\frac{\sum_{k=1}^{K} m_0(p, A_k) |\ln V_k - \ln \bar{V}|^{-\rho}}{\sum_{k=1}^{K} m_0(p, A_k)} \right]^{-1/\rho} . \tag{8.3.1}
$$

The first term in the social welfare functions (8.3.1) corresponds to an average of individual welfare levels over all consuming units

$$
\ln \bar{V} = \frac{\sum_{k=1}^{K} m_0(p, A_k) \ln V_k [pm(A_k)/M_k]}{\sum_{k=1}^{K} m_0(p, A_k)} ,
$$

$$
= \ln p' \left(\alpha_p + \frac{1}{2} B_{pp} \ln p \right) - D(p) \frac{\sum_{k=1}^{K} m_0(p, A_k) \ln [M_k/m_0(p, A_k)]}{\sum_{k=1}^{K} m_0(p, A_k)} .
$$

The second term in (8.3.1) is a linear homogeneous function of deviations of levels of individual welfare from the average. This is a measure of dispersion in individual welfare levels.[11] Since both terms are homogeneous of degree one in individual welfare levels, the social welfare functions (8.3.1) provide cardinal measures of social welfare.[12]

The Pareto principle requires that an increase in individual welfare must increase social welfare. This condition implies that the first term in (8.3.1), representing the average level of individual welfare, must increase by more than the second term, representing the dispersion in individual welfare, whatever the initial distribution of individual welfare. We assume that the function $\gamma(x)$ in (8.3.1) must take the maximum value consistent with the Pareto principle, so that

$$\gamma(x) = \left\{ \frac{\sum_{k \neq j}^{K} m_0(p, A_k)}{\sum_{k=1}^{K} m_0(p, A_k)} \left(1 + \left[\frac{\sum_{k \neq j}^{K} m_0(p, A_k)}{m_0(p, A_j)} \right]^{-(\rho+1)} \right) \right\}^{1/\rho} \qquad (8.3.2)$$

where

$$m_0(p, A_j) = \min_k m_0(p, A_k), \qquad (k = 1, 2, \ldots, K).$$

The social welfare functions (8.3.1) incorporate a notion of horizontal equity. In particular, we require that no individual is given greater weight in the social welfare function than any other individual with an identical individual welfare function. We also incorporate a notion of vertical equity by requiring that the social welfare functions (8.3.1) are equity-regarding in the sense of Hammond (1977). This amounts to imposing a version of Dalton's (1920) principle of transfers. This principle requires that a transfer from a rich household to a poor household that does not reverse their relative position must increase the level of social welfare.

At this point we have generated a class of social welfare functions capable of expressing the implications of a variety of ethical judgments. In order to choose a specific social welfare function, we must narrow the range of possible ethical judgments by imposing further requirements on the class of social welfare functions. The parameter ρ in the representation (8.3.1) determines the curvature of the social welfare function in the individual welfare functions $\{W_k(x)\}$. We refer to this parameter as the *degree of aversion to inequality*. By selecting an appropriate value of this parameter, we can incorporate ethical judgments about inequality in the distribution of individual welfare.

To provide a basis for comparisons among social states $\{x_{nk}\}$ we formulate a money measure of social welfare. Following Pollak (1981), we can define the *social expenditure function* as the minimum level of total expenditure $M = \sum_{k=1}^{K} M_k$ required to attain a given level of social welfare, say W, at a specified price system p. More formally, the social expenditure function $M(p, W)$ is defined by

$$M(p, W) = \min \left\{ M : W(u, x) \geq W; M = \sum_{k=1}^{K} M_k \right\}. \qquad (8.3.3)$$

The social expenditure function and the social welfare function can be employed in assessing the impacts of changes in prices and the distribution of total expenditures on social welfare.

We can translate any level of social welfare into monetary terms by evaluating the social expenditure function at that level of welfare for a given price system p. Two different levels of social welfare can be compared with reference to a single price system by determining the minimum level of aggregate expenditure required to attain each level of social welfare for the reference prices.

In order to determine the form of the social expenditure function $M(p, W)$ (8.3.3), we can maximize the social welfare function (8.3.1) for a fixed level of aggregate expenditure by equalizing total expenditure per household equivalent member $\{M_k/m_0(p, A_k)\}$ for all consuming units. For the translog indirect utility function the maximum value of social welfare for a given level of aggregate expenditure takes the form

$$\ln \bar{V} = \ln p'\left(\alpha_p + \frac{1}{2} B_{pp} \ln p\right) - D(p) \ln\left[M \Big/ \sum_{k=1}^{K} m_0(p, A_k)\right]. \qquad (8.3.4)$$

This is the maximum level of welfare that is potentially available and can be taken as a measure of efficiency.

If aggregate expenditure is distributed so as to equalize total expenditure per household equivalent member, the level of individual welfare is the same for all consuming units. For this distribution of total expenditure the social welfare function reduces to the average level of individual welfare $\ln \bar{V}$. The value of social welfare is obtained by evaluating the translog indirect utility function (8.2.1) at total expenditure per household equivalent member $M \Big/ \sum_{k=1}^{K} m_0(p, A_k)$ for the economy as a whole.

We can express aggregate expenditure as a function of the level of social welfare and prices

$$\ln M(p, W) = \frac{1}{D(p)} \left[\ln p'\left(\alpha_p + \frac{1}{2} B_{pp} \ln p\right) - W\right] + \ln\left[\sum_{k=1}^{K} m_0(p, A_k)\right].$$

$$(8.3.5)$$

The value of aggregate expenditure is obtained by evaluating the social expenditure function (8.3.5) at the level of social welfare W and the number of household equivalent members $\sum_{k=1}^{K} m_0(p, A_k)$ for the economy as a whole.

8.4   Standard of Living Index

In this section we present methods for translating changes in the price system p and the distribution of total expenditure $\{M_k\}$ into measures of change in the standard of living. We first define the social standard of living index, say Q_A, as the ratio of two levels of aggregate expenditure per capita

$$
Q_A(p^0, W^0, W^1) = \left[M(p^0, W^1) \Big/ \sum_{k=1}^{K^1} m_0(p^0, A_k) \right]
$$
$$
\Big/ \left[M(p^0, W^0) \Big/ \sum_{k=1}^{K^0} m_0(p^0, A_k) \right]. \tag{8.4.1}
$$

The numerator of our social standard of living index (8.4.1) is the aggregate expenditure per capita required to attain the current level of social welfare W^1 at the base period price system p^0. The denominator of the index (8.4.1) is the expenditure per capita required to attain the base period level of welfare W^0 at this price system. Our measure of the size of the population in each period is the number of household equivalent members for society as a whole. The current number of households is K^1, while the base period number of households is K^0.

The social welfare function (8.3.1) and the translog social expenditure function (8.3.5) can be employed in implementing the social standard of living index (8.4.1). First, to obtain the base level of social welfare W^0, we evaluate the social welfare function (8.3.1) at the base period price system p^0 and the base period distribution of total expenditure $\{M_k^0\}$. We can express the current level of social welfare W^1 in terms of the social welfare function by replacing the base period price system and distribution of total expenditure with the current price system p^1 and the current distribution of total expenditure $\{M_k^1\}$.

Next, we decompose our social standard of living index (8.4.1) into the product of an index of efficiency and an index of equity. For this purpose we first determine the maximum level of welfare, say W^3, that can be attained through lump-sum redistributions of aggregate total expenditure $M^1 = \sum M_k^1$. As before, aggregate expenditure must be distributed so as to equalize individual expenditure per capita, so that the social welfare function (8.3.1) reduces to average individual welfare (8.3.4)

$W^3 = \ln \bar{V}^1$

$$= \ln p^{1'}\left(\alpha_p + \frac{1}{2} B_{pp} \ln p^1\right) - D(p^1) \ln\left[M^1 \Big/ \sum_{k=1}^{K^1} m_0(p^1, A_k)\right]. \quad (8.4.2)$$

This is the maximum level of social welfare that is potentially available in the current period and can be taken as a measure of efficiency.

We can define the quantity index of efficiency, say Q_P, as the ratio of two levels of aggregate expenditure per capita

$$Q_P(p^0, W^2, W^3) = \left[M(p^0, W^3) \Big/ \sum_{k=1}^{K^1} m_0(p^0, A_k)\right]$$

$$\Big/ \left[M(p^0, W^2) \Big/ \sum_{k=1}^{K^0} m_0(p^0, A_k)\right]$$

$$= \left[M(p^0, W^3) \Big/ \sum_{k=1}^{K^1} m_0(p, A_k)\right]$$

$$\Big/ \left[M^0 \Big/ \sum_{k=1}^{K^0} m_0(p, A_k)\right], \quad (8.4.3)$$

where M^0 is the base period level of total expenditure.

The numerator of our quantity index of efficiency (8.4.3) is the aggregate expenditure per capita required to attain the potential level of social welfare in the current period W^3 at the base period price system p^0. The denominator of our index is the expenditure per capita required to attain the potential level of welfare in the base period W^2 at this price system. The quantity index of efficiency (8.4.3) is the ratio of money measures of efficiency in the current period and the base period, both evaluated at the base period price system p^0.

Finally, we can define a quantity index of equity, say Q_E, as the ratio of the index of social welfare to the index of efficiency

$$Q_E = \frac{Q_A}{Q_P} = \frac{M(p^0, W^1)/M(p^0, W^3)}{M(p^0, W^0)/M^0}. \quad (8.4.4)$$

The numerator of our quantity index of equity (8.4.4) is a money measure of equity in the current period, evaluated at the base period price system p^0. Similarly, the denominator is the money measure of equity in the base period, evaluated at this same price system.[13]

To illustrate the social standard of living index (8.4.1), we can assess the impact of changes in the price system p and the distribution of total expenditure $\{M_k\}$ on the standard of living for the U.S. economy as a whole. In table 8.1 we present the standard of living index (8.4.1) and its rate of growth for the period 1947–1985 corresponding to degree of aversion to inequality ρ equal to minus one. This value of the parameter gives the greatest possible weight to equity considerations. We use prices of 1972 as the base period price system. Over the thirty-eight-year period, the index has risen from 0.445 to 1.370 with 1972 equal to 1.000.

To illustrate the decomposition of the social standard of living index into indexes of efficiency (8.4.3) and equity (8.4.4) we present these indexes for the U.S. economy as a whole and their rates of growth for the period 1947–1985 in table 8.1. As before, we employ prices for 1972 as the base period price system. Over the thirty-eight-year period, the index of efficiency has risen from 0.499 to 1.311, while the index of equity has risen from 0.893 to 1.045. Both indexes are equal to 1.000 in 1972.

For the period as a whole, the average annual rate of growth of the standard of living is 2.96 percent. The growth rate of efficiency during this period is 2.54 percent, while the growth rate of equity is 0.42 percent. Growth in equity is 14.2 percent of growth in welfare, while growth in efficiency is 85.8 percent. Inspection of the index of equity (8.4.4) presented in table 8.1 reveals that most of the growth in equity occurred during the period 1958–1978, twenty years out of the thirty-eight-year period 1947–1985.

During the twenty-year period 1958–1978, the average annual rate of growth of the standard of living is 3.91 percent. The growth rate of efficiency is 3.11 percent, while the growth rate of equity is 0.79 percent. Growth in equity is 20.2 percent of the growth in welfare, while growth in efficiency is 79.8 percent. By contrast the contribution of equity to growth in welfare during the periods 1947–1958 and 1978–1983 is slightly negative.

8.5   Real Expenditure per Person

In the preceding section we have analyzed the growth of a social standard of living index for the U.S. economy. This index is defined in terms of the social welfare function (8.3.1) and reflects changes in the price system p and the distribution of total expenditure $\{M_k\}$. An alternative measure of social welfare is the level of real aggregate expenditure per person, where the size of the population is the

Table 8.1
Standard of living indexes

	Standard of living indexes (1972 = 1.000)			Annual growth rates (percent)		
Year	Standard of living	Efficiency	Equity	Standard of living	Efficiency	Equity
1947	0.445	0.499	0.893	0.00	0.00	0.00
1948	0.447	0.505	0.886	0.37	1.16	−0.80
1949	0.456	0.520	0.877	2.03	2.98	−0.96
1950	0.480	0.538	0.893	5.18	3.39	1.79
1951	0.499	0.561	0.888	3.72	4.31	−0.59
1952	0.514	0.579	0.888	3.14	3.13	0.01
1953	0.521	0.591	0.881	1.24	1.98	−0.74
1954	0.518	0.588	0.881	−0.60	−0.56	−0.04
1955	0.526	0.600	0.877	1.52	2.01	−0.50
1956	0.551	0.624	0.883	4.71	3.95	0.76
1957	0.551	0.630	0.874	0.00	1.09	−1.09
1958	0.563	0.636	0.886	2.24	0.92	1.32
1959	0.614	0.667	0.920	8.53	4.72	3.81
1960	0.640	0.689	0.929	4.19	3.16	1.03
1961	0.654	0.699	0.935	2.16	1.56	0.60
1962	0.664	0.710	0.935	1.50	1.46	0.04
1963	0.687	0.726	0.947	3.51	2.30	1.21
1964	0.715	0.757	0.945	3.92	4.13	−0.21
1965	0.756	0.793	0.954	5.64	4.68	0.96
1966	0.803	0.829	0.969	6.01	4.46	1.55
1967	0.827	0.849	0.975	2.97	2.31	0.66
1968	0.871	0.888	0.981	5.18	4.55	0.63
1969	0.903	0.916	0.986	3.59	3.11	0.48
1970	0.934	0.942	0.992	3.40	2.78	0.62
1971	0.953	0.958	0.995	2.00	1.74	0.26
1972	1.000	1.000	1.000	4.78	4.25	0.53
1973	1.033	1.030	1.003	3.27	2.97	0.30
1974	1.049	1.039	1.010	1.50	0.84	0.66
1975	1.078	1.061	1.015	2.70	2.16	0.54
1976	1.123	1.099	1.022	4.16	3.49	3.67
1977	1.173	1.139	1.030	4.34	3.60	0.74
1978	1.230	1.184	1.038	4.71	3.85	0.86
1979	1.255	1.216	1.033	2.07	2.64	−0.57
1980	1.240	1.204	1.030	−1.22	−1.01	−0.20
1981	1.246	1.207	1.032	0.47	0.29	0.18
1982	1.261	1.215	1.038	1.19	0.62	0.57
1983	1.292	1.245	1.038	2.44	2.47	−0.02
1984	1.332	1.278	1.043	3.03	2.58	0.45
1985	1.370	1.311	1.045	2.82	2.55	0.27

number of persons. In this section we evaluate the biases involved in substituting an index of real aggregate expenditure per person for the standard of living index (8.4.1).

We first define an index of nominal aggregate expenditure per capita, as follows

$$\ln \frac{M^1 / \sum_{k=1}^{K^1} m_0(p^1, A_k)}{M^0 / \sum_{k=1}^{K^0} m_0(p^0, A_k)} = \ln \frac{M(p^1, W^3) / \sum_{k=1}^{K^1} m_0(p^1, A_k)}{M(p^0, W^2) / \sum_{k=1}^{K^0} m_0(p^0, A_k)} . \qquad (8.5.1)$$

The base period level of aggregate expenditure M^0 is a money measure of potential social welfare, evaluated at base period prices p^0. Similarly, the current level of aggregate expenditure M^1 is a measure of potential welfare at current prices p^1.

Next, we decompose our index of nominal aggregate expenditure (8.5.1) into the product of an index of efficiency and a social cost-of-living index. We can rewrite the nominal expenditure index (8.5.1), as follows

$$\ln \frac{M^1 / \sum_{k=1}^{K^1} m_0(p^1, A_k)}{M^0 / \sum_{k=1}^{K^0} m_0(p^0, A_k)} = \ln Q_P + \ln P ,$$

where Q_P is the index of efficiency (8.4.3) and

$$\ln P = \ln \frac{M(p^1, W^3)}{M(p^0, W^3)} .$$

The index P is the *social cost-of-living index* introduced by Jorgenson and Slesnick (1983), evaluated at the current level of potential social welfare W^3.[14] This index is the ratio of the aggregate expenditure required to attain the potential level of welfare in the current period W^3 at current prices p^1 to the expenditure required to attain this level of welfare at base period prices p^0. If the social cost-of-living index is greater than unity and aggregate expenditure is constant, then social welfare is decreased by the change in prices.

Finally, we can express the index of efficiency (8.4.3) as the ratio of nominal aggregate expenditure per capita (8.5.1) to the social cost-of-living index. For this purpose we first introduce an index of the number of household equivalent members of society as a whole, as follows

$$\ln (H^1 / H^0) = \ln \frac{\sum_{k=1}^{K^1} m_0(p^1, A_k)}{\sum_{k=1}^{K^0} m_0(p^0, A_k)} .$$ (8.5.2)

The current number of household equivalent members is H^1, while the base period number is H^0.

The index of efficiency (8.4.3) is the ratio of nominal aggregate expenditure to the index of household equivalent members (8.5.2), divided by the social cost-of-living index

$$\ln Q_P = \ln \frac{M^1}{M^0} - \ln \frac{H^1}{H^0} - \ln P.$$ (8.5.3)

Our overall conclusion is that the index of efficiency (8.4.3) is a measure of real aggregate expenditure per capita.

As an alternative to the index of efficiency (8.4.3) we can consider real aggregate expenditure per person, say Q, defined as the ratio of nominal aggregate expenditure to an index of the number of persons in the population, divided by the consumer price index of the Bureau of Labor Statistics

$$\ln Q = \ln \frac{M^1}{M^0} - \ln \frac{N^1}{N^0} - \ln \text{CPI} .$$ (8.5.4)

The current number of persons in the population is N^1, while the base period number is N^0. The consumer price index is denoted CPI.

We can express the bias, say B_Q, in using the real expenditure index (8.5.4) in place of the index of efficiency (8.4.3) by subtracting the logarithm of the real expenditure index from the index of efficiency, obtaining

$$\ln B_Q = \ln Q_P - \ln Q = \ln B_N + \ln B_P ,$$ (8.5.5)

where B_N is the bias in the population size index and B_P is the bias in the price index

$$\ln B_N = \ln \frac{N^1}{N^0} - \ln \frac{H^1}{H^0} ,$$
$$\ln B_P = \ln \text{CPI} - \ln P.$$

To illustrate the magnitude of the bias B_Q in real aggregate expenditure per person (8.5.4) as a measure of efficiency, we present this bias for the period 1947–1985 in table 8.2. We use prices of 1972 as the base

Table 8.2
Biases in real aggregate expenditure per person

Year	Efficiency bias	Population bias	Price bias	Welfare bias	Equity index
1947	0.917	0.937	0.979	0.819	0.893
1948	0.933	0.944	0.988	0.826	0.886
1949	0.951	0.967	0.984	0.835	0.877
1950	0.951	0.973	0.977	0.849	0.893
1951	0.976	0.978	0.998	0.866	0.888
1952	0.979	0.984	0.995	0.870	0.888
1953	0.969	0.991	0.978	0.855	0.881
1954	0.954	0.978	0.975	0.840	0.881
1955	0.933	0.967	0.965	0.818	0.877
1956	0.942	0.972	0.969	0.832	0.883
1957	0.946	0.972	0.973	0.827	0.874
1958	0.950	0.970	0.979	0.841	0.886
1959	0.961	0.992	0.969	0.884	0.920
1960	0.976	1.006	0.970	0.907	0.929
1961	0.978	1.007	0.971	0.914	0.935
1962	0.968	1.000	0.968	0.906	0.935
1963	0.969	1.004	0.965	0.917	0.947
1964	0.969	1.005	0.964	0.916	0.945
1965	0.974	1.013	0.962	0.930	0.954
1966	0.977	1.011	0.966	0.946	0.969
1967	0.973	1.002	0.972	0.949	0.975
1968	0.982	1.005	0.978	0.964	0.981
1969	0.989	0.999	0.990	0.976	0.986
1970	1.002	0.998	1.003	0.994	0.992
1971	1.002	0.997	1.005	0.997	0.995
1972	1.000	1.000	1.000	1.000	1.000
1973	1.003	0.999	1.003	1.006	1.003
1974	1.013	0.994	1.019	1.022	1.010
1975	1.028	0.997	1.031	1.043	1.015
1976	1.029	0.999	1.030	1.051	1.022
1977	1.033	1.003	1.030	1.064	1.030
1978	1.045	1.007	1.038	1.085	1.038
1979	1.074	1.011	1.063	1.109	1.033
1980	1.088	0.992	1.096	1.121	1.030
1981	1.099	0.992	1.108	1.134	1.032
1982	1.103	0.995	1.109	1.145	1.038
1983	1.090	0.992	1.099	1.132	1.038
1984	1.090	0.991	1.100	1.137	1.043
1985	1.094	0.988	1.108	1.144	1.045

period price system. Over the thirty-eight-year period, the bias B_Q has risen from 0.917 to 1.094 with 1972 equal to 1.000. The average annual rate of growth of the bias is 0.46 percent for the period as a whole. This is 18.1 percent of growth in efficiency. We conclude that real aggregate expenditure per person (8.5.4) is seriously biased as a measure of efficiency.

We can also illustrate the decomposition of the quantity bias B_Q into components associated with biases in population size and prices in table 8.2. The bias in population size B_N has risen from 0.937 to 0.988 and the bias in the price index B_P has risen from 0.979 to 1.108. Both indexes are equal to 1.000 in 1972. The average annual rate of growth is 0.14 percent for the bias in population size and 0.32 percent for the bias in the price index. The population bias is 30.4 percent and the price bias is 69.6 percent of the bias in real aggregate expenditure per person (8.5.4) as a measure of efficiency.

Although the index of real aggregate expenditure per person Q is best regarded as a measure of efficiency, it can be misinterpreted as a social standard of living index. Using the decomposition (8.4.4) of the standard of living index Q_A into components corresponding to efficiency Q_P and equity Q_E, we obtain

$$\ln Q_A = \ln Q_P + \ln Q_E . \tag{8.5.6}$$

We can express the bias, say B, in real aggregate expenditure per person (8.5.4) as a standard of living index by subtracting the logarithm of the real expenditure index from the standard of living index (8.5.6), as follows

$$\ln B = \ln Q_A - \ln Q = \ln B_N + \ln B_P + \ln Q_E . \tag{8.5.7}$$

To illustrate the magnitude of the bias B in real aggregate expenditure per person (8.5.4) as a measure of the standard of living, we present this bias for the period 1947–1985 the fourth column of table 8.2. The bias has risen from 0.819 to 1.144 over the thirty-eight-year period with 1972 equal to 1.000. For the period as a whole the average annual rate of growth of this bias is 0.88 percent or 29.7 percent of the growth of welfare. The growth of the bias is nearly as great as the growth of real aggregate expenditure per person. The price bias is 37.0 percent of the bias in the measurement of welfare. Omission of equity is 47.1 percent and the population bias is 15.9 percent of the overall bias.

We conclude that the social standard of living index (8.4.1) differs substantially from real aggregate expenditure per person. First, the standard of living index incorporates a measure of equity in the distribution of individual welfare as well as the measure of efficiency implicit in real expenditure. Second, the standard of living index includes a social cost-of-living index rather than the consumer price index employed in real aggregate expenditure. Finally, the standard of living index reflects changes in the number of household equivalent members for society as a whole, rather than the number of persons in the population.

Our overall conclusion is that the social standard of living index (8.4.1) provides an interesting new approach to translating changes in the price system and the distribution of total expenditure into a measure of social welfare. The primary advantage of this measure over alternative measures based on national accounting data alone is that it incorporates both equity and efficiency considerations. The advantage of an econometric approach over alternatives based on the distribution of income or total expenditure is that differences in the demographic composition of the population and variations in prices over time can be incorporated in the normative analysis of economic growth.

Notes

1. Muellbauer (1974b, p. 498), has shown that measures of social welfare based on "income" coincide with measures based on individual welfare if and only if preferences are identical and homothetic for all consuming units. See also: Roberts (1980c).
2. The literature on standard of living indexes is summarized by Deaton and Muellbauer (1980b, pp. 179–190), Diewert (1981), and Sen (1987).
3. For further discussion, see Lau (1977b, 1982) and Jorgenson, Lau, and Stoker (1982).
4. The translog indirect utility function was introduced by Christensen, Jorgenson, and Lau (1975) and extended to encompass determinants of expenditure allocation other than prices and total expenditure by Jorgenson and Lau (1975).
5. The translog household equivalence scale is discussed by Jorgenson and Slesnick (1987a). Alternative approaches are summarized by Deaton and Muellbauer (1980b).
6. The 1972–1973 Survey of Consumer Expenditures is discussed by Carlson (1974).
7. We employ data on the flow of services from durable goods rather than purchases of durable goods. Personal consumption expenditures in the U.S. National Income and Product Accounts are based on purchases of durable goods.
8. This series is published annually by the U.S. Bureau of the Census.
9. A detailed discussion of the stochastic specification of our model is presented by Jorgenson, Lau and Stoker (1982, section 6). Econometric methods for pooling time-series and cross-section data are discussed by Jorgenson and Stoker (1986).
10. For further discussion, see Jorgenson and Slesnick (1984a).

11. It is important to note that the social welfare functions (8.3.1) exemplify the single profile approach to social choice of Bergson (1938) and Samuelson (1947, 1982). The literature on single profile social welfare functions is summarized by Roberts (1980d) and Samuelson (1982).

12. Blackorby and Donaldson (1982) refer to homogeneous social welfare functions as *distributionally homothetic*.

13. For further discussion, see Jorgenson and Slesnick (1984a).

14. See Jorgenson and Slesnick (1983, pp. 290–293).

9   Carbon Taxes and Economic Welfare

Dale W. Jorgenson,
Daniel T. Slesnick, and
Peter J. Wilcoxen

9.1   Introduction

The possibility that increased concentrations of carbon dioxide in the atmosphere might lead to global warming has emerged as a leading environmental concern. Many nations, including the United States, are considering policies to reduce emissions of carbon dioxide.[1] The policy instrument for reducing carbon dioxide emissions most often recommended by economists is a carbon tax.[2] A carbon tax levied on fossil fuels in proportion to the amount of carbon dioxide they produce during combustion would stimulate firms and households to reduce fossil fuel use and shift the fuel mix toward less carbon-intensive fuels, such as natural gas.

A carbon tax would internalize the externality associated with carbon dioxide emissions.[3] However, this externality affects the whole planet, while carbon taxes are the responsibility of individual governments. Furthermore, carbon taxes would interact with taxes levied to achieve other objectives, such as taxes on motor fuels used to generate revenues for highway construction and maintenance. The design of an appropriate level for carbon taxes would involve international coordination and consideration of interactions among different tax and expenditure programs within each nation. Finally, benefits of a carbon tax would have to be weighed against losses in efficiency resulting from distortions in resource allocation.

Jorgenson and Wilcoxen (1992) have measured the efficiency cost to the U.S. economy of carbon taxes required to achieve alternative restrictions on carbon dioxide emissions.[4] For this purpose they simulated U.S. economic growth under different tax regimes by means of an intertemporal general equilibrium model of the U.S. economy. In this paper we analyze the distributional impact of carbon taxes that would stabilize U.S. carbon dioxide emissions at 1990 levels. To achieve this objective we disaggregate the overall economic impact of carbon taxes to the level of individual households.

An evaluation of the impact of taxes to reduce carbon emissions must consider not only the resulting efficiency losses but also the effects of these taxes on equity in the distribution of welfare among households. A carbon tax has potentially significant distributional consequences, because it would affect the relative prices faced by consumers. The impact of this change in relative prices could vary widely among consumers groups with different expenditure patterns. For example, an increase in the price of energy, resulting from the imposition of a carbon tax, would adversely affect those consumers who devote a larger share of their total expenditures to energy.

Our paper is not the first to examine the distributional impact of carbon taxes. Poterba (1991b) has employed a static, partial equilibrium approach to estimate the impact of a $100-per-ton carbon tax on U.S. households with different levels of total expenditure. He concludes that such a tax would be regressive. DeWitt, Dowlatabadi and Kopp (1991) have conducted a similar study for a range of carbon taxes, using a detailed econometric model of U.S. household energy consumption to estimate the response of energy consumption patterns to the tax.[5] They find that there would be substantial differences in the economic effect among regions of the United States.

Our analysis of the welfare effect of carbon taxes differs from these previous studies in two important ways. First, we employ a general equilibrium approach in analyzing these taxes. A partial equilibrium analysis is limited to the effects of changes in energy prices. As Poterba (1991b) and DeWitt, Dowlatabadi and Kopp (1991) point out, nonenergy prices will also change, so a general equilibrium approach is required to assess the full impact. Second, because a carbon tax will alter saving, investment, and interest rates, as well as relative prices, we measure changes in economic welfare throughout the lifetime of consumers. Jorgenson and Wilcoxen (1992) have shown that it is essential to incorporate changes in the U.S. economy over time into the evaluation of a carbon tax.

To estimate the distributional effects of carbon taxes on the lifetime welfare of consumers, we consider a population of infinitely lived households. We refer to different household types, cross-classified by demographic characteristics and levels of wealth, as "dynasties." Each household type is linked to a similar household type in the future through intergenerational altruism in preferences.[6] We evaluate the effect of carbon taxes on each dynasty through willingness to pay to avoid the consequences of the tax. Our measures of willingness to pay are variations in dynastic wealth that are the monetary equivalent of changes in dynastic welfare.[7] We consider the distributional impact of carbon taxes on more than 16,000 different types of households.

The measurement of welfare levels of individual households is an essential first step in the evaluation of policies to control carbon dioxide emissions. An overall evaluation, however, must combine individual welfare levels into a measure of social welfare.[8] We define a social welfare function on distributions of individual welfare over households. An explicit social welfare function facilitates the decomposition of changes in social welfare into two components: changes in efficiency and changes in equity. Our social welfare function is consistent with principles of consistent social choice under measurability and comparability of individual preferences. It is sufficiently flexible to incorporate alternative normative assumptions for ranking distributions.

In this paper we first describe the intertemporal general equilibrium model of the U.S. economy employed in our evaluation of the effect of carbon taxes. Next, we outline the framework for measuring the welfare of individual households and combining these measures into an overall measure of social welfare. The effects of taxes required to hold U.S. carbon dioxide emissions constant at 1990 levels are analyzed, and the growth of the U.S. economy with these taxes is compared with a "base case" with no controls on emissions. Finally, we evaluate the distributional effect of carbon taxes and summarize our conclusions.

9.2   An Overview of the Model

Our analysis of the incidence of carbon taxes is based on simulations of U.S. economic growth, using an intertemporal general equilibrium model of the U.S. economy described in detail by Jorgenson and Wilcoxen (1990b). This model has been used to measure the cost of all U.S. environmental regulations imposed at the federal level before 1990. Here, we outline the key features of the model and describe its application to policies for the control of carbon dioxide emissions.

9.2.1   Producer Behavior

Our submodel of producer behavior is disaggregated into 35 industrial sectors, listed in table 9.1. The model determines levels of output for 35 separate commodities, each produced by one or more industries. The industries correspond, roughly, to two-digit industry groups in the Standard Industrial Classification (SIC). This level of industrial detail makes it possible to measure the effect of changes in tax policy on relatively narrow segments of the economy. Because carbon dioxide emissions are generated by fossil fuel combustion, a disaggregated model is essential for modeling sectoral differences in the response to policies for controlling these emissions.

We represent the technology of each of the 35 industries in our model by means of a hierarchical tier structure of models of producer behavior. At the highest level, the price of output in each industry is represented as a function of prices of energy, materials, and capital and labor services. Similarly, the price of energy is a function of prices of coal, crude petroleum, refined petroleum, electricity, and natural gas; the price of materials is a function of the prices of all other intermediate goods. We derive demands for inputs of capital and labor services and inputs of the 35 intermediate goods into each industry from the price function for that industry.

Table 9.1
Industries used in the model

Agriculture, forestry, and fisheries	Paper and allied products	Electrical machinery
Metal mining	Printing and publishing	Motor vehicles
Coal mining	Chemicals and allied products	Other transportation equipment
Crude petroleum, natural gas extraction	Petroleum refining	Instruments
Nonmetallic mineral mining	Rubber and plastic products	Miscellaneous manufacturing
Construction	Leather and leather products	Transportation and warehousing
Food and kindred products products	Stone, clay, and glass products	Communication
Tobacco manufactures	Primary metals	Electric utilities
Textile mill products	Fabricated metal products	Gas utilities
Apparel and other textile products	Machinery, except electrical	Trade
Lumber and wood products		Finance, insurance, and real estate
Furniture and fixtures		Other services
		Government enterprises

We have estimated the parameters of production models for the 35 industries econometrically. For this purpose we have constructed a set of consistent interindustry transactions tables for the U.S. economy for the period 1947 through 1985.[9] Our econometric method for parameterization stands in sharp contrast to the calibration method used in almost all applied general equilibrium models. Calibration involves choosing parameters to replicate the data for a particular year.[10]

The econometric approach to parameterization has several advantages over the calibration approach. First, by using an extensive time series of data rather than a single data point, we are able to derive the response of production patterns to changes in prices from historical evidence.[11] The calibration approach imposes these responses on the data through the choice of functional forms. Elasticities of substitution, for example, are set equal to unity by imposing the Cobb-Douglas functional form or zero by imposing the Leontief form. Similarly, all elasticities of substitution are set equal to each other by imposing the constant elasticity of substitution functional form.

A second advantage of the econometric approach is that parameters estimated from time series are much less likely to be affected by the peculiarities of the data for a particular time period. By construction, parameters obtained by calibration are forced to absorb all the random errors present in the data for a single benchmark year. This poses a severe problem when the benchmark year is unusual in some respect. Parameters calibrated to data for 1973, for example, would incorporate into the model all the distortions in energy markets that resulted from price controls and rationing of energy during the first oil crisis. Econometric parameterization greatly mitigates this problem by reducing the influence of random errors for any particular time period.

The third important feature of our producer submodel is the endogenous determination of productivity growth.[12] Other models used to study global warming, for example, Manne and Richels (1990), take productivity growth to be exogenous. In our model the rate of productivity growth for each industry is determined endogenously as a function of input prices. In addition, an industry's productivity growth can be biased toward some inputs and away from others. Biased productivity growth is a common feature of historical data but is often excluded from models of production. By allowing for biased productivity growth, our model is able to capture the evolution of input patterns much more accurately.

In summary, the salient features of our production model are, first, that it is disaggregated into 35 industries. Second, all parameters of the model are estimated econometrically from an extensive historical data base developed specifically for this purpose. Third, the model determines rates of productivity growth endogenously and allows for biased productivity change in each industry. Fourth, the model incorporates extensive historical evidence on the price responsiveness of input patterns, including changes in the mix of fossil fuels. We turn next to a brief discussion of our modeling of final demands—consumption, investment, government expenditure, and foreign trade.

9.2.2   Consumption

Our model of household behavior is generated by a three-stage optimization process. At the first stage, each household allocates full wealth, defined as the sum of human and nonhuman wealth, across different time periods. We formalize this decision by introducing a representative agent who maximizes an additive intertemporal utility function, subject to an intertemporal budget constraint. The optimal allocation satisfies a sequence of necessary conditions that can be summarized by means of a Euler equation.[13] This allocation is determined by the rate of time preference and the intertemporal elasticity of substitution.

After households have allocated full wealth to the current time period, they proceed to the second stage of the optimization process—choosing the mix of leisure and goods. We represent household preferences for leisure and goods by means of a representative agent with an indirect utility function that depends on the prices of leisure and goods. We derive demands for leisure and goods as functions of these prices and the wealth allocated to the period. This implies an allocation of the household's exogenously given time endowment between leisure time and the labor market, so that this stage of the optimization process determines labor supply.

The third stage of the household optimization problem is the allocation of total expenditure among capital and labor services and the 35 commodity groups included in the model. At this stage, we replace the representative consumer approach by the approach of Jorgenson, Lau and Stoker (1982) for deriving a system of demand functions for each household. We distinguish among household types cross-classified by attributes such as the number of household members and the geographic region in which the household is located. For each type of household we employ a hierarchical tier structure of models of consumer behavior to represent demands for individual commodities.[14] These features of our household model are described in greater detail in the following sections.

As with production, the parameters of the behavioral equations for all three stages of our consumer model are estimated econometrically.[15] This includes the Euler equation, demand functions for leisure and personal consumption expenditures, and demand functions for individual commodities. Our household model incorporates extensive time-series data on the price responsiveness of demand patterns by consumers and detailed cross-section data on demographic effects on consumer behavior. An important feature of our household model is that demands need not be homothetic. As levels of total expenditure increase, patterns of expenditure on individual commodities change, even in the absence of price changes. This captures an important feature of cross-section data on household expenditure patterns that is usually ignored in applied general equilibrium modeling.

9.2.3 Investment and Capital Formation

Our investment model is based on perfect foresight or rational expectations. In particular, we require that the price of new investment goods is always equal to the present value of future capital services.[16] The return on a unit of capital is determined by the economy-wide rental price of capital services. The price of investment goods and the discounted value of future rental prices are brought into intertemporal equilibrium by adjustments in prices and the term structure of interest rates. This intertemporal equilibrium incorporates the forward-looking dynamics of asset pricing by producers.

For tractability, we assume there is a single capital stock in the economy that is perfectly malleable, so that it can be reallocated among industries and between industries and final demand categories at zero cost. Under this assumption imposition of a carbon tax can affect the distribution of capital and labor supplies among sectors, even in the short run. In each time period the supply of capital in our model is completely inelastic, since the stock of capital is determined by past investment. Investment during the period is determined by the savings made available by households. The relationship between capital stock and past investment incorporates backward-looking dynamics into our model of intertemporal equilibrium.

We assume that new capital goods are produced from individual commodities, so that the price of new capital depends on commodity prices. We have estimated the price function for new capital goods using final demand data for investment over the period 1947–1985. Thus, our model incorporates substitution among inputs in the composition of the capital. This feature can play an important role in the evaluation of environmental policies. Jorgenson and Wilcoxen (1990a) have found, for example, that an increase in the price of automobiles resulting from mandatory installation of pollution control devices shifts investment away from motor vehicles and toward other types of capital.

In summary, capital formation in our model is the outcome of intertemporal optimization by households and firms. Optimization by households is forward-looking and incorporates expectations about future prices, wages and interest rates. Optimization by producers is also forward-looking and depends upon these same expectations. Both types of optimization are important for modeling the impact of future restrictions on carbon dioxide emissions. The effects of these restrictions will be anticipated by households and firms, so that future policies will have important consequences for current decisions.

9.2.4   Government and Foreign Trade

The two final demand categories remaining in our model are the government and foreign sectors. We determine final demands for government consumption from the income-expenditure identity for the government sector. The first step is to compute total tax revenue by applying exogenous tax rates to appropriate transactions in the business and household sectors. We then add the capital income of government enterprises, determined endogenously, and nontax receipts, determined exogenously, to tax revenue to obtain total government revenue.

We assume the government budget deficit can be specified exogenously. We add the deficit to total revenue to obtain total government spending. To arrive at government purchases of goods and services, we subtract interest paid to domestic and foreign holders of government bonds together with government transfer payments to domestic and foreign recipients. We allocate the remainder among commodity groups according to fixed shares constructed from historical data. Finally, we determine the quantity of each commodity by dividing the value of government spending on the good by its price.

Foreign trade has two components—imports and exports. We assume that imports are imperfect substitutes for similar domestic commodities.[17] The goods actually purchased by households and firms reflect substitution between domestic and imported products. The price responsiveness of these purchases is estimated econometrically from historical data. In effect, each commodity is assigned a separate elasticity of substitution between domestic and imported goods. Because the prices of imports are given exogenously, intermediate and final demands implicitly determine imports of each commodity.

Exports, on the other hand, are determined by a set of export demand equations, one for each commodity, that depend on exogenously given foreign income and the foreign price of U.S. exports. Foreign prices are computed from domestic prices by adjusting for subsidies and the exchange rate. The demand elasticities in these equations are estimated from historical data. Without an elaborate model of international trade, it is impossible to determine both the current account balance and the exchange rate endogenously. In the simulations reported below, we take the current account to be exogenous and the exchange rate to be endogenous.

9.2.5 Estimating Carbon Emissions

The most important remaining feature of the model is the way in which carbon dioxide emissions are calculated. For tractability we assume that carbon dioxide is emitted in fixed proportion to fossil fuel combustion. This implicitly assumes that nothing can be done to reduce the carbon dioxide produced by a given combustion process.[18] For comparability with other studies, we measure carbon dioxide emissions in tons of contained carbon. To convert to tons of carbon dioxide, the reader can multiply contained carbon by 3.67.

We have calculated the carbon content of each fossil fuel by multiplying the heat content of the fuel by the carbon emitted. From the Energy Information Administration (1990), we obtained the average heat content of each fuel in millions of British thermal units (BTUs) per quantity unit. We then obtained data from the Environmental

Table 9.2
Carbon emissions data, 1987

Item	Coal (tons)	Oil (barrels)	Gas (thousands of cubic feet)
Heat content (million BTUs per unit)	21.94	5.80	1.03
Emissions rate (kg per million BTUs)	26.9	21.4	14.5
(kg per unit)	590.2	124.1	14.9
Total domestic output (billion units)	0.9169	0.3033	17.8
Total carbon emissions (million tons)	595.3	414.1	268.6

Source: Authors' calculations; Energy Information Administration (1990), and Environmental Protection Agency (1988).

Protection Agency (1988) on the amount of carbon emitted per million BTUs generated from each fuel. Multiplying the emissions figures by the heating value gives the carbon content of each fuel. Total carbon emissions can then be calculated from data on fuel production. Table 9.2 gives data for each fuel in 1987.

All prices in our model are normalized to unity in a common base year, so quantities do not correspond directly to physical units. Moreover, the model has a single sector for oil and gas extraction. To convert the data for this industry into a form appropriate for the model, we have added carbon production for crude petroleum and natural gas and divided by the industry's output for 1987 to obtain the carbon coefficient for this industry. Similarly, the coefficient for coal was obtained by dividing total carbon production from coal by the model's 1987 value for coal mining output. These coefficients were used to estimate carbon emissions in each simulation. We now turn to a brief discussion of the model's base case.

9.2.6   The Base Case

To simulate the U.S. economy we must provide values of the exogenous variables for all time periods. We have accomplished this in two steps. First, we have adopted a set of default assumptions about the time path of each exogenous variable in the absence of changes in government policy. These assumptions are used in generating a simulation of U.S. economic growth called the "base case." The second step is to change certain exogenous variables to reflect the introduction of a carbon tax and simulate U.S. economic growth again to produce an "alternative case." We then compare the two simulations to assess the impact of the policy change. Obviously, the assumptions underlying the base case are important in interpreting the results.

Because our model is based on agents with perfect foresight, we must solve the model indefinitely far into the future. To do this we project values for all exogenous variables over the period 1990–2050. After 2050 we assume the variables remain constant at their 2050 values, which allows the model to converge to a steady state by the year 2100.[19] First, we set all tax rates to their values in 1985, the last year in our sample period. Next, we assume that foreign prices of imports in foreign currency remain constant in real terms at 1985 levels before U.S. tariffs are applied.

We project a gradual decline in the government deficit through the year 2025, after which the nominal value of the government debt is maintained at a constant ratio to the value of the national product. Finally, we project the current account deficit by allowing it to fall gradually to zero by the year 2000. After that we project a current account surplus sufficient to produce a stock of net claims on foreigners by the year 2050 equal to the same proportion of national wealth as in 1982.

The most important exogenous variables are those associated with growth of the U.S. population and corresponding changes in the economy's time endowment. We project population by age, sex and educational attainment through the year 2050, using demographic assumptions consistent with Social Security Administration projections.[20] We hold population constant after 2050, which is approximately in line with these projections. In addition, we project the educational composition of the population by holding the level of educational attainment constant, beginning with the cohort reaching age 35 in the year 1985. We transform our population projection into a projection of the time endowment by holding relative wages across different types of labor input constant at 1985 levels. Because capital formation is endogenous in our model, our projections of the time endowment effectively determine the size of the economy in the more distant future.

9.3 Welfare Economics

In assessing the welfare effects of a carbon tax we have focused on three closely related questions. First, how does the tax affect the welfare of different types of households? Second, how can these individual effects be aggregated to provide a summary measure of the effect of the tax? Third, is the tax progressive or regressive? This section presents the analytical framework used to answer each of these questions.

9.3.1 Dynastic Welfare

We begin by assuming that the household sector comprises a number of infinitely lived households, which we refer to as dynasties. Each household takes commodity prices and rates of return as given and is endowed with perfect foresight. All dynasties face the same vector of consumer goods prices at time t, p_t, and the same nominal interest rate, r_t. The quantity of commodity n consumed by dynasty d in period t is x_{ndt}, and the total expenditure of dynasty d on consumption in period t is M_{dt}.

$$M_{dt} = \sum_{n=1}^{N} p_{nt} x_{ndt} \, ,$$

where N is the number of commodities.

We assume that each dynasty maximizes an additive intertemporal utility function of the form

$$V_d = \sum_{t=0}^{\infty} \delta^t \ln V_{dt} \, , \tag{9.1}$$

where $\delta = 1/(1 + \rho)$ and ρ is the subjective rate of time preference. The intratemporal indirect utility function V_{dt} is taken to be of the form

$$\ln V_{dt} = \alpha'_p \ln p'_t + \frac{1}{2} \ln p_t \, B_{pp} \ln p_t - D(p_t) \ln (M_{dt}/N_{dt}) \, . \tag{9.2}$$

In this representation α_p and B_{pp} are unknown parameters, $N_{dt} = K_{dt} \, m_0(p_t, A_d)$ is the number of household equivalent members in the dynasty at time t and $D(p_t)$ has the form

$$D(p_t) = -1 + \iota' B_{pp} \ln p_t .$$

The number of household equivalent members is

$$\ln m_0(p, A_d) =$$

$$\frac{\ln m(A_d)' \alpha_p + 1/2 \ln m(A_d)' B_{pp} \ln m(A_d) + \ln m(A_d)' B_{pp} \ln p}{D(p)} ,$$

where the function $\ln m(A_d) = B_{pp}^{-1} B_{pA} A_d$ is a vector of commodity-specific equivalence scales.[21] We allow dynasties to differ by a vector of attributes A_d. These attributes allow for differences in preferences among households.

The dynasty maximizes the intertemporal utility function V_d over the time path of the intratemporal utility levels $\{V_{dt}\}$ subject to the budget constraint

$$\sum_{t=0}^{\infty} \gamma_t M_{dt}(p_t, V_{dt}, A_d) = \Omega_d ,$$

where

$$\gamma_t = \prod_{s=0}^{t} (1 + r_s)^{-1} ,$$

and Ω_d is the wealth of the dynasty. In this representation $M_{dt}(p_t, V_{dt}, A_d)$ is the intratemporal expenditure function and takes the form

$$\ln M_{dt}(p_t, V_{dt}, A_d) = \frac{\alpha'_p \ln p_t + 1/2 \ln p'_t B_{pp} \ln p_t - \ln V_{dt}}{D(p_t)} + \ln(N_{dt}) . \quad (9.3)$$

The necessary conditions for a maximum of the intertemporal utility function, subject to the wealth constraint, are given by the discrete time Euler equation

$$\ln V_{dt} = \frac{D_t}{D_{t-1}} \ln V_{dt-1} + D_t \ln\left(\frac{D_{t-1}\gamma_t N_{dt} P_t}{\delta D_t \gamma_{t-1} N_{dt-1} P_{t-1}}\right), \quad (9.4)$$

where we have used D_t to denote $D(p_t)$ and

$$P_t = \exp\left(\frac{\alpha'_p \ln p_t + 1/2 \ln p_t B_{pp} \ln p_t}{D_t}\right).$$

The Euler equation implies that the current level of utility of the dynasty can be represented as a function of the initial level of utility and the initial and future prices and interest rates

$$\ln V_{dt} = \frac{D_t}{D_0} \ln V_{d0} + D_t \ln\left(\frac{D_0 \gamma_t N_{dt} P_t}{\delta^t D_t N_{d0} P_0}\right). \tag{9.5}$$

Equation (9.5) enables us to represent dynastic utility as a function of wealth and initial and future prices and interest rates. We begin by rewriting the intertemporal budget constraint as

$$\sum_{t=0}^{\infty} \gamma_t N_{dt} P_t V_{dt}^{-1/D_t} = \Omega_d . \tag{9.6}$$

Substituting (9.5) into (9.6) and simplifying yields the following

$$\ln V_{d0} = - D_0 \ln\left(\frac{\Omega_d}{N_{d0}R}\right), \tag{9.7}$$

where

$$R = \frac{P_0}{D_0}\left(\sum_{t=0}^{\infty} \delta^t D_t\right).$$

This enables us to evaluate dynastic utility in terms of dynastic wealth

$$V_d = \sum_{t=0}^{\infty} \delta^t \ln V_{dt}$$

$$= \sum_{t=0}^{\infty} \delta^t \left[\frac{D_t}{D_0} \ln V_{d0} + D_t \ln\left(\frac{D_0 \gamma_t N_{dt} P_t}{\delta^t D_t N_{d0} P_0}\right)\right]$$

$$= \sum_{t=0}^{\infty} \delta^t \left[-D_t \ln (\Omega_d/R) + D_t \ln\left(\frac{D_0 \gamma_t N_{dt} P_t}{\delta^t D_t P_0}\right)\right]$$

$$= S \ln R - S \ln \Omega_d + \sum_{t=0}^{\infty} \delta^t D_t \ln\left(\frac{\gamma_t N_{dt} P_t D_0}{\delta^t D_t P_0}\right), \tag{9.8}$$

where

$$S = \sum_{t=0}^{\infty} \delta^t D_t .$$

Solving for wealth as a function of prices and utility yields the intertemporal expenditure function[22] of the dynasty

$$\ln \Omega_d(\{p_t\}, \{\gamma_t\}, V_d) = \frac{1}{S}\left[S \ln R + \Sigma \delta^t D_t \ln\left(\frac{\gamma_t N_{dt} P_t D_0}{\delta^t D_t P_0}\right) - V_d\right], \qquad (9.9)$$

where $\{p_t\}$ indicates a profile of prices and $\{\gamma_t\}$ is a profile of discount factors. We employ this expenditure function in measuring the monetary equivalent of a change in welfare resulting from the imposition of a carbon tax. We let $\{p_t^0\}$ and $\{\gamma_t^0\}$ be the profiles of prices and interest rates under the base case and V_d^0 be the resulting level of welfare. If the welfare of the dynasty after the imposition of a carbon tax is denoted V_d^1, the equivalent variation in dynastic wealth is

$$\Delta W_d = \Omega_d(\{p_t^0\}, \{\gamma_t^0\}, V_d^1) - \Omega_d(\{p_t^0\}, \{\gamma_t^0\}, V_d^0) . \qquad (9.10)$$

The equivalent variation in wealth (9.10) is the wealth required to attain the welfare associated with imposition of a carbon tax at prices in the base case, less the wealth required to attain the welfare of the base case at these prices. If this equivalent variation is positive, the carbon tax produces a gain in welfare; otherwise, the policy change results in a welfare loss. Equivalent variations in wealth enable us to rank the policy of the base case and any number of alternative policies in terms of a money metric of dynastic welfare.

9.3.2   Social Welfare

Although the distribution of equivalent variations across dynasties is useful for policy analysis, it is also important to assess the change in social welfare that results from the imposition of a carbon tax. For this purpose, we define an intertemporal social welfare function over the distribution of dynastic welfare functions given in equation (9.8). Following Jorgenson and Slesnick (1990) we take the intertemporal social welfare function to be a weighted sum of the average dynastic welfare and a measure of deviations from the average

$$W = \bar{V} - \eta \left(\sum_{d=1}^{D} a_d |V_d - \bar{V}|^{-\mu} \right)^{-1/\mu},$$
(9.11)

where

$$\bar{V} = \sum_{d=1}^{D} a_d V_d .$$

In this representation of the social welfare function, the parameter η is chosen to ensure that social welfare is increasing in the levels of individual welfare; this is the familiar Pareto principle. The parameter μ is a measure of social aversion to inequality and can take values ranging from minus one to minus infinity. The maximum value of minus one gives the greatest weight to equity relative to efficiency. Allowing this parameter to go to minus infinity generates a utilitarian social welfare function and gives the least relative weight to equity considerations.

If we require that all transfers of wealth from rich dynasties to poor dynasties must increase social welfare, then the weights on the individual welfare levels must be given by

$$a_d = \frac{\exp\left\{ \left[\sum_t \delta^t D_t \ln(N_{dt}) \right] / S \right\}}{\sum_{l=1}^{D} \exp\left\{ \left[\sum_t \delta^t D_t \ln(N_{lt}) \right] / S \right\}} .$$

The maximum level of social welfare for fixed prices and fixed total wealth is attained by reallocating wealth among dynasties to equalize dynastic welfare. This occurs when the wealth of dynasty d is $\Omega_d^* = a_d \Omega$, where Ω is total wealth.

The maximum level of social welfare can be represented as:

$$W_{\max} = S \ln R - S \ln \Omega + S \ln N + \sum_{t=0}^{\infty} \delta^t D_t \ln\left(\frac{\gamma_t P_t D_0}{\delta^t D_t P_0} \right),$$
(9.12)

where

$$N = \sum_{l=1}^{D} \exp\left\{ \left[\sum_t \delta^t D_t \ln(N_{lt}) \right] / S \right\} .$$

This is a representative agent version of equation (9.8) above and can be interpreted as the welfare level of a dynasty with size equal to the number of household equivalent members in the whole population.

To derive a money measure of social welfare, we define the social expenditure function as the minimum level of total wealth required to attain a specified level of social welfare at given prices and interest rates

$$\Omega(\{p_t\}, \{\gamma_t\}, W) = \min \left[\Omega: W(u, x) \geq W; \Omega = \sum_{d=1}^{D} \Omega_d \right].$$

Our representation of the social expenditure function is obtained by solving the welfare function for the representative agent shown in equation (9.12) for aggregate wealth as a function of social welfare and the initial and future prices and interest rates

$$\ln \Omega(\{p_t\}, \{\gamma_t\}, W) = \frac{1}{S} \left[S \ln R + S \ln N + \sum \delta^t D_t \ln \left(\frac{\gamma_t P_t D_0}{\delta^t D_t P_0} \right) - W \right]. \quad (9.13)$$

This is the expenditure function of a representative agent with welfare level given by equation (9.12).

The social expenditure function enables us to evaluate the monetary equivalent of the change in social welfare that results from the imposition of a carbon tax. Let W^0 be the level of social welfare under the base case and let W^1 be the corresponding level of social welfare after the imposition of a carbon tax. The monetary measure of the change in social welfare is given by:

$$\Delta W = \Omega(\{p_t^0\}, \{\gamma_t^0\}, W^1) - \Omega(\{p_t^0\}, \{\gamma_t^0\}, W^0). \quad (9.14)$$

This is the variation in wealth equivalent to imposition of the tax. If this equivalent variation is positive, then social welfare has increased as a result of the tax. Otherwise, the tax decreases social welfare or leaves it unaffected.

Policies for control of carbon dioxide emissions are often evaluated solely in terms of their impact on economic efficiency. Accordingly, we can define the change in efficiency to be the change in social welfare at a perfectly egalitarian distribution of wealth. For this distribution social welfare is a maximum for a given level of wealth and corresponds to the potential level of welfare associated with a particular policy. This measure of efficiency is independent of the distribution of welfare among dynasties. If W_{max}^0 is the maximum level of social welfare in the base case and W_{max}^1 is the corresponding level after the imposition of a carbon tax, our monetary measure of the change in efficiency is

$$\Delta E = \Omega(\{p_t^0\}, \{\gamma_t^0\}, W_{max}^1) - \Omega(\{p_t^0\}, \{\gamma_t^0\}, W_{max}^0) . \tag{9.15}$$

The definition of the change in efficiency shown in equation (9.15) suggests a decomposition of the change in social welfare shown in equation (9.14) into efficiency and equity components

$$\Delta W = \Delta E + \Delta EQ , \tag{9.16}$$

where ΔEQ is a monetary measure of the change in equity. The difference between the level of potential welfare and the level of actual welfare is the loss due to an inequitable distribution of dynastic welfare. Our measure of equity is the monetary value of the change in this welfare loss due to a carbon tax:

$$\begin{aligned}
\Delta EQ &= [\Omega(\{p_t^0\}, \{\gamma_t^0\}, W^1) - \Omega(\{p_t^0\}, \{\gamma_t^0\}, W_{max}^1)] \\
&\quad - [\Omega(\{p_t^0\}, \{\gamma_t^0\}, W^0) - \Omega(\{p_t^0\}, \{\gamma_t^0\}, W_{max}^0)] .
\end{aligned} \tag{9.17}$$

A positive value of ΔEQ indicates that equity has increased due to the imposition of the carbon tax.

9.3.3   Tax Progressivity

We have developed a framework for evaluating the impact of a carbon tax on the level of social welfare. A separate but closely related issue is the progressivity of such a tax. Following Slesnick (1986) we can classify a tax as progressive if it induces greater equality in the distribution of welfare. Equality, however, can be measured in absolute or relative terms. In the context of the model presented above, an absolute index of equality is given by

$$\begin{aligned}
AEQ(\{p_t^0\}, \{\gamma_t^0\}, W, W_{max}) &= [\Omega(\{p_t^0\}, \{\gamma_t^0\}, W) \\
&\quad - \Omega(\{p_t^0\}, \{\gamma_t^0\}, W_{max})] .
\end{aligned} \tag{9.18}$$

This measure of equality is the monetary value of the loss in social welfare due to an inequitable distribution of welfare. It is nonpositive and invariant to equal absolute additions to the money measures of potential and social welfare.

A relative measure of equality can be defined as the ratio of money metric social welfare to the monetary measure of potential welfare

$$REQ(\{p_t^0\}, \{\gamma_t^0\}, W, W_{max}) = \frac{\Omega(\{p_t^0\}, \{\gamma_t^0\}, W)}{\Omega(\{p_t^0\}, \{\gamma_t^0\}, W_{max})} \, . \tag{9.19}$$

This measure of equality lies between zero and one and attains the value of unity when the actual distribution of welfare is the perfectly egalitarian distribution. The measure of relative equality is invariant to equal proportional changes in money metric potential and social welfare. This will occur with equal proportional changes in the wealth of all dynasties.

An absolute measure of progression of a carbon tax is the change in the absolute measure of equality

$$AP = AEQ(\{p_t^0\}, \{\gamma_t^0\}, W^1, W_{max}^1) - AEQ(\{p_t^0\}, \{\gamma_t^0\}, W^0, W_{max}^0) \, . \tag{9.20}$$

The measure of absolute progressivity is identical to the measure of the change in equation (9.17). A positive value indicates that the carbon tax is absolutely progressive. A negative value indicates absolute regressivity. The corresponding relative measure of progressivity is defined similarly

$$RP = REQ(\{p_t^0\}, \{\gamma_t^0\}, W^1, W_{max}^1) - REQ(\{p_t^0\}, \{\gamma_t^0\}, W^0, W_{max}^0) \, . \tag{9.21}$$

It is easily demonstrated that a carbon tax that is absolutely progressive need not be relatively progressive and, *vice versa.*

9.4 The Impact of a Carbon Tax

We next consider the economic impact of adopting a sequence of carbon taxes that holds U.S. carbon dioxide emissions constant at the 1990 level of 1,576,000,000 tons. To measure this impact we have constructed two alternative simulations of U.S. economic growth. The base case simulates U.S. economic growth without a carbon tax. The alternative case simulates growth with emissions of carbon dioxide held constant.[23]

To hold the level of carbon dioxide emissions constant, we introduce an endogenous tax applied to primary fuels in proportion to their carbon content. Since this tax produces substantial revenue, we hold government spending constant at its base-case level and allow the average tax rate on labor income to adjust to keep the government deficit constant. We hold the marginal tax rate on labor income constant, so that adjustments in the average rate reflect changes in the implicit zero-tax threshold. This tax adjustment is equivalent to a lump-sum transfer to the household sector.

9.4.1   Long-Run Effects

The direct effect of introducing a carbon tax is to increase purchasers' prices of coal and crude oil. In the year 2020, for example, the tax needed to hold emissions at 1990 levels is $17.65 per ton of carbon.[24] Using the data in table 9.2, this amounts to a tax of $11.46 per ton of coal, $2.41 per barrel of oil or $0.29 per thousand cubic feet of gas. The rising price of fossil fuels results in substitution away from fossil fuels and toward other energy and nonenergy commodities by both firms and households. Total energy consumption falls to about 68 quadrillion BTUs or by twelve percent, relative to the base case. This substitution toward nonenergy inputs results in a drop of 0.7 percent in the capital stock and 0.5 percent in the national product by the year 2020.

The impact of a carbon tax differs considerably among different types of fossil fuels. Figure 9.1 shows changes in the supply price of the 35 commodities, measured as percentage changes relative to the base case. The largest change occurs in the price of coal, which rises by 40 percent. This, in turn, increases the price of electricity by about 5.6 percent. Electricity prices rise considerably less than coal prices because coal accounts for only about 13 percent of total electric utility costs. Other prices showing significant effects are those for crude and refined petroleum and gas utilities. These rise, directly or indirectly, because of the tax on the carbon content of oil and natural gas.

Changes in relative prices affect demands for energy and nonenergy commodities and lead to a restructuring of industry outputs. Figure 9.2 gives percentage changes in quantities produced by the 35 industries by the year 2020. Although most sectors show only small changes in output, the output of coal falls by 25 percent. Coal is strongly affected because its demand is elastic. Most coal is purchased by electric utilities. In our model these utilities can substitute other fuels for coal when its price rises. Moreover, the utilities also have some ability to substitute other inputs for energy, such as labor and capital services, further reducing the demand for coal. Finally, users of electricity reduce their demands substantially when the price of electricity rises.

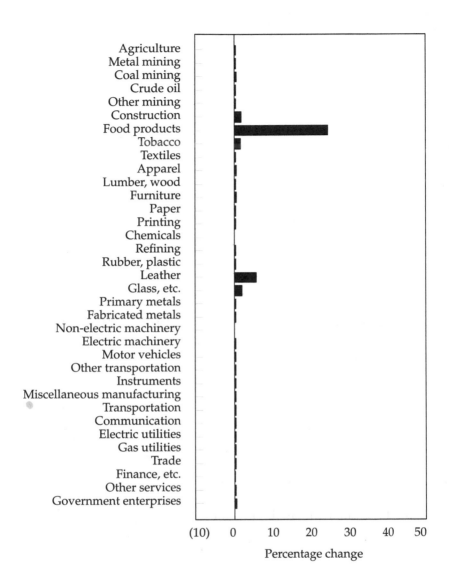

Figure 9.1
Effect of a carbon tax on prices in 2020.
Source: authors' calculations

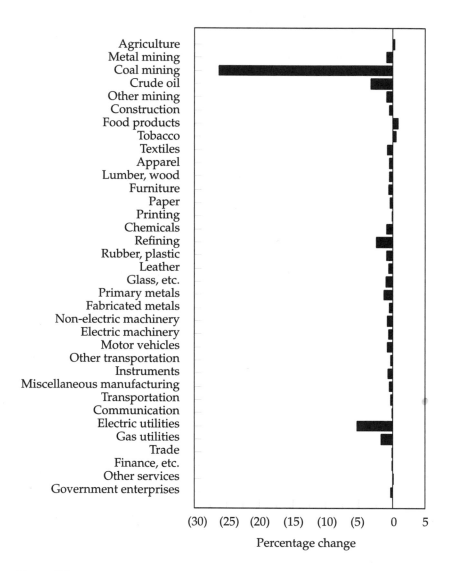

Figure 9.2
Effect of a carbon tax on quantities in 2020.
Source: authors' calculations

9.4.2   Economic Dynamics

Carbon restrictions adopted today will have effects far into the future through their influence on capital formation. At the same time, anticipated future restrictions will have effects today through expectations of future prices, wages, and interest rates incorporated into current prices of investment goods. To assess the intertemporal effects of carbon taxes, we now examine the dynamics of the transition to an economy with lower emissions of carbon dioxide.

The time path of the carbon taxes needed to maintain 1990 emissions is shown in figure 9.3. Base-case emissions increase over time, so the tax grows gradually over the next several decades. Holding carbon dioxide emissions constant lowers emissions relative to the base case, as shown in figure 9.4. By the year 2020 emissions are about fourteen percent lower than they would have been without the tax.

The rising price of energy reduces the rate of capital formation. The outcome is shown in figure 9.5, which gives percentage changes in the capital stock from the base case. The capital stock does not decline immediately; instead, it remains near its base-case level for the first few years. This reflects intertemporal optimization by households. The household regards carbon taxes as reductions in future earnings and reacts by lowering consumption in all periods. In the early years, household income is largely unaffected. However, the drop in consumption leads to an increase in saving and helps to maintain capital formation. Eventually, the impact of the tax reduces capital stock relative to the base case.

The decline in growth of the capital stock leads to a drop in economic growth, as shown in figure 9.6. The national product falls gradually, relative to the base case, by about half a percent. The capital stock, however, is not the only factor contributing to the decline. Higher energy prices reduce the rate of productivity growth, leading to slower growth of output. Under the carbon tax average annual growth of output between 1990 and 2020 is 0.02 percentage points lower than in the base case. About half of this is due to slower productivity growth and half due to reduced capital formation.

1990 $/ton

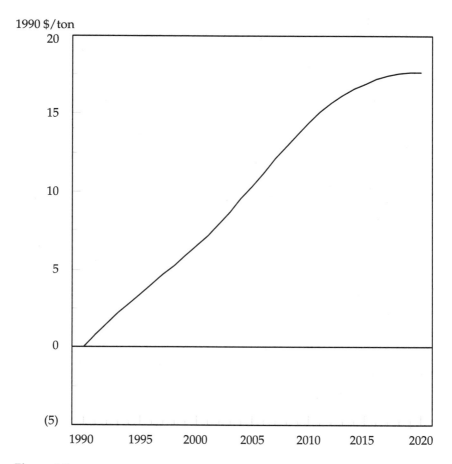

Figure 9.3
Carbon tax required to maintain 1990 emission levels, 1990–2020.
Source: authors' calculations

Percentage change

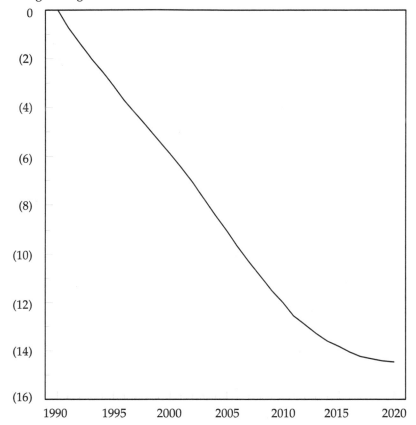

Figure 9.4
Change in carbon emissions as a result of carbon tax, 1990–2020.
Source: authors' calculations

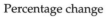

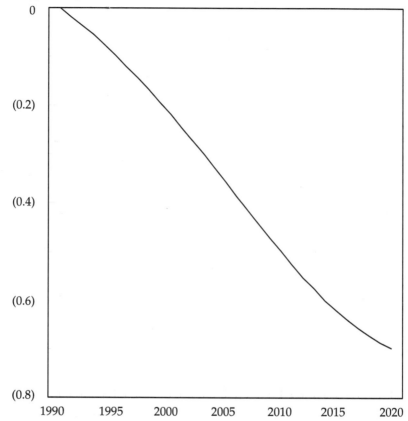

Figure 9.5
Change in capital stock as a result of carbon tax, 1990–2020.
Source: authors' calculations

Percentage change

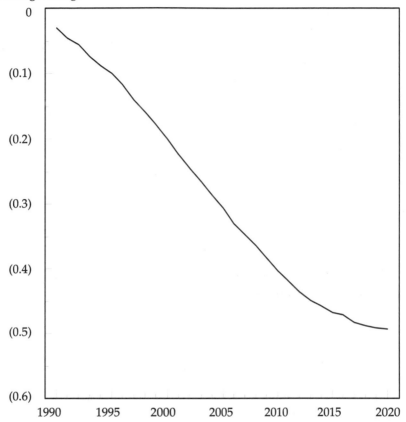

Figure 9.6
Change in real GNP as a result of carbon tax, 1990–2020.
Source: authors' calculations

9.5   The Effect of Welfare

We now evaluate the welfare impact of the carbon tax, using the framework we have presented above. Within each period households allocate total expenditure among five broad commodity groups:

1. *Energy:* expenditures on electricity, natural gas, heating oil, and gasoline.

2. *Food:* expenditures on all food products, including tobacco and alcohol.

3. *Consumer goods:* expenditures on all other nondurables.

4. *Capital services:* the service flow from consumer durables and housing.

5. *Consumer services:* expenditures on consumer services.

Each of these commodity groups is an aggregate of several consumer goods and services.

Our model contains 35 consumer goods and services, as shown in table 9.3. Each consumer good is produced from the primary output of one or more industries. Gasoline, for example, is produced by combining the output of petroleum refining with outputs of transportation services and retail trade. The price changes consumers face are a transformation of the changes in the prices of industry outputs. Figure 9.7, for example, gives changes in prices of consumer goods and services in the year 2020.

In figure 9.8 we present the percentage changes of prices of the five commodity groups resulting from the imposition of carbon taxes. Although all prices increase relative to the base case, the changes are quite small except for energy prices, which exhibit the largest price

Table 9.3
Consumer goods used in model

Food	Toys	Transportation
Meals	Stationary	Medical services
Employee meals	Imports	Medical insurance
Shoes	Reading	Personal services
Clothing	Rental	Financial services
Gasoline	Electricity	Other services
Coal	Gas	Recreation
Fuel	Water	Foreign travel
Tobacco	Communications	Private education
Cleaning	Labor	Housing maintenance
Furnishings	Other household	Durables
Drugs	Own transportation	

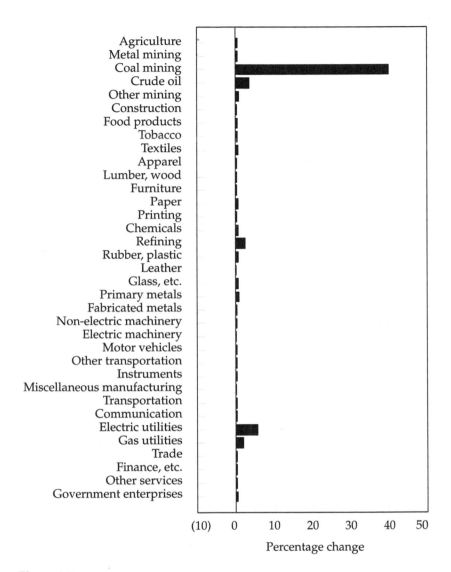

Figure 9.7
Effect of a carbon tax on consumer prices in 2020.
Source: authors' calculations

Percentage change

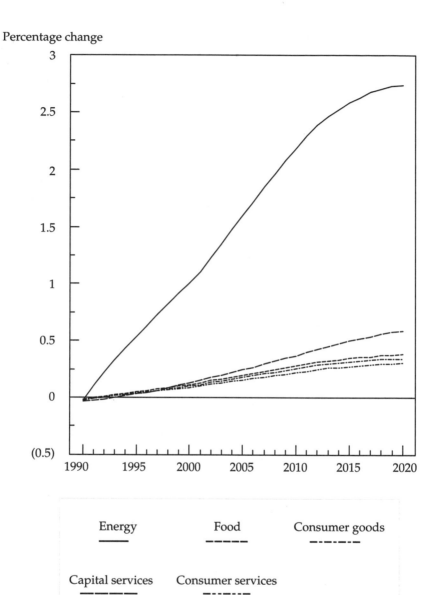

Figure 9.8
Change in prices of aggregate goods as a result of a carbon tax, 1990–2020.
Source: authors' calculations

increases over the entire period. The next largest increase is in the price of capital services. This demonstrates the importance of analyzing the general equilibrium effects of carbon taxes rather than focusing exclusively on the change in energy prices.

In figure 9.9 we present the time path of the change in nominal total expenditure under the carbon tax relative to the base case. In every year there is an increase in total expenditure after the imposition of the carbon taxes. As with the prices, however, the changes are quite small. The percentage increase in nominal total expenditure is smaller than the increase in commodity prices in most years. This implies that carbon taxes induce a decrease in efficiency.

9.5.1   Carbon Taxes and Dynastic Welfare

Given the projections of commodity prices and total expenditure we can evaluate the welfare changes induced by imposition of a carbon tax at various levels of aggregation. We begin by considering dynasties distinguished by the following demographic characteristics:

1. *Family size:* 1, 2, 3, 4, 5, 6, and 7 or more persons.

2. *Age of household head:* 16–24, 25–34, 35–44, 45–54, 55–64 and 65 and over.

3. *Region of residence:* Northeast, Midwest, South and West.

4. *Race:* White, nonwhite.

5. *Type of residence:* Nonfarm, farm.

6. *Sex of household head:* Male, female.

We consider 1,344 distinct types of households and twelve wealth categories within each household type, for a total of 16,128 household groups.

We require projections of the distribution of total expenditure over time across dynasties. For this purpose we assume that the distribution of total expenditure within each of the 1,344 household types is the same as in the Bureau of Labor Statistics' (1990) *Consumer Expenditure Survey* for 1989. The expenditure level of each dynasty increases at the rate given by the discrete time Euler equation (9.4).

We are now in a position to evaluate the welfare effects of a carbon tax for individual households. Since it is obviously impossible to present equivalent variations for each of 16,128 household groups, we have chosen a single reference household with family size four, and a white, male head of household, age 35 to 44, living in the urban

Percentage change

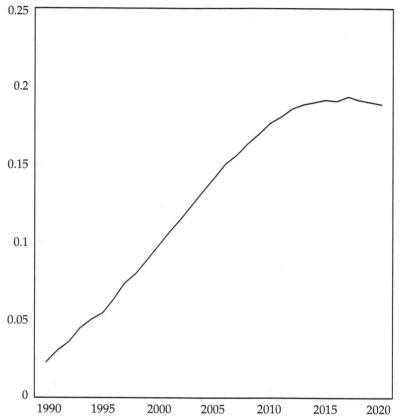

Figure 9.9
Change in consumer expenditure as a result of a carbon tax, 1990–2020.
Source: authors' calculations

Northeast. We present equivalent variations in wealth for the imposition of a carbon tax for this household type and other household types that differ in one of the demographic characteristics. We also evaluate these equivalent variations for low, medium and high levels of wealth. The results are presented in table 9.4.

The medium and high wealth levels correspond to time paths of total expenditure equal to average and double-the-average wealth levels. Households with low wealth have a time path of expenditure that is one-half average wealth. In table 9.4 we see that the equivalent variation in wealth is negative for all households. For a household of one member with a low level of wealth, the carbon tax is equivalent to a loss of $1,396. The equivalent variations increase with wealth, but less than in proportion to wealth. As an illustration, for a household of one member, the equivalent variation for medium wealth households is less than twice that of low wealth households but more than half that of high wealth households.

The demographic pattern of the equivalent variations is also of interest. The equivalent variations generally increase with family size. For a medium level of wealth, households of one member have an equivalent variation of –$2,545. Households of seven members with the same level of wealth have an equivalent variation of –$2,913. Thus, larger households are more adversely affected by imposition of a carbon tax than smaller households. The absolute size of the equivalent variations also decreases, with the age of the head of household. For a medium wealth household the equivalent variation is –$2,976 for heads of households under age 25 and –$2,845 for those aged 65 and above. Households in the West are affected least by the carbon tax, while those living in the Midwest have the greatest loss. Farm households experience substantially lower losses than do nonfarm households. Finally, nonwhite households and those headed by males have higher losses from imposition of a carbon tax.

Although the demographic pattern of equivalent variations in wealth from imposition of a carbon tax is interesting, an important feature of table 9.4 is that all of the losses are small. This can be seen more clearly in table 9.5, where the equivalent variations are divided by the corresponding wealth. For our reference dynasty—a four member household with medium wealth—imposition of a carbon tax is equivalent to a loss of slightly more than one-fourth of one percent (0.269%) of lifetime wealth. By this measure, nonwhite households with low levels of wealth are most affected by the tax—a loss of 0.325

Table 9.4
Equivalent variations in wealth upon imposition of a carbon tax (1990 dollars)

Wealth	Size 1	Size 2	Size 3	Size 4	Size 5	Size 6	Size 7+
Low	-1,396.22	-1,527.30	-1,570.84	-1,564.30	-1,586.36	-1,561.91	-1,580.02
Medium	-2,544.95	-2,807.17	-2,894.26	-2,881.19	-2,925.31	-2,876.39	-2,912.62
High	-4,594.80	-5,119.36	-5,293.58	-5,267.42	-5,355.69	-5,257.82	-5,330.29

Wealth	Age 16–24	Age 25–34	Age 35–44	Age 45–54	Age 55–64	Age 65+
Low	-1,611.60	-1,590.93	-1,564.30	-1,595.77	-1,600.36	-1,546.28
Medium	-2,975.80	-2,934.45	-2,881.19	-2,944.14	-2,953.30	-2,845.12
High	-5,456.68	-5,373.97	-5,267.42	-5,393.35	-5,411.69	-5,195.28

Wealth	Northeast	Midwest	South	West	Nonfarm	Farm
Low	-1,564.30	-1,646.41	-1,621.97	-1,514.02	-1,564.30	-1,471.77
Medium	-2,881.19	-3,045.43	-2,996.54	-2,780.60	-2,881.19	-2,696.08
High	-5,267.42	-5,595.98	-5,498.19	-5,066.21	-5,267.42	-4,897.12

Wealth	White	Nonwhite	Male	Female
Low	-1,564.30	-1,741.19	-1,564.30	-1,446.60
Medium	-2,881.19	-3,235.04	-2,881.19	-2,645.72
High	-5,267.42	-5,975.29	-5,267.42	-4,796.40

Source: Authors' calculations. Reference dynasty: size 4, age 35–44, Northeast, nonfarm, white, male.

Table 9.5
Equivalent variations as a percentage of wealth

Wealth	Size 1	Size 2	Size 3	Size 4	Size 5	Size 6	Size 7+
Low	-0.2608	-0.2853	-0.2935	-0.2922	-0.2964	-0.2918	-0.2952
Medium	-0.2377	-0.2622	-0.2704	-0.2691	-0.2733	-0.2687	-0.2721
High	-0.2146	-0.2391	-0.2472	-0.2460	-0.2501	-0.2456	-0.2490

Wealth	Age 16–24	Age 25–34	Age 35–44	Age 45–54	Age 55–64	Age 65+
Low	-0.3011	-0.2972	-0.2922	-0.2981	-0.2990	-0.2889
Medium	-0.2780	-0.2741	-0.2691	-0.2750	-0.2759	-0.2658
High	-0.2549	-0.2510	-0.2460	-0.2519	-0.2528	-0.2426

Wealth	Northeast	Midwest	South	West	Nonfarm	Farm
Low	-0.2922	-0.3076	-0.3030	-0.2829	-0.2922	-0.2750
Medium	-0.2691	-0.2845	-0.2799	-0.2597	-0.2691	-0.2518
High	-0.2460	-0.2614	-0.2568	-0.2366	-0.2460	-0.2287

Wealth	White	Nonwhite	Male	Female
Low	-0.2922	-0.3253	-0.2922	-0.2703
Medium	-0.2691	-0.3022	-0.2691	-0.2471
High	-0.2460	-0.2791	-0.2460	-0.2240

Source: Authors' calculations. Reference dynasty: size 4, age 35–44, Northeast, nonfarm, white, male.

percent of wealth—while unattached individuals with high wealth are affected least—a loss of 0.215 percent.[25]

9.5.2   Carbon Taxes and Social Welfare

The evaluation of policies to stabilize carbon dioxide emissions requires combining measures of changes in individual welfare into a measure of change in social welfare. For this purpose we estimate the changes in social welfare for two different representations of the social welfare function presented above. We take the inequality aversion parameter μ to be minus one and minus infinity, in turn. A value of minus one gives the greatest weight to equity, while a value of minus infinity gives the least weight to equity. The corresponding estimates of changes in social welfare are given in table 9.6.

Our first conclusion is that social welfare decreases as a result of imposing a carbon tax that would stabilize emissions of carbon dioxide at 1990 levels. This conclusion is independent of the choice of the inequality aversion parameter, since changes in social welfare are dominated by changes in efficiency. When inequality aversion is equal to minus one, its maximum value, money metric social welfare decreases by $187 billion (in 1990 dollars). When the inequality aversion parameter goes to minus infinity, the loss is $249 billion. These losses are very small proportions of aggregate wealth, 0.149 percent to 0.199 percent, respectively.

We can decompose the changes in social welfare into changes in efficiency and changes in equity. Our measure of efficiency is independent of the degree of aversion to inequality and is the same for both measures of social welfare. Imposition of a carbon tax reduces

Table 9.6
Change in social welfare

Inequality aversion parameter	Change in social welfare			Change in social welfare as a proportion of wealth		
	Welfare	Efficiency	Equity	Welfare	Efficiency	Equity
	(billions of 1990 dollars)			(percent)		
-1	-187	-234	47	$-.1495$	$-.1871$	$.0376$
$-\infty$	-249	-234	-15	$-.1991$	$-.1871$	$-.0120$

Source: Authors' calculations.

money metric efficiency by \$234 billions or 0.187 percent of total wealth. Our measures of equity vary from a gain of \$47 billions or 0.0376 of total wealth for the maximum value of aversion to inequality to a loss of \$15 billions or −0.0120 of total wealth for a utilitarian social welfare function.

Is the carbon tax regressive? The answer depends critically on whether equality is measured in absolute or relative terms, and on the inequality aversion parameter used in the social welfare function. The absolute measure of progression shown in equation (9.20) corresponds to the changes in equity reported in table 9.6. When the inequality aversion parameter is minus one, equity increases indicating that the carbon tax is absolutely progressive. When the social welfare function is utilitarian, however, equity decreases indicating that the same carbon tax is absolutely regressive. For both social welfare functions the change in equity induced by the carbon tax is small relative to the efficiency change.

The relative measure of progression shown in equation (9.21) indicates that the carbon tax is regressive for both social welfare functions. When the inequality aversion parameter is minus one, the index of relative progression is −0.0004. The utilitarian social welfare function implies an index of relative progression equal to −0.0005. The base-case measure of relative equality is equal to 0.58 so that, although a carbon tax is regressive in the relative sense, the impact on the relative distribution is extremely small.

In summary, the direct effect of imposing carbon taxes that would stabilize carbon dioxide emissions at 1990 levels is to increase the prices of fossil fuels. This increase induces changes in relative prices for all commodity groups in our model and results in changes in the industry composition of output through substitution away from fossil fuels by firms and households. Imposition of a carbon tax reduces carbon dioxide emissions quite substantially and depresses economic growth by a modest amount. These changes are spread over time, reflecting the backward-looking dynamics of capital accumulation and the forward-looking dynamics of intertemporal optimization by producers and consumers.

We have measured the impact of a carbon tax on social welfare and decomposed this impact into equity and efficiency components. The efficiency changes greatly predominate in the overall effect of the tax on social welfare. The equity changes are much smaller and depend on the degree of aversion to inequality in the social welfare function.

In addition, we find that the carbon tax is either mildly progressive or mildly regressive, depending on the the degree of inequality aversion and the measure of progression used.

Notes

1. Overviews of the economics of global warming have been given by Nordhaus (1991) and Schelling (1992).

2. A carbon tax was first analyzed by Nordhaus (1979) and has recently been discussed by the Congressional Budget Office (1990) and Poterba (1991b). Alternative policy options for stabilizing the global climate are described in detail by Environmental Protection Agency (1989).

3. The use of Pigouvian taxes to internalize environmental externalities is discussed by Laffont (1977) and Sandmo (1975). A very lucid exposition is provided by Laffont (1988, ch. 1, pp. 6–32).

4. Many estimates of the efficiency impact of restrictions on carbon dioxide emissions are now available. Detailed surveys are given by Hoeller, Dean and Nicolaisen (1991) and Nordhaus (1990).

5. This model was developed by Jorgenson, Slesnick, and Stoker (1987, 1988) and is similar in many respects to the model of the household sector used in this paper Jorgenson and Wilcoxen (1992).

6. Barro (1974) demonstrates the equivalence between a single consumer with an infinite time horizon and successive generations of consumers linked by intergenerational altruism. Laitner (1991) shows how similar household types are linked through time by assortative mating.

7. Our approach exemplifies the "lifetime incidence" approach discussed by Poterba (1989). Poterba (1991a) provides estimates of the lifetime incidence of gasoline taxes and references to the literature.

8. It is well known that unweighted or weighted sums of equivalent variations in wealth are inappropriate for this purpose. See Slesnick (1991) and the references given there.

9. Data on interindustry transactions are based on input-output tables for the United States constructed by the Bureau of Economic Analysis (1984). Income data are from the U.S. national income and product accounts, also developed by the Bureau of Economic Analysis (1986). The data on capital and labor services are described by Jorgenson (1990b). Additional details are given by Wilcoxen (1988, appendix C), and Ho (1989).

10. See Mansur and Whalley (1984) for more detail. An example of the calibration approach is Borges and Goulder (1984), who present a model of energy policy calibrated to data for the year 1973. Surveys of applied general equilibrium modeling are given by Bergman (1985, 1990).

11. A detailed discussion of our econometric methodology is presented by Jorgenson (1984, 1986).

12. Our approach to endogenous productivity growth was originated by Jorgenson and Fraumeni (1981). A general equilibrium model of production that incorporates both substitution among inputs and endogenous productivity growth is presented by Jorgenson (1984). This model has been analyzed in detail by Hogan and Jorgenson (1991).

13. The Euler equation approach to modeling intertemporal consumer behavior was originated by Hall (1978). Our application of this approach follows Jorgenson and Yun (1986).

14. Our model of personal consumption expenditures can be used to represent the behavior of individual households or the behavior of the household sector as a whole, as in Jorgenson and Slesnick (1987a) and Jorgenson, Slesnick, and Stoker (1987, 1988).

15. Details on the econometric methodology are given by Jorgenson (1984, 1990a). Additional details are provided by Wilcoxen (1988) and Ho (1989).

16. The relationship between the price of investment goods and the rental price of capital services is discussed in greater detail by Jorgenson (1989).

17. This is the Armington (1969) approach. See Wilcoxen (1988) and Ho (1989) for further details on our implementation of this approach.

18. This is largely the case in practice, since carbon dioxide is one of the natural products of combustion. Little can be done to change the amount produced when burning a particular fuel.

19. A more detailed discussion is given by Jorgenson and Wilcoxen (1992).

20. Our breakdown of the U.S. population by age, sex, and educational attainment is based on the system of demographic accounts compiled by Jorgenson and Fraumeni (1989). The population projections are discussed in detail by Wilcoxen (1988, appendix B).

21. Further details are given by Jorgenson and Slesnick (1987a).

22. The intertemporal expenditure function was introduced by Jorgenson and Yun (1991).

23. Jorgenson and Wilcoxen (1992) have considered the efficiency impact of imposing a number of alternative limits on carbon dioxide emissions by different sequences of carbon taxes.

24. All dollar amounts are in 1990 prices.

25. The results presented in table 9.4 are typical of findings for all 16,128 household types. For example, the minimum percentage loss is 0.186 percent of wealth and the maximum loss is 0.330 percent for all medium wealth households.

References

Advisory Commission to Study the Consumer Price Index 1995. *Toward a More Accurate Meausre of the Cost of Living.* Interim Report to the Committee on Finance, U.S. Senate, September 15.

Afriat, S.N. 1977. *The Price Index.* London: Cambridge University Press.

Allen, Roy G.D. 1949. The Economic Theory of Index Numbers. *Economica* 16, no. 63 (August): 197–203.

Armington, Paul S. 1969. The Geographic Pattern of Trade and the Effects of Price Changes. *IMF Staff Papers* 16 (July): 179–201.

Arrow, Kenneth J. 1963. *Social Choice and Individual Values.* New Haven, CT: Yale University Press, 2nd ed.

————. 1977. Extended Sympathy and the Possibility of Social Choice. *American Economic Review* 67, no. 1 (Feburary): 219–225.

Arrow, Kenneth J., Hollis B. Chenery, Bagicha S. Minhas, and Robert M. Solow. 1961. Capital-Labor Substitution and Economic Efficiency. *Review of Economics and Statistics* 43, no. 3 (August): 225–250.

Arrow, Kenneth J., and Gerard Debreu. 1954. Existence of an Equilibrium for a Competitive Economy. *Econometrica* 22, no. 3 (July): 265–290.

Arrow, Kenneth J., and J.P. Kalt. 1979. *Petroleum Price Regulation: Should We Decontrol.* Washington, DC: American Enterprise Institute.

d'Aspremont, Claude, and Louis Gevers. 1977. Equity and the Informational Basis of Collective Choice. *Review of Economic Studies* 44, no. 137 (June): 199–209.

Atkinson, Anthony B. 1970. On Measurement of Inequality. *Journal of Economic Theory* 2, no. 3 (September): 244–263.

————. 1983a. Bibliography 1970–1982. In *Social Justice and Public Policy,* ed. Anthony B. Atkinson, 31–36. Cambridge: MIT Press.

————. 1983b. Introduction to Part I. In *Social Justice and Public Policy,* ed. Anthony B. Atkinson, 3–13. Cambridge: MIT Press.

Atkinson, Anthony B., and François Bourguignon. 1982. The Comparison of Multi-Dimensioned Distributions of Economic Status. *Review of Economic Studies*, 49(2), no. 156 (April): 183–201.

Barro, Robert J. 1974. Are Government Bonds Net Wealth? *Journal of Political Economy* 82 (November–December): 1095–1117.

Barten, A. P. 1964. Family Composition, Prices and Expenditure Patterns. In *Econometric Analysis for National Economic Planning: 16th Symposium of the Colston Society*, eds. P. Hart, G. Mills, and J.K. Whitaker, 277–292. London: Butterworth.

———. 1977. The Systems of Consumer Demand Functions Approach: A Review. In *Frontiers of Quantitative Economics*, vol. IIIA, ed. Michael D. Intriligator, 23–58. Amsterdam: North Holland.

Becker, Gary S. 1981. *A Treatise on the Family*. Cambridge: Harvard University Press.

Bentzel, Ragnar. 1970. The Social Significance of Income Distribution Statistics. *Review of Income and Wealth* 16, no. 3 (September): 253–264.

Bergman, Lars. 1985. Extension and Applications of the MSG-Model: A Brief Survey. In *Production, Multi-Sectoral Growth, and Planning: Essays in Memory of Leif Johansen*, eds. Finn R. Forsund, Michael Hoel, and Sven Longva. Amsterdam: North-Holland.

———. 1990. The Development of Computable General Equilibrium Modeling. In *General Equilibrium Modeling and Economic Policy Analysis*, eds. Lars Bergman, Dale W. Jorgenson, and Erno Zalai. Oxford: Basil Blackwell.

Bergson, Abram. 1936. Real Income, Expenditure Proportionality, and Frisch's 'New Methods of Measuring Marginal Utility.' *Review of Economic Studies* 4, no. 1 (October): 33–52.

———. 1938. A Reformulation of Certain Aspects of Welfare Economics. *Quarterly Journal of Economics* 52, no. 2 (February): 310–334.

———. 1980. Consumer's Surplus and Income Redistribution. *Journal of Public Economics* 14, no. 1 (August): 31–47.

Berndt, Ernst R., Masako N. Darrough, and W. Erwin Diewert. 1977. Flexible Functional Forms and Expenditure Distributions: An Application to Canadian Consumer Demand Functions. *International Economic Review* 18: 651–676.

Blackorby, Charles, R. Boyce, and R.R. Russell. 1978. Estimation of Demand Systems Generated by the Gorman Polar Form: A Generalization of the S-Branch Utility Tree. *Econometrica* 46: 345–364.

Blackorby, Charles, and David Donaldson. 1978. Measures of Relative Equality and their Meaning in Terms of Social Welfare. *Journal of Economic Theory* 18, no. 1 (June): 651–675.

———. 1980. A Theoretical Treatment of Indices of Absolute Inequality. *International Economics Review* 21, no. 1 (February): 107–136.

———. 1982. Ratio-Scale and Translation-Scale Full Interpersonal Comparability without Domain Restrictions: Admissible Social-Evaluation Functions. *International Economic Review* 23, no. 2 (June): 249–268.

———. 1985. Consumers' Surpluses and Consistent Cost-Benefit Tests. *Social Choice and Welfare* 1: 251–262

Borges, Antonio M., and Lawrence H. Goulder. 1984. Decomposing the Impact of Higher Energy Prices on Long-Term Growth. In *Applied General Equilibrium Analysis*, eds. Herbert E. Scarf and John B. Shoven. Cambridge, England: Cambridge University Press.

Bureau of the Census. Various dates. *Current Population Reports*, Series P-60, Consumer Income. Washington, DC: U.S. Department of Commerce.

Bureau of Economic Analysis. 1984. The Input-Output Structure of the U.S. Economy, 1977. *Survey of Current Business* 64 (May): 42–78.

———. 1986 *The National Income and Product Accounts of the United States, 1929–1982: Statistical Tables*. Washington, DC: U.S. Department of Commerce.

Bureau of Labor Statistics. 1990. Consumer Expenditures Survey 1989. Washington, DC: Department of Labor. Magnetic tapes.

Carlson, Michael D. 1974. The 1972–1973 Consumer Expenditure Survey. *Monthly Labor Review* 97, no. 12 (December): 16–23.

Chipman, John S., and J.C. Moore. 1973. Aggregate Demand, Real National Income, and the Compensation Principle. *International Economic Review* 14: 153–181.

———. 1980a. Compensating Variation, Consumer's Surplus, and Welfare. *American Economic Review* 70, no. 5 (December): 933–949.

———. 1980b. Real National Income with Homothetic Preferences and a Fixed Distribution of Income. *Econometrica* 48: 401–422.

Christensen, Laurits R., Dale W. Jorgenson, and Lawrence J. Lau. 1975. Transcendental Logarithmic Utility Functions. *American Economic Review* 65, no. 3 (June): 367–383.

Congressional Budget Office. 1990. *Carbon Charges as a Response to Global Warming: The Effects of Taxing Fossil Fuels*, August. Washington, DC: Government Printing Office.

Dalton, Hugh. 1920. The Measurement of Inequality of Income. *Economic Journal* 30, no. 119 (September): 361–384.

Danziger, Sheldon H., Robert H. Haveman, and Robert D. Plotnick. 1986. Antipoverty Policy: Effects on the Poor and the Nonpoor. In *Fighting Poverty*, eds. S.H. Dansiger and D.H. Weinberg. Cambridge, MA: Harvard University Press.

Dasgupta, Partha, Amartya K. Sen, and David Starrett. 1973. Notes on the

Measurement of Inequality. *Journal of Economic Theory* 6, no. 2 (April): 180–187.

Deaton, Angus S. 1986. Demand Analyis. In *Handbook of Econometrics*, eds. Zvi Griliches and Michael D. Intriligator, vol. 3. Amsterdam: North-Holland.

Deaton, Angus S., and John S. Muellbauer. 1980a. An Almost Ideal Demand System. *American Economic Review* 70: 312–326.

———. 1980b. *Economics and Consumer Behavior*. Cambridge, England: Cambridge University Press.

———. 1986. Measuring Child Costs: With Applications to Poor Countries. *Journal of Political Economy* 94, no. 4 (August): 720–744.

Deschamps, Robert, and Louis Gevers. 1978. Leximin and Utilitarian Rules: A Joint Characterisation. *Journal of Economic Theory* 17, no. 2 (April): 143–63.

DeWitt, Diane E., Hadi Dowlatabadi, and Raymond J. Kopp. 1991. Who Bears the Burden of Energy Taxes? Discussion Paper QE91–12. Washington, DC: Resources for the Future.

Diamond, P.A., and Daniel McFadden. 1974. Some Uses of the Expenditure Function in Public Finance. *Journal of Public Economics* 3, no. 1 (February) 3–21.

Diewert, W. Erwin. 1976. Exact and Superlative Index Numbers. *Journal of Econometrics* 4, no. 2 (May): 115–145.

———. 1980. Duality Approaches to Microeconomic Theory. In *Handbook of Mathematical Economics*, eds. Kenneth J. Arrow and Michael D. Intriligator, vol. 3. Amsterdam: North-Holland.

———. 1981. The Economic Theory of Index Numbers: A Survey. In *Essays on Theory and Measurement of Consumer Behavior in Honor of Sir Richard Stone*, ed. Angus S. Deaton, 163–208.

———. 1984. Group Cost-of-Living Indexes: Approximations and Axiomatics. *Methods of Operations Research* 48: 23–45.

Dupuit, Jules. 1969. On the Measurement of the Utility of Public Works. In *Readings in Welfare Economics*, eds. Kenneth J. Arrow and T. Scitovsky, Homewood: Richard D. Irwin, pp. 255–283 (originally published in French in 1844).

Energy Information Administration. 1990. *Annual Energy Review 1989*. Washington, DC: Department of Energy.

Engel, E. 1895. Die Lebenskästen Belgischer Arbeiterfamilien früher und jetzt—Ermittelt aus Familienhaushaltsrechnungen. *Bulletin of the International Statistical Institute* 9.

Environmental Protection Agency. 1988. The Potential Effects of Global Climate Change in the United States. Draft report to Congress. October.

———. 1989. Policy Options for Stabilizing Global Climate, vol. 2. Draft report to Congress. Frebruary

Foster, James E. 1984. On Economic Poverty: A Survey of Aggregate Measures. In *Advances in Econometrics*, eds. Robert L. Basmann and G.F. Rhodes, Jr., vol. 3, 215–252. Greenwich, CT: JAI Press.

Foster, James E., Joel Greer, and Erik Thorbecke. 1984. A Class of Decomposable Poverty Measures. *Econometrica* 52, 761–766.

Frisch, Ragnar. 1936. Annual Survey of Economic Theory: The Problem of Index Numbers. *Econometrica* 4, no. 1 (January): 1–39.

Gill, P.E., W. Murray, M.A. Saunders, and M. Wright. 1983. User's Guide for SOL/NPSOL: A Fortran Package for Nonlinar Programming. Systems Optimization Laboratory, Stanford University, Technical Report SOL 83–12, July.

Goettle, Richard J., IV, and Edward A. Hudson. 1983. The Macroeconomic Consequences of Oil Price and Tax Policies. Cambridge, MA: Dale W. Jorgenson Associates.

Goettle, Richard J., IV, Edward A. Hudson, Dale W. Jorgenson, and Daniel T. Slesnick. 1983. The Macroeconomic Consequences of Alternative Natural Gas Policies. Cambridge, MA: Dale W. Jorgenson Associates.

Gorman, William M. 1953. Community Preference Fields. *Econometrica* 21: 63–80.

———. 1976. Tricks with Utility Functions. In *Essays in Economic Analysis: Proceedings of the 1975 AUTE Conference, Sheffield*, eds. M.J. Artis and A.R. Nobay, 211–243. Cambridge, England: Cambridge University Press.

Hall, Robert E. 1978. Stochastic Implications of the Life Cycle-Permanent Income Hypothesis: Theory and Evidence. *Journal of Political Economy* 86 (December): 971–987.

Hammond, Peter J. 1976. Equity, Arrow's Conditions and Rawl's Difference Principle. *Econometrica* 44, no. 4 (July): 793–804.

———. 1977. Dual Interpersonal Comparisons of Utility and the Welfare Economics of Income Distribution. *Journal of Public Economics* 7, no. 1 (February): 51–71.

———. 1978. Economic Welfare with Rank Order Price Weighting. *Review of Economic Studies* 45: 381–384.

Harberger, Arnold C. 1971. Three Basic Postulates for Applied Welfare Economics: An Interpretative Essay. *Journal of Economic Literature* 9, no. 3 (September): 785–797.

Hardy, Godfrey H., John E. Littlewood, and George Polya. 1959. *Inequalities.* 2d ed. Cambridge: Cambridge University Press.

Harsanyi, John C. 1976. *Essays on Ethics, Social Behavior and Scientific Explanation.* Dordrecht: D. Reidel.

Hausman, Jerry A. 1981. Exact Consumer's Surplus and Deadweight Loss. *American Economic Review* 71, no. 4 (September): 662–676.

Hicks, John R. 1940. The Valuation of Scoial Income. *Economica* N.S. 7: 105–124.

———. 1942. Consumers' Surplus and Index Numbers. *Review of Economic Studies* 9, no. 2 (Summer): 126–137.

Hicks, John R., and Roy G. D. Allen. 1934. A Reconsideration of the Theroy of Value, I, II. *Economica*, N.S. 1, nos. 1, 2 (February, May): 52–75, 196–219.

Ho, Mun Sing. 1989. The Effects of External Linkages on U.S. Economic Growth: A Dynamic General Equilibrium Analysis. Ph.D. dissertation, May, Harvard University: Department of Economics.

Hoeller, Peter, Andrew Dean, and John Nicolaisen. 1991. Macroeconomic Implications of Reducing Greenhouse Gas Emissions: A Survey of Empirical Studies. *OECD Economic Studies*, 16 (Spring): 45–78.

Hogan, William W., and Dale W. Jorgenson. 1991. Productivity Trends and the Costs of Reducing Carbon Dioxide Emissions. *The Energy Journal* 12 (January): 67–85.

Hotelling, Harold S. 1938. The General Welfare in Relation to Problems of Taxation and of Railway and Utility Rates. *Econometrica* 6, no. 3 (July): 242–269.

Houthakker, Hendrik S. 1957. An International Comparison of Household Expenditure Patterns Commemorating the Centenary of Engel's Law. *Econometrica* 25, no. 4 (October): 532–551.

———. 1960. Additive Preferences. *Econometrica* 28, no. 2 (April): 244–257.

Hudson, Edward A., and Dale W. Jorgenson. 1974. U.S. Energy Policy and Economic Growth, 1975–2000. *Bell Journal of Economics and Management Science* 5, no. 2 (Autumn): 461–514.

———. 1976. U.S. Tax Policy and Energy Conservation. *Econometric Studies of U.S. Energy Policy*, ed. Dale W. Jorgenson, 7–94. Amsterdam: North-Holland.

———. 1978a. Energy Prices and the U.S. Economy, 1972–1976. *Natural Resources Journal* 18, no. 4: 877–897.

———. 1978b. The Economic Impact of Policies to Reduce U.S. Energy Growth. *Resources and Energy* 1, no. 3 (November): 205–230.

Hurwicz, Leonid and Hirofumi Uzawa. 1971. On the Integrability of Demand Functions. *Preferences, Utility and Demand*, eds. J.S. Chipman *et al.*, 114–148. New York: Harcourt Brace.

Jorgenson, Dale W. 1984. Econometric Methods for Applied General Equilibrium Analysis. In *Applied General Equilibrium Analysis*, eds. Herbert E. Scarf and John B. Shoven, 139–203. Cambridge, England: Cambridge University Press.

———. 1986. Econometric Methods for Modeling Producer Behavior. In

Handbook of Econometrics, eds. Zvi Griliches and Michael D. Intriligator, vol. 3, 1841–1915. Amsterdam: North-Holland.

————. 1989. Capital as a Factor of Production. In *Technology and Capital Formation*, eds. Dale W. Jorgenson and Ralph Landau, 1–35. Cambridge, MA: MIT Press.

————. 1990a. Aggregate Consumer Behavior and the Measurement of Social Welfare. *Econometrica* 58 (September): 1007–1040.

————. 1990b. Productivity and Economic Growth. In *Fifty Years of Economic Measurement*, eds. Ernst R. Berndt and Jack E. Triplett, 19–118. Chicago: University of Chicago Press.

Jorgenson, Dale W., and Barbara M. Fraumeni. 1981. Relative Prices and Technical Change. In *Modeling and Measuring Natural Resource Substitution*, eds. Ernst R. Berndt and Barry C. Field, 17–47. Cambridge, MA: MIT Press.

————. 1989. The Accumulation of Human and Nonhuman Capital, 1948–1984. In *The Measurement of Saving, Investment, and Wealth*, Robert E. Lipsey and Helen S. Tice, 227–282. Chicago, IL: University of Chicago Press.

Jorgenson, Dale W., and Jean-Jacques Laffont. 1974. Efficient Estimation of Nonlinear Simultaneous Equations with Additive Disturbances. *Annals of Social and Economic Measurement* 3, no 1 (January): 615–640.

Jorgenson, Dale W., and Lawrence J. Lau. 1975. The Structure of Consumer Preferences. *Annals of Social and Economic Measurement* 4, no. 1 (January): 49–101.

————. 1979. The Integrability of Consumer Demand Functions. *European Economic Review* 12, no. 2 (April): 115–147.

————. 1986. Testing the Integrability of Consumer Demand Functions, United States, 1947–1971. In *Advances in Econometrics*, vol. V, ed. Daniel Slottje, 3–48. Greenwich, CT: JAI Press.

Jorgenson, Dale W., Lawrence J. Lau, and Thomas M. Stoker. 1980. Welfare Comparison Under Exact Aggregation. *American Economic Review* 70, no. 2 (May): 268–272.

————. 1981. Aggregate Consumer Behavior and Individual Welfare. In *Macroeconomic Analysis*, eds. D. Currie, R. Nobay, and D. Peel, 35–61. London: Croom-Helm.

————. 1982. The Transcendental Logarithmic Model of Aggregate Consumer Behavior. In *Advances in Econometrics 1*, eds. Robert L. Basmann and G.F. Rhodes, Jr., vol. 1, 97–238. Greenwich, CT: JAI Press.

————. 1986. Nonlinear Three Stage Least Squares Pooling of Time Series and Cross-Section Data. In *Advances in Statistical Analysis and Statistical Computing*, ed. R.S. Mariano, 87–115. Greenwhich, CT: JAI Press.

Jorgenson, Dale W., and Daniel T. Slesnick. 1983. Individual and Social Cost-of-Living Indexes. In *Price Level Measurement*, eds. W. Erwin Diewert and C. Montmarquette, 241–323. Ottawa: Statistics Canada.

————. 1984a. Aggregate Consumer Behavior and the Measurement of Inequality. *Review of Economic Studies* 51(3), no. 166 (July): 369–392.

————. 1984b. Inequality in the Distribution of Individual Welfare. In *Advances in Econometrics*, eds. Robert L. Basmann and G.F. Rhodes, Jr., vol. 3, 67–130. Greenwich, CT: JAI Press.

————. 1985a. Efficiency versus Equity in Petroleum Taxation. *The Energy Journal* 6: 171–188.

————. 1985b. Efficiency versus Equity in Natural Gas Price Regulation. *Journal of Econometrics* 30: 301–316.

————. 1985c. General Equilibrium Analysis of Economic Policy. In *New Developments in Applied General Equilibrium Analysis*, eds. John Piggott and John Whalley. Cambridge, England: Cambridge University Press.

————. 1987a. Aggregate Consumer Behavior and Household Equivalence Sales. *Journal of Business and Economic Statistics* 5 (April): 219–232.

————. 1987b. General Equilibrium Analysis of Natural Gas Price Regulation. In *Public Regulation*, ed. E.E. Bailey. Cambridge, MA: MIT Press.

————. 1989. Redistributional Policy and the Measurement of Poverty. In *Research on Economic Inequality*, ed. Daniel Slottje, vol. 1. Greenwich, CT: JAI Press.

————. 1990a. Inequality and the Standard of Liveing. *Journal of Econometrics* 43: 103–120.

————. 1990b. Individual and Social Cost-of-Living Indexes. In Price Level Measurement, ed. W. Erwin Diewert. Amsterdam: North-Holland.

Jorgenson, Dale W., Daniel T. Slesnick, and Thomas M. Stoker. 1987. Two-Stage Budgeting and Consumer Demand for Energy. In *Advances in the Economics of Energy and Natural Resources*, ed. John R. Moroney, vol. 6. Greenwich, CT: JAI Press.

————. 1988. Two-Stage Budgeting and Exact Aggregation. *Journal of Business and Economic Statistics* 6 (July): 313–326.

Jorgenson, Dale W., and Thomas M. Stoker. 1986. Nonlinear Three Stage Least Squares Pooling of Time-Series and Cross-Section Data. In *Advances in Statistical Analysis and Statistical Computing*, ed. R.S. Mariano, vol. 1, 87–115. Greenwich, CT: JAI Press.

Jorgenson, Dale W., and Kun-Young Yun. 1986. The Efficiency of Capital Allocation. *Scandinavian Journal of Economics* 88: 85–107.

————. 1991. The Excess Burden of U.S. Taxation. *Journal of Accounting, Auditing, and Finance* 6: 487–509.

Jorgenson, Dale W., and Peter J. Wilcoxen. 1990a. Environmental Regulation and U.S. Economic Growth. *RAND Journal of Economics* 21 (Summer): 314–340.

———. 1990b. Intertemporal General Equilibrium Modeling of U.S. Environmental Regulation. *Journal of Policy Modeling* 12 (Winter): 715–744.

———. 1992. Reducing U.S. Carbon Dioxide Emissions: The Cost of Different Goals. In *Advances in the Economics of Energy and Natural Resources*, ed. John R. Moroney, vol. 7, 126–158. Greenwich, CT: JAI Press.

Kakwani, Nanak C. 1977. On the Estimation of Consumer Unit Scales. *Review of Economics and Statistics* 59, no. 4 (November): 507–510.

King, Mervyn A. 1983a. An Index of Inequality: With Applications to Horizontal Equity and Social Mobility. *Econometrica* 51, no. 1 (January): 99–115.

———. 1983b. Welfare Analysis of Tax Reforms Using Household Data. *Journal of Public Economics* 21: 183–214.

Kolm, Serge C. 1969. The Optimal Production of Social Justice. In *Public Economics*, eds. Julius Margolis and Henri Guitton, 145–200. London: Macmillan.

———. 1976a. Unequal Inequalities I. *Journal of Economic Theory* 12, no. 3 (June): 416–442.

———. 1976b. Unequal Inequalities II. *Journal of Economic Theory* 13, no. 1 (August): 82–111.

Konüs, A.A. 1939. The Problem of the True Index of the Cost of Living. *Econometrica* 7, no. 1 (January): 10–29; originally published in 1924.

Laffont, Jean-Jacques. 1977. *Effets externes et théorie économique*. Paris: Centre National de Recherche Scientifique.

———. 1988. *Fundamentals of Public Economics*, transl. by John P. Bonin and Helene Bonin. Cambridge, MA: MIT Press.

Laitner, John. 1991. Modeling Marital Connections among Family Lines. *Journal of Political Economy* 99 (December): 1123–1141.

Lau, Lawrence J. 1977a. Complete Systems of Consumer Demand Functions Through Duality. In *Frontiers of Quantitative Economics*, vol. IIIA, eds. Michael D. Intriligator and David A. Kendrick, 59–86. Amsterdam: North-Holland.

———. 1977b. Existence Conditions for Aggregate Demand Functions: The Case of a Single Index. Technical report no. 248 (October). Stanford, CA: Institute for Mathematical Studies in the Social Sciences, Stanford University (Revised 1980 and 1982).

———. 1979. On Exact Index Numbers. *Review of Economics and Statistics* 61, no. 1 (February): 73–82.

———. 1982. A Note on the Fundamental Theorem of Exact Aggregation. *Economics Letters* 9, no. 2: 119–126.

———. 1986. Functional Forms in Econometric Model-Building. In *Handbook*

ʟ

of Econometrics, ed. Zvi Griliches and Michael D. Intriligator, vol. 3. Amsterdam: North-Holland.

Lau, Lawrence J., Wou-Long Lin, and Pan A. Yotopoulos. 1978. The Linear Logarithmic Expenditure System: An Application to Consumption-Leisure Choice. *Econometrica* 46, no. 4 (July): 843–868.

Lazear, Edward P., and Robert T. Michael. 1980. Family Size and The Distribution of Real Per Capita Income. *American Economic Review* 70, no. 1 (March): 91–107.

Leser, Conrad E.V. 1963. Forms of Engel Functions. *Econometrica* 31, no. 4 (October): 694–703.

Manne, Alan S., and Richard G. Richels. 1990. CO_2 Emission Limits: An Economic Analysis for the USA. *The Energy Journal* 11 (April): 51–79.

Mansur, Ahsan H., and John Whalley. 1984. Numerical Specification of Applied General Equilibrium Models: Estimation, Calibration, and Data. In *Applied General Equilibrium Analysis*, eds. Herbert E. Scarf and John B. Shoven, 69–127. Cambridge, England: Cambridge University Press.

Marshall, Alfred. 1920. *Principles of Economics*, 8th ed. London: Macmillan.

Martos, Bela. 1969. Subdefinite Matrices and Quadratic Forms. *SIAM Journal of Applied Mathematics* 17: 1215–1223.

Maskin, Eric. 1978. A Theorem on Utilitarianism. *Review of Economic Studies* 42, no. 139 (February): 93–96.

McKenzie, George W. 1982. *Measuring Economic Welfare: New Methods*. Cambridge, England: Cambridge University Press.

McKenzie, Lionel W. 1957. Demand Theory without a Utility Index. *Review of Economic Studies* 24: 185–189.

Mirrlees, James A. 1971. An Exploration in the Theory of Optimal Income Taxation. *Review of Economic Studies* 38, no. 114 (April): 175–208.

Muellbauer, John. 1974a. Household Composition, Engel Curves and Welfare Comparisons between Households: A Duality Approach. *European Economic Review* 5, no. 2 (August): 103–122.

———. 1974b. Inequality Measures, Prices and Household Composition. *Review of Economic Studies* 41(4), no. 128 (October): 493–504.

———. 1974c. Prices and Inequality: The United Kingdom Experience. *Economic Journal* 84, no. 333 (March): 32–55.

———. 1975. Aggregation, Income Distribution and Consumer Demand. *Review of Economic Studies* 42: 525–543.

———. 1976a. Economics and the Representative Consumer. In *Private and Enlarged Consumption*, eds. L. Solari and J.N. Du Pasquier, 29–54. Amsterdam: North-Holland.

———. 1976b. Community Preferences and the Representative Consumer. *Econometrica* 44: 979–999.

———. 1977. Testing the Barten Model of Household Composition Effects and the Cost of Children. *Economic Journal* 87, no. 347 (September): 460–487.

———. 1980. The Estimation of the Prais-Houthakker Model of Equivalence Scales. *Econometrica* 48, no. 1 (January): 153–176.

Muellbauer, John and Panos Pashardes. 1982. Testing the Barten Equivalence Scale Hypothesis in a Flexible Functional Form Context. Birkbeck College, University of London, Discussion Paper no. 112 (January).

Nordhaus, William D.. 1979. *The Efficient Use of Energy Resources.* New Haven, CT: Yale University Press.

———. 1990. The Cost of Slowing Climate Change: A Survey. *The Energy Journal* 12 (January): 37–65.

———. 1991. To Slow or Not to Slow: The Economics of the Greenhouse Effect. *Economic Journal* 101 (July): 920–937.

Ng, Yew-Kuang. 1975. Bentham or Bergson? Finite Sensibility, Utility Functions and Social Welfare Functions. *Review of Economic Studies* 42, no. 4 (October): 545–569.

Orshansky, M. 1965. Counting the Poor: Another Look at the Poverty Profile. *Social Security Bulletin* 28, no. 1 (January): 3–29.

———. 1966. Recounting the Poor: A Five Year Review. *Social Security Bulletin* 29, no. 1 (January): 20–37.

Parks, Richard W., and A.P. Barten. 1973. A Cross Country Comparison of the Effects of Prices. Income and Population Compensation on Consumption Patterns. *Economic Journal* 83, no. 331 (September): 834–852.

Plotnick, Robert D., and Felicity Skidmore. 1975. *Progress Against Poverty: A Review of the 1964–1974 Decade.* New York: Academic Press.

Pollak, Robert A. 1971. The Theory of the Cost-of-Living Index. Research Discussion Paper no. 11, Office of Prices and Living Conditions. Washington, D.C.: U.S. Bureau of Labor Statistics.

———. 1981. The Social Cost-of-Living Index. *Journal of Public Economics* 15, no. 3 (June): 311–336.

Pollak, Robert A., and Terence J. Wales. 1978. Estimation of Complete Demand Systems from Household Budget Data: The Linear and Quadratic Expenditure Systems. *American Economic Review* 68, no. 3 (June): 348–359.

———. 1979. Welfare Comparisons and Equivalent Scales. *American Economic Review* 69, no. 2 (May): 216–221.

———. 1980. Comparison of the Quadratic Expenditure System and Translog Demand Systems with Alternatives Specifications of Demographic Effects. *Econometrica* 48, no. 3 (April): 595–612.

————. 1981. Demographic Variables in Demand Analysis. *Econometrica* 49, no. 6 (November): 1533–1552.

Poterba, James M. 1989. Lifetime Incidence and the Distributional Burden of Excise Taxes. *American Economic Review* 79 (May): 325–330.

————. 1991a. Is the Gasoline Tax Regressive? In *Tax Policy and the Economy*, ed. David Bradford, vol. 5. Cambridge, MA: MIT Press.

————. 1991b. Tax Policy to Combat Global Warming: On Designing a Carbon Tax. In *Global Warming: Economic Policy Responses*, eds. Rudiger Dornbusch and James M. Poterba, 71–97. Cambridge, MA: MIT Press.

Prais, S.J., and Hendrik S. Houthakker. 1971. *The Analysis of Family Budgets.* Cambridge, England: Cambridge University Press (1st ed., 1955).

Pyatt, Graham. 1987. Measuring Welfare, Poverty, and Inequality. *Economic Journal* 97: 459–467.

Ray, Robert. 1982. The Testing and Estimation of Complete Demand Systems on Household Budget Surveys: An Application of AIDS. *European Economic Review* 17, no. 3 (March): 349–370.

Robbins, Lionel. 1938. Interpersonal Comparisons of Utility: A Comment. *Economic Journal* 48, no. 4 (December): 635–641.

Roberts, Kevin W.S. 1980a. Possibility Theorems with Interpersonally Comparable Welfare Levels. *Review of Economic Studies* 47, no. 147 (January): 409–420.

————. 1980b. Interpersonal Comparability and Social Choice Theory. *Review of Economic Studies* 47, no. 147 (January): 421–439.

————. 1980c. Price-Independent Welfare Prescriptions. *Journal of Public Economics* 13, no. 3 (June): 277–298.

————. 1980d. Social Choice Theory: The Single-Profile and Multi-Profile Approaches. *Review of Economic Studies* 47, no. 147 (January): 441–450.

Ross, Christine, Sheldon H. Danziger, and Eugene Smolenski. 1985. The Level and Trend of Poverty 1939–1979. Discussion Paper no. 790–85, December. Madison: University of Wisconsin.

Roy, René. 1943. *De l'Utilité: Contribution à la Théorie des Choix.* Paris: Hermann et Cie.

Russell, R. Robert. 1983. Comments. In *Price Level Measurement*, eds. W. Erwin Diewert and C. Montmarquette. Ottawa: Statistics Canada.

Samuelson, Paul A. 1947. *Foundations of Economic Analysis.* Cambridge, MA: Harvard University Press.

————. 1950. Evaluation of Real National Income. *Oxford Economic Papers* N.S. 1: 1–29.

————. 1956. Social Indifference Curves. *Quarterly Journal of Economics* 70, no. 1 (February): 1–22.

————. 1974. Complementarity—An Essay on the 40th Anniversary of the Hicks-Allen Revolution in Demand Theory. *Journal of Economic Literature* 12, no. 4 (December): 1255–1289.

————. 1982. Bergsonian Welfare Economics. In *Economic Welfare and the Economics of Soviet Socialism: Essays in Honor of Abram Bergson*, ed. S. Rosefielde, 223–266. Cambridge, England: Cambridge University Press.

Samuelson, Paul A., and S. Swamy. 1974. Invariant Economic Index Numbers and Canonical Duality: Survey and Synthesis. *American Economic Review* 64, no. 4 (September): 566–593.

Sandmo, Agnar. 1975. Optimal Taxation in the Presence of Externalities. *Swedish Journal of Economics* 77: 86–98.

Schelling, Thomas C. 1992. Some Economics of Global Warming. *American Economic Review* 82 (March): 1–14.

Sen, Amartya K. 1970. *Collective Choice and Social Welfare*. San Francisco: Holden-Day.

————. 1973. *On Economic Inequality*. Oxford: Clarendon Press.

————. 1976a. Real National Income. *Review of Economic Studies* 43, no. 133 (February): 19–40.

————. 1976b. Poverty: An Ordinal Approach to Measurement. *Econometrica* 44, 219–231.

————. 1977. On Weights and Measures: Informational Constraints in Social Welfare Analysis. *Econometrica* 45, no. 7 (October): 1539–1572.

————. 1979a. The Welfare Basis of Real Income Comparisons: A Survey. *Journal of Economic Literature* 17, no. 1 (March): 1–45.

————. 1979b. Personal Utilities and Public Judgements: Or What's Wrong with Welfare Economics. *Economic Journal* 89, no. 763 (September): 537–558.

————. 1979c. Issues in the Measurement of Poverty. *Scandinavian Economic Journal* 81: 285–307.

————. 1981. *Poverty and Famines: An Essay in Entitlement and Deprivation*. Oxford: Oxford University Press.

————. 1987. *The Standard of Living*. Cambridge, England: Cambridge University Press.

Slesnick, Daniel T. 1986. The Measurement of Effective Commodity Tax Progressivity. *Review of Economics and Statistics* 68 (May): 224–231.

————. 1991a. Normative Index Numbers. *Journal of Econometrics* 50, nos. 1/2 (October/November): 107–130.

————. 1991b. The Standard of Living in the United States. *Review of Income and Wealth* 37, no. 4 (December): 363–386.

————. 1991c. Aggregate Deadweight Loss and Money Metric Social Welfare. *International Economic Review* 32 (February): 123–146.

————. 1993. Gaining Ground: Poverty in the Postwar United States. *Journal of Political Economy* 101, no. 1 (February): 1–38

————. 1994. Consumption, Needs, and Inequality. *International Economic Review* 35, no. 3 (August), 677–703.

Statistics Canada. 1982. *The Consumer Price Index Reference Paper*. Ottawa: Statistics Canada.

Stone, Richard. 1954. Linear Expenditure Systems and Demand Analysis: An Application to the Pattern of British Demand. *Economic Journal* 64: 511–527.

Takayama, Noriyuki. 1979. Poverty, Income Inequality, and their Measures: Professor Sen's Axiomatic Approach Reconsidered. *Econometrica* 47: 747–760.

Törnqvist, Leo. 1936. The Bank of Finland's Consumption Price Index. *Bank of Finland Monthly Bulletin*, no. 10: 1–8.

Tinbergen, Jan. 1970. A Positive and Normative Theory of Income Distribution. *Review of Income and Wealth* Series 16, no. 3 (September): 221–234.

van der Gaag, Jacques, and Eugene Smolensky. 1982. True Household Equivalence Scales and Characteristics of the Poor in the United States. *Review of Income and Wealth* 28, no. 1 (March): 17–28.

Watts, Harold. 1968. An Economic Definition of Poverty. In *On Understanding Poverty*, ed. Daniel P. Moynihan, 316–329. New York: Basic Books.

Wilcoxen, Peter J. 1988. The Effects of Environmental Regulation and Energy Prices on U.S. Economic Performance. Ph.D. Dissertation, December. Harvard University: Department of Economics.

Wolak, Frank A. 1989. Local and Global Testing of Linear and Nonlinear Inequality Constraints in Nonlinear Econometric Models. *Econometric Theory* 5: 1–35.

Index

Note: Pages tagged with *t* locate tables.

Aggregate consumer behavior models, 2–3. *See also* Econometric model of aggregate consumer behavior
labor-leisure choice, 34
transcendental logarithmic, 35–36*t*
Aggregate demand function, 100. *See also* Individual demand function; Preferences
derived from individual demand function, 5
representative consumer model, 1–2
Aggregate expenditure. *See also* Consumer expenditures; Real aggregate expenditure per person
as function of prices and social welfare level, 24, 308–309, 350
model, unknown parameters, 19–20
as money measure of efficiency, 144–145
needed to eliminate poverty, 333
to reach base level of social welfare, 74
Aggregate expenditure shares, 16, 179, 224, 257. *See also* Individual expenditure shares
applied to exact translog cost-of-living index, 89–90
calculating, 50–51
under exact aggregation, 306
individual shares recovered from, 157
model for all commodities, 233–234
obtaining, 111
source of random error of measurement, 230
AIDS specification, 222
Alternative economic policy
based on consumer welfare impact, 165
individual welfare impact, 168, 262
ordering of, 165–169
petroleum prices and taxation, 186–194
poverty measures, 328–335, 336
for reducing carbon dioxide emissions, 361
regulation of natural gas prices, 264–271, 268–270*t*, 283–287
social welfare impact, 206, 210–211
Anonymity property, 120, 198, 202, 274
Arrow, Kenneth J., 120, 344
alternative policy evaluation, 66
impossibility theorem, 3, 64–65, 117, 118–119, 196–197, 273
mean value function, 202
social welfare function, 63, 64, 167, 199, 203
d'Aspremont, Claude, 65
cardinal unit comparability, 3, 197
nondictatorial social orderings, 119
Atkinson, Anthony B., 120, 166
inequality measurement, 66, 99, 198
social welfare function, 32, 343

Barten, A.P., 47, 107, 167, 170
effective quantities consumed, 175, 219, 225, 258
expenditure allocation, 223
household equivalence scale, 222
Becker, Gary S., 7
Bergson, Abram
mean value function, 202
social welfare function, 32, 166, 199, 253, 291, 343
Between-group inequality. *See also* Group inequality; Within-group inequality
money measure, 148, 151, 154–155, 156*t*, 322, 324–326

Between-group inequality (*cont.*)
   relative, 140
   translog index, 139, 140
Between-group welfare function, 138. *See
   also* Group welfare function;
   Household welfare function; Social
   welfare function
   efficiency and equity measures, 139–140
   equity-regarding, 139
   as measure of within-group equality,
      139
   money measure, 147–148, 151
Blackorby, Charles R., 123, 201

Capital formation
   impact of carbon tax on, 383, 386
   substitution among inputs, 368
Carbon dioxide emissions
   estimating, 369–370
   holding constant, 379, 383, 384
   impact of carbon tax on, 383, 385, 397
   policies for reducing, 361
   sectoral differences, 364
Carbon tax
   consumer price effect, 388–391
   distributional impact, 362
   dynamics of transition, 383–387
   dynastic economic effects, 363
   economic impact, 379–387
      dynamics of transition, 383–387
      long-run effects, 380, 382*t*
   efficiency cost, 361, 377–378
   equity vs. efficiency changes, 396–397
   expenditure effect, 391, 392
   objectives, 361
   progressivity, 378–379, 396–398
   regressivity, 396–398
   social welfare impact, 396–398
   welfare effects, 362, 372–379, 388–398
      demographic differences, 393,
         394–395*t*
   willingness to avoid consequences of,
      363
Cardinal full comparability, 64, 66–67, 118,
   120–121, 196, 273, 344
Cardinal noncomparability, 65, 119, 197
Cardinal unit comparability, 3, 65,
   119–120, 198, 199
Carlson, Michael D., 181, 237
CES. *See* Survey of Consumer
   Expenditures

Chenery, Hollis B., 202
Chipman, John S., 25, 165
Christensen, Laurits R., 170, 223
Cobb-Douglas functional form, 365
Compensation principle, 25
Consumer behavior models, 13–20
Consumer equilibrium, 107, 175
   at base price system, 57
   with elimination of poverty, 305
   impact of economic policy on, 264,
      281–282, 283
   indirect utility function, 220
   after price changes, 57
Consumer expenditures
   commodity groups, 18–20, 51, 53–55*t*,
      112, 180, 236, 237, 262, 346–347
   impact of carbon tax on, 391, 392
Consumer Price Index, 87
   vs. social cost-of-living index, 31–32
Cost of living
   impact of price changes and
      distribution of total expenditure
      on, 30*t*
   measurement of, 25, 41
   U.S., 1958–1978, 86
Cost-of-living index. *See also* Group cost-
      of-living index; Individual cost-of-
      living index; Social cost-of-living
      index
   base level of individual welfare, 40
   based on econometric model of
      aggregate consumer behavior, 39
   exact number approach, 88–89
   index number vs. econometric
      approach, 41, 86–89
   social, 355–359
Covariance matrix of transformed
   disturbances, 230, 231
Current Population Reports, 113, 237, 263,
   347
Current Population Survey, 87, 222

Dalton, Hugh, 99
Dalton's (1920) principle of transfers, 10,
   71, 125, 204, 275, 297, 349
Deaton, Angus S., 170, 171
   expenditure allocation, 223
   household equivalence scale, 49, 220,
      222, 227
   social welfare function, 33, 343
Deschamps, Robert, 65, 119, 197

DeWitt, Diane E., 362
DGEM. *See* Dynamic General Equilibrium
     Model of U.S. economy
Diewert, W. Erwin, 88
Donaldson, David, 123, 201
Dowlatabadi, Hadi, 362
Dupuit, Jules, 165, 166
Dynamic General Equilibrium Model of
     U.S. economy, 168
   natural gas price regulation, 266–271,
      284–287
   petroleum policy analysis, 188–194, 213
Dynastic welfare, 372–375. *See also* Group
     welfare; Social welfare
   impact of carbon tax on, 375, 377, 391,
      393, 395–396t
   intertemporal expenditure function,
      375
   intratemporal expenditure function,
      373
   number of household equivalent
      members, 373
   utility function, 374–375
Dynasty, defined, 362

Econometric model of aggregate
     consumer behavior, 1, 254–263
   based on exact aggregation, 42,
      102–112, 169–180, 222–228, 306
   commodity groups, 51
   cost-of-living index based on, 39–40
   demographic characteristics, 51–52,
      53–55t
   empirical results, 112–116, 180–185,
      236–239
   estimation and identification, 221–222,
      228–236
   expenditure coefficients, 19, 52, 113,
      181, 347
   implementation, 167–168
   indirect utility functions, 13, 14–15
   inequality measurement based on,
      99–159
   integrability condition, 85
   integrable demand function, 293
   normalization of parameters, 43
   for policy evaluation, 167
   pooled cross-section and time-series
      data, 52, 112–113, 114–116, 167–
      168, 180–181, 221, 232, 235, 237,
      238, 245–250, 254–255, 262–263

price coefficients, 181, 237
   unknown parameters, 19–20, 52, 113,
      181, 263, 347
Economic growth
   without carbon tax, 379
   as percent of U.S. standard of living, 31
Effective prices, 47, 107, 175, 225, 259
Effective quantities consumed, 47, 107,
     175, 225, 258
Effective quantity, defined, 219–220
Efficiency index. *See* Quantity index of
     efficiency; Translog index of
     efficiency
Efficiency measure. *See also* Quantity
     index of efficiency; Translog index of
     efficiency
   aggregate total expenditure as, 144–145,
      355–356
   for between-group welfare function,
      139–140
   of carbon tax, 377–378
   demographic differences, 1958–1978,
      135, 160t
   of group welfare, 101, 134–135, 146, 147,
      160t
   within and between groups, 147–148
   for index of nominal aggregate
      expenditure, 355–356
   in individual welfare distribution, 158
   in inequality index, 100, 127, 128
   money, 10–11, 34
   of money metric social welfare,
      207–210, 212
   in quantity index of social welfare, 26
   in social standard of living index,
      351–353, 354t
   of social welfare, 24, 144, 277, 278–279,
      350
Elimination of poverty
   alternative measures, 336
   within groups, 314–322
   lump-sum transfers in, 296, 315, 333,
      334t
   optimal policy for, 34
   societal benefits from, 298, 299–300,
      335
   society's willingness to pay for, 335–336
Engel curve, linearity of, 2
Engel, E., 220
Equity growth, 344–345
   as percent of U.S. standard of living, 31

Equity measure
    of between-group welfare, 139–140
    of carbon tax, 378
    of group welfare, 101, 134–135, 146, 147
    of individual welfare distribution, 158
    in inequality index, 100
    money, 10–11, 34
    in social standard of living index,
        351–353, 354t
    of social welfare, 127–129, 130–131, 144,
        207–210, 212, 277, 278–279
Ethical assumptions. See Horizontal
    equity; Vertical equity in social
    welfare
Euler equation, 366, 367, 373–374
    discrete time, 391
Exact aggregation, 13–14, 42, 102, 169
    conditions for, 44, 104, 171–172, 224,
        256–257
    econometric model based on, 14–15,
        222
    formulations, 14
    indirect utility function under, 104–105
    individual demand function under, 345
    individual expenditure shares under,
        306
    restrictions on individual preferences
        ·for, 254
Expenditure function. See also Group
    expenditure function; Individual
    expenditure function; Social
    expenditure function
    between-group, 147
    for household equivalence scale, 261
    for individual cost-of-living index,
        56–57, 58
    translog, 21, 49, 56–57, 58, 109, 177, 227,
        260, 306
Expenditure shares. See Aggregate
    expenditure shares; Individual
    expenditure shares
Export demand equation, 369

Fertility choice, 34
Foreign trade, 369
Foster, James E., 336
Full wealth, 366

Gephardt bill, 266
Gevers, Louis, 65
    cardinal unit comparability, 3, 197

nondictatorial social orderings, 119
Gill, P.E., 20, 235
Global warming models, 365
Goettle, Richard J. (IV), U.S., 189
Gorman, William M., 14, 25, 170
    household equivalence scale, 222
    representative consumer concept, 2
Government consumption demand,
    368–369
Group cost-of-living index, 78–85. See also
    Cost-of-living index
    defined, 41, 80
    demographic differences, 81, 82–84t, 85,
        94–96t
    exact number approach, 89–90
    impact of price changes on, 81
    translog, 81, 86, 89–90
    U.S., 1958–1978, 81, 82–84t
Group expenditure function, 41, 79–80, 86.
    See also Expenditure function;
    Individual expenditure function;
    Social expenditure function
    incorporating ethical judgments,
        317–318
    to measure within group poverty,
        315–316
    for money metric inequality, 145–146
    translog, 80, 81, 146, 151
Group inequality
    money measure, 101, 146, 151
    relative vs. actual levels, 135
Group relative inequality
    demographic differences, 318, 319–321t
    money metric measure, 317
Group welfare. See also Dynastic welfare;
    Social welfare
    actual vs. potential level, 137–138
    demographic differences, 135, 159t
    efficiency and equity measures,
        134–135
    as function of price system and group
        expenditure, 81
    money measure, 146–147
Group welfare function, 41. See also
    Between-group welfare function;
    Social welfare function
    defined, 79
    to determine within-group inequality,
        133
    equity-regarding, 134
    in inequality index, 100–101

invariance for positive affine
    transformation, 138–139
to measure poverty and remaining
    inequality, 294
to measure within group poverty, 314,
    317
for translog indirect utility function, 80

Hammond, Peter J., 10, 25, 71, 117, 275, 297
    social welfare function, 63, 195, 272, 349
    vertical equity notion, 204
Harsanyi, John C., 66, 120
Head-count ratio, 295
    bias in, 32
    defined, 328
    household equivalent, 329–330, 331t
    poverty as function of, 294
Head-count ratio of the poor. See Head-
    count ratio
Heteroscedasticity adjustment, 231, 233,
    234
Hicks, John R., 25, 33, 165
Homogeneity of individual expenditure
    shares, 17, 45, 105, 173
Horizontal equity
    in anonymity property, 120
    in individual welfare function, 22
    among individuals, 5–6
    in social ordering, 66, 198
    in social welfare, 10, 70, 124, 202, 274,
        297, 349
Household behavior model, 7
    three-state optimization process, 366
Household equivalence scale. See also
    Translog household equivalence
    scale
    commodity-specific, 176–177, 219–221,
        226, 238–240, 239t, 258–260, 373
    defined, 48
    demographic characteristics, 240,
        241–242t, 243t
    diseconomies of scale, 238
    estimating, 219, 221
    general, 49–50, 109–110, 177–178, 220,
        227, 238–240, 260–261, 336
    translog indirect utility function in
        terms of, 47, 107–108, 175–176,
        225–226, 259
Household welfare function. See also
    Group welfare function; Social
    welfare function

as cardinal measure of individual
    welfare, 295
maximization of, 102, 169, 255
Houthakker, Hendrik S., 166, 171, 220
Hudson, Edward A.
    Dynamic General Equilibrium Model
        of U.S. Economy, 168, 188, 266
    projections for alternative petroleum
        policies, 189

Identical homothetic preferences, 1–2,
    33
Independence of irrelevant alternatives,
    64, 118, 196, 272
Index number approach
    vs. econometric approach, 86–89
    exact, 88–90
    social applications, 89–90
Index of equality, absolute vs. relative,
    378–379
Index of equity, 31
Index of poverty, 298, 299–300
    basis for, 328
    utilitarian, 328–329
Indirect utility function, 220, 254, 293
    for all consuming units, 13, 14–15
    as cardinal measure of individual
        welfare, 346
    as cardinal measure of utility, 51, 105,
        258, 263
    to define individual welfare, 40, 168,
        305, 336
    for each consuming unit, 42
    in econometric model of consumer
        behavior, 169–170, 222
    under exact aggregation, 44, 104–105,
        172, 257–258
    for general translog household
        equivalence scale, 110, 228, 261
    for group inequality, 149–150
    with household equivalent scales only,
        176
    to implement individual cost-of-living
        index, 56
    individual comparability, 20
    individual demand function derived
        from, 221
    with ratios of price to total expenditure,
        176
    to represent individual preferences,
        102–103, 255

Individual cost-of-living index, 40, 56–62.
    See also Cost-of-living index
    to analyze price changes from
        1958–1978, 58–59, 60–62*t*,
        91–93*t*
    defined, 41, 85–86
    economic theory of measurement, 39
Individual demand function
    aggregate demand function derived
        from, 5
    exact aggregation conditions, 345
    integrability conditions, 17–18, 293, 345
Individual expenditure function, 4–5, 7–8,
        86, 166, 254. *See also* Translog
        individual expenditure function
    applications, 206
    to construct measure of household
        standard of living and cost, 8–9
    in cost-of-living index, 40
    to raise poor household to poverty
        threshold, 296
    to reach threshold of affluence, 298
    social expenditure function and, 73,
        205–206, 277, 303
    to translate individual welfare to
        money metric social welfare, 168
Individual expenditure shares, 15–16, 43,
        103–104. *See also* Aggregate
        expenditure shares
    for all commodities, 229
    conditions for, 256–257
    for consuming units with identical
        demographic characteristics, 111,
        179
    exact aggregation conditions, 224, 306
    for five commodity groups, 181
    integrability, 16–18, 45–46, 85, 105–106,
        157, 172–174, 217
    monotonicity of, 226, 260, 263
    normalization of parameters, 104, 171,
        223–224, 256
Individual households
    demographic characteristics, 19, 51–55,
        112, 180, 220, 221, 236, 262, 347
Individual preferences
    exact aggregation conditions, 254
    homothetic, 165–166
    represented by indirect utility function,
        102–103, 255
    social choice theory vs. econometric
        modeling, 4

Individual welfare. *See also* Money metric
        individual welfare
    cardinal measures of, 20, 345
    defined in terms of indirect utility
        function, 40, 336
    distribution, inequality index, 129–130,
        131*t*, 158
    econometric model, 305, 345–347
    ethical judgments in distribution of, 274
    impact of alternative policy on, 185,
        262, 264
    increase in social welfare with increase
        in, 23
    inequality in distribution of, 99–159,
        179–180
    measures of, 254, 292
        at intuitive level, 22
    natural gas price policy affecting, 264,
        267, 271
Individual welfare function, 4–5, 111. *See
        also* Group welfare function;
        Household welfare function; Social
        welfare function
    cardinal full comparability, 66–67,
        120–121, 344
    cardinal unit comparability, 65,
        197–198, 199
    to construct measure of household
        standard of living and cost, 8–9
    defined on set of social states, 347–348
    homogeneous function of deviations of,
        3
    indirect utility function, 5
    invariance for positive affine
        transformation, 71, 124–125, 134,
        203, 275
    to measure social welfare, 346
    in measuring social welfare, 306–307
    ordinal noncomparability assumption,
        3–4, 197–198
    set of admissible, 63, 117, 196, 272
    social welfare function and, 22
    to translate price changes into cost-of-
        living changes, 56
Inequality
    analysis of, 179
    degree of aversion to, 23, 69–70, 123,
        202, 274, 308, 328
        gain from redistributional policy, 335
    ethical judgments, 308, 317
    money measure, 34

Inequality index, 127–132. *See also*
    Remaining inequality
    absolute vs. relative, 100, 127, 129
    to define measure of remaining
        inequality, 299
    distributional homotheticity, 129
    between group, 101
    within group, 101, 133–136
    between group, 137–142
    within group, 137*t*, 140
    between group, 141*t*
    within group, 141*t*
    between group, 147–148
    within group, 147–148
    between group, 158
    within group, 158
    in population subgroups, 100–101
Inequality measure, 291. *See also* Money
        metric inequality
    based on econometric model of
        consumer behavior, 99–100
    group, 101
    income- vs. welfare-based, 99
    in individual welfare distribution, 100,
        129–130, 131*t*, 158
Inequality remaining after elimination of
    poverty. *See* Remaining inequality
Inflation rate
    calculated from translog group cost-of-
        living indexes, 81, 82–84*t*, 85
    demographic differences, 59, 60–62*t*,
        78*t*, 81–85
Integrability conditions, 45–46, 105–106,
    157, 172–174, 293, 345
    of individual expenditure shares, 85,
        217
Intertemporal general equilibrium model
    of U.S. economy
    applied to carbon emissions policy,
        363–371
    base case, 370–371
    consumer goods and services, 388–390
    consumption, 366–367
    government and foreign trade,
        368–369
    investment and capital formation,
        367–368
    producer behavior, 364–366
Intertemporal indirect utility function,
    372. *See also* Indirect utility function
    wealth constraint, 373

Investment model, 367–368

Jorgenson, Dale W., 368
    commodity group classification, 18
    Dynamic General Equilibrium Model
        of U.S. Economy, 168, 188, 266
    econometric model of consumer
        behavior, 13, 221, 254
    efficiency cost of carbon tax, 361, 362,
        363
    equality measurement, 291
    general household equivalence scale,
        336, 346
    index of within group inequality, 323,
        324
    least squares estimator, 20
    money metric individual welfare, 33
    money metric measure of inequality,
        293, 303, 316, 317
    money metric social welfare, 33–34
    net equivalent variation concept, 186
    NL3SLS estimator, 234, 235
    social cost-of-living index, 28–29,
        355–359
    social welfare function, 22–23, 307, 348,
        375
    translog indirect utility function, 170,
        223

Kalt, J.P., 120
    alternative policy evaluation, 66
    utilitarian social welfare function, 203
King, Mervyn A., 33
Kolm, Serge C., 120, 166
    inequality measurement, 66, 99, 198
    social welfare function, 32, 343
Konüs, A.A., 40, 56
Kopp, Raymond J., 362
Kronecker product form, 230, 231

Labor leisure choice, 34
Laffont, Jean-Jacques
    least squares estimator, 20
    NL3SLS estimator, 234
Lau, Lawrence J., 2, 167
    econometric model of consumer
        behavior, 13, 221, 254
    exact aggregation theory, 42, 224
    household equivalence scale, 222
    money metric individual welfare, 33
    net equivalent variation concept, 186

Lau, Lawrence J. (*cont.*)
    translog indirect utility function, 170, 223
Lazear, Edward P., 222
Least squares estimator, 233
    ordinary, 232
    for pooling time-series and cross-section data, 20
Leontief form, 365
Lin, Wou-Long, 222
Lump-sum taxes, 297, 315, 323
    to reach margin of affluence, 298
Lump-sum transfer, 292, 296, 315
    within and between groups, 323
    maximum level of social welfare through, 297
    needed to eliminate poverty, 333, 334*t*
    to reach poverty threshold, 298

McKenzie, Lionel W., 4, 33, 166
Manne, Alan S., 365
Margin of affluence, 297
    between groups, 323
Martos, Bela, 18, 106, 174
Maskin, Eric, 65, 119, 197
Maximum likelihood estimator, 232, 233
Mean value function, 202
Michael, Robert T., 222
Minhas, Bagicha S., 202
Mirrlees, James A., 66, 120
MLE. *See* Maximum likelihood estimator
Money metric efficiency, 34, 148, 207–210, 212
    under alternative petroleum policies, 214–215
    with carbon tax, 396–397
    group, 146, 147, 153, 162*t*
    for social welfare, 278–279, 280–287
    U.S., 1958–1978, 151, 152*t*, 153, 161*t*
Money metric equity, 34, 145, 207–210, 212
    under alternative petroleum policies, 215–216
    with carbon tax, 396–397
    group, 146, 147
    for social welfare, 279, 280–287
Money metric group inequality, 101, 146, 147–148, 151, 316. *See also* Group inequality; Within-group inequality
    between-group, 154–155, 156*t*, 324–326
    defined, 153
    relative, 151, 153–154, 155*t*, 316, 317

U.S., 1958–1978, 152–154, 154*t*
    within-group, 154–155, 156*t*, 324
Money metric individual welfare, 5, 7, 33, 195, 296. *See also* Individual welfare
    under alternative petroleum policies, 189, 190*t*, 191–192*t*
    for alternative policy analysis, 263–271
    application, 217
    to assess alternative policy impact, 185–194
    definition, 185–186
    as a monotone increasing transformation of individual welfare, 195
    natural gas price regulation affecting, 264–267, 268–270*t*
    Pareto principle applied to, 271
    provided by expenditure function, 9
    social welfare function based on, 167
Money metric inequality, 34, 142–149. *See also* Group inequality; Inequality; Money metric relative inequality; Relative inequality
    applications, 149–156
    defined, 101, 149, 152, 159
    U.S., 152, 153*t*, 309, 311*t*, 312
Money metric poverty, 292, 301–302, 304–305, 309–313. *See also* Elimination of poverty; Poverty measures
    defined, 330
    demographic differences, 318, 319–321*t*
    group relative, 316
    within groups, 316, 318, 319–321, 323
    between groups, 324, 326
    within groups, 326
    between groups, 327*t*
    within groups, 327*t*
    relative, 302, 312, 313*t*, 326
    social expenditure function, 303
    U.S., 1947–1985, 311*t*, 312, 313*t*
    utilitarian, 330, 332*t*, 333
Money metric relative inequality, 151
    within and between groups, 148–149, 150, 325–326
Money metric remaining inequality, 292–293, 302, 304–305, 309–313, 311*t*
    within groups, 316, 318, 319–321*t*, 323
    between groups, 325–326
    within groups, 326
    between groups, 327*t*

within groups, 327t
relative, 302–303, 326
U.S., 1947–1985, 309, 311t
utilitarian, 330, 332t, 333
Money metric social welfare, 33–34, 145,
    279–287, 349. See also Social welfare
    actual vs. potential levels, 151, 209
    for alternative policy analysis, 168–169,
        205–212, 217, 218
    corresponding to degree of aversion to
        inequality, 309, 310t
    effect of natural gas price policies on,
        284–286t
    efficiency and equity measures, 10–11,
        207–210, 212, 280–287
    to evaluate impact of carbon tax, 377
    within groups, 147–148
    impact of alternative petroleum policies
        on, 212–216
    resulting from elimination of poverty,
        309, 310t
    U.S., 1958–1978, 151, 152t
    in units of second commodity, 212,
        283
Monotonicity of individual expenditure
    shares, 18–19, 46, 48, 106, 174, 181,
    263
Moore, J.C., 25, 165
Muellbauer, John, 14, 170, 171
    expenditure allocation, 223
    household equivalence scale, 49,
        109–110, 220, 221, 227
    inequality measurement, 99
    representative consumer concept, 2
    social welfare function, 33, 167
Murray, W., 20, 235

Natural gas price regulation, alternative
    policy analysis, 264–271, 283–287
Net equivalent variation, 186
Ng, Yew-Kuang, 66, 120
NIPA. See U.S. National Income and
    Product Accounts
NL3SLS estimator, 234, 235–236
Nominal aggregate expenditure index,
    28–29, 355–356
Nondictatorship, 118–119, 197, 273
    impossibility of, 63, 64–65
Nonhomotheticity of preferences, 166
Nonimposition, 64, 67, 118, 121, 196, 199,
    200, 272

Nonnegativity of individual expenditure
    shares, 18, 46, 106, 174
Normative economics
    econometric approach, 343
    ethical assumptions, 5

Ordinal noncomparability, 3–4, 64, 118,
    196–197, 273
    replacing with cardinal
        noncomparability, 119
Orshansky, M., 328

Pareto principle, 23, 119, 376
    conditions of, 307–308
    individual welfare conditions, 348–349
    in ordering of economic policies, 33,
        166, 195, 253, 271
    replaced by positive association and
        nonimposition, 121
    social ordering under, 9, 65, 273
    in social welfare function, 197
Parks, Richard W., 167, 222
Pashardes, Panos, 222
Petroleum price control
    alternative policy analysis, 186–194
    impact on social welfare, 212–216
PIGL demand system, 221
PIGLOG demand system, 221
Plotnick, Robert D., 335
Pollak, Robert A., 4–5, 7, 102, 167, 169, 303
    fertility choice, 34
    household equivalence scale, 222
    household welfare function, 255, 295
    social cost-of-living index, 75, 76
    social expenditure function, 205–206,
        276, 349
Poor household, 296
Population bias, 358
Positive association condition, 64, 67, 70,
    72, 118, 121, 124, 126, 196, 199, 200,
    203, 205, 272, 276
Poterba, James M., 362
Poverty. See also Elimination of poverty;
        Index of poverty
    defined, 291
    social welfare and, 295–301
    statistics, 328, 336
Poverty gap, 296, 300
    aggregate, 296
    defined, 295
    distribution of, 335

Povery gap (*cont.*)
 individual, 296
 money measure, 296, 314
Poverty measures. *See also* Index of
  poverty
 alternative approaches, 294–295,
  328–335
 econometric model, 305
 as function of head-count ratio, 294, 328
 between groups, 294
 within groups, 294, 314–322
 between groups, 322–328
 incorporating changes in prices and
  total expenditure distribution, 292
 individual welfare functions, 305–309
 relative, 335
 social welfare function, 293, 295,
  305–319
Poverty threshold, 300, 309, 315, 328, 335
 defined by individual welfare, 292, 295
 demographic characteristics, 336
 households with welfare levels below,
  295–296
 lump-sum transfer to reach, 298
 relative, 335
 threshold of affluence as function of,
  298
Prais, S.J., 166, 170, 220
Preferences. *See also* Individual
  preferences
 differences among consumers, 47
 homothetic, 99
 identical, 99, 166–167
 identical homothetic, 167
 intergenerational altruism in, 362
 for leisure and goods, 366
 nonhomotheticity, 166
 restrictions on, 343–344
Price bias, 358
Production model
 endogenous determination of
  productivity growth, 365–366
 parameterization, econometric vs.
  calibration approach, 365
Pyatt, Graham, 336

Quantity index, 13
Quantity index of efficiency, 26–27, 344,
  352, 353. *See also* Efficiency measure;
  Translog index of efficiency
Quantity index of equity, 27–28, 352–353

Quantity index of social welfare, 6
 efficiency and equity indexes, 26
 postwar period, 25
 social expenditure function, 26

Ray, Robert, 167, 222
Real aggregate expenditure per person
 biases in, 356, 357*t*, 358
 as measure of efficiency, 356, 358
 as measure of social welfare, 353,
  355–359
 vs. social standard-of-living index, 359
Real expenditure per capita as a measure
  of standard of living, 31
Redistribution locus, 299
Redistributional policy
 degree of aversion to inequality and,
  335
 within vs. between groups, 294, 326, 328
 impact on social welfare, 328
 with lump-sum transfers, 323
 optimal, 292, 297
 societal benefits from, 34, 291, 293, 335
 society's willingness to pay for, 294,
  335–336
Relative inequality
 within and between groups, 148–149,
  151
 money measure, 145, 148–149, 151
Remaining inequality. *See also* Money
  metric remaining inequality
 elimination of, 300–301, 335–336
 within groups, 315
 between groups, 322–328
 within groups, 322, 323
 index of, 299–300, 301, 328
 social welfare as measure of, 293, 295
 transfers needed to eliminate, 333, 334*t*,
  335
Representative consumer concept, 11
Rich household, 297
Richels, Richard G., 365
Roberts, Kevin W.S., 3, 65, 67, 121
 cardinal full comparability, 120–121
 cardinal unit comparability, 197, 199
 individual welfare distribution, 180
 inequality measurement, 99
 nondictatorial social ordering, 117, 119
 preference restrictions, 167, 343
 social choice framework, 63
 social welfare function, 33

Roy's (1943) Identity, 15, 171, 256, 306
  applied to translog indirect utility
      function, 43, 223
  logarithmic form, 103

Samuelson, Paul A., 7, 25, 76, 102, 166,
      169, 303
  household welfare function, 255, 295
  money metric utility concept, 186
  social welfare function, 32, 199, 253,
      291, 343
Saunders, M.A., 20, 235
Sen, Amartya K., 3, 119
  cardinal noncomparability, 65
  ordinal noncomparability, 197
  poverty measure, 335, 336
  social welfare function, 63, 66, 117, 121,
      195, 272
  welfarism, 200
Skidmore, Felicity, 335
Slesnick, Daniel T.
  commodity group classification, 18
  equality measurement, 291
  general household equivalence scale,
      336, 346
  measure of group inequality, 293, 303,
      316, 317, 323, 324
  money metric social welfare, 33–34
  progressive tax, 378
  social cost-of-living index, 28–29,
      355–359
  social welfare function, 22–23, 307, 348,
      375
Social choice
  axiomatic framework, 63, 117
  individual preferences, 2–3
  theory of, 1, 2–3
Social cost-of-living index, 75–78. *See also*
      Cost-of-living index
  defined, 28, 41, 75
  econometric approach, 87–88
  exact number approach, 89–90
  impact of price changes on, 40–41, 77
  social expenditure function, 72–73
  translog, 76, 77–78, 89–90
  U.S., 1958–1978, 77, 78*t*
Social expenditure function, 24, 349. *See
      also* Group expenditure function;
      Translog social expenditure function
  for analysis of natural gas price policy,
      284

to assess alternative policy impact, 280
defined, 4–5, 10, 40, 101, 205–206,
      276–277
to determine money metric social
      welfare, 168, 217, 344
equity and efficiency measures, 10–11,
      145
to evaluate impact of carbon tax, 377
to express quantity index of social
      welfare, 26
for gains from elimination of poverty,
      301
individual expenditure function and,
      73, 277, 303
for inequality indexes, 158–159
money measures, 10–11, 145, 168
for money metric inequality, 142–143
in social cost-of-living index, 72–73
in social standard-of-living index,
      11–13, 351
Social ordering, 195
  cardinal full comparability, 3
  class of nondictatorial, 197–198
  group, 78–79
  within group, 133
  between group, 138
  horizontal equity, 120
  impossibility of nondictatorial, 63,
      64–65, 117, 118–119, 196–197, 273
  to measure within group poverty,
      314–315
  for measuring poverty, 297, 307
  for measuring social welfare, 348–349
  notion of horizontal equity, 66
  by real-valued social welfare function, 7
  for set of all social states, 200
  in terms of social welfare function,
      22–23, 63–64, 117–118, 196–198,
      272–274
Social standard-of-living index, 344,
      351–354, 358–359. *See also* Standard-
      of-living index
  defined, 344
  efficiency and equity measures, 344
  translog, 26
Social state, 195
  characteristics of alternative, 201
  definition, 272
  individual welfare function, 347–350
  nonwelfare characteristics, 67–69, 122,
      200

Social state (*cont.*)
  ordering of, 9, 117, 200
Social welfare. *See also* Money metric
    social welfare; Quantity index of
    social welfare
  actual vs. potential level, 151, 301
  alternative policy effects, 279
  efficiency and equity measures, 277,
      396–397
  as function of price system and
      aggregate expenditure, 74, 76, 127,
      144
  impact of carbon tax on, 375–378,
      396–398
  impact of petroleum policy on, 206, 208,
      210–211, 212–216
  impact of transfers on, 46, 106–107, 174,
      258
  individual welfare and, 23, 346
  maximum level attained through lump-
      sum transfer, 12–13, 315
  maximum vs. potential level, 129
  redistributional policy effects, 34, 328
  resulting from elimination of poverty,
      295–301, 304–305, 309, 310*t*
Social welfare function, 9–10, 40, 63–74,
    271–279. *See also* Group welfare
    function; Household welfare
    function; Utilitarian social welfare
    function
  in alternative policy analysis, 195–205,
      206, 278
  anonymity property, 66, 70, 120, 198,
      202, 274
  assumption of identical homothetic
      preferences, 33, 99
  based on utilitarian social welfare
      function, 120, 198
  as cardinal measure of social welfare,
      28, 348–349
  components of, 3
  defined, 6, 63, 117, 167, 272, 291, 343
  degree of aversion to inequality, 23,
      69–70, 100, 127–128, 328
  dictatorial, 344
  in distribution of individual welfare,
      157, 363
  distributionally homothetic, 69, 123,
      201
  efficiency and equity measures,
      127–129, 130–131, 144, 278–287

equity-regarding, 71, 124, 125, 204,
    275–276, 297, 349
  in evaluation of redistributional policy,
      335
  expressing ethical judgments, 23, 68,
      117, 122, 168, 200–201, 217, 274,
      308, 349
  function $g(x)$, 69–70, 121, 122, 123, 199,
      200, 201–202
  between group, 139
  group welfare function and, 79
  horizontal equity, 10, 22–23, 70, 198,
      202, 274, 297, 349
  in implementing social welfare index,
      25–26
  income distribution vs. individual
      welfare measures, 32–33, 166
  incorporating individual welfare
      measures, 39
  incorporating nonwelfare
      characteristics, 67–69, 122
  individual welfare function and, 22
  inequality aversion parameter, 397
  intertemporal, 375–376
  limiting form, 328–329
  to measure poverty and remaining
      inequality, 293
  for measuring poverty, 307
  for money metric inequality, 144
  to order economic policies, 165–169, 195
  origin, 253
  properties of, 63–65, 117–119, 196–198
  restrictions on, 167, 343–344
  single vs. multiple profile approach, 199
  in social cost-of-living measurement,
      11–13, 63, 73, 75–76
  social ordering in terms of, 272–274
  in social standard-of-living index, 351
  translog indirect utility function, 128
  vertical equity, 10, 23, 71, 204, 275, 297,
      349
SOL/NPSOL algorithm, 20, 235
Solow, Robert M., 202
Standard of living. *See also* Cost of living
  actual to potential ratio, 13
  alternative measures, 31–32
  equity considerations, 32
  household, 8–9
  impact of price changes and
      distribution of total expenditure
      on, 29–32, 30*t*

measurement of, 25
social, 11–13
U.S, postwar period, 6
Standard-of-living index
defined, 351
efficiency and equity measures, 351–353, 359
vs. real aggregate expenditure per person, 359
U.S., postwar period, 1947–1985, 353, 354t
Stoker, Thomas M.
commodity group classification, 18
econometric model of consumer behavior, 13, 221, 254
exact aggregation theory, 42
money metric individual welfare, 33
net equivalent variation concept, 186
NL3SLS estimator, 235
Strictly merely positive subdefinite matrix, 18, 46, 106, 174
Summability of individual expenditure shares, 17, 45, 105, 173
Survey of Consumer Expenditures, 1972–1973, 19, 52, 86, 112, 181, 222, 237, 263, 347
Symmetry of individual expenditure shares, 17–18, 45–46, 105–106, 173

Tax progressivity of carbon tax, 378
Threshold of affluence, 297, 300
as function of poverty threshold, 298
individual expenditure function, 298
Törnqvist, Leo, 88–89, 90
Translog cost-of-living index, 57. See also Cost-of-living index
demographic differences, 59, 60–62t
Translog household equivalence scale, 260. See also Household equivalence scale
commodity-specific, 21, 48, 108–109, 176–177, 238, 306
general, 21, 50, 110, 177–178, 227, 261, 305–306, 346
Translog index of efficiency, 128. See also Efficiency measure; Quantity index of efficiency
for between-group welfare function, 139
within groups, 134
for money metric inequality, 147
U.S., 1958–1978, 131, 132t

Translog index of inequality, 128–129, 132, 135. See also Inequality index
defined, 131, 158
demographic differences, 1958–1978, 136, 137t
within groups, 134, 135, 139
between groups, 140–142
within groups, 140–142
between groups, 142t, 158
within groups, 158
relative, 131–132
Translog indirect utility function, 43, 85, 103, 106, 170, 223, 255–256. See also Indirect utility function
in alternative policy analysis, 263
as cardinal measure of individual welfare, 125, 275
as cardinal measure of utility, 112
determined from individual expenditure shares, 157, 216–217
as efficiency measure, 132, 158
exact aggregation conditions, 346
group welfare function for, 80
is assessing alternative policy impacts, 185
maximum level of welfare for, 24, 74, 146, 206, 277–278, 308, 350
measures of compensating variations, 186
social welfare function for, 128
in terms of household equivalence scales, 47, 107–108, 175–176, 225–226, 259
Translog individual expenditure function, 85. See also Individual expenditure function
in alternative policy analysis, 185, 263
to determine money metric individual welfare, 217
translog social expenditure function and, 149
Translog social expenditure function, 74, 76, 86, 207, 278. See also Social expenditure function
to implement social cost-of-living index, 75–76
to implement social welfare index, 25–26
for money metric inequality, 147
translog individual expenditure function and, 149

U.S. Bureau of the Census, poverty
    statistics, 328, 336
U.S. Department of Energy
    natural gas price regulation policy,
        265–266
    petroleum price control policy, 187–188
U.S. National Income and Product
        Accounts, 19, 52, 112–113, 181, 222,
        237, 263, 347
Unobservable random disturbances for all
        commodities, 229–230
Unrestricted domain, 64, 118, 196, 272
Utilitarian social welfare function, 3, 203,
        294
    applications, 66, 120, 198
    distributional considerations, 66, 120
    index of poverty for, 328–329
    to measure carbon tax impact, 397
    welfare economics, 66

Vertical equity in social welfare, 10, 71,
        125, 204, 275, 297, 349
    among individuals, 6

Wales, Terence J., 34, 167, 222
Welfare distribution. See also Inequality
        measure
    alternative policy impacts, 168
    inequality of, 99–100
Welfare economics
    of carbon tax, 372–379, 388–398
    utilitarian social welfare function in,
        66
Welfare measurement. See also Individual
        welfare function; Social welfare
        function
    based on distribution of real
        expenditure, 179–180
    between-group, 137–138, 141
    Dupuit approach, 166
Welfarism, 68, 121, 200
Wilcoxen, Peter J., 361, 362, 363, 368
Windfall profits tax
    impact of eliminating, 187, 191t, 193t,
        194, 213–215
    impact of reform, 187, 191t, 193t, 194,
        213–215
Within-group inequality, 151
    index of, 323
    money metric, 154–155, 156t
Wright, M., 20, 235

Yotopoulos, Pan A., 222

1968

A HUSBAND
IN BOARDING SCHOOL

GIOVANNI GUARESCHI IS THE AUTHOR OF

The Little World of Don Camillo

Comrade Don Camillo

My Home, Sweet Home

A Husband in Boarding School

husband
in
boarding
school

GIOVANNI
GUARESCHI

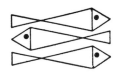

Farrar, Straus and Giroux

New York

A HUSBAND
IN BOARDING SCHOOL

Introduction

Someone once remarked to Signor Sappho Madellis that there were two possibilities: either he'd mistaken his name or he'd mistaken his sex. What reply the gentleman made is not known; what is known is that Signor Sappho Madellis succeeded in finding a certain Leonida Foulard, a girl of a very good family, and he married her, thus reestablishing a kind of equilibrium.

Sappho and Leonida then brought into the world two charming little girls, whom they named Elisabetta and Flaminia. With the passing years, Elisabetta and Flaminia became, naturally enough, enchanting young ladies, and then it was time to find husbands for them.

At this point we must note that the forebears of both the Madellis and the Foulards had taken part in the most important crusades, handing down to their descendants country seats and castles and noble blood. Though the castles and the country seats vanished in the course of the centuries, the noble blood remained intact and uncorrupted.

It was only reasonable, therefore, that when Sappho and Leonida began to seek a husband for their first-born daughter, Elisabetta, they looked among the descendants of the noblest families, and they found Gastone Food, whose ancestors had taken part in all the crusades, indiscriminately. After they took note of the fact that, with the worldly goods of the Madellis, the Foulards, and the Foods all put together, there was still nothing to live on, they sacrificed their second daughter, Flaminia, marrying her off to Tommaso Wonder, whose ancestors had not even looked on while the noble gentlemen went off on the crusades, so occupied were they selling sausages and sauerkraut, but who had nevertheless handed on to *their* descendants a small fortune which slowly, as the years went by, grew bigger and bigger until it became a large fortune. The Madellis and the Foods did Tommaso the honor of moving into his house and living there, at his expense, for some twenty years.

During this time, the House of Wonder was gladdened by the births of Robinia Food and of Edo Food and then of Carlotta Wonder. At this point, suddenly, Signor Tommaso Wonder was removed to another world, leaving the following characters in our story: Sappho Madellis, seventy;

Leonida Madellis, seventy; Gastone Food, forty-seven; his wife Elisabetta, forty-eight; his daughter Robinia, eighteen; his son Edo, sixteen; Flaminia Wonder, forty; and her daughter Carlotta, fourteen.

Next there came on the scene Casimiro Wonder, brother of the departed Tommaso. Casimiro Wonder had spent most of his life traveling, and he came home every once in a while, only to make sure that his large and untouched patrimony was still in order. He was alone in the world, and had no relations except those that Tommaso had got for him, so he decided to grant the Madellis, Foulards, etc., a fine house to live in and a monthly allowance.

"I'm giving you the money," he said, "but the house and everything in it remain mine. The day you get on my nerves, I'll kick you out, and then you won't get on my nerves any more."

At the time our story begins, Carlotta had just become twenty-two, which means that the noble family of Madellis and so on had now been living for eight years at the expense of Signor Casimiro Wonder—with the exception, that is, of Sappho Madellis, who, at seventy-seven, abandoned the affairs of this world to join his ancestors, the crusaders.

chapter 1

Donna Leonida Foulard Madellis had just rung for the coffee when the old butler, Giusmaria, came into the room and said, in an agitated voice: "He's here!"

Donna Leo grew pale, as did her daughters Elisabetta and Flaminia and her granddaughter Robinia. Signor Gastone Food frowned menacingly. Young Edo Food shrugged, and Carlotta cried: "Oh!"

Signor Casimiro Wonder had returned unexpectedly after an absence of almost two years, and in a very little while he entered the dining room as usual, his filthy old hat on his head and a cigar between his teeth. He cast an all-embracing

6

glance at the family seated around the table, and then he said: "What on earth could have happened to the old man to make him miss his dinner?"

"Signor Sappho Madellis is dead," replied Donna Leo haughtily.

"He might have let me know," Casimiro muttered. "I've told you a hundred times that in my house no one does anything without my permission."

"Sir!" cried the old lady in a tone of noble pride. "No permission is required—for centuries the Madellis have been dying perfectly well by themselves."

"The trouble is they don't know how to live by themselves," Casimiro observed with a shrug. Then, turning to Carlotta, he demanded: "Well? Am I going to meet that scamp of a husband?"

Everyone looked at Carlotta in astonishment; embarrassed, she lowered her head.

"The last time I was here, I told Carlotta that when I came back I wanted to meet the man she'd chosen for her husband, so if I liked him, the wedding could take place before I went away again. It looks to me as if Miss Carlotta hasn't paid the slightest attention to my orders!"

Donna Flaminia exclaimed angrily that she had no intention of giving her daughter a husband.

"But I do!" cried Casimiro. "Since I have no family and am going to leave my money to my niece when I die, I want to see what kind of man she's going to marry. I'll never let her marry a crook who's going to steal her money. Either she marries somebody I like or I leave all my money to charity."

"But, Uncle," Carlotta interrupted, "I don't see why there has to be such a rush. You're young and healthy and I don't think you have any intention of dying soon."

Casimiro replied that his intentions were his own business and that this was something else altogether: his orders had been disobeyed. Furthermore, he warned: "If by the day after tomorrow you're not married to a man I approve of, I'll not only leave everything I have to the poor, I'll kick you all out of the house and cut off your income."

Carlotta knew her uncle well, and she knew that he meant what he said. "But Uncle Casimiro," she moaned in despair, "how can I find a husband in two days?"

"That's a woman's business," Casimiro replied. "Work it out—you've had plenty of time already."

It was a serious matter, and old Donna Leo looked at Flaminia. Flaminia nodded and looked at her sister Elisabetta. Elisabetta indicated she had understood and looked at her husband Gastone. Gastone glanced at his daughter Robinia, and Robinia whispered something into her brother Edo's ear.

Edo rose. His face was pallid with the depth of his emotion. "Signor Wonder," he said, breaking the profound silence, "I ask for the hand of your niece in marriage."

"They grew up together," explained Elisabetta, "and they've always been fond of one another."

Casimiro looked at Edo, then took Carlotta by the shoulders.

"Is it true," he asked indignantly, "that you love that idiotic-looking creature?"

Carlotta shook her head, and Casimiro calmed down.

"So much the better," he said. "And that's enough of this silly chatter. Either you're married by evening the day after tomorrow or I throw the lot of you out. Tomorrow I'll stay home, at the Palazzetto. When you've got something ready, bring it around and show it to me. Just remember I don't want any blonds, and redheads are even worse. Better if they're bald!"

Then Casimiro growled at the butler to stop sleeping all the time and look after things, and pulling a chair out from under Gastone, he said: "Have this fixed! Can't you see one of the legs is about to come off?"

Then he went out and they all looked after him, slumped dispiritedly in their chairs, except Gastone, who remained standing, ill-treated and ignored but proud.

Around the coffee table there occurred the most dramatic of meetings of the House of Madellis. Having barred the doors, Donna Leo raised her arms to the heavens and cried: "That man is insane!"

"Criminally insane," added Robinia, who, unmarried at twenty-six, had no patience with the idea that a girl of twenty-two should be required to marry within two days.

"Insane or not, if Carlotta isn't married by the day after tomorrow, we'll all end up on the sidewalk," said Edo, who did not lack a certain common sense.

All were quiet as they peered around at Carlotta. Carlotta, at last, rose.

"I'm going," she said.

"Where?"

"To find a husband, for I will never let it be said that because of me an entire family has been hurled to ruin. And then after all, when you come down to it, a husband may be a chronic nuisance but never a fatal illness."

"A husband?" repeated Donna Flaminia, in an anguished tone. "And how are you going to find yourself one, in a few hours, if you don't have, and never have had, a fiancé?"

Carlotta shrugged.

"Aha!" Donna Flaminia pressed on. "Do you mean to say that without the knowledge of your grandmother or the approval of your family you have been carrying on clandestine flirtations with one, two, or maybe even three young men, as is the habit of the badly brought up girls of today? In God's name, Carlotta, answer me!"

"No," Carlotta answered, "I have no secret fiancé. I know a few boys that I like, that's all."

"What a pity," breathed the loving mother. "If only you had a few fiancés, everything would have been a lot easier."

"I am going," Carlotta repeated.

The ladies began to sob, protesting that Carlotta must not sacrifice herself in this way and that they would never allow her to commit such an act of folly, and meanwhile they accompanied her to the door.

"What a kind and generous soul!" Gastone murmured admiringly.

Edo meanwhile breathed heavenward a passionate prayer:

"Dear God, I thank you for having saved me from Carlotta. Dear God, I would rather be condemned to the most terrible punishment than to a wife like Carlotta. You could even make me work. . . ."

After she left the house, Carlotta made her way to the Old Park, a lonely neighborhood and not at all suitable for finding husbands in, but it was well thought of by people who wanted to be alone to consider their own affairs in peace and quiet.

And this remarkable young lady felt an urgent need to think things over and reach some kind of conclusion.

It will suffice to report here the conclusion that Carlotta, after deep deliberation, arrived at: "There are five men who, despite their failure to become my boyfriends, have nonetheless continued to desire to marry me: Count Donalot, Doctor Grimal, Signor De Parpay, Flamel, and Gigi. Of these five, the first three are not of the slightest interest to me, but I like Flamel and Gigi very much. Gigi particularly I feel I might quite easily fall in love with. Flamel particularly, too. Yes, particularly the first and the second—particularly both of them, in fact. So as far as marriage goes, Gigi and Flamel are out of the question, because if I married the first I'd be ready to cut my head off for not having married the second, and vice versa. And to marry both of them is beyond me. But I could marry one of the other three and become engaged secretly one day to Gigi and one day to Flamel. . . ."

It may not have been a magnificent piece of logic, ethically speaking, but there was a certain reasonableness about it.

And, as Carlotta remained convinced of the correctness of her judgment, she left the Old Park and took a taxi to the Palazzetto. She found Uncle Casimiro in his study, busily turning over the pages of account books.

"Uncle Casimiro," she said sweetly, "you are absolutely right, and I will do all I can to be married by the day after tomorrow. But you'll have to help me."

"I'm not a matrimonial agency," Uncle Casimiro replied brusquely.

"I'm not suggesting you are," said Carlotta, "and I'm not asking you to find me a husband either. I'll find him myself without very much difficulty. In fact, three gentlemen have already asked for my hand time and again. All we have to do now is find out which of the three you like."

"I've already told you," said Uncle Casimiro. "Bring him here and we'll see."

Carlotta explained that one could not say point blank to a gentleman: "Come with me, Uncle Casimiro wants to see what you're like—if he approves, you can marry me." To do things right, they had to find a good excuse to bring the three to meet Uncle Casimiro. That way he could have a look at the birds and make his choice.

"We might," Carlotta said, "have a little party to celebrate your return. I could invite the three gentlemen and introduce them to you, and you could study them at your leisure. Of course you'd have to make an effort for two or three hours and try to be nice."

Uncle Casimiro grumbled in an angry tone that he'd been

around and didn't need instructions on how to behave, but he agreed to the idea.

"Tomorrow night at nine," he said, "I'll be at your house, and we'll see what's what. But you better be ready by tomorrow night because no matter how you rush things you still need a day to get married in."

"It's up to you, Uncle Casimiro. You choose the one you like, I'll do exactly what you say."

"Very well," said Uncle Casimiro approvingly.

Carlotta ran home to tell her family about her plan and then to write the invitations and then to get things ready for the fatal party.

chapter 2

PART ONE

The next morning, the principal protagonists of the Madellis family began to suffer the torments of purgatory.

"God only knows how that savage will behave," moaned Donna Leo, as she held her smelling salts to her nose.

"I wouldn't be surprised," Elisabetta wailed, "if he came dressed as a cowboy."

"He'll spit on the ceiling!" cried another.

"He'll curse in seven languages!"

"He'll poke his finger at the young ladies!"

Uncle Casimiro, however, did not come dressed as a

14

cowboy but instead wore a well-cut dinner jacket, and he did not spit on the ceiling or poke his finger at the young ladies. He almost seemed well brought up.

There were a number of guests; among them, naturally, the three candidates for Carlotta's hand. She handled them very carefully. She managed to withdraw into a quiet corner first with one, then with the other, and then with the third; she was noncommittal with all three, and she let all three know that Uncle Casimiro possessed a peculiar power over her.

"It is he," she said, "who rules my life. I could never marry a man he didn't like. It must seem a very peculiar thing indeed that in order to marry Carlotta a man must pay court not to Carlotta but to Uncle Casimiro."

When she finished speaking, first one, then the other, and then the third pressed the dainty little hand that Carlotta had absent-mindedly left in theirs, after which they took off to confront Uncle Casimiro.

Following the introductions and a bit of amiable chatter, Uncle Casimiro decorously withdrew to the little Japanese room to smoke his cigar, and it was there that Count Donalot, first of the three suitors for Carlotta's languorous hand, found him.

"Sir," he said politely to Uncle Casimiro, "shall we help each other to eliminate boredom by a hand at cards?"

Uncle Casimiro accepted with good grace and played cards and chatted with Count Donalot. Then an opportune hint from Carlotta called the Count elsewhere, and he was succeeded by Doctor Grimal, who in turn was followed by

Signor De Parpay. In brief, Carlotta managed things so well that her three suitors had the chance, one after the other, to try to enchant her authoritarian uncle.

Which one of the three succeeded in winning the affections of Signor Wonder became known only later, when Uncle Casimiro called Carlotta to him, and asked her harshly: "Well? Am I to see the three famous champions, or not?"

"Uncle Casimiro," Carlotta replied smiling, "you've already seen them—they are the three gentleman with whom you have just spent so much time. Now all you have to do is choose—which of the three do you prefer?"

"Not any one of them!" Uncle Casimiro barked in his most peremptory tone. "Show me some others or it's all off."

Carlotta gently tried to explain to him that her collection of admirers was now exhausted, and she saw no immediate way to replenish it.

"Grant me an extension," she asked. "I have no other candidates to offer you at the moment."

Uncle Casimiro looked at his watch. "It's almost midnight," he said, "and I am aware of the difficulties you might encounter in getting hold of some new numskulls. I will therefore grant you an extension of twelve hours. If you haven't found a husband I like by noon tomorrow, you're just out of luck."

"But Uncle Casimiro!" Carlotta implored him. "Please remember that I live in a fashionable world where men never get up before noon. Would you force me to go around getting young men in pajamas out of their beds?"

"Well, another five hours of extension then," grumbled Uncle Casimiro. "Zero hour is now five o'clock in the afternoon. Good night to you. And the devil take all the other nitwits that are here."

"Where shall I bring the candidates to you?" Carlotta sounded frightened.

"Not here, that's for sure. At my house."

Uncle Casimiro departed, and a little later, after the guests had departed too, Carlotta gave her family an account of what had happened.

"Now what?" said Signor Gastone, much worried. "Where do we find any more candidates?"

"I certainly didn't ask your help to find the first batch," Carlotta told him, "and I'm not going to ask it for the second."

Carlotta retired to her room and fell asleep soon after making this new decision: "Tomorrow I'll throw Flamel and Gigi into the assault on Uncle Casimiro. If he likes Gigi, I'll marry Gigi and get engaged to Flamel. If he likes Flamel, I'll marry Flamel and get engaged to Gigi. And if he likes them both . . ." Carlotta laughed to herself. "If he likes them both, I'll marry them both."

"And if he doesn't like either one?" asked an inner voice.

"Then let all three of them go to the devil—Flamel, Gigi, and Uncle Casimiro.

PART TWO

"Heads for Gigi, tails for Flamel," said Carlotta, as she tossed a coin in the air.

Tails came up as it fell on the rug. Carlotta jumped out of bed, dressed with special care, and as it was already past noon, ate heartily.

"You're taking it awfully easy," observed Edo, who was not without a certain degree of common sense. "Will you still have time to call a general assembly of your boyfriends? Wouldn't it be better to print an order and summon them here, say, according to their draft cards?"

"I forbid you to make jokes about such a serious subject," said Donna Leo. "I'm sure that you, even for the good of your family, couldn't do as well."

"That's true," Edo admitted honestly, for he was not without a certain degree of common sense. "I'd never be able to find a husband in three hours."

Carlotta got up from the table.

"There's no point," she said, "in going anywhere before two. Only after two do I know where to find them, those chickens of mine."

From two in the afternoon on (that is to say, until two the next morning), Gigi and Flamel were available respectively at the Hunt Club and the White Rose, where they could always be found around the baccarat and poker tables.

Carlotta calmly went to her usual café in the Old Park, and from there telephoned the White Rose, asking for

Flamel. The gentleman came to the phone at once but had very little time to say anything. Carlotta came to the point at once.

"Flam, this is Carlotta. I'll meet you at the café in the Old Park in ten minutes. Very urgent, maximum importance." She hung up.

Then she telephoned the Hunt Club and asked for Gigi. She wanted to know his precise location so she could rush him to Uncle Casimiro should her first candidate flunk out.

She was told that Gigi had just gone out, but Carlotta wasn't worried. "Lazy as he is, he couldn't have gone very far," she thought. "He'll be back soon." She didn't think about him for long, however, for Flamel arrived shortly.

"Flam," cried Carlotta, putting her hands on his shoulders and staring into his eyes. "Flam, do you really love me, or don't you?"

"I'll do anything," Flamel panted, "no matter how crazy, to prove it."

"This is your chance then. Go to my uncle Casimiro and ask for my hand in marriage."

"From your uncle Casimiro?"

"Yes, from him. He wants me to get married before tomorrow or—I can tell you this—he'll cut me out of his will. I don't have anyone else in the world but you, Flam . . ."

"I'll fly to your uncle, Carlotta! Oh, how happy I am! Oh, the immeasurable joy of it!"

"Take it easy, Flam," Carlotta warned him. "Don't build

too many castles in the air. We can get married only if my uncle likes you. And he's so very strange . . ."

"Oh, I've tamed wild animals a lot wilder than that wild uncle of yours," boasted Flamel gaily.

Uncle Casimiro was in his study and remained seated at his desk when Carlotta came in with Flamel. He did not rise when Carlotta presented the gentleman to him.

"Signor Flamel wants to speak to you, Uncle Casimiro," Carlotta murmured and backed out into the adjoining room to await the results of the examination.

"I have," said Flamel as soon as he found himself alone with Signor Wonder, "the honor of requesting the hand of your niece Carlotta."

"You're an odd kind of guy," Uncle Casimiro grumbled. "You've only just met me and you're already asking me for something. But, tell me now, why do you want to marry Carlotta?"

"Because—because I love her!" Flamel stammered, embarrassed.

"And does she love you?"

"Yes, of course."

"That's a pack of lies, my fine young fellow. If that's the way things were, you'd have married her without asking my permission. Love doesn't think about uncles. Therefore, you're a liar."

"Not at all," Flamel explained. "We haven't married because until today Carlotta didn't want to. If it were up to me, we'd have got married two years ago."

"Then you have no pride. When a woman puts too high a price on herself, then you should tell her to go to the devil. Let's see your hands."

Flamel held out his hands.

"The index finger and the middle finger of your right hand are stained with nicotine. You smoke too many cigarettes, one after the other. Say 'thirty-three.'"

"Thirty-three," said Flamel, as Uncle Casimiro put his ear against the young man's back.

"Weak lungs," grumbled Uncle Casimiro. "You've been sitting around in closed rooms. You're as white as a sheet. Do you know how to play *scopa*?"

"I play very little," lied Flamel, for he didn't want to seem like a wastrel.

"So much the worse for you. I always let luck decide. Take that deck of cards and sit down here. We'll have a game—if you win, I'll give you the hand of Carlotta; if you lose, you don't get anything."

It was a lightning-quick game. Flamel, who thought he was an experienced *scopa* player, lost so fast and so thoroughly he could only sit there looking at Uncle Casimiro with his mouth open.

"I've played twenty thousand games," he cried at last, "but I've never played against anyone as good as you are."

"While I," said Uncle Casimiro, "have cheated at least forty thousand times but never against a player as dumb as you are." And he began to draw sevens out of his sleeves, his pockets, his collar, and the cuffs of his trousers. "A player as obstinate and as stupid as you would go through my niece's inheritance in a couple of years."

"But, sir," Flamel protested, "you've judged me wrongly —I'm a gentleman and I spend only my own money."

"We'll soon find out about *that,* young man. I'll give you the hand of my niece on condition that you renounce her dowry entirely."

"I accept!" cried Flamel, with a noble light in his eyes.

Uncle Casimiro shook his head.

"Do you perhaps doubt my sincerity, Signor Wonder?"

"On the contrary, Signor Flamel. It's quite obvious that you are speaking in perfectly good faith. And that's the whole trouble. Only a romantic fool would give up an inheritance like that. No, you're not the man for us."

He accompanied Flamel to the door, where, in a loud voice, Uncle Casimiro called, "Send in another!"

Carlotta and Flamel looked at each other for a long time; then Flamel shrugged his shoulders and left, while Carlotta went into her uncle's study.

"Hurry up," said Uncle Casimiro, without raising his head from his papers. "Let's cut out the compliments and get to the point—why do you want to marry my niece?"

"This is me, Uncle, Carlotta."

"Oh? Then where are the others? It's now four-fifteen," growled Uncle Casimiro. "Your time runs out, my girl, in three quarters of an hour."

"Then let me have a few more hours," begged Carlotta. "It's not so easy to scrape a lot of suitors together. Be nice for once in your life!"

Uncle Casimiro grumbled a bit, then said he would wait until eight o'clock that evening. But after eight there would be no possibility of changing anything.

Carlotta rushed over to the Hunt Club and in a voice trembling with anxiety asked for Gigi, for Gigi by now was her last hope. They told her that Gigi had left about two o'clock and had not yet come back. A gentleman explained the situation to her, "Gigi's at home. It's useless to call him because I myself have just put the telephone inside the safe. Gigi's asleep and doesn't want to be disturbed."

By now it was six-thirty in the evening, and time was of the essence. Carlotta had herself driven to Gigi's house and began to hammer on the door.

An old nurse tried to stop her, but Carlotta talked her way into the house and succeeded in finding Gigi's bedroom.

The wretch was stretched out with an ice bag on his head and so deeply asleep that Carlotta had to smack him soundly in order to wake him.

"I pass," muttered Gigi. Carlotta went on shaking him, and when he opened his eyes at last, he said: "I didn't get any sleep last night. I was playing cards and drinking and smoking until two in the morning. When I finally got to bed, my eyes were on fire and my head was thumping like a hammer. Let me sleep, Gelsomina."

"I'm not your nurse," cried the girl, shaking him and sprinkling water in his face. "I'm Carlotta!"

"Carlotta? My God, what's happened?"

"Get up!" said Carlotta. "And go straight to my uncle,

and if you love me as much as you claim, ask him if you can marry me!"

"But how can I, my darling?" moaned Gigi. "Don't you see I can't even stand up? What would your uncle think of me if I turned up in this miserable condition?"

All that was true enough, but Carlotta did not yet give up the ship.

"Pretend that you're really sick," she said. "I'll persuade my uncle to come here, and when he sees how things are, he'll let me have another extension."

"All right, Carlotta," said Gigi, "and may God have mercy on us."

And so Carlotta appeared once again before her uncle Casimiro, who began at once to holler that this was nothing but an excuse and that he couldn't possibly do it, but after an impassioned plea by his niece, he agreed to visit the sick man. Twenty minutes later, preceded by Carlotta, he entered Gigi's room.

The wretch had fallen asleep again and was snoring in the most disgusting fashion.

Carlotta shook him. "Gigi," she implored, "here is my uncle—open your eyes for a minute."

"The hell with all uncles," muttered Gigi.

"He's delirious," Carlotta said to Uncle Casimiro.

Then to Gigi she said gently: "Gigi, it's me, Carlotta. Wake up for a minute, don't torture me this way."

The wretch did at last wake up but could open only half an eye.

"I am very ill," he mumbled. "Please excuse me, sir, but I am very very ill and here on my bed of pain I ask your hand in marriage—"

"You," said Uncle Casimiro, "are the most shamelessly drunk human being I have ever seen in my entire life. You are disgusting."

"I mean," said Gigi, "I want to marry the hand of your niece," and promptly fell asleep again and resumed his snoring.

Carlotta found herself in a carriage beside her uncle. "Wonderful merchandise you offer," said Signor Wonder, in a disgusted tone. "Well, anyway, it's over and done with now. Your time runs out in half an hour. And I swear to you I will have no more pity on you."

"I understand, Uncle," Carlotta remarked bitterly. "It's precisely what you wanted. You must always have your way."

"All right, all right!" said Uncle Casimiro. "I'll let you have until ten o'clock tomorrow morning. But if by ten o'clock tomorrow morning you don't bring me the man you're going to marry within the day, I'll cancel your allowance and I'll throw you all out. And then I'll change my will."

When she got back home, Carlotta refused to make a report on the situation as it then was. She postponed it all until morning.

"Set the alarm for six," she told Giusmaria. When the old butler asked if the alarm was only for her, she replied: "No, it's for everybody except me. I won't need to be awakened."

And that night, truthfully enough, Carlotta slept not a wink, and at five in the morning she was already walking in the garden.

The meeting was held in the drawing room, and the sleepy eyes of the delegates were hardly open, but after Carlotta retold the events of the previous evening, they flew wide apart and the last traces of sleep vanished with a wink. A prolonged and animated discussion followed.

"It's inhuman," cried Gastone Food indignantly, "to suppose that a poor little girl could find a husband in four hours."

"In one hour," corrected Edo Food, who was not without a certain degree of common sense.

The clock, confirming his announcement, struck nine.

"Well, then," said Edo, breaking the silence, "do we pack our bags?"

"Not yet!" cried Carlotta, rising. "Let me think."

"In God's name, think fast!" begged her aunt Elisabetta. "Time is flying!"

Carlotta ran up the stairs to her room, closed and locked the door, and went to the window that looked out onto the garden. At the very moment that she rested her elbows on the cold marble of the sill, she felt something damp and pungent cross her face.

The house that Signor Wonder had assigned to the Madellis family was one of those great old mansions that may still be seen today in streets which the unwholesome mania for orderly rows of floors and the frenzied imagination of the new architects have not yet succeeded in destroying. They are long, one-storied buildings with great ornaments on the façade, with bulging gratings over the ground-floor windows, and with a huge door in the center. The plan of these buildings is almost invariably a U. The base of the U is the front of the house and looks onto the public street; in the middle is a great courtyard; beyond it stands a garden. When the sun strikes the back of the house, the huge door in the darkened façade opens like a great eye full of a soft green light.

Onto the ample garden of the Madellis' house opened the window of Carlotta's room, which was at the end of the right wing of the building. When she was in her room, Carlotta could see whoever happened to be on the other side of the wall in the neighboring garden. And vice versa: whoever happened to be on the other side of the wall, in the neighboring garden, could see, if nothing more, at least the window from which Carlotta often leaned. It is because of this that Camillo Debrai, Carlotta's neighbor and the melancholy hero of this tale, often saw Carlotta leaning on her sill. Too often, to be precise.

Camillo Debrai, at this time, was twenty-five years old; he had a very pleasing and attractive air but—aside from his profession of woodcarver—possessed nothing else. He worked in a small room on the ground floor of the house next door to that of the Madellis, and when he had to carve large pieces of wood moved his workroom out into the garden because of lack of space.

The ancestors of Camillo Debrai had not gone off to the crusades, like the maternal forebears of Carlotta: but this did not prevent Camillo from falling in love with Carlotta Wonder. For her part, Carlotta Wonder was not even aware of the existence of the unhappy lover: however, she was aware, and had been for almost two years, of a mysterious bunch of flowers that appeared daily in her room.

Carlotta might find the flowers on the bed or on the floor, or perhaps on the dressing table. She had often wondered about the source of this sweet-smelling homage: but she discovered who it was only that morning when she leaned out the window. The homage, in fact, struck her right in the face—and the man who bestowed it had no time to hide.

Thus Carlotta discovered that she had a fourth suitor, perhaps the most tenacious of the lot.

Camillo wore a big gray apron from whose pocket stuck out the handle of a hammer and the blade of a chisel. On his head was the battered crown of an old hat, as greasy as a pancake. But by then it was twenty minutes past nine o'clock, and Carlotta could no longer quibble.

"A gift from God!" said Carlotta to herself, and a minute later was down in the garden, where she climbed up a ladder and leaned over the wall onto the neighboring garden.

Terrified by all that had happened, Camillo was still standing there, with his mouth open, staring up at Carlotta's window. He paled when he saw the head of Carlotta herself appear miraculously above the garden wall.

"What kind of work do you do?" Carlotta asked him.

"Woodcarving," Camillo stammered.

"Excellent! There's some very urgent work for you at the Palazzetto Wonder, in Piazza Tokai. Wash your hands and face, put your best clothes on, and hurry to the Palazzetto. You'll find me in front of the door. Be polite—don't keep me waiting."

"Yes, ma'am," said Camillo, in a trembling voice.

chapter 3

The minute Signor Wonder saw Carlotta, he asked her what she had decided.

"I've brought you a new candidate," she said.

"Only one?" barked Casimiro. "That's not a very wide assortment."

"It's the best I can do, Uncle. May I present him to you?"

Uncle Casimiro advised her to get a move on, for her time was getting short, and Carlotta ran down the stairs with a prayer in her heart that that shabby-looking creature wouldn't keep her waiting.

But the shabby-looking creature was already in the doorway, still out of breath from having run all the way.

Carlotta looked at him in astonishment. Cleaned up now, he seemed—except for the terrible cut of his clothes—a very handsome young man. But that, in any case, was of secondary importance.

"What's your name?" Carlotta asked.

"Camillo Debrai."

"Come with me, then, Signor Debrai. I want to introduce you to my uncle."

"Yes, ma'am," stammered Camillo, following her up the stairs.

Uncle Casimiro was writing and calmly went on writing when Carlotta came in with Camillo in tow.

"This is Signor Camillo Debrai," said Carlotta.

"All right," answered her uncle. "Leave him here. And meanwhile you go over and have a look at my bags—they're packing them for me."

Camillo stood stiff as a board in front of Signor Wonder's desk. He could not manage to persuade himself that there was any reality in all the things that had happened to him so suddenly. In any event, connecting it all with the unfortunate bunch of roses that had struck Carlotta in the face, he could only pray God that he wasn't going to get into too much trouble.

Uncle Casimiro put down his pen, rose, and looked Camillo over carefully.

"All right, you," he said, at last, in a severe tone, "what kind of work do you do?"

"Woodcarving," Camillo replied, growing even paler.

"Furniture, statuettes, candelabra, ceilings, and cabinets. I also do some inlaying."

Uncle Casimiro drew closer to the unhappy youth and wagged a menacing finger under his nose.

"And you," he growled, "you with an income of two francs a day, you have the nerve to think you can marry Carlotta Wonder, heiress to fifteen farms, six large houses, a forest, and two stables!"

"Sir," Camillo said, trembling, "I haven't done anything wrong. I came here because the young lady said you had some urgent work for me. I can leave right away if you like."

"How did you come to meet my niece?" asked Uncle Casimiro.

"It was an accident, sir."

"An accident?"

"Yes, sir. A bunch of flowers fell out of my hands onto the young lady's head. Then the young lady told me to come here because of some urgent work."

Somewhat bewildered, Uncle Casimiro looked at the unhappy Camillo. "Where was she when the flowers fell?"

"At the window of her room."

"And you?"

"Down in the garden of my house."

Uncle Casimiro nodded gravely.

"Strange kind of flowers," he said, "that fall up from below. Is it the first time that's happened to you?"

Camillo was confused. First he said, "No, sir," and then

he said, "Yes, sir," and he ended up with the announcement that he was an honest man.

"I get it," said Uncle Casimiro. "This is what they do so as not to lose out. They pick the first thing that comes along and they think that in order to avoid ridicule to the family I'll put it all off till doomsday. I'll show them!"

Uncle Casimiro had Carlotta called.

"Excellent, my dear Carlottina," he cried. "I'm fully satisfied with your choice. Now I'll have my secretary get everything in order."

Carlotta grew pale. "Yes, Uncle Casimiro," she managed to stammer out.

Camillo inquired timidly if they had any further need of him.

"No," answered Uncle Casimiro. "You hurry up and get the wedding certificate and bring it to me here before noon."

"Wedding certificate? Yes, sir. Whose wedding?"

"Yours, by God!"

Camillo wondered who was crazy, he or the others. "Excuse me, sir," he said daringly, at last, "but who is it I'm supposed to marry?"

"My niece Carlotta!" shouted Uncle Casimiro. "Why? Have you changed your mind? Isn't it true you're so madly in love with her you throw bunches of flowers secretly into her room every morning?"

"But, sir, I don't have any money—"

"Money, I've got money! And I'll give it to whomever I

like. So hurry up—and get back here before noon with the wedding certificate."

Camillo went toward the door, where he stopped, turned around, and looked first at the uncle and then at the niece. Then he vanished.

"Hard to get everything done in one day," observed Uncle Casimiro. "I'll put off my departure in any case. Never fear, my little Carlottina, Uncle Casimiro only wants his little niece to be happy and will stay by her side till her dream of love comes true. Are you satisfied?"

In the Madellis house, the second conference of the day took place that afternoon. It was highly dramatic.

"What?" shrieked Donna Flaminia when Carlotta had told her story. "My daughter marry a miserable woodcutter!"

"Our house will be loaded with ridicule," moaned Donna Elisabetta, while Gastone, with his eyes fixed on the ceiling, kept saying over and over: "Madness . . . Madness . . ."

"Now what man will come near me," sobbed Robinia, "when they know my cousin has married a beggar?" It was a relief to Robinia at last to find a reason why no man had yet asked for her hand in marriage, not even by mistake.

"If he's a good woodcarver," said Edo cheerfully, for he was not without a degree of common sense, "I'll have my cousin carve me a magnificent decorated pipe to put over my fireplace."

Thereupon the meeting continued more calmly under the direction of Donna Leo, and at last a somewhat satisfying conclusion was reached. The wedding would be celebrated secretly—there was no need to publish the banns. Then afterwards . . . but Donna Leo did not care to go into the subject any further.

"I have my own idea," she said, "and it's the best idea of all. Given time, everything will work out all right. Meanwhile, and most important, we'll change the staff. We'll keep only Giusmaria. Giusmaria can be trusted."

So spoke Donna Leo, and the Madellis-Foulard-Wonder-Food family breathed a sigh of relief.

Meanwhile, in a room at the Palazzetto, Camillo Debrai, weakened by a high fever, allowed a considerable number of specialists to measure him with impunity for suits, hats, shoes, shirts, and gloves.

chapter 4

The Debrai-Wonder wedding was celebrated so discreetly that Camillo Debrai himself—although, in his capacity as bridegroom, he was unquestionably present—knew very little about it. Even later, after he'd had a chance to think the whole thing over, he could recall only that one evening, in an unfamiliar little country church, an old priest had asked him suddenly if he took this woman Carlotta Wonder to be his wife; and that he, after he'd turned his head and discovered, to his astonishment, that this woman was indeed Carlotta Wonder, had replied: "Yes, sir."

Except for Signor Casimiro Wonder and the members of the Madellis family, nobody was aware that the noble Signorina Carlotta Wonder had been united in the bonds of matrimony to Signor Camillo Debrai, woodcarver.

When the ceremony was ended, Camillo and Carlotta got into a railway carriage for their honeymoon, planned by Signor Casimiro Wonder, but the first-class compartment reserved for the wedding couple was arranged in a rather unusual fashion: on the left, Carlotta Wonder Debrai, her mother Flaminia Madellis Wonder, her aunt Elisabetta Madellis Food, and her cousin Robinia Food; on the right, her grandmother Donna Leonida Foulard Madellis, her uncle Gastone Food, and her cousin Edo Food.

The bridegroom, Camillo, was therefore, quite properly, asked to find accommodation in a neighboring compartment.

This separation from Carlotta by a mere wooden partition lasted only during the train trip. After they reached their destination, Carlotta, her mother, her grandmother, her aunt, her uncle, and her cousin took rooms in one hotel, while Camillo and his cousin Edo had their rooms in a hotel in the opposite quarter of the city.

On the return trip it was hardly different. Since all the other compartments were occupied, Camillo stood in the corridor of the coach and every once in a while caught a glimpse—through glass doors—of his wife.

It would be interesting, certainly, to describe Camillo's state of mind, but that, alas, is impossible, for Camillo, even at the end of his honeymoon with the Madellis family, did not possess a state of mind. That he had loved Carlotta for such a long time makes little difference. History relates how the Marquis of Toupie fell passionately in love with the daughter of Count Veramon, and passed back and forth under the balcony where his beloved used to sit and look out. Even though the Marquis of Toupie, unlike Camillo Debrai, had taken regular courses in theology and mathematics and was the possessor, therefore, of a solid culture, on the day that the balcony collapsed and the lovely girl fell on his head, he too, just like Camillo, found himself quite unexpectedly without a state of mind. And not only that one day, but for another two months.

When the group honeymoon was over, the Madellis family returned to its place of residence. More precisely, it returned there and it didn't return there, since they temporarily left the big house in the city and settled in the Trebotton villa, where they customarily went for the summer. The staff, save for Giusmaria, the old and very discreet butler, was completely changed, so all that was necessary now was to bring Giusmaria up to date. This faithful servant was received one day in private audience by Donna Leo.

"As you will have observed," she said, "we have something new. Do you by any chance recall having seen before the person who is with us now?"

"If my memory is correct," Giusmaria replied, "the person to whom you are referring is the young man who a month ago was a woodcarver living in the house whose garden is next to that of your old house in the city."

"Excellent, Giusmaria," said Donna Leo. "But from now on you will recall nothing of the sort."

"Very well, madam. May I ask then how the person of whom you are speaking is to be treated? As a guest?"

Donna Leo thought for a moment.

"More or less," she replied at last.

"More or less in the sense of 'less' or in the sense of 'more'?"

"In the sense of 'more.'"

"How painful," sighed Giusmaria, with sincere regret. "And how do I refer to the person under discussion? I don't even know his name."

"His name is Camillo Debrai," breathed Donna Leo.

"Then he may be referred to simply as Camillo."

Donna Leo sighed. "Signor Camillo," she corrected.

"How painful," said Giusmaria. "May I say that the title seems unsuited to his rank? I should think that permitting him to be called Signor Debrai would already be a considerable concession for a guest."

"I said 'more than a guest,'" Donna Leo insisted. "He must be regarded as almost a member of the family."

"How *very* painful," said Giusmaria.

"It's painful also for us."

"But 'almost,'" said Giusmaria, "in the sense of 'much' or in the sense of 'little'?"

"In the sense," Donna Leo felt herself obliged to admit, "of 'rather.'"

"I refuse to believe it, madam!" cried Giusmaria.

Donna Leo shook her head. "You must obey instructions, Giusmaria," she said.

"I hope madam will excuse me," Giusmaria continued, "if

I go on with a discussion so obviously painful. But I should like to know how I am to explain to the staff the position of the person of whom you have been speaking."

"As a poor and distant relation."

"Very well, madam. A poor and distant relation."

"A distant rich relation," Donna Leo said, "might be better."

"Yes, madam. A rich and distant relation."

Donna Leo remained lost in thought for a moment; then she came to a decision. "A distant and simple-minded relation," she said.

Giusmaria nodded. " 'Simple-minded,' " he asked, "in the sense of 'much' or 'little'?"

"In the sense of 'rather,' Giusmaria. It's less binding."

A verbatim transcription of the historic colloquy held in the green room has been recorded here not out of pedantry but in order to give a clear idea of the cordiality with which Camillo Debrai, partially married to Carlotta Wonder, was received in the Madellis house. The colloquy is important also because, while it was occurring in the green room, another and no less important event took place not very far away: Camillo was experiencing the first suggestions of a state of mind.

He was standing motionless in the center of a small single room. "I said I was willing to marry Signorina Carlotta," he thought, "and I was. But how do I know if she was willing to marry me or not, since I haven't yet been able to speak to her?"

He realized that by now a month had passed since the nocturnal ceremony in the little church, and that an explanation of sorts was in order.

"Maybe," he thought, "she's mad at me because I said I was willing to marry her without first asking her whether she was willing that I should be willing to marry her. But how could I do it, when Signor Casimiro wouldn't even let me go out of my room? Anyway, is it my fault if I love her?"

Quite clearly, these were the first symptoms of a state of mind. Very faint symptoms, for otherwise Camillo would have wondered why he let them treat him like the stupidest man in creation. Instead he fell asleep, concluding with easy optimism, "You'll have to understand it, esteemed Signorina Carlotta, for yourself. That's the way love is."

chapter 5

Once they had accepted, so far as Camillo Debrai was concerned, the provision that he was a distant and simple-minded relation, in the sense of "rather," the servants in the Madellis house found it only natural that he should spend his days and eat his meals in his room.

The one who found it less than natural was Camillo Debrai. After four more extremely dismal days had passed, Camillo decided that the situation was no longer bearable.

"I'll speak to her," he said to himself. "And if she won't listen to me, then I'll write her!"

Having, in this state of mind, reached the bottom of the stairway, he stood perplexed, wondering in what direction to set his uncertain feet, when the good Lord caused Giusmaria, the omnipresent butler, to appear in front of him.

"Excuse me," said Camillo, "but may I speak to my wife?"

"Doubtless, sir," replied Giusmaria. "If you have a wife, no one can prevent your speaking to her."

"Thank you," stammered Camillo. "But where will I find her?"

"I am not in a position to tell you, sir," Giusmaria said. "As I am unaware of the identity of your wife, it is quite impossible for me to inform you of her whereabouts."

Camillo plucked up his courage. "I," he said, "I am the husband of Signorina Carlotta."

Giusmaria made no reply. Proudly he raised the head that for sixty-five years he had carried bent forward, in his professional capacity, and marched firmly to the green room, where Donna Leo was working at a very complicated game of patience.

"Madam!" Giusmaria cried. "The person whom I have agreed, out of respect for you, to call 'Signor Camillo' now claims to be the husband of Signorina Carlotta, whom I had the honor to watch being born. I beg you to let me put him out of the house."

"I should like to," murmured Donna Leo. "However, you must realize that his highly offensive statement bears a certain relation to the truth."

"Even admitting that the person in question is only partially the husband of Signorina Carlotta, this is too much!"

"You must make the sacrifice, Giusmaria," said Donna

Leo sadly, "even as we must all of us sacrifice ourselves. Be as discreet as always. I assure you that the question is one of a transitory nature."

Giusmaria bowed his head as a tear furrowed a silver thread across his cheek, lined by years of faithful service. "What shall I tell Signor Camillo?" he asked.

"Tell him the signorina has gone out and will be back in a couple of hours."

Meanwhile, Camillo, alone at the foot of the stairs and unsure of what move to make next, found nothing better to do than to sit down in a red armchair and wait to see what happened.

The message that Giusmaria brought gave heart to Camillo, who till then had seen himself confined to the apprehensions of the armchair for an indefinite period.

"Very good," said Camillo, as he started back along the road to his room. "Very good."

Meanwhile, in the green room, Donna Leo called an urgent meeting of the family.

It was extraordinarily dramatic.

"The woodcutter is showing his nails," Donna Leo began. "He's begun to put forward his claims—he's asked to speak to Carlotta."

"He's a brute!" cried Flaminia.

"He's an adventurer," said Elisabetta.

"He's a fellow," Gastone affirmed, indignantly.

"He's an idiot," asserted Robinia.

"He's a poor fool," sighed Carlotta.

"He's your husband," concluded Edo, with his degree of common sense.

Donna Leo summed up: "He's married to Carlotta, and he can make even more terrible claims than seeing his wife and speaking to her. We must put our plan in operation at once."

This, quite obviously, was a case of the royal "we," for nobody else had a plan but Donna Leo.

"We must see to it," she affirmed, "that Camillo Debrai, now that he's married to Carlotta, does not become her husband. We must keep Debrai dangling till the day that cursed Signor Casimiro Wonder makes his departure from this sad world of ours. Once Carlotta comes into possession of her inheritance, it will be easy to annul a marriage that has not been consummated."

It was an ingenious plan, and Carlotta began to skip around the room in her joy.

"What if Camillo consummates?" observed Edo.

"He will not consummate!" declared Donna Leo. "First of all, Carlotta will pack her bags and go with her mother to some secluded spot on the Riviera. Our family doctor will give us the excuse that her health is seriously impaired. That ought to hold Debrai at bay."

"We might also," Carlotta suggested, "put it to him as a bit of good business. I don't believe that, when faced with half a million cash, any artistic woodcutter would have enough self-respect to say no."

Donna Leo bowed her head gravely in approval. "Naturally," she said. "However—*extrematio!*"

Presumably the learned lady meant to say *extrema ratio,* but no one took offense at it: what's important is the Latin quotation in itself. Latin is, in fact, so miraculous a language that even if Donna Leo had said *sursum corda* instead of *extrema ratio,* everyone would have understood perfectly what she meant: there's always time to pay and to die.

The family decided to have a farewell tea for Carlotta and her mother, so tea and cakes were served. Then came Giusmaria to announce that everything was ready, and then at last came evening.

When he saw the sun sink behind the trees in the garden, Camillo knew that it must be about nine o'clock. He knew he had had his conversation with Giusmaria precisely at two, and that somewhere in those seven hours the two of which Giusmaria had spoken must surely have passed. He ventured outside his room, and finding the butler at the foot of the stairway, asked if Signorina Carlotta had returned.

"Signorina Carlotta and her mother," replied Giusmaria, "have left for a health resort."

This time Camillo did not say, "Very good." He wanted to know, uneasily, who was ill.

"Signorina Carlotta," said Giusmaria, according to instructions. "It isn't serious, but it's going to take a long time, and my advice to you is not to worry about it. Signorina Carlotta is able to recover her health by herself."

"I want to know at once," Camillo cried, "where my wife has gone! I must join her."

Frightened by this unexpected vigor on Camillo's part, Giusmaria hurried off to request the intervention of Donna Leo, and Donna Leo intervened.

"My granddaughter is ill," she said in a severe tone to Camillo. "She needs absolute quiet, so there's no sense in your getting upset—her mother is with her, and she is the best person to look after her and take care of her."

"I won't say anything to her," replied Camillo stubbornly, "but I want to know where she's gone. I've got to go after her. You must excuse me, ma'am, but I'm her husband."

How often the best laid plans go wrong because of some slight imprudence! He who would put his own designs into effect must always forget that he possesses such things as nerves. Donna Leo, alas, considering her imposing proportions, possessed so many of those nerves it was humanly impossible to forget them all. In a voice full of challenge, she cried: "Husband? Not yet, young man!"

When she realized what she had said, it was already too late: the damage had already been done. Camillo understood all. Somewhat more precisely, this sturdy young man understood nothing: but it's at the very moments when one understands nothing that so often one understands all.

"Very good," replied Camillo. He ran down the hall and out of the house.

Twenty minutes later he was still running, and night had by then descended on the silent countryside. A cart passed, with its lamps lit, and Camillo asked for a lift.

"Which way are you going?" asked the man in the cart.

"The same way you are," said Camillo.

"Jump in," said the man.

Camillo left the cart at the outskirts of the city. By now there were lights behind every window. The trees were black against the sky. Camillo felt he was looking at a world that no longer belonged to him. He sat down on a small bench that was already damp with dew. On the other side of the avenue stood a very black building with but one window lit, and through that window Camillo saw a carved ceiling.

For a long time he looked at that ceiling until it seemed to him that he had seen those huge carved roses before. He tried to remember where, and at last he succeeded. He ran across the avenue and tugged desperately at the bell that swayed in the evening breeze beside the big door.

Signor Casimiro Wonder was turning over one of his account books when Camillo appeared before him.

"How did you get here?" he demanded, in an extremely annoyed tone of voice.

"I don't know, Signor Wonder," whispered the very humbled Camillo.

Signor Casimiro wanted a detailed account of the events, and Camillo recounted them in detail, and Casimiro lost his patience. "Bravo!" he cried. "Is that the best you could do?"

"How could I do better?" protested Camillo. "They were seven against one."

"Seven against one fool," Signor Casimiro added. "Then you're not her husband?"

"Not yet, Signor Wonder," sighed Camillo. "Signora

Leonida also pointed it out, so I got mad, and then I ran away."

"That's the one thing you shouldn't have done!" exclaimed Signor Casimiro. "Desertion! That's exactly what those people want. That way it will be even easier for them to annul your marriage and send you off about your business. Don't you see that that's their idea?"

"No, sir, all I see is, I can't stay in that house any more."

Signor Casimiro sat in silence for quite some time, then in an almost gentle voice he asked: "How about you, young man, how do you feel about your wife?"

"Yes, sir," sighed Camillo, lowering his head.

"Will you tell me what you're talking about, you stupid fool?" roared Signor Casimiro. "What do you mean by 'yes, sir'?"

Camillo was ashamed to speak of things so sweet to a person so severe. He spread his arms and shrugged his shoulders.

"More in love than before," said Signor Casimiro, in a disgusted tone.

"Yes, sir."

Signor Casimiro called a servant and told him to have the the horses hitched up to the carriage. Then he turned to Camillo. "Go back to the house," he said, "and stay in your room. Don't come down till you're asked to come down."

"Yes, sir."

"The devil with this 'yes, sir'! Run, man, and learn how to be a husband."

"You'll have to excuse me, Signor Wonder, but it's the first time I've done it . . ."

After Camillo left, Uncle Casimiro summoned his lawyer.

"I want to remake my will," he said, when the lawyer arrived, "to this effect: I leave all my goods not only to my niece Carlotta but also to the children of my niece Carlotta Wonder Debrai and her husband Camillo Debrai. Should there be no children, my niece Carlotta Wonder Debrai may come into possession of her inheritance at the age of fifty. In the meanwhile all the income will go to the Brachette foundation, save for the sum of fifty thousand lira monthly to be divided between my niece and her husband Camillo Debrai."

"Very well," said the lawyer. "Shall I make the change tomorrow?"

"No, at once. I wouldn't want to die tonight, furious that I hadn't paid this last service to the family of the crusades."

"Once the change is made, do I communicate it to Donna Carlotta?"

"Of course! How else can the game be won?"

chapter 6

When the Madellis family became acquainted with the latest clause inserted in Uncle Casimiro's will, Donna Leo suffered a nervous crisis comparable, in intensity and duration, to that historic one she suffered in 1910 on the occasion of Flaminia's marriage to the late Tommaso Wonder, the eventual father of Carlotta to be sure, but first of all the descendant of sausage-makers.

"No!" cried the noble lady. "I shall not permit the low-born Camillo Debrai to make me a great-grandmother. Better death!"

Signor Gastone Food, approving in the highest degree

the proud decision of Donna Leo, pointed out nevertheless that the situation was not quite desperate.

"Haven't we always got along," he asked, "on the monthly income that this so-called Signor Wonder gives us? Is the monthly income tied up with the birth of this proposed child? I hope you will forgive so inelegant a phrase, but while there's life there's hope."

"The trouble is," observed young Edo Food, with his degree of common sense, "that the life in question is not ours but that of Signor Wonder. In fact, the moment that Signor Wonder stops living, we stop getting the income, which is the result of his personal generosity and has no legal sanction. In the absence of the aforesaid child, our family will have to learn to live on the fifty thousand lira a month that have been granted 'in the meanwhile' to Carlotta and her husband."

"That wouldn't even pay for my clothes!" exclaimed Donna Elisabetta, horror-struck.

"So," Edo concluded, "we must have ready the child of which the will speaks, so as not to be taken by surprise."

The argument was convincing: it was received with gravity and meditated in silence.

The first to speak was Signor Gastone Food, descended from the most famous crusaders in history: beneath his peace-loving exterior beat a heart of stone. Signor Gastone rose. "So be it then," he said, with utter simplicity. "Personal pride must give way to the common good. If sacrifices must be made for the well-being of the family, then I am ready to sacrifice myself. I agree to become the uncle of a Debrai."

Edo shrugged. It was not a matter that interested him very much, and when a matter didn't interest Edo very much, he always accepted the majority decision.

"It's horrible!" murmured Donna Flaminia, Donna Elisabetta, and Donna Robinia, crushed by the crude reality of life.

Donna Leo said nothing.

Carlotta rose from her armchair and decisively spoke her first word. She said, "No!"

Donna Leo looked proudly at her granddaughter. "Neither I nor Carlotta," she declared, "will be parties to such an abomination. While we admit the necessity of having a child by our union with Signor Debrai, we are not prepared to dishonor the family by presenting to the world a husband of the caliber of Debrai!"

"A clandestine child, then?" suggested Signor Gastone.

"People who are prominent," said Donna Leo, "cannot have clandestine children. And the children must be recognized by the husband. If we presented a husband like Debrai to the world, the world would laugh at us. We must invent for Carlotta a husband worthy of our traditions."

"But the husband," Signor Gastone observed, "already exists, and exchanging him is impossible."

"The raw material exists. Out of this a husband may be made. Signor Debrai is attractive-looking and of a suitable age. If he were properly educated, he could become—at least in appearance—a man of our class, acceptable in the best society. We must mold him, we must shape his mind and his spirit, and when the moment comes we may present him as our husband without having to fear the derision of the world."

All gave their tacit approval—save Carlotta.

"Grandmother," she said, "it's impossible. I don't like him, and I could never love him!"

"My daughter," breathed Donna Leo, "this is not a question of love, it's a question merely of marriage. God has sentenced us to a husband unworthy of us—we must try to make the sentence as little painful as possible. We are all its victims."

"All the same," said Carlotta, rather annoyed, "I'm the one who has to have the husband. And the child—"

"Carlotta!" Donna Leo broke in, in a severe tone. "That is not a suitable topic of conversation for a young girl. Don't worry about it—we'll take care of it."

"Very well," sighed Carlotta. But if anyone had dared say that she was convinced everything was going well, he would have been lying in the most barefaced way.

And what, during the time that elapsed between his visit to Uncle Casimiro and the knocking at his door, were Camillo's thoughts?

Few enough, in all truth. In fact, only one—but that one highly important, both in intensity and in duration. Camillo thought about nothing but Carlotta.

"I," said Camillo to himself at last, "am not only head over heels in love with Carlotta but I am also her husband, so if I put my foot down, I could force her to be my wife."

Then he had to make a sad confession.

"But I could never put my foot down. I will always do what the others want. And I will do it not because I'm a dumbbell but because I know Carlotta detests me. Uncle Casimiro may be able to make a woman marry a man, he may even be able to make her live with him, but he can never make her love him. Only I can make myself loved—but how can I do it if God doesn't help me?"

Having heard Camillo's argument, the reader will have no choice but to be cheered by it, for everything has now become clear and open: Camillo is no longer a strange character thrust by fate into a stranger situation. He is now a normal man, endowed with good sense and a rational mind. Just another dumbbell, in other words.

It has already been noted, however, that someone has knocked on Camillo's door. All personal considerations must be abandoned, then, to see who it is that knocked.

"Come in!" called Camillo.

"Sir," Giusmaria announced, peering in discreetly, "you are wanted below."

Camillo threw on a jacket and headed for the door. But Giusmaria respectfully detained him.

"May I take the liberty," he said, "of observing that a dark suit would be preferable to the light gray one. I have the impression that it would be more suitable to the present circumstances."

"Oh!" stammered Camillo. "Did someone die or something?"

"No, sir. Had it been a case of mourning, I would have suggested a black suit, not a dark one."

"Then is somebody sick maybe?" Camillo asked, making his own interpretation of the distinction in tonality.

"It is now evening," said Giusmaria, "and a dark suit would be more acceptable to the ladies and gentlemen who are awaiting you for dinner."

When Camillo entered the dining room and saw the Madellis family seated gravely around the table, he prayed for God's mercy.

It must be noted, in all honesty, that Giusmaria did all he could to help Camillo through the dinner. But even an admirable butler cannot perform miracles. He cannot prevent the person entrusted to his care from eating soup with a fork, or shucking an oyster with the nutcracker, or peeling an apple with a carving knife.

Finally, when Camillo, having made his excuses to everyone, had returned to his room, the Madellis family drew its conclusions.

"The preliminary examination," said Donna Leo," proves the man is a brute. We'll have to start from scratch."

Various methods were proposed; Edo's was approved at last.

"His is a virgin mind," said Edo, who was not without a certain degree of common sense, "and one must not overload it. One must proceed slowly. It's no good pretending that he can learn to handle twenty different plates at the same time. We'll begin with the easiest plate and continue slowly until he's master of the material."

Thus, the following morning, Camillo began to eat apart, in a small room, and for breakfast had a cup of consommé with croutons. At lunch he had three cups of consommé with croutons.

For three days Camillo lived exclusively on cups of broth with croutons, and at last, thanks to Edo's detailed instructions, succeeded in getting them down with decency. For the next three days, Camillo fed exclusively on antipasto, and since it seemed to Robinia (his antipasto instructor) that this subject was particularly difficult, Camillo had rehearsals between meals.

Then came the steak lessons, under the direction of Gastone; then the pasta lessons from Donna Flaminia; then the roast lessons from Signorina Robinia; then the fruit lessons from Donna Elisabetta. Finally, after two weeks, Camillo reached dessert and stabbed away at it for three days under the personal supervision of Donna Leo herself.

Camillo waited anxiously, wondering if Carlotta might conduct the coffee lessons.

But when he timidly asked Edo about it, Edo replied, "A gentleman is known by his table manners. Carlotta must recognize that you are a gentleman in order to respect you as you must certainly desire. When you are able to eat a meal with total self-possession, you will join us at the table and see Carlotta. Not before."

After nearly three weeks, Donna Leo determined to submit Camillo to a comprehensive trial.

At this point the basic flaw in the educational system was revealed: for three days in a row, Camillo had eaten nothing but steak; for another three, nothing but spaghetti and such. Now, when all the materials were set before him simultaneously, havoc resulted. He managed the fish fork irreproachably, but he used it on the roast partridge; and so it went throughout the meal up to the moment when he tried to peel a grape after having speared it on a fork.

Carlotta watched Camillo in disgust during the entire meal, and at the end, when her face was splattered with bits of the oyster that Camillo was trying to slice with his knife, she burst forth. "You're coming along!" she cried. "First you only threw flowers in my face. Now it's oysters! Keep it up and you'll soon have the whole table on my head!"

Camillo lowered his head and left the room, ashamed of his miserable failure. Another conference was called.

"It is impossible," said Donna Leo, "to get any satisfactory results out of the person in question by following these empirical systems. We need a more rational method, and constant supervision. He must be educated by specialists, or we'll never make a presentable husband out of him."

"I don't think it can be done," declared Gastone, spreading his hands. "With my instruction, even a horse would have learned to eat a steak correctly."

"We must come to grips with the problem," said Donna Leo. "There is one correct method, and I know what it is."

They all looked at her.

"We'll send him to school!" she cried.

"At his age?" asked Gastone in astonishment. "No school would accept him."

"For Donna Leonida Madellis there are always people willing to make exceptions."

"The question is whether *he*'ll agree," said Edo, with his degree of common sense.

"For Carlotta Wonder there are always people willing to make fools of themselves," said Carlotta. "I'll take care of him—I'll go up and talk to him now."

As she went toward the door, Donna Flaminia cried, in a shocked tone, "Carlotta! Alone in a man's room?"

"Don't worry, Mama," said Carlotta. "He's not a man, he's my husband."

chapter 7

The head of the famous Pipet School was an elderly man with much dignity and starched linen, and the boys detested him most respectfully. Thus, when they saw him coming unexpectedly into the large study hall, they promptly got to their feet, but managed at the same time to make a most infernal racket.

"Boys," he said, once the noisy scraping of the chairs had stopped, "of the things of this world that are still veiled in deep mystery, electricity and the human brain must be counted among the first. Even though we are acquainted with a thousand machines that electricity operates and with a thousand acts that the brain causes the human machine to do, we are still unable to explain, even today, what, precisely, electricity and the human brain are. Let us not be surprised, then, if sometimes we come across cases that defy all analysis. Let us, instead, accept them without unnecessary wonder and without making a great fuss about it. Let us avoid all gossip. The present case has nothing to do with novelties in the field of electricity. No, the novelty, or the oddity, that interests us today pertains to the human brain. It is, in a word, a human being who suddenly, because of a grave illness, lost his true personality of a respectable and cultured man and assumed that of someone who is coarse and crude. The person under discussion has already passed his twenty-fifth year; he belongs to a very noble family, and so that he may return worthy of being presented as a scion of such noble stock, he must be reeducated. This reeducation has, quite naturally, been entrusted to the Pipet School, world famous for outstanding methods of teaching. Welcome then, my dear boys, your new comrade with the warmth and affection that his particular case deserves. Don't burden him with your curiosity, but be a friend to him, in the most intelligent and sympathetic meaning of the word."

Here was a discourse, obviously, of the highest importance; and its unquestioned persuasive power was put immediately to the test.

When a solidly built young man, in his twenty-fifth year, entered the study hall, all the scholars, without a single exception, guffawed as loud as their lungs would permit.

After their guffaws died down, they welcomed their more seasoned comrade with the respect and affection the headmaster requested.

"Hi, grandpa!"

Of the things of this world that are still veiled in deep mystery, electricity and the human brain must be counted among the first. How otherwise to account for the fact that Camillo Debrai had the courage to smile? Or was it in truth an electrical phenomenon? Did Camillo have a Ruhmkorff coil instead of a brain?

No, Camillo Debrai had a brain that was a brain from top to toe. The trouble was, he also had a heart that was more heart than ever, and Carlotta's criminal plan succeeded easily.

When Carlotta appeared in Camillo's bedroom, it was like a miracle, and Camillo, naturally enough, looked at her as if that were truly what she was.

"Shall we have a little talk, Signor Camillo?" said Carlotta with a smile.

Camillo gave up all thought of undertaking a reply.

"No?" Carlotta went on. "Are you sorry you married me?"

"No!" cried Camillo.

"Well, I am," said the girl. "But there's no use in crying over spilt milk. It's done now. I'm your wife and you're my husband, isn't that right?"

"That's what Signor Casimiro says. Your grandmother, on the other hand, says no."

"Let us not bring my relatives into it, Signor Camillo, I beg of you. The fact of our marriage is of interest only to us."

"That's not how it seems to me, signorina," Camillo stammered. "I have the impression that it's of more interest to all the others."

"Don't be impressed by appearances," Carlotta warned him. "Appearances are always deceiving. We are the interested people, and the affair ought to be settled between us. Do you agree?"

"Yes, ma'am."

"Exactly! Then let's speak frankly. We're alone, so we can. When you married me, did you marry me for love or for money?"

"For love, signorina, I swear to you. For two years I waited hidden in the garden every morning for you to come to your window so I could see you, and once I had seen you I was happy for the rest of the day. You'll have to excuse me, Signorina Carlotta, but I've always loved you."

"I'm sincerely sorry," Carlotta sighed. "For I, on the other hand, have never loved you, and I married simply for money. I had to get married within a few hours or lose my inheritance from Uncle Casimiro, and I married you—the first man that came along. I hope you appreciate my frankness?"

"I'm very grateful for it. Anyway, I never dared to think

that you were even aware of my existence. I was satisfied just to look at you. I married you because you said you were willing to marry me—otherwise, I would never have allowed myself to do it."

Carlotta began to laugh: poor Camillo amused her.

"You're a kind soul, Signor Debrai," Carlotta resumed. "But the important fact is this: we *are* married, married for life, and therefore we will have to live together and even have children."

"Signorina!" Camillo began to blush. "I assure you that my intentions—"

"I believe you, Signor Debrai. But the law is the law, and we, as we're married, will have to live together and have children. When husband and wife love each other, everything works out well—trouble comes when the husband and wife don't love each other."

"I love you," Camillo protested.

"That's a beginning, Signor Debrai. It means this love business is already fifty percent settled. There remains only the other fifty percent—in a word, me. For everything to work properly, I'll have to love you too. A little at least is indispensable. And I can assure you that I'm ready to do my very best to love you."

"I always knew," Camillo cried, much moved, "that you had a noble soul!"

"But the way things are," Carlotta went on, "I can't love you. I would first have to see you as a man worthy—through education, culture, and knowledge of life—of the traditions of my noble family. How could I love a man I'd be ashamed to introduce to my friends? First of all, I would have to respect you—and that depends entirely on you, Signor Camillo."

The unhappy Camillo spread wide his arms. "Then tell me, signorina, what I must do. With all the good will in the world, I just couldn't learn how to eat fish or steak in a few days. I'll begin over, I promise. I'll study, I'll even eat at night—"

"But it's not only that. In fact, that's the least of it. You must acquire culture, you must refine your mind. You must learn how to live both materially and spiritually. But I have every confidence in your intelligence and your love."

"I'll do anything!" Camillo cried.

"Will you agree to go away and complete your education at a school?"

"A school? But I'm over twenty-five years old!"

"But it's not a school for children, it's for young men. Furthermore, the only acceptable method for learning rapidly and definitively the essential things that you don't know is the scholastic one. Even if we recruited an army of private instructors, we would never succeed. And, what's more, if the thing were done at home, it would leak out and we'd be laughed down. The school of which I am speaking is in Switzerland—no one will have to know anything about it."

"But do I have to stay shut up there the whole time without ever seeing you?"

"No. I'll visit you every once in a while."

"But won't they laugh at me? It sounds so crazy—a boarding-school husband!"

"It's a sublime sacrifice. A sublime proof of your love that I will value at its true worth and that will help me to grow fonder of you."

When Carlotta returned, the conference stared at her in silence.

"I thought he was stupid," said Carlotta, "but instead. . . ."

"Instead?" cried the conference, alarmed.

"Instead he's an absolute idiot," Carlotta concluded. "He said he's even ready to go back to kindergarten."

"Carlotta," cried Donna Leo, embracing her grand-daughter, "I admire you."

"You are a great woman," said Uncle Gastone.

"You're marvelous!" said Donna Flaminia, Carlotta's mother.

"You're splendid!" said Aunt Elisabetta.

"You're diabolic!" said Cousin Robinia.

"You should be sympathized with for having the most idiotic husband in the universe," said Cousin Edo, with his degree of common sense.

"No, to be envied!" cried Signora Food. "That would be the ideal husband."

Suddenly Signor Food remembered how he had always been pleased when Signora Food said to her friends: "I'm happy—my Gastone is the ideal husband."

"Yours," said Signora Food to him now, having guessed his thought, "yours is a special case."

Signor Food relaxed. "I have never doubted it, my dear," he said.

It will not be necessary to explain how Donna Leo succeeded in interesting the headmaster of the Pipet School in the "Debrai case," or how the situation was rationalized for the other boys. The discourse of the headmaster has already been given.

Nor will it be necessary to detail here the sufferings of Camillo Debrai at the initial approaches made by his young comrades: the subject of Camillo will be resumed somewhat later. More urgent matters intervene. The trouble that everyone knew lay in the future grew even more complex.

No one could have foreseen the appearance of one Signor Meditato Filet, a formidable man, indeed.

chapter 8

Before describing the entrance of Signor Meditato Filet into the present history, and in the hope of establishing a term of reference, the adventure of a certain young Dester may be considered.

One morning young Dester put on his best suit and presented himself at the house of a Signor Wagoon. After saluting Signor Wagoon correctly, he said, "Sir, I have the honor to request the hand of your daughter in marriage."

"No," replied Signor Wagoon. He then informed the young man that the exit was on the right.

Young Dester took advantage of this helpful information,

and as he was crossing the room adjoining Signor Wagoon's study, he met Signora Wagoon.

"Signora," said the young Dester in an impassioned tone of voice, "I have been madly in love with you for about a year, and I would like to tell you so at greater length. Can we make an appointment?"

"No," replied Signora Wagoon, and furnished the young man with useful information about the direction of the exit.

As he was crossing a hall, young Dester ran into the governess of the smallest of the Wagoons, and bending toward her he said with warmth: "Signorina, for a long time now I have been living for the moment when I could speak to you alone. Where may I meet you tonight?"

"Nowhere," replied the governess and called the maid to escort the young man to the door.

The maid wasn't much, but she wasn't altogether impossible either, so young Dester said to her, "Honey, I've been after you for a long time. Let's go to the movies tonight."

"No," replied the girl as she opened the door to the front hall. Then, as someone called her, she explained to young Dester that if he slammed the front door after he left, it would lock by itself.

Alone in the front hall, Dester saw an umbrella in the stand. He put the umbrella under his arm and left, murmuring to himself: "Well, it's better than nothing!"

Signor Meditato Filet, as he was passing in front of the Madellis villa, saw a pretty rosebush and reached his arm between the bars of the iron gate to try to pick one of the flowers.

"Hey!" cried one of the maids.

Signor Meditato Filet closed the gate behind him and entered the garden. Holding out his arms toward the attractive girl, he cried: "Of the two roses, I naturally choose the prettier."

"Keep your hands to yourself!" cried the girl, continuing with a laugh into the garden. Signor Filet followed her but was soon blocked by Donna Elisabetta Food, a woman of mature but worthwhile quality.

"I hope you will forgive my boldness," said Signor Filet gallantly, "but for a long time I've been awaiting the moment when I can tell you all I—"

"Sir," Donna Elisabetta interrupted, "I am married and I have two children. The gate for leaving is the same you entered by."

Signor Filet started to withdraw but passing the arbor met Donna Flaminia, the younger of the two sisters and notably more worthwhile.

"Signora," cried Meditato, "will you never let me tell you that for six months I have been racked with pain on your account?"

"Leave at once, I beg of you," said Donna Flaminia. "I am a respectable widow! Do you want to embarrass me in front of my daughter, who is coming this very minute with my mother?"

Signor Filet continued on and after a moment or two

found himself face to face with Carlotta and Donna Leonida.

Of all the roses in the garden, Carlotta was certainly the freshest and the sweetest. Donna Leo, however, though a very faded rose indeed, was still full of thorns, and it was to her that Signor Filet turned.

"Signora," he said, "I have the honor to ask the hand of your granddaughter in marriage."

As Donna Leo and Carlotta looked at him in absolute astonishment, Signor Filet added: "I am Meditato Filet of the noble house of Altavianda, I have land and houses at home and I possess eighteen fazendas in Brazil. I place all my wealth and my life itself at your feet and at the feet of your granddaughter."

"I hope that you will be on time to take tea with us on Sunday at five," said Donna Leo, with a smile. "We don't like unpunctual people."

Signor Meditato Filet made his way back to the street in the highest of spirits, and he didn't, unlike young Dester, say, "Well, it's better than nothing!"

Before replying to Carlotta's unspoken question, Donna Leo sent the faithful Giusmaria, the cautious Signor Gastone, and the enterprising Signorina Robinia on the trail of the aforementioned Filet. Later that evening she compared the three versions and discovered they were substantially the same: Signor Filet, who had recently acquired the former Villa Pricot, led a most expensive life, his bank account was substantial, he had land and houses in the province of Tunnel, and people of the utmost reliability were willing to swear that the eighteen estates he had in Brazil gave the highest returns in all Latin America.

At that point Donna Leo was ready to reply to Carlotta's quite natural but unspoken question.

"No, my child," said Donna Leo, "I'm not crazy. This is our salvation. Signor Filet's income will allow us to give up the legacy of that so-called Signor Wonder. Signor Filet's the husband for us."

"But, Grandmother," objected Carlotta, "you forget that I already have a husband."

"We have no husband, my child. There is, to be sure, a man presently in school who married us but only to a certain degree. To annul that marriage will be easier now than ever. The said marriage, which is far from perfect from the material point of view, is highly imperfect from the moral point of view. Who would consider a man sane who goes back to boarding school at the age of twenty-five? The easiest thing would be to move him direct from the school to the lunatic asylum."

"That seems to me a little too much, Grandmother," said Carlotta. "I'd feel guilty."

"Very well," replied Donna Leo expansively. "We'll leave him free, but only out of respect to you. Be careful of him, though, he's a scoundrel."

Carlotta then asked advice on how to behave.

"Leave it all to me. Be gracious but reserved with Signor Filet. When the time comes, I'll do the talking."

The other members of the family were requested to remain silent observers of the scene and not to ask for explanations of events that might seem strange but that would become clear before too long.

That night Donna Leo saw repeatedly in her dreams a sort of three-dimensional picture: an imposing woman, her head surrounded by a resplendent light, her left foot placed firmly on the head of a man lying face down in the dust. The man was Casimiro Wonder, the overthrown tyrant. The woman was Donna Leo, liberator of the Madellis family. Poor Camillo wasn't in the allegory at all, not even as a figure in the background.

But Camillo must not be forgotten: he has finished his first month at the school. While Donna Leo composes allegories in a velvet-hung drawing room, Camillo is in his little schoolboy's room, laboriously composing a letter that he has been working on for days.

Dear Sig. Carlotta,

I have now been in school a month, and time passes slowly.

The first days were very unpleasant because the boys called me grandpa and made fun of me. But after I took sixteen of the largest ones and threw them into the fish pond in the garden, they have been very respectful and have helped me with my work once I got out of the detention cell.

Also I have become captain of the school soccer team, and as I am pretty good at it we have beaten the best teams in the city.

Arithmetic and composition don't bother me, but Latin and philosophy I don't get at all. Do I really have to learn all this crazy stuff to have the right to what you so kindly promised?

As for the table, I'm trying to do my best. I have made great progress in fish and vegetables, but I'm best at steaks, since this requires a certain amount of strength and I am getting a lot of training because all the boys want me to cut their steaks too.

I have to admit that I'm still having trouble with chicken, even though Swiss chickens are very skinny. Anyway, whatever I can't manage with a knife and fork, I don't use my hands, I throw it under the table.

Considering my long experience as a woodcarver and my skill with the chisel and the gouge, I am having very good success with boiled beef, which is hard and substantial.

I don't know how pleased you'll be with me. The teachers may have told you I don't pay much attention during lessons, but that's not because I don't want to. The fact is, I'm always thinking about you, and if I stop thinking about you for a minute, I feel guilty, as though I'd forgotten you.

I am proud to tell you that the drawing master is enthusiastic about me, but that's really not my own ability, it's just my profession of woodcarver. I am making a picture of you in color, and as soon as it's finished I'll send it to you. I hope you won't be angry if instead of being a blonde I made your hair a little greenish because I ran out of yellow.

Please come and see me, otherwise in a weak moment I will jump over the wall and run to your house. Waiting for your reply, I greet you with unchangeable devotion.

chapter 9

Giusmaria accepted with admirable restraint instructions from all members of the Madellis family—but he executed only those from Donna Leo. It was, in fact, impossible for him to believe that anything could take place in the Madellis family without the consent of Donna Leo. In 1907 an earthquake caused some damage in the town residence of the Madellis, and Giusmaria, when he went to report it to Donna Leo, who was summering in the country, had tears in his eyes.

"I hope Madam will forgive it," said Giusmaria, in a very humble tone, "but an earthquake has partially demolished the partition in the green room and has completely destroyed the old porcelain service."

"Indeed?" replied Donna Leo severely. "Don't let it happen again."

It is hardly surprising, therefore, that Giusmaria would announce to Donna Leo: "The barber for Madam is in the waiting room." Or: "The delivery boy from the Such-and-such Company has brought a racing bicycle for Madam." There was nothing in the Madellis house that was not "Madam's" or "for Madam." So everything flowed toward Madam in order to be shunted away from Madam and assigned to the proper person. Thus, when Camillo's letter arrived at the Madellis villa, Giusmaria laid it in the center of a tray and, having approached Donna Leo respectfully, said, "A letter for Madam."

It is necessary, at this point, to explain that when Giusmaria brought the letter to her, Donna Leo was not alone: otherwise, it would be impossible to say how it happened that, with the envelope in her hands, she asked in the politest of tones for permission to open it. Mention must also be made of the fact that among those present were Carlotta and Meditato Filet.

Every afternoon for almost a month now, Signor Meditato Filet had been given the opportunity to explain to Carlotta the reasons that impelled him to consider her the most fascinating woman in the world.

Preceded by glorious bunches of flowers and handsome gifts, Signor Meditato Filet made his triumphal daily entry into the Madellis house. There, while Donna Leo and the other inhabitants pretended to be aware of nothing, he settled himself comfortably in an armchair and supplied Carlotta with interesting information about the passion that made him seem more and more fascinating to her.

Meditato Filet, around thirty-five years old, tall and extremely elegant, with dark hair and a splendid mustache, was the kind of man who always excites feminine curiosity. Carlotta was no exception: her interest was evident, and she was able to forget without the slightest difficulty that she had a husband at school.

This is not to accuse Carlotta of immorality. Agreed, women ought not to be interested in men who aren't their husbands. And agreed also that a woman whose husband is still alive ought not to embrace wholeheartedly a project for becoming engaged. Carlotta, however, although a married woman before the law, was still unmarried in the sight both of God and of men.

Then, too, it must be remembered that for Carlotta husbands were like life-preservers thrown to a woman floundering in the water: what harm is there if she sees one that's better than the one she already has and holds out her arms for it? And isn't it reasonable for her, before getting a firm hold on the second, to hang on to the first?

Given Carlotta's way of thinking, therefore, it is reasonable to hold on to the life belt called Camillo until one has a firm hold on the life belt called Meditato.

After having read the letter, Donna Leo rose.

"I beg of you to excuse me, Signor Filet," she said, "but

unexpected and unsettling news about the health of a family connection forces me to deprive myself of your most agreeable company."

It was only natural that if Donna Leo left the drawing room, everyone else should leave the drawing room too. It was Giusmaria's belief that on the day Donna Leo leaves this sad world, no one within the Madellis coterie ought to be allowed to remain on earth.

"I trust that it is nothing serious," said Signor Meditato Filet sadly, and then, after giving Carlotta a last, significant glance, he left.

"Who among our relatives," asked Signor Gastone Food when they were alone, "is ill?"

"We are!" cried Donna Leo darkly. Then she handed Camillo's letter over to Carlotta to read aloud.

Carlotta read it aloud, and when she had finished, everyone expressed his own personal opinion.

"Ridiculous," said Signor Gastone.

"Idiotic," said Donna Flaminia.

"Puerile," said Aunt Elisabetta.

"Disgusting," said Cousin Robinia.

"Schoolboy love," said Cousin Edo, with a certain degree of common sense.

Carlotta shook her head. "It's distressing," she said.

"He is a hardened criminal sunk deep in vice!" cried Donna Leo. "He threatens to descend on us like a vulture and ruin irreparably our forthcoming marriage with Signor Filet!"

"But if Carlotta," said Signor Gastone, "is going to marry Signor Filet, we will have to explain to him his fiancée's matrimonial situation. Or were you planning to get an annulment without letting Signor Filet know anything about it?"

"No, of course not—Signor Filet will have to know, and I myself will speak to him. But this is still a little too soon. When Signor Filet asks us permission to become officially engaged, that will be the time. Up until now he's spoken only to Carlotta, and we officially know nothing about it. So on what basis would we mention to him the existence of this damned husband? We'll have to work it out so that he waits another month before expressing his desire, and by that time his attraction to Carlotta will have become a passion. And passion knows no obstacles. What's more, Signor Filet can then give us the financial help we will need to settle this woodcutter definitively. What we must prevent is having the villain descend on our house—there's the trouble."

"I'll go and talk to him at school," said Carlotta, "as he asks. I'll tame him down."

Her mother, Donna Flaminia, wrung her hands in anguish. "Carlotta!" she cried. "Remember that you're almost engaged! Be careful not to compromise yourself!"

"He isn't the kind of husband," Carlotta assured her, "who could compromise a woman of my temperament."

Her departure was agreed upon, and two hours later Carlotta was sitting in her comfortable first-class compartment traveling at high speed toward the nearby Swiss frontier.

Carlotta took Camillo's letter from her purse and reread it, concluding to herself: "He's a fool."

This definition, however, did not quite satisfy her, and she reread the letter another couple of times. She amended her definition: "He's a romantic fool."

At this point she felt a slight doubt. "A romantic fool, or a foolish romantic?" A fifth reading led her to decide on "a foolish romantic."

The question to be decided now was whether Camillo was a fool as a result of his romanticism or independently of it. That is to say, was he touched in the heart or in the head?

But the distinctions, thought Carlotta, between heart and head are literary ones. The fact that the heart beats stronger on certain occasions does not mean the heart is the seat of the emotions. If one is a fool and if one's brain doesn't react on particular occasions, one's heart nevertheless continues to beat in its rhythm. Camillo therefore was a fool as a result of his romanticism: his emotions had clouded his reason. The letter, reread for the sixth time, demonstrated that Camillo, rather than a foolish romantic, was a victim of romanticism.

"Poor thing," thought Carlotta, and she felt faintly distressed.

Some little while later, surprising herself rereading the letter for the seventh time, Carlotta impatiently crumpled the sheet into a ball and stuck it into her purse.

"He's a penniless woodcutter," she grumbled, "who has

dared to become the husband of a Madellis-Wonder! Let him go to the devil!"

Carlotta interested herself in the scenery until the journey ended. She arrived in early afternoon and went at once to the school. She was in a hurry now to get the thing over with.

A servant conducted her respectfully into the parlor and left her there. "I will tell the master at once," he said.

It was a bright sunny day in early September. Carlotta went to the open window to draw the cord of the curtains and cut out a bit of the light that filled the room. The window gave onto a large courtyard in which two school teams were furiously contesting a game of soccer, while a noisy public, composed of the other schoolboys, crowded about.

At a certain point, one, ten, a hundred furious cries were raised: "Millone! Millone!" A large young man headed the ball toward the enemy goal, which stood some fifteen yards away from the parlor window. The large young man, wearing a white jersey with the sleeves rolled up, seemed made of bronze, his skin was so burned by the sun and covered with sweat. Soccer teams are composed of eleven players, but at least fifteen hurled themselves at the young man with the ball, trying to get it away from him: this was a case, evidently, when even the reserves went into the field to defend their colors. But no one succeeded in stopping the advance: he was a strong devil, and very quick, and the ball seemed to belong to him.

The cries of the crowd grew louder: "Millone! Millone!"

The aforesaid Millone discharged a mighty kick and the ball sailed off like a dream: it passed hissing through the posts of the goal, struck a tremendous blow against the trunk of a horse chestnut a couple of yards behind, and then ricocheted, still full of fury, to the parlor window. An inch or two lower and Carlotta would have got it smack in the face; as it was, it lifted off her hat and left it on the floor some ten feet away.

When Camillo entered, Carlotta was still arranging her hat.

"Who," she asked through clenched teeth, "is that Millone who was playing a few minutes ago in the courtyard?"

"That was me," said Camillo. "The boys call me Camillone. Millone for short."

"So I thought," said Carlotta. "First bunches of flowers, then oysters, now footballs. We're making progress, it seems to me, Signor Camillo. Have you taken a vow to destroy my face? Does it annoy you that much?"

"Excuse me, signorina. I—"

The headmaster came in and paid his compliments to Signorina Wonder, who was Camillo Debrai's cousin (according to Donna Leo), then in a pleased voice said: "This happens to be the hour for free time, and as our student has been behaving so very well, I have no objection to your accompanying your cousin on a little walk. It's a beautiful day, and I think the change will be good for him, as he has seemed rather unhappy lately."

Astonished, Carlotta stammered, "Of course, of course . . ."

Camillo went off for a moment to change. The headmaster whispered: "Please tell Donna Leo that the patient is visibly improving. We're on the right road, there's no question of that. Remarkable progress . . ."

"Thank you," whispered Carlotta back.

Camillo returned after a moment or two.

Soon they found themselves walking side by side along a handsome avenue that bordered a lake.

"We must avoid compromising ourselves with this imbecile," said Carlotta to herself, recalling the wise words of her mother.

They sat down at a little table in a lonely café, under a vine. The blue water of the lake trembled from leaf to leaf.

"Well, here I am," said Carlotta brusquely. "May I now know what was so urgent that you had to threaten to run away to make me come up here?"

"I wanted to see you," said Camillo sweetly. "I hope you're not annoyed."

Camillo was dripping with sweat. After playing soccer for an hour in a scorching sun, a man does not stop sweating at once merely because he finds himself in the company of a lovely young lady; and it would be wrong to pretend that he does.

"I see you're dying of the heat," said Carlotta. "Take off your jacket."

"Impossible!" declared Camillo. "A gentleman never takes off his jacket in public. Especially if he's with a lady."

"Bravo!" cried Carlotta. "I see you're profiting by the lessons you've been getting. I give you permission to take off your jacket."

"Sometimes," replied Camillo, "out of the great kindness of her heart, or moved to pity at seeing the man who is with her uncomfortably warm, the lady may suggest that he remove his jacket. Even so, the gentleman must firmly but courteously refuse, because he knows that the fleeting pleasure he may derive from the relief could never repay him for the mortification of seeing, in the face of the lady, the distaste that must be provoked in her sensitive soul by the sight of an undressed man—"

"Undressed?"

"Yes, signorina, undressed in the sense of being in his shirt sleeves."

Camillo obviously had an excellent memory and if requested could have furnished the number of the page on which these instructions were to be found. Carlotta, on the other hand, was remembering the bronzed arms that gleamed so brightly in the sun, bathed in sweat.

"That's all very well," she said. "But I *order* you to take your jacket off."

Camillo took off his jacket, and his splendid bronze arms emerged from the very short sleeves of his white shirt.

"The arms of a porter," thought Carlotta. "He could pick Signor Filet up by the neck and toss him twenty yards. God save me from a beast like that!"

"I'm tired of being at school," murmured Camillo.

"But you've only been here a little over a month! Aren't you all right here? It's a very good school, and comfortable, and the countryside is beautiful. Don't you ever watch the lake as it reddens in the light of the setting sun?"

"Yes, but I'd rather look at you. You too, after all, redden in the light of the setting sun. Everything reddens in the light of the setting sun."

"I didn't know they gave you lessons in humor at school too," returned Carlotta. "Doesn't it interest you to know that I regard you with growing affection rather than with dislike?"

"Don't talk that way, Signorina Carlotta," Camillo protested. "You know I love you very much."

"Good!" Carlotta cut him short. "And now, instead of being naughty like a schoolboy, why don't you tell me something about the place. Do you do a lot of studying? Did you finish my portrait?"

Camillo brightened. He looked in his jacket and brought out a roll of paper that he opened very carefully. "Here it is!"

Carlotta looked at it breathlessly—for it was indeed an excellent bit of painting.

"And in your opinion," she said in a tone of pleased protest, "I am that very beautiful woman."

"Yes, signorina. That beautiful, and more. You can't see yourself, so you don't know it."

"But I do see myself! I've seen myself a million times in the mirror with these very eyes!"

"Yes, but not with these," murmured Camillo, touching his own eyes.

Carlotta felt a flash of annoyance: for maybe the distinction between heart and brain did really exist, and Camillo was both a romantic and a fool, the one independently of the other—a romantic emotionally and a fool mentally. He would have to be treated carefully, and kindly.

She was careful and kind. "I am very grateful," she said, "for your charming compliments. But you still haven't told me how your studies are going. I'm very interested—you know that everything depends on them."

Camillo talked about his studies. He had, indeed, learned quite a lot in a month, and Carlotta expressed her satisfaction.

"We'll see," she concluded, "what your report card says at the end of the first term."

"Do you think I can get out of here pretty soon?"

"It all depends on you. But you must promise me not to do anything silly. I've committed myself to my family, I've told them you're a man of good sense and intelligence, don't make a liar out of me."

"I swear to you," cried Camillo, "that I won't leave here till you want me to!"

It was full afternoon: the lake sparkled in the sunlight.

"Would it amuse you," Camillo asked timidly, "to go out in a boat for a little while?"

"Surely," thought Carlotta, "that won't compromise me. In his shirt sleeves and suntanned, everyone will take him for a boatman."

They went for a long ride in a boat, and the oars bent in Camillo's strong hands.

Carlotta thought: If he knew I was playing with him like a big doll, he could wring my neck with two of his fingers. When he does know it, it will be too late. He's the ideal man to marry a barmaid or a fishwife. With a husband like him, I'd have to fight all the servant girls in the neighborhood."

They parted in the school parlor.

"When will you be back?" Camillo asked sadly.

"That depends on you," Carlotta replied, giving him her hand.

Then she cried out.

"Signor Camillo," she said, "a brief review of the chapter on hand-clasping would not, I think, be wasted."

"No need for it, I know it all by heart."

"Then you think the correct procedure is to crush a poor woman's hand?"

"No, of course not, but you'll have to forgive me—it's the first time I've taken the hand of a woman I was married to, and I'm confused. I'll do better next time."

"You'll have a long wait," laughed Carlotta to herself, as she made her way to the station.

She reached home late at night. The entire family was still up, awaiting her return with anxiety.

"Well?" cried Donna Leo, in a full voice.

"The enemy has been driven back," Carlotta assured her, "beyond the horizon."

"Did you have to make many concessions to the brute?" asked Donna Flaminia.

"None, Mama. We didn't even leave the parlor, and I didn't even shake hands with him."

"What? Did he indicate that he wanted to shake hands with you? The monster!"

"Yes, but I pretended not to see. 'Good evening, Signor Debrai,' I said, that's all. One must never be intimate with a husband."

chapter 10

A month has passed.

The Madellis family was living through one of the most historic days of its life.

Ostensibly the gala dinner decreed by Donna Leo was to honor Carlotta on her name day, but the importance of the event depended on something else altogether.

"I judge Signor Filet to be in an emotional condition favorable to our plan," Donna Leo solemnly decreed. "His passion for Carlotta has reached a more than satisfying intensity, and all that we must do is insure a suitable atmosphere for it to be revealed in all its power. The opportunity will be supplied by Carlotta's name day: we will invite Signor Filet to dinner, we will let him breathe our sweet family air, we will refresh him with our best wine, and on rising from the table Signor Filet will not be able to resist asking, in the most official manner, permission to become engaged to Carlotta."

"A nice kettle of fish," Carlotta remarked. "Even if we receive his request favorably, I doubt whether my husband will allow me to become engaged to another man."

Donna Leo became annoyed. "I find it most unsuitable," she said, "that a lady in whose veins runs the pure blood of the Madellis should, on the eve of her betrothal to a gentleman, make public mention of her unworthy relations with a plebeian."

"But, Grandma, he's my husband!"

Donna Leo cut her short. "Between an officious husband and an official fiancé, it's the official fiancé that counts. Furthermore, no one has suggested that you occupy yourself with whatever possible complications may arise. I will take care of those. Signor Filet will ask for our hand, and we'll become engaged—then, after a certain period of time has elapsed, we will explain the state of affairs and induce Signor Filet to lend us his valuable help in the elimination of the obstacle. Once the marriage is annulled, our victory will be complete."

"And what if Signor Filet," Carlotta objected, "when he hears of the existence of this so-called obstacle, doesn't want to hear another word about me?"

"You will always have the other husband," Donna Leo replied.

"And what if the other husband hears about our plans and gets annoyed and leaves me? He could have the marriage annulled and then we'd lose the legacy."

"He will never hear about it. We will act with the utmost caution."

When the day of the party arrived, the rooms of the Madellis villa were filled with flowers. Marvelous, priceless flowers, in enormous bunches, bushes, baskets: for Signor Meditato Filet, in his gratitude at being the only stranger invited to share the intimate entertainment, had sent a thousand perfect orchids.

Carlotta spent the morning reading the hundreds of names on the cards that accompanied flowers sent by relatives.

"Everybody remembered," she said at last. "Everybody— even Uncle Casimiro."

Uncle Casimiro had sent a bunch of cyclamen. The envelope that accompanied them contained, not his visiting card, but a rather generous check.

"What a boor!" cried Donna Leo. "He never loses an opportunity to offend us, showing off his filthy money!" Gingerly she tucked the check away in her strongbox, locked it, and put the key in her pocket.

She called Giusmaria. "Take the cyclamen," she said, "and hide them away in the bathroom."

"In the *bathroom?*" asked Giusmaria.

"Those," replied Donna Leo, "are the flowers of our so-called Signor Casimiro Wonder."

Giusmaria said that in that case he understood.

Considering the refinement of atmosphere that has been created, it is not possible to say precisely where the flowers sent by Signor Casimiro Wonder made their miserable end; perhaps the reader will understand, nonetheless.

Carlotta, having made her inspection of the floral offerings, withdrew to be by herself in the blue room, but she was soon joined by the entire family.

"Lucky girl!" sighed Donna Leo. "No woman has ever had such a gift from her sweetheart as a thousand orchids all at one time!"

"A plebiscite of love!" said Donna Flaminia, Carlotta's mother, in a happy tone.

"The fact that we have retired here," said Signor Gastone Food proudly, "away from the world, has not prevented our friends from remembering the day. A great satisfaction for you, Carlotta, and for the family."

"A triumph!" cried Aunt Elisabetta.

"Everyone remembered—it's enough to make one burst with happiness!" remarked Cousin Robinia Food, with obvious resentment.

"It's only the husbands who forget their absent wives," said Cousin Edo Food, with his degree of common sense.

Carlotta shrugged. "If he knew how to behave," she cried, laughing, "we wouldn't have sent him to school!"

The others laughed with her.

"Giusmaria," Donna Leo said, after the laughter had died down, "it is not necessary, I think, to tell you what to do with any flowers that may arrive from Signor Debrai."

"It is not necessary, madam," said Giusmaria. "They will naturally join Signor Casimiro's cyclamens."

This remark provoked further laughter from everyone. Carlotta's laughter, however, was not entirely convincing, for which she had very good reasons indeed: granted that she didn't care a hoot for Camillo; and granted also that Camillo's flowers would have had the same sad end as Uncle Casimiro's; nevertheless, she was annoyed that her boor of a husband should not have remembered the name day of his wife.

Officious or official, respected or despised, loved or hated, husbands always have certain obligations toward their wives. It is a question of principle.

The Viscount of Lapipe, according to the eighteenth-century chronicles, after having suffered a shipwreck, found himself on a rock with one of his lackeys, a certain Patton. After six days of abject hunger, the Viscount of Lapipe seized the lackey and ate him. The viscount did not like this particular servant of his; in fact, he detested him heartily. Nevertheless, the viscount was much annoyed, because, when he began to dine, the servant did not say, "Bon appétit!"

It is a question of principle.

The festive meal was a triumph of Donna Leo's thesis: Signor Meditato Filet's eyes soon became very languorous, and he looked at nothing and nobody but Carlotta. This he was able to do with great ease, as they sat facing each other, and his sighs had no difficulty reaching the consignee.

"I've wandered about the whole world," cried Signor Filet at one point. "I've lived in a hundred different houses, I've eaten my meals in a thousand hotels, in the company of a hundred thousand different people. I've lunched in the shadow of the Pyramids and dined at the foot of Vesuvius, and the following morning, opening the window of my room, I've seen the ruins of the Acropolis and the Parthenon. That's the way it's always been, always, because it seemed to me that to stop meant to die. But today I believe that to stop means to live. I've had a thousand houses, but today I believe that I've never yet had a home."

Meditato Filet's voice was low, and he kept looking into Carlotta's eyes. Then he sighed again.

"I've had a thousand extraordinary adventures," he said. "Yet today I realize I've never had the one extraordinary adventure that makes having lived worthwhile: the adventure that begins with meeting a girl in a garden by a wide avenue and ends with meeting the same girl every second of the day within the walls of a house."

Carlotta's smile was very gentle.

He went on: "I've always wondered with the greatest astonishment how a man could ever tie himself down to a woman. Today I wonder with the same astonishment how a man could not tie himself down to a woman."

Silent as a ghost, Giusmaria carried away the soup course, which still stood untouched before Signor Filet.

94

"That," Carlotta replied, "isn't what other men say, Signor Filet."

With that, Carlotta spoke the greatest lie in the book: what man hasn't said exactly the same thing as Signor Filet to the woman he wanted to marry? Could he have said anything more banal?

But all this is of no importance. The fact is, Carlotta said what she said, and even more important, she had a truly languid air about her as she looked at him.

"Carlotta," sighed Signor Filet, "the first day I saw you, I asked you to marry me. It was a touch of madness—I behaved like someone in a book. But in these past two months I've thought it over, and now I ask you again, in a much humbler fashion: will you one day do me the great honor of becoming my wife?"

Meditato Filet was in truth a fascinating man, and Carlotta quite forgot a few rather important details about her civil status. Gently, sweetly, she nodded her head.

"May I speak to your family?" asked Signor Filet.

Yes, repeated the unfortunate Carlotta. Meditato Filet could hold out no longer: a state of affairs to be communicated at the end of the meal could surely be communicated during the partridge course.

Meditato rose. "Ladies and gentlemen," he said, "I have some sensational news for you. Signorina Carlotta and I—"

"Signor Camillo Debrai!" announced Giusmaria.

Meditato Filet stopped, annoyed at the interruption. The Madellises paled in terror.

Carlotta spoke promptly, "It's one of our relations," she said with a smile to Signor Filet, "who's a little eccentric. If you'll forgive me for just a moment?"

She rose and marched with decision on the invader.

"Why did you come here?" she said, when she found herself facing the enemy. Her voice was steel. "How does it happen that despite your promise you haven't stayed in school?"

"I brought you some flowers," Camillo said, "and my best wishes on your name day."

"I appreciate your kind thought," Carlotta said reluctantly. "It would have been equally appreciated if sent through the post."

"I could have sent you my best wishes," said Camillo, "but not the flowers."

"All you had to do was send word to any florist, and the flowers too would have been delivered."

With a smile, Camillo held up his thin little bouquet.

"Not these," he said. "I cut these in the same garden where I used to cut the flowers I threw into your room. The ones you got right in your face that famous day. I thought you'd like them because of their, so to speak, symbolic significance. You couldn't order these at any florist's."

He's a romantic fool, I've always said it, thought Carlotta. Then, making a great effort, she succeeded in smiling.

"I'm very grateful," she said. "It was a sweet thought. I hope you won't throw the flowers in my face this time. But how did you scuff your shoes so shamefully?"

"There were no more trains," said Camillo, "so I walked."

"Thirty-two kilometers?" cried Carlotta in horror. "Have you gone mad?"

"No, I love you, and so—"

"Please! Tell me instead how you got permission to leave from the headmaster?"

"I ran away. I couldn't do anything else."

"Ran away? That I didn't expect from you." Panic-stricken, she remembered that the others were waiting. "We'll talk about it again later," she said. "Come in with me now, sit down at the table, and try to behave as well as possible. Don't talk. We have an important guest."

"What do I have to eat?" asked Camillo in a worried tone.

Carlotta shrugged. "Partridge pie, scaloppine with madeira, chicken Gutenberg."

"Dessert?"

"Of course. Paradise cake and cream puffs."

"That's all right, then," said Camillo. "Those are all subjects I've studied. I'll pass."

Camillo was introduced as "our Camillo" to Meditato Filet, who had obviously been thrown off his stride, then a place was made for Camillo next to Robinia.

The conversation was resumed with animation, and everyone undertook to ignore Camillo's existence. Only Robinia was worried about him: no one had said anything, but as they put him beside her, she understood that they wanted her to look after him.

"Signor Debrai," she whispered, "I advise you to handle the scaloppine carefully. Try not to make it slide into anyone's face. You're a blackmailer!"

"A blackmailer?"

"Yes, a blackmailer! You're taking advantage of the presence of a stranger to accomplish your evil designs. Go easy with the knife! Wipe your mouth."

"I brought flowers for her name day," said Camillo.

"A fine reason! If everyone who sent flowers had come in person, we'd have had to borrow an army kitchen."

"But I had to come, Signorina Robinia! I'm her hus—"

"Shh!" cried Robinia. "Don't say such silly things." And then she asked several dozen questions about the teaching system of the school, the distribution of time, the technique of woodcarving, and the international political situation. Thus she succeeded in neutralizing Camillo.

Meanwhile, Signor Meditato Filet had resumed his state of grace and with the help of the excellent wine of the Madellis house his expression had grown remarkably relaxed. He looked at Carlotta impassioned and spoke to her in a low voice, with a sweet smile.

"Who's that one in front of your cousin?" asked Camillo.

"Signor Debrai," whispered Robinia, "I beg you, for the love of God, not to stare at him! It's the worst manners to keep staring at people. Tell me, is the technique of the woodcarver the same as the xylographer's?"

"No, the xylographer's is something else entirely." Camillo continued to stare at Carlotta, and even craned his neck so as to see her better. "And I don't think it's such good manners," he said, "to lean your elbows on the table and whisper to somebody when there are other people at the table."

"If a guest commits a breach of manners, it's obligatory for well-brought-up people to pretend not to have noticed. How about Switzerland? Is it a beautiful country?"

"Beautiful! Too bad it's all in the mountains. What's it all about?"

"You must know what it's all about. I've never been to Switzerland."

Camillo shook his head. "I'm asking you what *that* one's all about, not what Switzerland's all about."

"How on earth did Signor Filet come into it? We were talking about Switzerland. Have you fallen asleep?"

"No, signorina. Signor Filet comes into it because right now he's taking an interest in Carlotta. Switzerland does not take an interest in Carlotta."

Robinia pretended to find this remark excrutiatingly funny. Then she said that Signor Filet was a government official who had known Carlotta when she was a little girl, and all went well till the sparkling wine arrived.

At this point Signor Meditato, who felt he had matters under control again, rose suddenly and announced: "Ladies and gentlemen, I have sensational news for you—"

Donna Leo counterattacked. "Please, Signor Filet," she said. "If the sensational announcement is the one you suggested two months ago in the garden, there is no need to repeat it. We all know what it is by now, and we are all in agreement on the subject."

Meditato Filet's smile was a pleased one: everything had gone all right then!

He sat down again. "You guessed, Donna Leo," he cried, with a laugh.

"Three cheers!" called out Signor Gastone, raising his glass of sparkling wine.

"Three cheers," they all echoed as they drank.

Camillo was the only one who said nothing, and Robinia told him to say three cheers like everybody else.

"Three cheers for what?" he asked in a whisper.

"Three cheers for the sensational news. What else?"

"What sensational news?"

Robinia got mad. "I wish I knew where they teach good manners if they don't teach them at school! Do you think it's well-bred to want to know someone else's business?"

"And I don't want to know it," Camillo returned. "But if I'm supposed to holler three cheers for something, I've got to know what it is. Otherwise, I don't holler three cheers."

Terror-struck, Robinia saw that Filet was putting out his hand with the obvious intention of pressing Carlotta's hand. She put her mouth to Camillo's ear.

"The sensational news," she whispered, "is that the cabinet is about to fall and that the left-wing faction threatens to take over!"

"Why didn't Donna Leo want him to say it?"

Robinia put her ear even closer to his ear. "Politics is politics. All our servants are new—it's best to be careful."

Signor Filet, flushed with pleasure, was returning his glass to the table when Camillo turned in his direction.

"Three cheers!" he cried, raising his glass. The isolated cry sounded menacing in the silence. "I've never liked the present cabinet," he whispered to Robinia, who was looking at him with her mouth open.

"Don't pay any attention to him, Signor Filet," Carlotta whispered, having just lived through a moment of terrible anguish. "As I told you, he's a bit eccentric. Don't be offended by him."

"Offended?" Signor Meditato Filet laughed. "On the contrary. His cheers were the result of long reflection and are therefore the sincerest of all. Your eccentric relation observed us carefully—I was aware of it—and now he understands that we love each other very much, and he is gratified that we are happy."

"How well you understand people!" cried Carlotta, admiringly.

The company reassembled in the garden to enjoy the last moments of warmth of that splendid autumn day.

"Give me your arm," Robinia instructed, as Camillo seemed upset by the fact that Signor Filet had sat down with Carlotta on the most remote bench in the garden.

"I don't understand," said Camillo in an annoyed tone, "what he's got to say to her that he has to be always whispering in her ear."

"He's telling her," said Robinia, "about the new cabinet."

"And I don't understand why a man, when he's talking to a woman about politics, has to press her arm that way."

"—The swing!" cried Robinia enthusiastically, drawing

Camillo away. "I'm going to sit in the swing and you're going to push me."

Camillo assented, but stopped when Robinia gave a shriek.

"Murderer!" she cried. "Do you want to kill me?"

Furiously, she jumped down.

"Another push," she said, "and I'd have made a complete circle. I'd like to know what you think about when you push young ladies on the swing."

"I think about a young lady who is not on a swing," said Camillo. "I'm sorry," he stammered. "I'm terribly sorry."

Robinia looked at him in disgust. "Are you jealous of an old friend of the family because he's sitting next to your wife?"

Camillo declared that that was furthest from his mind.

"What's more, Signor Filet doesn't know that you're married to Carlotta. Was it not arranged that Carlotta would not introduce you as her husband until you had shown yourself worthy to be married to a descendant of the Madellis? And did you not approve? Now do you want to spoil everything? Do you want to make us all look ridiculous? What are you going to say to him? 'Hey, get away, I'm Carlotta's husband'?"

Camillo dropped onto the swing and put his hands to his head. "You're right," he cried. "Everybody's right. Except I'm in love with Carlotta. So I'm in serious trouble, because when I think about Carlotta I can't think about anything else. Have you ever tried being in love with your wife?"

Robinia laughed. "I can imagine what it's like. And don't think I'm blaming you. One must admit that Carlotta isn't behaving at all well right now—it almost looks as though she's doing whatever she can to make you angry."

There were a few moments of silence as Robinia stared at Camillo's shining hair and powerful neck. A strange, new sensation came over her, and she abruptly exclaimed: "You're the dumbest man in the world!"

Camillo raised his head and looked at her: in his eyes could be read a courteous request for an explanation.

"Your wife is flirting to get you mad and you just sit here without moving a finger."

"But what can I do?" asked Camillo.

"Pay her back in her own coin. She's flirting with a man, so you flirt with a woman. That's the way to do it!"

Camillo shrugged. "You're right, but where can I find a woman now?"

"Do I look like a member of the Swiss Guard?"

"But you—"

"I feel sorry for you, I feel so sorry for you that in spite of the fact that I find you outrageous, I'll agree to play the comedy for you. Let's go and sit down on that bench over there."

Robinia pointed to an empty bench and took Camillo by the arm.

"Sit down beside me," said Robinia, "and whisper into my ear. I'll laugh loud enough for Carlotta and Signor Filet to hear me. Just say anything that comes into your head. It's only a game. But get closer, dear boy! What's the matter? Are you afraid I'll eat you? Come on!"

"Today is Wednesday," Camillo whispered into Robinia's ear.

Robinia laughed. "Splendid, Signor Camillo!"

The two benches were about thirty feet apart, and between them stood a few bushes, but the bushes were thin, and so Carlotta, when she heard Robinia's laughter and raised her head, could perfectly well see what she was meant to see.

"Thirty days hath September," whispered Camillo meanwhile, "April, June, and November. All the rest have thirty-one . . ." And Robinia giggled again, and again Carlotta raised her head to have a look. "Excepting February—"

"Do you really think so, Signor Camillo?"

Robinia's laughter grew softer and softer till after a little while Meditato Filet could not help remarking, "He doesn't waste time, that eccentric cousin of yours. Look how he's getting along with your cousin."

Carlotta looked over with unconcern: Robinia was resting her head on Camillo's shoulder, as Camillo whispered in her ear.

"The gate is open," he was whispering, "the door is closed, snow is white, wheels turn, grass is green, the morning's clear. Twelve, fifteen, forty-nine. The sky is blue, tomorrow it will rain, open the umbrella."

"Carlotta," murmured Meditato Filet, "what would you say if we followed their example?"

Carlotta did not bother to raise her head again, for

Robinia and Camillo interested her not in the slightest; nevertheless, she could see perfectly well that Robinia and Camillo were kissing.

"Let's go inside," said Carlotta. "The wine has given me a headache."

They went into the house, and a short while later Signor Filet took his leave of the Madellis family.

"May I have the honor," he asked, turning toward Carlotta, "of coming to pay my respects tomorrow?"

"Of course," said Donna Leo, taking advantage of her granddaughter's silence.

As Meditato Filet was saying his goodbyes, Camillo and Robinia returned to the villa.

"More and more," said Robinia, "I'm convinced that you're an ill-bred lout. You didn't even return the kiss I gave you."

"Forgive me, signorina, but we were only acting a comedy."

"Exactly, Signor Debrai. Comedies must be acted right, or they're no good at all. Let's hope that Carlotta wasn't aware that you didn't return my kiss. Otherwise it will all be wasted."

"Let's hope so," agreed the poor wretch.

And here this fascinating conversation came to an end, for Giusmaria came to Camillo and said: "The gentleman is expected in the blue room."

"You're a monster!" cried Carlotta, as Camillo crossed the blue room.

Camillo paled. "But I ate the scaloppine perfectly!" he cried. "And never once did I drink when I had my mouth full. And even with the cake and the cream puffs I behaved honorably. Signorina Robinia will bear witness—"

"You're a monster!" Carlotta cried more loudly. "And now you're trying to make jokes. You're ungrateful too—while your wife makes all kinds of sacrifices to keep you in school and give you the education you never had, you act like a villain and run away and come down on us treacherously and put us all through the most terrible tortures!"

"I brought you flowers for your name day," Camillo pointed out humbly.

Carlotta grew calmer. What was the point of it all, after all? The idea was to get Camillo back to school and keep him there till Donna Leo had brought her project to completion. What good did it do to get angry?

Her voice grew soft. "You made me uneasy," she said with a smile, "chiefly for the bad impression you've created in the family. How can they believe me when I tell them that you're a reasonable man? And that you love me so well you would undertake any sacrifice?"

"Forgive me, Carlotta," Camillo murmured more cheerfully. "I didn't do it out of spite, I swear to you, but I had to see you again . . ." He blushed, he shook his head. "And I can't tell you how I suffered watching Signor Filet whispering in your ear—"

Carlotta began to laugh. "My God, what a joke!" she cried. "Weren't you whispering in my cousin's ear? It would be very odd indeed if that made me suffer. We're only married to the smallest possible degree, so we can still enjoy our liberty, can't we? Still and all, in spite of what I say, it's not a very gentlemanly thing to let your wife watch you while you kiss her cousin. It's a question of taste."

"I swear to you, Carlotta," Camillo said unhappily, putting his hands together as in prayer, "I swear to you that I did not kiss your cousin."

"How odd! I'll have to have my eyes checked. I could have sworn that the two people I saw kissing on the bench were Signor Camillo and Signorina Robinia."

"On my word of honor, it wasn't me."

"Oh, no?"

"It was her. To help me."

"To help you?"

Camillo told her the story of the comedy that he had played with Robinia. "I know," he concluded, "that Signorina Robinia doesn't like me at all, but I was suffering so deeply that she took pity on me. You have pity on me too, Carlotta, and forgive me."

"I'm getting a clear picture of the whole thing," said Carlotta, "and I do not hold you to blame in any way. However, I advise you not to go on with those little games— they're never in the best of taste."

"I never would have done it, but Signorina Robinia was so nice about it and offered so politely—"

"I understand. Robinia is always very nice and polite and ready to sacrifice herself—but one mustn't take advantage of her."

"I swear I'll never do it again."

Carlotta expressed her satisfaction. Then she said: "Would you like to leave on the five o'clock train, or the nine o'clock? Let me know, so I can have the carriage take you to the station at Breslette."

Camillo looked at her open-mouthed.

"I'll write an excuse for you," she went on, "to the headmaster. But you must promise to write me every day. I want you to tell me everything you do and everything you think. And I'll come up to see you soon. Will you take me out in the boat again, like the other time?"

This was the first time Carlotta had spoken so gently to him, and Camillo could feel his heart melt away into nothing. "Yes, of course, Carlotta," he murmured. "We'll go out in the boat, wherever you like. And when we're alone, in the middle of the lake, I'll tell you everything that I . . ." Camillo had taken hold of Carlotta's hand.

"If you leave on the five o'clock train, which is what I suggest, you can just make it." Carlotta's voice was as gentle as it could be.

"You're right," Camillo admitted. Then firmly he added: "I'm going—but on one condition."

"Blackmail?"

"Just a tiny little bit. Promise you'll come to see me on Sunday."

"Next Sunday," Carlotta repeated solemnly. "I promise to come to see you."

Then she called Giusmaria and ordered the carriage. A few moments later Camillo was dashing off to the station at Breslette, and the Madellis family invaded the blue room.

"Was it much work," Robinia asked with studied indifference, "to get him to go back?"

"When an imbecile is madly in love with a woman like me," Carlotta declared, "it's always easy to get him to do anything."

"You know," said Robinia, still in the same indifferent tone, "I don't find him quite as much of an imbecile as you do."

"As far as I'm concerned, he's an imbecile." Carlotta's tone was as indifferent as her cousin's. "I can't speak for anyone else. Everyone must decide for himself."

"Tomorrow," said Donna Leo in a worried tone, "I'll have to speak to Signor Filet. We've got to move a little faster."

"I agree, Grandma," said Carlotta. "Camillo is so in love with me I wouldn't be surprised to see him turn up again in a couple of days."

"I wouldn't either," added Robinia softly, perfidiously.

chapter 11

The following afternoon Signor Meditato Filet was received in the green room, but not by Carlotta. He found himself face to face with Donna Leo.

"Signor Filet," this remarkable lady began in the gravest tone, "at the table yesterday I made you a promise that I knew I couldn't keep. I owe you therefore an explanation."

"But I don't understand," stammered Meditato Filet. "Have you perhaps some doubt that—"

"No doubt at all," sighed Donna Leo, "but absolute certainty. Carlotta cannot marry you."

"Why not?"

"Because she is married already."

Signor Meditato Filet put his head in his hands in a gesture of desperation.

"Yes," Donna Leo continued, "she is married and at the same time she is not married. She is a married woman in the eyes of the law but a maiden in the sight of God."

Meditato Filet looked at her in astonishment and said he did not quite understand.

"The marriage was celebrated but not consummated," said Donna Leo. "That's all there is to it."

"In the name of God, don't keep me on tenterhooks! Tell me what happened."

"For a variety of reasons that there is no point in going into, Carlotta was married six months ago. The wedding took place in great secrecy, because the groom desired it. No one, therefore, knew anything about it. But that very same day we discovered a ghastly fact—the bridegroom was insane!"

"Insane?"

"Insane, Signor Filet. Not violently so, but insane."

"Truly ghastly!"

"We did not of course permit him to have any sort of relations with Carlotta. Rather, we succeeded in persuading him to go away to make his recovery."

"In an asylum?"

"No. We persuaded him that there were serious gaps in his education. He is now at a boarding school."

Meditato Filet began to laugh. "A husband at school! It sounds like the title of a farce."

"But it's really the title of a tragedy."

"I don't agree with you, Donna Leo." Meditato Filet's tone of voice was a pleased one. "It would be the easiest thing in the world to have the marriage annulled. But tell me—who is this peculiar schoolboy?"

"Signor Camillo Debrai—the young man you met yesterday. He had just run away from school. He's gone back now and with God's help will stay there. Oh, it's a terrible thing!" cried Donna Leo. "Here we are, such unworldly people, with no influence, and with a terror of scandal. What can we do?"

"Signora," exclaimed Meditato Filet, "I am at your service. What needs to be done, I will do, and you may rest assured that I will do it because my happiness depends on its outcome. That marriage will be annulled—I promise you."

"But there'll be a scandal!"

"No scandal at all. I shall act with the greatest circumspection. If necessary, we'll leave the country for a while, as so many have done, and come back when everything is in order. No one will know anything about it. Where is this schoolboy?"

"In Switzerland. The Pipet School."

"That's all I need to know, Donna Leo. Look on me as your son-in-law!"

Meditato Filet rushed away, and Donna Leo, much moved, called the Madellis family to conference.

"Everything has worked out for the best!" she announced. "Signor Meditato Filet has undertaken to have the marriage annulled. We'll soon be free! Signor Meditato Filet is willing to do it all."

Donna Flaminia, Donna Elisabetta, and Signor Gastone cried out in their joy.

"A bit of a fool too," remarked Edo, who was not without a certain degree of common sense.

"Let's hope he succeeds," said Carlotta unenthusiastically.

"Yes," murmured Robinia, "he's a good boy and didn't deserve a wife like you."

Carlotta smiled her sweetest smile. "If one can't find a husband of one's own, it's always amusing to find someone else's husband."

"There's a boy in the kitchen," said Robinia, "who's painting the new cabinet. You've had so much experience, Carlotta, couldn't you show me how to make love to a workman? I'd like to get married too."

Carlotta went outside to walk in the garden. She felt warm. Very warm.

The reader may have noticed a rather remarkable fact: he has never been alone with Signor Meditato Filet. He has seen him only when there were other people present; his acquaintance with him, therefore, can only be of the most superficial kind.

Then perhaps the reader would like to make an unexpected call on Signor Filet and find him alone with his thoughts. Up the monumental stairway, down the long hall on tiptoe, into the very study of Signor Filet.

But he is not alone. Signor Meditato Filet is talking to his butler.

"What a mess!" cried the butler. "It's all going up in smoke."

"In smoke my eye," replied Meditato Filet. "It's *got* to work! I've got to marry that girl—not only because she's beautiful but because she's rich. She's Casimiro Wonder's sole heir, and he's got enough dough to drive anybody crazy. No, chum, I've got to get away with it!"

"If you don't, we'll have to pack up our tent and move silently away. The jig'll be up, and we'll be in trouble."

"I know. But there isn't as much of a rush as you think there is. Do you know how much our debts come to?"

"But, Jim, I—"

"Eight hundred and fifty-seven thousand francs!" Signor Meditato Filet groaned. "It's too much for them to begin wondering about me just yet. It'll take another six months at least. If I can just announce the marriage within six months, they'll come on their knees and beg me to accept more credit from them."

The butler sank into an armchair and put his feet on the desk. He wasn't convinced. What's more, he wasn't well brought up either.

"It's one husband too many, my boy," he said. "Even if it's a crazy husband and a secret husband, it's still a husband."

"We'll make him vanish!" cried Meditato Filet gaily. "When a man goes for a ride in a carriage, all sorts of terrible accidents can happen. He can end his days in, for instance, a Swiss ravine."

"That's right," agreed the butler. "And another man might end his days in a prison of undetermined nationality."

Meditato Filet gave the butler a strange look.

The butler spread his arms. "I'm tired, Jim," he said. "I'm tired of getting into these messes—and getting out again just by the skin of our teeth. I'm not afraid, Jim, it wouldn't bother me to chuck a nut down a well—it's just that I'm tired."

"Me, too, Flick. This will be the last time. Then it'll be all over, and we can live in peace and comfort. And you can have a big farm, with cows and horses."

"A threshing machine too?"

"Even a threshing machine."

"A red one?"

"A red one."

"Okay, Jim—we'll marry the girl no matter what."

The reader will already have observed that his journey to the Filet house was not in vain. Signor Meditato is not quite the gentleman the reader thought. Nor is he the brilliant match that's in Donna Leo's mind. But then neither is Carlotta the brilliant match that's in Meditato Filet's mind. So it looks as if Donna Leo and Signor Filet are each, if the reader will pardon a rather vulgar expression, about to con the other.

chapter 12

The large first-form study hall, for the older boys, was deadly silent. The master slept, unfeigned and whole-heartedly, beside his desk; the boys were huddled over their desks, their heads sunk in their books.

It was the last study hour on Saturday morning, and though the instructor may have slept, the first article of the rules of behavior (chapter on "Duties") stood guard, sleep-less and relentless: "Any student who, at noon on the day preceding a holiday, is unable to present on request the entire week's work written out with the greatest care will not be allowed to enjoy the scheduled free time."

A folded bit of paper landed, with admirable precision, on

the notebook of the student Nicolino Grissin. The airmail missile read: "Pass me at once the problem, the exercise in logical analysis, the Latin translation, and the history summary. Otherwise I'm done for! Yours, C.D."

Nicolino turned toward C.D., who was sitting at a desk in another part of the room, and nodded. Nicolino was fourteen years old but even when he stood on tiptoe was no taller than a ten-year-old; hence he could crawl, unseen by the sleepy eyes of the instructor, past the legs of his fellow students across the room to a particular door.

The student C.D. went to the same door, but in a more legal manner: first he raised two fingers and received permission from the proctor.

Next to the toilet was the storeroom for firewood, and there the two students sought refuge.

"The whole week's work!" said Nicolino. "May I ask what you've been doing up to now?"

"Nicolino," begged the student C.D. (who is unquestionably Camillo Debrai), "give it to me to copy or I'm done for. If I don't have it ready in an hour, they won't let me out tomorrow—and I'm expecting a very important visit."

"Who's coming?" asked gossipy Nicolino.

"Somebody I'm interested in," Camillo replied.

"I know! It's that little cousin of yours that you went out on the lake with one Sunday. I saw you. She's not bad, that little cousin of yours."

"Give me the work, Nicolino!" cried Camillo impatiently. "Don't be like that."

"Only," said Nicolino artfully, "if you tell me who the girl is."

"I've already told you, haven't I? She's my cousin."

"Nuts! Nobody's that interested in cousins. More likely she's your girlfriend."

"All right, she's my fiancée. Now let's have the work."

"But fiancées don't come alone to Switzerland to see their prospective husbands and go out with them in a boat and so on. Tell the truth, Camillo—she's a . . ." Nicolino winked.

Camillo was furious. "Nicolino!" he cried. "How dare you? She's my wife!"

At that point, as may be imagined, there might have been violence, but Nicolino only stood with his mouth open and his eyes wide. "It never occurred to me," he stuttered. "I'm sorry, Camillo . . . Here's the work!"

Somewhat later, during the half hour of liberty before lunch, they met in a corner of the courtyard.

"Nicolino," said Camillo, "please don't make things tough for me—don't say anything to anybody. You understand, it might be a little embarrassing."

Nicolino was fourteen years old. However, even when he stood on tiptoe, he didn't look more than ten. He smiled in a superior manner and said, "We're not boys, after all, Camillo!" And then he went on, in a serious tone: "Camillo, everyone likes you, because you're a good football player, or because you're a good guy, or else because they think you're a poor nut, as the head said, who's lost his memory. But not me—I've always liked you because you're an artist and you've got a sweet nature and you're intelligent, and I always thought they were playing a trick on you. But now I don't know. You've got a wife and yet you're willing to stay quietly here in school with a lot of boys learning logical analysis. Tell me the truth, Camillo. Are you crazy?"

"No, Nicolino," sighed Camillo, "I'm in love."

He needed to unburden himself to somebody, and so he told Nicolino briefly about his strange adventure, about his overwhelming love for Carlotta, and how he had agreed to stay in school because it seemed the only way to make himself an acceptable husband for his wife. "There are men who kill themselves for love," Camillo concluded. "And no one marvels at it. So why should anybody be astonished if a man goes to school for love?"

Nicolino shook his head. "If I had guessed," he said, "that the lessons I gave you would help get you into a boat with that woman you were talking about, I wouldn't have given them to you. She's a kind of Lucrezia Borgia."

Camillo laughed.

But Nicolino had read a lot of historical novels and was first in philosophy. His ideas were very clear. "Her plan," he declared, "is to make you seem crazy in the eyes of the world. Then one fine day she'll have you shut up in an asylum, and that way she'll be rid of you."

"Nicolino," Camillo said with great assurance, "you talk that way because you don't know her."

"Personally no. But I know women."

"Whoever's late to the table goes without fruit," said one of the masters who happened to be passing.

The two boys hurried off to the dining hall.

After lunch, they met again in the same corner of the courtyard, but Nicolino was unable to impart his wise counsel to Camillo, for a porter interrupted: "Signor Debrai to the parlor right away."

"But today is Saturday," stammered Camillo. "Tomorrow is Sunday."

Maybe, thought Camillo, as he headed toward the parlor, she wanted to see me so much she couldn't wait till tomorrow.

And his heart, as usual, burst into a thousand bits.

As he crossed the room, he heard a rude voice say, "Here's our famous idiot!"

He heard a gentle voice say, "How's our famous husband?"

He grew pale as he looked at Signor Casimiro Wonder and Robinia Food.

There are always people in novels that are born by mistake. There are such people in real life too, but the thing isn't so serious as it is in novels, especially serials. The celebrated Lapin De La Casse, the author of very fast moving serial stories, was the victim of one of these characters born by mistake. De La Casse was writing a story of love and adventure for an important newspaper. When he reached the seventh installment, he realized that three installments back he had left a certain Jeremy Slapp waiting, after having met the hero, in a back room at the Café de la Patonne.

"Now, what am I going to do with that idiot?" asked the annoyed author. He tried to find some solution to the problem, but the best he could do was to have him write a letter beginning, "I waited in vain for you in a back room at the Café de la Patonne," and ending, "In any case, my address is . . ."

For another three installments, Jeremy Slapp was left peacefully at home, and then letters began to arrive from readers annoyed that little use was being made of someone as likable as Jeremy Slapp and that he was allowed to be completely idle.

The writer was forced therefore to bring Jeremy out of the darkness every now and then and with superhuman effort make him do something or other, at which Jeremy would behave in the most eccentric and undependable manner possible. Poor Lapin De La Casse, when he reread the installment in the newspaper, blushed with shame and bit his fingernails. But there seemed to be no other, less crazy way of employing Jeremy.

Meanwhile, the flow of letters increased, and all spoke with wild enthusiasm of Jeremy Slapp: women and men both were madly in love with Jeremy Slapp. "He's divine . . . He has a most original personality . . . He's a breath of fresh air in the contemporary novel . . . Dickens's characters are pale and lifeless when compared with Jeremy Slapp . . ."

Poor Lapin De La Casse howled in rage, and fought with both logic and his conscience to find something to do with

Jeremy Slapp. When God willed, the serial ended, and a very important publishing house offered Lapin De La Casse a large sum of money for the rights to publish the installments in book form; their sole condition was that the title be changed to *Jeremy Slapp*. "You understand," they said, "the main interest of the book is Jeremy."

De La Casse, gnashing his teeth, agreed; and when the book came out, the critics reviewed it exclusively as a vehicle for Jeremy Slapp. The history of literature today lists Lapin De La Casse as "the immortal creator of the immortal Jeremy Slapp."

It is always possible to tell a character born by mistake because he remains unemployed for a long period of time, then suddenly leaps into the book, and the reader cries, "Well! Look who's here!"

This is not, however, the case with Signor Casimiro Wonder. There's been no sign of life from Signor Casimiro Wonder for a long time quite simply because he has had a lot of things to do: personal matters that are none of the reader's business. But when he does return, it will not be as a background figure from some old, forgotten chapter but as an important character with a position of his own.

Life in the Madellis house was unusually quiet. Donna Leo, Carlotta, Donna Flaminia, Donna Elisabetta, Signor Gastone, and Signorino Edo had all left on Friday afternoon to spend Saturday with the Bigoudis-la-Lumme, and Robinia had remained alone to look after the deserted house.

Robinia did her looking-after in a figurative, rather than an absolute, sense: it consisted, in the main, in having a good long sleep, though the clock had already sounded ten.

When Uncle Casimiro found her in bed, he was furious.

"Only one member of this loathsome family here," he screamed, "and she's sleeping like a log!"

Robinia opened an eye and asked if the house was on fire. Then she opened both eyes.

"And is this the way to wake respectable people?" she inquired indignantly.

"No," cried Uncle Casimiro, "this is the way to wake up a do-nothing like you and all the other Madellises in the world! Where's Carlotta?"

"Good morning, Uncle. Carlotta is a guest of the Bigoudis-la-Lumme, and will be back this evening."

"Is that miserable husband of hers with her?"

"Of course not. Why should he be?"

"Because he's her husband!" shrieked Uncle Casimiro. "Where is he then, if he's not with his wife?"

Robinia pretended great surprise. "Didn't you know, Uncle? Didn't you know that Camillo's going to school?"

"School? To do what?"

"Why, to learn." Robinia laughed. "He's learning all sorts of little things."

Uncle Casimiro advised Robinia that if she didn't explain what was going on, she'd get a smacking, and Robinia declared that all she wanted to do was explain, and in a few words she did explain.

"What is this, some kind of stupid joke you're trying to play on me?" Uncle Casimiro's tone was threatening.

But Robinia was not frightened. "Not at all, Uncle Casimiro," she said. "It's so absolutely true that I'll go with you myself to Camillo's school. We can be back by this evening—it's only about three hours."

"Be careful, Robinia."

"If everything I've told you isn't the truth, I hereby authorize you to throw me into the lake beside the Pipet School."

Uncle Casimiro did not say a word throughout the journey. Nor did he speak when they reached the school and Robinia asked that her cousin, the student Debrai, be summoned. He did not speak until he saw Camillo. Then, as has already been noted, he cried: "Here's our famous idiot!"

"Good afternoon, Uncle Casimiro," stammered Camillo.

"Is this the way to play the husband?" roared Uncle Casimiro.

Robinia interrupted softly: "Let's go some place where you can bellow, Uncle, without making a scandal. Wait a minute while I get permission from the headmaster for our student to leave the grounds."

The three of them walked silently through the town and at last arrived at a lonely, deserted café, whose tables were set up beside the blue waters of the lake.

"Is it possible," asked Uncle Casimiro after they were seated, "for a human being to be any more of an idiot? Would you mind explaining what this lunacy is all about?"

"No lunacy, Uncle Casimiro," said Camillo sadly. "My

only lunacy was marrying Carlotta. Now that I've done that, whatever other crazy things I do to try to make her love me are justifiable. Unless you think it's best to break up our marriage and let everybody go his own way."

Uncle Casimiro did not berate Camillo; perhaps he realized that he was to blame for all the misfortunes that had befallen the humble woodcarver.

"Yours is not," he remarked, "a wholly false line of reasoning. Yet bear in mind that there is always a minimal amount of dignity which must be preserved. If you're willing to come here and learn logical analysis and how to eat chicken, tomorrow will you be ready to dress up like a little girl and learn how to crochet or make lace because that's what your lunatic wife wants?"

Robinia began to laugh outrageously, and Uncle Casimiro gave her a stern look. "What's so funny?" he shouted.

"The thought of Camillo crocheting!" She dissolved into laughter again. "Or making filet!"

The unhappy Camillo, hearing the name Filet, turned pale. "You're wicked, Robinia," he whispered.

Uncle Casimiro, who had been lost in his thoughts, now turned again to Camillo. "Basically, my boy," he said warmly, "you're right. If this is what you want to do, no one's going to stop you. Besides, there's always the possibility that your sacrifice will be appreciated by your wife and make her like you better. Stay here then as long as you want, and if you need anything write me. Shall we take Camillo back to school, Robinia?"

"There's something I'd like to tell him," replied Robinia.

"I'll take him back. We still have a couple of hours—wait for me in the Imperial lobby. I'll be there soon."

Uncle Casimiro walked off, and when he was far enough away, he ground his teeth and kicked a cat that happened to be passing.

So, he said to himself, they're trying to lead Casimiro Wonder by the nose! To the devil with the crusader's family! I'll teach them to send a husband to school. They'll find out, they'll find out now, at once! I'll change my will again. We'll see who gets the last laugh!"

When Uncle Casimiro reached the Imperial, he was in very good humor.

"And if Camillo," he murmured aloud, "isn't an absolute fool, he can make them all drop dead of sheer fury. What a picture!"

Once they were alone, neither Camillo nor Robinia could think of anything to say for quite some time.

"Camillo," Robinia said at last, "will you permit me to ask you something?"

"I am at your service, Signorina Robinia."

"Well, then, here it is," said Robinia sweetly. "Do you know that you're the greatest fool of the century?"

"Yes," replied Camillo sadly. "Yes, I know it."

"But I," declared Robinia, "say that you don't know it."

"No, no, I know it, Signorina Robinia. I know it, you know it, everybody knows it, even Nicolino knows it."

"You don't know a thing," Robinia laughed, "you and your Nicolino. Do you remember last Saturday, when you ran away from school, what happened at the table at home?"

"Yes, I remember it all."

"At the end, then, whom did you drink to and cry three cheers for?"

"The health of the new cabinet."

Robinia laughed. "You drank to the health of the future bride and groom."

"Future what?"

"Carlotta Wonder and Meditato Filet. That was the sensational news Grandma Leo didn't want anyone to mention."

"You're joking!" cried Camillo. "You're making it all up to hurt me."

With absolute clarity Robinia expounded Donna Leo's plan. "What I've done now," she concluded, "is not very friendly toward my cousin, but is very friendly toward you. I'd rather help you than my cousin. I like you better."

Camillo looked at Robinia in complete astonishment.

"But I," he stammered, "I—I don't know how to thank you for your kindness—"

"Don't put yourself out," said Robinia with a smile, as she rose. "I know how to thank myself."

Leaning down, she gave Camillo a memorable kiss right on the lips.

Signorina Robinia, having paid herself for her trouble, left Camillo, but before abandoning him altogether to his fate, put some money into the hands of a sturdy boatman and said, "Keep an eye on that young man there by the edge of the lake. If he jumps in, fish him out again."

But Camillo only sat down on the ground, with his legs dangling over the water, and there he stayed chewing bits of grass for so long that the sturdy boatman, who had been patiently waiting with his oars ready, approached the bank and held out the bank note Robinia had given him.

"If you're going to throw yourself in, do it right away," said the honest boatman. "Otherwise, here's the money, and you throw yourself in when you want, on your own hook. I can't just sit around here waiting."

Camillo rose and went back toward the school, muttering to himself, "Poor fool, poor fool."

"Well?" said Nicolino, when he saw him coming back.

"It seems you're right, Nicolino," he replied sadly, but said no more. He closed himself in his room, and no one could get him out till the following morning.

They say that the Prince of Condé slept well during the night that preceded some battle or other; so they say. Camillo Debrai, on the other hand, didn't close an eye during the night that preceded Sunday. He clutched the grating on his window and stared out into the night. He watched the yellow moon turn white, and the sky grow whiter, and the stars disappear one by one. Then he realized he hadn't even got undressed, and he waited for the alarm to ring.

"Well?" asked Nicolino again, when he saw him at breakfast.

Camillo nodded gloomily. "Today she's supposed to come to see me, and I'll tell her what I have to."

"Good!" said Nicolino. "And you better give her a smack or two."

"Carlotta? A smack or two?"

"Sure. That's the way to treat women, my boy," declared Nicolino, who was fourteen years old but even when he stood on tiptoe didn't look more than ten.

"A smack or two," repeated Camillo. "Think of that!"

When, a few hours later, a porter came to tell Camillo he was wanted in the parlor, he headed there with only one thought in mind: he would see Carlotta, he would talk to her, he would tell her that he loved her very much.

"I knew those stories of Robinia's were lies," he assured himself as he crossed the room, and to beg her pardon for having doubted her, he would unquestionably have thrown himself on his knees at her feet—but for one detail. The person waiting for him was not Carlotta but a man, who handed him a note. Camillo read it in astonishment:

I'm staying with the Countess Luisella De Sambot, who ran into me as I was coming out of the station and insisted I come with her. You come too, then you can meet my dearest friend.

Yours,
Carlotta

"I'm the countess's secretary," said the man. "The car is outside. It's only a few miles—the countess's villa is at Melinette."

"Let's go!" cried Camillo.

"You can't leave," shouted the porter, "without permission from the headmaster."

"I've got my wife's permission!" cried Camillo as he jumped into the car. "That's a lot better!"

The car moved along at a good clip and was soon climbing a very pretty stretch of road.

After about half an hour, the car entered a courtyard. "Here we are," said the secretary.

Camillo jumped down, and as he did, a heavy sack was put over his head, and while his hands were being tied, he heard someone say: "Lock him up down in the basement."

chapter 13

"Damn all the weekends in the world!" cried Carlotta, in reply to Donna Leo's request to know the reason for her ill-humor.

The remark was made in the historic green room of the famous country house of the Madellis, in the presence of all members of the family: it called forth a chorus of disapproval for the inelegance of its style as well as for the rudeness of its concept, both previously unheard of in Carlotta's conversation.

"It seems odd to me," Donna Leo observed coldly, "that you should acquire so sudden an aversion to end-of-the-week country entertainments. What is even odder is the tone in which you express that aversion."

"Odd, my hat!" cried Carlotta. Mouths stood agape at this new barbarity, even that of Giusmaria, who was watching and listening behind the service entrance, as a good butler should.

"I do not understand," announced Donna Leo, pale and trembling.

"It's quite simple," replied Carlotta. "In order to spend the weekend with the Bigoudis-la-Lumme, we left Friday afternoon, and we've just returned, late Sunday afternoon. So damn all weekends in the world for being a waste of time and making one miss appointments!"

"Carlotta," said Donna Flaminia, "is it possible that my daughter, my only daughter, has appointments of which I am ignorant? With whom, if I may be permitted to inquire."

"With my husband, naturally!" said Carlotta, annoyed.

"I do not find it at all natural," returned Donna Flaminia, "that you should be making appointments with your husband. Are you determined to compromise yourself irreparably?"

Carlotta wrung her hands. "Are we determined," she cried, "to behave like the Tarantines, who, when Attila was at their gate, went on arguing about whether cherubim have wings or not?"

"I beg your pardon," said Uncle Gastone, "it was not the Tarantines, it was the Byzantines. And it wasn't Attila, it was some other barbarian. Furthermore, that subject was rather more subtle. Isn't that true, Edo?"

"Yes, of course," agreed Edo, who, as he did not lack a certain degree of common sense, took no interest in the discussion.

"Quite right, quite right," said Gastone Food. "Nevertheless, it has not yet emerged precisely what subject was being discussed by the Byzantines while the enemy stood at their gates—"

"A subject on a level with this one!" cried Carlotta. "Go on, go right on! And meanwhile, Signor Debrai, whom I promised to visit today, will think that he has been fooled again. Unable to withstand the passion that devours him, he will have jumped over the wall of the school and will even now be on his way by forced marches to our very house. And that's why I said damn all weekends that prevented me from going to pay him the promised visit today."

"Forgive me, Carlotta," said Donna Flaminia, embracing her daughter. "My suspicions of you were unjust. It was indeed imprudent to offer further provocation to that madman."

"He must be kept away," said Donna Leo, "at any cost. "We require complete freedom of action just now. Furthermore, so long as Debrai remains voluntarily in the boys' school it will be much easier for us to demonstrate that he is off his head and therefore incapable of playing the husband. He must be kept away at any cost."

"Unfortunately I would not be surprised to see him turning up here tonight," said Carlotta. "He's insanely in love with me, poor thing."

"Do you really think so?" said Robinia. "I don't have that impression."

"I know my husband!" cried Carlotta, rather annoyed.

"So do I," said Robinia with a smile.

At this point the reader may well wonder what strange thoughts had been passing through the mind of Signorina Robinia. Who would have expected her to help Camillo by playing out the comedy in the garden? And what about yesterday's strange expedition with Uncle Casimiro? And the revealing of the plan that was being worked out against poor Camillo?

Does Robinia hate her cousin Carlotta, then? Or is it not hate for someone but a love of justice that inspires Robinia to aid the weak and the oppressed?

Or is it something else? The reader may have forgotten the scene in the garden, but he couldn't possibly forget the scene beside the lake, when Robinia declared that she was accustomed to paying for herself and gave Camillo that memorable kiss. When a woman goes around giving kisses to a man, she doesn't do it out of hate for some other woman or out of love of justice.

No, it seems very likely that Robinia was in love with Camillo. The reader must not be surprised, then, however wildly Robinia behaves: a woman in love is capable of anything. Even of hating the man she loves. It is not necessary to seek the reason for this in the place where such reasons are usually sought. On the contrary. People say, "You can never tell what a woman in love is going to do because a woman in love is not capable of reasoning." That is incorrect. The truth is that a woman does not normally reason, she lives and behaves by instinct; but a woman in love begins to reason—and to reason, alas, as only a woman can.

Carlotta was not forced to reply to her cousin's insinuation: Giusmaria saved her.

"Signor Morbillier," he announced, as everyone stared at him in astonishment, wondering what on earth Uncle Casimiro's lawyer wanted with them.

"Perhaps," said Edo, giving voice to the general silence, "the good man has come to announce Signor Wonder's retirement from this world."

But quite obviously Signor Casimiro Wonder was still benefitting from uncommonly good health; unfortunately for the Madellises as they were soon to find out.

"My client," said the lawyer, "Signor Casimiro Wonder, has made a slight change in his will and desires me to make you acquainted with it."

"We are very grateful to Signor Wonder," Donna Leo replied with great dignity. "Not on our own behalf, for the matter is of interest to us only incidentally, but on behalf particularly of our little Carlotta, presumably the only interested party."

The lawyer brought the will out of his briefcase and now proceeded to read the slight modification: "I leave all my worldly goods to the children that my niece Carlotta Wonder Debrai may bear to her husband Camillo Debrai. If within one year from today there should be no children of this union, my entire estate is to go unconditionally to the Brachette Foundation, which is pledged to pay the sum of five thousand francs monthly, during their natural lives, to my niece Carlotta Wonder and her husband Camillo Debrai, beginning the day after the birth of their first child—and only then."

The lawyer laid a copy of the testament down on a table.

"Signor Casimiro Wonder," he said, "has charged me with informing you that, precisely one year from today, he will suspend payment of all moneys to the family and will assign it instead, with a suitable accretion, to the child that he expects to be born within the year."

"What happens," asked Signor Gastone, "if this child refuses to obey the commands of Signor Wonder?"

"Then nobody gets anything," said the lawyer, and he left them.

The family looked at one another in dismay.

"Monstrous!" exclaimed Donna Leo. "Abominable! To expect us to give him a child within twelve months!"

"To be precise," said Edo, who was not without a certain degree of common sense, "he doesn't expect us to produce the child, he expects it of Carlotta."

"How," sobbed Donna Flaminia, "how can he require such a horrible thing of a poor girl who knows nothing of life? How can he?"

"Don't you see, Aunt Flaminia," said Edo, with his degree

of common sense, "he doesn't expect Carlotta to produce the child by herself. That would really be too demanding. No, Signor Wonder expects it to result from a collaboration between Carlotta and her husband."

"No!" cried Donna Leo grandly. "We shall never permit such shame to befall us!"

"I wouldn't have the courage to raise my head," said Signor Gastone Food, "if I gave birth to a nephew who answered to the name of Debrai."

"Indeed not!" said Donna Elisabetta. "No wretched Debrai will ever make *me* an aunt!"

"A child of shame!" said Donna Flaminia darkly.

Robinia merely smiled a highly ambiguous smile.

Behind the door, Giusmaria wept. "I could never bear it!" he sobbed.

Abruptly Carlotta broke her silence. "I beg of you," she said, "not to begin all these academic discussions over again. This peculiar business will have to be ended once and for all. There's no time to lose—tomorrow morning I'll go up to see him by the first train."

"I don't feel," said Donna Leo, "that the matter is quite so urgent as you pretend. I know that you like things to be settled without delay. Nevertheless, bear in mind that we have a year ahead of us. The so-called Signor Wonder has assured us that for one more year he will give us our allowance, and in a year we'll be able to arrange something calmly and quietly."

Carlotta's voice was annoyed. "I'm afraid I can't agree," she said, "with your way of thinking, Grandma Leo. You claim there's time to arrange things, whereas I don't see how Uncle Casimiro is going to have a grandnephew within a year unless—well—unless it gets going right away."

Carlotta blushed as she spoke these last words. Donna Leo, her aunt, her mother, and Signor Gastone looked at her in great surprise.

"My poor little Carlotta!" cried Donna Leo, opening wide her arms. "I'm afraid all these silly mix-ups have upset you. You have forgotten the most important thing of all! What does this so-called Signor Wonder matter to us anyway? We won't need him once you're married to Signor Filet."

It was at this moment that Carlotta spoke the first historic sentence of her life. "I don't give a damn," she said, "for Signor Meditato Filet!"

The meeting opened wide its eyes.

"You don't give a damn," Donna Leo repeated, horrified, "for Signor Meditato Filet? The man you're going to marry?"

"I haven't the slightest intention of marrying him," declared Carlotta.

Donna Leo spread her arms in consternation. "If you don't want to marry Signor Filet," she said, "whom do you want to marry?"

"I want to marry Camillo!" cried Carlotta, clenching her fists.

"She wants to marry her husband," muttered Donna Leo. "How shocking!"

The rest of the family looked suitably shocked.

"Despite the fact," said Carlotta vigorously, "that our sweet little Robinia keeps smiling at me in that very odd way, there is nothing romantic about my decision. I am aware that my husband has the kind of good looks that might be called 'popular' and that attract girls of easy taste and limited intelligence. Thus I can see how a little fool like Robinia could fall in love with him—"

"Grandma Leo!" cried Robinia, with feigned dismay. "Her husband's wife, and jealous! How horrible! Poor Carlotta!"

"Your lofty irony does not disturb me," said Carlotta, with a bitter laugh. "As I was saying, this is not a question of romance. Quite simply, I am not going to give up a sure husband for a probable one, and a certain legacy for uncertain wealth. With the danger of ending up without either husband or money. We must all make our sacrifices for the common good, and if I sacrifice my ideals and my freedom and agree that a Debrai become the father of my child, you can sacrifice a little of your family pride and agree to it too. Basically, after all, I'm the victim, not you. You reap the benefit of my sacrifice. Even if I hadn't married, Uncle Casimiro would always have given me enough for myself and my needs."

This was not just rebellion but outright revolution, and the Madellis family watched with dismay as Carlotta, red-faced and with eyes bright with unshed tears, spoke so sternly and so forcefully.

Donna Leo rose. "Has God let me live so long," she wept,

"only to give me the pain of hearing a Madellis, someone of my own blood, talk like a sausage-maker? How lucky you are, Sappho Madellis! Heaven has shielded you from this blow!" Donna Leo wiped away a tear.

"My daughter," cried Donna Flaminia, "you, my daughter, a Madellis—"

"Enough of that!" said Carlotta. "I'm not a Madellis after all, I'm a Wonder. And my father, if I'm not mistaken, did not descend from the crusades but from sausages. And what's more you, Mother, you, a Madellis, you married him!"

"Oh! That she should judge me!" sobbed Donna Flaminia. "That she should condemn me!"

"Silence, heartless wretch!" commanded Donna Leo. "Do you belittle your mother's sacrifice?"

There was a moment of profoundest silence.

Then Signor Gastone sighed. "The sins of the fathers," he said, "fall on their innocent sons. It's fate. . . ." But then, as he saw that Donna Elisabetta was looking at him with obvious disapproval, he corrected himself. "The sins of the mothers fall on their innocent daughters. . . ." But he saw the look in Donna Elisabetta's eye, so he sighed again and made another correction: "The sins of the uncles fall on their innocent nieces. . . . Casimiro Wonder, you're a monster!"

Silence fell again.

Carlotta saw her mother weeping; her grandmother sitting with her head bent; her uncle looking pale; her aunt staring off into space, her lips pressed; and her cousin smiling scornfully. She also saw that her cousin Edo, who was not without a certain degree of common sense, was working a crossword puzzle. Nonetheless, she felt like an ungrateful daughter, a corrupt granddaughter, a guilty niece.

She was just about to cry and beg pardon for her wickedness, when Giusmaria interrupted again. He turned on the lights, it now being nine o'clock in the evening, and he handed Donna Leo a telegram.

How often a single stroke of color against a dull background is sufficient to change the composition of the whole picture. The little yellow square gave new warmth to the icy meeting.

Everyone raised his head and looked at Donna Leo.

"Read it," she said, handing the telegram to Signor Gastone.

Signor Gastone read: "STUDENT DEBRAI ESCAPED. FLED EARLY AFTERNOON COMPANY UNKNOWN PERSON IN AUTO-MOBILE. NOTHING MORE KNOWN. PLEASE TELEGRAPH WHETHER RETURNED HOME OR NOT. REGARDS. HEADMASTER PIPET."

"I knew he'd run away," said Carlotta. "He'll be here tomorrow morning."

"Let's hope," said perfidious Robinia.

"The matter is no longer of interest to us," said Donna Leo, in a tone of disgust. "It is of interest only to Carlotta." She called Giusmaria back. "Giusmaria," she said, "the apartment in the left wing is to be put in order. Open it, air it, prepare a double bedroom. Signorina Carlotta is marrying and will move to the left wing with her husband."

"Very good, madam. And when will the happy event take place, if I may ask?"

"Tonight, or tomorrow."

"Very good, madam. Then the matter is a very urgent one."

"Irreparable, Giusmaria."

"Very good, madam."

"Very bad, Giusmaria."

"Very bad, madam, very bad indeed."

"If Signor Filet calls tomorrow, tell him that we have gone away and will return in a month. I'll write a note this evening that you may give to him."

"Very good, madam."

"Very bad, Giusmaria."

"Very bad indeed, madam."

As Giusmaria withdrew, he seemed more bent than ever. Donna Leo shook her head. "Poor old thing," she murmured. "How he must be suffering too . . ."

"It's humiliating," said Signor Gastone, "when servants have a greater sense of dignity than their masters."

This bitter remark was aimed at Carlotta, but Carlotta gave no sign of having heard it. She continued to stand by the window, looking at the autumn night that had by now descended on the warm garden.

Donna Flaminia clasped her hands and, looking up at the carved ceiling, called heaven to witness such filial impiety.

"In love," she muttered, through clenched teeth. "In love with her husband!"

Carlotta turned suddenly.

"In love with my uncle's legacy!" she said crossly. "That's something entirely different."

It was, indeed, something entirely different, but basically it was the same old thing.

chapter 14

But was any one of them able to sleep that wretched Sunday night? Were any of these gravely preoccupied people able to surrender themselves to the sweetness of dreams?

Not Carlotta certainly, who awaited with fear and trembling the impending arrival of her unbalanced husband.

Or Donna Leo, who, already disheartened by the failure of her superb plan for the redemption of the family, was now faced with the bitter necessity of showing Signor Filet the door.

Or Robinia, tortured by her unrequited passion.

Or Donna Flaminia, or the Foods, who now saw their last

hope vanish of being ever freed from bondage to Signor Casimiro.

Or Giusmaria, who had heard all and who watched with terror the advancing horde of barbarians.

And not Camillo certainly, last seen under the most frightful circumstances, locked in a cellar.

Two people might, however, have enjoyed a tranquil sleep that night: Edo and Meditato Filet. But Edo, though he was totally disinterested in the affairs that so agitated the others, had a toothache; while Meditato Filet, though he had received the very important telegram he was expecting, was kept awake by a minor incident that had nothing to do with the Madellis matter.

Early Monday morning, then, when Giusmaria went to deliver the letter that Donna Leo had written, he found Signor Filet already working at the papers on his desk. Signor Filet seemed worried.

"Have we had some disagreeable news, Giusmaria?" he asked, as he opened the envelope.

This is what he read:

Dear Signor Filet,

Because of certain unexpected and highly unpleasant complications that have arisen, on the subject of which I beg you to question no further, I regret to tell you that all connections between us must be immediately and irreparably broken.

Out of the friendship that you have always shown us and

the affection that bound you to our unhappy granddaughter, I must ask you to put an end to your highly agreeable visits.

I assure you that if you could, for one moment, imagine the anguish that the writing of these words causes us, you would have no difficulty in forgiving

Your unhappy

Leo Madellis

For a moment or two, Meditato Filet found himself unable to breathe; then, as he looked questioningly at Giusmaria, the butler sighed deeply, and Filet decided that the man knew quite a bit about the affair. Somehow or other, he said to himself, I must get this old fool to talk.

It turned out to be far easier than he thought.

Though Giusmaria, probably the most discreet servant who ever lived, would never have revealed even the tiniest secret concerning the Madellis household to a stranger, he did not consider Signor Filet a stranger. He had liked Signor Filet since the very first day; he began by thinking of him as the ideal employer, then as a probable employer and no less ideal, and finally as a future and welcome employer. Now unexpectedly forced to give up an employer like Signor Filet for one of the contemptible caliber of Camillo, Giusmaria was upset and indignant.

"Giusmaria," said Meditato gravely, "for once in your life forget to be the most perfect butler that I have ever known. Remember only that you are a man—and listen to another man who is speaking to you out of the depths of his anguish.

What dreadful thing have I done that I am forbidden to cross the threshold of the house where I had hoped to find happiness?"

Giusmaria wiped away a tear with his spotless cuff.

"No, sir!" he cried. "I protest. You have done nothing! We are all most unhappy about this, and Madam didn't sleep a wink last night. . . . Oh, sir, it's a terrible thing."

"Giusmaria," said Meditato Filet solemnly, "do you trust me? Do you love the people with whom you've worked for so many years?"

"Yes, sir."

"Then tell me all you know. For I would like—and I am able—to help Donna Leo and Carlotta. So tell me all. And if this does not fall within your duties as a butler, obey your obligations as a man."

"Once upon a time," said Giusmaria, without hesitation, "the Madellis family were very rich, but they were also very openhanded, and at last came to live on a monthly stipend that was given them by Signor Casimiro Wonder, brother of the deceased husband of Donna Flaminia. Everything belongs to him: the house, the villa, the furniture, the carriages. Signor Wonder, who is arrogant, vulgar, and eccentric, required Signorina Carlotta to marry within forty-eight hours or else he would cut off her inheritance, make the family leave the house, and give them nothing to live on. For that reason, Signorina Carlotta married Signor Debrai, who, as Donna Leo told you, was discovered to be unbalanced. . . ."

Meditato Filet could not help smiling, and Giusmaria understood why.

"Sir," he declared, "among the duties of a good butler, the first is to listen at doors. Only by knowing what is going on may he avoid making mistakes that might be irreparable. Had I not eavesdropped, I would not now be in a position to offer, through your kindness, a helping hand to Donna Leo and to Signorina Carlotta."

"I am in full approval, Giusmaria!" cried Filet. "Please continue."

"You know better than I what Donna Leo's intention was—to annul the marriage, not yet by great good luck, consummated, and to give you the hand of Signorina Carlotta. Yesterday, however, most unexpectedly, Signor Wonder's lawyer informed us of a new, and highly criminal, clause introduced by Signor Wonder into his will, whereby Signorina Carlotta may inherit his fortune only if she has a child within one year by her husband Signor Debrai. Otherwise, within one year, Signor Wonder will throw them all out, and cut off their allowance, giving Signorina Carlotta only the minimum necessary for existence."

"So that's the way it is!" cried Filet.

"That is exactly the way it is," declared Giusmaria. Anyone who does not realize that servants listen at doors not only with their ears but also with their eyes glued to the keyhole might be surprised by Giusmaria's next remark: "I heard this, sir, with my own eye!"

Meditato Filet remained for some time sunk in thought, then with honest indignation he cried, "What an abomi-

nable thing!" He was thinking, however, not of the requirements that Signor Casimiro had imposed, but of how nearly
he had come to marrying a woman without a penny. After a
moment he went on: "But why do they now, instead of
counting on my help more than ever, refuse it?"

"Donna Leo," Giusmaria explained, "had every intention
of asking you for the full extent of your help, but Signorina
Carlotta, I'm sorry to say, was of little faith. She felt she ran
the risk of finding herself one day without either husband or
inheritance, and she preferred security, no matter how great
the sacrifice."

"Which is?"

"To, shall we say, complete the marriage." Giusmaria
blushed.

Meditato Filet shook his head sadly. "And Signor Debrai," he said, "must be coming very soon if they ask me to
give up my visits immediately."

"They expect him from one moment to the next. It
appears he has already left school. It may be that he has
arrived."

"You're right," said Signor Filet, in a distant voice, "he
has no doubt arrived."

In the next room, on a dressing table, the yellow telegram
square glittered in the sun. This is what it said: "WINE
BOTTLED AS REQUESTED. NO BOTTLES BROKEN. AWAITING INSTRUC-
TIONS FOR FINAL ARRANGEMENTS. RESPECTFULLY, GIUSEPPE."

Of course the telegram had nothing to do with wine. It
meant: "That nut of a schoolboy with a mustache is locked
in the cellar as you said. Nothing out of the way happened,

nobody suspects anything. Waiting for your permission to get rid of him by knocking him on the head and chucking him into a ravine like a sack of potatoes. Yours, Flick."

It was because of this telegram that Signor Filet, as has already been remarked, ought to have been able to sleep the sleep of the satisfied. What more could he have hoped for? At the right moment, Signor Camillo Debrai would be found at the bottom of a ravine, along with the wreck of an automobile—the victim of an accident; and his widow, Carlotta, would be able to marry Signor Filet.

Here was reason enough to sleep soundly. Yet that night Signor Filet did not sleep—and the cause is to be found in an unexpected event that has nothing to do with the mainstream of the story.

Before going home, Meditato Filet had gone to a late café where he had seen a face that was familiar to him although he could not remember exactly who the person was.

Many of life's smaller problems are more perplexing and time-consuming than the big ones. Does it not happen sometimes that a man, after he has gone to bed, begins to wonder whether he has locked the door or not? He thinks about it for a long time, he tries to recall everything he did in the last quarter of an hour, and at last, in desperation, he gets up and goes to find out whether the door is locked or not.

Then he goes back to bed.

Five minutes later comes the question: "Is the door locked or not?"

"I just got up a second ago to make sure!"

"So you say. But have you any proof that you got up?" asks the other voice in this inner dialogue. "You thought of getting up—"

"For heaven's sake! I'm not out of my mind!"

"Don't get angry about it. Do as you think best. And if in fact the door *was* left open . . ."

After a little while, he sneaks out of bed to see whether the door is locked or not. Finding that it is, he pulls back the bolt and then pushes it to again with a loud bang.

He goes back to bed.

Some ten minutes later, the doubt rises in his mind: "Is the door locked or not?"

This time he gets really angry: how can there be any question, he asks, since he distinctly pulled back the bolt and then pushed it to again? "Or have I lost my mind?"

"For heaven's sake," says the other voice again, "there is no doubt that you distinctly pulled back the bolt. The only real question is, did you push it to again?"

It's maddening, but after some five minutes of this, he gets out of bed again to see whether the door is locked or not.

And so it goes, on and on.

There are even smaller problems. One might, for instance, be alone five thousand feet up a mountain and begin to wonder how many *c*'s there are in "necessary." This is the kind of problem that can be discussed for hours on end, since there is not the slightest possibility of solving it.

Another of the same sort is that of the familiar face, and

that is the problem that kept Signor Filet awake during the night. "Yes," he muttered a thousand times, "I'm sure I saw him in prison, but was he in the cell with me, or was he one of the guards?"

But surely by now it's time to leave Signor Filet's bedroom, having read the telegram on the dressing table, and return to the study, where Meditato Filet is having his discussion with Giusmaria.

The study is empty!

It would probably be easier to locate Giusmaria than Meditato Filet.

The Madellis house: nine o'clock. The family has breakfasted and is now in the red room, each with a morning newspaper before him and each reading the strangest things.

"How shocking!" Donna Leo reads. "What will Signor Filet think of us? What a dreadful girl! And how she'll pay for it! And why doesn't Giusmaria come back?"

"What will people say," reads Donna Flaminia Food, "when we have to introduce that husband of hers to society? What a dreadful girl! And how she'll pay for it!"

Robinia: "I'd marry him myself, just to spite Carlotta. And he hasn't turned up yet! Oh, oh, oh!"

Carlotta: "What's the matter with that fool? No sign of him yet! Where has he got to?"

Edo Food: "A rich English planter treated his twenty black slaves worse than usual, so one day the unhappy creatures ran away and hid in the forest. The planter tracked them down and from behind a tree watched the twenty Negroes cutting up a long rope with the obvious intention of hanging themselves so as to escape further mistreatment. The planter realized that the death of twenty slaves would ruin him, so he came out and asked them to give him a piece of rope too, so he could hang himself as well. At that point, the Negroes, in terror of finding themselves on the other side with their ferocious owner, gave up the idea of hanging themselves and went back to the plantation. . . ."

It was only Edo, obviously, who was reading the words in front of him; the others were reading the words that were imprinted in their brains.

There was a long silence.

It was broken, at last, by Robinia, who suffered greatly when she was unable to speak. "Mama," she said, rather loudly, "you've got the local newspaper. Look at the lost and found section and see whether a husband who disappeared yesterday has been recovered."

"It's easier to recover a husband," said Carlotta, "than to get one in the first place."

"Sharp reply of young wife to bitter old maid," said Edo, "for teasing about non-arrival of schoolboy-husband."

Robinia was about to continue her attack, much annoyed, when Giusmaria entered, out of breath and white as a sheet.

Everyone knew at once that something absolutely terrible had happened: Giusmaria had entered *without knocking!*

"Madam!" he sobbed. "Madam! How terrible!"

Donna Leo ordered him to speak.

"Signor Filet," said Giusmaria, "was so kind as to ask me to convey his compliments to you, when suddenly several strange men entered the room. One of them laughed coarsely. 'No,' he said, 'I didn't make a mistake when I saw you last night in the café. You're Jim Lapatte, and we've been looking for you in the matter of the Brenton jewels. This time you won't get away.'"

Giusmaria wiped away the sweat that streamed from his forehead as though he were a gardener or a stableboy. Then he went on: "Signor Filet began to laugh. 'Either you're having a joke,' he said, 'or you're the victim of some strange misapprehension. In any event, the thing can be cleared up at the police station. I am naturally willing to accompany you, but I trust you will allow me to put on a jacket and a topcoat. I don't believe you would ask me to go out in my dressing gown.' The other man said all right, but went with him into the dressing room, and then into the next room. A little while later we heard a loud noise. The others ran in and found a man with a chair over his head."

Giusmaria fell silent.

"And who on earth was he?" asked Signor Gastone.

"He was not Signor Filet," said Giusmaria. "When the man came to, he said Signor Filet must have got away through a door hidden behind a hanging. They all ran off to follow him."

Donna Leo did not even have time to faint, things moved so quickly. A frightened servant girl ran in, screaming, "Police!" Then right on her heels came a man with a forthright expression.

"Signora Leo Madellis?" he asked.

"Yes?" murmured Donna Leo.

"My name is Percot, police inspector. In the house of the man calling himself Meditato Filet, a well-known confidence man and thief, we have found this letter of yours in which you ask him not to call here any more. Has he perhaps tried something on you?"

"No," said Donna Leo, with great dignity. "But I realized that there was something not quite right about him and I determined not to allow him to frequent my house any longer."

"You were wise. There is an allusion in this letter to an attachment with your granddaughter. Is there anything to that?"

"He was paying court to my granddaughter Robinia," said Donna Leo. "He had asked for her hand in marriage."

Robinia blushed in annoyance but had sufficient self-control to say nothing.

The inspector began to laugh. "You had a lucky escape!" he cried. "You'd better thank God for it."

"Have you arrested him?" asked Gastone.

"He got away again," grumbled the inspector. "But we'll find him, don't worry."

After he left, Donna Leo took time to faint for a few minutes. When she came to, she was attacked by Robinia.

"So I'm the one," cried Robinia, "that escaped convicts pay court to! Why didn't you tell him the truth?"

"The truth is always what is said," Donna Leo declared, "not what ought to be said. Furthermore, I cannot permit objections to my behavior—I act always for the common good."

Then Donna Leo turned to Carlotta.

"You may thank your poor old grandmother, my child," she said. "If I hadn't made you behave with the utmost caution, you might be in some ghastly situation now. Dishonored perhaps, with no husband, no legacy. Next time, remember to listen to the voice of experience. Remember it, Carlotta."

"Yes, Grandma Leo," said Carlotta simply, with no surprise in her voice, for she was used to Grandma Leo. "And thank you."

After a hasty lunch, the family reconvened in the historic green room, where Donna Leo made an overall appraisal of the situation.

"The infamous clause," she concluded, "that the so-called Signor Wonder has imposed on us fills us with indignation. Nevertheless we must, though with bleeding hearts, accept it. Within a year we must present that contemptible person with a great-nephew. We shall do it. Time presses, therefore, and we must recover Signor Debrai as soon as possible."

"I agree," remarked Signor Gastone. "But how are we going to recover him if we don't know where he is?"

"He won't be much longer," said Carlotta, easily. "After all, it's only twenty-four hours since he left school."

"But so many things can happen in twenty-four hours," murmured Robinia, with an ambiguous smile.

"The other day," said Edo Food, who was not without a

degree of common sense, "I borrowed three thousand francs from the man calling himself Meditato Filet. Should I give them back?"

"I forbid any child of mine to have further relations with such a person," said Gastone Food, who had borrowed seven thousand francs from the man calling himself Meditato Filet.

chapter 15

"The silly old fool came just in time," snickered the man eating bread and cheese at a table in a humble kitchen.

"I don't see the connection," observed the man watching him eat, "between a silly old fool and your getaway."

"I know, I'd have got here safe even if he hadn't turned up. But I wouldn't have known I owned a million francs."

"Joking, Jim?"

"No, Flick, I'm not. Don't you get it yet? The girl inherits only if she and that other fool you've got locked up in the cellar downstairs have a kid inside a year. Casimiro Wonder's fortune being enormous, it means that the fool downstairs is worth at least a cool million."

Open-mouthed, the man called Flick stared at the man calling himself Meditato Filet. The latter continued: "We change step, that's all. First we wanted to get rid of Debrai, now we've got to hold on to him carefully till the girl slips us the million. Nobody knows us here in Switzerland. I tell you, Flick, we've got it made."

"Okay," said Flick, "but we haven't got any time to waste."

"Right. We'll go down now and get him to write the letter. They'll bring the money to us, don't worry. And they won't say a word—for one thing, they're worried about the inheritance, and for another, they don't want to get laughed at. Flick, bring a lantern."

The cellar door was fastened by a huge bolt, which took a minute or two to draw. Once that was done, and the door thrown wide, the man calling himself Filet took the opportunity to launch the most colorful stream of invective he had ever launched in his life.

The fool worth a million francs was gone. Through a large hole in the wall could be seen the moonlight on the garden outside.

A shadow moved in the darkness of the garden wall.

"There he is!" cried the man calling himself Filet.

Flick drew his revolver and shot into the darkness as he ran across the garden.

There were traces of blood on the low wall: the fugitive, clearly, had been wounded.

"He won't get very far!" cried Filet. He and Flick set off in pursuit.

The fugitive wasn't running, he was rolling down the slope of the hill on which the house was built. At the bottom of the dell, a stream of water glittered in the moonlight, and perhaps the fugitive hoped to reach it and let the water carry him away.

The other two were close on his heels.

"Stop!" cried Flick. "Unless you want a couple of holes in your back!"

A shot was heard, and Flick, wounded in the leg, fell screaming to the ground.

"Over here!" said a voice.

The fugitive obeyed, there was a footbridge, he crossed it to the other side of the stream.

That love is blind is a well-known thesis, and generally accepted. Yet when Camillo Debrai found himself unable to see, it was not because of the coils of love in which he was enmeshed. Far more blinding than love is a good thick sack tied around the head, and that was the unfortunate predicament of poor Camillo Debrai.

His first thought was not a very bright one. Is this, he wondered, the singular manner in which countesses receive their guests? His second thought, somewhat less foolish and slightly more realistic, was that in his present situation he would have very little opportunity to satisfy his burning desire to *see* Carlotta. His third thought was more complex. Robinia was right, he said to himself, as he was pushed, hooded and tied, to the cellar. Robinia was right—they're trying to get rid of me so Carlotta can marry that damned Filet. I've been a shocking fool, but they won't get away with it any more. I'm going to keep my eyes open!

But it was too late. What good would it do Camillo to keep his eyes open if his head was buried in an impenetrable sack? Or, once the sack was taken off, in an unlighted cellar?

He cursed the moment he first caught a glimpse of Carlotta at the window of her room. Nicolino too, he thought, though somewhat tardily, was right: she was a kind of Lucrezia Borgia! Oh, if only, he thought, I were free again! And he considered the various things he would do were he to find himself in that happy situation. He reached, at last, a rather comforting conclusion: since all he wanted was to be free of Carlotta and her damned family, and since all they wanted was to be rid of him, why couldn't they all come to some kind of agreement? Groping his way in the darkness, he found a bit of straw and lay down tranquilly to sleep.

If Camillo decided not to await the arrival of Filet, the fault was Flick's, for he was a man of no imagination and took no thought for his prisoner. He had been told to get hold of him and lock him up in the cellar, and that is what he did. He did not bother to wonder whether the prisoner might be hungry or thirsty. Midnight of that unhappy Sunday came and went, and then midnight of an even more unhappy Monday, and still Camillo saw no sign of life.

He kicked the door, he shouted as loud as he could, but he

got no response. I understand now, he said. They're going to starve me to death here.

Thanks to his quite remarkable strength, he managed to free his hands from the ropes that bound them. Then he found a huge nail and set to work. The house was built on a slope, so that the front of the cellar was underground while the back of it gave on to a small garden.

The walls of the cellar were made of large stones. A small air hole guided Camillo to make the correct choice, and while the first stone was difficult, the rest was relatively easy. He worked all day Tuesday, so that by the time Filet arrived, tired and hungry after a perilous journey, Camillo was almost finished with his work. He could see the low white wall of the garden, the deep blue sky, and the yellow moon.

When he heard steps approaching, he was just loosening the last stone. He managed to hurl himself out and ran toward the garden wall.

The shots Flick fired did not even graze Camillo, although there was indeed blood on the garden wall. Camillo had banged his head against a rock, and was having a nosebleed.

Having heard Flick's threat, then the pistol shots, and then Flick's cries of pain, Camillo decided he was mortally wounded. But then it seemed to him improbable that if he had indeed been wounded, others would be crying out in pain, so he took heart again, and when he heard an unknown voice pointing out the way, he ran toward it and was across the footbridge in a flash.

Someone took him by the arm and led him, through rocks and bushes, to a cave where four shadowy figures sat on sacks around a little fire. Camillo threw himself panting on the ground. The man who had fired the shot muttered something to the others, handed a little flask of grappa to Camillo, and went out. A few drops of that delicious liquor were sufficient to make Camillo feel a great deal better.

Now the man returned and said, "They're in retreat, those two. The one who wanted to put a couple of holes in your back must have got a pretty good-sized hole himself in the leg. The other one's carrying him on his shoulders."

"I don't," Camillo began, "know how to thank you—"

"Let it go!" interrupted the other. "Did you want to bring stuff in or only get through?"

"I—uh, I was escaping," said Camillo, somewhat embarrassed. "I had just made a hole in the wall—"

"In for long?"

"Three days."

"Here, you must be hungry." The man handed him bread and cheese. "Even Swiss jails don't rate three stars."

Camillo thought he had better explain. "You've made a mistake," he said. "Actually, I'm an honest man—"

"Sure, sure," said the other brusquely. "If I hadn't known right away you were one of us, do you think I'd have gone looking for trouble putting holes in people's legs? We're all honest men in this profession. Does the Bible say it's a sin to buy stuff in one place and sell it a couple of miles away? Robbing's a sin, not buying and selling. That's a respectable business, don't you agree?"

"Of course," said Camillo, as he went on eating greedily. "Of course!"

"Let's move on," said the man, after he'd finished his pipe. They all hoisted sacks on their shoulders.

Camillo proffered his own rather remarkable shoulders, and soon he too had a load on his back. The words of the leader had fully reassured him. As he walked on with the others, and went on stuffing food inside himself to try to make up for three foodless days, he thanked God that he had been lucky enough to fall in with honest peddlers who thought nothing of citing important passages of the Scriptures.

For some time they followed the rocky stream. Every once in a while, the ringleader told them to watch out, and then they all dropped behind some rocks to wait further orders. Camillo decided there must be a good many landslides in this neighborhood, and thought it was wise to be so careful about rocks.

After they left the stream, they entered a kind of narrow passage through the rocks, with the sky for a ceiling.

Here there occurred something rather unpleasant.

"Stop!" cried a voice suddenly from the top of a high rock.

"Stop or we shoot!" cried another voice from behind.

It was a classic ambush: the peddlers were trapped. But they did not lose heart; they threw themselves to the ground and undertook a furious defense, scattering shots to right and left.

The attackers too began to shoot, and Camillo, who had remained standing, felt the bullets whistle past his head.

"We're lucky," whispered one of the men to the ring-leader. "The Wolf's Hole's only about fifteen feet away."

"I saw it," said the leader. "Everybody that way," he ordered in a whisper. "One every two minutes. Head for Bicheville by the usual way. Meet at Witlon's."

One by one, as the others intensified their fire, the men entered a kind of cleft in the rock and slipped down. Camillo followed. Cursing the robbers that seemed to infest the neighborhood, he followed a narrow path through the bushes and at last came out on the other side to find a fine wide road heading downhill. By this time his load of sacks was enormous, for he kept coming across them lying on the ground and piled them on top of his own. "The devil!" he cried. "They left all their stock behind, to get away faster."

Suddenly, at a turn in the road, Camillo saw that he was at the entrance to a town: a wide, deserted street shone under the rows of lamplight.

"Thank God!" cried the miserable wretch, as he read a large sign saying: "Bicheville 500 feet." This, he thought, is the very town the peddlers said to go to. Now all I have to do is find Witlon's.

His steps echoed on the frosty sidewalk, and the sacks he carried got heavier with every passing moment. If only he could find someone to ask!

As he was crossing a little square, he came at last upon two policemen.

"Please," he said, "would you tell me where Witlon's is? If I don't find it soon, I'll drop dead."

The older policeman laughed. "You look more like a moving company than a porter," he said. "Go straight, then take the first turn on your right. Fifty feet in all."

"Thanks. Good night."

"Good morning!"

At last he saw a sign that said *Hotel Witlon*. But he realized he couldn't unload the sacks himself, so he gave the door a good kick. "Hey! Hey there in the hotel!" he shouted.

A man pale as death opened the door.

"Did the others get here?" asked Camillo. "Quick! This stuff's heavy!"

"Holy smoke!"

He was shown down a steep stairway into a cellar where he saw the ringleader and all the others.

"This isn't a man," said the leader, as they all helped unload the sacks from Camillo's shoulders. "It's a tidal wave! He's brought it all. How did you manage not to be seen?"

"There wasn't a soul around," said Camillo, with a laugh. "Who could have seen me?"

"How did you find my place?" asked Witlon. "Do you know Bicheville?"

"Never been here," said Camillo. "I asked two policemen in the square."

They all began to groan.

"He's crazy!" cried Witlon.

The ringleader shrugged. "With all that stuff on his back, could he have tried to run away? He'd have been arrested right away. He did the only right thing. Now quick, Witlon, get our suitcases. We'll put the stuff in and we'll drift off quietly, one by one, just as if we were ordinary travelers. That way they won't find anything even if they do come here."

"But," said Camillo, "I—"

"You stay well hidden, my boy. The two cops saw your face, they know you now. We'll take care of getting you away when the time comes. Hurry up!"

But Camillo still did not quite understand. "Excuse me," he said, "but even if they recognize me, what have I done?"

The ringleader laughed. "Nothing." he replied. "But how would you prove that you didn't shoot the customs officers and that you aren't an accomplice of ours since they saw you with the smuggled goods on your back?"

"Oh!" said Camillo. Sinking down on a bundle of rags, he lay back and closed his eyes.

"Leave him alone, Witlon," said the ringleader. "He must be dead tired, poor devil."

But Camillo wasn't asleep, he lay like a stone, unconscious, not because he was so tired but because he was frightened to death: the wretch at last understood.

"Look after him, Witlon," said the leader, as he was leaving. "God knows what he was up to, but he's a bright boy and I like him. We'll have to get him out of this mess he's in—it's to our own interest too."

"Yeah," grumbled Witlon. "You're taking off and leaving me stuck with this guy."

To Camillo, it seemed that he would be spending the rest of his life in Swiss cellars.

chapter 16

Bicheville is a town of some 43,000 souls in the French-speaking part of Switzerland—but anyone who goes looking for it will be wasting his time.

First of all, he won't find it; and second of all, it isn't worth a visit because it's the least interesting town in the world. It enters this story only because of Camillo, who escaped the cellar of the faithless Filet to end up in that of Witlon, the innkeeper of Bicheville.

Should a traveler, however, have found himself there on the morning of November 30, 19–, he could not have failed to notice the innumerable groups of people standing staring up at huge placards affixed during the night to all the street corners.

And had the traveler approached each of these groups, he would have heard the most disparate comments. He would also, of course, have wasted the best part of the morning, to the detriment of his own affairs, so there is no reason to detain him longer and abuse his patience. It seems likely, in any case, that the most interesting opinion was that expressed by a man wearing a cloak who was walking with a friend not far from Witlon's.

"I'm sure of it," he said. "It's the man who was carrying all that stuff and asked us where Witlon's was. Don't you remember, Patter?"

"Sure, Sergeant, I remember," said the man called Patter. "We had a good laugh too, that morning. And all the time he was making fools of us. No doubt at all, it's the same man."

"Let's keep our eyes open, Patter. Fifty of those big thousand-franc notes would come in very handy."

"Let's hope we have the luck to run into him. Because this hasn't been much of a job so far, Sergeant. For two weeks we've been stuck here and haven't picked up a thing except rheumatism and a bad cold. What's the idea, Sergeant?"

"Well, we know that Witlon's in contact with all the smugglers in the area—that's why we want to keep our eye on all the people who go into and come out of his hotel. Something will come of it, you'll see—we'll meet an old friend or two, or maybe make a new friend. But it takes patience."

"We've got that, Sergeant."

"And it'll pay off, Patter, I'm sure of it. The six smugglers that pulled that job and shot up the three customs officers hid out at Witlon's. This Witlon's the key to the whole thing. And the crazy man with the bundles too, don't you think he's got a connection with Witlon?"

It must be obvious by now who the crazy man with the bundles is, and to explain how he gets mixed up with the placard that was of so much interest to the two plain-clothes policemen, it will be easiest to reproduce the wording of the placard itself:

HAVE YOU SEEN THIS MAN?
Camillo Debrai
Age 27. Height 5'10". Dark eyes. Black hair,
with black mustache. Wearing gray-flannel
trousers and black jacket when last seen.
Disappeared from Geneva, November 7.
50,000 FRANCS REWARD
to whoever brings him back alive to the Manager,
Hotel Wurstel, Geneva

Obviously, this singular placard didn't spring up of its own accord on the street corners of Bicheville. Somebody must have composed it. But who? And who is supplying the fifty thousand francs?

Signor Casimiro Wonder, at four o'clock in the afternoon of November 11, felt more like Nero than ever. Four days had passed since he had tossed his incendiary bomb into the enemy camp, and with each passing moment his desire grew stronger to see for himself the effects of the new provision he had had written into his will. By four o'clock in the afternoon of November 11 he could hold out no longer; he decided to invade the Madellis house.

Donna Leo, right after the Filet thunderbolt struck, moved her family to its winter quarters: it was, therefore, at the door of the town house that Uncle Casimiro ungraciously banged. As usual, he pushed aside the servant who opened the door for him, and with his hideous old hat firmly planted on his head he marched toward the drawing room, where, at that hour of the day, he knew the enemy would be encamped.

He kicked open the door and found himself facing the saddest and quietest assembly there had ever been.

"Well?" shouted Uncle Casimiro, in his accustomed style. "Is this the way the Crusaders greet the master of the house?"

He pulled the chair out from under Signor Gastone and called Giusmaria. "Are you in your second childhood?" he shouted. "Have you forgotten I told you those legs were loose? Take that chair away and have it fixed at once!"

Donna Leo, Donna Elisabetta, and Donna Flaminia rose to their feet together, like three ghostly automatons, and with head erect walked proudly to the door, never so much as glancing at Uncle Casimiro. Signor Gastone, who was already on his feet, had only to trail after them. Edo, Robinia, and Carlotta remained seated where they were.

Uncle Casimiro laughed heartily. "What about you?" he said, turning toward Edo. "Doesn't my presence offend you, young Crusader? You don't seem to be any less of an idiot than the rest!"

"No," said Edo quietly, for he was not without a degree of common sense, "I'm an idiot too, but on my own."

"And you, Carlotta," said Uncle Casimiro in a friendlier voice, "what's the matter that you don't even speak to me?"

Carlotta rose and went to the window, where she stood looking out.

"She's suffering, poor thing," said Robinia with a sigh. "She's been seduced and abandoned and now she's waiting for someone who will never come again."

"Silly ass!" said Carlotta, without turning.

Uncle Casimiro required an explanation.

"It's a very sad affair," said Edo. "Four days ago Carlotta's husband ran away from school, and despite all our efforts there hasn't been a sign of him since. We are all naturally much worried. As you know, Signor Debrai is very highly thought of by the entire family."

"How funny!" Uncle Casimiro snickered. "That's why the old guard marched off in such fury at the sight of me— they think I arranged the disappearance in order to complicate the new clause in the will."

Carlotta wheeled around. "Of course!" she cried. "This can only be one of your happy inspirations—like making me get married in forty-eight hours. Well, have a good time, Uncle Casimiro—we're only puppets in your hands!"

She looked at him for a moment in anger.

"However, my dear uncle," she went on, "if I hadn't been thinking about the others, I'd have told you to go to hell long ago, you and your damned inheritance! At least I can do it now. I don't need your money to live on, I can always look after myself—and I will in spite of you!"

"Good!" cried Uncle Casimiro. "That's the way I like to hear a Wonder talk. But I'd like you to know I haven't had anything to do with this. Robinia, you're a witness that I told Camillo to stay quietly at school. But you're a mean little devil—who knows what you told him when you were alone with him!"

Carlotta looked at Robinia in astonishment.

Robinia began to laugh. "Don't look at me with those great big eyes!" she cried. "It's all true. Saturday, Uncle Casimiro and I went to see Camillo and I told him the whole story."

"The whole story?" Carlotta repeated. "What whole story?"

"That you wanted to get rid of him so you could marry the man calling himself Meditato Filet."

"That's a lie!" cried Carlotta.

"Oh, no, it's not. What about the arrangement you made with Grandma Leo? The flowers, the presents, the daily visits? And all the loving words, and the engagement supper, and Grandma Leo talking to Signor Filet about helping to have the marriage annulled—what about all that?"

"I can be accused," said Carlotta, "of not having had the courage to stand up against my grandmother, and my mother, and my aunt, and all of you, and of agreeing to play a game that disgusted me, but that's all I can be accused of. When the time came, I spoke my mind clearly enough."

"Tell it to the marines," said Robinia. "Maybe they'll be able to flush Camillo out."

On a little table beside Carlotta stood a pleasant little porcelain group representing a shepherd on his knees handing a bunch of violets to a splendidly dressed lady in crinoline. It seemed to recall the sweetly perfumed verses of Arcadia. Carlotta looked at it for a moment, but Uncle Casimiro's hand was quicker and the porcelain didn't end its days smashed on Robinia's head.

Uncle Casimiro nodded, and Robinia and her brother left the room.

After Uncle Casimiro was alone with Carlotta, he turned to her and asked brusquely, "What kind of dirty trick is this?"

"There's only been one dirty trick, my dear uncle," said Carlotta, "and you're the one who played it. Making a girl get married in forty-eight hours!"

For a moment Uncle Casimiro made no reply. He too went to the window and looked out. Then he turned. "I don't want to scold you," he said. "Let's have the marriage annulled, and we won't say another word about it."

Carlotta's cheeks flushed in annoyance. "I wouldn't dream of it!" she cried.

Uncle Casimiro lost his patience. "Then for the love of God," he cried, "will you tell me what you want?"

"I want my husband!" screamed Carlotta, brandishing the unfortunate shepherd. "You made me marry him, now you find him for me!"

"No one's ever got anything out of Casimiro Wonder talking to him that way! I'm going to get rid of the lot of you!" He kicked the door open and left the house and that same day the head of the best detective agency in Europe was summoned and told to find Camillo Debrai even if it cost a million.

Two weeks passed with no developments at all. So Uncle Casimiro had the placards put up all over Switzerland.

He even wrote the text himself. Carlotta, looking over the rough copy, added the words: "Dark eyes."

"That's an idiotic thing to put down," Uncle Casimiro remarked. "Who remembers whether that idiot has dark eyes or light eyes? I certainly don't!"

"But I do," said Carlotta, with a sigh.

In Bicheville, they were still speaking of it late that same evening. If the traveler, in fact, around midnight of that November 30, had happened to wander into Witlon's, he'd have heard the placard being discussed at more than one table in the large, smoky hall.

At the table nearest the door sat two men: one was tall and slender and elegant in appearance; the other, old but strong and rather common-looking.

"Fifty thousand francs!" sneered the tall man. "Why, I'd give a hundred thousand myself to have him delivered to the house. But we'll get him, don't worry."

"Are you really sure he's here?" asked the other, in a doubtful tone.

"Flick, my friend, I'm not a poet—I don't say things just because the words happen to be in my mouth. The evening they shot you, I followed those five smugglers, and when they were trying to get through the ravine at Lapipe they were stopped by border guards. I was a long way off, but there was a very bright moon, if you remember, and I could see clear as day. They exchanged shots, and the three guards were wounded. Then I saw the five disappear, one after the other, and our blockhead with them, all as though they'd been swallowed up by the earth. Later I saw them reappear again on the road that goes down to Bicheville. Evidently there's some sort of cave that leads down from the Lapipe ravine, and the smugglers got back that way.

"I slid down like an avalanche and got on the trail of one of them and followed him here. When they opened the door for him, I slipped in right behind him before they had a chance to close the door, and asked for a room. Witlon said there were no rooms and got me out, but I had a good look at the man, who was standing there like a statue, so frightened he couldn't move.

"So I left, but I didn't go very far. I hid out in an alley and kept my eye on this door. After about half an hour I saw the last of the smugglers arrive, loaded down with sacks of stuff. Then later they came out one by one carrying suitcases as though they were regular travelers, and I stuck to my man like a shadow. He took a train and then a bus to his house, so I knew who he was. The same day, though, he got away without my being able to stop him. All I could do then was wait here for him to come back, which he did after about three days.

"So I stopped him just as he was coming out of the hotel, and he very kindly told me the whole story. He said the blockhead was here, hidden out in the cellar, and they wouldn't let him out because they were afraid he'd be recognized by two policemen, and they weren't taking any chances. That's why I wrote you to come here."

"But even assuming that the smuggler told you the truth, what's to prevent him warning the others once he got over the shock?"

"What's the matter with you, Flick, are you losing your mind? That one will never talk again after the fright I gave him. What may complicate the matter now is this damned placard—fifty thousand francs can make people do silly things. We've got to keep an eye on Witlon—the guy he's talking to now, for instance, looks like one of the five smugglers."

Meditato Filet was, as a matter of fact, right: Witlon was talking to the leader of the gang.

"It's still too dangerous to bring him out," Witlon was saying. "There are two of them wandering around, often in plain clothes, but they don't fool me—it's always the same two cops. And now, with the picture on the placard, the fool's face is well known, everybody wants to get hold of him and pick up fifty thousand francs. If the two cops see him, we've had it—the minute they start questioning him, we'll be in the soup."

"I don't think he'll talk. After all, I saved his life."

"Listen, whether they recognize him as the man who carried the stuff here the night of the fight with the border guards, or whether they recognize him as the Debrai on the poster, we're done for."

"We'll have to take a chance. Fifty thousand francs aren't hay. And I'm here, they didn't get me, did they?"

"That was dangerous too, coming here. You know they've got their eye on you at the Central Police Station, someone must have been talking plenty."

"Yes, but it's a question of fifty of the big notes. And we'd better hurry, or the other four will get in on the deal . . ."

At a table near the stove, three peaceful gentlemen were drinking beer.

"Be careful," said the oldest of the three. "Ten minutes ago our man was joined by another one, tall, slender, and elegant."

"Is he the one?" asked the others, who did not want to turn to look.

"I'd swear it. He's the spitting image of the picture we've got in our pockets. Since he's called for his pal, that means there's something doing for both of them. We'll have to keep our eyes open."

A fourth gentleman sat down at the table.

"Sensational news!" he cried. "I've just been talking to a friend in the police and he tells me the guy in the placard is the same one that asked where Witlon's was the night of the tenth. The two cops remember him perfectly because he was carrying a mountain of sacks on his back. I also learned that Witlon is being watched for smuggling activities."

"Witlon is being watched by the police," said another. "We know now that there is a connection between Camillo and Witlon. Meditato Filet tells his partner to meet him here at Witlon's. This seems to be the key to the whole thing—so why shouldn't Signor Debrai be here too?"

What a peculiar rhythm marks the story now! It can't take a single step forward without taking ten back, but this, if God wills, is the last backward step. From now on, the story moves straight to the end.

Then who *were* these four peaceful gentlemen? Four representatives of the best private detective agency in Europe, the one that Uncle Casimiro had hired.

Having got to work at once, the four had made a preliminary investigation at the Madellis house and had found Robinia the most meticulous source of information. At the end they asked: to whose interest was it that Camillo should disappear? The inevitable answer was Meditato Filet.

It was necessary, then, to find Filet. Though his new place of residence had not been discovered, despite thorough investigations by the police, the four private bloodhounds could follow a trail with a nearer point of departure: Pipet School, Geneva.

There they discovered that Camillo had left in a car, and they pestered everybody in the neighborhood until they discovered what kind of car it was, who was driving it, and where he and Camillo went. When they got to the house of the two criminals, they saw a man who bore a very marked resemblance to a photograph they had on which was noted, "Federico Molk, known as Flick, servant of the man calling himself Filet."

Without letting themselves be seen, they waited patiently for someone to come and join the lonely crook, who, they noticed, limped rather badly. They were confident that something was bound to turn up here. And sure enough, two weeks later Flick received a letter which made him leave at once, lovingly followed by the four bloodhounds.

When they got to Bicheville, one of the four went off to talk to an old friend in the police department, while the others kept their eyes on Flick, who led them, late that evening, to Witlon's hotel. At that point, one went out to telephone the fourth, as they had agreed.

Then, as has already been remarked, someone came to join Flick at his table.

Camillo, meanwhile, was lying in a hammock at the bottom of a dry well, swinging slowly back and forth. He was picturing his sudden return to daylight: he saw himself walking down a fine, deserted street and meeting Carlotta Wonder Debrai and taking hold of her by the nape of the neck and the part of the body that in a man is called the "seat of the trousers" and holding her thus for a while over a deep river before abandoning her to her fate.

"Bitch!" he cried after her, as he saw her disappear into

the muddy water. Then he thought further and repeated the finale, shouting, as he threw Carlotta into the river, "Agrippina!"

However, he didn't like the effect of that either, nor was he satisfied with "Lucrezia Borgia." He did the whole scene over again, and this time when he threw Carlotta into the water he said nothing. He merely slapped his hands together, as though to clean them, and spat into the swirling river.

On the subject of revenge, Camillo was probably a perfectionist, for the last scene did not satisfy him either. I need something more symbolic, he thought; and did the whole thing over from the beginning. After meeting Carlotta, he bowed to her and said, "I beg your pardon, you viper, if I mistook you for a lady." Then, his head held high, he left.

No, he thought, it isn't properly symbolic, and anyway a viper is too powerful—if I call her a viper, it means I recognize how strong she is, I admit she's somebody.

He went off to meet Carlotta again, and again he bowed. "I beg your pardon," he said, "if I mistook you for a lady, you mosquito." A mosquito was symbolic enough, signifying a being that had tried to do Camillo wrong but had succeeded merely in stinging him. But it wasn't offensive enough. Maybe a flea would have been better. No, a flea wasn't right either.

Camillo got down from the hammock and tried to walk up and down despite being at the bottom of a well. The only light was that of a single candle. Camillo threw himself back into the hammock, very depressed because he'd been unable to find exactly the right thing.

He wondered if maybe it wouldn't have been better to smack her across the face a couple of times and leave her without any further symbolism. So this time when he met her he smacked her twice and then walked away with his head down, glaring at her. He went back, tried giving her a boot, then tried a smack again. But no, he decided, that sort of thing didn't do any good. A sentence of some sort was what was needed: words were what hurt the most. He wondered if maybe it wouldn't be a good idea to prance by in front of her riding a white horse—until he recalled that he didn't know how to ride. He tried it on a bicycle, but the effect wasn't quite right.

Back on his feet again, when he met Carlotta this time, he abused her soundly, with all the rude names he could think of, then turned his back and left.

"Camillo!" he heard someone call.

"Drop dead," he replied, without moving.

"Watch it, Camillo! I'm throwing down the ladder," the voice went on.

"Ladder," called Camillo. "What are you talking about?"

"Watch it now!"

A rope ladder dangled in front of Camillo's nose.

"Climb up! Hurry!" said the voice from above.

It was Witlon, and when Camillo realized it, he thought in dismay: Now they're taking me out and I still don't know what to say to her! What will I do?

He climbed up. Witlon and the gang leader were waiting for him. They gave him a cloak with a fur collar and a big fur hat.

"Now's the time," said Witlon. "It's one in the morning. In twenty minutes there's a train to Geneva—we'll take you there, and then you'll be free!"

At last! Camillo's heart felt as though it was about to burst with joy: for tomorrow he would see the sun again. And maybe tomorrow he would also see Carlotta again . . . "I beg your pardon, you viper, if I mistook you for a lady!" No, better not think about it now, there's still plenty of time.

They came out into the cold night and walked slowly, the three of them, along the little street that led to the main avenue, their loudly beating hearts the only sound.

"Stop!" cried a voice as they turned into the broad boulevard. Two men slipped out of a doorway.

Witlon shot away like a skyrocket, while the gangleader knocked one of the men down with a good, solid punch, then disappeared in the opposite direction. Camillo didn't even try to free himself from the grip of the man who was holding him.

"Damn it, Sergeant!" cried the man who had fallen, as he rose to his feet again. "They got away before we had a look at them."

"Never mind, Patter," said the sergeant. "We've still got one of them. He'll talk. Let's go!"

Camillo walked meekly on between the two policemen,

contemplating his sad story: out of a cellar, into a well in a cellar, out of the well, into a prison . . . probably into the cellar of a prison.

They hadn't walked more than a hundred yards when a closed carriage pulled up alongside.

"I beg your pardon," said the coachman, "but I must take my employer, who is on the point of death, to the Kemineth Clinic, and I don't know where it is. For the love of God, gentlemen, help me! Listen to the poor man in his agony!"

Groans of pain came from inside the carriage. The sergeant and Patter drew nearer, holding tightly to Camillo, and began to explain to the coachman how to get to the clinic. Suddenly Camillo saw something come out of a window of the carriage, and the sergeant, hit over the head by a blackjack, fell to the ground. Patter turned instinctively toward him, which was enough for the coachman to strike him across the back of the neck with a stick.

"Get in! Hurry!" The door opened and shut; the carriage shot away at a gallop and was soon out of Bicheville.

Camillo, recovering from his surprise, took heart again: he was free once more, thanks to the cleverness of Witlon and the gangleader.

"That was really something," said Camillo in admiration.

"It doesn't take much to get away from a couple of cops," said the man beside him. But the voice was not Witlon's or of the gangleader's.

"And as for you, young fellow, take better care of other people's cellar walls if you have any respect for your skin."

"But you," Camillo stammered, "you're Signor Filet!"

"Brilliant!" said the voice mockingly. "Just as I knew you were Signor Camillo Debrai as soon as I saw you come out of the dark with Witlon and that other one. We'll soon reach an agreement. Meanwhile, don't move around too much, you might press against the trigger of my revolver. There's so little space here."

Camillo was ready to believe that he had lost his mind: smugglers, innkeepers, policemen, Filet. How did Filet know that he had got away from the cellar?

"Flick," said Filet meanwhile, "how far are we from the car?"

"Couple of miles," replied the man on the coachman's seat. "We'll be there in a few minutes."

Camillo started, for the voice was that of the man who had pushed him down into the cellar the first time. Cellar, well, cellar: there was something to laugh at. Then this Filet was so determined to marry Carlotta he didn't hesitate to ally himself with thieves and brigands and to assault policemen.

"Excuse me, Signor Filet," said Camillo timidly. "Is all this on account of Carlotta?"

"You guessed it."

"Well, if that's all you want, there's no sense in a lot of bad blood. I'm ready to give her up whenever you like. In fact, I didn't even marry her on purpose—"

"Imagine that, Signor Debrai!" cried Filet. "But that's not the way it's going to be. You have no idea how eager I am to see you reunited with your wife. All I want you to do is write a little note to your wife telling her you're my guest, and then I'll explain how she's to send the money in order to get you back."

"Money to get me back?" said Camillo. "But she wouldn't take me for nothing—"

"Damn!" cried Flick. A car had overtaken the carriage and was blocking the road. Flick tried to go around.

"Hands up!" cried a voice behind the barrel of a gun.

"Damn it to hell!" said Flick, raising his arms.

A hand removed the huge old fur hat Camillo was wearing. Several voices cried, "That's the one!"

The carriage had been stopped on the brow of a hill across which ran the road. Some ten yards down, amid the bushes, glittered the water of a stream. Camillo, who was sitting on that side, felt the door giving way to the pressure of his foot. He made a sudden decision: he crouched down and jumped out. For how was he to know that the new arrivals were Uncle Casimiro's detectives?

He rolled down the hill, crossed the stream jumping from stone to stone, and kept on running as long as he could. When he came upon an abandoned hut, he sank down on the straw.

He awoke trembling with the cold. It was daylight now; he lit a fire and was soon feeling better. A few hundred yards away he saw a large town in a valley and he headed toward it. He still had a little money in his pocket, and he wanted something to eat. Then, it was clear, he ought to take the train and go to the nearest consulate: but his poor mind had stopped working; three attacks in one night were too many—police, blackmailers, and Lord knows who else. What did all those people want of him?

When he got to the town, the first thing he saw was a large placard with a photograph on it.

I know that idiotic face, said Camillo to himself, bad-tempered. Then he read that fifty thousand francs were being offered to anyone who brought the possessor of that idiotic face to Geneva—and he thought he understood.

That's what they all wanted of me, he thought. There's a price on my head! Who could have put it there? And what terrible thing did I do to make someone put a price on my head?

He decided to put an end to it. He bought bread and cheese and walked firmly to the railroad station.

"A ticket to Geneva," he said, his face buried in his jacket collar. "I'm going to find out what this is all about. Third class."

chapter *17*

When he arrived at the Hotel Wurstel, Camillo said he
wanted to speak to the person who was interested in Signor
Debrai.

He was accompanied to the door of Apartment 115, which
the porter opened for him. Camillo entered ready for a fight.

"You finally got here, you damned nuisance!" said Uncle
Casimiro Wonder in a tone of considerable annoyance as he
came into the room. "Would you mind telling me where
you've been hiding all this time?"

"I—"

"You're a damned fool!"

"Yes, sir."

chapter 18

It was a dark December morning, and Carlotta had for some time been trying to make strange shapes out of the cracks in the ceiling above her bed, when the door opened and the maid came in.

"Your coffee, signora," she said.

"Signora?" Carlotta repeated, surprised. "Up until last night you called me signorina."

"Yes, I know, but this morning Signor Giusmaria issued instructions to call you signora."

"Very well. Leave the coffee on the table. I'm getting up."

She slipped out of bed and stood for a moment looking at herself in the large mirror of the wardrobe.

"Poor Signora Carlotta!" she sighed, with a sad shake of her head.

On the tray were two newspapers and three postcards: no news then. For almost a month now, not a word had come from the school.

She turned again to look at Carlotta in the glass.

"May one ask," she said, "why you're so upset just because that person doesn't come back?"

"You know why," said Carlotta in the glass.

"Ah, yes!" cried the other hurriedly. "It's because of that silly provision in the will. My lunatic uncle has to have a grand-nephew within a year or he won't leave me a penny, so naturally I'm worried—"

"No, Signora Carlotta," said Carlotta in the glass. "Those little stories you can tell the rest of the world but not me. I'm you. And I know you don't care a fig for the inheritance— what interests you is that person himself."

"A likely story!" laughed Carlotta. "He interests me just about as much as any husband could interest his wife."

"Oh, sure, I know," said Carlotta in the glass. "But I hope you realize that there's more than one wife in the world who's in love with her husband."

"How silly!" Carlotta's tone was incredulous. "A wife who's in love with her husband! I've never known one—"

"I have," said Carlotta in the glass. "Her name is Carl—"

"Absurd!" cried the flesh-and-blood Carlotta nervously, turning away.

A ray of sunlight brightened the gray rectangle of the window. The air in the room was warm and scented;

Carlotta, wearing a heavy dressing gown, opened the window. Suddenly she recalled another time when she had looked out the window and had got a bouquet of flowers in her face.

"What a lot of nonsense," she said, leaning her elbows on the windowsill. Then she drew back with a cry, as something whistled through the air and landed in her room.

It was a slipper.

Carlotta leaned out.

"Sorry!" she heard someone call up from the garden of the neighboring house. "A cat stole my steak, but I guess I got my aim wrong—"

"Please don't mention it," said Carlotta with as much sarcasm as she was capable of. "I'm quite used to your throwing things in my face. Are you well?"

"Very well," said Camillo Debrai.

For it was indeed Camillo. He had returned home, home to his own house, and he was busy once again in his workroom that opened onto the garden next door to the Madellis garden. Camillo was wearing a rough, heavy coat and slippers; one slipper, actually; the other has already been spoken of.

"What's new?" Carlotta went on, in her friendliest tone. "What are you working on?"

"Something in full relief," murmured Camillo. "I've got a lot to do, too, if you'll excuse me, and I'm a bit cold, with only one slipper—"

"Of course! Get right back to your study. I hope the work

goes well!" Carlotta cried, making every effort to keep from banging the window shut. She closed it gently to hide the fury that was gnawing her.

She stood in front of the wardrobe with the slipper in her hand, looking at it with disgust.

"Junk like this flying through the window!" she cried.

"Why don't you take it down to him," said Carlotta in the glass, "instead of throwing it back?"

"Me? Are you out of your mind?"

A half hour later, Carlotta went out of the house with an elegant package dangling from her little finger.

Camillo's workroom had a large glass door that gave onto the garden, so Carlotta, before she entered, was able to observe her husband working.

"Very attractive," she exclaimed at last, opening the door.

Camillo turned with a start. The work he was doing now was very special—a kind of artistic revenge in wood. It was a group consisting of a number of figures, all still in a rough state except one, which was almost finished: a wicked caricature of Donna Leo.

"Very attractive," Carlotta repeated. "I suppose that these figures will eventually represent all the members of my family. Which one is me?"

"You're not any of them," said Camillo, rather embarrassed. "Signor Casimiro doesn't want you."

"So you're filling an order for Signor Wonder?"

"Yes."

"How marvelous! That way I can be ashamed at the same time of being both your wife and his niece. Well, let's talk about something else. Here, I brought your slipper back."

"How kind of you! I must ask you once again to excuse my clumsiness . . ."

Camillo went on working, taking care never to meet Carlotta's glance. Carlotta sat on a stool and watched him in silence. The room smelled sweetly of wood, and the fire in the stove gave off an odor of resin.

He is exactly the kind of man, Carlotta thought, that a woman like Robinia would fall in love with. Then suddenly she blushed, for it seemed to her she could hear the Carlotta of the looking glass giggling at her: "Lady, you're not telling *me* that, are you? I'm you!"

After half an hour Carlotta rose.

"We've said nothing on a variety of fascinating subjects," she remarked. "Yours is exactly the kind of conversation I like, Signor Debrai. Good morning."

"Good morning," stammered Camillo, opening the door for her.

After he was alone, he shook his head decisively, and to himself he said: I agree, she was very nice to bring the slipper back, and she was very friendly. And all the things that happened weren't her fault but her family's. And I agree that this Filet business wasn't arranged by her, as Robinia would have liked me to believe. Filet, I agree, was trying to get away with something on his own hook. And maybe Uncle Casimiro was right about how worried she was when they couldn't find me. All right, I agree with it all, but what's been decided is decided. This ridiculous farce has to come to an end. The marriage will have to be annulled—all the more so as I am now completely indifferent to Carlotta.

As he made this last statement, Camillo felt a kind of burning in his cheeks: apparently he couldn't even tell himself a lie.

"The devil with them all!" he cried.

He was annoyed, and the one who suffered most was Donna Leo, as the revengeful gouge drew out two of her teeth and gave her a squint.

When she got home, Carlotta found her family in the empire drawing room. Apparently there had been an animated discussion, and the moment she appeared, Carlotta was confronted by Donna Leo.

"Carlotta!" she cried, highly alarmed. "Giusmaria asserts that he saw that person this morning in the adjacent garden."

"Yes, madam," Giusmaria said. "That's why I immediately gave orders to the staff to call the signorina signora. I had hoped up till the last—"

"Well done," said Donna Leo.

"Yes, I see," said Carlotta, thinking about the maid who had brought her coffee.

"Well, what are we going to do, Carlotta?" asked Donna Leo in a very worried tone. "This man is still our husband, we have admitted it to the staff, and already one month of the twelve granted us by the will has passed. There is nothing else to be done now—he must take up regular residence in this house, and everything, everything I say, must proceed in the regular manner. I hope you understand what I mean?"

"Oh-ho-ho!" giggled Robinia, winking an eye. "We understand, Grandma Leo."

Edo, who was not without a degree of common sense, although every now and then seemed to be, began to laugh stupidly, while Carlotta blushed and much annoyed went to the window to look out.

"This is not a joking matter, Robinia," said Donna Leo. "Nor a laughing matter either, Edo. It is a matter of the utmost seriousness which concerns the entire family. Carlotta, come here and stop pouting. You must take immediate action."

"I?"

"Of course. Bring him here at once. It's absurd for your husband to live in the house next door and to go on carving wood instead of living respectably in our house."

"If I have time, I'll write him a postcard," said Carlotta in a bored voice.

"Carlotta!" cried Donna Flaminia, rebuking her.

"Let us not take things quite so lightly," said Signor Gastone severely.

"You must not be thinking only of yourself all the time," Aunt Elisabetta told her, "but of your family as well."

"My sense of dignity," Carlotta announced, "prevents me from frequenting a boor who has been wandering around Lord only knows where for almost a month!"

"Let's not get started," said Signor Gastone, "on this dignity nonsense."

"Yet until recently," said Carlotta, "thousands of tragedies occurred on account of the dignity of the family."

"*We* are responsible for the family and its honor," announced Donna Leo in severe tones. "And only we know when the question of dignity should be raised. There is no such thing as your personal dignity, my girl. There is only the common dignity of the family, and that is in our charge!"

"But there is such a thing as my will!" cried Carlotta violently. "And I assure you that I will never set foot in that miserable creature's pigsty. He will have to come here to ask my pardon. And he will, too."

"I rather doubt it," Robinia remarked slyly. "If you will permit me to do so."

Carlotta laughed contemptuously in her face. "He's tried to get away from me," she said. "He's made every effort to forget me, but he had to come back. One word from me and he'll come flying up here—but I won't say that word, and yet he'll come all the same."

That same afternoon, after having taken a long and angry walk, Carlotta went without knocking into Camillo's workroom.

"I forgot to ask you," she said with admirable nonchalance, "if you had seen Uncle Casimiro lately. And as I was passing, I thought I'd stop in."

"I saw him three days ago in Geneva," said Camillo, after having tried vainly to lie.

"In Geneva? How come?"

Camillo felt humiliated. I swore I wouldn't say anything to her, he thought. I said I wouldn't give her the slightest explanation, and now just because she asks an idle question I'm going to tell her the whole story. I'm a fool!

Camillo narrated his frightful adventures from the very beginning, and Carlotta listened wide-eyed and breathless. And bit by bit, as events followed one another, she experienced a sensation that could only be pity for the poor, unfortunate creature—but it was a very gentle pity, which made her heart beat more slowly and languidly.

She had never felt that kind of pity for anybody, she was sure of it. Even when, two years ago, the old gardener had told her about his misfortunes, the illness in his family, the fire in his house, the death of his wife, his father's accident, Carlotta recalled very clearly the great pity she had felt for him and the money she had given him; but she had felt no burning desire to put her arms around the unfortunate creature and kiss him passionately on the lips, which is what she felt now, listening to Camillo.

She restrained herself only because, as she well knew, men are coarse creatures who might easily mistake a gesture of pity for one of weakness, or even worse, of affection.

"Poor Camillo," she sighed at last, and told him how indignant the entire family felt about Filet. "Think how they'll feel when they hear the latest!" she cried. Then she glanced at her wristwatch. "It's already eight-fifteen," she said, "and we eat at a quarter to eight at home. Everything will be ice-cold or overcooked. And I'm so hungry tonight, too! It's all your fault."

"But I—uh," Camillo stammered, "I often lose track of time."

"You'll just have to take me out to dinner—some place where I can have hot, well-cooked food."

"Me take you out to dinner?" Camillo repeated, astonished. "In a good restaurant?"

"Of course. After all the money we spent sending you to school, you ought to be able to behave properly at a restaurant now."

Hearing her speak of the school, Camillo gritted his teeth, and his face darkened.

But Carlotta insisted. "Come on," she said, "get cleaned up. Hurry up! You're my husband, aren't you?"

"Only to a certain point," muttered Camillo with a frown, going into the other room.

Carlotta, who heard him, felt suddenly cold.

Dinner passed in silence. At last Carlotta asked angrily if Camillo had turned into a deaf-mute, since he couldn't even answer her questions.

"I've been out of training for twenty-three days," was his

asinine reply. "Unless I pay attention, I make terrible mistakes. Why, I started to eat the roast chicken with just a fork. I don't know whether I'll ever get all this straight . . ."

Camillo accompanied Carlotta to the door of her house.

"Will you come in?" asked Carlotta.

"Thank you, I think I'll go straight home."

"This is your home too, if I'm not mistaken."

"Yes, but less than mine. Good night."

"Good night. And thank you so much."

The entire Madellis family was seated in the smoking room awaiting the culprit who had not come to dinner and who was now returning home at such a late hour.

"Where have you been, Carlotta?" asked Donna Leo in her most frightening voice.

"Movies, dinner with friends, a café, lots of places," Carlotta replied nonchalantly.

Donna Flaminia jumped to her feet. "Is that the way you speak to the mother of your mother?" she cried. "To the mother of your mother who has asked you to account for your scandalous behavior?"

"But I'm married," said Carlotta. "And I account for what I do only to my husband."

The entire Madellis family grew pale. Was this, then, total rebellion? The breaking up of the family circle?

In the frigid silence that followed, there could be heard the sound of a slap: Donna Leo, promptly and decisively, had struck the rebellious cheek. Carlotta broke out into a sob and threw herself on the sofa, her face in the cushions.

"Tomorrow," said Donna Leo firmly, "you will go to your husband and bring him here."

Carlotta nodded.

The Madellis family smiled: the rebellion had been put down, Donna Leo had resumed control of the situation.

chapter 19

As Camillo worked on his group of figures, he thought about his problems; and when at last he put the finishing touch to Donna Leo's double chin, he reached the following conclusion: There's no doubt that Carlotta's going to try to trap me once more, but never again in my life will I cross the threshold of that damned house. Furthermore, if that kind lady should be so rash as to come here again, I will tell her in no uncertain terms what my plan is: annulment! Camillo Debrai may be a damned fool a hundred times, but not a hundred and one!

At that moment the kind lady entered.

"I hope," said Carlotta, "you are not going to make me

leave home every time I want to have the pleasure of seeing your face."

"It's not a very difficult sort of face," said Camillo, offhandedly. "You could easily commit it to memory and save yourself a lot of trouble."

"It would be a lot nicer of you," said Carlotta, "to move into our apartment, so I could be your wife, instead of making all these silly jokes."

"I see no necessity to be nice to you," said Camillo with a smile.

Camillo, obviously, was no longer the little lamb he once had been: and Carlotta knew it. His troubles had matured him, and school had sharpened his wits. It is remarkable how harmful the company of boys may be to ingenuous adults. Lady, don't send your husband to school!

"Please be serious," said Carlotta. "Your duty is to live next door, with your wife. If people hear about this, we'll be the talk of the town!"

Camillo sighed. "I've got something terrible to confess to you," he said. He took a piece of paper out of a drawer and handed it to her. "It's my report card," he said. "As you see, I got a four in history, a three in geography, a one in analytical logic, and a five in philosophy. With such horrible grades, how could I dare to cross the threshold of your house? Don't you understand, I've flunked out!"

Carlotta understood very well that the situation was now reversed: it was now she who did the begging, he who did the joking.

"Everyone's against me," she said sadly. "Uncle Casimiro

makes me get married in forty-eight hours, my mother doesn't understand me, my cousin slanders me, my grandmother forces me to do things that are unworthy of me and then slaps me afterward. Now you too have become my enemy, and you sit there making fun of me and laughing at me. Did I do something wicked to you when I said I'd marry you? Do you think I'd ever have married you if I hadn't felt something for you right from the start? Oh, you're a monster!" she sobbed, and fell silent.

Camillo clasped his hands. "Calm yourself," he cried, "for the love of God! I'll come back. I'll eat my meals and I'll sleep in your house—though I'll go on working here. But please note that I don't intend to change my mind. Anyway, I'm sure that you will soon be asking me to leave."

"No one," said Carlotta, drying her tears, "will force you to do anything you don't want to do."

After Carlotta left, Camillo paced up and down the room, kicking furiously at any object that happened to get in the way of his feet.

"Trapped again!" he cried. "Everything was going fine, I had the upper hand—and now, because of a couple of crocodile tears, it's all topsy-turvy again. And I missed my cues like the most amateur actor in the world! When she said, 'It's your duty to live with your wife,' I should have told her, 'It's my firm intention to live as far as I possibly can from my wife.' Then I should have told her I wanted the marriage annulled. Instead I've spoiled everything—just because I wanted to have my joke about the report card!"

Camillo stopped. Soon he was able to reaffirm his self-respect. "Never mind, my dear Carlotta," he cried, "it doesn't make any difference—it's still no dice! Camillo Debrai may be a damned fool a hundred times, but not a hundred and one!" He thought for a moment and then made a correction: "Well, yes, maybe a hundred and one times, but never, never a hundred and two!"

I'll begin by not keeping my word, he said to himself. Did I promise to move to her house? Well, so much the worse for her—I won't go.

And to tell the truth, Camillo did manage to stay away until late that evening. Then he decided it would be ill-mannered to force a lady to return to beg him to go back with her, so he headed for the Madellis house, saying to himself: Oh, well, a damned fool, yes, but a gentleman.

The Madellis family was finishing in silence the most silent meal of its life, when Giusmaria entered, much agitated.

"The signorina's husband," he announced, "has arrived."

Camillo, on his heels, muttered a greeting, to which the family replied in chorus.

"Do sit down," said Donna Leo with a smile. "We'll have something brought for you at once."

"Thank you, I've already eaten," said Camillo. "If you would just tell me where my room is—"

"I'll go with you," said Carlotta, rising and heading toward the door.

"But—"

"Don't worry, I've eaten."

"Yes, yes, she's eaten," said Donna Leo. To be honest, however, she had not.

Camillo and Carlotta went up a flight of steps and down a long corridor. Then Carlotta opened a door.

"Here's the room," she said.

It was in fact a very fine room indeed: magnificently furnished, splendidly heated, beautifully illuminated. Yet it had a defect—it was a room with a double bed.

"A great big bed like that isn't necessary," Camillo remarked. "Any little old bed would do."

"But," said Carlotta, blushing in spite of herself, "a large bed is more comfortable for two people."

"Ah, yes!" said Camillo, as though he had just remembered the very same fact.

He took off his coat and began to unknot his tie.

Carlotta couldn't blush, since she was already blushing, but in her embarrassment she went hurriedly to the door, stammering her excuses. "I'll have to go downstairs for a minute," she said, "to say good night to Grandma . . ."

But she didn't go downstairs at all; she went to her old room and shut herself in. "Barbarian!" she cried, sitting down in front of the looking glass. "If I'd stayed a minute longer, I'd have seen him in his undershirt. Is that the way to behave? What does he take me for?"

"For his wife," said the looking-glass Carlotta.

"Just because he finds himself alone for the first time with his wife," returned the flesh-and-blood Carlotta, angrily, "doesn't mean that he has to take his clothes off. That shows a lack of respect."

"Up to a certain point. It would have been a lack of respect if he'd been an ugly old brute—but, as a matter of fact, he's a handsome man with an athletic body—"

"How do you know? Have you taken a bath with him, or something?"

"No, dear," replied Carlotta in the mirror. "But we did see him in that short-sleeve shirt and we were much impressed with his arms."

"Don't be so idiotic," said the flesh-and-blood Carlotta. "The fact is, he was being his usual boorish self. And his undressing the minute we entered the room was intended to be offensive."

"That could be. But this is hardly the moment for finding fault. What you've got to do now is go back to the room, get undressed, and get into bed."

"Into bed with him? I get into bed with a man I know only because he happens to be my husband? Never!"

"You know something?" giggled the looking-glass Carlotta. "You really make me laugh. You—who've always pretended to be a woman who laughs at everything—now you're afraid to sleep with your husband."

"If it was only a question of sleeping!" whimpered the flesh-and-blood Carlotta. "But who knows what desires that brute may have! Didn't you see how he tore his jacket off?"

"You're a silly little girl! You're the kind of silly little girl who's very bold and cynical when it comes to words but who's ready to die of fright the minute a man gives her the eye!"

The discussion continued for quite some time and ended only when the flesh-and-blood Carlotta drew away from her mirror, saying, "I don't care what I think about myself! I'm going to sleep here, in my room, alone. And it will show him that I asked him to come back only to have peace in the house again."

So she got undressed and went to bed. But she couldn't sleep. She heard midnight sound, then one, then two, then three, then four, then five. At six she saw the sky begin to lighten: it was dawn. Day had come, and all fears left her. She got determinedly out of bed and headed for the nuptial chamber.

I'll get very quietly into bed, she thought. It will be fun to watch him sleeping and to see his embarrassment when he wakes up. I'll bet he looks silly in his pajamas."

Turning the knob of the door with the utmost care, she stopped suddenly and stood without breathing for a second or two, for she had heard something that tickled her so she could hardly keep from laughing: Camillo Debrai was snoring like a whole orchestra of double basses.

As she opened the door, the desire to laugh deserted her. The great bed was empty. Not only Camillo was missing, but one of the mattresses, one of the covers, and one of the pillows. The poor fool had taken refuge in the dressing room. Carlotta, guided by the double basses, peeked through the keyhole and saw him sound asleep on a folding bed that he had found on top of one of the wardrobes.

He'll have to go this way to get out, said Carlotta to herself, as she sat down on the bed and opened a book. She hadn't very long to wait. At a quarter to seven, the door to the dressing room opened, and preceded by a mattress, Camillo entered.

"I'll put everything in order," he said, laying the mattress on the bed. "That way nobody will know anything."

Carlotta laughed. "All this changing around was quite unnecessary," she said. "As it happens, I slept peacefully in my own room."

"Well," said Camillo, "you can never take too many precautions."

Carlotta only just managed to keep her hand from smacking him across the face. Instead, she laughed. "Don't worry, Signor Camillo," she said. "No one will make any attacks on your virtue. In fact, to show you how well we agree, I'll make up your bed every night. Unhappily, I shall have to sleep in this bed, but you may snore to your heart's content all the same."

Camillo blushed. "Can you hear me with the door shut?"

"Yes. Instead of the door, you ought to keep your mouth shut."

"If it disturbs you, give me a place to sleep in a room farther away."

"I wouldn't dream of it! People will have to see us going into the same room if I'm to have any peace in this house.

What happens afterward in that room, no one has to know but you and me. Anyway, don't worry—you snore very pleasantly. In C sharp Minor, like Beethoven's Moonlight Sonata. I adore Beethoven!"

"I'm going to work," said Camillo with a bow. "Good morning."

Around eleven, Carlotta went downstairs and found the family in a meeting.

"It's done," said Donna Leo happily. "The invitations were sent out last night, while you were asleep. All you'll have to do is see that your consort is in order."

"What do you mean?" said Carlotta.

"We're giving a little party tonight," said Donna Leo. "After all, we have to give an explanation for this man's presence in our house."

"Quite right," said Donna Flaminia. "I shall be able to say to the world, 'This is my daughter's husband,' not just some nobody."

"Better say right out he's your husband," cried Robinia. "I wouldn't want anyone to think he was mine!"

"Obviously," said Donna Elisabetta. "There must be no misunderstanding."

"Indeed," added Signor Gastone, "people must know that although there's a strange-looking ruffian in the Madellis house, nobody may say a word, because he's Carlotta's husband."

"Otherwise," said Edo, with his degree of common sense, "people might think he was one of my creditors who has come to live here in the hope of getting his money back."

"Well," said Carlotta, "what am I supposed to do?"

"Make him understand that both your happiness and our good will depend on his behavior tonight. Teach him how to act properly, tell him not to talk very much, prepare a few subjects for him to—"

"Madam is served," Giusmaria announced, and the Madellis family moved to the table. Shortly after, they were joined by Camillo, who ate correctly: a fact that was noted with pleasure by the entire family.

After lunch was over, Camillo tried to slip quietly away, but Carlotta took hold of him and led him to another room.

"Tonight," Carlotta began, "we're having a little party—"

"I'm glad you told me," cried Camillo. "If there's one thing I hate, it's family parties. I'll sleep in my own house so I won't have to hear the noise of your chatter."

Carlotta explained to him that the party was being given in his honor, to present him officially as the husband of Carlotta Wonder, and so he could hardly not come.

"The trouble is," said Camillo, with evident irony, "I don't want to be presented as the husband of Carlotta Wonder."

"Nor do I want to be presented as your wife! But, on the other hand, it's got to be done. I ask this favor of you on behalf of my family."

"All right," said Camillo, "if it's a question of doing a favor for your family, I'll make the sacrifice."

"I'd like to tell you a little bit about how to behave—"

"Not one word! I know it all. They told us at school how to behave at family parties. From how to dress to how to get spots of soup off of shirt fronts or cuffs. After all, that school ought to be of some use."

After Camillo left, Carlotta was joined by her family.

"Well?" asked Donna Leo.

"Everything in order," said Carlotta. "He's got his instructions, and he understands them."

"Excellent!" cried Signor Gastone.

"Nevertheless, it might be a good idea for us to ask God's help," murmured Edo, who was not without a certain degree of common sense.

chapter 20

"May I ask," whispered Donna Leo to Carlotta, "what that idiot is waiting for?"

"He had to clean his hands, Grandma, and with hands like his, that takes time. And then," Carlotta went on, "he said to me, 'I'll come down after everybody's here, and Edo can announce the surprise: Carlotta's husband, Signor Camillo Debrai!' I could hardly say no."

"Well," sighed Donna Leo, "let's hope for the best."

Donna Leo's little party had become a gala reception, to which everybody came, even the Duke of Vigatto, who hadn't gone out into the world for six years. The flower of the city's aristocracy was there, in the rooms of the Casa Madellis, and since it was the first reception of the season, the ladies were dressed with much grandeur and fantasy.

The Madellis family was ready to die of both pride and fear. Who knew whether Camillo was going to behave or not?

By now all the guests had arrived, and the dancing was about to start (there was even a small but very loud orchestra), when a breath of cold wind swept through the glittering ballroom, and all the guests stood motionless, in shocked silence.

An athletic young man had appeared out of nowhere and was now moving boldly toward Carlotta: he was wearing a light-colored sports jacket, a heavy red sweater, and yellow shoes.

"You beast!" cried Carlotta in a whisper, when Camillo reached her side.

Donna Leo and the other ladies of the Madellis household retired to one of the upper rooms so as to be able to faint comfortably.

Edo broke the icy silence that had fallen. His voice, despite the icy silence, was loud as he announced: "I have a surprise for all of you. May I present to you Carlotta's husband, Signor Camillo Debrai?"

"Hooray for Signor Debrai!" cried Camillo, shaking hands with himself. "Congratulations and best wishes! Three cheers for Signor Debrai!"

It could be seen a mile away: the beast was drunk as a lord.

"Three cheers!" cried the Duke of Vigatto, who was very fond of alcohol.

"Three cheers!" cried all the others, ladies and gentlemen, counts and duchesses, all of them amused by the amiable lunacy of that splendid hunk of young man.

"I am Maria Del Castello," said the Countess Del Castello with a smile, as she held out her hand to Camillo.

"Hi, auntie!" cried Camillo, embracing her and then kissing her three times, once on each cheek and once on the lips.

Now, mature countesses of a certain age are not at all averse to being greeted informally and kissed soundly by a handsome young man. The Countess Del Castello laughed enthusiastically. Then the other wellborn ladies also laughed and presented themselves to Camillo.

Camillo kissed them all, one after the other: cute little aunts and cute little cousins and cute little sisters. Then he also kissed the Duke of Vigatto on the forehead, and the Duke of Vigatto, who by now was rather well tanked up on old cognac, kissed him back and called him "my little flower."

Donna Leo, Donna Elisabetta, and Donna Flaminia were still in an upper room, where, with the assistance of Signor Gastone, they took turns swooning, and this was how Edo, when he came to report, found them.

"What is that horrible creature doing now?" sobbed Donna Leo.

"Well, just at the moment," replied Edo, "he's doing double somersaults from a standing start in the tapestry room."

"Oh, good God!" cried the ladies. "Has anyone ever heard the like?"

"No," said Edo, "not even Count De Pistis, who's traveled all over the world. He says he's never seen anyone do double somersaults from a standing start—"

"Silence!" cried Donna Leo. "This is the most horrible thing I've ever heard of! We are completely dishonored!"

"I think not, Grandma," said Edo, who was not without a certain degree of common sense. "Everyone's having a good time."

"At our expense! They're laughing at us! That drunken idiot is enough to make anyone sick!"

"I think not, Grandma," said Edo again. "All the ladies, young and old, were happily letting him kiss them."

"That too?" shrieked Donna Leo. "The ladies let him kiss them?"

"Yes, Grandma," Edo said. "And you had better give your granddaughter Robinia a good bawling out, for she took advantage of Camillo's tipsiness and introduced herself to him at least fifteen times under different names in order to be kissed. Carlotta was very annoyed about it."

"A tragedy!" cried Donna Leo. "A total tragedy! Dishonor and ridicule for the entire family. Well, whatever it costs, we must pretend to be strong and enjoy the joke. Later we'll have our reckoning."

The family descended and joined their guests.

Camillo had calmed down and was dancing with Donna Gisella Marodolis, the prettiest woman in the city.

"What an extraordinary young man!" began the Countess Del Castello to Donna Leo.

But Donna Leo did not take up the gambit. "Giusmaria!" she called. "The ices!"

The dance had ended, and Camillo, unfortunately, overheard her instructions.

"Well, ladies and gentlemen," cried Camillo, "Giusmaria will have the honor of offering you ices while I will have the honor of offering you Giusmaria."

With that he disappeared, and the guests waited eagerly to see what was going to happen.

When they reappeared, Giusmaria was carrying an enormous silver tray loaded with ices, and Camillo was carrying Giusmaria. He had his left hand on Giusmaria's neck and his right on the seat of Giusmaria's trousers, and he walked about holding Giusmaria out as though it was the most natural thing in the world. Nor did he show the least sign of fatigue when, after the tray was empty, he carried Giusmaria back into the kitchen.

Donna Leo, who had run back upstairs, remained unconscious until the end of the party. Donna Flaminia and Donna Elisabetta, however, forced themselves to stand by.

The reception ended around six in the morning. Even

then, the guests hated to leave. Weeping, Camillo embraced all the ladies and kissed them affectionately as he said goodbye to them, calling them his dear little aunt or his dear little cousin, his dear little sister or his dear little niece; and they all returned his embrace.

Edo remarked later that a certain Robinia said goodbye to Camillo at least six or seven times.

And Carlotta?

Carlotta went on laughing. Everyone, men and women both, assured her that her husband was the most attractive young man in the world, and Carlotta laughed with pleasure.

To keep from weeping with rage.

At dawn, before retiring, the Madellis family met to strike their balance.

Said Donna Leo: "Having thought the matter over somewhat more calmly, and having seen the final results, we conclude that the wretch has been hoist on his own petard. He got himself disgustingly drunk and he dressed himself up like a teddy boy in the hope of heaping dishonor on our house, but instead of being taken for the boor he is, he has been accepted as an attractive eccentric, and more than one of the ladies envies us such a husband. We must nourish this misunderstanding, then, and speak of him publicly as a madcap. It is unnecessary to reiterate that for our own internal use, Debrai will always be an unmitigated boor."

"He's an absolute monster!" cried Carlotta.

"I solemnly protest!" Donna Leo announced. "The fault is

yours, after all. It was you, with your disagreeable character, who did not allow this healthy and affectionate young man to open his heart to you. We have all of us always thought of him, and think of him still, with the greatest affection. Only you have been consistently his enemy. *In vino veritas,* my girl! This evening your husband, after a glass or two of champagne, kissed all the ladies affectionately—the only lady he didn't kiss, my dear girl, was you, Carlotta!"

"True enough," said Donna Elisabetta and Donna Flaminia, who, in the general farewells, had also been kissed by Camillo and called his "dear little cousins."

"And he didn't kiss you," Donna Leo went on, "because his subconscious mind, which takes control after a few drinks, told him you were his enemy. Take care, my dear girl, not to find yourself in a situation from which you cannot be extricated save to your own disadvantage, and bear in mind that we expect a grandchild as soon as possible."

Before throwing herself into bed, Carlotta kicked the door of the dressing room. "Monster!" she cried.

"Hi, duke," muttered Camillo in his sleep, and then resumed his snoring with a will.

chapter 21

"Coffee or tea?" asked Giusmaria very respectfully.

"Fried eggs and onions," replied Camillo, without lifting his eyes from his newspaper.

Donna Leo and the other members of the Madellis family gave a start, sat motionless for a moment with their heads down, then returned to their coffee.

Giusmaria failed to catch anyone's eye with his own frightened glance, and so, to gain time, he asked, "Did you say coffee, sir?"

"I said fried eggs and onions!" Camillo repeated decisively.

After Giusmaria received an affirmative nod from Donna Leo, he ran to the kitchen to give the cook the frightful order. "He wants fried eggs and onions!"

"That's not so bad," said the cook. "Yesterday he asked for boiled eggplant with *pesto;* the day before, apple fritters with anchovies; and the day before that, fried salami with zabaione. So this morning it's not so bad."

As Camillo, whistling softly, finished his newspaper, Carlotta came into the room, said good morning to everyone and sat down beside her husband.

Donna Leo, Donna Elisabetta, Donna Flaminia, Signor Gastone, and Robinia raised their heads: ten eyes stared imperiously, unwaveringly at Carlotta.

"Haven't you served Signor Camillo?" said Carlotta to Giusmaria, in an attempt to divert the silent inquisition.

"Signor Camillo," said Donna Leo with a smile, "is waiting for his fried eggs and onions."

Carlotta lowered her head.

The eggs and onions arrived. The Madellis family watched with growing horror as Camillo breakfasted, then Donna Leo rose and the company dispersed in silence.

"If they want me," said Camillo to Giusmaria, "I'll be in the workroom, as usual." He took his cap and left.

Carlotta was summoned to Grandma Leo's boudoir, where she found her mother and her aunt Elisabetta as well.

The ladies transfixed Carlotta with the same terrible questioning glance that had so harried her at the table. "Well?" rumbled Donna Leo threateningly.

Carlotta blushed and felt an almost irresistible desire to sweep all the porcelain ornaments to the floor, but she merely lowered her head.

"Not yet, eh?" said Donna Leo through clenched teeth, and then added sarcastically: "Well done!"

The other two ladies were content to put their hands together as though in prayer and stare imploringly up at the ceiling.

"You may leave," said Donna Leo in a mocking tone.

Carlotta left.

Signor Gastone, who had been pacing nervously up and down in front of the door, entered.

Donna Leo looked at him and spread her arms. "Not yet," she said.

"Unheard of!" cried Signor Gastone.

Then Robinia came in, took one look at her father's disconsolate expression, and went out again.

Edo was stretched out on a sofa, reading his newspaper.

"It's going badly," Robinia whispered to him. "Nothing new. *Consummatum non est!*"

"What have the points of the compass got to do with it?" muttered Edo, who knew no Latin.

"Imbecile!" cried Robinia, scornfully.

"Agreed," said Edo, who was not without a degree of common sense. He did not raise his eyes from his newspaper. "An imbecile, but an independent one."

It would be foolish to suggest that Edo asked the same question every morning about the points of the compass.

Yet, roughly the same scenes occurred every morning in the Madellis house for some twenty-five days.

In the historic plenary session held after the termination of the famous "little party," the fact was established that Camillo was a nice boy and that the person who was at fault was Carlotta.

Every morning thereafter, the family demanded precise information from Carlotta on the interesting question of the grandnephew imposed by Uncle Casimiro, and every morning Carlotta, humiliated and ashamed, lowered her head, and Robinia hissed maliciously to Edo: *Consummatum non est!*

What a to-do there would have been if the family had discovered that every night, night after night, Carlotta slept in the large bed and Camillo barricaded himself in the dressing room . . .

Carlotta spent a most unhappy morning. She did not come down for lunch at noon, nor did she appear at dinner. As Camillo went through the bedroom on his way to the dressing room, he found her lying on the big bed, still completely dressed.

"What's the matter?" he asked with feigned indifference. "Aren't you feeling well?"

"I can't go on any more," Carlotta replied, her voice low and sad.

"It's not my fault. I told you I was coming here against my will. These people get on my nerves and I go too far."

"The way you behave," said Carlotta, "is my only consolation. I love it when I hear you ask for pickled peppers with whipped cream for breakfast, or when I see you cutting up your fish at lunch into little pieces with a knife and then eating them with your dessert spoon, or when Uncle Gastone and my cousin come down to dinner in black suits and you wear your sports coat and your heavy sweater. I love it, I admire your style. The whole day long, you don't say more than eight of the most ordinary words, and yet they're enough to poison the whole family's blood. I'm grateful to you for all that. However, every time you annoy them, they pass it on to me, they make me feel the weight of their displeasure, and I have to spend the whole day here alone. You work all day and at night you go to sleep before I do, and I never see you any more. We don't even talk together— I won't say like friends—but like husband and wife. That all makes me very sad."

Camillo looked into Carlotta's glistening, sad eyes and decided she was telling the truth. He felt upset. "Your life is too monotonous," he said, in an effort to console her. "You ought to go out more, see people, wander through crowded streets. You ought to go to the movies, or the theater, to a musical."

Carlotta shook her head, smiling.

"You don't like any of those things?" asked Camillo.

"Yes, I like them," Carlotta replied. "But I'm not a girl any more, I'm a married woman, and married women don't go out alone, nor can they ask some other member of the family to go with them while they've got a husband who goes to bed."

Camillo made no reply.

Carlotta threw herself back on the bed, with her face in the pillows. Camillo looked at the slender, delicate nape of her neck and at her fine, soft hair, and he began to pace up and down. At last he paused.

He tried to keep his voice as indifferent as possible. "Do you like musical reviews?" he asked.

"Very much," replied Carlotta with a sigh.

"All right. Hurry up, put on your coat, we'll just be in time. They're playing *Klo-Klo* at the Fenice."

"You'll really take me?"

"Of course." Then Camillo remembered. "But how do we get out? Do we have to pass the whole lot of them?"

"No, we can't do that," said Carlotta, throwing herself disconsolately back on the bed. "We can't give them that satisfaction."

"I've got it!" cried Camillo, who had been standing by the window. "Just below there's a big pile of leaves. I'll jump down and then I'll help you down. That way we can go through the garden of the house next door—my house, in fact, and I've got the key. So we get out and the Madellis family gets foxed."

"You should have more respect for my family," said Carlotta, putting on her coat.

They bolted the door from the inside and covered the keyhole. They turned out the light.

Camillo jumped lightly down and held up his arms for Carlotta. He deposited her gently on the ground. They went across the other garden and out through the door of the other house.

"And that's how the Madellis family is foxed!" cried Carlotta happily, when she found herself out in the street.

"You should have a little more respect for your family," said Camillo.

They laughed, both of them, like a pair of heedless children.

They enjoyed *Klo-Klo* very much; it was highly diverting; and when it was over and they were leaving, Camillo said, "There's a nightclub downstairs, with a show, and you can dance till morning."

"When did you go?"

"Never. A friend told me."

"But . . . Who knows what kind of place it is?"

"You're with me, you don't have to worry."

"That's what you men always say."

"I beg your pardon. I'm your husband—"

"Ooh! Husbands are even worse. But you do dance well . . ."

By that time they had got there and were already dancing. They returned at five, the same way they'd left. They closed the window very quietly.

"I had a good time," sighed Carlotta.

"Me too," said Camillo. "And they didn't know a thing about it."

They talked for a bit in whispers, then Camillo took his mattress and carried it into the dressing room. "Good night, Carlotta," he said.

"Good night, Camillo."

The next morning Camillo asked for scrambled salami and chocolate cream for breakfast.

The family paled.

Carlotta bit her lip to keep from laughing.

"May I point out, sir," said Giusmaria, "that it is usually the eggs that are scrambled, not the salami?"

"Doesn't matter. Scramble it all the same."

That afternoon Carlotta heard a noise at the window of her room. When she looked out, she discovered it was Camillo, who had thrown a stone and was now motioning to her to come down. She told her family she was going to the dressmaker's.

He was waiting for her in his workroom, which seemed much gayer than usual. It had a festive air.

"What a wonderful smell!" cried Carlotta as she came in.

"I've been roasting chestnuts," said Camillo.

"How marvelous! We never have them at home because everyone says they're indigestible."

"We'll eat chestnuts and drink wine," said Camillo.

They filled themselves up on chestnuts and they drank spumante from a pot because it was the only glassware Camillo had.

Carlotta returned while the family was at dinner but went directly up to bed because, she said, she wasn't hungry. After trying for an hour to sleep stretched out on the bed in the dark, she saw Camillo tiptoe in.

Before continuing into his little room, Camillo touched her forehead to see if she had a fever, and asked her softly if the chestnuts and the wine had made her sick.

"No!" whispered Carlotta. "They've made me feel awfully well!"

Three other escapades followed: the movies, the theater, and an operetta. Then, a week later, came the Grand Canary Ball. They had agreed to go, and they went.

They left by way of the window, as they had before. They drank champagne and danced as though possessed.

They came home around three, arm-in-arm: that is to say, Camillo had his arm around Carlotta's slender waist, and Carlotta rested her head on his shoulder.

"We look like a couple of lovers," said Camillo.

"But instead we're only husband and wife," sighed Carlotta.

After they reached home, Carlotta said, "I'm tired tonight, I don't think I want to try getting in through the window. Let's be very quiet and use the door tonight. They won't hear a thing."

"All right," said Camillo. "I'm tired too."

They took off their shoes, and nobody heard a thing. But

as they passed the empire drawing room, they saw the lights still on. The door was ajar.

"Giusmaria," said Donna Leo, "claims he saw them jumping down from the balcony. One can't just go and knock on the door. What if they're there? It would look very odd."

"I want to know what's going on," said Aunt Elisabetta. "I'm not going to bed. If they come in through the window, Giusmaria, who's hiding in the garden, will see them. And if they come this way, we'll hear them."

"We might go to bed," said Donna Flaminia. "It's three o'clock. Tomorrow morning I'll talk to Carlotta."

Camillo felt Carlotta's hand clasp his.

"Let's go," whispered Camillo.

They retraced their steps and found themselves in the street again.

"Now we can put our shoes back on," said Camillo.

"Damn them all!" cried Carlotta.

They hurried through the December night to a doorway where both of them pulled the cord of the bell, making a frightful racket.

A terrified servant let them in. At the top of the stairs stood a man in a dressing gown, armed with a candle and a pistol. "So it's you!" he growled. "Tiresome wretches!"

"Yes, Uncle Casimiro."

"Do you intend to stay here?"

"Yes, Uncle Casimiro."

"For long?"

"Forever, Uncle Casimiro."

And so ends the story—an odd story, no doubt, but one with a moral: love is powerful, and when a man and a woman love each other, they end up by marrying even though they may already be husband and wife.

A *Husband in Boarding School* is Giovanni Guareschi's most recent and
most enjoyable farce.

Dom Casimiro Wonder, an unmarried Italian of great wealth but ques-
tionable lineage (he is descended
from a long line of sausage-makers),
has promised to leave his fortune to
his attractive niece, Carlotta, provided
she is married by the time he next
returns from his extensive travels.
When he shows up unexpectedly and
finds that Carlotta is still single, Dom
Casimiro gives her an ultimatum—produce a husband or be cut out of his
will.

In desperation Carlotta marries the
first adult male she can find: a handsome, uncouth woodworker named
Camillo Debrai who eats his soup
with a fork. Carlotta packs him off to
boarding school to learn some man-